Rick Steves®

BEST OF ITALY

Contents

South Italy

Italy
Luzern
Lake Luzern
Vaduz
LIECH.
Brenner Pass
Vipiteno
Bern
Murten
REIFENSTEIN CASTLE
SWITZERLAND
Fribourg
Spiez
Interlaken
Merano
Castelrotto
GLACIER EXPRESS
St. Moritz
Lausanne
BERNER OBERLAND
Samedan
Bolzano
ALPE DI SIUSI
Lake Geneva
Montreux
Gimmelwald
TICINO
Pontresina
Glurns
Adige
BERNINA EXPRESS
Locarno
TRENTINO ALTO ADIGE
Saas Fee
Domodossola
Lago di Como
Trento
Matterhorn
Zermatt
Lugano
Menaggio
Varenna
Chamonix
AIGUILLE DU MIDI
Lago Lugano
Bellagio
Riva
Mont Blanc
Lago Maggiore
Breuil-Cervinia
Stresa
Como
Lecco
Lago d'Iseo
Lago di Garda
VEN
Courmayeur
Lago di Orta
Chiasso
Bergamo
Pré-St Didier
Aosta
Orio al Serio
Vicenza
AOSTA
Malpensa
Monza
Sirmione
Verona
Linate
Brescia
Milan
Desenzano
Catullo
LOMBARDY
Mantua
Modane
Adige
Po
Cremona
Turin
Piacenza
Po
Briançon
PIEDMONT
Asti
Parma
Santa Margherita Ligure
EMILIA
Alba
Modena
MONTE VISO
Barolo
Reggio Emilia
ROMAGNA
Bologna
Genoa
Sestri Levante
Cuneo
Levanto
ITALY
Camogli
Monterosso
Colle di Tonda Pass
Savona
Vernazza
APUAN ALPS
LIGURIA
La Spezia
Finale
CINQUE TERRE
Carrara
Portofino
FRANCE
Alassio
Pistoia
Amerigo Vespucci
Porto Venere
Viareggio
Lucca
Ventimiglia
Florence
Arno
Pisa
MONACO
Ligurian Sea
Galileo
CHIANTI
Nice
Villefranche
Livorno
San Gimignano
Antibes
Cannes
Volterra
TUSCA
St-Tropez
Siena
COTE D'AZUR
Montalcino
Capraia
VIA AURELIA
Piombino
Portoferraro
Grosseto
Bastia
Elba
L'Ile Rousse
Monte Argentario
To Marseille, France
CORSICA (France)
Tyrrhenian
Ajaccio
Propriano
Mediterranean Sea
Bonifacio
Maddalena
S.Teresa
EMERALD COAST
Asinara
Olbia
Porto Torres
Olbia
SARDINIA (Italy)
Sassari
GROTTO OF NEPTUNE
50 kilometers
50 miles
A-1
A-3
A-2
A-12
A-9
A-40
A-5
A-8
A-4
A-43
A-32
A-7
A-21
A-6
A-26
A-15
A-13
A-14
A-10
A-11
A-22
S-222
S-68
S-2

AUSTRIA
LEGEND
Freeway/Autostrada
Major Road
Major Rail Line
Airport
National Park/ Natural Wonder
Ruin, Museum, Other Point of Interest
Cruise Port
To Vienna
Spittal
Klagenfurt
San Candido
Cortina
Tarvisio
DOLOMITES
JULIAN ALPS
Bled
Lake Bled
Lake Bohinj
Brnik
Calalzo
Ljubljana
FRIULI
Belluno
Udine
SLOVENIA
Palmanova
Postojna Caves
Škocjan Caves
Asolo
AQUILEIA
Grado
Lipica
Treviso
Trieste
Piran
Mestre
Marco Polo
Venice
Padua
Rijeka
Pazin
ISTRIA
Krk
Chioggia
Rovinj
Po
Pula
Cres
Rab
BOSNIA-HERZ.
Ferrara
Adriatic Sea
CROATIA
Ravenna
Zadar
Faenza
Rimini
Dugi Otok
SAN MARINO
Pesaro
Šibenik
Split
San Leo
Trogir
Urbino
Rubicon
Falconara
Ancona
LE MARCHE
Brač
Sansepolcro
Arno
Loreto
Hvar
Arezzo
Gubbio
Macerata
To Dubrovnik, Croatia
Cortona
Monte-pulciano
L. Trasimeno
Assisi
Perugia
Spello
Ascoli Piceno
San Benedetto
Pienza
Deruta
Bevagna
Montelfalco
Chiusi
UMBRIA
Orvieto
Todi
Spoleto
To Patra, Greece
Bagnoregio & Civita
Mt. Gran Sasso
Pescara
Lago di Bolsena
Terni
Viterbo
Rieti
L'Aquila
ABRUZZO
Chieti
Orte
Tiber
TARQUINIA
LAZIO
Termoli
Civitavecchia
Tivoli
Vieste
CERVETERI
HADRIAN'S VILLA
ABRUZZO NAT'L PARK
GARGANO PENINSULA
VATICAN CITY
Rome
MOLISE
Manfredonia
Fiumicino / da Vinci
Ciampino
Isernia
Campobasso
To Bari
OSTIA ANTICA
ABBEY & BATTLE SITE
Foggia
Montecassino
Latina
To Bari
Sea
Anzio
PUGLIA
Formia
Caserta
CAMPANIA
BASILICATA
Mt. Vesuvius
Naples
POMPEII
Potenza
Ponza
HERCULANEUM
Positano
Salerno
Ischia
To Matera
Sorrento
Amalfi
Batti-paglia
Capri
AMALFI COAST
PAESTUM
To Sicily
A-2
A-23
A-27
A-4
E-45
S-423
A-14
SP-146
S-2
A-1
A-24
S-1
A-12
A-25
A-16
A-3

Introduction

B*ella Italia!* Italy has Europe's richest, craziest culture. It bubbles with art, emotion, corruption, and irate ranters shaking their fists one minute and walking arm-in-arm the next. Accept Italy as a package deal—from the exquisite to the exasperating. It's the sum of its amazing parts that makes it my favorite country.

Savor your cappuccino, dangle your feet over a canal, and imagine what it was like centuries ago. Ramble through the rubble of Rome and mentally resurrect those ancient stones.

Italy is the cradle of European civilization—established by the Roman Empire and carried on by the Roman Catholic Church. Here you'll stand face-to-face with some of the world's most iconic images from this 2,000-year history: the ancient Colosseum, Michelangelo's *David,* Botticelli's *Venus,* the playful Baroque exuberance of the Trevi Fountain, and the island city of elegant decay: Venice.

Beyond these famous sights, traditions live within a country that is modern, vital, and passionate. Join the locals for their ritual evening stroll—the *passeggiata.* Seek out homemade gelato, dodge motor scooters and pickpockets, and make time for *il dolce far niente* (the sweetness of doing nothing). Write a poem over a glass of wine in a sun-splashed village. Italy is for romantics.

THE BEST OF ITALY

This book focuses on Italy's top destinations, from its thriving cities to its authentic towns. The biggies on everyone's list are Venice, Florence, and Rome. But no visit to Italy is complete without seeing the countryside, from the coastal villages of the Cinque Terre to the hill towns of the heartland. For a dose of southern Italy, dip down past Rome to gritty Naples, seaside Sorrento, historic Pompeii, and the scenic Amalfi Coast.

Beyond the major destinations, I also cover what I call the Best of the Rest—great destinations that don't quite make my top cut, but are worth seeing if you have more time or specific interests: Milan, Varenna (on Lake Como), Verona, Padua, and Pisa. And I'm throwing in Pisa for its iconic tower.

To help you link the top sights, I've designed a two-week itinerary (see page 26), with tips to help tailor it to your interests and available time.

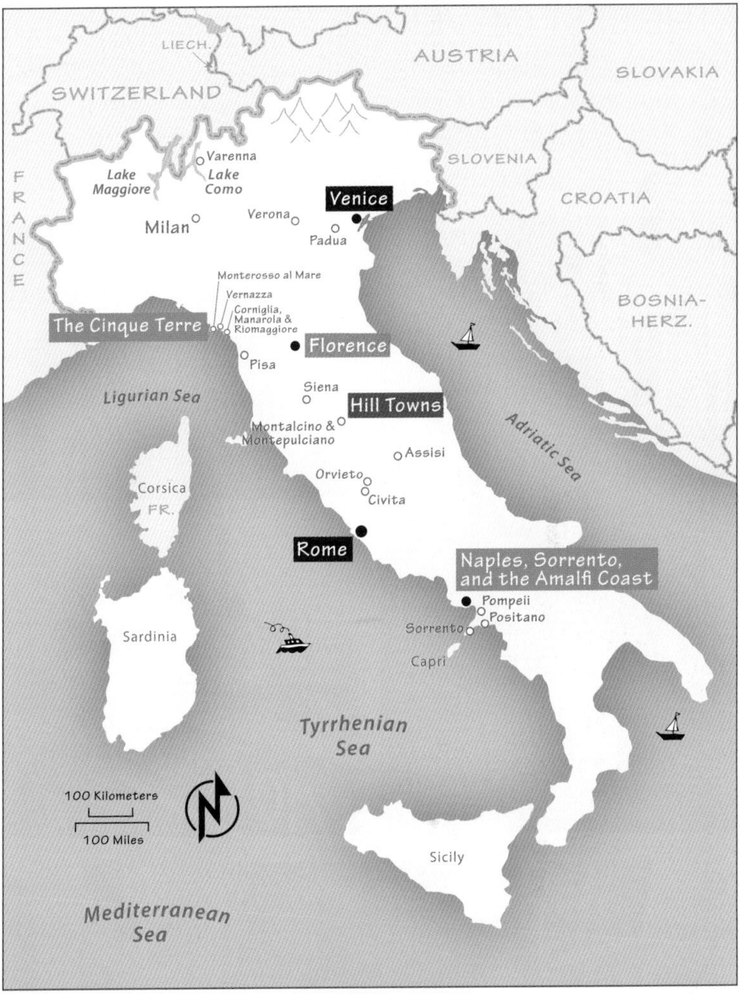

AUSTRIA
SLOVAKIA
LIECH.
SWITZERLAND
SLOVENIA
CROATIA
BOSNIA-HERZ.
FRANCE
Varenna
Lake Maggiore
Lake Como
Milan
Verona
Venice
Padua
Monterosso al Mare
Vernazza
Corniglia, Manarola & Riomaggiore
The Cinque Terre
Florence
Pisa
Siena
Hill Towns
Ligurian Sea
Montalcino & Montepulciano
Adriatic Sea
Assisi
Corsica FR.
Orvieto
Civita
Rome
Naples, Sorrento, and the Amalfi Coast
Pompeii
Positano
Sorrento
Capri
Sardinia
Tyrrhenian Sea
100 Kilometers
100 Miles
Sicily
Mediterranean Sea

THE BEST OF VENICE

Frozen in time, the island city of Venice—speckled with fanciful domes and spires—still looks much as it did centuries ago. It's a city of churches, sensuous paintings, powdered-wig Vivaldi concerts, faded grandeur, and eternal romance.

❶ *Explore the **back lanes and canals** to find a Venice without tourists.*

❷ *Ascend the **Campanile** bell tower for a sky-high view of Venice.*

❸ *Hiring a **gondolier** can be worth the splurge. You'll pay more at night, but the experience is dreamy.*

❹ *Long an emblem of the city, fanciful masks capture the anything-goes spirit of **Carnevale,** celebrated with gusto in Venice.*

❺ *Exotic inside and out, **St. Mark's Basilica** sports bulbous domes topping a church slathered with gold mosaics inside.*

❻ *Ride a vaporetto water bus down the **Grand Canal**—Venice's grandest thoroughfare—passing gondolas and a parade of palaces.*

❼ *Spanning the Grand Canal with style, the **Rialto**—Venice's signature bridge—leads to a lively open-air market.*

THE BEST OF THE CINQUE TERRE

This string of five villages dotting the coast of the Italian Riviera is a marvelous place to take a vacation from your vacation. The villages, which each have a distinct and engaging personality, are connected by trains, hiking trails, and boats. There's no checklist of sights—just a scenic hike, succulent seafood, delightful towns, and sparkling Mediterranean views.

❶ ***Vernazza,*** *the cover-girl town of the Cinque Terre, has long been my favorite.*

❷ *Seek out the* ***regional specialties:*** tegame *(fresh anchovies with potatoes and tomatoes), pesto, and* antipasti frutti di mare *(mixed seafood).*

❸ ***Manarola*** *poses for your picture.*

❹ *Enjoy a stroll along Vernazza's breakwater at* ***sunset*** *when colors deepen and glow.*

❺ *Splash!*

❻ *Little groceries make* ***picnicking*** *easy.*

❼ *Spend a day* ***hiking*** *trails that connect the towns.*

❽ *The most resort-like town on the Cinque Terre,* ***Monterosso*** *has the longest beach and best nightlife.*

4
5
6
BITE
FRESCHE
ACQUA
36
7
CORNIGLIA
CONTROLLO
8

THE BEST OF FLORENCE

Florence hosts the Uffizi Gallery's world-class collection of Renaissance art, Brunelleschi's dome-topped cathedral, and Michelangelo's *David*. Its compact core offers the greatest hits of the Renaissance against a lively urban backdrop of high fashion, zippy Vespa scooters, and Italy's best gelato.

❶ *Look into the eyes of* ***Michelangelo's David*** *to see the quintessential Renaissance Man.*

❷ *Florence's cathedral, the* ***Duomo,*** *is topped with a strikingly graceful dome—the biggest since Rome's Pantheon—thanks to architect Brunelleschi.*

❸ ***Palazzo Vecchio,*** *on Florence's main square, has a soaring tower you can climb.*

❹ *The wide Arno River is spanned by the historic* ***Ponte Vecchio,*** *with central Florence on the left and the unvarnished Oltrarno neighborhood on the right.*

❺ *The city is famous for having Italy's finest* ***gelato.*** Artiginale *means made on the premises.*

❻ *You can reserve ahead for the* ***Uffizi Gallery's*** *wonderful collection of Renaissance art, starring Botticelli's lovely* Birth of Venus.

THE BEST OF THE HILL TOWNS

The top towns of the country's heartland are proud Siena, saintly Assisi, and classic Orvieto. Siena is the biggest, with the most sights, from the magnificent red-brick Il Campo square, towering city hall, and massive cathedral, to the frenzied Palio horse race. Spiritual Assisi is graced by the art-filled Basilica of St. Francis. Orvieto and its tiny hill village neighbor, Civita, are small, cute, and perched on pinnacles.

❶ *Adorable* ***Civita di Bagnoregio,*** *high atop a hill, is reachable only by a path.*

❷ *Pilgrims and art lovers come to* ***Assisi's Basilica of St. Francis,*** *drawn by the saint's divine message and Giotto's down-to-earth frescoes.*

❸ ***Tuscan cuisine*** *is reason alone to visit. This chef serves cheese with tasty toppings.*

❹ ***Orvieto*** *is famous for its ceramics, Classico wine, and cathedral (interior pictured here).*

❺ *The* ***Tuscan countryside*** *offers sublime views.*

❻ *During Siena's* ***Palio horse race,*** *each neighborhood waves its flags and cheers wildly for its horse to win.*

❼ *Conversation flows with* ***Classico wine.***

❽ *The facade of Siena's* ***Duomo*** *is lively and colorful.*

THE BEST OF ROME

Rome, Italy's capital, is studded with Roman ruins and floodlit-fountain squares. From the Vatican to the Colosseum, with crazy traffic in between, Rome is wonderful, huge, and exhausting. The crowds, the heat, and the weighty history of the Eternal City where Caesars walked can make tourists wilt. Recharge by taking siestas, gelato breaks, and after-dark walks, strolling from one atmospheric square to another in the refreshing evening air.

❶ *The much-admired* ***Pantheon****—which had the world's largest dome until the Renaissance—is nearly 2,000 years old (and doesn't look a day over 1,500).*

❷ *Raphael's* School of Athens *in the* ***Vatican Museums*** *embodies the humanistic spirit of the Renaissance.*

❸ *In the* ***Colosseum,*** *gladiators fought wild animals and one another, entertaining crowds of up to 50,000.*

❹ *Smiles are free at this Rome* **ristorante.**

❺ *Brightly garbed guards at* ***St. Peter's Basilica*** *take their work seriously.*

❻ *At the* ***Trevi Fountain,*** *toss in a coin and make your wish to return to Rome. It's always worked for me.*

❼ *Michelangelo's dome tops* ***St. Peter's Basilica.***

3

4

5

6

THE BEST OF NAPLES, SORRENTO, AND THE AMALFI COAST

This region south of Rome is worth a three- or four-day excursion. The colorful port of Naples, with its impressive Archaeological Museum (containing Pompeii's best artifacts), makes a fascinating half-day stop between Rome and Sorrento. The seaside resort of Sorrento serves as a fine home base, with connections to nearby sights: ancient Pompeii, the island of Capri, and the Amalfi Coast—Italy's Coast with the Most.

➊ ***Naples** has a vibrant street scene.*

➋ *Enjoy **pizza** in its birthplace—Naples.*

➌ *The cliff-hanging road along the **Amalfi Coast** offers thrilling views of villages spilling toward the Mediterranean.*

➍ *Three generations straddle one motorbike.*

➎ *Explore ancient **Pompeii,** the Roman town buried and preserved in volcanic ash for centuries.*

➏ ***Mt. Vesuvius** looms over Naples and the surrounding region.*

6

THE BEST OF THE REST

With extra time or interest, splice any of these destinations in northern Italy into your itinerary. You might fly into or out of bustling Milan, which has Leonardo's *The Last Supper.* The laid-back village of Varenna on Lake Como is relaxing. Engaging Verona has an ancient Roman amphitheater, plus *Romeo and Juliet* sights (the play was set here). Padua features the pre-Renaissance genius of Giotto's art, a pilgrimage site, and market squares bubbling with life. Pisa's tipsy tower is an icon we all remember from our childhood—now you can climb to the top.

❶ *In* ***Milan,*** *Leonardo's* **The Last Supper** *is still compelling, even as it fades.*

❷ *Ascend the rooftop of* ***Milan's Duomo*** *for views of the spires, buttresses, and cityscape.*

❸ *The music-loving town of* ***Verona*** *stages operas in its ancient Roman Arena.*

❹ *The peaceful village of* ***Varenna on Lake Como*** *whispers honeymoon.*

❺ ***Pisa's famous tower*** *leans out from behind the Duomo.*

❻ ***Padua****'s market squares are fun for browsing.*

❼ *In Padua, Giotto's groundbreaking, realistic frescoes in the* ***Scrovegni Chapel*** *beautifully illustrate the lives of Mary and Jesus.*

4

5

6

7

TRAVEL SMART

Approach Italy like a veteran traveler, even if it's your first trip. Design your itinerary, get a handle on your budget, make advance arrangements, and follow my travel strategies on the road. For my best advice on sightseeing, accommodations, restaurants, and transportation, see the Practicalities chapter.

Designing Your Itinerary

Decide when to go. Peak season (roughly May-Oct in the north and May-June and Sept-Oct in the south) comes with crowds, heat, and higher prices. The heat in July and August can be oppressive, especially in the south. Between November and April, expect cool weather, shorter hours at sights, and fewer crowds and activities. If you're traveling in winter when waves batter the shores, skip the Cinque Terre and Amalfi Coast.

Choose your top destinations. My itinerary (on page 26) gives you an idea of how much you can reasonably see in 14 days, but you can adapt it to fit your own interests and timeframe. Romantics linger in Venice. For hiking and beach fun, the Cinque Terre is tops. Art lovers are drawn to Florence and Rome. If rolling hills, charming towns, and wine tastings sound like paradise, you'll find it heavenly to spend a week exploring Italy's hill towns. Pilgrims make tracks to Assisi, while honeymooners hide out at Lake Como. Historians could marvel at Rome's sights for days. Stretching out a southern loop from Rome—from a few days to a week or more—offers a lot of variety: Naples (Italy in the extreme), ancient Pompeii, jet-setting Capri, friendly Sorrento, and the wildly scenic Amalfi Coast, with the beach village of Positano. Photographers want to go everywhere.

Draft a rough itinerary. Figure out how many destinations you can comfortably fit in the time you have. Don't overdo it—few travelers wish they'd hurried more. Allow enough days per stop: Figure on at least two or three days for major destinations.

Staying in a home base—like Sorrento—and making day trips can be more time-efficient than changing locations and hotels. Minimize one-night stands, especially consecutive ones; it can be worth taking a late-afternoon train ride or drive to get settled into a town for two nights.

Connect the dots. Link your destinations into a logical route. Determine which cities you'll fly into and out of; begin your search for transatlantic flights at Kayak.com.

Decide if you'll travel by car or public transportation, or a combination. A car is particularly helpful for exploring the hill-town region, where public transportation can be sparse. But a car is useless in cities, and it's not necessary for connecting far-apart destinations (easier by train), unless you plan to make a lot of stops along the way. Compared to trains, buses are slower yet cheaper and can reach a few places that trains can't (but note that buses run less frequently on Sundays).

Allot sufficient time for transportation in your itinerary. Whether you travel by train, bus, or car, it'll take a half-day to get between most destinations.

To determine approximate transportation times between your destinations, study the driving chart (on page 504) or train schedules (at www.trenitalia.it or www.italotreno.it for domestic journeys, www.bahn.com for international trips). Compare the cost of any long train ride with a budget flight; check Skyscanner.com for cheap flights within Europe.

Average Daily Expenses Per Person: $170

Cost	Category	Notes
$80	Lodging	Based on two people splitting the cost of a $160 double room
$45	Meals	$5 for breakfast, $15 for lunch, and $25 for dinner
$35	Sights and Entertainment	This daily average works for most people
$10	City Transit	Buses, Metro, or vaporetti (Venice)
$170	**Total**	Applies to cities, figure on less for towns

Plan your days. Fine-tune your itinerary; write out a day-by-day plan of where you'll be and what you want to be sure to see. To help you make the most of your time, I've suggested day plans for destinations. But check the opening hours of sights; avoid visiting a town on the one day a week that your must-see sight is closed. Also look into whether any holidays or festivals will occur during your trip—these attract crowds and can close sights (for the latest, visit Italy's tourist website, www.italia.it).

Give yourself some slack. Nonstop sightseeing can turn a vacation into a blur. Every trip, and every traveler, needs downtime for doing laundry, picnic shopping, relaxing, people-watching, and so on. Pace yourself. Assume you will return.

Ready, set... You've designed the perfect itinerary for the trip of a lifetime.

Trip Costs per Person

Run a reality check on your dream trip. You'll have major transportation costs in addition to daily expenses.

Flight: A round-trip flight from the US to Milan or Rome costs about $1,000-2,000, depending on where you fly from and when.

Public Transportation: For a two-week trip, allow $370 for second-class trains ($500 for first class) and buses. You'll usually save money buying train tickets in Italy, rather than buying a rail pass before you leave home.

Car Rental: Allow roughly $250 per week, not including tolls, gas, parking, and insurance (theft insurance is mandatory in Italy). Rentals and leases (an economical way to go if you need a car for at least three weeks) are cheaper if arranged from the US.

Budget Tips: You can cut my suggested daily expenses by taking advantage of the deals you'll find throughout Italy and mentioned in this book.

City transit passes (for multiple rides or all-day usage) decrease your cost per ride. Avid sightseers buy combo-tickets or passes that cover multiple museums. If a town doesn't offer deals, visit only the sights you most want to see, and seek out free sights and experiences (people-watching counts).

THE BEST OF ITALY IN 2 WEEKS

Here's an itinerary for an unforgettable two-week trip that'll show you the very best that Italy has to offer. It's geared for public transportation (mainly trains and a few buses), given Italy's good transit system, but can be traveled by car, even just partway: For example, you could rent a car when leaving Siena to more fully explore the hill-town region, then drop it off in Orvieto, which has good train connections with Rome.

DAY	PLAN	SLEEP IN
	Arrive in Venice	Venice
1	Sightsee Venice	Venice
2	Venice	Venice
3	Travel to the Cinque Terre (6 hours by train)	Cinque Terre
4	Cinque Terre	Cinque Terre
5	More Cinque Terre, then travel in the evening to Florence (3 hours by train)	Florence
6	Florence	Florence
7	More Florence, then travel in the evening to Siena (1.25 hours by bus)	Siena
8	Siena	Siena
9	Travel to Assisi (1.75 hours by bus)	Assisi
10	More Assisi, then travel to Orvieto (2-3 hours by train)	Orvieto
11	Orvieto and Civita	Orvieto
12	Travel in the morning to Rome (1-1.5 hours by train)	Rome
13	Rome	Rome
14	Rome	Rome
	Fly home	

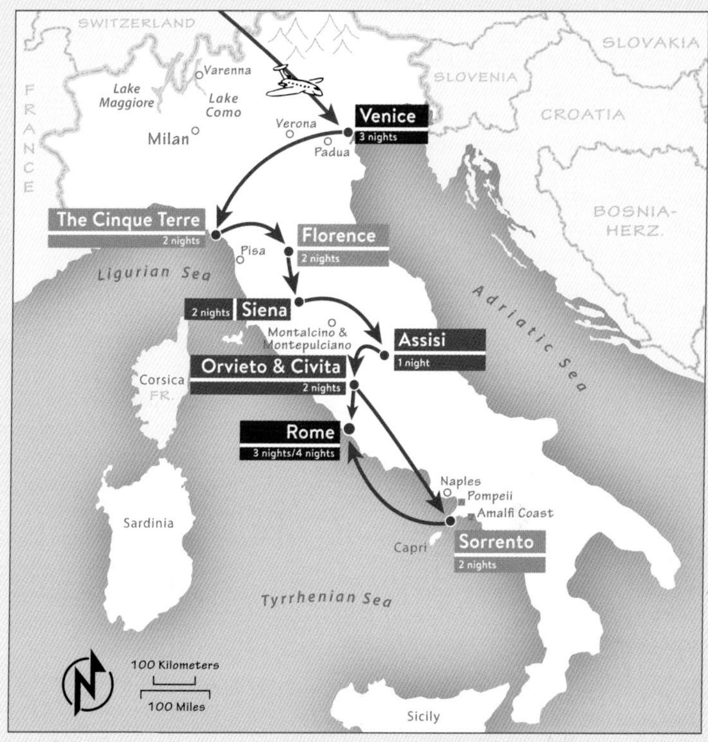

Adding Naples, Sorrento, and the Amalfi Coast

To add these southern destinations (and lengthen your trip), insert them after Orvieto. After your southern loop, enjoy a grand trip finale in Rome, which has good flight connections to the US.

DAY	PLAN	SLEEP IN
12	Travel in the morning from Orvieto to Sorrento, with a midday stop in Naples (total of 5 hours by train)	Sorrento
13	Sightsee the Amalfi Coast (by bus or minibus) or Capri (by boat). Or add a day to do both.	Sorrento
14	Visit Pompeii en route to Rome (3 hours by train)	Rome
15	Rome	Rome
16	Rome	Rome
17	Rome	Rome
	Fly home	

Alternatively, to fit this southern loop into a 14-day trip, drop whatever destination (such as museum-packed Florence, sleepy hill towns, or weather-dependent coastal towns) isn't a must-see for you.

Some businesses—especially hotels and walking-tour companies—offer discounts to my readers (look for the RS% symbol in the listings in this book).

Book your rooms directly with the hotel via email or phone for the best rates. Some hotels offer discounts if you pay in cash and/or stay three or more nights (it pays to check online or ask). Rooms cost less outside of peak season (roughly Nov through March). And even seniors can stay in hostels (some have double rooms) for about $30 per person. Or check Airbnb-type sites for deals.

It's no hardship to eat cheap in Italy. You can get tasty, inexpensive meals at delis, bars, takeout pizza shops, ethnic eateries, and Italian restaurants, too. Cultivate the art of picnicking in atmospheric settings.

When you splurge, choose an experience you'll always remember, such as a gondola ride, a concert, or a food-tasting tour. Minimize souvenir shopping—how will you get it all home? Focus instead on collecting wonderful stories, vivid memories, and new friends.

Stick This Guidebook in Your Ear!

My free Rick Steves Audio Europe app makes it easy for you to download my audio tours of many of Europe's top attractions and listen to them offline during your travels. For Italy, these include major sights and neighborhoods in Milan, Venice, Florence, Assisi, Rome, Naples, and Pompeii. Sights covered by audio tours are marked in this book with this symbol: ♫. The app also offers insightful travel interviews from my public radio show with experts from Italy and around the globe. It's all free! You can download the app via Apple's App Store, Google Play, or Amazon's Appstore. For more info, see www.ricksteves.com/audioeurope.

Before You Go

You'll have a smoother trip if you tackle a few things ahead of time. For more info on these topics, see the Practicalities chapter and check www.ricksteves.com for book updates, more travel tips, and helpful talks.

Make sure your passport is valid. If it's due to expire within six months of your ticketed date of return, you need to renew it. Allow up to six weeks to renew or get a passport (www.travel.state.gov).

Arrange your transportation. Book your international flights. Figure out your main form of transportation within Italy. Consider buying train tickets online in advance, getting a rail pass, renting a car, or booking cheap European flights. (You can wing it once you're there, but it may cost more.) Drivers may want to bring an International Driving Permit (sold at AAA offices in the US, www.aaa.com), along with their US license.

Book rooms well in advance, especially if your trip falls during peak season or any major holidays or festivals.

Reserve or buy tickets ahead for major sights. To avoid waiting in long ticket-buying lines, it's smart to reserve for Florence's Uffizi Gallery (Renaissance paintings) and Accademia (Michelangelo's *David*)—or buy a Firenze Card upon arrival. To climb inside Florence's cathedral dome, you must make a reservation (online or in person), and if you have a Firenze Card, it must be in person. For Pisa, you can book a time online to climb the Leaning Tower. For Milan, reserve three months ahead for Leonardo's *The Last Supper.* For Padua, book at least two days in advance for Giotto's Scrovegni Chapel. For Rome, book a week ahead for the Borghese Gallery (Bernini sculptures).

You can make reservations for Rome's Vatican Museums (Sistine Chapel), and buy a Roma Pass or advance tickets for quick entry into the Colosseum and Forum. Details are in the chapters.

Consider travel insurance. Compare the cost of the insurance to the cost of your potential loss. Check whether your existing insurance (health, homeowners, or renters) covers you and your possessions overseas.

Call your bank. Tell them you'll be using your debit and credit cards in Europe. Ask about transaction fees, and get the PIN number for your credit card. You won't need to bring euros for your trip; you can withdraw euros from cash machines in Europe.

Use your smartphone smartly. Sign up for an international service plan to reduce your costs, or rely on Wi-Fi in Europe instead. Download any apps you'll want on the road, such as maps, translation, transit schedules, and Rick Steves Audio Europe (see sidebar).

Pack light. You'll walk with your luggage more than you think. Bring a single carry-on bag and a daypack. Use the packing checklist in Practicalities as a guide.

Travel Strategies on the Road

If you have a positive attitude, equip yourself with good information, and expect to travel smart, you will.

Read—and reread—this book. To have an "A" trip, be an "A" student. Study up on sights, noting opening hours, closed days, crowd-beating tips, and whether reservations are required or advisable. Check the latest at www.ricksteves. com/update.

Be your own tour guide. As you travel, get up-to-date info on sights, reserve tickets and tours, reconfirm hotels and travel arrangements, and check transit connections. Find out the latest from tourist-information offices (TIs), your hoteliers, checking online, or phoning ahead. Upon arrival in a new town, lay the groundwork for a smooth departure; confirm the train, bus, or road you'll take when you leave.

Give local tours a spin. Your appreciation of a city or region and its history can increase dramatically if you take a walking tour in any big city or even hire a private guide. If you want to learn more about any aspect of Italy, you're in the right place with experts happy to teach you.

Try alternatives to restaurants. Italian restaurants are often closed when we're hungry, particularly for dinner. Compared to our standards, Italians eat late, having lunch—their biggest meal of the day—around 13:00 to 16:00, and dinner starting about 20:00. To cope, try picnics, delis, cafeterias, pizzerias, or the ubiquitous corner bar (for *panini* sandwiches and more). Note that bar pricing is tiered: If you stand at the bar, you'll pay less than

A little Italian goes a long way.

Takeaway sandwiches save time and money.

One of the best ways to connect with Italian culture is through its food.

customers who are seated at tables and served by waitstaff. In the bigger cities, consider taking a food-tasting tour; they're pricey, but think of it as a tasty meal peppered with cultural insight.

Outsmart thieves. Pickpockets abound in crowded places where tourists congregate (at sights, on buses, getting on and off trains, and so on). Treat commotions—such as people bumping into you—as smokescreens for theft. Keep your cash, cards, and passport secure in a money belt tucked under your clothes; carry only a day's spending money in your front pocket. Don't set valuable items down on counters or café tabletops, where they can be quickly stolen or easily forgotten. In case of theft or loss, see page 478.

To minimize potential loss, keep your expensive gear to a minimum. Bring photocopies or take photos of important documents (passport and cards) to aid in replacement if they're lost or stolen. While traveling, back up your digital photos and files frequently.

Beat the summer heat. If you wilt easily, choose a hotel with air-conditioning, start your day early, take a midday siesta at your hotel, and resume your sightseeing later. Churches offer some amazing art and a cool haven (but note that a modest dress code—no bare shoulders or shorts for anyone—is enforced at larger churches, such as Venice's St. Mark's and the Vatican's St. Peter's). Try a different gelato flavor every day. Join in the *passeggiata,* when locals stroll in the cool of the evening.

Guard your time and energy. Taking a taxi can be a good value if it saves you a long wait for a cheap bus or an exhausting walk across town. To avoid long lines at sights, take advantage of the crowd-beating tips in this book, such as making reservations in advance, or sightseeing early or late. In Rome and in Venice, you can buy combo-tickets at lesser visited sights (like Rome's Palatine Hill) to get into more popular sights (like the Colosseum) without a long wait.

Be flexible. Even if you have a well-planned itinerary, expect changes, closures, sore feet, sweltering weather, and

Welcome to Rick Steves' Europe

Travel is intensified living—maximum thrills per minute and one of the last great sources of legal adventure. Travel is freedom. It's recess, and we need it.

I discovered a passion for European travel as a teen and have been sharing it ever since—through my tours, public television and radio shows, and travel guidebooks. Over the years, I've taught thousands of travelers how to best enjoy Europe's blockbuster sights—and experience "Back Door" discoveries that most tourists miss.

This book offers you a balanced mix of Italy's lively cities and cozy towns, from brutal but *bella* Rome to *tranquillo,* traffic-free Riviera villages. And it's selective—rather than listing dozens of hill towns, I recommend only the best ones. My self-guided museum tours and city walks give insight into the country's vibrant history and today's living, breathing culture.

I advocate traveling simply and smartly. Take advantage of my money- and time-saving tips on sightseeing, transportation, and more. Try local, characteristic alternatives to expensive hotels and restaurants. In many ways, spending more money only builds a thicker wall between you and what you traveled so far to see.

We visit Italy to experience it—to become temporary locals. Thoughtful travel engages us with the world, as we learn to appreciate other cultures and new ways to measure quality of life.

Judging from the positive feedback I receive from readers, this book will help you enjoy a fun, affordable, and rewarding vacation—whether it's your first trip or your tenth.

Buon viaggio! Happy travels!

Rick Steves

so on. Your Plan B could turn out to be even better. And when problems arise (if your hotel is disappointing, you were overcharged at a restaurant, or your must-see sight is closed for restoration), keep things in perspective. You're on vacation in a beautiful country.

Attempt the language. Many Italians—especially those in the tourist trade and in big cities—speak English, but if you learn some Italian, even just a few phrases, you'll get more smiles and make more friends. Practice the survival phrases near the end of this book, and even better, bring a phrase book.

Connect with the culture. Interacting with locals carbonates your experience. Enjoy the friendliness of the Italian people. Ask questions—many locals are as interested in you as you are in them. Slow down, step out of your comfort zone, and be open to unexpected experiences. When an interesting opportunity pops up, say *"Si!"*

Hear the gondolier singing? Taste the pasta and chianti? Your next stop...Italy!

Venice

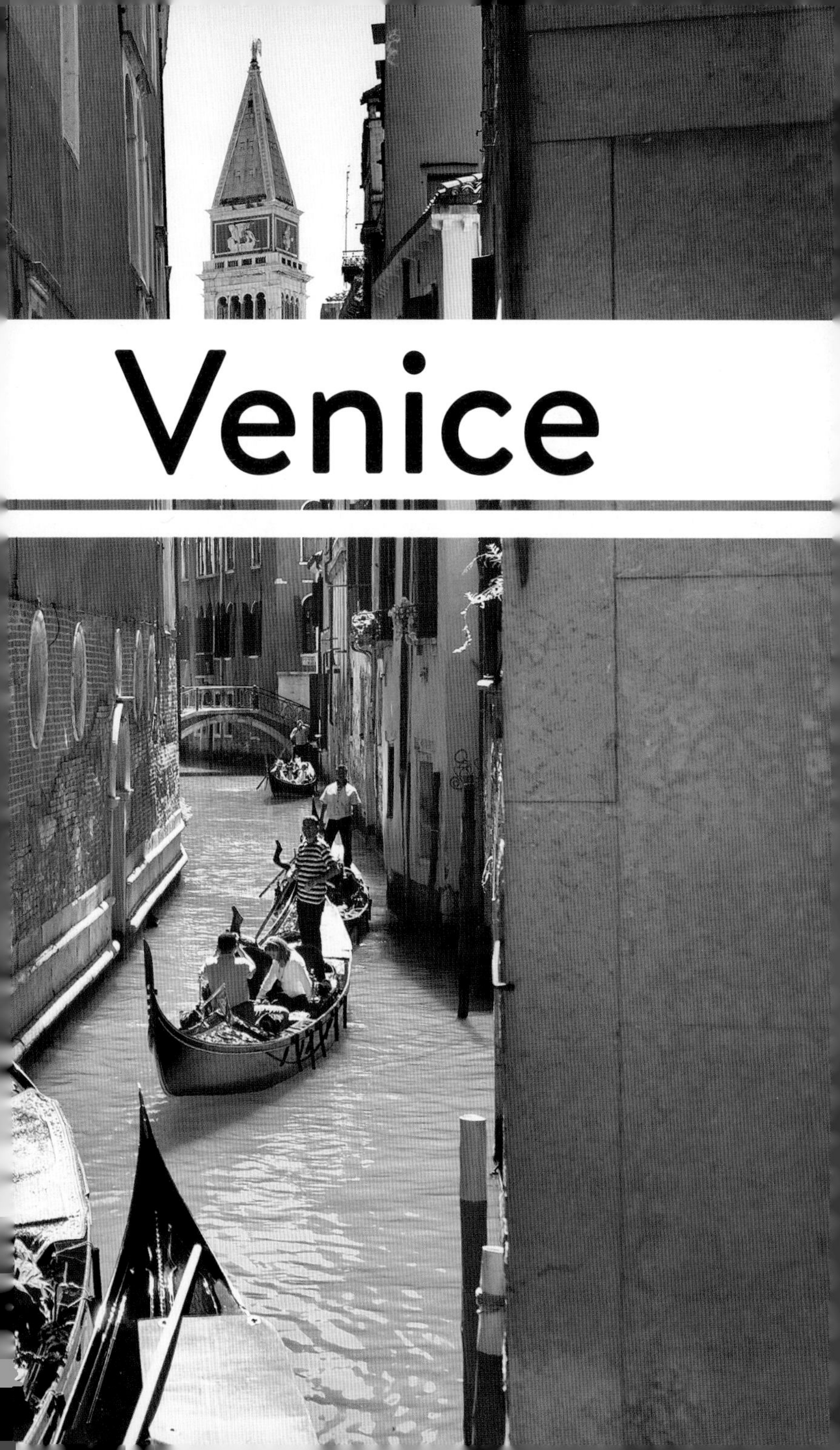

Venice is a world apart. Built on a hundred islands, its exotic-looking palaces are laced together by graceful bridges over sun-speckled canals. Romantics revel in the city's atmosphere of elegant decay, seeing the peeling plaster as a metaphor for beauty in decline. And first-time visitors are often stirred deeply, waking from their ordinary lives to a fantasy world unlike anything they've ever seen.

Those are strong reactions, considering that Venice today, frankly, can also be an overcrowded tourist trap. While there are about 270,000 people in greater Venice (counting the mainland, not counting tourists), the old town has a small-town feel. To see Venice away from the touristic flak, escape the Rialto-San Marco tourist zone and savor the town early and late. At night, when the hordes of day-trippers have gone, another Venice appears. Glide in a gondola through quiet canals. Dance across a floodlit square. Pretend it's Carnevale, don a mask—or just a clean shirt—and become someone else for a night.

VENICE IN 2 DAYS

Venice's greatest sight is the city itself, easily worth two days. It can be Europe's best medieval wander if you make time to stroll and explore.

Day 1: In the morning, take the slow vaporetto #1 from the train station down the Grand Canal to St. Mark's Square. Stop off midway at the Rialto market (Rialto Mercato) to grab an early lunch at the *cicchetti* (appetizer) bars nearby. Resume your ride down the Grand Canal to St. Mark's Square. Spend the afternoon on the square, visiting your choice of St. Mark's Basilica, Doge's Palace, Bridge of Sighs, the Correr Museum, and Campanile bell tower (open late in summer).

On any evening: Do a pub crawl for dinner (except on Sun, when most pubs are closed), or dine later at a restaurant. Enjoy a gondola ride (or, the budget version, a moonlit vaporetto, ideally one with open-air front seats). Catch a Vivaldi concert. Hum along with the dueling orchestras on St. Mark's Square, whether you get a drink or just stroll.

Day 2: Spend the morning shopping and exploring as you make your way over the Rialto Bridge to the Frari Church for the art. Afterward, head to the Dorsoduro neighborhood for lunch, then devote the afternoon to more art—select from the Accademia (Venetian art), Peggy Guggenheim Collection (modern art), and Ca' Rezzonico (18th-century palace).

Too many museums? Go on a photo safari through back streets and canals.

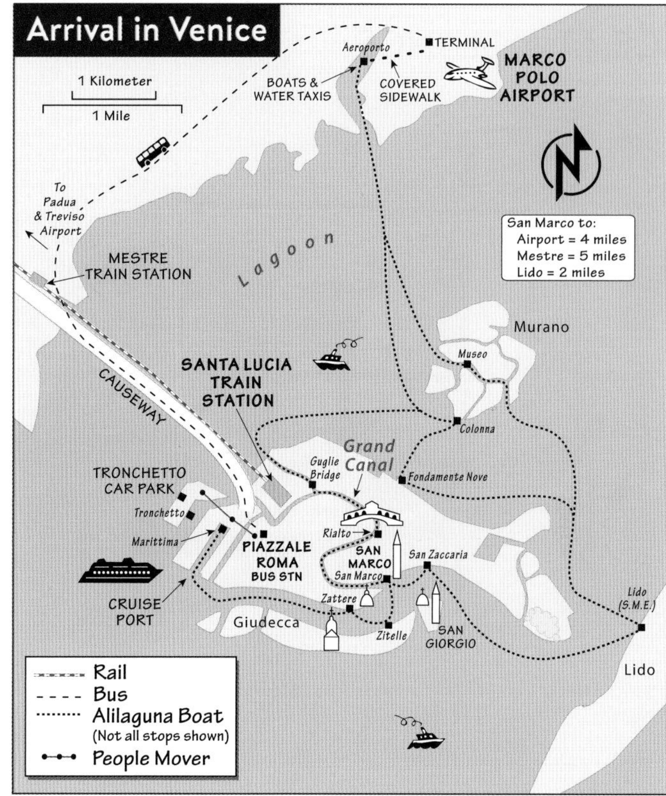

Or take a short vaporetto trip to the San Giorgio Maggiore island for a sublime skyline view of Venice.

With extra time: Visit the lagoon islands of Murano, Burano, and Torcello. For beach time, it's the Lido (across the lagoon via vaporetto). The nearby towns of Padua (with Giotto's frescoed Scrovegni Chapel—reserve ahead) and Verona (with a Roman amphitheater) make great day trips or stops to or from Venice.

Rick's Tip: *Venice is* **crowded with cruise-ship passengers and day-trippers** *daily from 10:00 to about 17:00. Major sights are busiest in the late morning, which makes that a delightful time to explore the back lanes. The sights that have crowd problems get even more packed when it rains.*

ORIENTATION

Venice is shaped like a fish. Its major thoroughfares are canals. The Grand Canal winds through the middle of the fish, starting at the mouth where all the people and food enter, passing under the Rialto Bridge, and ending at St. Mark's Square (Piazza San Marco). Park your 21st-century perspective at the mouth and let Venice swallow you whole.

Venice has six districts *(sestieri):* **San Marco** (from St. Mark's Square to the Accademia Bridge), **Castello** (the area east of St. Mark's Square), **Dorsoduro** (the "belly" of the fish, on the far side of the Accademia Bridge), **Cannaregio** (between the train station and the Rialto Bridge), **San Polo** (west of the Rialto Bridge), and **Santa Croce** (the "eye" of

VENICE AT A GLANCE

▲▲▲**St. Mark's Square** Venice's grand main square. **Hours:** Always open. See page 54.

▲▲▲**St. Mark's Basilica** Cathedral with mosaics, saint's bones, treasury, museum, and viewpoint of square. **Hours:** Mon-Sat 9:45-17:00, Sun 14:00-17:00 (until 16:00 Nov-Easter). See page 54.

▲▲▲**Doge's Palace** Art-splashed palace of former rulers, with an attached prison. **Hours:** Daily April-Oct 8:30-19:00, Nov-March 8:30-17:30. See page 60.

▲▲▲**Rialto Bridge** Distinctive bridge spanning the Grand Canal, with a market nearby. **Hours:** Bridge—always open; market—souvenir stalls open daily, produce market closed Sun, fish market closed Sun-Mon. See page 65.

▲▲**Correr Museum** Venetian history and art. **Hours:** Daily April-Oct 10:00-19:00, Nov-March 10:00-17:00. See page 62.

▲▲**Accademia** Venice's top art museum. **Hours:** Mon 8:15-14:00, Tue-Sun 8:15-19:15. See page 63.

▲▲**Peggy Guggenheim Collection** Popular display of 20th-century art. **Hours:** Wed-Mon 10:00-18:00, closed Tue. See page 65.

▲▲**Frari Church** Franciscan church featuring Renaissance masters. **Hours:** Mon-Sat 9:00-18:00, Sun 13:00-18:00. See page 66.

▲▲**Scuola San Rocco** "Tintoretto's Sistine Chapel." **Hours:** Daily 9:30-17:30. See page 66.

▲**Campanile** Dramatic bell tower on St. Mark's Square with elevator to the top. **Hours:** Daily April-mid-Oct 8:30-21:00, mid-Oct-April 9:30-17:30. See page 62.

▲**Bridge of Sighs** Famous enclosed bridge, part of Doge's Palace, near St. Mark's Square. **Hours:** Always viewable. See page 63.

▲**La Salute Church** Striking church dedicated to the Virgin Mary. **Hours:** Daily 9:00-12:00 & 15:00-17:30. See page 65.

▲**Ca' Rezzonico** Posh Grand Canal palazzo with 18th-century Venetian art. **Hours:** Wed-Mon 10:00-18:00, Nov-March until 17:00, closed Tue year-round. See page 65.

Nearby Islands

▲▲**Burano** Sleepy island known for lacemaking and lace museum. **Hours:** Museum open Tue-Sun 10:00-18:00, Nov-March until 17:00, closed Mon year-round. See page 68.

▲**San Giorgio Maggiore** Island facing St. Mark's Square, featuring church with Palladio architecture, Tintoretto paintings, and fine views back on Venice. **Hours:** daily 9:00-19:00, Nov-March 8:30-18:00. See page 63.

▲**Murano** Island famous for glass factories and glassmaking museum. **Hours:** Glass Museum open daily 10:00-18:00, Nov-March until 17:00. See page 67.

▲**Torcello** Near-deserted island with old church, bell tower, and museum. **Hours:** Church—daily March-Oct 10:30-18:00, Nov-Feb 10:00-17:00; museum—closed Mon. See page 69.

▲**Lido** Family-friendly beach. See page 70.

San Michele Cemetery island on the lagoon. **Hours:** Daily 7:30-18:00, Oct-March until 16:30. See page 67.

the fish, across the canal from the train station).

The easiest way to navigate is by landmarks. Many street corners have a sign pointing you to (*per*) the nearest major landmark, such as San Marco, Accademia, Rialto, Ferrovia (train station), and Piazzale Roma (bus station). Determine whether your destination is in the direction of a major signposted landmark, then follow the signs through the maze. Obedient visitors stick to the main thoroughfares as directed by these signs...but miss the charm of back-street Venice.

Beyond the city's core lie several other islands, including San Giorgio Maggiore (with great views of Venice), San Michele (old cemetery), Murano (famous for glass), Burano (lacemaking), Torcello (old church), and the skinny Lido (with Venice's beach). The island that matters to drivers is Tronchetto, with the huge parking lot at the entrance to Venice.

Rick's Tip: *It's OK to* **get lost in Venice.** *Remind yourself, "I'm on an island, and I can't get off." When it comes time to find your way, just follow the arrows on building corners or simply ask a local,* **"Dov'è San Marco?"** *("Where is St. Mark's?") Most Venetians speak some English. If they don't, listen politely, watch where their hands point, say* **"Grazie,"** *and head in that direction. If you're lost, pop into a hotel and ask for their business card—it probably comes with a map and a prominent "You are here."*

Tourist Information

Venice's TIs are understaffed and don't have many free printed materials. Their website, www.veneziaunica.it, can be more helpful than an actual TI office. If you need to check or confirm something, try phoning the TI information line at 041-2424. Other useful websites are www.museicivicivenezianі.it (city-run museums in Venice), www.unospitedivenezia.it/en (sights and events), www.venicexplorer.net (detailed maps), www.veniceforvisitors.com (general travel advice), and www.venicelink.com (travel agent selling public and private transportation tickets).

If you must visit a TI, you'll find offices near **St. Mark's Square** (daily 9:00-19:00, in the far-left corner with your back to the basilica), at the **airport** (daily 9:00-20:00), next to the **bus station** (daily 7:30-19:30, inside the huge white Autorimessa Comunale parking garage), and at the **train station** (across from track 2, daily 7:00-21:00).

Rick's Tip: *Beware of* **travel agencies that masquerade as TIs** *but serve fancy hotels and tour companies. They're in the business of selling things you don't need.*

Maps: Venice demands a good map. Hotels give away freebies, but it's worth investing in a good one (around €5) that shows all the tiny alleys; they're sold at bookstores and newsstands. Also consider a mapping **app** for your smartphone. The **City Maps 2Go** and **Google Maps** apps have good maps that are searchable even when you're not online.

Sightseeing Passes

Venice offers an array of passes for sightseeing and transit. For most people, the best choice is the **Museum Pass,** which covers entry into the Doge's Palace, Correr Museum, Ca' Rezzonico (Museum of 18th-Century Venice), and sights on the islands: the Glass Museum on Murano, and the Lace Museum on Burano. At €24, this pass is the best value if you plan to see the Doge's Palace and Correr Museum and even just one of the other covered museums. Buy it at any TI, the participating museums, or their websites.

Note that some major sights are not covered on any pass, including the Accademia, Peggy Guggenheim Collection, Scuola San Rocco, and the Campanile, along with the three sights within St. Mark's Basilica that charge admission.

Light sightseers could get by with just a €20 **combo-ticket** that covers both the Doge's Palace and the Correr Museum. To bypass the long line at the palace, buy your combo-ticket at the never-crowded Correr or online (but not at TIs).

I'd skip the **Venice Card** (a.k.a. "city pass," covers 12 city-run museums and 16 churches) and the cheaper **San Marco Pack** (covers Doge's Palace and several sights). It's hard to make either of these passes pay off (valid for 7 days, www.veneziaunica.com).

Rolling Venice is a youth pass offering discounts at dozens of sights and shops, but its best deal is for transit. If you're under 30 and want to buy a 72-hour transit pass, it'll cost you just €22 with the pass—rather than €40 (€6 pass for ages 14-29, sold at TIs, vaporetto ticket offices, and VèneziaUnica shops, www.veneziaunica.com).

Tours

🎧 To sightsee on your own, download my **free audio tours** that illuminate some of Venice's top sights (see page 28).

Avventure Bellissime Venice Tours offers several two-hour walks, including a St. Mark's Square tour called the "Original Venice Walking Tour" (€25, includes church entry, most days at 11:00, Sun at 14:00); a 65-minute private boat tour of the Grand Canal (€48, daily at 16:00, 10 people maximum); and a Rialto Market-area food-and-wine tour (€69, in summer 3/week at 11:15; tel. 041-970-499, www.tours-italy.com, info@tours-italy.com). For a 10 percent Rick Steves discount, contact them before booking for a promo code.

Debonair guide **Alessandro Schezzini** organizes two-hour Venetian bar tours, including appetizers and wine at three pubs (€35/person, most nights at 18:00), plus a 1.5-hour Backstreets Tour that gets you into offbeat Venice (€20/person, most nights at 16:30). Tours depart nearly daily when six or more sign up (book by email—alessandro@schezzini.it—or by phone, mobile 335-530-9024, www.schezzini.it). Meet 50 yards north of the Rialto Bridge under the big clock on Campo San Giacomo.

Artviva Tours offers many intro and themed tours (Grand Canal, Venice Walk, Doge's Palace, Gondola Tour), plus a private "Learn to Be a Gondolier" tour. Rick Steves readers get a 10 percent discount (at www.artviva.com/ricksteves, username "ricksteves" and password "reader").

Walks Inside Venice is enthusiastic about teaching in Venice and outlying destinations (€270/3 hours per group up to 6; or €62.50 for a 2.5-hour walking tour offered Mon-Sat at 14:30; Roberta: mobile 347-253-0560; Sara: mobile 335-522-9714; www.walksinsideitaly.com, info@walksinsidevenice.com). Ask about Rick Steves discounts.

Tour Leader Venice, a.k.a. Treviso Car Service, offers transfers (e.g., to/from airport) and tours outside of Venice, including the Dolomites (mobile 348-900-0700; www.trevisocarservice.com, tvcarservice@gmail.com).

Helpful Hints

Theft and Safety: The dark, late-night streets of Venice are generally safe. Even so, pickpockets (often well dressed) work the crowded main streets, docks, and **vaporetti**. Your biggest risk is inside St. Mark's Basilica, near the Accademia and Rialto bridges (especially if you're preoccupied with snapping photos), or on a tightly packed vaporetto.

A handy *polizia* station is on the right side of St. Mark's Square as you face the basilica (at #63, near Caffè Florian). To call the police, dial 113. The Venice TI handles complaints—which must be submitted in writing—about crooks, including gondoliers, restaurants, and hotel rip-offs (fax 041-523-0399, complaint.apt@turismovenezia.it).

It's illegal for street vendors to sell knockoff handbags, and it's also illegal for

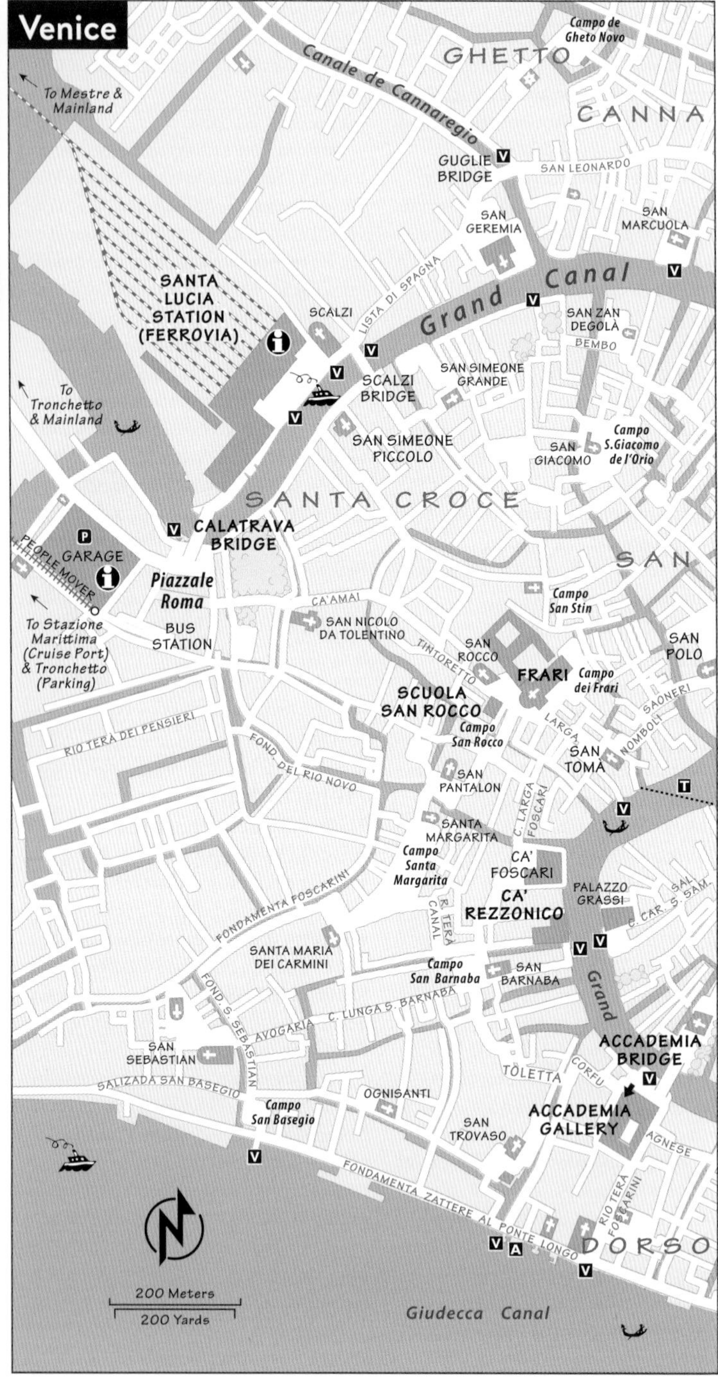
Venice
Canale de Cannaregio
GHETTO
Campo de Gheto Novo
CANNA
GUGLIE BRIDGE
SAN LEONARDO
SAN GEREMIA
SAN MARCUOLA
Grand Canal
SANTA LUCIA STATION (FERROVIA)
SCALZI
LISTA DI SPAGNA
SAN ZAN DEGOLÀ
BEMBO
SCALZI BRIDGE
SAN SIMEONE GRANDE
SAN SIMEONE PICCOLO
SAN GIACOMO
Campo S.Giacomo de l'Orio
To Mestre & Mainland
To Tronchetto & Mainland
SANTA CROCE
CALATRAVA BRIDGE
GARAGE
PEOPLE MOVER
Piazzale Roma
BUS STATION
To Stazione Marittima (Cruise Port) & Tronchetto (Parking)
SAN
CA'AMAI
SAN NICOLO DA TOLENTINO
Campo San Stin
SAN ROCCO
TINTORETTO
FRARI
Campo dei Frari
SAN POLO
SCUOLA SAN ROCCO
Campo San Rocco
SAONERI
NOMBOLI
LARGA
SAN TOMÀ
RIO TERÀ DEI PENSIERI
FOND. DEL RIO NOVO
SAN PANTALON
C. LARGA FOSCARI
SANTA MARGARITA
Campo Santa Margarita
CA' FOSCARI
CA' REZZONICO
PALAZZO GRASSI
SAL. S. SAM.
C. CAR.
R. TERÀ CANAL
FONDAMENTA FOSCARINI
SANTA MARIA DEI CARMINI
Campo San Barnaba
SAN BARNABA
Grand
FOND. S. SEBASTIAN
AVOGARIA
C. LUNGA S. BARNABA
SAN SEBASTIAN
ACCADEMIA BRIDGE
TOLETTA
CORFU
SALIZADA SAN BASEGIO
Campo San Basegio
OGNISANTI
SAN TROVASO
ACCADEMIA GALLERY
AGNESE
FONDAMENTA ZATTERE AL PONTE LONGO
RIO TERÀ FOSCARINI
DORSO
200 Meters
200 Yards
Giudecca Canal

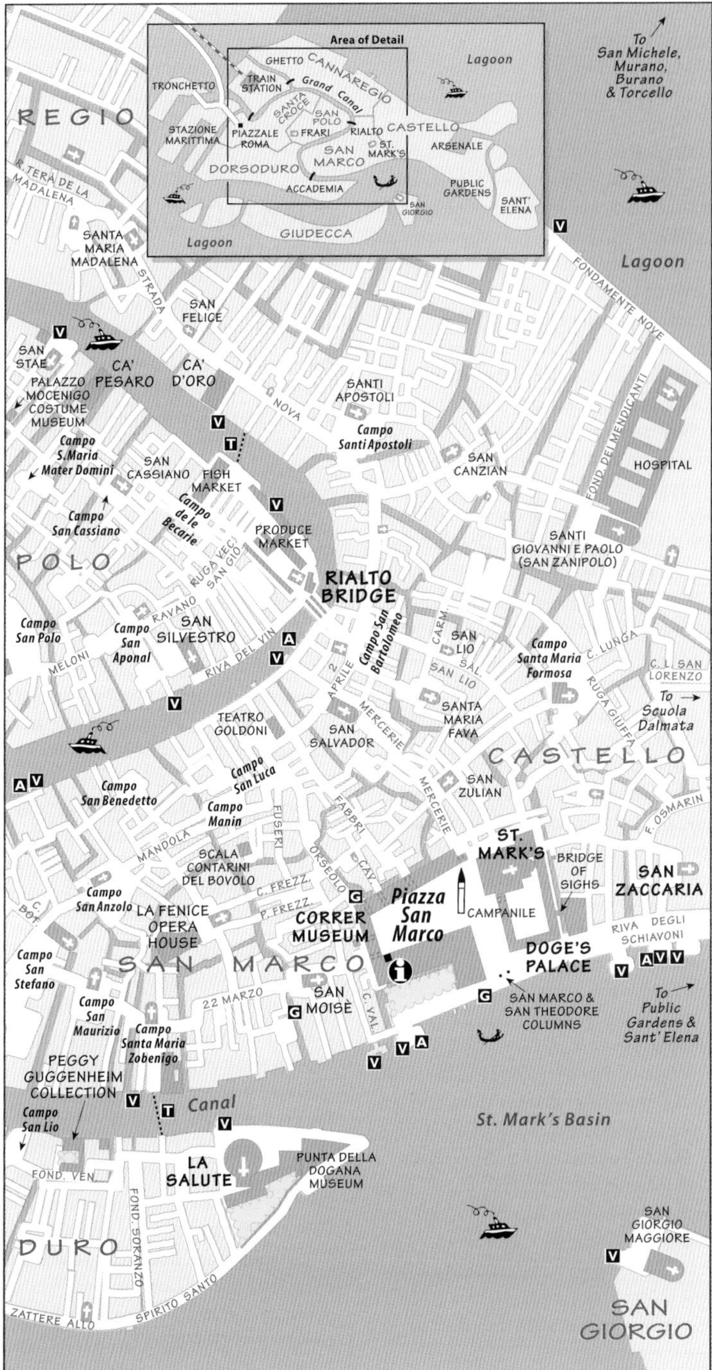
Area of Detail
GHETTO
CANNAREGIO
TRAIN STATION
TRONCHETTO
Grand Canal
SANTA CROCE
SAN POLO
STAZIONE MARITTIMA
PIAZZALE ROMA
FRARI
RIALTO
CASTELLO
SAN MARCO
ST. MARK'S
ARSENALE
DORSODURO
ACCADEMIA
PUBLIC GARDENS
SANT' ELENA
SAN GIORGIO
GIUDECCA
Lagoon
To San Michele, Murano, Burano & Torcello
REGIO
R. TERA DE LA MADALENA
SANTA MARIA MADALENA
STRADA
SAN FELICE
FONDAMENTE NOVE
SAN STAE
PALAZZO MOCENIGO COSTUME MUSEUM
CA' PESARO
CA' D'ORO
NOVA
SANTI APOSTOLI
Campo Santi Apostoli
FOND. DEI MENDICANTI
HOSPITAL
Campo S.Maria Mater Domini
SAN CASSIANO
FISH MARKET
SAN CANZIAN
Campo de le Becarie
Campo San Cassiano
PRODUCE MARKET
SANTI GIOVANNI E PAOLO (SAN ZANIPOLO)
POLO
RUGA VEC. SAN GIO.
RIALTO BRIDGE
Campo San Bartolomeo
CARM.
Campo San Polo
RAVANO
Campo San Aponal
SAN SILVESTRO
SAN LIO
Campo Santa Maria Formosa
C. LUNGA
C. L. SAN LORENZO
MELONI
RIVA DEL VIN
2 APRILE
SAL. SAN LIO
RUGA GIUFFA
To Scuola Dalmata
TEATRO GOLDONI
MERCERIE
SANTA MARIA FAVA
SAN SALVADOR
CASTELLO
Campo San Luca
Campo San Benedetto
SAN ZULIAN
F. OSMARIN
Campo Manin
FUSERI
FABBRI
MERCERIE
MANDOLA
SCALA CONTARINI DEL BOVOLO
ORSEOLO
CAV.
ST. MARK'S
BRIDGE OF SIGHS
SAN ZACCARIA
C. FREZZ.
P. FREZZ.
Piazza San Marco
CAMPANILE
C. BOT.
Campo San Anzolo
LA FENICE OPERA HOUSE
CORRER MUSEUM
RIVA DEGLI SCHIAVONI
DOGE'S PALACE
Campo San Stefano
SAN MARCO
22 MARZO
SAN MOISÈ
C. VAL.
SAN MARCO & SAN THEODORE COLUMNS
To Public Gardens & Sant' Elena
Campo San Maurizio
Campo Santa Maria Zobenigo
PEGGY GUGGENHEIM COLLECTION
Canal
St. Mark's Basin
Campo San Lio
LA SALUTE
PUNTA DELLA DOGANA MUSEUM
FOND. VEN.
FOND. SORANZO
SAN GIORGIO MAGGIORE
DURO
SPIRITO SANTO
ZATTERE ALLO
SAN GIORGIO

you to buy them; both you and the vendor can get big fines.

Medical Help: A first-aid station staffed by English-speaking doctors is on St. Mark's Square (at #63, same address as the **polizia** station, daily 8:00-20:00). Venice's **Santi Giovanni e Paolo hospital** (tel. 118) is a 10-minute walk from both the Rialto and San Marco neighborhoods, located behind the big church of the same name on Fondamenta dei Mendicanti (toward Fondamente Nove). You can take vaporetto #4.1 from San Zaccaria, or #5.2 from the train station or Piazzale Roma, to the Ospedale stop.

Sightseeing Tips: To avoid the worst of the crowds at **St. Mark's Basilica,** go early or late, or reserve a time online. You can usually bypass the line if you have a large bag to check (see page 55). At the **Doge's Palace,** purchase your ticket at the never-crowded Correr Museum across St. Mark's Square, or visit later in the day. For the **Campanile,** ascend first thing in the morning or go late (it's open until 21:00 July-Sept), or skip it entirely if you're going to the similar San Giorgio Maggiore bell tower.

Wi-Fi: Almost all hotels have Wi-Fi, many have a computer that guests can use, and most provide these services for free. A few shops with pricey Internet access can be found on back streets (€5/hour, marked with an @ sign).

Laundry: The full-service Lavanderia Gabriella is a few streets north of St. Mark's Square (closed Sat-Sun, on Rio Terà de le Colonne, San Marco 985, tel. 041-522-1758, Elisabetta).

Water: Carry a water bottle to refill at public fountains fed by pure, safe water piped in from the foothills of the Alps.

Public Toilets: Public pay WCs are near major landmarks, including St. Mark's Square (behind the Correr Museum and at the waterfront park, Giardinetti Reali), Rialto, and the Accademia Bridge. Use free toilets in any museum or any café you're eating in, or get a drink at a bar and use their WC for free.

Travel Agencies: Agenzie 365, in the train station's main lobby, sells vaporetto and train tickets and has shorter lines than the ticket windows (9 percent surcharge on train tickets, daily 8:00-19:30, tel. 041-275-9412).

GRAND CANAL CRUISE

Take a joyride and introduce yourself to Venice by boat, an experience worth ▲▲▲. Cruise the Grand Canal all the way to St. Mark's Square, starting at the train station (Ferrovia) or the bus station (Piazzale Roma).

If it's your first trip down the Grand Canal, you might want to stow this book and just take it all in—Venice is a barrage on the senses that hardly needs narration. But these notes give the cruise a little meaning and help orient you to this great city.

You can break up the tour by hopping on and off at various sights described in greater depth later in the chapter. Just remember: a single-fare vaporetto ticket is good for just 75 minutes; passes let you hop on and off all day.

I've organized this tour by boat stop. I'll point out both what you can see from the current stop, and what to look forward to as you cruise to the next stop.

Orientation

Length of This Tour: Allow 45 minutes.

Cost: €7.50 for a 75-minute vaporetto ticket, or covered by a transit pass—the best choice if you want to hop on and off.

Getting There: This tour starts at the Ferrovia vaporetto stop (at Santa Lucia train station). If you want to board upstream at the less-crowded Piazzale Roma, it's a five-minute walk over the Calatrava Bridge from the Ferrovia stop.

Catching Your Boat: This tour is designed for **slow boat #1** (which takes about 45 minutes). The **express boat #2** travels the same route, but it skips some

Grand Canal

stops and takes 25 minutes, making it hard to sightsee. Also, early and late in the day, the vaporetto #2 terminates at Rialto; you'll have to get off and switch to #1 to do the whole tour.

Where to Sit: You're more likely to find an empty seat if you catch the vaporetto at Piazzale Roma. Try to snag a seat in the bow—in front of the captain's bridge—for the perfect vantage point for spotting sights left, right, and forward. Not all boats have seats in the bow, but some of the older vaporetti do. Otherwise, your options are sitting inside (and viewing the passing sights through windows); standing in the open middle deck (where you can move from side to side if the boat's not crowded—especially easy after dark); or sitting outside in the back (where you'll miss the wonderful forward views). The left side of the boat has a slight edge, with more sights and the best light late in the day.

Stops to Consider: Some interesting stops are Rialto Mercato (fish market and famous bridge), Ca' Rezzonico (Museum of 18th-Century Venice), Accademia (art museum and the nearby Peggy Guggenheim Collection), and Salute (huge art-filled church).

Audio Tour: 🎧 If you download my free audio tour (see page 28), you won't even have to look at the book. Because it's hard to see everything in one go, you may want to do this tour twice (perhaps once in either direction).

Overview

The Grand Canal is Venice's "Main Street." At more than two miles long, nearly 150 feet wide, and nearly 15 feet deep, it's the city's largest canal, lined with its most impressive palaces. It's the remnant of a river that once spilled from the mainland into the Adriatic. The sediment it carried formed barrier islands that cut Venice off from the sea, forming a lagoon.

Venice was built on the marshy islands of the former delta, sitting on wood pilings driven nearly 15 feet into the clay (alder was the preferred wood). About 25 miles of canals drain the city, dumping like streams into the Grand Canal. Technically, Venice has only three canals: Grand, Giudecca, and Cannaregio. The 45 small waterways that dump into the

Grand Canal are referred to as rivers (e.g., Rio Novo).

Venice is a city of palaces, dating from the days when the city was the world's richest. The most lavish palaces formed a grand architectural cancan along the Grand Canal. Once frescoed in reds and blues, with black-and-white borders and gold-leaf trim, they made Venice a city of dazzling color. This cruise is the only way to truly appreciate the palaces, approaching them at water level, where their main entrances were located. Today, strict laws prohibit any changes in these buildings. So while landowners gnash their teeth, we can enjoy Europe's best-preserved medieval/Renaissance city—slowly rotting. Many of the grand buildings are now vacant. Others harbor chandeliered elegance above mossy, empty, often flooded ground floors.

➲ Self-Guided Cruise

Start reading the tour when your vaporetto reaches Ferrovia.

❶ *Ferrovia*

The **Santa Lucia train station,** one of the few modern buildings in town, was built in 1954. It's been the gateway into Venice since 1860, when the first station was built. "F.S." stands for "Ferrovie dello Stato," the Italian state railway system.

More than 20,000 people a day commute in from the mainland, making this the busiest part of Venice during rush hour. The **Calatrava Bridge,** just upstream, was built in 2008 to alleviate some of the congestion.

❷ *Riva de Biasio*

Venice's main thoroughfare is busy with all kinds of boats: taxis, police boats, garbage boats, ambulances, construction cranes, and even brown-and-white UPS boats. Somehow they all manage to share the canal in relative peace.

About 25 yards past the Riva de Biasio stop, look left down the broad **Cannaregio Canal** to see what was the **Jewish Ghetto.** The twin, pale-pink, six-story "skyscrapers"—the tallest buildings you'll see at this end of the canal—are reminders of how densely populated the community was. Founded in 1516 near a copper foundry (a *geto*), this segregated community gave us our word "ghetto."

❸ *San Marcuola*

At this stop, facing a tiny square just ahead, stands the unfinished Church of San Marcuola, one of only five churches fronting the Grand Canal. Centuries ago, this canal was a commercial drag of expensive real estate in high demand by wealthy merchants. About 20 yards ahead on the right (across the Grand Canal) stands the stately gray **Turkish Exchange (Fondaco dei Turchi),** one of the oldest houses in Venice. Its horseshoe arches and roofline of triangles are reminders of its Byzantine heritage. Turbaned Turkish

Ferrovia vaporetto stop

Calatrava Bridge

traders docked here, unloaded their goods into the warehouse on the bottom story, then went upstairs for a home-style meal and a place to sleep. Venice in the 1500s was cosmopolitan, welcoming every religion and ethnicity—so long as they carried cash. (Today the building contains the city's Museum of Natural History—and Venice's only dinosaur skeleton.)

Just 100 yards ahead on the left, Venice's **Casinò** is housed in the palace where German composer Richard Wagner *(The Ring)* died in 1883. See his distinct, strong-jawed profile in the white plaque on the brick wall. In the 1700s, Venice was Europe's Vegas, with casinos and prostitutes everywhere. *Casinòs* ("little houses" in Venetian dialect) have long provided Italians with a handy escape from daily life. Today, they're run by the state to keep Mafia influence at bay. Notice the fancy front porch, which greets high rollers arriving by taxi or hotel boat.

❹ *San Stae*

The San Stae Church sports a delightful Baroque facade. Opposite the San Stae stop is a little canal opening. On the second building to the right of that opening, look for the peeling plaster that once made up **frescoes** (you can barely distinguish the scant remains of little angels on the lower floors). Imagine the facades of the Grand Canal at their finest. Most of them would have been covered in frescoes by the best artists of the day. As colorful as the city is today, it's still only a faded, sepia-toned remnant of a long-gone era, a time of lavishly decorated, brilliantly colored palaces.

Just ahead, on the right with blue posts, is the ornate white facade of **Ca' Pesaro,** which houses the International Gallery of Modern Art. *"Ca'"* is short for *casa* (house).

In this city of masks, notice how the rich marble facades along the Grand Canal mask what are generally just simple, no-nonsense brick buildings. Most merchants enjoyed showing off. However, being smart businessmen, they only decorated the side of the buildings that would be seen and appreciated. But look back as you pass Ca' Pesaro. It's the only building you'll see with a fine side facade. Ahead, on the left (just before the next stop), is Ca' d'Oro with its glorious triple-decker medieval arcade.

❺ *Ca' d'Oro*

The lacy **Ca' d'Oro** (House of Gold) is the best example of Venetian Gothic architecture on the canal. Its three stories offer different variations on balcony design, topped with a spiny white roofline. Venetian Gothic mixes traditional Gothic (pointed arches and round medallions stamped with a four-leaf clover) with Byzantine styles (tall, narrow arches atop thin columns), filled in with Islamic

All kinds of boats ply the canal.

A classic canal view

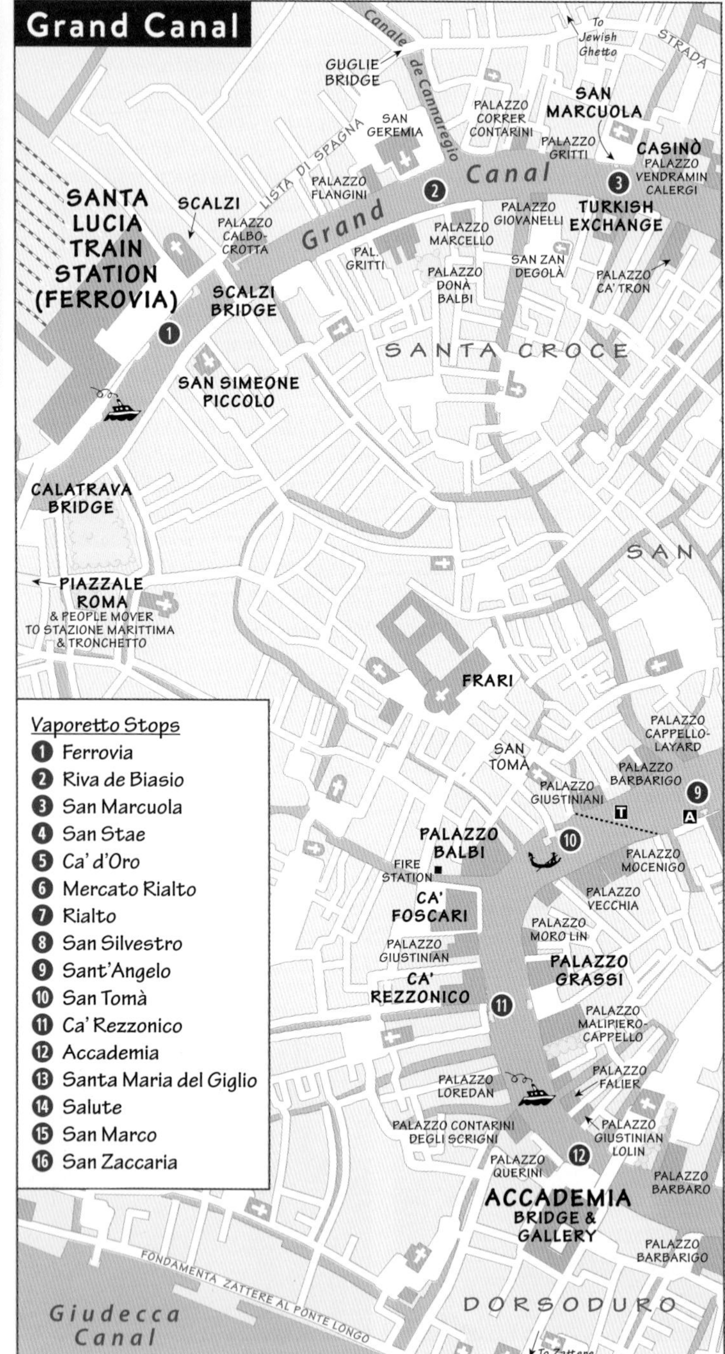
Grand Canal
Canale de Cannaregio
GUGLIE BRIDGE
To Jewish Ghetto
STRADA
SAN MARCUOLA
PALAZZO CORRER CONTARINI
SAN GEREMIA
LISTA DI SPAGNA
PALAZZO GRITTI
CASINÒ
PALAZZO VENDRAMIN CALERGI
PALAZZO FLANGINI
Grand Canal
SANTA LUCIA TRAIN STATION (FERROVIA)
SCALZI
PALAZZO CALBO-CROTTA
PALAZZO GIOVANELLI
TURKISH EXCHANGE
PALAZZO MARCELLO
PAL. GRITTI
SAN ZAN DEGOLÀ
PALAZZO DONÀ BALBI
PALAZZO CA' TRON
SCALZI BRIDGE
SANTA CROCE
SAN SIMEONE PICCOLO
CALATRAVA BRIDGE
SAN
PIAZZALE ROMA
& PEOPLE MOVER TO STAZIONE MARITTIMA & TRONCHETTO
FRARI
Vaporetto Stops
1 Ferrovia
2 Riva de Biasio
3 San Marcuola
4 San Stae
5 Ca' d'Oro
6 Mercato Rialto
7 Rialto
8 San Silvestro
9 Sant'Angelo
10 San Tomà
11 Ca' Rezzonico
12 Accademia
13 Santa Maria del Giglio
14 Salute
15 San Marco
16 San Zaccaria
PALAZZO CAPPELLO-LAYARD
SAN TOMÀ
PALAZZO BARBARIGO
PALAZZO GIUSTINIANI
T
A
PALAZZO BALBI
FIRE STATION
PALAZZO MOCENIGO
CA' FOSCARI
PALAZZO VECCHIA
PALAZZO MORO LIN
PALAZZO GIUSTINIAN
PALAZZO GRASSI
CA' REZZONICO
PALAZZO MALIPIERO-CAPPELLO
PALAZZO LOREDAN
PALAZZO FALIER
PALAZZO CONTARINI DEGLI SCRIGNI
PALAZZO GIUSTINIAN LOLIN
PALAZZO QUERINI
PALAZZO BARBARO
ACCADEMIA BRIDGE & GALLERY
PALAZZO BARBARIGO
FONDAMENTA ZATTERE AL PONTE LONGO
Giudecca Canal
DORSODURO
To Zattere

Lagoon
200 Meters
200 Yards
FONDAMENTE NOVE
NOVA
PALAZZO MARCELLO
PALAZZO MOLIN
PALAZZO ZULLAN
4
SAN STAE
PALAZZO BARBARIGO
PALAZZO FONTANA
PALAZZO GIUSTI
CANNAREGIO
PALAZZO SAGREDO
STRADA NOVA
PALAZZO DONÀ
CA' D'ORO
CA' PESARO
PALAZZO FAVRETTO
PALAZZO MICHIEL COLONNE
5
PALAZZO CORNER DELLA REGINA
PALAZZO BRANDOLIN
T
PALAZZO VALMARANA
PALAZZO CA' DA MOSTO
FISH MARKET
6
PRODUCE MARKET
PALAZZO CIVRAN
POLO
FONDACO DEI TEDESCHI (FORMER GERMAN EXCHANGE)
RIALTO BRIDGE
A
7
SAL. S. LIO
S. MARIA FORMOSA
PALAZZO PAPADOPOLI
PALAZZO BARZIZZA
PALAZZO DOLFIN-MANIN
PALAZZO BEMBO
MERCERIE
PALAZZO DONÀ
8
PALAZZO CORNER-CONTARINI
PALAZZO BERNARDO
PALAZZO FARSETTI-DANDOLO
CASTELLO
PALAZZO GRIMANI
PALAZZO BENZON
PALAZZO MARTINENGO
MERCERIE
FABBRI
PALAZZO CORNER-SPINELLI
ST. MARK'S BASILICA
CAMPANILE
BRIDGE OF SIGHS
SAN MARCO
DOGE'S PALACE
SAN MARCO
16
CALLE LARGA XXII MARZO
SAN MARCO & SAN THEODORE COLUMNS
HARRY'S AMERICAN BAR
GRITTI PALACE HOTEL
A
15
CA' GRANDE
PALAZZO FLANGINI
To Lido
13
Canal
Grand
T
14
LA SALUTE CHURCH
St. Mark's Basin
PALAZZO DARIO
PALAZZO GENOVESE
PUNTA DELLA DOGANA MUSEUM
PEGGY GUGGENHEIM COLLECTION
To San Giorgio Maggiore & Giudecca

frills. Like all the palaces, this was originally painted and gilded to make it even more glorious than it is now. Today the Ca' d'Oro is an art gallery.

Look at the Venetian chorus line of palaces in front of the boat. On the right is the arcade of the covered **fish market,** with the open-air **produce market** just beyond (closed Sun). It bustles in the morning but is quiet the rest of the day. This is a great scene to wander through—even though European Union hygiene standards have made it cleaner but less colorful than it once was.

Find the ***traghetto*** gondola ferrying shoppers—standing like Washington crossing the Delaware—back and forth. There are three *traghetto* crossings along the Grand Canal, each one marked by a classy low-key green-and-black sign. Piloting a *traghetto* isn't these gondoliers' normal day jobs. As a public service, all gondoliers are obliged to row a *traghetto* a few days a month. Make a point to use them. At €2 a ride, *traghetti* offer the cheapest gondola rides in Venice (but at this price, don't expect them to sing to you).

❻ *Mercato Rialto*

Boats stop here to serve the busy market. The long and officious-looking building at this stop is the Venice courthouse. Straight ahead in the distance, rising above the roofline, is the tip of the Campanile (bell tower), crowned by its golden angel at St. Mark's Square, where this tour will end. The **Fondaco dei Tedeschi** (former German Exchange, a building just beyond, on the left) was the trading center for German metal merchants in the early 1500s. Today it's a shopping center with great views from its small rooftop terrace (free).

You'll cruise by some trendy and beautifully situated wine bars on the right, but look ahead as you round the corner and see the impressive Rialto Bridge come into view.

A major landmark of Venice, the **Rialto Bridge** is lined with shops and tourists. Constructed in 1588, it's the third bridge built on this spot. Until the 1850s, this was the only bridge crossing the Grand Canal. With a span of 160 feet and foundations stretching 650 feet on either side, the Rialto was a massive engineering feat in its day. Earlier Rialto Bridges could open to let big ships in, but not this one. When this new bridge was completed, much of the Grand Canal was closed to shipping and became a canal of palaces.

When gondoliers pass under the fat arch of the Rialto Bridge, they take full advantage of its acoustics: *"Volare, oh, oh..."*

❼ *Rialto*

Rialto, a separate town in the early days of Venice, has always been the commercial district, while San Marco was the reli-

Ca' d'Oro—the House of Gold

Mercato Rialto

gious and governmental center. Today, a winding street called the Mercerie connects the two, providing travelers with human traffic jams and a mesmerizing gauntlet of shopping temptations. This is the only stretch of the historic Grand Canal with landings upon which you can walk. They unloaded the city's basic necessities here: oil, wine, charcoal, iron. Today, the quay is lined with tourist-trap restaurants.

Venice's sleek, black, graceful **gondolas** are a symbol of the city. With about 500 gondoliers joyriding amid the churning **vaporetti,** there's a lot of congestion on the Grand Canal. Pay attention—this is where most of the gondola and vaporetto accidents take place. While the Rialto is the highlight of many gondola rides, gondoliers understandably prefer the quieter small canals. Watch your vaporetto driver curse the better-paid gondoliers.

❽ *San Silvestro*

We now enter a long stretch of important ***merchants' palaces,*** each with proud and different facades. Because ships couldn't navigate beyond the Rialto Bridge, the biggest palaces—with the major shipping needs—line this last stretch of the navigable Grand Canal.

Palaces like these were multifunctional: ground floor for the warehouse, offices and showrooms upstairs, and the living quarters above the offices on the "noble floors" (with big windows designed to let in maximum light). Servants lived and worked on the top floors (with the smallest windows). For fire-safety reasons, the kitchens were also located on the top floors. Peek into the noble floors to catch a glimpse of their still-glorious chandeliers of Murano glass.

The **Palazzo Grimani** (across from the San Silvestro dock) sports a heavy white Roman-style facade—a reminder that the Grimani family included a cardinal and had strong Roman connections.

The **Palazzo Papadopoli,** with the two obelisks on its roof (50 yards beyond the San Silvestro stop on the right, with the blue posts), is the very fancy Aman Hotel where George and Amal Clooney were married in 2014.

❾ *Sant'Angelo*

Notice how many buildings have a foundation of waterproof white stone *(pietra d'Istria)* upon which the bricks sit high and

Rialto Bridge

dry. Many canal-level floors are abandoned as the rising water level takes its toll.

The **posts**—historically painted gaily with the equivalent of family coats of arms—don't rot underwater. But the wood at the waterline, where it's exposed to oxygen, does. On the smallest canals, little blue gondola signs indicate that these docks are for gondolas only (no motorized craft).

⑩ *San Tomà*

Fifty yards ahead, on the right side (with twin obelisks on the rooftop) stands **Palazzo Balbi,** the palace of an early-17th-century captain general of the sea. This palace, like so many in the city, flies three flags: Italy (green-white-red), the European Union (blue with ring of stars), and Venice (a lion on a field of red and gold).

Just past the admiral's palace, look immediately to the right, down a side canal. On the right side of that canal, before the bridge, see the traffic light and the **fire station** (the 1930s Mussolini-era building with four arches hiding fireboats parked and ready to go).

The impressive **Ca' Foscari,** with a classic Venetian facade (on the corner, across from the fire station), dominates the bend in the canal. This is the main building of the University of Venice, which has about 25,000 students. Notice the elegant lamp on the corner—needed in the old days to light this intersection.

Best Views in Venice

- A slow vaporetto ride down the **Grand Canal**—ideally very early or just before sunset—is a shutterbug's delight.
- On St. Mark's Square, enjoy views from the soaring **Campanile** or the balcony of St. Mark's Basilica (both require admission).
- The **Rialto** and **Accademia Bridges** provide free, expansive views of the Grand Canal, along with a cooling breeze.
- The luxury "mall" **Fondaco dei Tedeschi**, just north of the Rialto bridge, has great views—but as the space is small and free, it can be crowded, especially near sunset.
- Get off the main island for a view of the Venetian skyline: Ascend **San Giorgio Maggiore's bell tower,** or venture to **Giudecca Island** to visit the swanky bar of the Molino Stucky Hilton Hotel (the free-to-"customers" shuttle boat leaves from near the San Zaccaria-B vaporetto dock).

The grand, heavy, white **Ca' Rezzonico,** just before the stop of the same name, houses the Museum of 18th-Century Venice (see page 65). Across the canal is the cleaner and leaner **Palazzo Grassi,** the last major palace built on the canal, erected in the late 1700s. It was purchased

Navigational posts

Ca' Foscari

by a French tycoon and now displays a contemporary art collection.

⓫ *Ca' Rezzonico*

Up ahead, the Accademia Bridge leads over the Grand Canal to the **Accademia Gallery** (right side), filled with the best Venetian paintings (see page 63). The bridge was put up in 1934 as a temporary structure. Locals liked it, so it stayed. It was rebuilt in 1984 in the original style.

⓬ *Accademia*

From here, look through the graceful bridge and way ahead to enjoy a classic view of **La Salute Church,** topped by a crown-shaped dome supported by scrolls. This Church of Saint Mary of Good Health was built to thank God for delivering Venetians from the devastating plague of 1630 (which had killed about a third of the city's population).

The low, white building among greenery (100 yards ahead, on the right, between the Accademia Bridge and the church) is the **Peggy Guggenheim Collection.** The American heiress "retired" here, sprucing up a palace that had been abandoned mid-construction. Peggy willed the city her fine collection of modern art (see page 65).

As you approach the next stop, notice on the right how the line of higgledy-piggledy palaces evokes old-time Venice. Two doors past the Guggenheim, Palazzo Dario has a great set of characteristic **funnel-shaped chimneys.** These forced embers through a loop-the-loop channel until they were dead—required in the days when stone palaces were surrounded by humble, wooden buildings, and a live spark could make a merchant's workforce homeless. Three doors farther is the **Salviati building,** which once served as a glassworks. Its Art Nouveau mosaic, done in the early 20th century, features Venice as a queen being appreciated by the big shots of society.

⓭ *Santa Maria del Giglio*

Back on the left stands the fancy **Gritti Palace hotel.** Hemingway and Woody Allen both stayed here (but not together).

Take a deep whiff of Venice. What's all this nonsense about stinky canals? All I smell is my shirt.

⓮ *Salute*

The huge **La Salute Church** towers overhead as if squirted from a can of Catholic Reddi-wip.

As the Grand Canal opens up into the lagoon, the last building on the right with the golden ball is the 17th-century **Customs House,** which now houses the Punta della Dogana contemporary art museum. Its two bronze Atlases hold a statue of Fortune riding the ball. Arriving ships used to stop here to pay their tolls.

⓯ *San Marco*

Up ahead on the left, the green pointed tip of the Campanile marks **St. Mark's Square,** the political and religious center of Venice... and the final destination of this tour. You could get off at the San Marco stop and go straight to St. Mark's Square (and you'll

La Salute Church

Is Venice Sinking?

Venice has battled rising water levels since the fifth century. Several factors, both natural and artificially-constructed, cause Venice to flood about 100 times a year—usually from October until late winter—a phenomenon called the *acqua alta.*

Venice sits atop sediments deposited at the ancient mouth of the Po River, which are still settling. Early industrial projects, such as offshore piers and the bridge to the mainland, affected the sea floor and tidal cycles, making the city more vulnerable to flooding. Twentieth-century industry pumped massive amounts of groundwater out of the aquifer beneath the lagoon for nearly 50 years before the government stopped the practice in the 1970s. In the last century, Venice has sunk by about nine inches.

Meanwhile, the waters around Venice are rising, especially in winter. The notorious *acqua alta* happens when an unusually high tide combines with strong winds and a storm. When a storm—an area of low pressure—travels over a body of water, it pulls the surface of the water up into a dome. As strong sirocco winds from Africa blow storms north up the Adriatic, they push this high water ahead of the front, causing a surging tide. Add the worldwide sea-level rise that's resulted from climate change, and the high sea gets that much higher.

During the *acqua alta,* the first puddles appear in the center of paved squares, pooling around the limestone grates. These grates cover cisterns that long held Venice's only source of drinking water. Surrounded by the lagoon and beset by constant flooding, this city had no natural source of fresh water. For centuries, residents carried water from the mainland. In the ninth century, they devised a way to collect rainwater by using paved, cleverly sloped squares as catchment systems, with limestone filters covering underground clay tubs. Venice's population grew markedly once citizens could access fresh water from these "wells." Several thousand cisterns provided the city with drinking water up until 1884, when an aqueduct was built. Now the wells are capped, and rain drains from squares into the lagoon—or up from it, as the case may be.

In 2003, a consortium of engineering firms began construction on the MOSE Project. Named for the acronym of its Italian name, *Modulo Sperimentale Elettromeccanico,* it's also a nod to Moses and his (albeit temporary) mastery over the sea. Underwater gates are being installed on the floor of the sea at the three inlets where it enters Venice's lagoon. When the seawater rises above a certain level, air will be pumped into the gates, causing them to rise and shut out the Adriatic. The first gates are already installed, but, in good Italian fashion, corruption and scandal have surrounded the project. Combined with technical challenges, the completion date continues to get pushed into the future—the latest estimate is 2021. You can learn more about the project at www.mosevenezia.eu.

have to if you're on vaporetto #2, which terminates here). But I'm staying on the #1 boat for one more stop, just past St. Mark's Square (it's a quick walk back).

Survey the lagoon. Opposite St. Mark's Square, across the water, the ghostly white church with the pointy bell tower is **San Giorgio Maggiore,** with superb views of Venice's skyline (see page 63). Next to it is the residential island Giudecca, stretching from close to San Giorgio Maggiore to the Hilton Hotel (good nighttime view, far-right end of island).

Still on board? If you are, as we leave the San Marco stop, look left and prepare for a drive-by view of St. Mark's Square. First comes the bold white facade of the old mint (marked by a tiny cupola, where Venice's golden ducat, the "dollar" of the Venetian Republic, was made) and the library facade. Then come the twin columns, topped by St. Theodore and St. Mark, who have welcomed visitors since the 15th century. Between the columns, catch a glimpse of two giant figures atop the **Clock Tower**—they've been whacking their clappers every hour since 1499. The domes of **St. Mark's Basilica** are soon eclipsed by the lacy facade of the **Doge's Palace.** Next you'll see many gondolas with their green breakwater buoys, the **Bridge of Sighs** (leading from the palace to the prison—check out the maximum-security bars), and then the grand harborside promenade—the **Riva.**

Follow the Riva with your eye, past elegant hotels to the green area in the distance. This is the largest of Venice's few **parks,** which hosts the now-annual Biennale festival. Much farther in the distance is the **Lido,** the island with Venice's beach. Its sand and casinos are tempting, though its car traffic disrupts the medieval charm of Venice.

⑯ *San Zaccaria*

OK, you're at your last stop. Quick—muscle your way off this boat! (If you don't, you'll eventually end up at the Lido.)

At San Zaccaria, you're right in the thick of the action. A number of other vaporetti depart from here (see page 91). Otherwise, it's a short walk back along the Riva to St. Mark's Square. Ahoy!

The Campanile and Doge's Palace dominate the view of Venice from San Giorgio Maggiore.

SIGHTS

Venice's city museums offer youth and senior discounts to Americans and other non-EU citizens. Also, when you see a 🎧 in a listing, it means the sight is covered in a free audio tour (via my Rick Steves Audio Europe app—see page 28).

San Marco District

▲▲▲ST. MARK'S SQUARE (PIAZZA SAN MARCO)

This grand square is surrounded by splashy, historic buildings and sights: St. Mark's Basilica, Doge's Palace, the Campanile bell tower, and Correr Museum. The square is filled with music, lovers, tourists, and pigeons by day. It's your private rendezvous with the Venetian past late at night, when it becomes Europe's most romantic dance floor.

St. Mark's Basilica dominates the square with its Eastern-style onion domes and glowing mosaics. Mark Twain said it looked like "a vast warty bug taking a meditative walk."

With your back to the church, survey one of Europe's great urban spaces, and the only square in Venice to merit the title "Piazza." Nearly two football fields long, it's surrounded by the offices of the republic. On your right are the "old offices" (16th-century Renaissance). On your left are the "new offices" (17th-century High Renaissance). Napoleon called the piazza "the most beautiful drawing room in Europe," and added to the intimacy by building the final wing, opposite the basilica.

🎧 For a detailed explanation of St. Mark's Square, download my free **audio tour.**

Rick's Tip: *If you're* **bombed by a pigeon,** *resist the initial response to wipe it off immediately—it'll just smear into your hair. Wait until it dries, and it should flake off cleanly. But if the poop splatters on your clothes, wipe it off immediately to avoid a stain.*

▲▲▲ST. MARK'S BASILICA (BASILICA DI SAN MARCO)

Built in the 11th century, this basilica's distinctly Eastern-style architecture underlines Venice's connection with Byzantium (which protected it from the ambition of Charlemagne and his Holy Roman Empire). It's decorated with booty from returning sea captains—a Venetian trophy chest. The interior glows mysteriously with gold mosaics and colored marble. Since about A.D. 830, the saint's bones have been housed on this site. The San Marco Museum within holds the original bronze horses (copies of these overlook the square), and a balcony offering a remarkable view over St. Mark's Square.

Rick's Tip: *To* **avoid crowds** *at* **St. Mark's Basilica,** *go early or late or book a time online.*

Cost: Basilica entry is free, but you can pay €2 for an online reservation that lets you skip the line (well worth it).

Three separate exhibits within the church charge admission: the **Treasury** (€3, includes audioguide); **Golden Altarpiece** (€2); and **San Marco Museum** (€5). The San Marco Museum has the original bronze horses (copies of these overlook the square), a balcony offering a remarkable view over St. Mark's Square, and various works related to the church.

Hours: Church open Mon-Sat 9:45-17:00, Sun 14:00-17:00 (Sun until 16:00 Nov-Easter), interior brilliantly lit daily 11:30-12:30; museum open daily 9:45-16:45, including on Sunday mornings when the church itself is closed; if considering a Sunday visit, note that the museum has a balcony that provides a fine view down to the church's interior. The treasury and the Golden Altarpiece are both open Easter-Oct Mon-Sat 9:45-17:00, Sun 14:00-17:00; Nov-Easter Mon-Sat 9:45-16:00, Sun 14:00-16:00. On St. Mark's Square, vaporetto: San Marco or San Zaccaria, tel. 041-270-8311, www.basilicasanmarco.it.

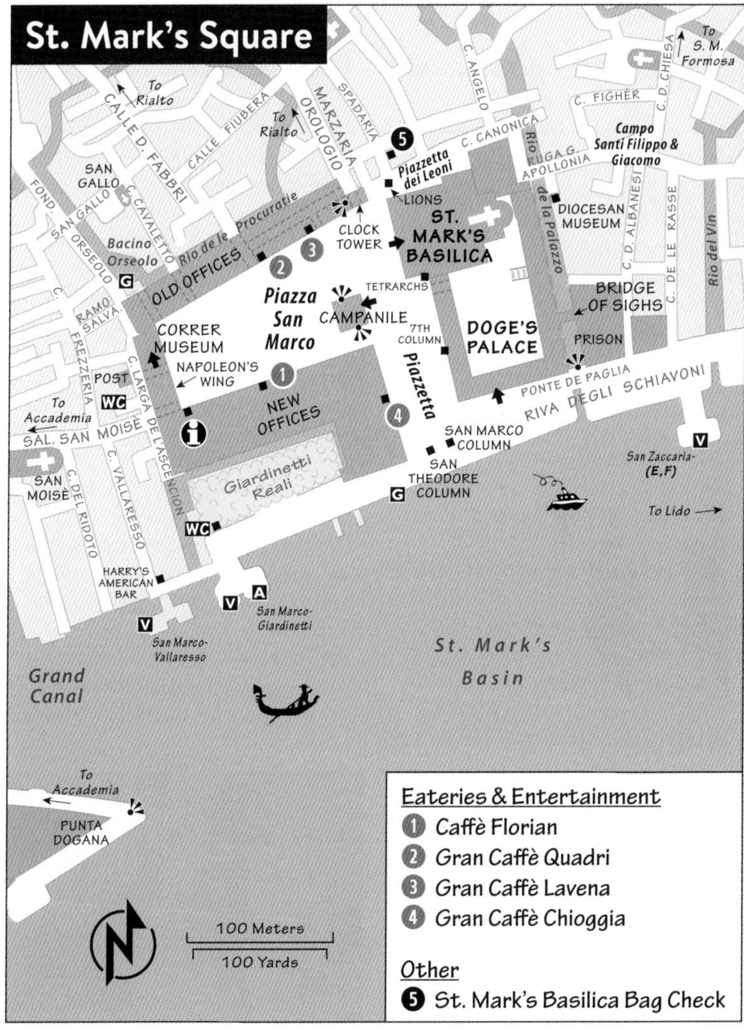

Theft Alert: St. Mark's Basilica is the most notorious place in Venice for pickpocketing—inside, it's always a crowded jostle.

Dress Code: Modest dress (no bare knees or bare shoulders) is strictly enforced for men, women, and even kids. Shorts are OK if they cover the knees.

Tours: Free, hour-long English **tours** (heavy on the mosaics' religious symbolism) are offered many days at 11:30 (meet in atrium, schedule varies, see schedule board just inside entrance).

Download my free St. Mark's Basilica **audio tour.**

Bag Check: Small purses and shoulder bags are usually allowed inside, but larger bags and backpacks are not. Check them for free for up to one hour at the nearby church called Ateneo San Basso, 30 yards to the left of the basilica, down narrow Calle San Basso (daily 9:30-17:00). Note that you generally can't check small bags that would be allowed inside.

Photography: No photos are allowed inside.

Rick's Tip: *Those* **checking large bags** *usually get to* **skip the line,** *as do their companions (at the guard's discretion). Leave your bag at Ateneo San Basso and pick up your claim tag. Take your tag to the basilica's tourist entrance. Keep to the left of the railing where the line forms and show your tag to the gatekeeper. He'll generally let you in ahead of the line.*

➲ SELF-GUIDED TOUR

• *Start outside in the square, far enough back to take in the whole facade. Then zero in on the details.*

❶ Exterior—Mosaic of Mark's Relics: The mosaic over the far left door shows two men (in the center, with crooked staffs) bearing a coffin with the body of St. Mark. Seven centuries after his death, his holy body was in Muslim-occupied Alexandria, Egypt. In A.D. 828, two visiting merchants of Venice "rescued" the body from the "infidels," hid it in a pork barrel (which was unclean to Muslims), and spirited it away to Venice.

• *Enter the atrium of the basilica, and look up and to the right into an archway decorated with fine mosaics.*

❷ Atrium—Mosaic of Noah's Ark and the Great Flood: In the scene to the right of the entry door, Noah and sons are sawing logs to build a boat. Below that are three scenes of Noah putting all species of animals into the ark, two by two. Across the arch, the flood drowns the wicked. Noah sends out a dove twice to see whether there's any dry land where he can dock. He finds it, leaves the ark with a gorgeous rainbow overhead, and offers a sacrifice of thanks to God.

• *Climb seven steps, pass through the doorway, and enter the nave. Just inside the door, step to the far left, stop, and let your eyes adjust.*

❸ The Nave—Mosaics and Greek-Cross Floor Plan: These golden mosaics are in the Byzantine style, though many

St. Mark's Basilica

Gold mosaics cover every surface of St. Mark's interior.

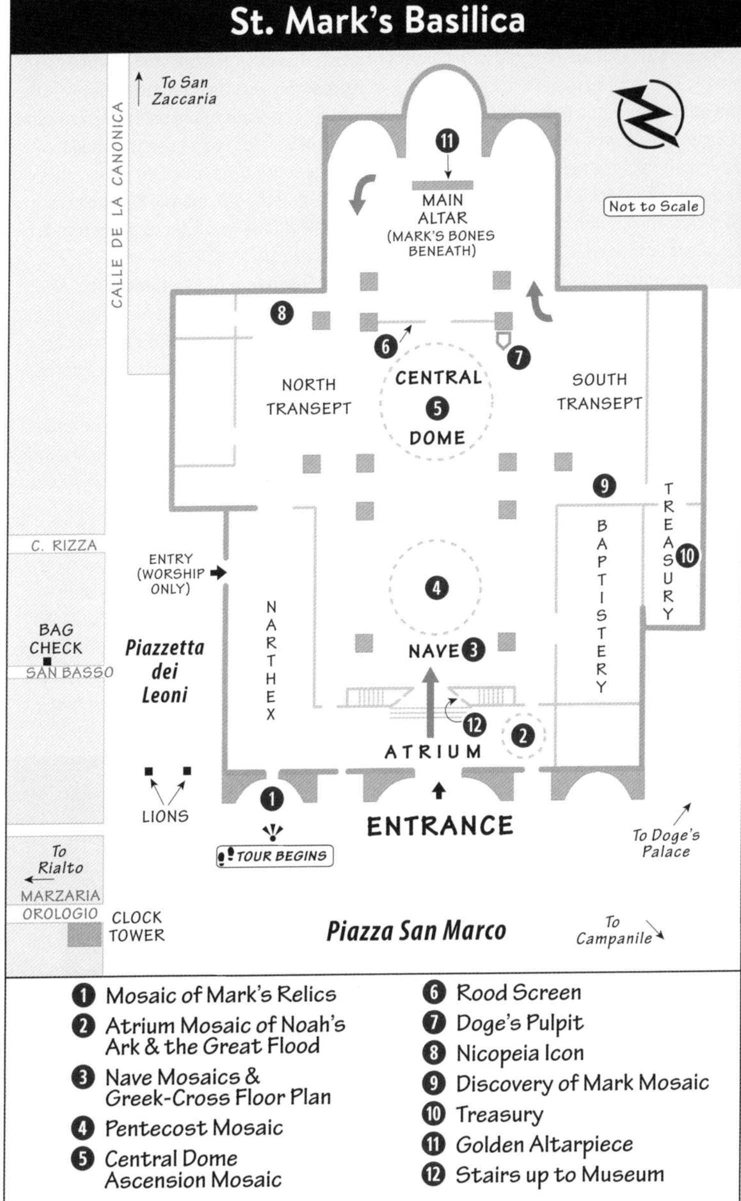

1. Mosaic of Mark's Relics
2. Atrium Mosaic of Noah's Ark & the Great Flood
3. Nave Mosaics & Greek-Cross Floor Plan
4. Pentecost Mosaic
5. Central Dome Ascension Mosaic
6. Rood Screen
7. Doge's Pulpit
8. Nicopeia Icon
9. Discovery of Mark Mosaic
10. Treasury
11. Golden Altarpiece
12. Stairs up to Museum

were designed by artists from the Italian Renaissance and later. The often-overlooked lower walls are covered with colorful marble slabs, cut to expose the grain, and laid out in geometric patterns. Even the floor is mosaic, with mostly geometrical designs. It rolls like the sea. Venice is sinking and shifting, creating these cresting waves of stone. The church is laid out with four equal arms, topped with domes, radiating from the center to form a Greek cross (+).

• *Find the chandelier near the entrance doorway (in the shape of a Greek cross cathedral space station), and run your eyes up the support chain to the dome above.*

❹ **Pentecost Mosaic:** In a golden heaven, the dove of the Holy Spirit shoots out a pinwheel of spiritual lasers, igniting tongues of fire on the heads of the 12 apostles below, giving them the ability to speak other languages without a Rick Steves phrase book. One of the oldest mosaics in the church (c. 1125), it has distinct "Byzantine" features: a gold background and apostles with halos, solemn faces, almond eyes, delicate hands, and rumpled robes, all facing forward.

• *Shuffle along with the crowds up to the central dome.*

❺ **Central Dome—Ascension Mosaic:** Gape upward to the very heart of the church. Christ—having lived his miraculous life and having been crucified for man's sins—ascends into the starry sky on a rainbow. In Byzantine churches, the window-lit dome represented heaven, while the dark church below represented earth.

Under the Ascension Dome: Look around at the church's furniture and imagine a service here. The ❻ rood screen, topped with 14 saints, separates the congregation from the high altar, heightening the "mystery" of the Mass. The ❼ pulpit on the right was reserved for the doge, who led prayers and made important announcements.

North Transept: In the north transept (to the left of the altar), today's Venetians pray to a painted wooden icon of Mary and Baby Jesus known as ❽ Nicopeia, or "Our Lady of Victory" (it's a small painting crusted over with a big stone canopy). In its day, this was the ultimate trophy—the actual icon used to protect the Byzantine army in war, looted by the Crusaders.

• *In the south transept (right of the main altar), find the dim mosaic high up on the three-windowed wall above the entrance to the treasury.*

❾ **Discovery of Mark Mosaic:** This mosaic isn't a biblical scene; it depicts the miraculous event that capped the construction of the present church. (It's high up and hard to read.)

It's 1094, the church is nearly complete (see the domes shown in cutaway fashion), and they're all set to re-inter Mark's bones under the new altar. There's just one problem: During the decades of construction, they forgot where they'd stored his body!

So (on the left), all of Venice gathers inside the church to bow down and pray for help finding the bones. The doge (from the Latin *dux*, meaning leader) leads them. Soon after (the right half),

San Marco Museum offers close-up views of mosaics.

(A) The altar and tomb of St. Mark

(B) Mosaic showing St. Mark's body being carried into the church

(C) Noah's Ark mosaic

(D) Central dome and the Ascension mosaic

the patriarch (far right) is inspired to look inside a hollow column where he finds the relics. Everyone turns and applauds, including the womenfolk, who stream in from the upper-floor galleries. The relics were soon placed under the altar in a ceremony that inaugurated the current structure.

Additional Sights: The ⓾ **Treasury** (Tesoro; ask for the included and informative audioguide when you buy your ticket) and ⓫ **Golden Altarpiece** (Pala d'Oro) give you the easiest way outside of Istanbul or Ravenna to see the glories of the Byzantine Empire. Venetian crusaders looted the Christian city of Constantinople and brought home piles of lavish loot (perhaps the lowest point in Christian history until the advent of TV evangelism). Much of this plunder is stored in the Treasury of San Marco. Most of these treasures were made in about A.D. 500, while Western Europe was stuck in the Dark Ages. Beneath the high altar lies the body of St. Mark ("Marce") and the Golden Altarpiece, made of 250 blue-backed enamels with religious scenes, all set in a gold frame and studded with 15 hefty rubies, 300 emeralds, 1,500 pearls, and assorted sapphires, amethysts, and topaz (c. 1100).

In the ⓬ **San Marco Museum** (Museo di San Marco) upstairs, you can see an up-close mosaic exhibition, a fine view of the church interior, a view of the square from the balcony with bronze horses, and (inside, in their own room) the original horses, which were stolen from Constantinople during the notorious Fourth Crusade. The staircase up to the museum is in the atrium, near the basilica's main entrance, marked by a sign in English.

▲▲▲DOGE'S PALACE (PALAZZO DUCALE)

The seat of the Venetian government and home of its ruling duke, or doge, this was the most powerful half-acre in Europe for 400 years. The Doge's Palace was built to show off the power and wealth of the Republic. The doge lived with his family on the first floor up, near the halls of power. From his once-lavish (now sparse) quarters, you'll follow the one-way tour through the public rooms of the top floor, finishing with the Bridge of Sighs and the prison. The place is wallpapered with masterpieces by Veronese and Tintoretto.

Cost and Hours: €20 combo-ticket includes Correr Museum, also covered by Museum Pass—see page 38, daily April-Oct 8:30-19:00, Nov-March until 17:30, last entry one hour before closing, café, photos allowed without flash, next to St. Mark's Basilica, just off St. Mark's Square, vaporetto stops: San Marco or San Zaccaria, tel. 041-271-5911, http://palazzoducale.visitmuve.it.

Rick's Tip: *To* **avoid long lines at the Doge's Palace,** *buy your combo-ticket at the* **Correr Museum** *across the square; then go straight to the Doge's Palace turnstile, skirting along to the right, entering at the "prepaid tickets" entrance. It's also possible to* **buy advance tickets online**—*at least 48 hours in advance—on the museum website (€0.50 fee). Or go later—crowds tend to diminish after 15:00.*

Tours: The **audioguide** tour is dry but informative (€5, 1.5 hours, need ID for deposit). For a 1.25-hour live **guided tour,** consider the Secret Itineraries Tour, which takes you into palace rooms otherwise not open to the public (€20, includes Doge's Palace admission but not Correr Museum admission; €14 with combo-ticket; three English-language tours each morning). Though the tour skips the palace's main hall, you're welcome to visit the hall afterward on your own. Reserve ahead for this tour in peak season—it can fill up as much as a month in advance. Book online (http://palazzoducale.visitmuve.it, €0.50 fee), or reserve by phone (tel. 848-082-000, from the US dial 011-39-041-4273-0892), or you can try just showing up at the info desk. Don't confuse this with the

Doge's Palace

Doge's Hidden Treasures Tour—it reveals little that would be considered a "treasure" and is a waste of money.

Visiting the Doge's Palace: You'll see the restored facades from the **courtyard.** Notice a grand staircase (with nearly naked Moses and Paul Newman at the top). Even the most powerful visitors climbed this to meet the doge. This was the beginning of an architectural power trip.

In the **Senate Hall,** the 120 senators met, debated, and passed laws. Tintoretto's large ***Triumph of Venice*** on the ceiling (central painting, best viewed from the top) shows the city in all its glory. Lady Venice is up in heaven with the Greek gods, while barbaric lesser nations swirl up to give her gifts and tribute.

The **Armory**—a dazzling display originally assembled to intimidate potential adversaries—shows remnants of the military might that the empire employed to keep the East-West trade lines open (and the Venetian economy booming).

The giant **Hall of the Grand Council** (175 feet by 80 feet, capacity 2,600) is where the entire nobility met to elect the senate and doge. It took a room this size to contain the grandeur of the Most Serene Republic. Ringing the top of the room are portraits of the first 76 doges (in chronological order). The one at the far end that's blacked out (in the left corner) is the notorious Doge Marin Falier, who opposed the will of the Grand Council in 1355. He was tried for treason, beheaded, and airbrushed from history.

On the wall over the doge's throne is Tintoretto's monsterpiece, ***Paradise,*** the largest oil painting in the world. Christ and Mary are surrounded by a heavenly

Tintoretto, Triumph of Venice

host of 500 saints. The painting leaves you feeling that you get to heaven not by being a good Christian, but by being a good Venetian.

Cross the covered **Bridge of Sighs** over the canal to the **prisons.** Circle the cells. Notice the carvings made by prisoners—from olden days up until 1930—on some of the stone windowsills of the cells, especially in the far corner of the building.

Cross back over the Bridge of Sighs, pausing to look through the marble-trellised windows at all of the tourists.

More Sights on the Square

▲▲CORRER MUSEUM (MUSEO CORRER)

This uncrowded museum gives you a good, easy-to-manage overview of Venetian history and art. The doge memorabilia, armor, banners, statues (by Canova), and paintings (by the Bellini family and others) re-create the festive days of the Venetian Republic. And it's all accompanied by English descriptions and breathtaking views of St. Mark's Square. The Correr Museum is a quiet refuge—a place to rise above St. Mark's Square when the piazza is too hot, too rainy, or too crowded.

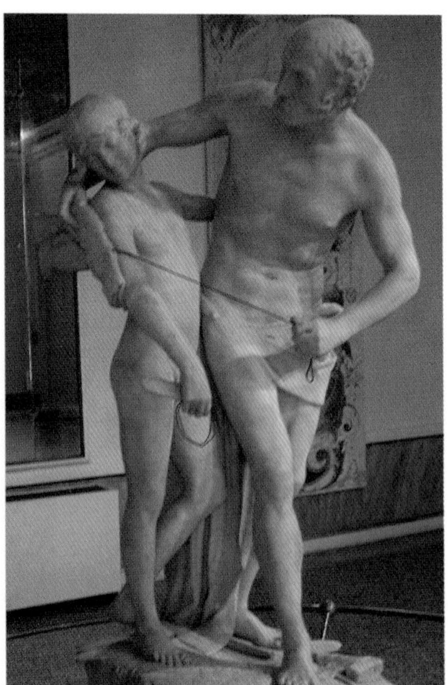

Canova, Daedalus and Icarus

Cost and Hours: €20 combo-ticket also includes the Doge's Palace; for €12 you can see the Correr Museum and tour the Clock Tower on St. Mark's Square, but this ticket doesn't include the Doge's Palace; daily April-Oct 10:00-19:00, Nov-March 10:00-17:00, last entry one hour before closing; bag check free and mandatory for bags bigger than a large purse, no photos, elegant café; enter at far end of square directly opposite basilica, tel. 041-240-5211, http://correr.visitmuve.it.

▲CAMPANILE (CAMPANILE DI SAN MARCO)

This dramatic bell tower replaced a shorter tower, part of the original fortress that guarded the entry of the Grand Canal. That tower crumbled into a pile of bricks in 1902, a thousand years after it was built. Ride the elevator 325 feet to the top for the best view in Venice (especially at sunset). For an ear-shattering experience, be on top when the bells ring. The golden archangel Gabriel at the top always faces into the wind. Avoid the crowds and enjoy the crisp morning air at 9:00 or the cool evening breeze at 18:00.

Rick's Tip: Beat the crowds *at* **the Campanile** *by going early or going late (it's open until 21:00 from spring through fall). Or head to the similar* **San Giorgio Maggiore bell tower** *across the lagoon. The lines are shorter and the view is just as good.*

Cost and Hours: €8, daily April-mid-Oct 8:30-21:00, mid-Oct-April 9:30-17:30, last entry 45 minutes before closing, may close during thunderstorms, audioguide-€3, tel. 041-522-4064, www.basilicasanmarco.it.

CLOCK TOWER (TORRE DELL'OROLOGIO)

The clock tower, built during the Renaissance in 1496, marks the entry to the main shopping drag, called the Mercerie (or "Marzarie," in Venetian dialect), which connects St. Mark's Square with the Rialto Bridge. From the square, you can see the bronze men (Moors) swing their huge clappers at the top of each hour. In the 17th century, one of them knocked an unsuspecting worker off the top and to his death—probably the first-ever killing by a robot. Notice one of the world's first "digital" clocks on the tower facing the square (the time flips every five minutes). You can go inside the clock tower with a pre-booked guided tour that takes you close to the clock's innards and out to a terrace with good views over the square.

Cost and Hours: €12 combo-ticket includes Correr Museum—where the tour starts—but doesn't cover Doge's Palace; €7 for the tour if you already have a Museum Pass or Correr/Doge's Palace combo-ticket; tours in English Mon-Wed at 10:00 and 11:00, Thu-Sun at 14:00 and 15:00; no kids under age 6.

Reservations: The mandatory tour requires reservations; call 848-082-000 or book online at http://torreorologio.visitmuve.it. You can also try dropping by the Correr Museum for same-day reservations.

Behind St. Mark's Basilica

▲BRIDGE OF SIGHS

This much-photographed bridge connects the Doge's Palace with the prison. Supposedly, a condemned man would be led over this bridge on his way to the prison, take one last look at the glory of Venice, and sigh—a notion popularized in the Romantic 19th century. Though overhyped, it's undeniably tingle-worthy—especially after dark, when the crowds have dispersed and it's just you and floodlit Venice.

Getting There: The Bridge of Sighs is around the corner from the Doge's Palace. From the palace, walk toward the waterfront, turn left along the water, and look up the first canal on your left. You can walk across the bridge (from the inside) by visiting the Doge's Palace. During the middle of the day, however, being immersed in the pandemonium of global tourism (and selfie sticks) can be a fascinating experience in itself.

Across the Lagoon from St. Mark's Square

▲SAN GIORGIO MAGGIORE

This is the dreamy church-topped island you can see from the waterfront by St. Mark's Square. The striking church, designed by Palladio, features art by Tintoretto, a bell tower, and good views of Venice.

Cost and Hours: Free entry to church; daily 9:00-19:00, Nov-March 8:30-18:00. The bell tower costs €6 and is accessible by elevator (runs until 20 minutes before the church closes but is not accessible Sun during services).

Getting There: To reach the island from St. Mark's Square, take the one-stop, five-minute ride on vaporetto #2 from San Zaccaria (single ticket-€5, 6/hour; direction: Tronchetto).

Dorsoduro District

▲▲ACCADEMIA (GALLERIA DELL'ACCADEMIA)

Venice's top art museum, packed with highlights of the Venetian Renaissance, features paintings by the Bellini family, Titian, Tintoretto, Veronese, Tiepolo, Giorgione, Canaletto, and Testosterone. It's just over the wooden Accademia Bridge from the San Marco action.

Cost and Hours: €15, free first Sun of the month, Mon 8:15-14:00, Tue-Sun 8:15-19:15, last entry one hour before closing, dull audioguide-€6, no flash photos allowed. At Accademia Bridge, vaporetto: Accademia, tel. 041-522-2247, www.gallerieaccademia.org.

Rick's Tip: *Just 400 people are allowed into the* **Accademia** *gallery at one time. It's most crowded on Tuesday mornings and whenever it rains;* **it's least crowded Wednesday, Thursday, and Sunday mornings** *(before 10:00) and late afternoons (after 17:00). It's possible to book tickets in advance (€1.50/ticket surcharge; online at www.gallerieaccademia.org or call 041-520-0345), but it's unnecessary if you avoid the busiest times.*

Renovation: The museum is nearing the end of a major, multiyear expansion and renovation. As a result, paintings come and go, and the actual locations of the pieces are hard to pin down. Still, the museum contains the best art in Venice. If you don't find a particular piece you'd like to see, check Room 23, which seems to be the holding pen for displaced art.

Visiting the Accademia: The Accademia is the greatest museum anywhere for Venetian Renaissance art and a good overview of painters whose works you'll see all over town. Venetian art is underrated and misunderstood. It's nowhere near as famous today as the work of the Florentine Renaissance, but it's livelier, more colorful, and simply more fun, with historical slices of Venice, ravishing nudes, and very human Madonnas. The Venetian love of luxury shines through in this collection, which starts in the Middle Ages and runs to the 1700s. Look for grand canvases of colorful, spacious settings, peopled with happy locals in extravagant clothes having a great time.

Medieval highlights include elaborate altarpieces and golden-haloed Madonnas, all painted at a time when realism, depth of field, and emotion were considered beside the point. Medieval Venetians, with their close ties to the East, borrowed techniques such as gold-leafing, frontal poses, and "iconic" faces from the religious icons of Constantinople (modern-day Istanbul).

Among early masterpieces of the Renaissance are Mantegna's studly *St. George* and Giorgione's mysterious *Tempest*. As the Renaissance reaches its heights, so do the paintings, such as Titian's magnificent *Presentation of the Virgin*. It's a religious scene, yes, but it's really just an excuse to display secular splendor (Titian was the most famous painter of his day—perhaps even more famous than Michelangelo). Veronese's sumptuous *Feast in the House of Levi* also has an ostensibly religious theme (in the middle, find Jesus eating his final

Bridge of Sighs

San Giorgio Maggiore

meal)—but it's outdone by the luxury and optimism of Renaissance Venice. Life was a good thing and beauty was to be enjoyed. (Veronese was hauled before the Inquisition for painting such a bawdy Last Supper...so he fine-tuned the title.) End your tour with Guardi's and Canaletto's painted "postcards" of the city—landscapes for visitors who lost their hearts to the romance of Venice.

▲▲PEGGY GUGGENHEIM COLLECTION

The popular museum of far-out art, housed in the American heiress' former retirement palazzo, offers one of Europe's best reviews of the art of the first half of the 20th century. Stroll through styles represented by artists whom Peggy knew personally—Cubism (Picasso, Braque), Surrealism (Dalí, Ernst), Futurism (Boccioni), American Abstract Expressionism (Pollock), and a sprinkling of Klee, Calder, and Chagall.

Cost and Hours: €15, usually includes temporary exhibits, Wed-Mon 10:00-18:00, closed Tue, audioguide-€7, pricey café, 5-minute walk from Accademia Bridge, vaporetto: Accademia or Salute, tel. 041-240-5411, www.guggenheim-venice.it.

▲LA SALUTE CHURCH (SANTA MARIA DELLA SALUTE)

This impressive church with a crown-shaped dome was built and dedicated to the Virgin Mary by grateful survivors of the 1630 plague.

Cost and Hours: Free entry to church, €4 to enter sacristy; daily 9:00-12:00 & 15:00-17:30, 10-minute walk from Accademia Bridge, vaporetto: La Salute, tel. 041-274-3928.

▲CA' REZZONICO (MUSEUM OF 18TH-CENTURY VENICE)

This Grand Canal palazzo offers the most insightful look at the life of Venice's rich and famous in the 1700s. Wander under ceilings by Tiepolo, among furnishings from that most decadent century, enjoying views of the canal and paintings by Guardi, Canaletto, and Longhi.

Cost and Hours: €10, Wed-Mon 10:00-18:00, Nov-March until 17:00, closed Tue year-round, audioguide-€4; last entry one hour before closing, no flash photography, café, vaporetto: Ca' Rezzonico, tel. 041-241-0100, http://carezzonico.visitmuve.it.

San Polo District

▲▲▲RIALTO BRIDGE

One of the world's most famous bridges, this distinctive and dramatic stone structure crosses the Grand Canal with a single confident span. The arcades along the top of the bridge help reinforce the structure... and offer some enjoyable shopping diversions, as does the **market** surrounding the bridge (produce market closed Sun, fish market closed Sun-Mon).

Veronese, Feast in the House of Levi

FONDACO DEI TEDESCHI (GERMAN EXCHANGE)

This luxury "mall," with fantastic views from its roof terrace, occupies a block-long building that was once the long-ago home to Germanic traders (*tedeschi*) in the city, and more recently the main post office. The ground floor features gourmet food shops, ritzy cafés, classy Venetian souvenirs, and free WCs.

Cost and Hours: Free, daily 10:00-20:00, longer hours in summer, less crowded in the morning, most crowded near sunset, north side of Rialto Bridge, www.tfondaco.com.

▲▲FRARI CHURCH (BASILICA DI SANTA MARIA GLORIOSA DEI FRARI)

My favorite art experience in Venice is seeing art in the setting for which it was designed—as it is at the Frari Church. The Franciscan "Church of the Brothers" and the art that decorates it are warmed by the spirit of St. Francis. It features the work of three great Renaissance masters: Donatello, Giovanni Bellini, and Titian—each showing worshippers the glory of God in human terms.

Cost and Hours: €3, Mon-Sat 9:00-18:00, Sun 13:00-18:00, modest dress recommended, no flash photos, on Campo dei Frari, near San Tomà vaporetto and *traghetto* stops, tel. 041-272-8618, www.basilicadeifrari.it.

Tours: You can rent an **audioguide** for €2, or ⓘ download my free Frari Church **audio tour.**

Visiting the Frari Church: In **Donatello's wood statue of *St. John the Baptist*** (just to the right of the high altar), the prophet of the desert—dressed in animal skins and nearly starving from his diet of bugs 'n' honey—announces the coming of the Messiah. Donatello was a Florentine working at the dawn of the Renaissance.

Bellini's *Madonna and Child with Saints and Angels* painting (in the sacristy farther to the right) came later, done by a Venetian in a more Venetian style—soft focus without Donatello's harsh realism. While Renaissance humanism demanded Madonnas and saints that were accessible and human, Bellini places them in a physical setting so beautiful that it creates its own mood of serene holiness. The genius of Bellini, perhaps the greatest Venetian painter, is obvious in the pristine clarity, rich colors (notice Mary's clothing), believable depth, and reassuring calm of this three-paneled altarpiece.

Finally, glowing red and gold like a stained-glass window over the high altar, **Titian's *Assumption of the Virgin*** sets the tone of exuberant beauty found in the otherwise sparse church. Titian the Venetian—a student of Bellini—painted steadily for 60 years...you'll see a lot of his art. As stunned apostles look up past the swirl of arms and legs, the complex composition of this painting draws you right to the radiant face of the once-dying, now-triumphant Mary as she joins God in heaven.

For many, these three pieces of art make a visit to the Accademia Gallery unnecessary (though they may whet your appetite for more). Before leaving, check out the Neoclassical pyramid-shaped Canova monument flanking the nave just inside the main entrance and (opposite that) the grandiose tomb of Titian. Compare the carved marble *Assumption* behind Titian's tombstone portrait with the painted original above the high altar.

▲▲SCUOLA SAN ROCCO

Sometimes called "Tintoretto's Sistine Chapel," this lavish meeting hall has some 50 large, colorful Tintoretto paintings plastered to the walls and ceilings. The best paintings are upstairs, especially the *Crucifixion* in the smaller room. View the neck-breaking splendor with the mirrors available in the Grand Hall.

Cost and Hours: €10, daily 9:30-17:30, no flash photography, next to the Frari Church, tel. 041-523-4864, www.scuolagrandesanrocco.it.

Venice's Lagoon

The island of Venice sits in a lagoon—a calm section of the Adriatic protected from wind and waves by the natural breakwater of the Lido. The Lido is Venice's beach—nice for a break on a sunny day.

Beyond the church-topped island of San Giorgio Maggiore (directly in front of St. Mark's Square), four interesting islands hide out in the lagoon: San Michele, Murano, Burano, and Torcello. These islands make a good, varied, and long day trip.

Getting to the Lagoon: You can travel to any of the islands by vaporetto. Because single vaporetto tickets (€7.50) expire after 75 minutes, getting a vaporetto pass (€20/24 hours) for a lagoon excursion makes more sense.

For a route that takes you to all four islands, start at the **Fondamente Nove** vaporetto stop on the north shore of Venice (the "back" of the fish). Lines #4.1 and #4.2 converge here before heading out to Murano. Catch either one (every 10 minutes); you'll first cross to San Michele (which has a stop called Cimitero) in six minutes, then continue another three minutes to Murano-Colonna. Stroll through Murano, then leave that island from a different stop: Murano-Faro, where you can board vaporetto #12 for the 30-minute trip to Burano. From Burano, you can side-trip to Torcello on vaporetto #12 (5-minute trip each way, make sure it stops at Torcello). To make a quick return to Venice from Burano, hop vaporetto #12 (some of these skip Torcello), which returns you to Fondamente Nove (45 minutes).

SAN MICHELE (A.K.A. CIMITERO)

This is the cemetery island—and the final resting place of a few foreign VIPs, from poet Ezra Pound to composer Igor Stravinsky. The stopover is easy, since **vaporetti** come every 10 minutes. If you enjoy wandering through old cemeteries, you'll dig this one—it's full of flowers, trees, and birdsong, and has an intriguing chapel (cemetery open daily 7:30-18:00, Oct-March until 16:30; reception to the left as you enter, free WC to the right).

▲MURANO

Murano is famous for its glassmaking. From the Colonna vaporetto stop, skip

Frari Church

Titian, Assumption of the Virgin

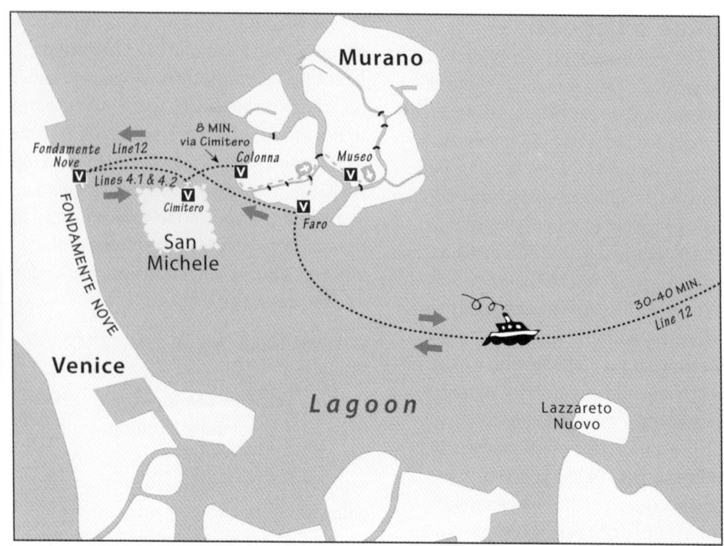

the glass shops in front of you, walk to the right, and wander up the street along the canal, **Fondamenta dei Vetrai** (Glassmakers' Embankment). The Faro district of Murano, on the other side of the canal, is packed with factories *(fabriche)* and their furnaces *(fornaci)*. You'll pass dozens of **glass shops.** Early along this promenade, at #47, is the venerable **Venini** shop, with glass a cut above the rest, and with an interior showing off the ultimate in modern Venetian glass design (Mon-Sat 9:30-18:00, closed Sun).

Murano's **Glass Museum** (Museo Vetrario) traces the history of this delicate art (€10, daily 10:00-18:00, Nov-March until 17:00, last entry one hour before closing, tel. 041-739-586, http://museovetro.visitmuve.it).

Rick's Tip: *Venetian glass blowers claim that much of the cheap glass you'll see in Venice is imported from China.* **Genuine Venetian glass** *comes with the Murano seal.*

▲▲BURANO

Known for lacemaking, Burano offers a delightful, vibrantly colorful village alternative to big, bustling Venice. The tight **main drag** is packed with tourists and lined with shops, selling lace or Burano's locally pro-

Murano's Fondamenta dei Vetrai

Firing up the glass furnace on Murano

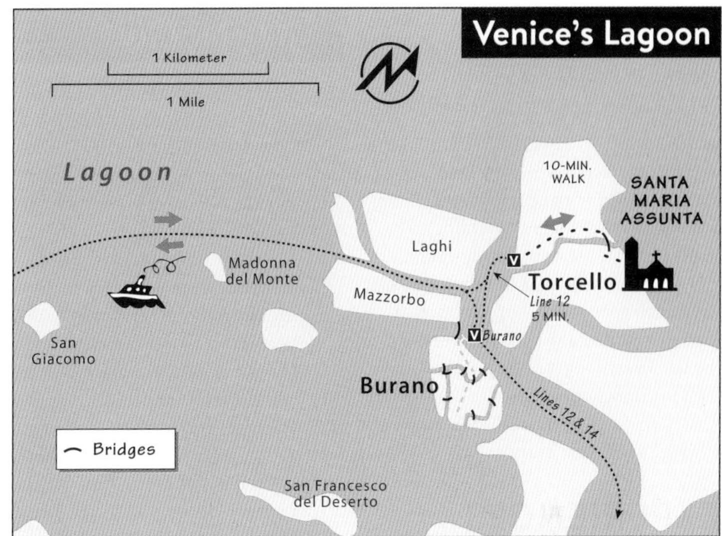

duced white wine. Wander to the far side of the island, and the mood shifts. Explore to the right of the leaning tower for a peaceful yet intensely colorful, small-town lagoon world. Benches line a little promenade at the water's edge—a pretty picnic spot.

Burano's **Lace Museum** (Museo del Merletto di Burano) shows the island's lace heritage (€5, Tue-Sun 10:00-18:00, Nov-March until 17:00, closed Mon year-round, tel. 041-730-034, http://museomerletto.visitmuve.it).

▲TORCELLO

This is the birthplace of Venice, where some of the first mainland refugees settled, escaping the barbarian hordes. Today, it's marshy and shrub-covered, the least-developed island (pop. 20). There's little to see except the church (a 10-minute walk from the dock; the oldest in Venice, and still sporting some impressive mosaics), a climbable bell tower, and a modest museum of Roman sculpture and medieval sculpture and manuscripts (€12 combo-ticket covers museum, church, and bell tower; €9 combo-ticket covers church and bell tower; both combo-tickets include audioguide; museum only—€3; church and bell tower—€5 each; church open daily March-Oct 10:30-18:00, Nov-Feb 10:00-17:00, museum

Colorful Burano

Burano lace is prized.

and campanile close 30 minutes earlier and museum closed Mon year-round; museum tel. 041-730-761, church tel. 041-730-119).

▲LIDO

Venice's nearest beach is the Lido, across the lagoon on an island connected to the mainland (which means car traffic). The sandy beach is pleasant, family-friendly, and good for swimming. Rent an umbrella, buy beach gear at the shop, get food at the self-service café, or have a drink at the bar. Everything is affordable and in the same building (vaporetto: Lido S.M.E., walk 10 minutes on Gran Viale S. Maria Elisabetta to beach entry).

EXPERIENCES

Gondola Rides

Riding a gondola is simple, expensive, and one of the great experiences in Europe. Gondoliers hanging out all over town are eager to have you hop in for a ride. It's a rip-off for cynics, but a must for romantics.

The price for a gondola starts at €80 for a 35-minute ride during the day. You can divide the cost—and the romance—among up to six people per boat, but only two get the love seat. Prices jump to €100 after 19:00—when it's most romantic and relaxing. Adding a singer and an accordionist will cost an additional €120. If you value budget over romance, save money by recruiting fellow travelers to split a

A gondola station

A Dying City?

Venice's population (fewer than 55,000 in the historic city) is half what it was just 30 years ago, and people are leaving at a rate of a thousand a year. Of those who stay, 25 percent are 65 or older.

Sad, yes, but imagine raising a family here: Apartments are small, high up, and expensive. Humidity and occasional flooding make basic maintenance a pain. Home-improvement projects require navigating miles of red tape, and you must follow regulations intended to preserve the historical ambience. Everything is expensive because it has to be shipped in from the mainland. You can easily get glass and tourist trinkets, but it's hard to find groceries or get your shoes fixed. Running basic errands involves lots of walking and stairs—imagine crossing over arched bridges while pushing a child in a stroller and carrying a day's worth of groceries.

With millions of visitors a year (150,000 a day at peak times), on any given day Venetians are likely outnumbered by tourists. Despite government efforts to subsidize rents and build cheap housing, the city is losing its residents. The economy itself is thriving, thanks to tourist dollars and rich foreigners buying second homes. But the culture is dying. Even the most hopeful city planners worry that in a few decades Venice will not be a city at all, but a museum, a cultural theme park, a decaying Disneyland for adults.

A gondola ride at night is worth the price.

gondola. Prices are standard and listed on the gondoliers' association website (go to www.gondolavenezia.it, click on "Using the Gondola," and look under "charterage").

Rick's Tip: *For* **cheap gondola thrills** *during the day, stick to the €2 one-minute ferry ride on a Grand Canal* traghetto. *At night, vaporetti are nearly empty, and it's a great time to cruise the Grand Canal on slow boat #1.*

Dozens of gondola stations *(servizio gondole)* are set up along canals all over town. Because your gondolier may offer narration or conversation during your ride, talk with several and choose one you like. Review the map and discuss the route; it's a good way to see if you enjoy the gondolier's personality and language skills. Establish the price, route, and duration of the trip before boarding, enjoy your ride, and pay only when you're finished. While prices are pretty firm, you might find them softer during the day. Most gondoliers honor the official prices, but a few might try for some extra euros, particularly by insisting on a tip. (While not required or even expected, if your gondolier does the full 35 minutes and entertains you en route, a 5-10 percent tip is appreciated; if he's surly or rushes through the trip, skip it.) While gondoliers can be extremely charming, locals say that anyone who falls for one of these Venetian Romeos "has slices of ham over her eyes."

If you've hired musicians and want to hear a Venetian song *(un canto Veneziano)*, try requesting *"Venezia La Luna e Tu."* Asking to hear *"O Sole Mio"* (which comes from Naples) is like asking a Chicago lounge singer to sing "Swanee River."

It's worth the extra cost to experience a gondola ride at night. The moon sails past otherwise unseen buildings and silhouettes gaze down from bridges while window glitter spills onto the black water. Put the camera down and make time for you and your partner to enjoy a threesome with Venice.

Festivals

Venice's most famous festival is **Carnevale,** the celebration Americans know as Mardi Gras (usually late Jan to early Feb, www.carnevale.venezia.it). Carnevale, which means "farewell to meat," originated as a wild, two-month-long party leading up to the austerity of Lent. In its heyday—the 1600s and 1700s—you could do pretty much anything with anybody from any social class if you were wearing a mask. These days it's a tamer 18-day celebration, culminating in a huge dance lit with fireworks on St. Mark's Square. Some Venetians don masks and join in the fun; others skip town.

Every year, the city hosts the world-class **Venice Biennale International Art Exhibition,** alternating between art in odd years (the main event) and architecture in even years (much smaller). The exhibition spreads over the Arsenale and Giardini park (take vaporetto #1 or #2 to Giardini-Biennale; for details and an events calendar, see www.labiennale.org). The actual exhibition usually runs from June through November, but other loosely connected events—film, dance, theater—are held throughout the year (as early as February) in various venues.

Nightlife

You must experience Venice after dark. The city is quiet at night, as many tour groups (not mine) stay on the mainland and day-trippers return to their beach resorts and cruise ships. Gondolas cost more, but are worth it.

Check at the TI or the TI's website (www.turismovenezia.it) for listings of entertainment and events, including church concerts. The free monthly Un Ospite di Venezia lists all the latest events in English (free at fancy hotels, or check www.unospitedivenezia.it/en).

St. Mark's Square

Streetlamp halos, floodlit history, and a ceiling of stars make St. Mark's Square magic at midnight. After dark, **dueling café orchestras** entertain. They feature similar food, prices, and a three- to five-

Carnevale is a masked extravaganza.

The evening café scene on St. Mark's Square

piece combo playing a selection of classical and pop hits. You can hang out for free behind the tables (allowing you to move on easily to the next orchestra when the musicians take a break). Dancing on the square is free—and encouraged.

If you spring for a seat to enjoy a concert, expect to pay €15 and up (for a drink and the cover charge for music)—money well spent. It's acceptable to nurse a drink for an hour—you're paying for the music with the cover charge. To save money (but forego proximity to the music), you can sip your coffee at the bar, because the law limits the charge for coffee at a bar.

Caffè Florian (on the right as you face the church) is the most famous Venetian café and was one of the first places in Europe to serve coffee. The outside tables are the main action, but walk inside through the richly decorated rooms where Casanova, Lord Byron, Charles Dickens, and Woody Allen have all paid too much for a drink (an espresso—your cheapest option—costs €12.50: €6.50 for the coffee and a €6 cover charge when the orchestra is playing, daily 10:00-24:00, shorter hours in winter, www.caffeflorian.com).

Gran Caffè Quadri, opposite the Florian, has equally illustrious clientele, including the writers Stendhal and Dumas, and composer Richard Wagner.

The scene at **Gran Caffè Lavena,** near the Clock Tower, can be great, despite its politically incorrect but dazzling chandelier.

Gran Caffè Chioggia, on the Piazzetta facing the Doge's Palace, charges no cover and has a few musicians playing—including a pianist—and a wider variety of tunes (no inside ambience, slightly cheaper than the others if you just want to sit on the square).

Rick's Tip: *You'll hear about the famous* **Harry's American Bar,** *which sells overpriced food and cocktails, but* **it's a tourist trap**...*and the last place Hemingway would drink today. It's cheaper to get a drink at any of the hole-in-the-wall bars just off St. Mark's Square.*

Concerts

Venice is a city of the Baroque era. For about €25, you can take your pick of traditional Vivaldi concerts in churches throughout town. You'll find young, frilly-costumed Vivaldis hawking concert tickets on many corners. Most shows start at 20:30 and generally last 1.5 hours. Hotels sell tickets at face-value.

Tickets can usually be bought the same day as the concert, so don't bother with websites that sell tickets with a surcharge. Musicians in wigs and tights offer better spectacle; musicians in black-and-white suits are better performers.

The **Interpreti Veneziani orchestra,** considered the best group in town, generally performs 1.5-hour concerts nightly at 21:00 inside the sumptuous San Vidal Church (€29, church ticket booth open daily 9:30-21:00, north end of Accademia Bridge, tel. 041-277-0561, www.interpretiveneziani.com).

Musica a Palazzo is an evening of opera at a Venetian palace on the Grand Canal. You'll spend about 45 delightful minutes each in three sumptuous rooms as eight musicians—usually four instruments and four singers—perform (about 2.25 hours total). They generally present three different operas on successive nights. With these surroundings,

under Tiepolo frescoes, you'll be glad you dressed up. There are only 70 seats, so book in advance by phone or online (€85, nightly at 20:30, Palazzo Barbarigo Minotto, Fondamenta Duodo o Barbarigo, vaporetto: Santa Maria del Giglio, San Marco 2504, mobile 340-971-7272, www.musicapalazzo.com).

EATING

While touristy restaurants are the scourge of Venice, my recommended places are popular with locals and respect the tourists who happen by.

First trick: Walk away from triple-language menus or laminated pictures of food. Second trick: Eat fish. Many seafood dishes are the catch-of-the-day. Note that seafood (and steak) may be sold by weight—per 100 grams or *etto*—rather than a set price; be savvy or be surprised. Third trick: Eat later. A place that feels touristy at 19:00 can be filled with locals at 21:00.

Budget Eating: Unique to Venice, *cicchetti* bars specialize in small appetizers that can combine to make a quick, tasty meal (see "The Stand-Up Progressive Venetian Pub-Crawl Dinner" later in this section).

Takeout pizza is one of the cheapest ways to eat in Venice. Small hole-in-the-wall shops in every neighborhood sell takeout pizza—round, by the slice, or by weight. Takeout prices increase dramatically as you near the Rialto and St. Mark's Square.

The Rialto open-air market is great for picnic gatherers (closed Sun), though any respectable grocery *(alimentari)* will do. As for supermarkets, a handy **Co-op** is between St. Mark's and Campo Santa Maria Formosa (daily 8:30-22:00, on the corner of Salizada San Lio and Calle del Mondo Novo at Castello 5817). A **Conad** supermarket is in Dorsoduro (daily 8:00-23:00, vaporetto: San Basilio).

Gelato: Venice isn't known for its quality gelato but you'll still find good *gelaterie* in every Venetian neighborhood. Several cafés on St. Mark's Square have gelato counters in summer, including **Gran Caffè Lavena** (at #134) and **Todaro** (on the corner of the Piazzetta at #5, near the water and across from the Doge's Palace). **Gelatoteca Suso** serves delectable flavors on the San Marco side of the Rialto Bridge (next to recommended Rosticceria San Bartolomeo, on Calle de la Bissa). **Il Doge** also sells Sicilian-style granita, slushy ice with fresh fruit (on bustling Campo Santa Margarita).

Near the Rialto Bridge

North of the Bridge

These restaurants and wine bars are located beyond Campo Santi Apostoli, on or near the Strada Nova, the main drag going from Rialto toward the train station.

$$$ Trattoria da Bepi, bright and alpine-paneled, feels like a classic, where Loris carries on his mother's passion for good, traditional Venetian cuisine. Ask for the seasonal specialties: The seafood appetizer plate and crab dishes are excellent. There's good seating inside and out. If you trust Loris, you'll walk away with a wonderful dining memory (Fri-Wed 12:00-14:30 & 19:00-22:00, closed Thu, reservations recommended, half a block

Venetian Cuisine

Venetian cuisine relies heavily on fish, shellfish, risotto, and polenta.

Antipasti: Popular choices include *antipasto di mare* (a marinated mix of fish and shellfish served chilled) and *sarde in saor* (sardines marinated with onions). *Cicchetti* are Venetian tapas, the finger-food appetizers served in some pubs.

First courses *(primi)*: Venice's favorite dish is risotto, a short-grain rice simmered in broth and often flavored with seafood (*risotto nero* is risotto made with squid and its ink; *risotto ai porcini* contains porcini mushrooms). Other first courses are *risi e bisi* (rice and peas), *pasta e fagioli* (pasta and bean soup), and *bigoli in salsa* (fat whole-wheat noodles with anchovy sauce). Pasta is commonly served *alla buzzara* (with a rich seafood-tomato sauce). You'll also see plenty of polenta—boiled cornmeal served soft or cut into firm slabs and grilled.

Second courses *(secondi)*: It's mostly *frutti di mare* (seafood). The most common fish are farmed, not wild—such as *branzino* (sea bass), *orata* (sea bream), *salmone* (salmon), and *rombo* (turbot, a flounder-like flatfish). The weirder the animal (eel, octopus, frogfish), the more local it is. *Baccalà* is dried Atlantic salt cod that's rehydrated and often served with polenta. Other choices are calamari, *cozze* (mussels, often steamed in broth), *gamberi* (shrimp), *moleche col pien* (fried soft-shell crabs), *pesce spada* (swordfish), *rospo* (frogfish, a small marine fish), *seppia* (cuttlefish, a squid-like creature; can be served in its own ink, often over spaghetti); *sogliola* (sole, served poached or oven-roasted), *vitello di mare* ("sea veal," like swordfish—firm, pink, mild, and grilled), and *vongole* (small clams, often steamed with herbs and wine). *Fritto misto di pesce* is assorted deep-fried seafood (often calamari and prawns). *Zuppa di pesce* is seafood stew.

Pasta with shellfish is a favorite.

Cocktails: The most popular *aperitivo* (pre-dinner drink) is *spritz,* which mixes white wine, soda or prosecco, and ice with either Campari (bitter) or Aperol (sweeter), garnished with an olive or skewer of fruit. Other options include the *bellini* (prosecco and white-peach puree) and *tiziano* (grape juice and prosecco). A popular *digestivo* (after-dinner drink) is *sgroppino:* squeezed lemon juice, lemon gelato, and vodka.

off Campo Santi Apostoli on Salizada Pistor, Cannaregio 4550, tel. 041-528-5031, www.dabepi.it).

$$$$ Vini da Gigio, a more expensive option, has a traditional Venetian menu and a classy but unsnooty setting that's a pleasant mix of traditional and contemporary (Wed-Sun 12:00-14:30 & 19:00-22:30, closed Mon-Tue, 4 blocks from Ca' d'Oro vaporetto stop on Fondamenta San Felice, behind the church on Campo San Felice, Cannaregio 3628a, tel. 041-528-5140, www.vinidagigio.com).

East of the Rialto Bridge

The next few places hide away in the

twisty lanes between the Rialto Bridge and Campo Santa Maria Formosa. Osteria da Alberto is a tad farther north of the others, in Cannaregio.

$ Rosticceria Gislon is a cheap—if confusing—self-service diner. This throwback budget eatery—kind of an Italian Mel's Diner—has a surly staff: Don't take it personally. Notice that the different counters serve up different types of food—pastas, *secondi,* fried goodies, and so on. You can get it to go, grab one of the few tiny tables, or munch at the bar—but I'd skip their upper-floor restaurant option (prices listed on wall behind counter, cheap glasses of wine, no cover and no service charge, daily 9:00-21:30, San Marco 5424, tel. 041-522-3569). To find it, imagine the statue on Campo San Bartolomeo walks backward 20 yards, turns left, and goes under a passageway. Follow him.

$$ Osteria al Portego is a small and popular neighborhood eatery near Campo San Lio. Carlo serves good meals, bargain-priced house wine, and excellent €1-3 *cicchetti* appetizers—best enjoyed early, around 18:00. The *cicchetti* here can make a great meal, but consider sitting down for a dinner from their menu. From 12:00-14:30 & 17:30-21:30, their six tables are reserved for those ordering from the menu; the *cicchetti* are picked over by 21:00. Reserve ahead if you want a table (daily 11:30-15:00 & 17:30-22:00, on Calle de la Malvasia, Castello 6015, tel. 041-522-9038, www.osteriaalportego.it, Federica).

$$ Osteria da Alberto, up near Campo Santa Maria Novo, is one of my standbys. They offer up excellent daily specials: seafood dishes, pastas, and a good house wine in a woody and characteristic interior. It's smart to reserve at night—I'd request a table in front (daily 12:00-15:00 & 18:30-22:30; on Calle Larga Giacinto Gallina, midway between Campo Santi Apostoli and Campo San Zanipolo/Santi Giovanni e Paolo, and next to Ponte de la Panada bridge, Cannaregio 5401; tel. 041-523-8153, www.osteriadaalberto.it, run by Graziano and Giovanni).

Rialto Market Area

The north end of the Rialto Bridge is great for menu browsing, bar-hopping, drinks, and snacks, as well as sit-down restaurants. You'll find lots of hardworking hole-in-the-walls catering to locals needing a quick, affordable, tasty bite. It's crowded by day, nearly empty early in the evening, and packed with Venetian hipsters later.

My listings below include a stretch of dark and rustic pubs serving *cicchetti* (Venetian tapas), a strip of trendy places fronting the Grand Canal, and several places at the market and nearby. All but the last eatery **(Osteria al Ponte Storto)** are within 200 yards of the market and each other.

***Cicchetti* Bars:** The 100-yard-long "*Cicchetti* Strip," which starts two blocks inland from the Rialto Market (along Sotoportego dei Do Mori and Calle de le Do Spade), is beloved for its conviviality and tasty bar snacks. These four $ places (listed in the order you'll reach them, if coming from the Rialto Bridge) serve food all day, but the spread is best around noon (generally open daily 12:00-15:00 & 18:00-20:00 or 21:00, but the first two are closed Sun). Scout these places in advance to see which ambience appeals most to you. At each place, look for the list of snacks (around €1.50-2) and wine by the glass (about €1-3) at the bar or on the wall. **Bar all'Arco,** a bustling one-room joint, is particularly enjoyable for its tiny open-face sandwiches (closed Sun, San Polo 436; Francesco, Anna, Matteo). **Cantina Do Mori** has been famous with locals (since 1462) and savvy travelers (since 1982) for its fine wine and *francobolli,* a spicy selection of 20 tiny, mayo-soaked sandwiches nicknamed "stamps." Go here to be abused in a fine atmosphere—the frowns are part of the shtick. Be aware that prices add up quickly (closed Sun, can be shoulder-to-shoulder, San Polo 430). **Osteria ai Storti** is more

The Stand-Up Progressive Venetian Pub-Crawl Dinner

My favorite Venetian dinner is a pub crawl *(giro d'ombra)*—a tradition unique to Venice, where no cars means easy crawling. (*Giro* means stroll, and *ombra*—slang for a glass of wine—means shade, from the old days when a portable wine bar scooted with the shadow of the Campanile bell tower across St. Mark's Square.)

Venice's residential back streets hide characteristic bars *(bacari)* with countless trays of interesting toothpick munchies *(cicchetti)* and blackboards listing wines served by the glass. The *cicchetti* selection is best early, so start your evening by 18:00. Most bars are closed on Sunday. For a stress-free pub crawl, take a tour with Alessandro Schezzini (see page 39).

***Cicchetti* bars** have a social stand-up zone and cozy tables where you can sit down with your *cicchetti* or order from a simple menu. Food generally costs the same price whether you stand or sit. Crowds sometimes happily spill into the street.

While you can order a plate, Venetians prefer going one-by-one...sipping their wine and trying this...then give me one of those...and so on. Try deep-fried mozzarella cheese, gorgonzola, calamari, artichoke hearts, and anything ugly on a toothpick. *Crostini* (small toasted bread with a topping) are popular, as are marinated seafood, olives, and prosciutto with melon. Meat and fish (*pesce;* PESH-ay) can be expensive; veggies *(verdure)* are cheap, at about €3 for a meal-sized plate. In many places, there's a set price per food item (e.g., €1.50). To get a plate of assorted appetizers for €8, ask for *"Un piatto classico di cicchetti misti da €8"* (oon pee-AH-toh KLAH-see-koh dee cheh-KET-tee MEE-stee dah OH-toh eh-OO-roh). Bread sticks *(grissini)* are free.

Bar-hopping Venetians enjoy an *aperitivo*—a before-dinner drink. Boldly order a Bellini, a *spritz con Aperol,* or a Prosecco, and draw approving looks from the natives. A small glass of house red or white wine *(ombra rosso* or *ombra bianco)* or a small beer *(birrino)* costs about €1. *Vin bon,* Venetian for fine wine, is €2-6 per little glass. A good last drink is *fragolino,* the local sweet wine—*bianco* or *rosso.* It often comes with a little cookie *(biscotto)* for dipping.

of a sit-down place (tables inside and on street). It's run by Alessandro, who speaks English and enjoys helping educate travelers (daily, around corner from Cantina Do Mori on Calle San Matio, San Polo 819). **Cantina Do Spade** is expertly run by Francesco and is also good for sit-down meals (30 yards down Calle de le Do Spade from Osteria ai Storti at San Polo 860, tel. 041-521-0583).

Canalside Seating: What I call the "Bancogiro Stretch," just past the Rialto Bridge, between Campo San Giacomo and the Grand Canal, has some of Venice's best canalside seating. Unless otherwise noted, all are open daily and serve drinks, *cicchetti,* and inventive, somewhat pricey sit-down meals. While you can get a drink anytime, dinner is typically served only after 19:00 or 19:30. During meals, they charge more and limit table seating to those ordering full lunches or dinners; but between mealtimes you can enjoy a drink or a snack at fine prices. After dinner, this stretch—especially in the surrounding alleys that house low-rent bars—becomes a trendy nightspot. I list them in the order you'll reach them from the Rialto Bridge. **$$$ Bar Naranzaria** serves Italian dishes with a few Japanese options. **$$ Caffè Vergnano** is your cheapest option (vegan dishes and a busy microwave oven). **$$$ Osteria al Pesador** has a friendly staff and serves local specialties. **$$$ Osteria Bancogiro** has the best reputation for dinner, a passion for the best cheese, and good *cicchetti* options at the bar (nice €17 cheese plate, closed Mon, tel. 041-523-2061, www.osteriabancogiro.it). The more modern **$$ Bar Ancòra** has a live piano player crooning lounge music during busy times (*cicchetti* at the bar).

At the Market: $ Al Mercà ("At the Market"), a few steps away and off the canal, is a lively little nook with a happy crowd. The price list is clear, and the youthful crowd seems to enjoy connecting with curious tourists (stand at bar or in square—there are no tables and no interior, Mon-Sat 10:00-14:30 & 18:00-21:00, closed Sun, on Campo Cesare Battisti, San Polo 213).

$$$$ Ristorante Vini da Pinto is a tourist-friendly eatery facing the fish market, with a large menu and relaxing outdoor seating (make sure you're sitting at the right restaurant and not their neighbors). Enjoy the lunch-only fixed-price, three-course seafood meal for €17. Rick Steves readers receive a welcoming prosecco and a farewell *limoncello* and homemade biscotti (daily 11:30-23:00, Campo de le Becarie, San Polo 367a, tel. 041-522-4599).

Farther Inland, off Campo San Aponal: $$ Osteria al Ponte Storto, on a quiet canalside corner a block off the main drag, is worth seeking out for its good-value main dishes, daily specials, and peaceful location (Tue-Sun 12:00-15:00 & 18:00-21:45, closed Mon, down Calle Bianca from San Aponal church, San Polo 1278, tel. 041-528-2144).

Near St. Mark's Square

At **$$$$ Ristorante Antica Sacrestia,** Pino greets you personally. His staff serves creative fixed-price meals (€35, €55, or €80), a humdrum *menù del giorno,* and wonderful pizzas. (Be warned: Order carefully. Pizza is your only budget escape. And there's no wine by the glass.) You can also order à la carte; their €22 antipasto spread looks like a lagoon aquarium spread out on a plate. My readers are welcome to a free *sgroppino* (lemon vodka after-dinner drink) upon request (Tue-Sun 11:30-15:00 & 18:00-23:00, closed Mon, behind San Zaninovo/Giovanni Novo Church on Calle

Romantic Canalside Settings

If you want a meal with a canal view, it generally comes with lower quality and/or a higher price. But if you're determined to take home a canalside memory, these places can be great.

Near the Rialto Bridge: The "Bancogiro Stretch" offers fine places to enjoy a drink or a snack.

You'll also see tourist-trap eateries lining the Grand Canal just south of the Rialto Bridge. These places usually offer lousy food and aggressive "service." If you really want to eat here, ask if there's a minimum charge before you sit down (most places have one). The budget ideal would be to get a simple pizza or pasta and a drink for €15, and savor the ambience without getting ripped off. But few restaurants will allow you to get off that easy. To avoid a dispute over the bill, ask if there's a minimum charge before you sit down (most places have one).

In the Dorsoduro Neighborhood: $$ Bar Foscarini, next to the Accademia Bridge, offers decent pizzas overlooking the canal with no cover or service charge. **$$$ Terrazza dei Nobili,** overlooking the wide Giudecca Canal, is nice just before sunset. Both are listed under "In Dorsoduro" eateries.

Corona, Castello 4463, tel. 041-523-0749, www.anticasacrestia.it).

For a quick meal just steps away from St. Mark's Square, try **"Sandwich Row"**—Calle de le Rasse. The lane is lined with places to get a decent sandwich at an affordable price with a place to sit (most places open daily 7:00-24:00, about €1 extra per item to sit; from the Bridge of Sighs, head down the Riva and take the second lane on the left). **$ Birreria Forst** serves busy local workers a selection of meaty €3 sandwiches (daily 9:30-23:00, air-con, Castello 4540, tel. 041-523-0557). **$ Bar Verde** is a more modern sandwich bar (also splittable salads, fresh pastries, at the end of Calle de le Rasse facing Campo Santi Filippo e Giacomo, Castello 4526). **$$ Ristorante alla Basilica,** just one street behind St. Mark's Basilica, serves a solid €16 fixed-price lunch, often amid noisy school groups (Wed-Mon 12:00-15:00, closed Tue, air-con, Calle dei Albanesi, Castello 4255, tel. 041-522-0524).

Rick's Tip: *Though* **you can't legally picnic on St. Mark's Square,** *you're allowed to munch your meal at nearby* **Giardinetti Reali,** *the small park along the waterfront, west of the Piazzetta.*

North of St. Mark's Square

For a marginally less touristy scene, walk a few blocks north to inviting Campo Santa Maria Formosa.

$$$$ Osteria alle Testiere is my top dining splurge in Venice. Hugely respected, Luca and his staff are dedicated to quality, serving up creative, artfully presented market-fresh seafood (there's no meat on the menu), homemade pastas, and fine wine. They have daily specials, 10 wines by the glass, and one agenda: a great dining experience. They're open for lunch (12:00-15:00), and reservations (by email only, info@osterialletestiere.it) are a must well in advance for their two dinner seatings: 19:00 and 21:30 (plan on €50 for dinner, closed Sun-Mon, on Calle del Mondo Novo, just off Campo Santa Maria Formosa, Castello 5801, tel. 041-522-7220, www.osterialletestiere.it).

$$$ Osteria al Mascaron is a rustic little bar-turned-restaurant where Gigi, Momi, and their food-loving band of ruffians dish up rustic-yet-sumptuous pastas with steamy seafood. The €16 *antipasto misto plate* and two glasses of wine make a terrific light meal (Mon-Sat 12:00-15:00 & 19:00-23:00, closed Sun, reservations smart Fri-Sat; on Calle Lunga Santa Maria Formosa, a block past Campo Santa Maria Formosa, Castello 5225; tel. 041-522-5995, www.osteriamascaron.it). While they advertise pastas only for two, you are welcome to have a half-order for half-price—still plenty big.

In Dorsoduro

All of these recommendations are within a 10-minute walk of the Accademia Bridge and well worth the walk.

Near the Accademia Bridge

$$ Bar Foscarini, next to the Accademia Bridge and Galleria, offers decent pizzas and *panini* in a memorable Grand Canal-view setting. The food is forgettable and drinks are pricey. But you're paying a premium for this premium location. They also serve breakfast (daily 8:00-23:00, until 20:30 Nov-April, on Rio Terà A. Foscarini, Dorsoduro 878c, tel. 041-522-7281, Paolo and Simone).

$ Al Vecio Marangon is tucked away from the frenzy of Venice, about 100 yards west of the Accademia. This stylishly rustic bar serves *cicchetti*-style dishes and pastas within its tight and picturesque interior or at a line of outdoor tables. Consider their splittable *piatto di cicchetti misti.* As they take no reservations, arrive early or be prepared to wait (daily 12:00-22:00, on Calle de la Toletta, Dorsoduro 1210, tel. 041-277-8554).

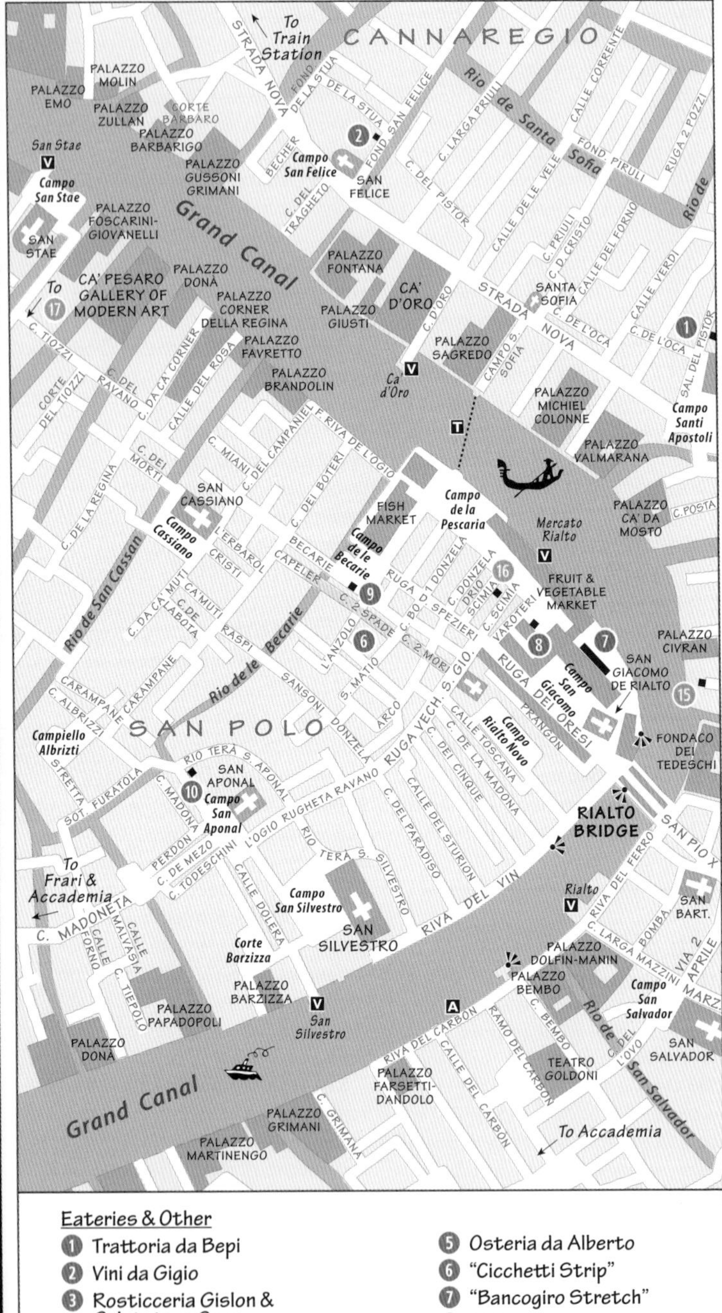

Eateries & Other

1. Trattoria da Bepi
2. Vini da Gigio
3. Rosticceria Gislon & Gelatoteca Suso
4. Osteria al Portego
5. Osteria da Alberto
6. "Cicchetti Strip"
7. "Bancogiro Stretch"
8. Al Mercà
9. Ristorante Vini da Pinto

Restaurants & Hotels near the Rialto Bridge

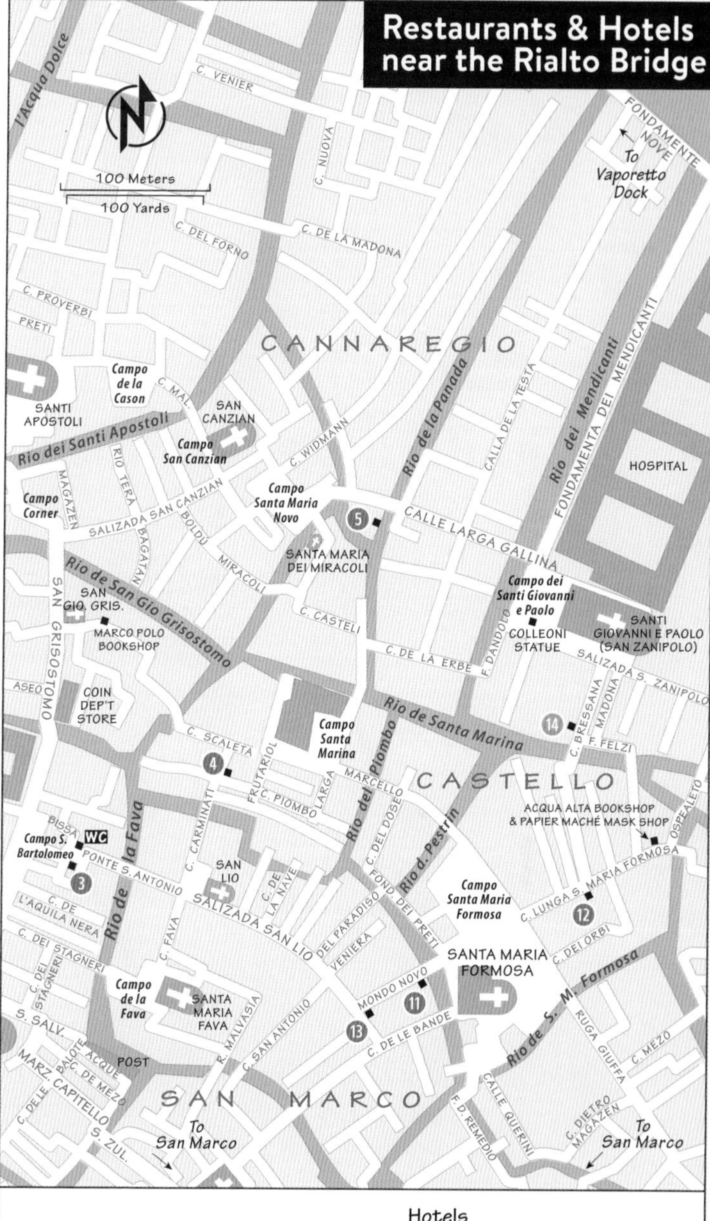

- ⑩ Osteria al Ponte Storto
- ⑪ Osteria alle Testiere
- ⑫ Osteria al Mascaron
- ⑬ Co-op Supermarket

Hotels

- ⑭ Locanda la Corte
- ⑮ Hotel al Ponte Antico
- ⑯ Pensione Guerrato
- ⑰ To Hotel al Ponte Mocenigo

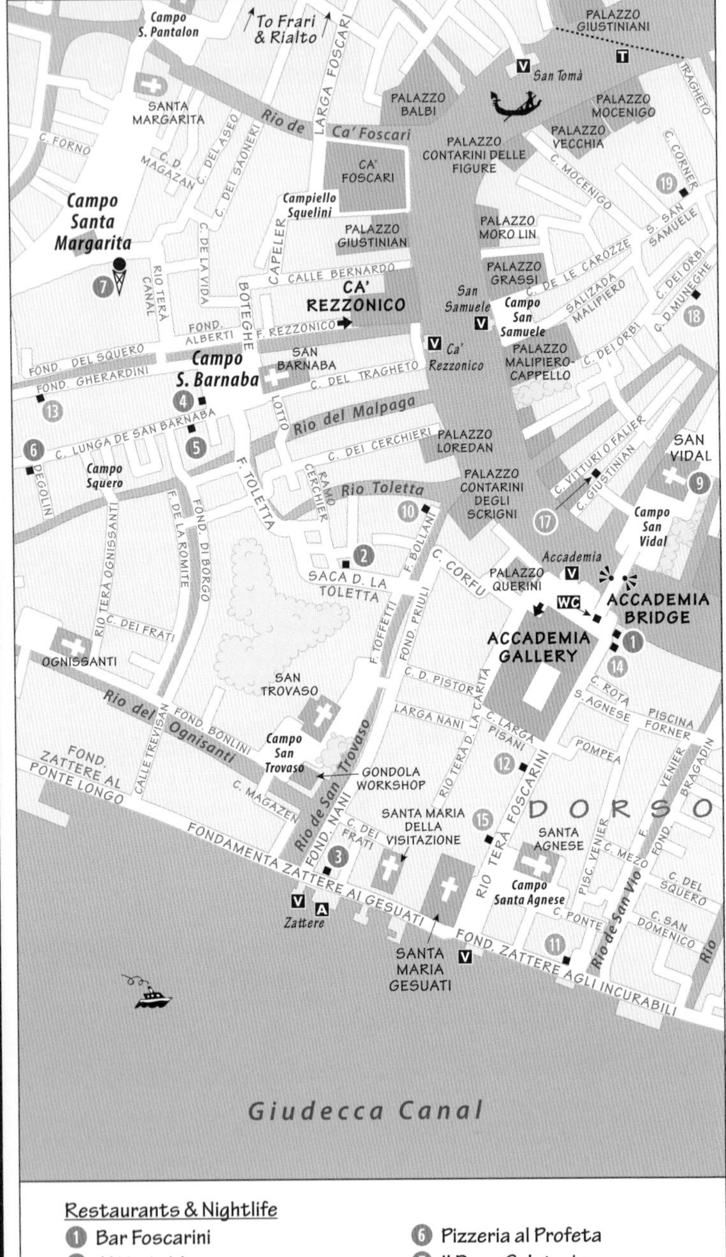

Restaurants & Nightlife

1. Bar Foscarini
2. Al Vecio Marangon
3. Terrazza dei Nobili
4. Ristoteca Oniga
5. Enoteca e Trattoria la Bitta
6. Pizzeria al Profeta
7. Il Doge Gelateria
8. Musica a Palazzo
9. Interpreti Veneziani Concerts

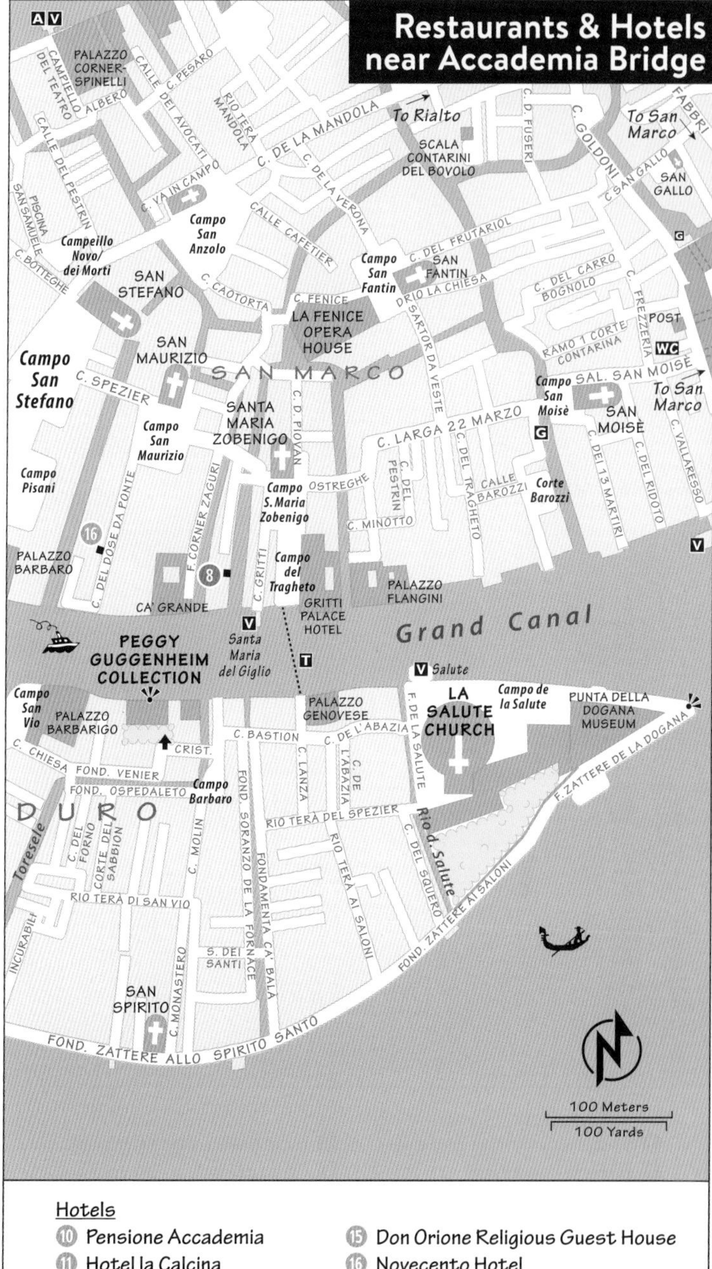

Hotels

10 Pensione Accademia
11 Hotel la Calcina
12 Hotel Belle Arti
13 Casa Rezzonico
14 Hotel Galleria
15 Don Orione Religious Guest House
16 Novecento Hotel
17 Foresteria Levi
18 Istituto Ciliota
19 Hotel San Samuele

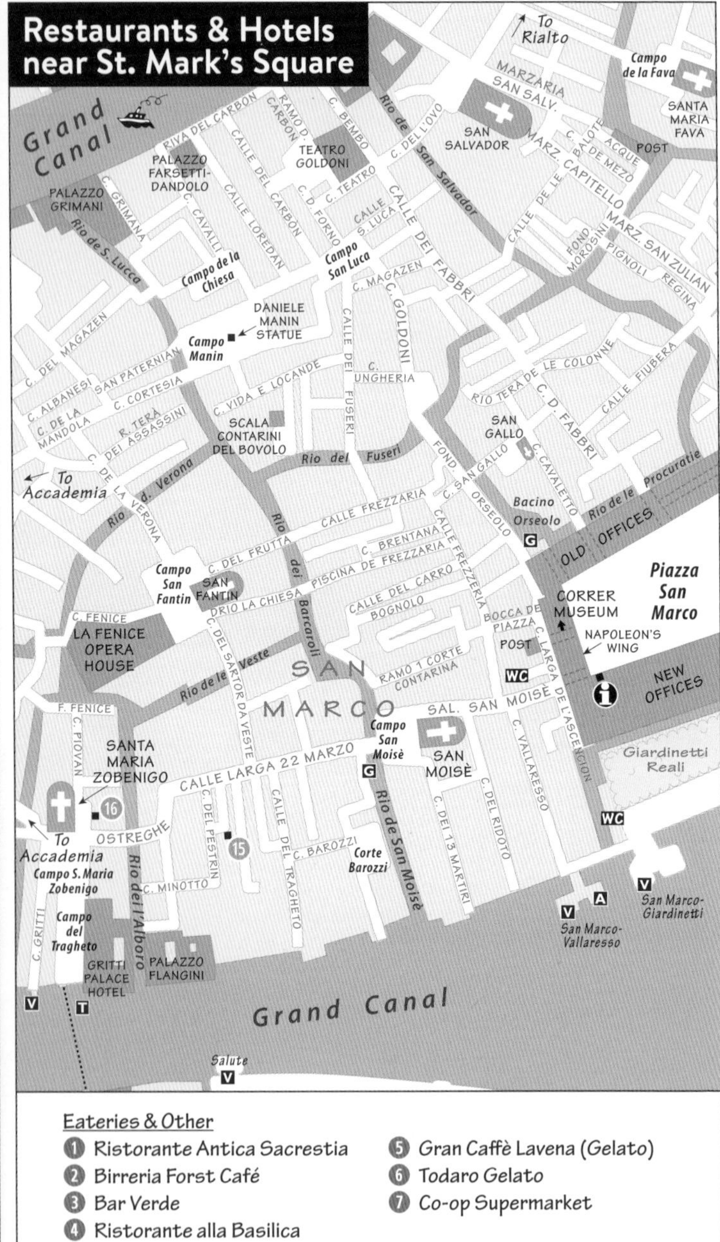

Eateries & Other

1. Ristorante Antica Sacrestia
2. Birreria Forst Café
3. Bar Verde
4. Ristorante alla Basilica
5. Gran Caffè Lavena (Gelato)
6. Todaro Gelato
7. Co-op Supermarket

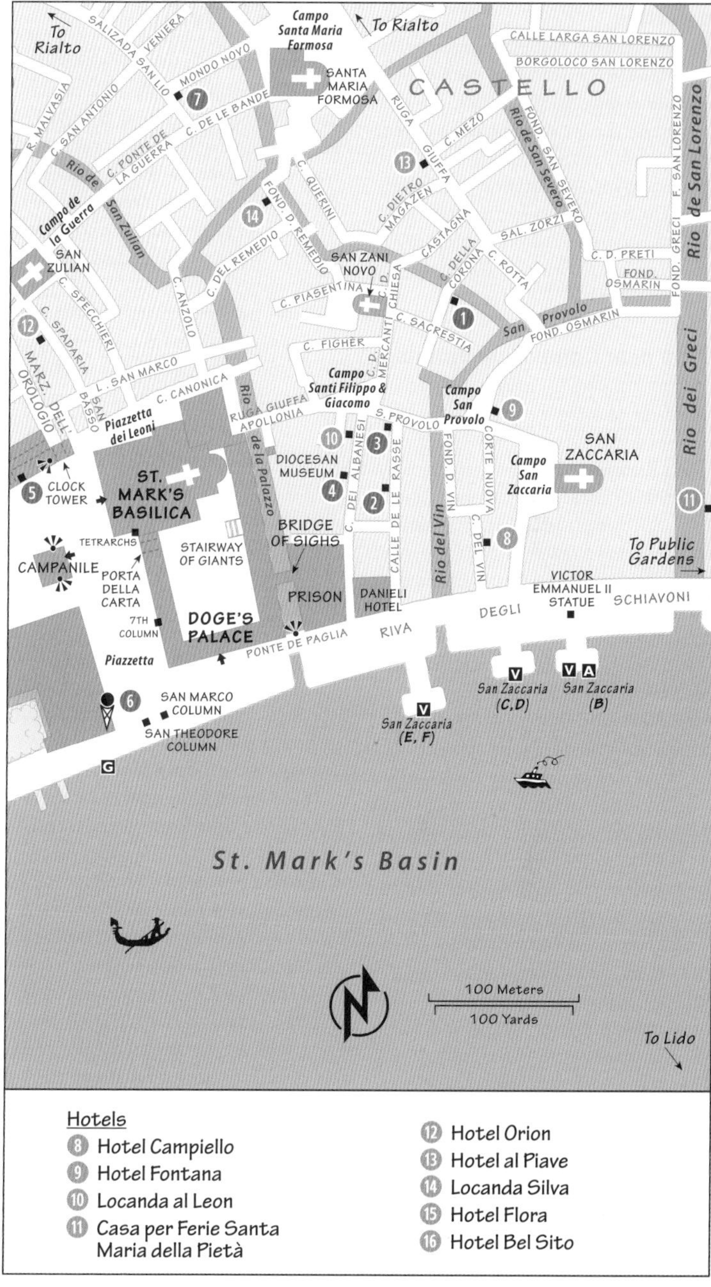

<u>Hotels</u>

8 Hotel Campiello
9 Hotel Fontana
10 Locanda al Leon
11 Casa per Ferie Santa Maria della Pietà
12 Hotel Orion
13 Hotel al Piave
14 Locanda Silva
15 Hotel Flora
16 Hotel Bel Sito

In Zattere

$$$ Terrazza dei Nobili takes full advantage of the warm, romantic evening sun. They serve regional specialties, along with pizza, at tolerable prices. The breezy and beautiful seaside seating comes with the rumble of vaporetti from the nearby stop. The interior is bright and hip (daily 12:00-24:00; from Zattere vaporetto stop, turn left to Dorsoduro 924; tel. 041-520-6895).

On or near Campo San Barnaba

This small square is a delight—especially for dinner. Make reservations to dine later in the evening.

$$$ Ristoteca Oniga has an eclectic yet cozy interior, great tables on the square, and is run by the enthusiastic Raffaele. The menu has a few vegetarian and meat dishes, but focuses on fresh fish and other sea creatures (daily 12:00-14:30 & 19:00-22:30, closed Tue in winter, reservations smart, Campo San Barnaba, Dorsoduro 2852, tel. 041-522-4410, www.oniga.it).

$$ Pizzeria al Profeta is a casual place popular for great pizza and steak. Its sprawling interior seems to stoke conviviality, as does its leafy garden out back (Wed-Mon 12:00-14:30 & 19:00-23:30, closed Tue; from Campo San Barnaba, a long walk down Calle Lunga San Barnaba to #2671, tel. 041-523-7466).

$$$ Enoteca e Trattoria la Bitta is dark and woody, with a soft-jazz bistro feel, tight seating, and a small back patio. They serve beautifully presented, traditional Venetian food with a "slow food" ethic. They do two dinner seatings (19:00 and 21:00) and require reservations (dinner only, Mon-Sat 19:00-23:00, closed Sun, cash only, just off Campo San Barnaba on Calle Lunga San Barnaba, Dorsoduro 2753a, tel. 041-523-0531, Debora and Marcellino).

SLEEPING

I've listed rooms in several neighborhoods: St. Mark's bustle, the Rialto action, and the quiet Dorsoduro area behind the Accademia. Note that hotel websites are particularly valuable for Venice, because they often include detailed directions that can help you get to your rooms with a minimum of wrong turns in this navigationally challenging city.

Prices can spike during festivals. Almost all places drop prices in July and August, and again from November through March (except during Christmas and Carnevale).

Near St. Mark's Square

To get here from the train station or Piazzale Roma bus station, ride the slow vaporetto #1 to San Zaccaria or the fast #2 (which also leaves from Tronchetto parking lot) to San Marco.

East of St. Mark's Square

Located near the Bridge of Sighs, just off the Riva degli Schiavoni waterfront promenade, these places rub drainpipes with Venice's most palatial five-star hotels.

$$$$ Hotel Campiello, lacy and bright, was once part of a 19th-century convent. Ideally located 50 yards off the waterfront on a tiny square, its 16 rooms offer a tranquil, friendly refuge for travelers who appreciate comfort and professional service (RS%, air-con, elevator, just steps from the San Zaccaria vaporetto stop, Castello 4647; tel. 041-520-5764, www.hcampiello.it, campiello@hcampiello.it; family-run for four generations, currently by Thomas, Nicoletta, and Monica). They also rent three modern family apartments, under rustic timbers just steps away.

$$$$ Hotel Fontana, two bridges behind St. Mark's Square, is a pleasant family-run place with 15 sparse but classic-feeling rooms overlooking a lively square (RS%, several rooms with terraces, family rooms, air-con, elevator, Wi-Fi in common areas, on Campo San Provolo at Castello 4701, tel. 041-522-0579, www.hotelfontana.it, info@hotelfontana.it, cousins Diego and Gabriele).

$$$$ Locanda al Leon, which feels a little like a medieval tower house, is conscientiously run and rents 12 rooms just off Campo Santi Filippo e Giacomo (RS%, some view rooms, family rooms, air-con, 2 apartments with kitchens, Campo Santi Filippo e Giacomo, Castello 4270, tel. 041-277-0393, www.hotelalleon.com, leon@hotelalleon.com, Giuliano and Marcella). Their annex down the street, B&B Marcella, has three newer, classy, and spacious rooms for the same rates (check in at main hotel).

$ Casa per Ferie Santa Maria della Pietà is a wonderful facility renting 53 beds in 15 rooms just a block off the Riva, with a fabulous lagoon-view roof terrace that could rival those at the most luxurious hotels in town. Institutional, with generous public spaces and dorm-style comfort, there are no sinks, toilets, or showers in any of its rooms, but there's plenty of plumbing down the hall (cash only, 2-night minimum on weekends in peak season, only twin beds, private rooms available, air-con, 100 yards from San Zaccaria-Pietà vaporetto dock, down Calle de la Pietà from La Pietà Church at Castello 3701, take elevator to third floor, tel. 041-244-3639, www.bedandvenice.it, info@bedandvenice.it).

North of St. Mark's Square

$$$$ Hotel Orion rents 21 simple, welcoming rooms in the center of the action. Steep stairs (there's no elevator) take you from the touristy street into a peaceful world high above (RS%—use code "RSTEVES," air-con, 2 minutes inland from St. Mark's Square, 10 steps toward St. Mark's from San Zulian Church at Calle Spadaria 700a, tel. 041-522-3053, www.hotelorion.it, info@hotelorion.it).

$$$ Hotel al Piave, with 27 rooms above a bright, tight lobby and breakfast room, is comfortable and cheery, and you'll enjoy the neighborhood (RS%, family rooms, lots of narrow stairs, air-con, on Ruga Giuffa at Castello 4838, tel. 041-528-5174, www.hotelalpiave.com, info@hotelalpiave.com; Mirella, Paolo, Ilaria, and Federico).

$$$ Locanda Silva is a well-located hotel with a functional 1960s feel and a peaceful terrace. It rents 23 simple rooms that are particularly worth considering if you're willing to share a bathroom to save some money (RS%, closed Dec-Jan, family rooms, air-con, lots of stairs, on Fondamenta del Remedio at Castello 4423, tel. 041-522-7643, www.locandasilva.it, info@locandasilva.it; Sandra, Katia, and Massimo).

Near Campo Santa Maria Formosa

Farther north, the quiet Castello area lies beyond inviting Campo Santa Maria Formosa.

$$$ Locanda la Corte is perfumed with elegance without being snooty. Its 14 attractive, high-ceilinged, wood-beamed rooms—Venetian-style, done in earthy pastels—circle a small, sun-drenched courtyard and a ground-level restaurant (RS%, family rooms, air-con, on Calle Bressana at Castello 6317, tel. 041-241-1300, www.locandalacorte.it, info@locandalacorte.it).

West of St. Mark's Square

These more expensive hotels are solid choices in a more elegant neighborhood.

$$$$ Hotel Flora sits buried in a sea of fancy designer boutiques and elegant hotels almost on the Grand Canal. It's formal, with uniformed staff and grand public spaces, yet the 40 rooms have a homey warmth and the garden oasis is a sanctuary for well-heeled, foot-weary guests (RS%, air-con, elevator, family apartment, on Calle Bergamaschi at San Marco 2283a, tel. 041-520-5844, www.hotelflora.it, info@hotelflora.it).

$$$$ Hotel Bel Sito offers pleasing Old World character, 34 smallish rooms, generous public spaces, a peaceful courtyard, and a picturesque location—facing a church on a small square between St. Mark's Square and the Accademia (RS%, some view rooms, air-con, elevator; near Santa Maria del Giglio vaporetto stop—line #1, on Campo Santa Maria Zobenigo/del Giglio at San Marco 2517, tel. 041-522-3365, www.hotelbelsitovenezia.it, info@hotelbelsitovenezia.it, graceful Rossella).

Near the Rialto Bridge

These places are on opposite sides of the Grand Canal, within a short walk of the Rialto Bridge. Express vaporetto #2 brings you to the Rialto quickly from the train station, the Piazzale Roma bus station, and the parking-lot island of Tronchetto, but you'll need to take the "local" vaporetto #1 to reach the minor stops closer to the last two listings (or take #2 and walk over Rialto Bridge to reach them).

$$$$ Hotel al Ponte Antico is exquisite, professional, and small. With nine plush rooms, a velvety royal living/breakfast room, and its own dock for water taxi arrivals, it's perfect for a romantic anniversary. Because its wonderful terrace overlooks the Grand Canal, Rialto Bridge, and market action, its rooms without a canal view may be a better value (air-con, 100 yards from Rialto Bridge at Cannaregio 5768, use Rialto vaporetto stop, tel. 041-241-1944, www.alponteantico.com, info@alponteantico.com, Matteo makes you feel like royalty).

$$$ Pensione Guerrato, right above the colorful Rialto produce market and just two minutes from the Rialto Bridge, is run by friendly, creative, and hardworking Roberto and Piero. Their 800-year-old building—with 22 spacious, charming rooms—is simple, airy, and wonderfully characteristic (RS%, cheaper rooms with shared bath, family rooms, air-con, on Calle drio la Scimia at San Polo 240a, take vaporetto #1 to Rialto Mercato stop to save walk over bridge, tel. 041-528-5927, www.hotelguerrato.com, info@hotelguerrato.com, Monica and Rosanna). My tour groups book this place for 90 nights each year. Sorry. The Guerrato also rents family apartments in the old center (great for groups of 4-8) for around €60 per person.

$$$ Hotel al Ponte Mocenigo is off the beaten path—a 10-minute walk northwest of the Rialto Bridge—but it's a great value. This 16th-century Venetian palazzo has a garden terrace and 15 comfy, beautifully appointed, and tranquil rooms (RS%, air-con, Santa Croce 1985, tel. 041-524-4797, www.alpontemocenigo.com, info@alpontemocenigo.com, Sandro and Valter). Take vaporetto #1 to the San Stae stop and head inland along the right side of the church.

Near the Accademia Bridge

As you step over the Accademia Bridge, touristy Venice is replaced by a sleepy village laced with canals. This quiet area is a 15-minute walk from the Rialto or St. Mark's Square. The fast vaporetto #2 to the Accademia stop is the typical way to get here from the train station, Piazzale Roma bus station, Tronchetto parking lot, or St. Mark's Square (early and late, #2 terminates at the Rialto stop, where you change to #1). For hotels near the Zattere stop, good options are vaporetto #5.1 or the Alilaguna speedboat from the airport.

South of the Accademia Bridge, in Dorsoduro

$$$$ Pensione Accademia fills the 17th-century Villa Maravege like a Bellini painting. Its 27 comfortable, elegant rooms gild the lily. You'll feel aristocratic gliding through its grand public spaces and lounging in its wistful, breezy gardens (family rooms, must pay first night in advance, air-con, no elevator but most rooms on ground floor or one floor up, on Fondamenta Bollani at Dorsoduro 1058, tel. 041-521-0188, www.pensioneaccademia.it, info@pensioneaccademia.it).

$$$$ Hotel la Calcina, the home of English writer John Ruskin in 1876, maintains a 19th-century formality. It comes with three-star comforts in a professional yet intimate package. Its 26 nautical-feeling rooms are squeaky clean, with nice wood furniture, hardwood floors, and a peaceful waterside setting facing Giudecca Island (some view rooms, air-con, no elevator and lots of stairs, rooftop terrace, buffet breakfast outdoors in good weather on platform over lagoon, near Zattere vaporetto stop at south end of Rio de San Vio at Dorsoduro 780, tel. 041-520-6466, www.lacalcina.com, info@lacalcina.com).

$$$$ Hotel Belle Arti, with a stiff, serious staff, is pricey and lacks personality but has an inviting garden terrace and 67 heavily decorated rooms (air-con, elevator, 100 yards behind Accademia art museum on Rio Terà A. Foscarini at Dorsoduro 912a, tel. 041-522-6230, www.hotelbellearti.com, info@hotelbellearti.com).

$$$$ Casa Rezzonico, a tranquil getaway far from the crowds, rents seven inviting, nicely appointed rooms with a grassy private garden terrace. All the rooms overlook either the canal or the garden (RS%, family rooms, air-con, near Ca' Rezzonico vaporetto stop—line #1, a few blocks past Campo San Barnaba on Fondamenta Gherardini at Dorsoduro 2813, tel. 041-277-0653, www.casarezzonico.it, info@casarezzonico.it, brothers Matteo and Mattia).

$$$$ Hotel Galleria has nine tight, old-fashioned, velvety rooms, most with views of the Grand Canal. Some rooms are quite narrow. It's run with a family feel by Lucio (breakfast in room, ceiling fans, 30 yards from Accademia art museum, next to recommended Foscarini pizzeria at Dorsoduro 878a, tel. 041-523-2489, www.hotelgalleria.it, info@hotelgalleria.it).

$$$$ Don Orione Religious Guest House is a big cultural center dedicated to the work of a local man who became a saint in modern times. With 80 rooms filling an old monastery, it feels cookie-cutter-institutional (like a modern retreat center), but is also classy, clean, peaceful, and strictly run. It's beautifully located, comfortable, and a good value supporting a fine cause: Profits go to mission work in the developing world (family rooms, groups welcome, air-con, elevator, on Rio Terà A. Foscarini, Dorsoduro 909a, tel. 041-522-4077, www.donorione-venezia.it, info@donorione-venezia.it).

North of the Accademia Bridge

These places are between the Accademia Bridge and St. Mark's Square.

$$$$ Novecento Hotel rents nine plush rooms on three floors, complemented by a big, welcoming lounge, an elegant living room, and a small breakfast garden. This boutique hotel is nicely located and has a tasteful sense of style, mingling Art Deco with North African and Turkish decor (air-con, lots of stairs, on Calle del Dose, off Campo San Maurizio at San Marco 2683, tel. 041-241-3765, www.novecento.biz, info@novecento.biz).

$$$ Foresteria Levi, run by a foundation that promotes research on Venetian music, offers 32 quiet, institutional yet comfortable and spacious rooms—some are loft quads, a good deal for families (RS%, air-con, elevator, on Calle Giustinian at San Marco 2893, tel. 041-277-0542, www.foresterialevi.it, info@foresterialevi.it).

$$$ Istituto Ciliota (a.k.a. Domus Ciliota) is a big, efficient, and sparkling-clean place—well-run, well-located, church-owned, and plainly furnished—with 30 dorm-like rooms and a peaceful courtyard. If you want industrial-strength comfort with no stress and little character, this is a fine value (air-con, elevator, on Calle de le Muneghe just off Campo San Stefano, San Marco 2976, tel. 041-520-4888, www.ciliota.it, info@ciliota.it).

$$$ Hotel San Samuele rents 10 rooms in an old palazzo near Campo San Stefano. It's in a great locale, and the rooms with shared bath can be a good deal (no breakfast, fans, some stairs, on Salizada San Samuele at San Marco 3358, tel. 041-520-5165, www.hotelsansamuele.com, info@hotelsansamuele.com, Judith).

TRANSPORTATION

Getting Around Venice

Narrow pedestrian walkways connect Venice's docks, squares, bridges, and courtyards. To navigate on foot, look for yellow signs on street corners pointing you to *(per)* the nearest major landmark (such as *Per Rialto*). Determine whether your destination is in the direction of a major signposted landmark, then follow the signs through the maze.

Some helpful street terminology: *Campo* means square, a *campiello* is a small square, *calle* (pronounced "KAH-lay" with an "L" sound) means "street," and a *ponte* is a bridge. A *fondamenta* is the embankment along a canal or the lagoon. A *rio terà* is a street that was once a canal and has been filled in. A *sotoportego* is a covered passageway. *Salizzada* literally means a paved area (usually a wide street). The abbreviations S. and S.S. mean "saint" and "saints," respectively. Don't get hung up on the exact spelling of street and square names, which may sometimes appear in Venetian dialect (which uses *de la, novo,* and *vechio*) and other times in standard Italian (which uses *della, nuovo,* and *vecchio*).

Every building in Venice has a house number. The numbers relate to the district (each with about 6,000 address numbers), not the street. If you need to find a specific address, it helps to know its district, street, house number, and nearby landmarks.

By Vaporetto

These motorized bus-boats run by the public transit system (ACTV) work like city buses except that they never get a flat, the stops are docks, and if you get off between stops, you might drown. You can purchase tickets and passes at docks and from ACTV affiliate VèneziaUnica (ACTV—tel. 041-2424, www.actv.it; VèneziaUnica—www.veneziaunica.com).

TICKETS AND PASSES

Individual Vaporetto Tickets: A single ticket costs €7.50 (kids under 6 travel free). Tickets are good for 75 minutes in one direction; you can hop on and off at stops and change boats during that time. Your ticket (a plastic card embedded with a chip) is refillable; put more money on it at the automated kiosks to avoid waiting in line at the ticket window. The fare is reduced to €5 for a few one-stop runs *(corsa semplice)* that are hard to do by foot, including from San Zaccaria to the island of San Giorgio Maggiore.

Vaporetto Passes: Because a single ticket costs €7.50, an unlimited-use *vaporetti* pass pays for itself quickly (€20/24 hours, €30/48 hours, €40/72 hours, €60/7-day pass). For example, the 48-hour pass pays for itself after just five rides (for example: to your hotel on your arrival, on a Grand Canal joyride, into the lagoon and back, and to the train station). Smaller and/or outlying stops, such as Sant'Elena and Biennale, are unstaffed—another good reason to buy a pass. It's fun to be able to hop on and off spontaneously, and avoid long ticket lines. On the other hand, many tourists just walk through Venice and rarely use a boat.

Passes are also valid on some of ACTV's mainland buses, including bus #2 to Mestre (but not the #5 to the airport or the airport buses run by ATVO, a separate company). Passholders get a discounted fare for all ACTV buses that originate or terminate at Marco Polo Airport (€6 one-way, €12 round-trip, must be purchased at the same time as the pass; otherwise, the airport shuttle costs €8 one-way, €15 round-trip).

Travelers between ages 14 and 29 can get a 72-hour pass for €22 if they also buy

Handy Vaporetti from San Zaccaria, near St. Mark's Square

Several vaporetti leave from the San Zaccaria docks, located 150 yards east of St. Mark's Square. There are four separate San Zaccaria docks spaced about 70 yards apart, with a total of six different berths, lettered A to F. While this may sound confusing, in practice it's simple: Check the big electronic board (next to the C/D dock), which indicates the departure time, line number, destination, and berth letter of upcoming vaporetti. Once you've figured out which boat you want, go to that letter berth and hop on. They're all within about a five-minute stroll of each other.

- **Line #1** goes up the Grand Canal, making all the stops, including San Marco, Rialto, Ferrovia (train station), and Piazzale Roma (but it does not go as far as Tronchetto). In the other direction, it goes from San Zaccaria to Arsenale and Giardini before ending on the Lido.
- **Line #2** zips over to San Giorgio Maggiore, the island church across from St. Mark's Square (5 minutes, €5 ride). From there, it continues on to stops on the island of Giudecca, the parking lot at Tronchetto, and then down the Grand Canal (dock B). Note: You cannot ride the #2 up the Grand Canal (for example, to Rialto or the train station) directly from this stop—you'll need to walk five minutes along the waterfront, past St. Mark's Square, to the San Marco-Giardinetti dock and hop on the #2 there.
- **Line #4.1** goes to San Michele and Murano in 45 minutes (dock D).
- **Line #7** is the summertime express boat to Murano (25 minutes, dock D).
- The **Molino Stucky shuttle boat** takes even nonguests to the Hilton Hotel, with its popular view bar (20-minute ride, 3/hour, from its own dock near the San Zaccaria dock B).
- **Lines #5.1** and **#5.2** are the *circulare* (cheer-koo-LAH-ray), making a loop around the perimeter of the island, with a stop at the Lido—perfect if you just like riding boats. Line #5.1 goes counterclockwise, and #5.2 goes clockwise. Both run less frequently in the evenings (#5.1 leaves from dock D, #5.2 from dock C).
- The **Alilaguna** shuttle to and from the airport stops here as well (dock D).

a **Rolling Venice** discount pass for €6 (offers discounts at sights and shops, too; www.veneziaunica.com).

Buying and Validating Tickets and Passes: Purchase tickets and passes from machines at most stops, from ticket windows at larger stops, or from the VèneziaUnica offices at the train station, bus station, and Tronchetto parking lot (Rolling Venice youth passes also sold at TIs).

Before you board, validate your ticket or pass at the small white machine on the dock. If you're unable to purchase a ticket before boarding, seek out the conductor immediately to buy a single ticket (or risk a big fine).

IMPORTANT VAPORETTO LINES

For most travelers, only two vaporetto lines matter: line #1 and line #2, which leave every 10 minutes or so and go up and down the Grand Canal, between the "mouth" of the fish at one end and St.

Mark's Square at the other. **Line #1** is the slow boat, taking 45 minutes and making every stop along the way. **Line #2** takes 25 minutes, stopping only at Tronchetto (parking lot), Piazzale Roma (bus station), Ferrovia (train station), Rialto Bridge, San Tomà (Frari Church), San Samuele (opposite Ca' Rezzonico), Accademia Bridge, and San Marco (west end of St. Mark's Square, end of the line).

Sorting out the different directions of travel can be confusing. Some boats run on circular routes, in one direction only (for example, lines #5.1 and #5.2, plus the non-Murano sections of lines #4.1 and #4.2). Line #2 runs in both directions and is almost, but not quite, a full loop. The #2 boat leaving from the San Marco stop goes in one direction (up the Grand Canal), while from the San Zaccaria stop—just a five-minute walk away—it goes in the opposite direction (around the tail of the "fish"). Make sure you use the correct stop to avoid taking the long way around to your destination.

To clear up any confusion, ask a ticket-seller or conductor on the dock for help. Get a copy of the most current ACTV map and timetable (in English and Italian, can be downloaded from www.actv.it, theoretically free at ticket booths but often unavailable). System maps are posted at stops, but it's helpful to print out your own copy of the map from the ACTV website before your trip.

BOARDING AND RIDING VAPORETTI

Many stops have two boarding platforms, and large stops—such as San Marco, San Zaccaria, Rialto, Ferrovia (train station), and Piazzale Roma—have multiple platforms. At these larger stops, electronic boards display which boats are coming next, when, and from which platform they leave; each platform is assigned a letter (clearly marked above the gangway). At smaller stops without electronic displays, signs on each platform show the vaporetto lines that stop there and the direction they are headed. As you board, confirm your destination by looking for an electronic sign on the boat or just asking the conductor.

You may notice some *vaporetti* sporting a *corsa bis* sign, indicating that they're running a shortened or altered route, and that riders may have to hop off partway (at Rialto, for example) and wait for the next boat. If you see a *corsa bis* sign, ask the conductor before you board if the boat is going to your desired destination (e.g., "San Marco?").

By Traghetto

Only four bridges cross the Grand Canal, but *traghetti* (shuttle gondolas) ferry locals and in-the-know tourists across the Grand Canal at three additional locations. Just step in, hand the gondolier €2, and enjoy the ride—standing or sitting. Some *traghetti* are seasonal, some stop running as early as 12:30, and all stop by 18:00. *Traghetti* are not covered by any transit pass.

By Water Taxi

Venetian taxis, like speedboat limos, hang out at busy points along the Grand Canal. Prices are regulated: €15 for pickup, then €2 per minute; €5 per person for more than four passengers; and €10 between 22:00 and 6:00. If you have more bags than passengers, the extra ones cost €3 apiece. Despite regulation, prices can be soft; negotiate and settle on the price or rate before stepping in. For travelers with lots of luggage or small groups who can split the cost, taxi

A traghetto *crossing*

boat rides can be a time-saving convenience—and a cool indulgence. For a little more than €100 an hour, you can have a private, unguided taxi-boat tour. You may find more competitive rates if you book through the Consorzio Motoscafi water taxi association (tel. 041-522-2303, www.motoscafivenezia.it).

Arriving and Departing

A two-mile-long causeway (with highway and train lines) connects the island to Mestre, the sprawling mainland section of Venice. Don't stop in Mestre unless you're changing trains or parking your car.

Marco Polo Airport

Venice's small, modern airport is on the mainland shore of the lagoon, six miles north of the city (airport code: VCE). There's one sleek terminal, with a TI (daily 9:00-20:00), car-rental agencies, ATMs, a bank, and a few shops and eateries. For flight info, call 041-260-9260, visit www.veniceairport.com, or ask your hotelier.

Treviso Airport, the next-closest airport, is described later.

GETTING BETWEEN MARCO POLO AIRPORT AND VENICE

There are several good options (including by boat) to get from the airport to Venice.

An advantage of the Alilaguna boats and water taxis is that you can reach my recommended hotels very simply, with no changes. Both kinds of boats leave from the airport's boat dock, an eight-minute walk from the terminal. Exit the arrivals hall and turn left, following signs along a paved, level, covered sidewalk.

Transport	Speed	Cost
Alilaguna boat	Slow	Moderate
Water taxi	Fast	Expensive
Airport bus to Piazzale Roma	Medium	Cheap
Land taxi to Piazzale Roma	Medium	Moderate

When flying out of Venice, plan to arrive at the airport two hours before your flight, and remember that just getting there can easily take up to two hours. Water transport can be slow, and small Alilaguna boats fill up quickly. In an emergency, hop in a water taxi and get to the airport in 30 minutes.

ALILAGUNA AIRPORT BOATS

These boats make the slow, scenic journey across the lagoon, shuttling passengers between the airport and the island of Venice (€15, €27 round-trip, €1 surcharge if bought on boat, discount if bought online, includes 1 suitcase and 1 piece of hand luggage, additional bags-€3 each, roughly 2/hour, 1-1.5-hour trip depending on destination). Alilaguna boats are not part of the ACTV vaporetto system, so they aren't covered by city transit passes. But they do use the same docks and ticket windows as the regular **vaporetti.** You can buy tickets for Alilaguna online at www.alilaguna.it or www.venicelink.com.

There are three key Alilaguna lines for reaching St. Mark's Square. From the airport, the **blue line** *(linea blu)* heads first to Fondamente Nove (40 minutes), then loops around to San Zaccaria and San Marco (about 1.5 hours) before continuing on to Zattere and the cruise terminal (almost 2 hours). The **orange line** *(linea arancio)* runs down the Grand Canal, reaching Guglie (45 minutes), Rialto (1 hour), and San Marco (1.5 hours). In high season, the red line *(linea rossa)* runs to St. Mark's in just over an hour. It circumnavigates Murano and then runs parallel to the blue line, ending at Giudecca Zitelle. For a full schedule, visit the TI, see the website (www.alilaguna.it), call 041-240-1701, ask your hotelier, or scan the schedules posted at the docks.

From the Airport to Venice: You can buy Alilaguna tickets at the airport's TI, the ticket desk in the terminal, and at the ticket booth at the dock. Any ticket seller can tell you which line you need. Blue- and orange-line boats from the airport run roughly twice an hour; red goes once an hour (blue line from 6:15, orange line from 7:45, red line from 9:40; blue and orange lines run until about midnight, the red line makes its last run at 18:40).

From Venice to the Airport: Ask your hotelier which dock and which line is best. Blue line boats leave Venice as early as 3:50 in the morning for passengers with early flights. Scope out the dock and buy tickets in advance to avoid last-minute stress.

WATER TAXIS

Luxury taxi speedboats zip directly between the airport and the closest dock to your hotel, getting you to within steps of your final destination in about 30 minutes. The official price is €110 for up to four people; add €10 for every extra person (10-passenger limit). You may get a higher quote—politely talk it down. A taxi can be a smart investment for small groups and those with an early departure.

From the airport, arrange your ride at the water-taxi desk or with the boat captains lounging at the dock. From Venice, book your taxi trip the day before you leave. Your hotel will help (since they get a commission), or you can book directly with the Consorzio Motoscafi water taxi association (tel. 041-522-2303, www.motoscafivenezia.it).

AIRPORT SHUTTLE BUSES

Buses between the airport and Venice are fast, frequent, and cheap. They drop you at Venice's bus station, at a square called Piazzale Roma. From there, you can catch a vaporetto down the Grand Canal—convenient for hotels near the Rialto Bridge and St. Mark's Square.

Two bus companies serve this route: ACTV and ATVO. ATVO buses go nonstop and take 20 minutes. ACTV buses make a few stops en route and take 30 minutes, but you get a discount if you buy a Venice vaporetto pass at the same time (see "By Vaporetto," above). The service is equally good (either bus: €8 one-way, €15 round-trip, ACTV bus with transit-pass discount: €6 one-way, €12 round-trip; runs about 5:00-24:00, 2/hour, drops to 1/hour early and late, check schedules at www.atvo.it or www.actv.it).

From the Airport to Venice: Both buses leave from just outside the arrivals terminal. Buy tickets from the TI, the ticket desk in the terminal, the kiosk near baggage claim, or ticket machines. ATVO tickets are not valid on ACTV buses and vice versa. Double-check the destination; you want Piazzale Roma. If taking ACTV, you want bus #5.

From Venice to the Airport: At Piazzale Roma, buy your ticket from the ACTV windows (in the building by the bridge) or the ATVO office (at #497g) before heading out to the platforms (although sometimes there's an attendant selling tickets near the buses). The newsstand in the center of the lot also sells tickets.

LAND TAXI OR PRIVATE MINIVAN

It takes about 20 minutes to drive from the airport to Piazzale Roma or the cruise port. A **land taxi** can do the trip for about €50. To reserve a private minivan, contact **Treviso Car Service** (minivan-€55, seats up to 8; car-€50, seats up to 3; mobile 338-204-4390 or 333-411-2840, www.trevisocarservice.com).

Treviso Airport

Several budget airlines, such as Ryanair and Wizz Air, use Treviso Airport, 12 miles northwest of Venice (airport code: TSF, tel. 042-231-5111, www.trevisoairport.it). The fastest option into Venice takes 40 minutes on the **Barzi express bus** to the Tronchetto parking lot—convenient if you'll be taking vaporetto #2 (€12, buy tickets on board, every 1-2 hours, www.barziservice.com). From Tronchetto, hop on a vaporetto, or take the People Mover monorail to Piazzale Roma for €1.50. **ATVO buses** are more frequent and drop you right at Piazzale Roma (saving you the People Mover ride), but take nearly twice as long (€12 one-way, €22 round-trip, about 2/hour, 70 minutes, buy tickets at ATVO desk in airport and stamp them on bus, www.atvo.it). **Treviso Car Service** offers minivan service to Piazzale Roma (minivan-€75, seats up to 8; car-€65, seats up to 3; mobile 338-204-4390 or 333-411-2840, www.trevisocarservice.com).

By Train

All trains to "Venice" stop at Venezia Mestre (on the mainland). Most continue on to **Santa Lucia Station** (a.k.a. Venezia S.L.) on the island of Venice itself. If your train happens to terminate at Mestre, you'll need to buy a Mestre-Santa Lucia ticket at a machine for €1.25 and validate it before hopping any nonexpress, regional train (with an R or RV prefix) for the ride across the causeway to Venice (6/hour, 10 minutes).

Santa Lucia train station is right on the Grand Canal, an easy vaporetto ride or fascinating 45-minute walk (with a number of bridges and steps) to St. Mark's Square. The station has a **baggage check** (daily 6:00-23:00, no lockers, along track 1). Pay **WCs** are at track 1. You'll find the **TI** across from track 2.

Before heading into town, confirm your departure plan (use the ticket machines or study the *partenze*/departures posters on walls). Minimize your time in the station—the banks of user-friendly ticket machines take euros and credit cards, display schedules, and issue tickets. There are two train companies and both have red ticket machines: **Trenitalia** has the most connections (toll tel. 892-021, www.trenitalia.it); the other is the high-speed **Italo** service (no rail passes accepted, cheaper in advance, tel. 06-0708, www.italotreno.it). **Ticket offices** for both Trenitalia and Italo are in the corner, near track 14. If you need international tickets or live help, head to the ticket windows (Trenitalia open 6:00-21:00; Italo open 8:30-20:00). Or take care of these tasks online or at a travel agency (extra ticket fee).

Getting from the Train Station to Downtown: Walk straight out of the station to the canal. You'll see vaporetto docks and ticket booths on both sides. The electronic signs show which boats are leaving when and from which platform. The slow boat down the Grand Canal is #1. The fast boat is #2; make sure that "Rialto" is among the destinations listed. If you're staying in the Dorsoduro neighborhood near the Zattere stop, take vaporetto #5.1. A water taxi from the train station to central Venice costs about €60-80 (the taxi dock is straight ahead).

TRAIN CONNECTIONS

Note that the departures listed below are operated by Trenitalia; a competing private rail company called Italo offers additional high-speed connections to major Italian cities including **Milan, Florence,** and **Rome,** but doesn't accept rail passes. When taking the train to nearby cities such as Padua and Verona, prices and journey times can vary greatly, depending on whether the train is express or regional.

From Venice by Train to: Padua (2/hour, 25-50 minutes); **Verona** (2/hour, 1.5-2.5 hours); **Bolzano/Dolomites** (to Bolzano about hourly, 3-3.5 hours, transfer in Verona; catch bus from Bolzano into mountains); **Milan** (2/hour, most direct on high-speed ES trains, 2.5 hours); **Cinque Terre/Monterosso** (5/day, 6 hours, change in Milan); **Florence** (hourly, 2-3 hours, often crowded so make reservations); **Rome** (hourly, 4 hours); **Naples** (almost hourly, 5.5 hours, some change in Bologna or Rome).

By Bus

Venice's "bus station" is actually an open-air parking lot called **Piazzale Roma.** The square itself is a jumble of different operators, platforms, and crosswalks over busy lanes of traffic, but bus stops are well-signed. The ticket windows for ACTV (local public buses, including #5 to Marco Polo Airport) are in a building between the bridge and vaporetto stop. The ATVO ticket office—for express buses to Marco Polo and Treviso airports and to Padua—is at #497g in the big white building, on the right side of the square as you face away from the canal (daily 6:45-19:30).

Piazzale Roma also has two big **parking garages** and the **People Mover monorail** (€1.50, links to cruise port and then the parking-lot island of Tronchetto). **Baggage storage** is next to the monorail at #497m (daily 6:00-20:00).

Getting from the Bus Station to Downtown: Find the vaporetto docks (just left of the modern bridge) and take #1 or the faster #2 down the Grand Canal to reach stops for the Rialto, Accademia, and San Marco (St. Mark's Square).

By Car

The freeway (monitored by speed cameras) dead-ends after crossing the causeway to Venice. At the end of the road you have two parking choices: garages at Tronchetto or Piazzale Roma. As you drive into the city, signboards with green and red lights indicate which lots are full.

The **Tronchetto garage** is much bigger, farther out, cheaper, and well-connected by vaporetto (€3-5/hour, €21/24 hours, discounts for longer stays, tel. 041-520-7555, www.veniceparking.it). After parking, cross the street to the brick building. While you can head left for a long walk to the People Mover monorail, it's easier to go right to the vaporetto dock (not well-signed, look for *ACTV*).

At the dock, catch vaporetto #2 in one of two directions: via the Grand Canal (more scenic, stops at Rialto, 40 minutes to San Marco), or via Giudecca (around the city, faster, no Rialto stop, 30 minutes to San Marco).

Don't be waylaid by **aggressive water taxi boatmen.** They charge €100 to take you where the vaporetto will take you for €7.50. Also **avoid the travel agencies masquerading as TIs;** deal only with the ticket booth at the vaporetto dock or the VèneziaUnica public transport office. If you're going to buy a local transport pass, do it now—to get maximum use out of it.

The two **Piazzale Roma garages** are closer in and more convenient—but more expensive and likelier to be full. Both face the busy square where the road ends. The big white building on your right is a 2,200-space public parking garage, **Autorimessa Comunale** (€26/24 hours, TI office in payment lobby open daily 7:30-19:30, tel. 041-272-7211, www.avmspa.it). In a back corner of the square is the private **Garage San Marco** (€32/24 hours, tel. 041-523-2213, www.garagesanmarco.it). At either of these, you'll have to give up your keys. Near Garage San Marco, avoid Parcheggio Sant'Andrea, which charges much higher rates.

BEST OF THE REST

MILAN

For every church in Rome, there's a bank in Milan. Italy's second city and capital of the Lombardy region, Milan is a hardworking, time-is-money powerhouse. And it's also an international fashion capital—the locals and the city itself are works of art.

Many tourists come to Italy for the past. But Milan is today's Italy. In this city of refined tastes, window displays are gorgeous, cigarettes are chic, and even the cheese comes gift-wrapped. Yet, thankfully, Milan is no more expensive for tourists than any other Italian city.

If you're flying in and out of Milan, you could save your exploration of this big, modern city for the end of your trip, by starting your journey softly at Lake Como, the Cinque Terre, or Venice. Then spend your last night or two in Milan before flying home.

Orientation

My coverage focuses on the old center. Most sights are within a 15-minute walk of the cathedral (Duomo), which is a direct eight-minute Metro ride from the Centrale train station. As in any big Italian city, be alert for pickpockets, particularly on the Metro and wherever tourists congregate.

Day Plan: On a short visit, tour the Duomo (exploring the cathedral's rooftop terraces and interior), have a scenic coffee in the Galleria Vittorio Emanuele II, dip into La Scala Opera House, and see *The Last Supper* (if you've reserved ahead). If you have more time, Milan has more to offer (including the Duomo Museum, Sforza Castle, and art museums).

Getting to Milan by Air: Most international flights land at **Malpensa Airport** (MXP, www.milanomalpensa-airport.com). Ride the **Malpensa Express train** into the city (€13, www.malpensaexpress.it): Take the Cadorna line to reach downtown (2/hour, 40 minutes) or the Centrale line to Milano Centrale train station (2/hour, 50 minutes). Airport **shuttle buses** cost about €8 for the one-hour trip downtown (www.malpensashuttle.it, www.terravision.eu, or www.autostradale.it). **Taxis** charge a fixed rate of €95.

Most European flights land at **Linate Airport** (LIN; www.milanolinate-airport.com), which is connected to downtown Milan by **shuttle bus** (€5, 35 minutes, www.airportbusexpress.it), **taxi** (about €25), and **public bus** #73 (€1.50, take it to the end of the line near the Duomo).

Getting to Milan by Train: Common connections are **Venice** (2/hour, 2.5 hours), **Florence** (Trenitalia: hourly, 2 hours; Italo: 2/hour, 2 hours), **Rome** (Trenitalia: 1-3/hour, 3.5 hours; Italo: 11/day nonstop, 3 hours, more with stops), **Cinque Terre/Monterosso al Mare** (8/day, 3 hours), **Varenna** on Lake Como (nearly hourly, 1 hour), and **Naples** (Trenitalia: 2/hour, 4-5 hours, more with change in Rome; Italo: 11/day, 4-5 hours).

Most trains arrive at the **Milano Centrale** station; to get downtown, follow signs for Metro yellow line 3 (direction: San Donato), go four stops to the Duomo stop, surface, and you'll be facing the cathedral. If you arrive at **Milano Cadorna** (served by the Malpensa Express from the airport), take Metro red line 1 to the Duomo. **Milano Porta Garibaldi** (used by high-speed trains from some international destinations and a few domestic trains) is on Metro green line 2, two stops from Milano Centrale.

Getting to Milan by Car: Park at lots at suburban Metro stops (see www.atm.it). There's a weekday congestion fee to drive in the center.

Tourist Information: The TI is in Galleria Vittorio Emanuele II, at the end nearest La Scala (Mon-Fri 9:00-19:00, Sat until

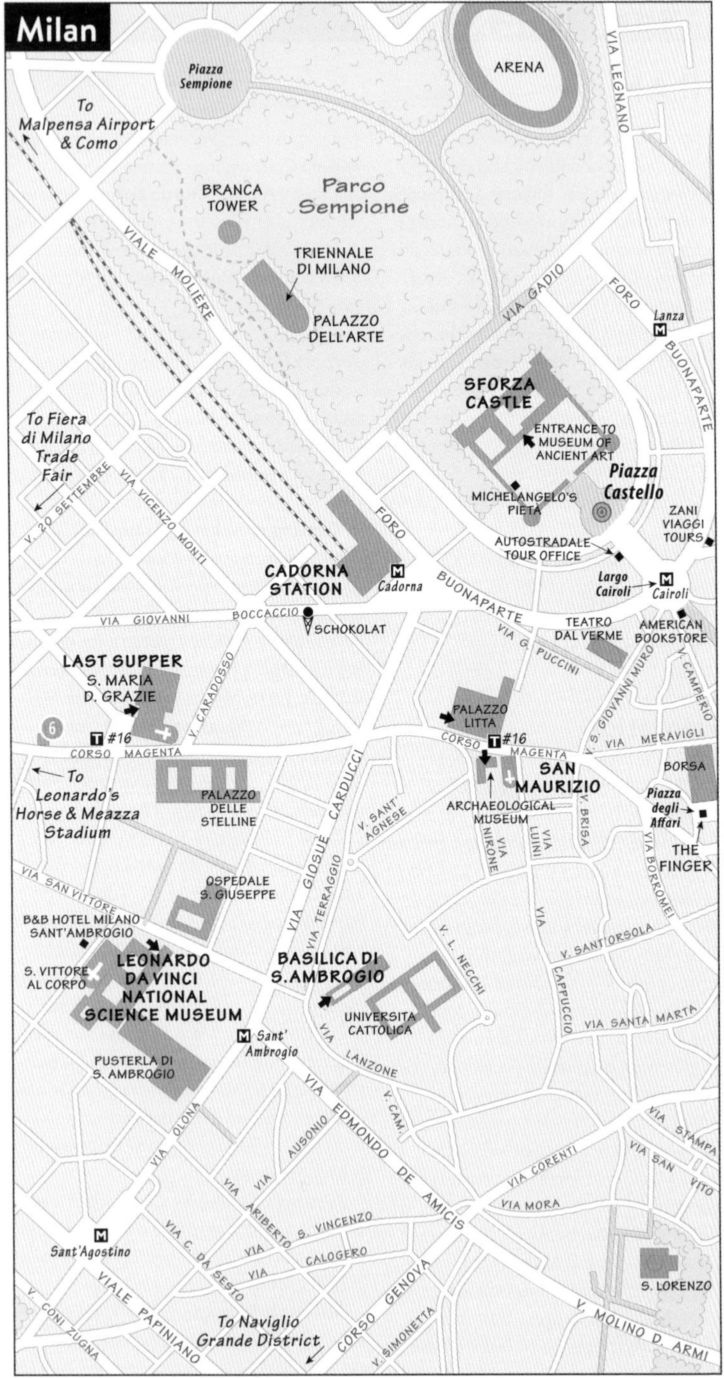
Milan
Piazza Sempione
To Malpensa Airport & Como
ARENA
VIA LEGNANO
BRANCA TOWER
Parco Sempione
TRIENNALE DI MILANO
PALAZZO DELL'ARTE
VIALE MOLIÈRE
VIA GADIO
FORO BUONAPARTE
Lanza
SFORZA CASTLE
ENTRANCE TO MUSEUM OF ANCIENT ART
Piazza Castello
MICHELANGELO'S PIETÀ
ZANI VIAGGI TOURS
AUTOSTRADALE TOUR OFFICE
To Fiera di Milano Trade Fair
V. 20 SETTEMBRE
VIA VICENZO MONTI
CADORNA STATION
Cadorna
Largo Cairoli
Cairoli
VIA GIOVANNI BOCCACCIO
SCHOKOLAT
TEATRO DAL VERME
AMERICAN BOOKSTORE
VIA G. PUCCINI
LAST SUPPER
S. MARIA D. GRAZIE
V. CARADOSSO
PALAZZO LITTA
VIA S. GIOVANNI MURO
V. CAMPERIO
#16
CORSO MAGENTA
VIA MERAVIGLI
BORSA
SAN MAURIZIO
To Leonardo's Horse & Meazza Stadium
PALAZZO DELLE STELLINE
VIA GIOSUÈ CARDUCCI
V. SANT' AGNESE
ARCHAEOLOGICAL MUSEUM
VIA NIRONE
VIA LUINI
V. BRISA
Piazza degli Affari
THE FINGER
VIA BORROMEI
VIA SAN VITTORE
OSPEDALE S. GIUSEPPE
VIA TERRAGGIO
B&B HOTEL MILANO SANT'AMBROGIO
S. VITTORE AL CORPO
LEONARDO DA VINCI NATIONAL SCIENCE MUSEUM
BASILICA DI S.AMBROGIO
V. L. NECCHI
VIA
V. SANT'ORSOLA
VIA CAPPUCCIO
VIA SANTA MARTA
UNIVERSITÀ CATTOLICA
Sant' Ambrogio
VIA LANZONE
PUSTERLA DI S. AMBROGIO
V. CAM.
VIA OLONA
VIA AUSONIO
VIA EDMONDO DE AMICIS
VIA STAMPA
VIA SAN VITO
VIA CORENTI
VIA MORA
VIA ARIBERTO
VIA S. VINCENZO
VIA CALOGERO
VIA C. DA SESTO
Sant'Agostino
VIALE PAPINIANO
V. CONI ZUGNA
To Naviglio Grande District
CORSO GENOVA
V. SIMONETTA
S. LORENZO
V. MOLINO D. ARMI

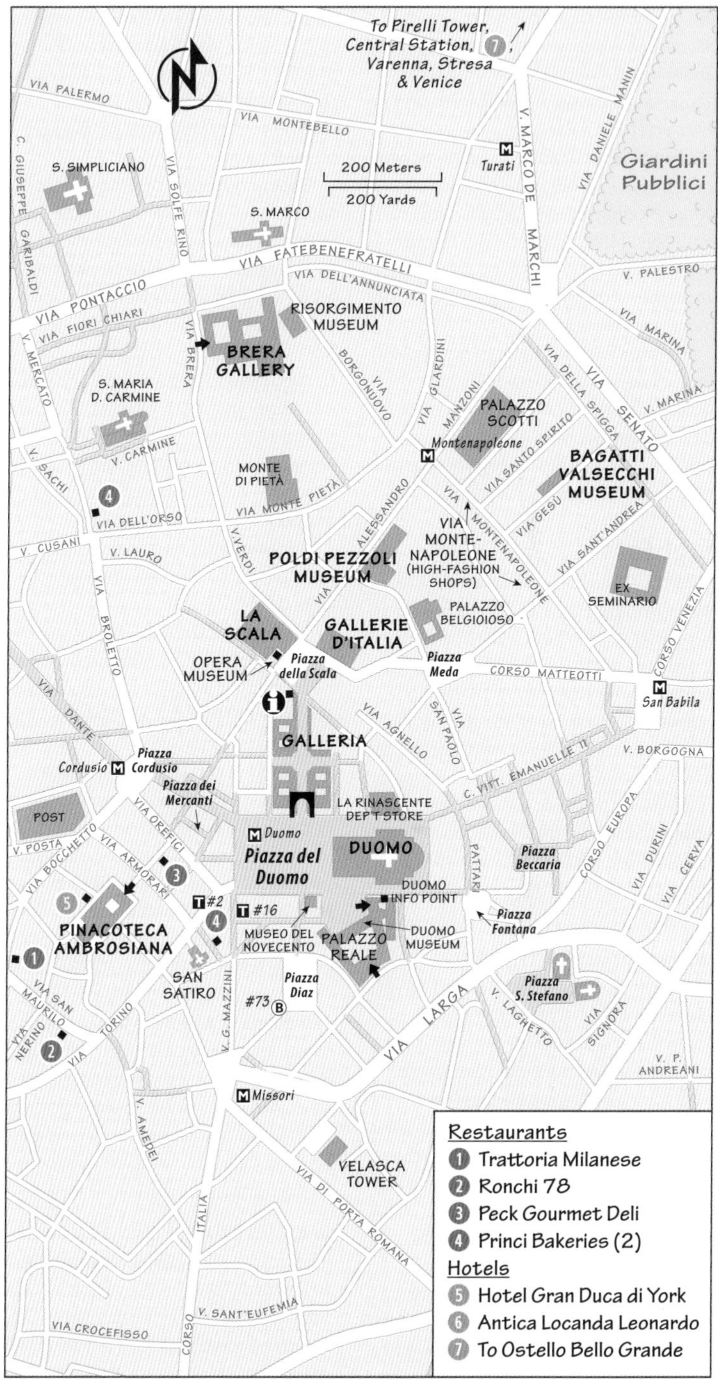
To Pirelli Tower, Central Station, 7, Varenna, Stresa & Venice
200 Meters
200 Yards
Turati
Giardini Pubblici
S. SIMPLICIANO
S. MARCO
VIA PALERMO
VIA MONTEBELLO
VIA SOLFERINO
C. GIUSEPPE GARIBALDI
V. MARCO DE MARCHI
VIA DANIELE MANIN
VIA FATEBENEFRATELLI
VIA DELL'ANNUNCIATA
VIA PONTACCIO
VIA FIORI CHIARI
V. PALESTRO
RISORGIMENTO MUSEUM
BRERA GALLERY
VIA BRERA
V. MERCATO
VIA BORGONUOVO
VIA GIARDINI
VIA MARINA
S. MARIA D. CARMINE
V. CARMINE
VIA MANZONI
PALAZZO SCOTTI
Montenapoleone
VIA DELLA SPIGA
VIA SENATO
V. MARINA
VIA SANTO SPIRITO
BAGATTI VALSECCHI MUSEUM
MONTE DI PIETÀ
VIA MONTE PIETÀ
V. SACHI
VIA DELL'ORSO
VIA ALESSANDRO
VIA MONTENAPOLEONE
VIA GESÙ
VIA SANT'ANDREA
V. CUSANI
V. LAURO
V. VERDI
VIA MONTE-NAPOLEONE (HIGH-FASHION SHOPS)
POLDI PEZZOLI MUSEUM
EX SEMINARIO
VIA BROLETTO
LA SCALA
GALLERIE D'ITALIA
PALAZZO BELGIOIOSO
CORSO VENEZIA
OPERA MUSEUM
Piazza della Scala
Piazza Meda
CORSO MATTEOTTI
San Babila
VIA DANTE
GALLERIA
VIA AGNELLO
VIA SAN PAOLO
Piazza Cordusio
Cordusio
V. BORGOGNA
C. VITT. EMANUELE II
Piazza dei Mercanti
LA RINASCENTE DEP'T STORE
POST
VIA OREFICI
Duomo
Piazza del Duomo
DUOMO
V. POSTA
VIA BOCCHETTO
VIA ARMORARI
VIA PATTARI
Piazza Beccaria
CORSO EUROPA
VIA DURINI
VIA CERVA
DUOMO INFO POINT
#2
#16
PINACOTECA AMBROSIANA
MUSEO DEL NOVECENTO
PALAZZO REALE
DUOMO MUSEUM
Piazza Fontana
SAN SATIRO
Piazza Diaz
#73
VIA SAN MAURILO
VIA NERINO
VIA TORINO
V. G. MAZZINI
VIA LARGA
Piazza S. Stefano
V. LAGHETTO
VIA SIGNORA
V. P. ANDREANI
Missori
V. AMEDEI
VELASCA TOWER
VIA DI PORTA ROMANA
CORSO ITALIA
V. SANT'EUFEMIA
VIA CROCEFISSO
Restaurants
1 Trattoria Milanese
2 Ronchi 78
3 Peck Gourmet Deli
4 Princi Bakeries (2)
Hotels
5 Hotel Gran Duca di York
6 Antica Locanda Leonardo
7 To Ostello Bello Grande

18:00, Sun 10:00-18:00, Metro: Duomo, tel. 02-884-5555, www.turismo.milano.it). Other helpful websites covering what's happening are www.hellomilano.it and www.wantedinmilan.com.

Using Public Transit: A **single ticket,** valid for 90 minutes, can be used for one ride, including transfers, on all forms of transport. Tickets must be run through the machines at Metro turnstiles when you enter and leave the station (€1.50, for more, see www.atm.it).

Private Guides: These guides know their city's history (€160-195/3 hours)—Lorenza Scorti (mobile 347-735-1346, lorenza.scorti@libero.it) and Sara Cerri (mobile 380-433-3019, www.walkingtour-milan.it, walkingtourmilan@gmail.com).

Sights

Milan's core sights—the Duomo, Duomo Museum, and Galleria Vittorio Emanuele II—cluster within easy walking distance. Download my free Milan's Duomo Neighborhood audio tour to link them in one convenient stroll (see page 28). Also in the Duomo area are the Piazza della Scala and La Scala Opera House.

Milan's other main sights—The Last Supper, Sforza Castle, and Brera Art Gallery—are scattered farther afield. It's easiest to reach them by public transportation.

▲▲▲DUOMO (CATHEDRAL)

The city's centerpiece is the third-largest church in Europe (after St. Peter's Basilica in Rome and Sevilla's Cathedral). At 525 by 300 feet, the place is immense, with more than 2,000 statues inside (and 1,000 outside) and 52 100-foot-tall pillars (representing the weekly liturgical calendar). If you do two laps, you've done your daily walk.

A visit here has several elements. First, take in the overwhelming exterior from various angles. Then go inside (requires a ticket) to see the church's vast nave, stained glass, historic tombs, and a quirky, one-of-a-kind statue of a flayed man. Nearby, visit the adjacent Duomo Museum. Finally, take an elevator ride (or long stair climb) up to the Duomo rooftop for city views and remarkable architecture.

Cost and Hours: Duomo and Duomo Museum—€3, includes skippable San Gottardo Church; rooftop terraces—€13 by elevator, €9 via stairs. To visit the archaeological area under the church, you'll need a separate €7 ticket or combo-ticket (€12-16); check website for details; Duomo and archaeological area—daily 8:00-19:00, last entry at 18:00; Duomo Museum—Thu-Tue 10:00-18:00, closed Wed, last entry at 17:00; rooftop terraces—daily 9:00-19:00, last ascent at 18:00.

Information: Church tel. 02-7202-2656, museum tel. 02-860-358, www.duomomilano.it.

Visiting the Duomo: Begin by circling the Duomo's pink marble exterior, then head inside to enjoy its remarkable bulk, fine 15th-century stained-glass windows, and Baroque altar. Napoleon crowned himself King of Italy under the altar's dome in 1805. The **▲Duomo Museum** helps to fill out the cathedral's story, and lets you see its original art and treasures up close. It's worth a walk-through if you have an interest in old church art. The collection lacks description (in any language), so get the audioguide (€5).

Strolling among the frilly spires of the cathedral's **▲▲rooftop terraces** is the most memorable part of a Duomo visit. You'll loop around the rooftop, wandering through a fancy forest of pinnacles with great views of the city, the square, and—on clear days—the crisp and jagged Alps to the north.

▲▲GALLERIA VITTORIO EMANUELE II

This breathtaking glass-domed arcade, next to Piazza del Duomo, is a symbol of Milan. Built during the 19th-century age of Eiffel, the iron-and-glass shopping mall showcased a new, modern era. It was the first

Two of Milan's top sights—the Duomo and the Galleria Vittorio Emanuele II (with flags)—are neighbors on the Piazza del Duomo.

building in town to have electric lighting and, from its inception, has been an elegant and popular meeting place. Luxury shops have had outlets here from the beginning.

At the venerable **Bar Camparino** (at the Galleria's Piazza del Duomo entry), turn an expensive cup of coffee into a good value by enjoying some of Europe's best people-watching (Tue-Sun 7:30-20:00, closed Mon and Aug).

▲▲LA SCALA OPERA HOUSE AND MUSEUM

Milan's famous Teatro alla Scala opened in 1778 with an opera by Antonio Salieri (Mozart's wannabe rival). Today, opera buffs can get a glimpse of the theater and tour the adjacent museum's extensive collection.

Cost and Hours: Museum—€8, daily 9:00-17:30, Piazza della Scala, tel. 02-8879-7473, www.teatroallascala.org.

Museum: The collection features Verdi's top hat, Rossini's eyeglasses, Toscanini's baton, Fettuccini's pesto, original scores, diorama stage sets, and death masks of great composers and musicians. But the main reason to visit is the opportunity (on most days) to peek into the actual theater. Take in the ornate red-velvet seats, white-and-gold trim, the huge stage and orchestra pit, and the massive chandelier made of Bohemian crystal.

Performances: The show goes on at the opera house every month except August. Seats sell out quickly. For schedules, online sales, and info on same-day tickets, see www.teatroallascala.org. You can also call Scala Infotel Service (daily 9:00-18:00, tel. 02-7200-3744).

▲▲BRERA ART GALLERY (PINACOTECA DI BRERA)

Milan's top collection of Italian paintings (13th-20th centuries) was established in 1809 to house Napoleon's looted art. Pick up an English map of the masterpieces. Highlights are Antonio Canova's nude statue of *Napoleon with Tinkerbell* (in the courtyard); Andrea Mantegna's tour-de-force *The Dead Christ* (a textbook example of feet-first foreshortening, in Room VI); Raphael's *Wedding of the Madonna* (Room XXIV); and the gritty-yet-intimate realism of Caravaggio's *Supper at Emmaus* (Room XXIX).

Cost and Hours: €10, Tue-Sun 8:30-19:15, closed Mon, last entry 45 minutes before closing, audioguide-€5 (useful, but museum has excellent English descriptions), Via Brera 28, Metro: Lanza or Montenapoleone, tel. 02-722-631, www.brera.beniculturali.it.

▲PINACOTECA AMBROSIANA

This oldest museum in Milan, inaugurated in 1618, features works by Botticelli, Caravaggio, and Titian—and, most important, a huge-scale sketch by Raphael (in Room 5) and a rare oil painting by Leonardo da Vinci (in Room 24, along with a big replica painting of *The Last Supper*).

Cost and Hours: €15, Tue-Sun 10:00-18:00, closed Mon, last entry one hour before closing, Piazza Pio XI 2, tel. 02-806-921, www.ambrosiana.eu.

▲▲LEONARDO DA VINCI'S *THE LAST SUPPER (L'ULTIMA CENA)*

Decorating the former dining hall of the Church of Santa Maria delle Grazie, this fresco by Leonardo da Vinci is one of the ultimate masterpieces of the Renaissance.

Cost and Hours: €12, includes €2 reservation fee (some visits cost €3.50 extra and include English tour); open Tue-Sun 8:15-18:45 (last entry), closed Mon; fine audioguide-€3.50. Show up 20 minutes before your scheduled entry.

Reservations: Reservations are mandatory, as only 30 tourists are allowed in, every 15 minutes, for exactly 15 minutes. Timed-entry reservations for each calendar month go on sale three months ahead. You can book **online** (www.vivaticket.it, type "Cenacolo Vinciano" in the search bar at the top of the page), but you may get a greater selection of time slots if you book by **phone** (from the US dial 011-39-02-9280-0360, office open Mon-Sat 8:00-18:30, closed Sun). A few scattered same-day spots may be available due to cancellations. It's a low-percentage play, but you can try just showing up and asking at the desk—even if the sold-out sign is posted.

Getting There: The church is a 10-minute walk from Metro: Cadorna or Conciliazione. Or take tram #16 from the Duomo (direction: San Siro or Piazzale Segesta).

Rick's Tip: *If you can't get a **reservation for The Last Supper,** consider a €60-75 tour that includes a guided visit to Leonardo's masterpiece (try **Veditalia,** www.veditalia.com, or **City Wonders,** www.citywonders.com). Other possibilities are year-round bus-and-walking tours (www.autostradaleviaggi.it or www.zaniviaggi.com) or seasonal hop-on, hop-off buses (www.milano.city-sightseeing.it) that charge extra for a reservation.*

Visiting *The Last Supper*: As your appointed time nears, you'll be herded between several rooms to reduce humidity before you reach the fresco, allowing you ample time to read this:

Hired by the ruling Sforza family, Leon-

La Scala Opera House

Leonardo da Vinci, The Last Supper

ardo worked on the fresco from about 1492 until 1498. It was essentially a bribe to the Dominican monks so that the Sforzas could place their family tomb in the church. Ultimately, the French drove the Sforzas out of Milan, they were never buried here, and the monks got a great fresco for nothing.

Deterioration began within six years of *The Last Supper's* completion because Leonardo painted on the wall in layers, as he would on a canvas, instead of applying pigment to wet plaster in the usual fresco technique. The church was bombed in World War II, but—miraculously, it seems—the wall holding *The Last Supper* remained standing. A 21-year restoration project (completed in 1999) peeled away 500 years of touch-ups, leaving Leonardo's masterpiece faint but vibrant.

The fresco is at one end of a big, vacant whitewashed room. Leonardo captures the psychological drama as the Lord says, "One of you will betray me," and the apostles huddle in stressed-out groups of three, wondering, "Lord, is it I?" Some are scandalized. Others want more information. Simon (on the far right) gestures as if to ask a question that has no answer. In this agitated atmosphere, Judas (fourth from left and the only one with his face in shadow) clutches his 30 pieces of silver and looks pretty guilty. With the extremely natural effect of the light and the drama of the faces, Leonardo created a tour de force.

▲▲SFORZA CASTLE (CASTELLO SFORZESCO)

The castle of Milan features a sprawling museum whose highlight is one of Michelangelo's final sculptures, the unfinished but powerful *Pietà*.

Cost and Hours: €5, free entry after 16:30 (Tue after 14:00); museum open Tue-Sun 9:00-17:30, closed Mon; castle grounds open daily 7:00-19:00, until 18:00 Nov-March; Metro: Cairoli or Lanza, tel. 02-8846-3700, www.milanocastello.it. If you walk here, take Via Dante, the pedestrian boulevard.

Visiting the Museum: It houses an array of exhibits, but I'd concentrate on the Michelangelo *Pietà* and the Museum of Ancient Art. Michelangelo died while still working on his fourth pietà—a representation of a dead Christ with a sorrowful Virgin Mary. While unfinished and seemingly a mishmash of corrections and reworks, it's a thought-provoking work by a genius at nearly 90 years old. The Museum of Ancient Art has an extensive collection of interesting medieval armor, furniture, early Lombard art, tapestries, and a room with the walls and ceiling painted by Leonardo—an intricate forest canopy woven with branches and rope in complicated knots.

Nightlife

For evening action, check out the artsy Brera area in the old center, with several swanky sidewalk cafés to choose from and lots of bars that stay open late. Another great neighborhood for nightlife, especially for a younger scene, is Naviglio Grande, Milan's "Little Venice" (Metro: Porta Genova).

Eating and Sleeping

$$$ Trattoria Milanese is family-run and traditional (Via Santa Marta 11). **$$$ Ronchi 78** has dependable Milanese classics (Via San Maurilio 7). **Peck Gourmet Deli** serves delectable fancy food for a superb though pricey picnic dinner (Via Spadari 9). **La Rinascente** department store, next to the Duomo, has a top-end food court with free city views and a WC on its seventh floor. **Princi** bakery is mobbed with locals vying for focaccia and luscious pastries (Via Speronari 6, also at Via Ponte Vetero 10).

If you're overnighting, **$$$$ Hotel Gran Duca di York** is modern, bright, and near the Duomo (www.ducadiyork.com).

$$$ Antica Locanda Leonardo, just down the street from *The Last Supper,* has a romantic, Old World vibe (www.anticalocandaleonardo.com). **¢ Ostello Bello Grande,** near the train station, is a well-priced hostel with hipster flair and some private rooms (www.ostellobello.com).

BEST OF THE REST

VARENNA ON LAKE COMO

Lined with stately 19th-century villas, crowned by snowcapped mountains, and busy with ferries and boats, Lake Como is a good place to take a vacation. It seems like half the travelers you'll meet have tossed their itineraries into the lake and are actually relaxing. And the best place for it is the lakeside village of Varenna. Other than watch visitors wash ashore with the landing of each ferry, there's wonderfully little to do. Varenna's volume goes down with the sun. At night, it whispers *luna di miele*—honeymoon.

Orientation

For the best mix of accessibility and scenery, Varenna can't be beat. On the quieter side of the lake, with a tiny harbor, narrow lanes, and dreamy views, Varenna is the ideal spot to munch a peach and ponder the place where Italy is welded to the Alps.

Day Plan: Spend time exploring Varenna, then take a ferry to admire the scenery and lakeside villas, or to poke around in the picturesque town of Bellagio.

Getting to Varenna by Train: From any destination covered in this book, you'll reach Lake Como via Milan. The quickest, easiest, and cheapest way is to take the train to Varenna (1-2/hour, 70 minutes) from Milan's central train station (Milano Centrale; catch train heading for Sondrio or Tirano and get off at Varenna-Esino-Perledo).

Getting to Varenna by Boat via Como: For a less convenient, much slower, but more scenic trip, take the train from Milan to the town of Como (2/hour, 30-60 minutes), walk 10 minutes to the dock, and catch a speedy hydrofoil or leisurely *battello* to Varenna (boats leave about every 2 hours).

Arrival in Varenna: Pretty much everything is within a 15-minute **walk** of the train station and boat dock. A **taxi** from the station costs about €10. **Drivers** can park at the multilevel lot at the south end of town.

Tourist Information: The TI is on Varenna's **main square** (closed Mon in season, open weekends only off-season, Via IV Novembre 7, tel. 0341-830-367, www.varennaturismo.com). The Tivano travel agency in the **train station** also operates as a TI, sells train tickets, and offers bus and boat tours of the region (open daily in season, www.tivanotours.com).

Sights

PASSERELLA

A generation ago, Varenna built this lovely lakeside promenade to connect the ferry dock with the old town center. Arcing past private villas guarded by wrought iron and wisteria, it's romantic. After dark, it's adorned with caryatid lovers pressing silently against each other in the shadows.

▲HIKE TO VEZIO CASTLE

A steep and stony trail leads to Varenna's ruined hilltop castle, Castello di Vezio. Take the small road, Via per Vezio (about 100 feet south of—and to the right of—Hotel Montecodeno), and figure on a 20-minute walk one-way to the peaceful hamlet of Vezio. There, follow *castello* signs to the bar that serves as the castle's ticket desk. Follow the little loop trail on the lake side of the castle for vistas over the rooftops, and climb the 62 steps of the castle tower for a 360-degree panorama of Lake Como. The castle hosts low-key falconry shows, usually around 15:30—but check the website or call in the morning for times.

Cost and Hours: €4, daily 10:00-18:00, closes at 17:00 March and Oct, closed Nov-Feb and in bad weather, www.castellodivezio.it.

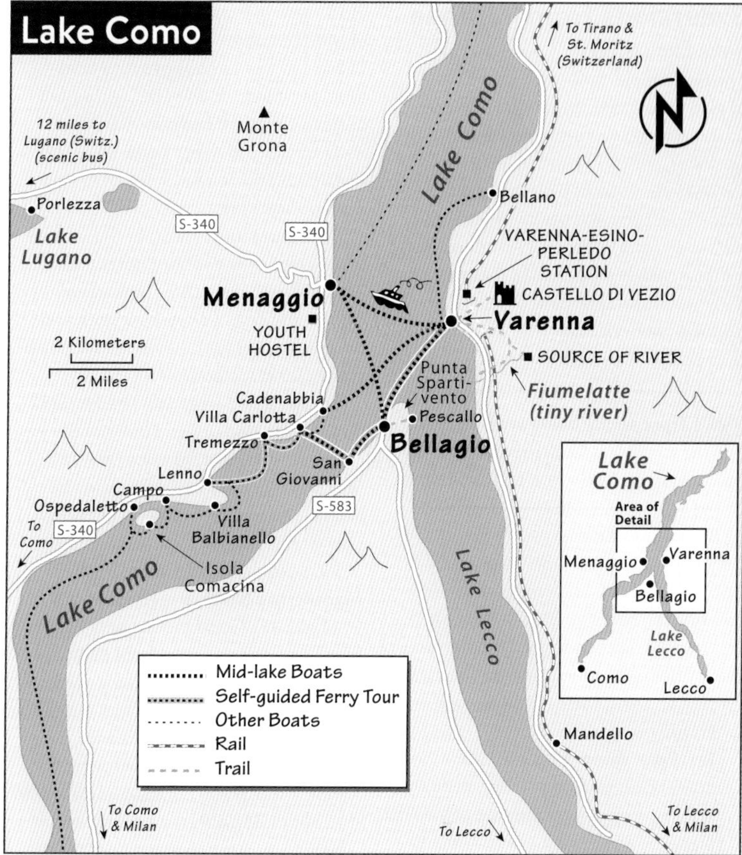

GARDENS

Two separate manicured lakeside gardens sit next door to each other just a short distance from the main square. The first are the small but lush terraces of **Villa Cipressi.** Just beyond are the more open grounds of **Villa Monastero,** which also admits visitors into the villa. The former residence of the De Marchi family, the villa is now a museum filled with ornate furnishings from the late 1800s. It's the handiest look inside one of the villas that line the lakeshore.

Cost and Hours: Villa Cipressi—€5, May-Nov daily 8:00-sunset, www.hotelvillacipressi.it. Villa Monastero—gardens—€5, gardens and museum—€8; gardens open March-Oct daily 9:30-19:00, museum open Fri-Sun only except in Aug, when it's open daily, www.villamonastero.eu. Both villas are closed off-season.

SWIMMING

There are three spots to swim in Varenna: the free little beach behind Hotel Royal Victoria off Piazza San Giorgio; the central lakefront area by Nilus Bar; and the *lido,* which is well-equipped for swimmers. Just north of the boat dock, it has showers, bathrooms, a restaurant/bar, and lounge chairs and umbrellas for rent (entry—€2).

Excursions from Varenna

Lake Excursions

The best simple day out on Lake Como is to take the *battello navetta* (mid-lake ferry) on its entire 50-minute Varenna-Bellagio-Villa Carlotta-Tremezzo-Lenno route. On the return trip, hop off at any sights that interest you: the beautiful Villa del Balbianello and its gardens (in Lenno, www.visitfai.it/villadelbalbianello), the impressive museum and gardens of the Villa Carlotta (www.villacarlotta.it), and/or the resort town of Bellagio (see next).

Rick's Tip: *Because* **boats are frequent** *and the schedule is hard to read, I just show up, buy a ticket for the next boat, and wait.*

Boats go about every 30 minutes between Varenna and Bellagio (€4.60/hop, cash only, 15-20 minutes; boat info: toll-free tel. 800-551-801 or tel. 031-579-211, www.navigazionelaghi.it). When you depart Bellagio (which has several docks), be sure you're at the right dock—ask when you buy your ticket.

Taxi Boat Varenna organizes one-hour central lake tours (€30/person); their 2.5-hour tour includes a guided stop at Villa del Balbianello (€55/person, www.taxiboatvarenna.com).

Boats2rent allows you to be your own skipper (motor boats from €60/hour for up to six people, no license required but €100 and ID needed for deposit, plus €10/hour kayaks, at harbor in front of Nilus Bar).

Bellagio Side-Trip

A classy combination of tidiness and Old World elegance, Bellagio is easy to reach by boat from Varenna. If you don't mind that "tramp in a palace" feeling, it's a fine place to surround yourself with posh travelers. Arcades facing the lake are lined with shops (heavy curtains hanging between the arches keep the visitors and their poodles from sweating).

The TI at the Bellagio boat dock has free brochures for well-crafted walking tours, varying from one to three hours, all of which explore the city and environs. Bellagio Water Limousines runs boat tours (at the dock, www.bellagiowaterlimousines.com) and Bellagio Water Sports rents kayaks and offers kayak tours (book ahead, 10-minute walk south of town, www.bellagiowatersports.com).

For wine tasting, step into the vaulted stone cellar of the funky **Enoteca Cava Turacciolo** to taste three regional wines with a sampling of cheeses, meats, and breads (€19 for Rick Steves readers, open long hours but closed Wed, Genazzini 3).

For lakeside dining, **$$$ The Florence** is nicely situated under a trellis of flowers (across from Hotel Florence on Piazza Mazzini). For dessert, try Bellagio's best gelato—hike up to **Gelateria del Borgo** (Via Garibaldi 46).

Picnickers can stock up at **Butti Macelleria e Salumeria** (closed Mon, Via Garibaldi 42). Good picnic spots are the benches along the waterfront in town and lining the promenade south of town.

An excellent viewpoint (that also works for a picnic) is **Punta Spartivento,** a park a few minutes' walk north of town. Its Renoir atmosphere comes complete with the inviting **$$ La Punta** bar-restaurant (open daily for lunch and dinner), a little harbor, and a chance to sit on a park bench and gaze north past the end of the lake to the Swiss Alps.

Varenna on Lake Como

Eating and Sleeping

For fancy lake-view dining in Varenna, try **$$$$ Ristorante la Vista** (Via XX Settembre 35) or **$$$$ Ristorante la Contrada** (Via IV Novembre 22). Two simple eateries, both with great views and lakefront seating, are on the harborfront: **$$ Nilus Bar** (closed Tue) and **$$ Bar Il Molo,** next door (daily). Varenna's two little grocery stores (at Via IV Novembre 2 and Via Venini 6) have all you need for a tasty balcony or breakwater picnic-dinner. **Gelateria Riva,** overlooking the water, makes its gelato fresh every day.

For overnighters, **$$$$ Villa Cipressi** sprawls gracefully along the lake in a centuries-old mansion (www.hotelvillacipressi.it), the romantic **$$$ Albergo Milano** offers extravagant views (www.varenna.net), and **$$$ Albergo del Sole** rents eight simple, comfortable rooms right on the town square (www.albergodelsolevarenna.it).

BEST OF THE REST

VERONA AND PADUA

If you want low-key Italian towns that have just enough sights and more than enough ambience, Verona and Padua make good stops. History buffs enjoy Verona's impressive Roman ruins. The town is also the pick for star-crossed lovers retracing Romeo and Juliet's steps. Art lovers head to Padua for Giotto's celebrated Scrovegni Chapel (reservations required).

The towns are nearly next-door neighbors. Connected by frequent trains (2/hour), Verona and Padua are only 40-80 minutes apart (depending on the speed of your train). Either town makes a fine day trip or a pleasant overnight. They're easy stops on the Milan-Venice train line.

Verona

Romeo and Juliet made Verona a household name, though the town's top attractions are its ancient Roman Arena, its pedestrian-only ambience, and its world-class opera festival, held each summer. If you like Italy but don't need blockbuster sights, this town is a joy.

Orientation

The enjoyable core of Verona lies along Via Mazzini between Piazza Brà (pronounced "bra") and Piazza Erbe, Verona's market square since Roman times.

Day Plan: For a good day in Verona, take my self-guided walk, beginning with a visit to the Roman Arena.

Getting There: Every hour, at least two trains connect Verona with Venice (and Padua). To save money, choose a cheaper regional train (R or RV, 1.5-2.5 hours) instead of the more expensive Frecce express, which gets you there only a bit faster.

Arrival in Verona: From Verona's Porta Nuova train station, catch a **bus** to Piazza Brà, the city center (bus #11, #12, #13, #51, or #52 from in front of the station, buy ticket from station tobacco shop). A **taxi** to Piazza Brà costs about €8-10. Because the old town is closed to traffic, **drivers** can park in one of the well-marked lots or garages just outside the center.

Tourist Information: Verona's helpful TI, just off Piazza Brà, offers walking tours on weekends (Sat-Sun at 11:30, 75 minutes, call to confirm schedule; open daily except closed Sun off-season, Via degli Alpini 9, tel. 045-806-8680, www.turismoverona.eu).

Verona Card: This tourist card covers entrance to all recommended Verona sights and city transportation (€18/24 hours, buy at TI or participating sights, www.tourism.verona.it).

Private Guides: These Verona guides will tailor tours of the town and region to your interests: **Marina Menegoi** (mobile 328-958-1108, mmenegoi@gmail.com) and **Valeria Biasi** (mobile 348-903-4238, valeria@veronatours.com).

Rick's Tip: *From mid-June through early September,* **Verona's opera festival** *brings the city to life, with music fans filling the Roman Arena. Cheap day-of-show tickets are often available at the box office at Via Dietro Anfiteatro 6B (www.arena.it).*

➲ *Verona Walk*

Allow two hours for this self-guided walk covering the essential sights in the town core, starting at Piazza Brà (at the Arena end) and ending at the cathedral.

If you're wondering about the name ❶ **Piazza Brà,** it means "big open space." Piazza Brà is all about strolling, by day or night. The broad, marble sidewalk circling the square was built by 17th-century Venetians, who made it big and wide so that promenading socialites could see and be seen.

The ❷ **ancient Roman Arena** looming over the piazza looks great in its pink marble (most of it is original). Over the centuries, crowds of up to 25,000 spectators have cheered Roman gladiator battles, medieval executions, rock concerts, and modern plays, all taking advantage of the arena's famous acoustics. This is where the popular opera festival is held every summer. Inside, if you climb to the top, you'll enjoy great city views (€10, skip combo-ticket with unimpressive Maffei Museum, Tue-Sun 8:30-19:30, Mon 13:30-19:30, closes earlier during opera season).

Find the ❸ **devotional column** (next to the arena and its ticket office) that blessed a marketplace held here in the Middle Ages. A **bronze plaque** in the sidewalk shows the Roman city plan—a town of 20,000 placed strategically in the bend of the Adige River.

Now, with your back to the arena, head down Via Oberdan (bearing left at the fork) and continue a couple of blocks until you see an ancient gate to your right, ❹ **Porta Borsari.**

Roman Arena

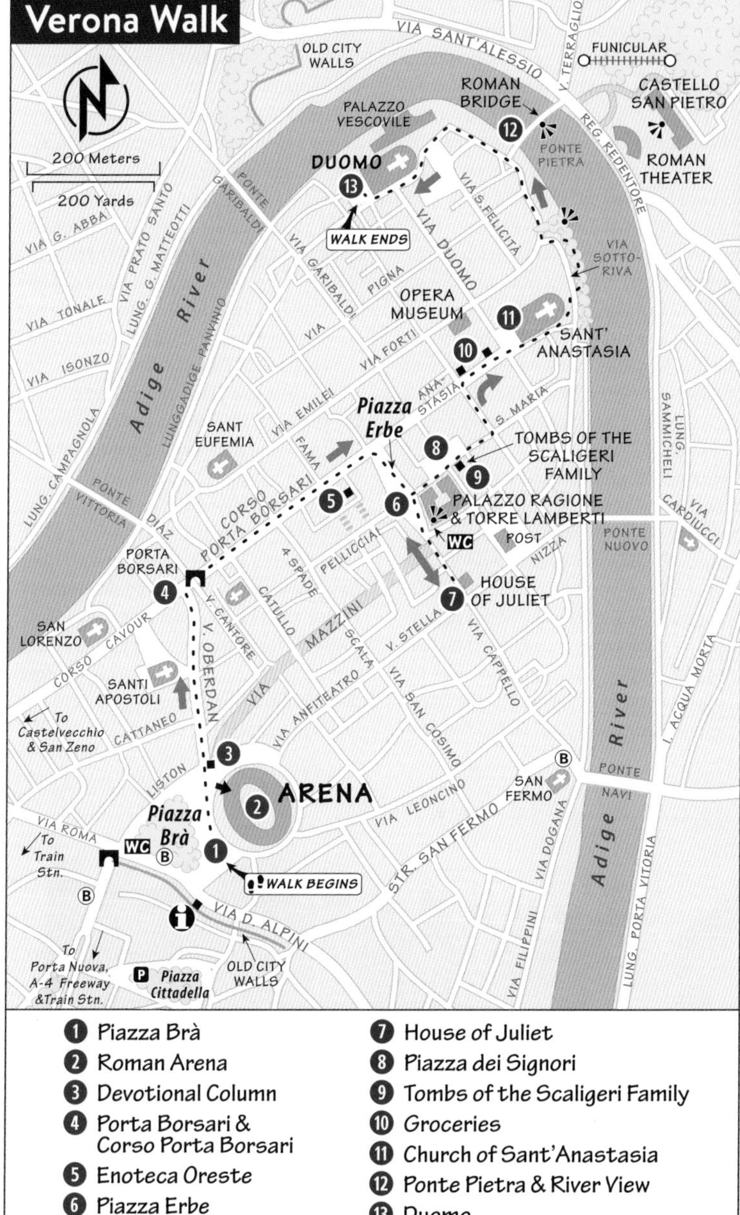
Verona Walk
200 Meters
200 Yards
OLD CITY WALLS
VIA SANT'ALESSIO
V. TERRAGLIO
FUNICULAR
ROMAN BRIDGE
CASTELLO SAN PIETRO
PALAZZO VESCOVILE
DUOMO
PONTE PIETRA
ROMAN THEATER
REG. REDENTORE
PONTE GARIBALDI
WALK ENDS
VIA S. FELICITÀ
VIA DUOMO
VIA SOTTO-RIVA
VIA G. ABBA
VIA PRATO SANTO
LUNG. G. MATTEOTTI
Adige River
VIA GARIBALDI
PIGNA
OPERA MUSEUM
VIA TONALE
LUNGADIGE PANVINIO
VIA
VIA FORTI
SANT' ANASTASIA
VIA ISONZO
ANASTASIA
S. MARIA
VIA EMILEI
Piazza Erbe
SANT EUFEMIA
FAMA
TOMBS OF THE SCALIGERI FAMILY
LUNG. SAMMICHELI
LUNG. CAMPAGNOLA
PONTE VITTORIA
CORSO PORTA BORSARI
DIAZ
PALAZZO RAGIONE & TORRE LAMBERTI
VIA CARDUCCI
WC
POST
PONTE NUOVO
PORTA BORSARI
4 SPADE
PELLICCIAI
NIZZA
HOUSE OF JULIET
SAN LORENZO
CORSO CAVOUR
V. CANTORE
CATULLO
MAZZINI
V. STELLA
VIA CAPPELLO
V. OBERDAN
SCALA
SANTI APOSTOLI
VIA
VIA ANFITEATRO
VIA SAN COSIMO
I. ACQUA MORTA
To Castelvecchio & San Zeno
CATTANEO
LISTON
ARENA
SAN FERMO
PONTE NAVI
Piazza Brà
VIA ROMA
VIA LEONCINO
STR. SAN FERMO
VIA DOGANA
To Train Stn.
WALK BEGINS
LUNG. PORTA VITORIA
VIA D. ALPINI
VIA FILIPPINI
To Porta Nuova, A-4 Freeway &Train Stn.
Piazza Cittadella
OLD CITY WALLS
1 Piazza Brà
2 Roman Arena
3 Devotional Column
4 Porta Borsari & Corso Porta Borsari
5 Enoteca Oreste
6 Piazza Erbe
7 House of Juliet
8 Piazza dei Signori
9 Tombs of the Scaligeri Family
10 Groceries
11 Church of Sant'Anastasia
12 Ponte Pietra & River View
13 Duomo

You're standing before the main entrance to Roman Verona. Back then, this gate functioned as a tollbooth (*borsari* means purse). Find the stone on the curb alongside Caffè Rialto—it's from a tomb. In Roman times, the roads outside the walls were lined with tombstones because burials were not allowed within the town itself.

Cross under the Roman gate into the ancient city. As you walk down **Corso Porta Borsari,** you'll discover bits of the town's illustrious past—chips of Roman columns, medieval reliefs, fine old facades, and fossils in marble. If you want to take a break, the old-style ❺ **Enoteca Oreste** is a fun wine and grappa bar (detour a few steps right to Vicolo San Marco in Foro 7).

Corso Porta Borsari flows into ❻ **Piazza Erbe,** a bustling market square. Its pastel buildings corral the fountains, pigeons, and people who have congregated here since Roman times, when this was a forum. The stone canopy in the center of the square held the scales where medieval merchants weighed the goods they bought and sold.

At the far end of Piazza Erbe, a market column features St. Zeno, the patron of Verona. He looks at the masses flushing into the city's silly claim to touristic fame: the ❼ **House of Juliet** (100 yards down Via Cappello to #23, on the left).

The tiny, admittedly romantic courtyard is a spectacle, with tourists from all over the world posing on the supposed balcony of Romeo and Juliet fame (free, gates open roughly 9:00-19:30, "museum" not worth the entry fee). Was there ever a real Juliet Capulet? You just walked down Via Cappello, the street of the cap makers—logically, the Capulets.

Backtrack to Piazza Erbe and head right on Via della Costa to the harmonious ❽ **Piazza dei Signori.** Locals call it Piazza Dante for the statue of **Dante Alighieri** that dominates it. Dante—always pensive—seems to wonder why the tourists prefer Juliet to him.

At Dante's two o'clock is the 12th-century Romanesque **Palazzo della Ragione.** Peek into its courtyard to see the only surviving Renaissance staircase in Verona. For a grand view, climb the palazzo's **Torre dei Lamberti** (€8, Tue-Fri 10:00-18:00, Sat-Sun 11:00-19:00, closed Mon).

Piazza dei Signori

Leave Piazza dei Signori, heading downhill (alongside the brick, crenellated palazzo). Just ahead, behind fine, original, wrought-iron protective cages, are the very Gothic 14th-century ❾ **tombs of the Scaligeri family.** The Scaligeri were to Verona what the Medici family was to Florence—and so powerful that they could buck the law about in-city burials. (For more on the Scaligeris, visit their residence-fortress, the ▲ **Castelvecchio,** at Corso Castelvecchio 2, museodicastelvecchio.comune.verona.it.)

At the next corner, take a left on Vicolo Cavalletto; then go right along Corso Sant'Anastasia. For a tasty diversion, pop into ❿ **two classic grocery stores:** Gastronomia, at #33, and Albertini, at #41.

Straight ahead is the big, unfinished brick facade of the ⓫ **Church of Sant'Anastasia** (€2.50, open daily). It's worth stepping inside this medieval church for its beautiful frescoes, especially Pisanello's *St. George and the Princess* (1438).

Go along the right side of the church to Via Sottoriva and jog left. You'll soon reach a small riverfront promenade that usually accommodates a few modern-day Romeos and Juliets. Belly up for the ⓬ **river and Ponte Pietra views.** The white stones of the footbridge are from the original Roman bridge that stood here. (The Veronese fished the marble chunks from the river after it was bombed in World War II.) From here, you can see across the river to an ancient Roman theater, built into the hillside. Way above the theater (behind the cypress trees) is a 15th-century fortress, Castello San Pietro.

Continue walking upriver (watch for the excellent **Gelateria Ponte Pietra,** at #13) toward the tall, white steeple of the ⓭ **Duomo** (€2.50, open daily). Started in the 12th century, this church was built over a period of several hundred years. Before entering, note the fine Romanesque carvings on its facade. Inside, the highlight is Titian's 16th-century ***Assumption of the Virgin*** (last chapel on the left). Mary calmly rides a cloud—direction up—to the shock and bewilderment of the crowd below.

Adjacent to the church is a fine **baptistery,** with clean Romanesque lines, a 14th-century crucifix, and a fine marble font. The peaceful **cloister** (around the left side of the church, as you face it) has the remains of a fifth-century mosaic floor.

Nightlife

The nighttime highlight of Verona is the ▲▲ ***passeggiata.*** Join the slow and elegant parade of strollers in making a big circle from Piazza Brà through the old town on Via Mazzini to the colorful Piazza Erbe, and then back down Corso Porta Borsari to Piazza Brà. To complement your stroll, try a *spritz* drink on Piazza Erbe (the most elegant bars are on the end farthest from Juliet's balcony).

Eating and Sleeping

Verona relishes its ***aperitivo*** ritual. All over town, locals enjoy a refreshing *spritz* (Campari and white wine), ideally on Piazza Erbe between 18:00 and 20:00. Choose a nice perch, and then, for about €4, you'll get the drink of your choice, a few nibbles (olives and/or potato chips), and a chance to feel very local as you enjoy the *passeggiata* scene.

For fine dining, **$$$$ Enoteca Cangrande** offers great, well-matched food and wine (closed Tue off-season, a block off Piazza Brà at Via Dietro Liston 19D). The bustling **$$$ Trattoria al Pompiere** serves classic regional specialties (closed Sun, Vicolo Regina d'Ungheria 5). Fun, family-run **$$ Osteria al Duca** has locals lining up for its affordable, traditional dishes (closed Sun, Via Arche Scaligere 2). **$ Brek Cafeteria,** a modern chain, makes eating on Piazza Brà affordable (Piazza Brà 20).

If you're staying overnight, try the stylish **$$$$ Hotel Giulietta e Romeo** (www.hotelgr.it), the homey **$$ Hotel Torcolo** (with a good family-style restaurant, www.hoteltorcolo.it), or the basic **$$ Albergo Arena** (www.albergoarena.it).

Padua

Lively Padua (Padova in Italian) is sprinkled with surprises, with its university adding a youthful vibe. Lovers of early Renaissance art make a pilgrimage here for the remarkable Scrovegni Chapel and its Giotto frescoes (reservations required). The religious faithful come for the cult relics of St. Anthony, preserved at the basilica dedicated to him.

Orientation

Padua's main tourist sights lie on a north-south axis through the heart of the city, from the train station to the Scrovegni Chapel to the market squares (the center of town) to the Basilica of St. Anthony.

Day Plan: Your plan will be based on when you get reservations to see the Scrovegni Chapel. Here's a possibility for a day trip: 9:00—Market action and sightseeing in town center, 11:00—Basilica of St. Anthony, 13:00—lunch, 15:00—Scrovegni Chapel tour. It's roughly a 10-minute walk between each of the sights.

Getting There: Trains from Venice are cheap, take 25-50 minutes, and run frequently (2/hour). Baggage check is available at Padua's station.

Arrival in Padua: To get from the train station to the city center, hop on the handy **tram** (purchase tickets inside station or from booth out front). A **taxi** into town costs €8-10.

Tourist Information: TIs are at the train station (open daily) and in the **center** (closed Sun, behind Caffè Pedrocchi, Vicolo Cappellatto Pedrocchi 9, tel. 049-201-0080, www.turismopadova.it).

Padova Card: This pass includes entry to my recommended sights plus unlimited tram rides and free parking near Prato della Valle (€16/48 hours, buy at either TI, the Scrovegni Chapel, or online, www.padovacard.it).

Private Guide: Cristina Pernechele is a great teacher (mobile 338-495-5453, cristina@pernechele.eu).

Sights

Padua's two main sights (Scrovegni Chapel and Basilica of St. Anthony) are, respectively, at the north and south end of downtown. But the city's atmospheric, cobbled core—with flourishing markets and inviting sun-and-café-speckled piazzas—is its own attraction.

▲▲MARKET SQUARES

The medieval Palazzo della Ragione provides a dramatic backdrop for Padua's produce market, which fills the surrounding squares—**Piazza delle Erbe** and **Piazza della Frutta**—each weekday morning and all day Saturday (closed Sun). This market has been renowned for centuries for its great selection of herbs, fruits, and vegetables. Stock up on picnic supplies here.

Don't miss the **indoor market** zone on the ground floor of the Palazzo della Ragione, where you'll find various butchers, *salumerie* (delicatessens), cheese shops, bakeries, and fishmongers at work. **Piazza dei Signori,** just a block away, is a busy clothing market in the morning and a popular gathering place for students in the evening.

▲▲▲SCROVEGNI CHAPEL (CAPPELLA DEGLI SCROVEGNI)

Giotto's beautifully preserved 14th-century fresco cycle covers the walls of the renovated Scrovegni Chapel. Its nearly 40 scenes from the lives of Jesus and Mary represent a turning point in European art and culture—away from scenes of heaven and toward a more down-to-earth, human-centered view. You must make reservations in advance to see the chapel. If you packed binoculars, bring them along for a better—and more comfortable—view of the uppermost frescoes.

Cost and Hours: €13 (also covers nearby Civic Museums). The chapel is open daily 9:00-19:00; Piazza Eremitani 8, tel. 049-201-0020, www.cappelladegliscrovegni.it. The nearest tram stop is Eremitani.

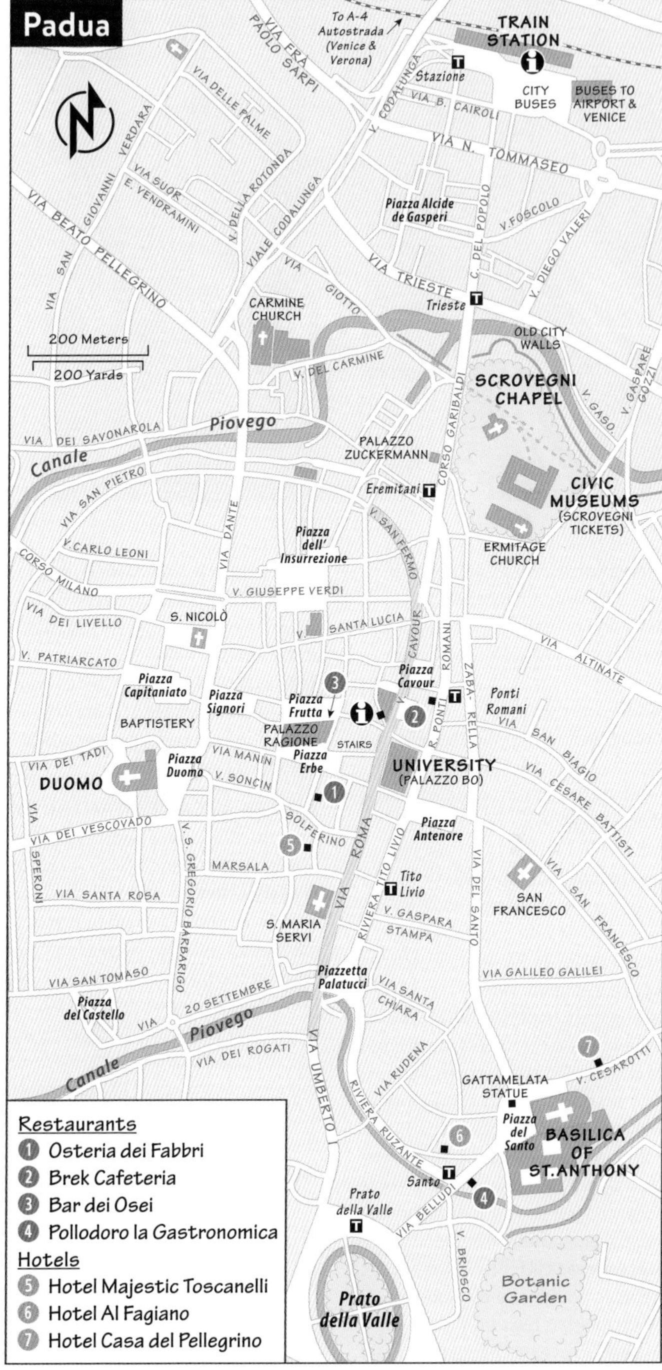
Padua
To A-4 Autostrada (Venice & Verona)
TRAIN STATION
Stazione
CITY BUSES
BUSES TO AIRPORT & VENICE
VIA FRA PAOLO SARPI
VIA DELLE PALME
V. CODALUNGA
VIA B. CAIROLI
VIA N. TOMMASEO
VIA GIOVANNI VERDARA
VIA SUOR E. VENDRAMINI
V. DELLA ROTONDA
VIALE CODALUNGA
Piazza Alcide de Gasperi
V. FOSCOLO
V. DIEGO VALERI
C. DEL POPOLO
VIA BEATO PELLEGRINO
VIA SAN GIOVANNI
VIA GIOTTO
VIA TRIESTE
Trieste
CARMINE CHURCH
200 Meters
200 Yards
OLD CITY WALLS
V. DEL CARMINE
SCROVEGNI CHAPEL
V. GASO
V. GASPARE GOZZI
VIA DEI SAVONAROLA
Piovego
Canale
PALAZZO ZUCKERMANN
CORSO GARIBALDI
VIA SAN PIETRO
Eremitani
CIVIC MUSEUMS (SCROVEGNI TICKETS)
VIA DANTE
Piazza dell' Insurrezione
V. SAN FERMO
V. CARLO LEONI
ERMITAGE CHURCH
CORSO MILANO
V. GIUSEPPE VERDI
VIA DEI LIVELLO
S. NICOLÒ
V. SANTA LUCIA
V. CAVOUR
ROMANI
VIA ALTINATE
V. PATRIARCATO
Piazza Cavour
ZABARELLA
Piazza Capitaniato
Piazza Signori
Piazza Frutta
Ponti Romani
BAPTISTERY
PALAZZO RAGIONE
STAIRS
R. PONTI
VIA SAN BIAGIO
VIA DEI TADI
VIA MANIN
Piazza Erbe
Piazza Duomo
UNIVERSITY (PALAZZO BO)
DUOMO
V. SONCIN
VIA CESARE BATTISTI
VIA DEI VESCOVADO
SOLFERINO
VIA ROMA
Piazza Antenore
VIA SPERONI
V. S. GREGORIO BARBARIGO
MARSALA
TITO LIVIO
Tito Livio
VIA DEL SANTO
VIA SAN FRANCESCO
VIA SANTA ROSA
S. MARIA SERVI
RIVIERA
V. GASPARA STAMPA
SAN FRANCESCO
VIA GALILEO GALILEI
VIA SAN TOMASO
Piazzetta Palatucci
VIA SANTA CHIARA
Piazza del Castello
VIA 20 SETTEMBRE
Piovego
Canale
VIA DEI ROGATI
VIA UMBERTO
VIA RUDENA
RIVIERA RUZANTE
GATTAMELATA STATUE
V. CESAROTTI
Piazza del Santo
BASILICA OF ST. ANTHONY
Santo
Prato della Valle
VIA BELLUDI
V. BRIOSCO
Prato della Valle
Botanic Garden
Restaurants
1 Osteria dei Fabbri
2 Brek Cafeteria
3 Bar dei Osei
4 Pollodoro la Gastronomica
Hotels
5 Hotel Majestic Toscanelli
6 Hotel Al Fagiano
7 Hotel Casa del Pellegrino

Scrovegni Chapel

Reservations: Only 25 people at a time are allowed in the chapel for 15-minute visits, and prepaid reservations are required. Reserve at least two days in advance at www.cappelladegliscrovegni.it or call 049-201-0020.

Getting In: To reach the chapel, enter through the Eremitani building, where you'll find the ticket office and a free but mandatory bag check.

Be at the chapel doors at least five minutes before your scheduled visit. If you're even a minute late, you'll forfeit your spot. At your appointed time, you first enter an anteroom to watch an instructive 15-minute video.

Visiting the Chapel: Although you have only 15 minutes in the chapel, it's divine. You're inside a Giotto time capsule, looking back at an artist ahead of his time.

Giotto painted the entire chapel in 200 working days over two years, from 1303 to 1305. In a sign of the Renaissance to come, Giotto placed real people in down-to-earth scenes, expressing human emotions. These frescoes were radical for their lively colors, light sources, emotion, and humanism.

The chapel was built from guilt. Reginaldo degli Scrovegni charged sky-high interest rates at a time when the Church forbade the practice. He even caught the attention of Dante, who placed him in one of the levels of hell in his *Inferno.* When Reginaldo died, the Church denied him a Christian burial. His son Enrico tried to buy forgiveness for his father's sins by building this superb chapel.

▲▲▲BASILICA OF ST. ANTHONY

Construction of this impressive Romanesque/Gothic church (with its Byzantine-style domes) started immediately after St. Anthony's death in 1231. As a mark of his universal appeal and importance in the medieval Church, he was sainted within a year of his death. For nearly 800 years, this glorious church has attracted pilgrims to Padua, both for the tomb and relics of its namesake saint and for the sumptuous main altar by the great Florentine sculptor Donatello. The basilica is a bigger hit with pilgrims than tourists. Enrich your experience by approaching it with a respectful mindset. Visit the holy relics with your hands folded, surrounded by others who came to Padua for this purpose. A modest dress code is enforced.

Basilica of St. Anthony

Cost and Hours: The basilica and chapel are free and open daily 6:20-19:45 (closes at 18:45 Nov-March; the chapel closes at lunchtime year-round), Via Orto Botanico 11, www.basilicadelsanto.org. The nearest tram stop is Santo.

Visiting the Basilica: On your way into the church, take note of the equestrian statue of a Venetian general by Donatello. Although it looks like a thousand other man-on-a-horse statues, it was a landmark in Italy's budding Renaissance—the first life-size, secular, equestrian statue cast from bronze in a thousand years.

Inside, gaze through the incense haze to Donatello's glorious crucifix and statues gracing the high altar. Donatello spent a decade in Padua (1444-1455) creating the ensemble.

You'll find Anthony's tomb in a side chapel decorated with marble reliefs showing scenes and miracles from the life of the saint. The Chapel of the Reliquaries (behind the altar) contains prized relics of the saint, including his miraculously unspoiled tongue.

Of the four cloisters, you can wander in three. In one, picnic tables invite pilgrims and tourists to enjoy meals (it's covered and suitable even when rainy, also has WCs).

Eating and Sleeping

$$ Osteria dei Fabbri, with shared rustic tables, offers a good mix of quality and price (Via dei Fabbri 13). The popular **$ Brek** self-service cafeteria is at Piazza Cavour 20 (a block from TI). **$ Bar dei Osei** is a sandwich bar with some of the best outdoor seats in town (Piazza della Frutta 1). **Pollodoro la Gastronomica** is my pick of the takeout delis near the basilica (Via Belludi 34).

If you're here in the early evening, get a **spritz** at a bar on Piazza dei Signori or Piazza della Erbe; grab a table, become part of the scene, and enjoy a discussion with smart, English-speaking students.

If staying the night, **$$ Hotel Majestic Toscanelli** is old-fashioned but well-located (www.toscanelli.com); **$$$ Hotel Al Fagiano** is bright and cheery (www.alfagiano.com); and the bare-bones **$ Hotel Casa del Pellegrino** is owned by the friars of St. Anthony (www.casadelpellegrino.com).

The Cinque Terre

Along a six-mile stretch of the Riviera lies the Cinque Terre (CHINK-weh TAY-reh), gently carving a good life out of difficult terrain. With a traffic-free charm—a happy result of their natural isolation—these five *(cinque)* towns are the rugged alternative to the glitzy resorts nearby. With sun, sea, sand (well, pebbles), and wine, this is pure, unadulterated Italy.

Each addictively photogenic village fills a ravine with a lazy hive of human activity—calloused locals and sunburned travelers enjoying a unique mix of culture and nature. Enjoy swimming, hiking, and evening romance in one of God's great gifts to tourism. While the Cinque Terre is now discovered (and can be crowded midday, when tourist boats and cruise ships drop by), I've never seen happier, more relaxed tourists. Most of the crowds are day-trippers, so make a point to get the most out of those cool, relaxed, and quiet hours early in the day and in the evening.

I cover the five towns in order from north to south—from Monterosso to Riomaggiore. Vernazza is my top choice for a home base, while Monterosso, the most resorty of the five towns, is an excellent runner-up, offering more amenities and activities. Avoid visiting in winter, when tall, crashing waves batter the charm out of the Cinque Terre.

THE CINQUE TERRE IN 2 DAYS

This string of five villages dotting the Italian Riviera makes an idyllic escape from the obligatory museums of turnstile Italy. The ideal stay is two full days (or three days to really relax). It's easiest to arrive and depart by train. If you have a car, park it in one of the few lots, then catch a shuttle bus into town.

Within the Cinque Terre, you can connect the towns in three ways: by train, boat, or foot. Trains are cheap, boats are more scenic, and hiking lets you enjoy more pasta. Consider supplementing the often frustratingly late trains with the sometimes more convenient boats.

Study your options, and piece together your best visit, mixing hiking, swimming, trains, boat rides, and a search for the best focaccia.

You could spend one day hiking from town to town (or take a boat or train partway, or as the return trip). For the best light, coolest temperatures, and fewest crowds,

start your hike early in the morning (or late in the afternoon). Cool off at a beach. Spend a second day visiting each town, comparing main streets, beaches, and gelato. And fit in another hike, if you like.

In the evenings, linger at a restaurant, enjoy live music at a low-key club, stroll any of the towns, or take a glass of your favorite beverage out to the breakwater to watch the sun slip into the Mediterranean.

Helpful Hints for the Cinque Terre

Book in Advance: It's essential to reserve rooms well in advance for these busy times—May, June, September, October, all summer weekends, and holidays (including Easter and April 25). Many accommodations in the Cinque Terre (especially in Vernazza) are *affittacamere,* or private rooms for rent. You get a key and come and go as you like, rarely seeing your landlord. Plan on paying cash. If you must cancel an *affittacamere* reservation, do it as early as possible. More formal places have strict cancellation policies.

Pickpocket Alert: At peak times, when the Cinque Terre is crowded, pickpockets (often female teens in groups of three or four) aggressively and expertly work the most congested areas. Be on guard, especially on train station platforms and while you're on trains and boats, particularly when getting on or off with a crush of people. Wear a money belt, and keep your things zipped up and buttoned down.

Money: You'll find banks and ATMs throughout the region.

Shuttle Buses: Each town has a helpful ATC shuttle bus route that generally runs through town and links the train station, nearest parking lot, and destinations farther up in the hills. Take a cheap joyride (€1.50 one-way, €2.50 from driver, free

THE CINQUE TERRE AT A GLANCE

▲▲**Monterosso al Mare** Resorty, flat, and spread out, with a charming old town, a modern new town, and the region's best beaches, swimming, and nightlife. See page 124.

▲▲▲**Vernazza** The region's gem, crowned with a ruined castle above and a lively waterfront cradling a natural harbor below. See page 134.

▲**Corniglia** Quiet hilltop village known for its cooler temperatures (it's the only one of the five villages set above the water), fewer tourists, and tradition of fine wines. See page 145.

▲▲**Manarola** Waterfront village dotted with a picturesque mix of shops, houses, and vineyards. See page 147.

▲**Riomaggiore** The biggest and most workaday of the five villages. See page 152.

with Cinque Terre park card required for coastal hikers—explained below). The buses don't connect Cinque Terre towns with each other.

Wi-Fi: All Cinque Terre train stations offer free Wi-Fi with a Cinque Terre park card.

Laundry: In Monterosso's new town, Wash and Dry Lavarapido offers full-service, same-day laundry at Via Molinelli 17 (also pick-up/drop-off service, daily, mobile 339-484-0940). In Vernazza, a small self-serve launderette is at the top of town next to the post office (daily).

Baggage Storage: You can store bags at the bar that also functions as the ***deposito bagagli*** office at Riomaggiore's train station; at the gift shop in Vernazza's train station, and in Monterosso at the TI next to the station or at Wash and Dry Lavarapido. All are open daily in season; for details, see individual town listings.

Services: Every train station has a free WC, but it's smart to bring your own toilet paper. Otherwise, pop into a bar or restaurant.

Tours: Arbaspàa, which has an office in Manarola, can arrange wine tasting at a vineyard, cooking classes (6-person minimum), fishing trips, and active adventures (office at Via Discovolo 204, tel. 0187-920-783, www.arbaspaa.com).

HIKING IN THE CINQUE TERRE

All five towns are connected by good trails, marked with red-and-white paint, white arrows, and some signs. The region has several numbered trails, but most visitors stick to the main coastal trail that connects the villages—that's trail #592 (also called SVA or the Blue Trail). You'll need a Cinque Terre park card to hike the main coastal trail.

Trail Closures: Trails can be closed in bad weather or due to landslides. Usually one or two trails are closed at any given time. These two segments will probably be closed when you visit: the trail between Riomaggiore and Manarola (a.k.a. the Via dell'Amore), and the trail between Manarola and Corniglia. Official closures are noted on the national park website (www.parconazionale5terre.it) and are posted at the park-information desks in each town's train station.

Hiking Conditions: Most of the main coastal trail is narrow, steep, rocky, and comes with lots of challenging steps. Readers often say the trail was tougher than they expected. The rocks can be slippery in the rain (avoid the steep Monterosso-Vernazza stretch if it's wet). Don't venture up on these rocky cliffs without sun protection or water.

When to Go: The coastal trail can be crowded (and hot) at midday. For the best light, coolest temperatures, and fewest crowds, start your hike early or late. If you want to hike in the evening, find out when the sun will set, and leave yourself plenty of time to arrive at your destination (no lighting on trails).

Navigation: Maps aren't necessary for the basic coastal hikes. But for more serious hikes in the high country, pick up a good hiking map (about €5, sold locally).

Give a Hoot: To leave the park cleaner than you found it, bring a plastic bag and pick up trail trash along the way.

Rick's Tip: *The Cinque Terre national park recently renamed and renumbered many local hiking trails. But you'll hear people using the old names/numbers, and many maps haven't caught up with the new system. Prepare to be confused!*

Cinque Terre Park Cards

The Cinque Terre—villages and all—is a national park. Each town has a park information office, which generally serves as an all-purpose town TI as well (listed throughout this chapter). The park's website—with up-to-date information on park cards, trail closures, and more—is www.parconazionale5terre.it.

Visitors hiking on the mainline coastal trails must buy a park card (good for one or two days, with an option covering trains). Cards can be purchased online, at train stations, TIs, and trailheads—good for 24 or 48 hours after validation. Those under 18 or over 70 get a discount, as do families with kids under age 13. The configuration and pricing of these cards is often in flux—the following details may change.

The **Cinque Terre Trekking Card** costs €7.50 for one day of hiking or €14.50 for two days (covers trails and ATC shuttle buses plus a few other extras but does not cover trains).

The **Cinque Terre Treno Multi-Service Card** covers what the Cinque Terre Trekking Card does, plus local trains connecting all Cinque Terre towns, Levanto, and La Spezia (€16/24 hours, €29/48 hours, validate card at train station by punching it in the machine). Even if you're not planning to hike, this card can be worth the price to avoid waiting in train ticket lines.

The Coastal Trail

If all of the main trails between the towns are open, the entire seven-mile coastal hike (which is very hilly between Corniglia and Monterosso) can be completed by fit hikers in about four hours; allow five or six for dawdling. Take it slow...smell the cactus flowers, notice the scurrying lizards, listen to birds singing in the olive groves, and enjoy vistas on all sides. You can tackle the hike in either direction, but remember that the coastal segments between Riomaggiore and Manarola and Corniglia are likely closed.

Of the hikes that are probably open: The trail from Corniglia to Vernazza is demanding, and the path from Vernazza to Monterosso is more challenging. Starting in Monterosso allows you to tackle the toughest section (with lots and lots of steep, narrow stairs) while you're fresh—and to enjoy some of the region's most dramatic scenery as you approach Vernazza.

Riomaggiore-Manarola (20 minutes): The popular, easy **Via dell'Amore** (Pathway of Love) was washed out by a landslide in 2012. If it's open, here's how to find the trailhead in Riomaggiore: Face the train station, go up the stairs to the right, following signs for *Via dell'Amore.* The photoworthy promenade winds along the coast to Manarola. A long tunnel and mega-nets protect hikers from

The trail views are worth the effort.

mean-spirited falling rocks. A recommended wine bar, Bar & Vini A Piè de Mà, is located at the Riomaggiore trailhead and offers light meals and awesome views. There's a picnic zone, a water fountain, and shade just above the Manarola station (and a WC at the station).

If the trail is closed, you can connect these towns by train, a scenic boat trip, or by taking the **alternative hiking route** (if it's open). Trail #531 goes up and over the mountain between these two towns (1.5 hours). But be warned: It's essentially stairs all the way up, then all the way down—it's more intense and dizzying than other parts of the coastal trail.

Manarola-Corniglia (45 minutes): The walk from Manarola to Corniglia is closed indefinitely due to landslides. If open, it's a little longer, more rugged, and steeper than the Via dell'Amore. To avoid the last stretch (switchback stairs leading up to the hill-capping town of Corniglia), end your hike at Corniglia's train station and catch the shuttle bus to the town center (2/hour, usually timed to meet trains).

If the trail is closed, you can connect the towns by train or this **alternative hiking route:** Hike between Manarola and Corniglia via Volastra (2.5 hours). The challenging trail leads from Manarola up to the village of Volastra, then north through high-altitude vineyard terraces, and steeply down through a forest to Corniglia (about four miles total). You can shave the two steepest miles off this route by taking the shuttle bus from Manarola up to Volastra (about hourly, 15 minutes).

Corniglia-Vernazza (1.5 hours): The scenic hike from Corniglia to Vernazza—the wildest and greenest section of the coast—is rewarding but hilly. From the Corniglia station and beach, zigzag up to the town (via the steep stairs, the longer road, or the shuttle bus). From Corniglia, you'll reach the trailhead on the main road, past Villa Cecio. You'll hike through vineyards and lots of fragrant and flowery vegetation. If you need a break before reaching Vernazza, stop by Bar la Torre, with a strip of shady tables perched high above the town.

Vernazza-Monterosso (1.5 hours): The trail from Vernazza to Monterosso is a challenging but scenic up-and-down-a-lot trek. Trails are narrow, steep, and crumbly,

Coastal trails are busiest at midday—hike early or late.

with a lot of steps, but easy to follow. The views just out of Vernazza, looking back at the town, are spectacular. From there you'll gradually ascend, passing little waterfalls. As you approach Monterosso, you'll descend steeply—on tall, knee-testing stairs—through vineyards, eventually following a rivulet to the sea. The last stretch into Monterosso is along a pleasant, paved pathway clinging to the cliff. You'll end right at Monterosso's old town beach.

More Hikes

While the national park charges a fee to use the coastal trails, they also maintain a free, far more extensive network of trails higher in the hills to each town's sanctuary and beyond (no park card required). Shuttle buses make the going easier, connecting coastal villages with distant trailheads. Ask for pointers at a TI or park office. Manarola-based **Cinque Terre Trekking** is a good resource (see page 149).

One of many good options is the hike between **Monterosso and Levanto** (about 3 hours one-way, moderately strenuous, take the train to or from Levanto one-way).

MONTEROSSO AL MARE

Monterosso al Mare is a resort with lots of hotels, rentable beach umbrellas, crowds, and more late-night action than the neighboring towns. Even so, don't expect full-blown Riviera glitz. The small, crooked lanes of the old town cradle Old World charm. Strolling the waterfront promenade, you can pick out each of the Cinque Terre towns decorating the coast. After dark, they sparkle.

The only Cinque Terre town built on flat land, Monterosso has two parts: a new town (called Fegina) with a parking lot, train station, and TI; and an old town (Centro Storico). A pedestrian tunnel connects the old with the new, but you can take a small detour around the point for a nicer walk.

Orientation

Arrival in Monterosso: Trains arrive in the new town. For hotels in the new town, turn right out of the station. For the old town, turn left; it's a scenic, flat, 10-minute stroll.

Shuttle buses run along the waterfront between the old town (Piazza Garibaldi, just beyond the tunnel), the train station, and the parking lot at the end of Via Fegina (*Campo Sportivo* stop). The bus saves you a 10-minute schlep with your bags but only runs twice an hour (€1.50 one-way, €2.50 on board, free with Cinque Terre park card).

Taxis usually wait outside the train station, though you may have to call one (€10 from station to the old town, mobile 335-616-5842, 335-616-5845, or 335-628-0933).

For **drivers,** Monterosso is 30 minutes off the freeway (exit: Carrodano-Levanto); at the fork in the road, follow signs for Fegina to reach the new town (with a huge beachfront guarded lot, €25/24 hours), or for *Monterosso Centro Storico* to get to the old town (Loreto parking garage on Via Roma, 10-minute downhill walk into town, cheaper prices). Only locals are allowed to drive between the old and new towns.

Medical Help: English-speaking **Dr. Vitone** charges €50-100 for a simple visit (less for poor students, mobile 338-853-0949, vitonee@yahoo.it).

Tourist Information: The TI Proloco is next to the train station (daily 9:00-18:30, shorter hours off-season, exit station and go left a few doors, tel. 0187-817-506, www.prolocomonterosso.it). For national park tickets and information, head upstairs within the station to the ticket office near platform 1 (likely daily 8:00-20:00, shorter hours off-season).

Baggage Storage: The TI stores bags (€6/day—but confirm closing time) and so does the laundry (see next).

Laundry: Wash and Dry Lavarapido is two blocks from the train station (daily 8:00-19:00, also offers €5 bag-check service, Via Molinelli 17, mobile 339-484-0940).

➲ Monterosso Walk

This easy, self-guided walk begins at the breakwater. Part 1, focusing on the mostly level town center, takes about 30 minutes; for Part 2, summiting the adjacent hill, allow another hour or so.

PART 1: MONTEROSSO HARBOR AND TOWN CENTER

• *Hike out from the dock in the old town and stand at the edge of the concrete...*

Breakwater: If you're visiting by boat, you'll start here anyway. From this point you can survey Monterosso's old town (straight ahead) and new town (stretching to the left, with train station and parking lot).

Looking to the right, you can see all *cinque* of the *terre* from one spot: Vernazza, Corniglia (above the shore), Manarola, and a few buildings of Riomaggiore beyond that.

The partial breakwater (a row of giant rocks in the middle of the harbor) is designed to save the beach from washing away, but sand erosion remains a major problem. While old-timers remember a vast beach, their grandchildren truck in sand each spring to give tourists something to lie on. (The Nazis liked the Cinque Terre, too—find two of their bomb-hardened bunkers, near left and far right.)

The four-star Hotel Porto Roca (pink building high on the hill, on the far right of the harbor) marks the trail to Vernazza. High above, you can see the roads that connect the Cinque Terre with the freeway over the hills.

Two prominent capes define the Cinque Terre. The farther cape is Punta di Montenero (to the right). The closer cape, Punta Mesco (to the left), marks a sea-life sanctuary, home to a rare grass that provides an ideal home for fish eggs. Buoys keep fishing boats away. The cape was once a quarry, providing employment to locals who chipped out the stones used to build the local towns (including

Monterosso al Mare

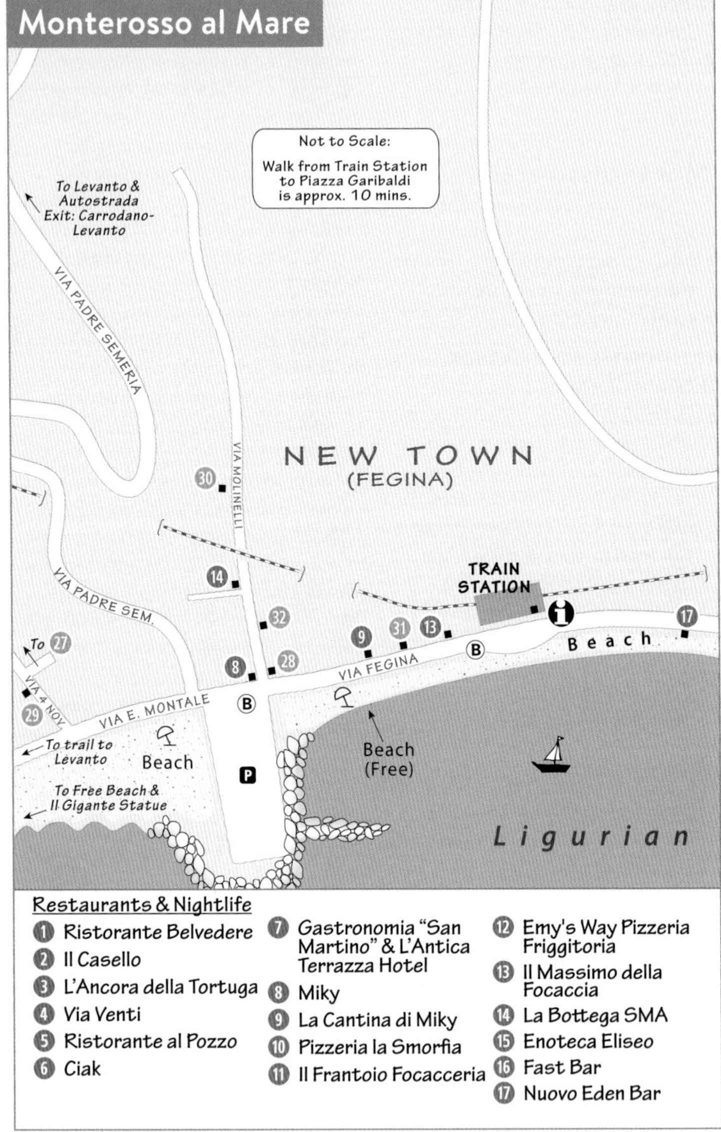

the greenish stones making up part of the breakwater below you).

On the far end of the new town, marking the best free beach around, you can just see the statue named *Il Gigante* (hard to spot because it blends in with the gray rock). It's 45 feet tall and once held a trident. Made of reinforced concrete, it dates from the early 20th century, when it supported a dance terrace for a *fin de siècle* villa. A violent storm left the giant holding nothing but memories.

• *From the breakwater, walk toward the old town and under the train tracks. Then ven-*

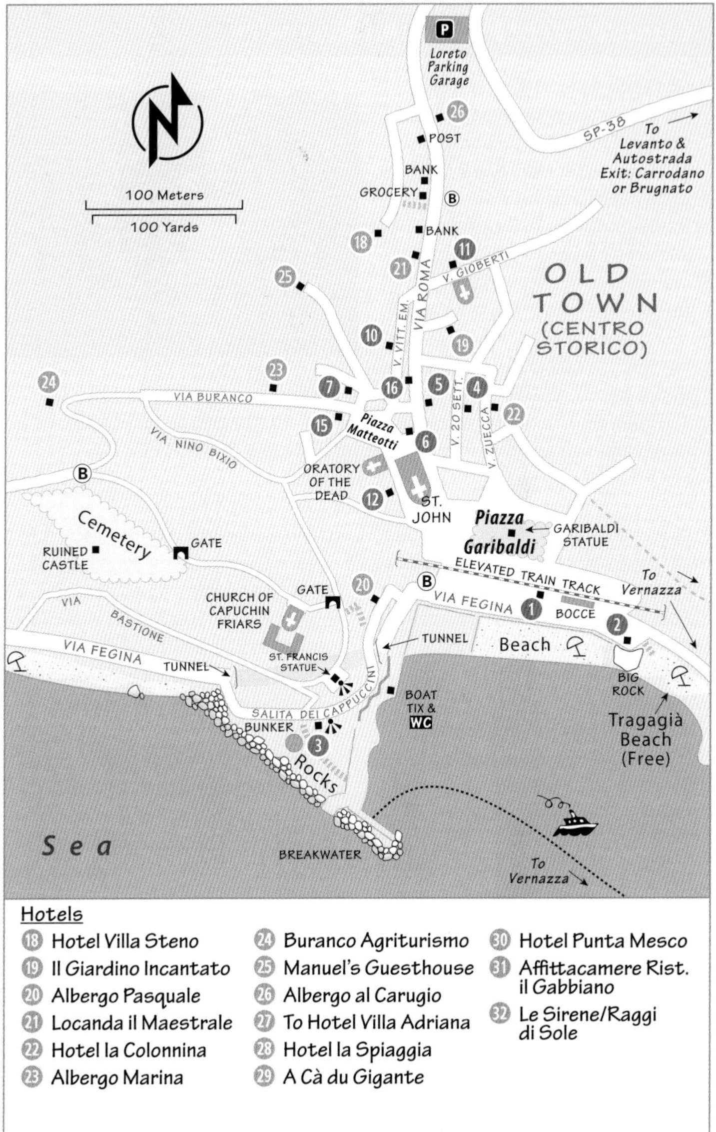

ture right into the square and find the statue of a dandy holding what looks like a box cutter (near the big playground).

Piazza Garibaldi: The statue honors Giuseppe Garibaldi, the dashing firebrand who, in the 1860s, helped unite the people of Italy. Facing Garibaldi, with your back to the sea, you'll see (from right to left) the orange city hall and a big home and recreation center for poor and homeless elderly. You'll also see A Ca' du Sciensa restaurant (with historic town photos inside and upstairs; you're welcome to pop in for a look).

Cinque Terre Flood and Recovery

On October 25, 2011, after a dry summer, a heavy rainstorm hit the Cinque Terre. Within four hours, 22 inches of rain fell. Flash floods rushed down the hillsides, picking up mud, rocks, trees, furniture, and even cars and buses in their raging, destructive path through the streets down to the sea. Part of Monterosso's old town and Vernazza's main drag were buried under a dozen feet of mud. Four villagers from Vernazza lost their lives.

Today, the Cinque Terre is back to normal. Strolling through these towns now, I appreciate the resilience of the human spirit.

Just under the bell tower (with your back to the sea, it's on your left), a set of covered arcades facing the sea is where the old-timers hang out. The crenellated bell tower marks the church.

• *Go to church (the entrance is on the inland side).*

Church of St. John the Baptist (Chiesa di San Giovanni Battista): Before entering, check out the facade. With white marble from Carrara and green marble from Punta Mesco, this church is typical of the Romanesque style. The marble stripes get narrower the higher they go, creating the illusion of a church that's taller than it really is. Note the delicate stone rose window above the entrance, with 18 slender mullions.

Church of St. John the Baptist

Step inside for more Ligurian Gothic: original marble columns with pointed arches to match. The octagonal baptismal font (in the back of the church) was carved from Carrara marble in 1359. In the chapel to the right of the high altar, look for the wooden statue of St. Anthony, carved about 1400, which once graced a church that stood atop Punta Mesco. The church itself dates from 1307—see the proud inscription on the left-middle column: "MilloCCCVII." Outside the church, on the side facing the main street, find the high-water mark from an October 1966 flood. Nearly half a century later, the October 2011 flood hit Monterosso. But the church's statues survived, thanks to townspeople who carried them through raging waters to safety.

• *Leaving the church, immediately turn left and go to church again.*

Oratory of the Dead (Oratorio dei Neri): During the Counter-Reformation, the Catholic Church offset the rising influence of the Lutherans by creating brotherhoods of good works. These religious Rotary clubs were called "confraternities." Monterosso had two, nicknamed White and Black. This building is the oratory of the Black group, whose mission—as the macabre interior decor indicates—was to arrange for funerals and take care of widows, orphans, the shipwrecked, and the souls of those who ignore the request for a €1 donation. It dates from the 16th century; membership has passed from father to son for generations. Notice the fine carved choir stalls (c. 1700) just inside the door, and the haunted-house chandeliers. Look up at the ceiling to find the symbol of the confraternity: a skull-and-crossbones and an hourglass...death awaits us all.

• *On that cheery note, if you're in a lazy mood, you can discreetly split off from our walking tour now to enjoy strolling, shopping, gelato, a day at the beach...or all of the above. If you're up for a hike, continue on to Part 2.*

PART 2: CAPUCHIN CHURCH AND HILLTOP CEMETERY

• *Return to the beach and find the brick steps that lead up to the hill-capping church (between the train tracks and the pedestrian tunnel, and passing in front of Albergo Pasquale). Approaching the bend in the path, watch for the stairs leading steeply and sharply to the right. This lane—Salita dei Cappuccini—is nicknamed Zii di Frati, or...*

Switchbacks of the Friars: Follow the yellow brick road (OK, it's orange...but I couldn't help singing as I skipped skyward). Pause at the terrace above the seaside castle at a statue of St. Francis and a wolf. Enjoy another opportunity to see all five of the Cinque Terre towns. From here, backtrack 20 yards and continue uphill.

• *When you reach a gate marked Convento e Chiesa Cappuccini, you have arrived at the...*

Church of the Capuchin Friars: The former monastery is now staffed by a single caretaker. The church's striped Romanesque facade is all fake: not marble, just cheap 18th-century stucco. Go inside and sit in the rear pew. The high altarpiece painting of St. Francis can be rolled up to reveal a statue of Mary behind it. Look at the statue of St. Anthony to the right and smile (you're on convent camera). Wave at the security camera—they're nervous about the precious painting to your left.

This fine painting of the **Crucifixion** is attributed to Anthony van Dyck, the 17th-century Flemish master (though art historians suspect that it was painted by someone in the artist's workshop). Notice

View from the Capuchin Church

the eclipsed sun in the painting, just to the right of the cross. When Jesus died, the earth went dark.

• *Leave and turn left through another gate to hike 100 yards uphill to the cemetery that fills the ruined castle. Reaching the cemetery's gate, look back and enjoy the view over the town.*

Cemetery in the Ruined Castle: In the Dark Ages, the village huddled within this castle. You're looking at the oldest part of Monterosso, tucked behind the hill, out of view of 13th-century pirates. Explore the cemetery, keeping in mind that cemeteries are sacred places. *Q.R.P.* is *Qui Riposa in Pace* (a.k.a. R.I.P.). Climb to the summit—the castle's keep, or place of last refuge.

• *Your tour is over—any trail leads you back into town.*

Experiences

Beaches

Monterosso's **new town** has easily the Cinque Terre's best—and most crowded—beach (immediately in front of the train station). Most of the beach is private, where you'll pay €25 to rent two chairs and an umbrella for the day (prices get soft in the afternoon). Light lunches are served by beach cafés to sunbathers at their lounge chairs. Various outfits along here rent kayaks and stand-up paddeboards (look for signs at the west end of the beach—near the parking lot—or ask around).

If there are no umbrellas on a stretch of beach, it's public, so you can spread out a towel anywhere. There's a free beach at the far-west end, near the Gigante statue.

The **old town** also has its own, predominantly private beach (rent umbrellas, chairs, kayaks, and paddleboats at the Beach Bar Alga, which is also a scenic spot for a drink). Tucked just beyond the private beach—under Il Casello restaurant at the east end of town—is the free public beach called Tragagià, which is gravelly and generally less crowded.

Boat Rides

In addition to the regularly scheduled boat service (see page 158), you can hire your own captain for transfers to other towns or for a full nautical tour. For example, Stefano has two six-person boats: the Matilde and the Babaah (about €100/hour, one hour is enough for a quick spin, two hours includes time for swimming stops; longer trips to Porto Venere and offshore islands possible; mobile 333-821-2007, www.matildenavigazione.com, info@matildenavigazione.com).

Wine Tasting

Buranco Agriturismo offers visits to their vineyard and cantina (reserve 2 days ahead). You'll taste some of their wines plus a grappa and a *limoncino,* along with home-cooked food (€20-30/person with snacks, English may be limited, follow Via Buranco uphill to path, 10 minutes above town, tel. 0187-817-677, www.buranco cinqueterre.it).

Nightlife

Enoteca da Eliseo, the best wine bar in town, comes with operatic ambience. Eliseo and his wife, Mary, love music as much as they love wine. Eliseo offers an education in *grappa,* stocking more than a hundred varieties (Wed-Mon 14:00-23:30, closed Tue, Piazza Matteotti 3, a block inland behind church, tel. 0187-817-308).

At **Fast Bar,** customers mix travel tales with cold beer. The crowd (and the rock 'n' roll) gets noisier as the night rolls on (cheap *panini* and salads usually served until midnight, Fri-Wed 9:30-late, closed Thu in winter; Via Roma in the old town).

La Cantina di Miky, in the new town just beyond the train station, is a trendy bar-restaurant with an extensive cocktail and *grappa* menu and occasional live music. They offer a fun "five villages" wine tasting with local meats and cheeses (€15/person for just wine, €20/person with food). It's the best place in

Cinque Terre Cuisine

Hanging out at a seaview restaurant while sampling local specialties could become one of your favorite memories.

The mainstay here is **anchovies** (*acciughe;* ah-CHOO-gay)—ideally served the day they're caught. Even if you've always hated American anchovies, try them fresh here. They can be prepared marinated, butterflied, and deep-fried (sometimes with a delicious garlic/vinegar sauce called *giada*). *Tegame alla vernazzana* is the most typical main course in Vernazza: a casserole-like dish of whole anchovies, fresh potatoes and tomatoes, white wine, oil, and herbs.

Antipasto here means *antipasti ai frutti di mare* (sometimes called simply *antipasti misti*), a plate of mixed "fruits of the sea." Splitting one of these and a pasta dish can be plenty for two people.

This region is the birthplace of **pesto.** Try it on *trenette* (the long, flat Ligurian noodle ruffled on one side) or *trofie* (short, dense twists made of flour with a bit of potato).

Pansotti are ravioli with ricotta and a mixture of greens, often served with a walnut sauce *(salsa di noci)*.

Focaccia, the tasty pillowy bread, also originates here. Locals say the best focaccia is made between the Cinque Terre and Genoa. It comes plain or with onions, sage, or olives and is sold in rounds or slices by weight (a portion is about 100 grams, or *un etto*).

The ***vino delle Cinque Terre,*** while not one of Italy's top wines, flows cheap and easy throughout the region. It's white—great with seafood. ***Sciacchetrà*** dessert wine is worth the splurge (€4-12 per small glass).

town for top-end Italian beers (Thu-Tue until late, closed Wed, Via Fegina 90, tel. 0187-802-525).

Nuovo Eden Bar, overlooking the beach by the big rock just east of the train station, is a fine place to enjoy a cocktail or ice cream with a sea view (€6 cocktails, drinks come with a light snack, good ice cream, closed Mon off-season).

Eating

With a Sea View

$$ Ristorante Belvedere, big and sprawling, is *the* place for a good-value meal indoors or outdoors on the harborfront. Their €48 *anfora belvedere* (mixed seafood stew) can easily feed four and the *misto mare* plate (2-person minimum, €15/person) can be an entire meal (Wed-Mon 12:00-14:30 & 18:00-22:00, closed Tue except Aug, on the harbor in the old town, tel. 0187-817-033).

$$ Il Casello, with outdoor tables on a rocky outcrop, is the only place for a fun meal overlooking the old town beach (daily April-Oct 12:00-22:00, closed Nov-March, mobile 333-492-7629).

$$$ L'Ancora della Tortuga is the top option in town for seaview elegance, with gorgeous outdoor seating high on a bluff and a lovely white-tablecloth-and-candles interior. The food doesn't quite live up to the fuss, and the service is uneven, but the setting is memorable (Tue-Sun 12:30-15:30 & 18:30-21:30, closed Mon, just outside the tunnel that connects the old and new town—or climb up the ramp in front of Albergo Pasquale, tel. 0187-800-065, mobile 333-240-7956).

In the Old Town

$$$ Via Venti is a quiet trattoria hidden in an alley deep in the heart of the old town. Imaginative seafood dishes use the day's catch and freshly made pasta. The outdoor tables are on a lane as nondescript as the humdrum interior—but you're here for the food (Fri-Wed 12:00-14:30 & 18:30-22:30, closed Thu, Via XX Settembre 32, tel. 0187-818-347).

$$$ Ristorante al Pozzo is a local favorite, with one of the best wine lists in town, homemade pasta, and wonderful seafood *antipasti misti* (Fri-Wed 12:00-15:00 & 18:30-22:30, closed Thu, Via Roma 24, tel. 0187-817-575).

$$$ Ciak is known for its huge, sizzling terra-cotta crock for two—crammed with the day's catch—and (sometimes) a bit of an attitude. Reservations are smart in summer (Thu-Tue 12:00-15:00 & 18:00-22:30, closed Wed, Piazza Don Minzoni 6, tel. 0187-817-014, www.ristoranteciak.net).

$ Gastronomia "San Martino" is a tiny, humble combination of takeaway and sit-down café with surprisingly affordable, quality dishes. Eat at one of the few tables—inside or out on a pleasant street—or find a driftwood log for a take-out feast to go (Tue-Sun 12:00-15:00 & 18:00-22:00, closed Mon, next to recommended L'Antica Terrazza hotel at Vicolo San Martino 3, mobile 346-109-7338).

In the New Town

$$$$ Miky is my Cinque Terre favorite, with well-dressed locals packed into a classy environment. Their elegantly presented, top-quality food celebrates local ingredients and traditions. Try their "pizza pasta"—finished in a bowl topped with a thin pizza crust and flambéed at your table. If I should want dessert, it would be their mixed sampler plate, *dolce misto* (Wed-Mon 12:00-15:00 & 19:00-23:00, closed Tue, reservations wise in summer, in the new town 100 yards from train station at Via Fegina 104, tel. 0187-817-608, www.ristorantemiky.it).

$$$ La Cantina di Miky, a few doors down toward the station, is more youthful and informal than Miky, yet serves artfully crafted Ligurian specialties in Miky's family tradition. Sit downstairs, in the garden, or overlooking the sea. They have creative desserts and large selection of Italian microbrews (Thu-Tue 12:00-24:00, closed Wed, Via Fegina 90, tel. 0187-802-525).

Light Meals, Takeout Food, and Breakfast

In the old town, shops and bakeries sell pizza and focaccia for an easy picnic. **$ Pizzeria la Smorfia** is the local favorite (Fri-Wed 11:00-24:00, closed Thu, Via Vittorio Emanuele 73, tel. 0187-818-395). Other options are **$ Il Frantoio** (Fri-Wed 9:00-14:00 & 16:30-20:00, closed Thu, just off Via Roma at Via Gioberti 1) and **$ Emy's Way Pizzeria Friggitoria,** which also serves deep-fried seafood to go (daily 11:00-20:00, later in summer, along the skinny street next to the church).

$ Il Massimo della Focaccia, right at the train station, is a good bet for a light meal with a sea view (Thu-Tue 9:00-19:00, closed Wed except June-Aug, Via Fegina 50 at the entry to the station). **La Bottega SMA** is a smart minimart with fresh produce, *antipasti,* deli items, and sandwiches; pay by weight (daily 8:00-13:00 & 16:30-19:30—except closed Sun afternoon, shorter hours off-season, near Lavarapido at Vittoria Gianni 21).

For breakfast, try **Fast Bar** on Via Roma in the old town. They serve an American-style breakfast for €12, or cheaper à la carte (Fri-Wed 9:30-late, closed Thu in winter).

Sleeping

Rooms in Monterosso are a better value than similar rooms in crowded Vernazza. The TI Proloco just outside the train station can give you a list of rooms for rent.

In the Old Town

$$$$ Hotel Villa Steno features great view

balconies, panoramic gardens, and a roof terrace with sun beds, and air-conditioning. Of their 16 rooms, 14 have view balconies (RS%, family rooms, hearty buffet breakfast, elevator, laundry service, ask about pay parking when you reserve, hike up to the panoramic terrace, closed Nov-March, Via Roma 109, tel. 0187-817-028 or 0187-818-336, www.villasteno.com, steno@pasini.com). It's a 15-minute climb (or €8 taxi ride) from the train station to the top of the old town. Readers get a free Cinque Terre info packet and a glass of local wine when they check in—ask for it.

$$$$ Il Giardino Incantato ("The Enchanted Garden") is a charming and cozy four-room B&B with impressive attention to detail in a tastefully renovated 16th-century Ligurian home in the heart of the old town. Sip their homemade limoncino upon check-in, and have breakfast under lemon trees in a delightful hidden garden (RS%, air-con, free minibar and tea and coffee service, laundry service, Via Mazzini 18, tel. 0187-818-315, mobile 333-264-9252, www.ilgiardinoincantato.net, giardino_incantato@libero.it).

$$$$ Albergo Pasquale, modern and comfortable, has 15 seaview rooms. Located right on the harbor, it's just a few steps from the beach, boat dock, and tunnel entrance to the new town. While there is some train noise, the soundtrack is mostly a lullaby of waves. It has an elevator and offers easier access than most (RS%, family room, same welcome drink as Villa Steno, air-con, laundry service, Via Fegina 8, tel. 0187-817-550 or 0187-817-477, www.hotelpasquale.it, pasquale@pasini.com, Felicita and Marco).

$$$ Locanda il Maestrale rents six small, stylish rooms in a sophisticated and peaceful little inn. Although renovated with all the modern comforts, it retains centuries-old character under frescoed ceilings. Its peaceful sun terrace overlooking the old town and Via Roma action is a delight. Guests enjoy free drinks and snacks each afternoon (RS%, air-con, Via Roma 37, tel. 0187-817-013, mobile 338-4530-531, www.locandamaestrale.net, maestrale@monterossonet.com, Stefania).

$$$ Hotel la Colonnina has 21 big rooms, generous and meticulously cared-for public spaces, a cozy garden, and an inviting shared seaview terrace with sun beds. It's buried in the town's fragrant and sleepy back streets (family rooms, many rooms with private terraces, cash preferred, air-con, fridges, elevator, a block inland from the main square at Via Zuecca 6, tel. 0187-817-439, www.lacolonninacinqueterre.it, info@lacolonninacinqueterre.it, Cristina).

$$$ Albergo Marina, creatively run by enthusiastic husband-and-wife team Marina and Eraldo, has 23 pleasant rooms and a garden with lemon trees. With a free and filling buffet featuring local specialties each afternoon, they offer a fine value (RS%, family rooms, elevator, air-con, free kayak and snorkel equipment, Via Buranco 40, tel. 0187-817-613, www.hotelmarina5terre.com, marina@hotelmarina5terre.com).

$$$ Buranco Agriturismo, a 10-minute hike above the old town, has wonderful gardens and views over the vine-covered valley. Its primary business is wine and olive-oil production, but they offer three apartments. It's a rare opportunity to stay in a farmhouse, but still be able to get to town on foot (air-con, €15 taxi from station, tel. 0187-817-677, mobile 349-434-8046, www.burancocinqueterre.it, info@buranco.it, informally run by Loredana, Mary, and Giulietta).

$$$ Manuel's Guesthouse, perched high above the town among terraces, is a garden getaway with six big, bright rooms and a grand view. After climbing the killer stairs from the town center, their killer terrace is hard to leave—especially after a few drinks (cash only, air-con, up about 100 steps behind church—you can ask them to carry your bags up the hill, Via San Martino 39, mobile 333-439-0809, www.manuelsguesthouse.com, manuelsguesthouse@libero.it).

$$ L'Antica Terrazza rents five tight, classy rooms right in town. With a pretty terrace overlooking the pedestrian street and minimal stairs, Raffaella and John offer a good deal (RS%, cheaper room with private bath down the hall, air-con, Vicolo San Martino 1, mobile 380-138-0082 or 347-132-6213, www.anticaterrazza.com, post@anticaterrazza.com).

$ Albergo al Carugio is a practical nine-room place in a big apartment-style building at the top of the old town. It's quiet, comfy, and a fine value for those on a budget (RS%, no breakfast, air-con—but only during the daytime June-Sept, Via Roma 100, tel. 0187-817-453, www.alcarugio.it, info@alcarugio.it, conscientiously run by Andrea).

In the New Town

$$$$ Hotel Villa Adriana is a big, contemporary, bright hotel on a church-owned estate set in a peaceful garden with a pool, free parking, and a no-stress style. They rent 54 rooms—some with terraces and/or sea views—ask for one when you reserve, but no guarantees (family rooms, air-con, elevator, free loaner bikes, affordable dinners, Via IV Novembre 23, tel. 0187-818-109, www.villaadriana.info, info@villaadriana.info).

$$$$ Hotel la Spiaggia is a venerable old 19-room place facing the beach. Half the rooms come with sea views (cash only, air-con, elevator, free parking—reserve in advance, Via Lungomare 96, tel. 0187-817-567, www.laspiaggiahotel.com, hotellaspiaggia@libero.it).

$$$ A Cà du Gigante, despite its name, is a tiny yet chic refuge with nine rooms. About 100 yards from the beach (and surrounded by blocky apartments and big hotels on a modern street), the interior is tastefully done with upscale comfort in mind (RS%, air-con, limited free parking, Via IV Novembre 11, tel. 0187-817-401, www.ilgigantecinqueterre.it, gigante@ilgigantecinqueterre.it).

$$$ Hotel Punta Mesco is a tidy, well-run little haven renting 17 quiet, casual rooms at a good price. While none have views, 10 rooms have small terraces (RS%, family room, air-con, parking, Via Molinelli 35, tel. 0187-817-495, www.hotelpuntamesco.it, info@hotelpuntamesco.it).

$$ Affittacamere Ristorante il Gabbiano, a touristy restaurant right on the beach, rents five basic, dated, but affordable rooms upstairs. Three rooms face the sea, with small balconies; two overlook a little garden at the back. The Gabbiano family restaurant serves as your reception (family rooms, cash only, air-con, Via Fegina 84, tel. 0187-817-578, www.affittacamereristoranteilgabbiano.com, affittacamereilgabbiano@live.it).

$ Le Sirene/Raggi di Sole, with nine simple rooms in two humble buildings, is a decent budget choice in this pricey town. It's run from a hole-in-the-wall reception desk a block from the station, just off the water. I'd request the Le Sirene building, which has smaller bathrooms but no train noise, and is a bit more spacious and airy than Raggi di Sole (RS%, family rooms, fans, Via Molinelli 10, mobile 331-788-1088, www.sirenerooms.com, sirenerooms@gmail.com).

VERNAZZA

With a ruined castle and a stout stone church, Vernazza is the jewel of the Cinque Terre. Only the occasional noisy train reminds you of the modern world.

Proud of their Vernazzan heritage, the town's 500 residents like to brag: "Vernazza is locally owned. Portofino has sold out." Fearing change, keep-Vernazza-small proponents stopped the construction of a major road into the town and region. Families are tight and go back centuries; you'll notice certain surnames (such as Basso and Moggia) everywhere. Leisure time is devoted to taking part in the *passeggiata*—strolling lazily together up and down the main street. Learn—and live—the phrase *"la vita pigra di Vernazza"* (the lazy life of Vernazza).

The action is at the harbor, where you'll find outdoor restaurants, a bar hanging on the edge of the castle, and a breakwater with a promenade, corralled by a natural amphitheater of terraced hills. In the summer, the beach becomes a soccer field, with teams fielded by bars and restaurants providing late-night entertainment.

Orientation

Arrival in Vernazza: The town's **train station** is only about three train cars long, but the trains are much longer—so most of the cars come to a stop in a long, dark tunnel. Open the door, get out, and walk through the tunnel to the station. From there the main drag flows through town right to the harbor. The **boats** dock at the harborfront square, at the base of main street. If arriving by **car,** don't drive to Vernazza. Roads are in terrible shape and parking is limited. If you're coming from the north, park in Levanto. If arriving from the south, park your car in La Spezia. From either town, hop on the train.

Rick's Tip: *A steep 10-minute hike in either direction from Vernazza gives you a* **classic village photo op.** *For the best light, head toward Corniglia in the morning—best views are just before the ticket booth for the national park—and toward Monterosso in the evening—best views are after the ticket booth.*

Tourist Information: At the train station, you can get answers to basic questions at the gift shop (daily 8:00-20:00, closed in winter), or the train ticket desk/park office (likely daily 8:00-20:00, shorter hours off-season, tel. 0187-812-533). Public WCs are just behind. Locals run their own helpful tourist board/website, called VisitVernazza.org.

Baggage Storage: You can leave your bags at the train-station gift shop near track 1 (€1/hour, €10/day, daily 8:00-19:30, closed in winter). Friendly Francesco and his staff will happily take your luggage from the train station to your hotel—and back (€3/piece).

Market: On Tuesday mornings (8:00-13:00), cars and trucks pull into town for a tailgate market offering produce and more.

Vernazza

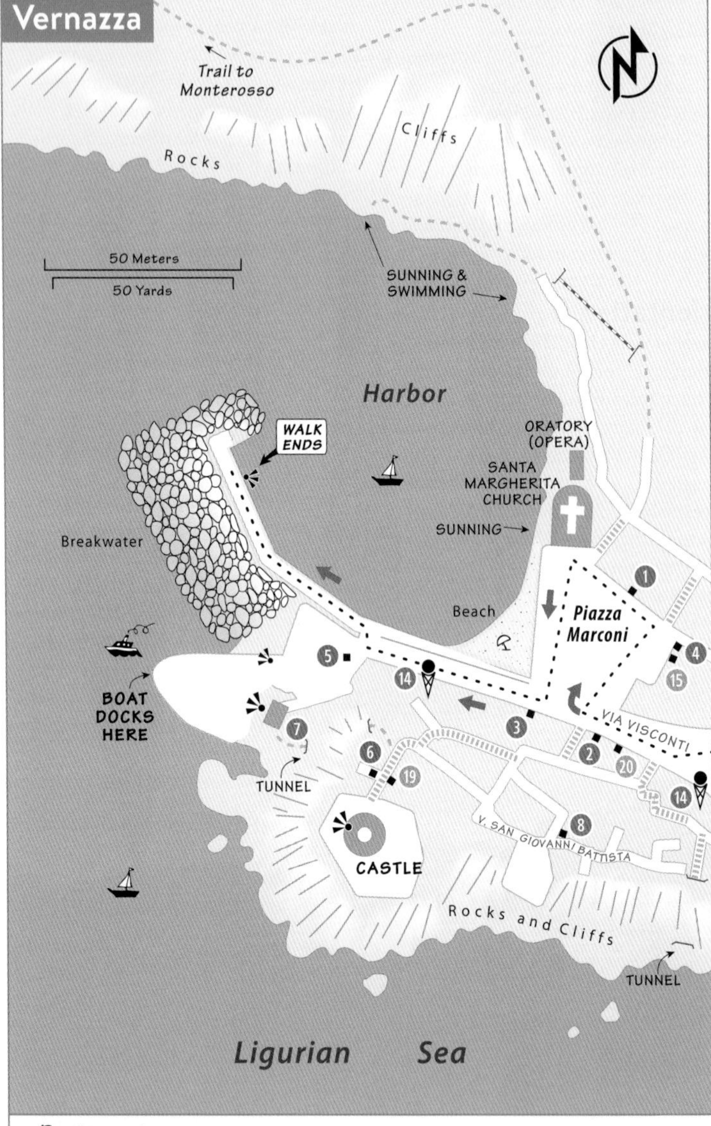

Restaurants

1. Trattoria del Capitano & Martina Callo Rooms
2. Gianni Franzi Ristorante/Reception
3. Gambero Rosso
4. Ristorante Pizzeria Vulnetia & Nicolina Rooms Reception
5. Pizzeria Baia Saracena
6. Ristorante al Castello
7. Ristorante Belforte
8. Vernazza Wine Experience
9. Trattoria da Sandro
10. Antica Osteria il Baretto
11. Blue Marlin Bar
12. Il Pirata delle Cinque Terre Café

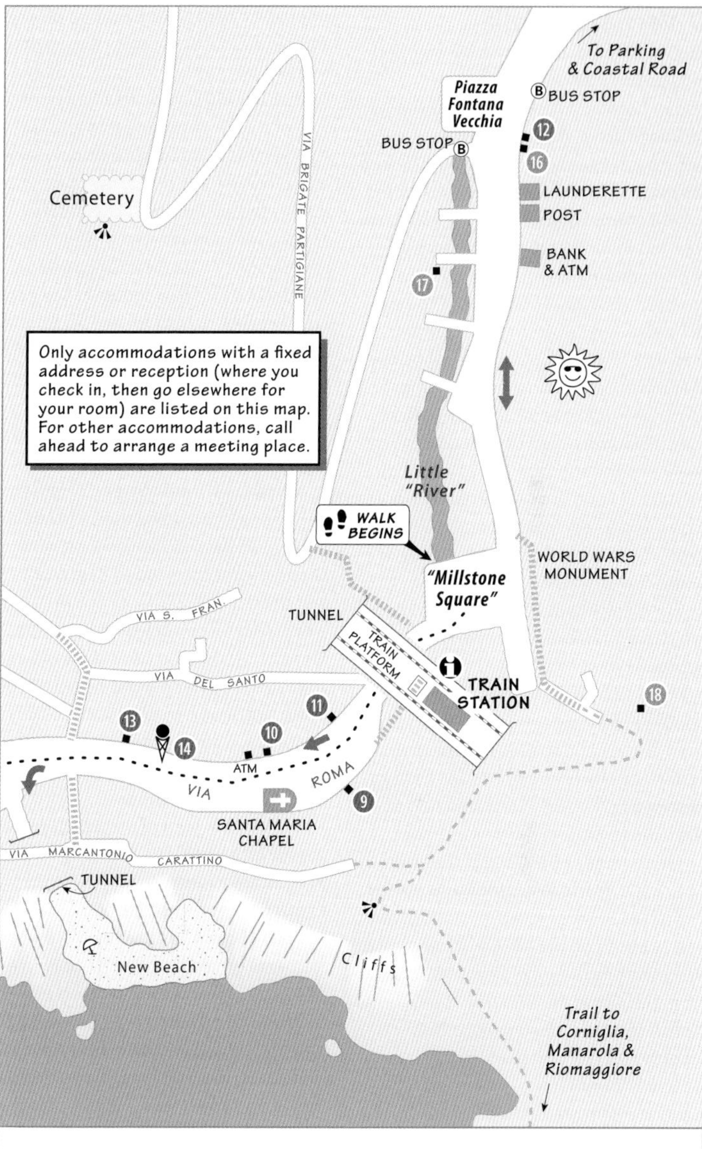

13 Forno Bakery
14 Gelaterias (3)

Hotels & Rooms

15 Albergo Barbara & Francamaria Reception
16 Tonino Basso Rooms & La Rosa dei Venti
17 Camere Fontana Vecchia
18 Giuliano Basso Rooms
19 Monica Lercari Rooms
20 Rosa Vitali Rooms

Vernazza Walk

This walk includes the town squares and ends on the scenic breakwater.

• *From the train station, walk under the tracks and uphill about 30 yards until you reach the sharp bend in the road. You'll see a tiny piazza with benches and big millstones.*

"Millstone Square": The big millstones are a reminder that the town stream (which goes underground here) once powered Vernazza's water mill. (You can still see its tiny "river" if you follow this road up a few steps.) Until the 1950s, the river ran openly through the center of town. Old-timers recall the days before the breakwater, when the river cascaded down and the surf sent waves rolling up Vernazza's main drag. (The name "Vernazza" is actually local dialect for "little Venice"—the town once had a string of bridges, evoking those in Venice.)

Corralling this stream under the modern street, and forcing it to take a hard right turn here, contributed to the damage caused by the 2011 flood. After the flood, alpine engineers were imported from Switzerland to redesign the drainage system, so any future floods will be less destructive. They also installed nets above the town to protect it from landslides.

On the wall at the bend in the road, notice the **World Wars Monument**—dedicated to those killed in World Wars I and II. Listed on the left are soldiers *morti in combattimento,* who died in World War I; on the right is the WWII section. Some were deported to *Germania;* others—labeled *Part* (for *partigiani,* or partisans, generally communists)—were killed while fighting against Mussolini.

Hikers take note: The **path to Corniglia** leaves from here (behind and above the plaque).

• *To see a more workaday part of Vernazza, you could wander a couple of minutes uphill from here, for a look at the...*

Top of Town: First you'll pass (on the left, at #7, with big brown garage doors and a *croce verde Vernazza* sign) the ambulance barn, where a group of volunteers is always on call for a dash to the hospital, 40 minutes away in La Spezia. Farther up, you'll come to a functional strip of modern apartment blocks facing the river. In this practical zone—the only place in town that allows cars—are a bank, the post office, a launderette, and the recommended tourist hub bar/café called Il Pirata delle Cinque Terre. The parking lot fills a square called Fontana Vecchia, named for an "old fountain" that's so old, it's long gone. Shuttle buses run from the post office to hamlets and sanctuaries in the hills above.

• *Whether or not you head up to the top of town, the next leg of our walk follows...*

Vernazza's "Main Street": Here you'll pass many locals doing their *vasche* (laps). Next you'll pass souvenir shops, wine shops, the recommended Blue Marlin Bar, and the tiny stone Chapel of Santa Marta, where Mass is celebrated only on special Sundays. Above and behind the chapel is the Vineria Santa Marta wine bar. Farther down, you'll walk by a gelateria, bakery, pharmacy, a grocery, and another gelateria. There are plenty of fun and cheap food-to-go options here.

• *On the left, in front of the second gelateria, a stone arch was blasted away by the 2011 flood. Scamper through the hole in the rock to reach Vernazza's shrinking...*

"New Beach": In the flood's aftermath, Vernazza's main drag and harbor were filled with mud and silt. Workers used the debris to fill in even more of this beach, and for several years Vernazza had a popular beach that felt a world away from the bustle of the main drag. But as time goes on, the erosion from the churning surf is taking it away.

• *Back on the main drag, continue downhill to the...*

Harbor Square (Piazza Marconi) and Breakwater: Vernazza, with the only natural harbor of the Cinque Terre, was established as the sole place boats could pick up the fine local wine. The two-foot-high square stone at the foot of the stairs (on the left) is marked *Sasso del Sego* (stone of tallow). Workers crushed animal flesh and fat in its basin to make tallow, which drained out of the tiny hole below. The tallow was then used to waterproof boats or wine barrels. Stonework is the soul of the region. Take some time to appreciate the impressive stonework of the restaurant interiors facing the harbor.

On the far side (behind the recommended Ristorante Pizzeria Vulnetia), peek into the tiny street with its commotion of arches. Vernazza's most characteristic side streets, called *carugi,* lead up from here. The narrow stairs mark the beginning of the trail that leads up to the quintessential view of Vernazza—and, eventually, on to Monterosso.

Located in front of the harborside church, the tiny piazza—decorated with a river-rock mosaic—is a popular hangout spot. The **church** is unusual for its strange entryway, which faces east (altar side), rather than the more typical western orientation. In the 16th century, the townspeople doubled the church in size, causing it to overtake a little piazza that once faced the west facade. From the square, use the "new" entry and climb the steps. Inside, the lighter pillars in the back mark the 16th-century extension. Three historic portable crosses hanging on the walls are replicas of crosses that (locals believe) Vernazza ships once carried on crusades.

• *Finish your town tour seated out on the breakwater. Face the town, and see...*

The Harbor: In a moderate storm, you'd be soaked, as waves routinely crash over the *molo* (breakwater, built in 1972). Waves can rearrange the huge rocks—depositing them onto the piazza and its benches. Freak waves have even washed away tourists. Enjoy the waterfront piazza—carefully.

The town's fishing fleet is down to just a few boats (with the net spools). Vernazzans are still more likely to own a boat than a car, and it's said that you stand a better chance of surviving if you mess with a local man's wife than with his boat. Boats are on buoys, except in winter or when the red storm flag (see the pole at the start of the breakwater) indicates bad seas. At these times, the boats are pulled up onto the square—which is usually reserved for restaurant tables.

The Castle (Castello Doria): On the far right, the castle, which is now a grassy park with great views (and nothing but stones), still guards the town (€1.50, not covered by Cinque Terre park card; daily 10:00-20:00, summer until 21:00, closed Nov-March; from harbor, take stairs by Trattoria Gianni and follow *Ristorante al Castello* signs, tower is a few steps beyond). This was the town's watchtower back in pirate days, and a Nazi lookout in World War II. The castle tower looks new because it was rebuilt after the British bombed it, chasing out the Germans.

Vernazza's harbor and breakwater

Sunbathing in Vernazza

The squat tower on the water (Ristorante Belforte) is a great spot for a glass of wine or a meal (from the breakwater, you can follow the rope to the restaurant and pop inside, past an actual submarine door; a photo of a major storm showing the entire tower under a wave—not uncommon in the winter—hangs near the bar).

The Town: Before the 12th century, pirates made the coast uninhabitable, so the first Vernazzans lived in the hills above (near the Reggio Sanctuary). The town itself—and its towers, fortified walls, and hillside terracing—are mostly from the 12th through the 15th centuries.

Vernazza has two halves. *Sciuiu* (Vernazzan dialect for "flowery") is the sunny side on the left, and *luvegu* (dank) is the shady side on the right. Houses below the castle were connected by an interior arcade. The square before you is locally famous for some of the area's finest restaurants. The big red central house—on the site where Genoan warships were built in the 12th century—used to be a guardhouse.

In the Middle Ages, there was no beach or square. The water went right up to the buildings, where boats would tie up, Venetian-style. Buildings had a water gate and a front door on the higher inland side. There was no pastel plaster—just fine stonework (traces survive above the Trattoria del Capitano).

Above the Town: The small, round tower above the red guardhouse reminds us of the town's importance in the Middle Ages. Back then, the enemies of key ally Genoa were Vernazza's enemies. Bar la Torre, just above and beyond the tower, welcomes hikers starting or finishing the Corniglia-Vernazza hike. That tower recalls a time when the entire town was fortified by a stone wall. Vineyards fill the mountainside beyond the town; notice the many terraces.

Castle at Vernazza

Santa Margherita Church

The Church, School, and City Hall: Vernazza's Ligurian Gothic church, built with black stones quarried from Punta Mesco (the distant point behind you), dates from 1318. The gray stone marks the church's 16th-century expansion. The gray-and-red house above the spire is the elementary school. Older students go to the "big city," La Spezia. The red building to the right of the schoolhouse, a former monastery, is the city hall.

Finally, on the top of the hill is the town cemetery. It's only fair that hardworking Vernazzans—who spend their lives climbing up and down the hillsides—are rewarded with an eternal world-class view.

Experiences

Beaches

The harbor's sandy cove has sunning rocks and showers by the breakwater. A ladder on the breakwater allows deep-water access. The sunbathing lane directly under the church has a shower. Vernazza's other beach (the "new beach") can be accessed through a hole halfway along the town's main drag.

Wine Tasting

Vernazza Wine Experience, at the top of town just under the castle, is run by Alessandro, a sommelier who enjoys explaining wines and the various €15 small plates matched with them (like a meat-and-cheese plate served on a slab of olive tree). You'll pay €15 for three very different wines. While the bill can add up, the quality is excellent, the setting is romantic, and the view is unforgettable (cash only, daily 17:00-21:00, hike from harborfront and turn left before castle, Via S. Giovanni Battista 31, tel. 331-343-3801).

Vineria Santa Marta is simpler and mellower, with less scenery and pretense. At this wine shop/tasting bar with a stone terrace, brothers Wolfgang and Michael offer a basic tasting of three local wines plus light snacks for €9 per person (also serves salads and *bruschette,* daily 9:30-20:30, above the little chapel on Via Roma—the main drag, tel. 0187-882-1084).

A Little Taste of Opera

My favorite Cinque Terre evenings are spent at Vernazza's summer opera. A big-name maestro from Lucca brings talented singers to town twice weekly for performances in the small, beautiful oratory tucked behind the town's big church (find the steps up and around, next to Ananasso Bar). Performances begin at 19:00 and last just over an hour (€13 in advance, €15 at the door, April-Oct Wed and Fri at 19:00 but confirm times locally, book tickets at Cinque Terre Riviera office at #24 on main street, tel. 0187-812-123, info@cinqueterreriviera.com).

"Voluntourism"

Save Vernazza, which began as a post-flood relief organization, has evolved into an advocacy group, emphasizing sustainable tourism. If you enjoy the Cinque Terre and would like to give something back, contact them to participate in a project designed to protect and promote Vernazza. "Voluntourism" activities, scheduled regularly through the high season, include rebuilding terrace walls and harvesting grapes (€29, reservations required, lunch and wine provided, generally 2/week late May-Oct 8:30-13:30, mobile 349-357-3572, www.savevernazza.com, workwithus@savevernazza.com).

Eating

Vernazza's restaurants take pride in their cooking. Wander around at about 20:00 and compare the ambience, but don't wait too long—many kitchens close at 22:00. To get an outdoor table on summer weekends, reserve ahead. Harborside restaurants and bars are easygoing. You're welcome to grab a cup of coffee or glass of wine and disappear somewhere on the **breakwater,** returning your glass when you're done.

Rick's Tip: *If you dine in Vernazza but are staying in Monterosso, be sure to* **check train schedules before sitting down to eat,** *as trains run less frequently in the evening.*

Harborside

$$$ Trattoria del Capitano serves a short menu of straightforward local dishes, including *spaghetti allo scoglio*—pasta entangled with seafood (Wed-Mon from 8:00 for breakfast, 12:00-22:00, closed Tue and Dec-Jan, tel. 0187-812-201).

$$$ Gianni Franzi is an old standby with well-prepared seafood and reliable, friendly service. While the outdoor seating is basic, the indoor seating is classy (check their *menù cucina tipica Vernazza,* Thu-Tue 12:00-15:00 & 19:00-22:00, closed Wed except in Aug, tel. 0187-812-228).

$$$$ Gambero Rosso is the priciest place on the square, but—ever since it was sold to a big-city restaurateur who runs it from afar—the quality can be hit-or-miss. Still, it has a fine interior and great outdoor tables (Fri-Wed 12:00-15:00 & 19:00-21:30, closed Thu and Dec-Feb, Piazza Marconi 7, tel. 0187-812-265).

$$$ Ristorante Pizzeria Vulnetia has a jovial atmosphere and serves regional specialties and affordable pizzas, making it a good choice for budget and family meals (Tue-Sun 12:00-22:00, closed Mon, Piazza Marconi 29, tel. 0187-821-193, Giuliano and Tullio).

$$ Pizzeria Baia Saracena ("Saracen Bay") is the budget option on the harbor, serving forgettable pizza and pastas out on the breakwater. Eat here not for high cuisine, but for a memorable atmosphere at reasonable prices (Sat-Thu 10:30-22:00, closed Fri, tel. 0187-812-113, Luca).

By the Castle

$$$ Ristorante al Castello is high above town, just below the castle, with commanding views. Reserve one of the dozen romantic cliff-side seaview tables for two, some of which snake around the castle, where you'll feel like you're eating all alone with the Mediterranean (Thu-Tue 12:00–15:00 & 19:00–22:00, closed Wed and Nov–April, tel. 0187-812-296).

$$$$ Ristorante Belforte serves a fine blend of traditional and creative cuisine, including a hearty *zuppa Michela* (a boatload of seafood), fishy *spaghetti alla Bruno, trofie al pesto* (hand-rolled noodles with pesto), and classic *antipasto misto di pesce.* Reserve ahead for tables on the view terrace (Wed-Mon 12:00-15:00 & 19:00-22:00, closed Tue and Nov-March, tel. 0187-812-222, Michela).

Rick's Tip: *After the restaurants close down, Vernazza is quiet except for a couple of* **nightspots: Blue Marlin Bar** *and* **Il Pirata delle Cinque Terre.** *All Vernazza bars must close by 24:00.*

On or near the Main Street

Several of Vernazza's inland eateries manage to compete without the harbor ambience, but with slightly cheaper prices.

$$ Trattoria da Sandro, on the main drag, mixes quality Genovese and Ligurian cuisine, including award-winning stuffed mussels, with friendly service (Wed-Mon 12:00-15:00 & 18:30-22:00, closed Tue, Via Roma 62, tel. 0187-812-223).

$$ Antica Osteria il Baretto is a solid bet for homey, reasonably priced traditional cuisine that's favored by locals (Tue-Sun 12:00-22:00, closed Mon, indoor and outdoor seating in summer, Via Roma 31, tel. 0187-812-381).

$$ Blue Marlin Bar, just below the train station, serves a short, creative menu of more casual dishes. It also serves breakfast and dominates the late-night scene with home-cooked food until 23:00, good drinks,

and occasional piano jam sessions. If you're young and hip, hang out here (Thu-Tue 7:00-24:00, closed Wed). If you're awaiting a train any time of day, the Blue Marlin's outdoor seating beats the platform.

$$ Il Pirata delle Cinque Terre, behind and above the train station, is popular for breakfast and attracts many travelers for lunch and dinner. Don't come here for the cuisine, but for a memorable evening with the Cannoli twins, who entertain while they serve, and aim their menu squarely at American taste buds (daily 6:30-24:00, Via Gavino).

Other main-street eateries offer a fine range of quick meals. **Forno Bakery** has good focaccia and veggie tarts (at #5). **Pino's grocery store** makes inexpensive sandwiches to order (generally Mon-Sat 8:00-13:00 & 17:00-19:30, closed Sun).

Gelato

Gelateria Vernazza, near the top of the main street, takes gelato seriously. **Gelateria Amore Mio** (midtown) has great people-watching tables but the least exciting gelato. Out on the harbor, **Gelateria Il Porticciolo** is arguably the best, with fresh ingredients and intense flavors.

Sleeping

People recommended here are listed for their communication skills—they speak English, have email, and are reliable with bookings. Anywhere you stay here requires some climbing, but keep in mind that more climbing means better views. Most do not include breakfast. Cash is preferred or required almost everywhere. Night noise can be a problem if you're near the station. Rooms on the harbor come with church bells (but only between 7:00 and 22:00).

Guest Houses (Pensiones)

$$$ Gianni Franzi, a busy restaurant on the harbor square, runs the closest thing to a big hotel that Vernazza has got. Its 25 small rooms are scattered across three buildings that are one hundred tight, winding stairs above the harbor square. Some rooms (including a few cheaper ones with shared bathrooms) are funky and decorated à la shipwreck, with tiny balconies and grand sea views; the comfy, newer rooms lack views. All rooms have access to a super-scenic cliff-hanging guests' garden and the panoramic terrace (where breakfast is served in season). Check-in before 16:00 or call to explain when you're coming. Emanuele, Simona, Caterina, and the staff speak a little English (RS%, closed Jan-Feb, Piazza Marconi 1, tel. 0187-812-228, tel. 0187-821-003, mobile 393-9008-155, www.giannifranzi.it, info@giannifranzi.it). Pick up your keys at the Gianni Franzi restaurant on the harbor square (on Wed, when the restaurant is closed, call ahead to make other arrangements).

$ Albergo Barbara rents nine basic-but-tidy top-floor rooms overlooking the square. Only a few rooms have real views; most have small windows and small views. It's a good value in a nice location, run by Alessio and Alberto (cheaper rooms with shared bath are a good value, more for views, closed Dec-Feb, reserve online with credit card but pay cash, piles of stairs, Piazza Marconi 30, tel. 0187-812-398, www.albergobarbara.it, info@albergobarbara.it).

Rooms for Rent (Affittacamere)

Vernazza lacks any real hotels, and almost all of my listings are *affittacamere* (private rooms for rent). I favor hosts who rent multiple rooms, speak just enough English, have email, and are reliable. Most places accept only cash and don't include breakfast. Some have killer views; some come with lots of stairs.

While a few places have all their beds in one building, most have rooms scattered over town. Some have an informal "reception desk" (sometimes at a restaurant or other business) where you can check in. But many places have no reception at all. (On the Vernazza map, I've marked only places that have a fixed address or reception office; if I say "reception," you'll check in there, then continue on to your actual room.)

Because this can be confusing, clearly communicate your arrival time (by phone or email) and get instructions on where to meet the owner and pick up the keys. In some cases, they'll meet you at the train station—but only if they know when you're coming.

INLAND

$$ Camere Fontana Vecchia, run by Annamaria, has eight bright and cheery rooms overlooking the ravine and its rushing river (cheaper room with shared bath, more for terrace, Via Gavino 15, tel. 0187-821-130, mobile 333-454-9371, www.cinqueterrecamere.com, m.annamaria@libero.it).

$$ Giuliano Basso's four carefully crafted, well-appointed rooms form a cozy little compound on the green hillside just above town, straddling a ravine among orange trees. Giuliano—the town's last stone-layer—proudly built the place himself (2 rooms have air-con, more train noise than others; follow the main road up above the station, take the ramp up toward Corniglia just before Pensione Sorriso, follow the path, and watch for a sharp left turn; mobile 333-341-4792, www.cameregiuliano.com, giuliano@cdh.it).

$$ Tonino Basso has four overpriced but colorful rooms in a drab, elevator-equipped, modern apartment block (air-con, Via Gavino 34, mobile 339-761-1651, www.toninobasso.com, Alessandra).

$ La Rosa dei Venti ("The Compass Rose"), run by Giuliana Basso, houses three airy, good-value rooms in her childhood home, on the third floor of an apartment building (call to arrange meeting time, air-con, Via Gavino 19, mobile 333-762-4679, www.larosadeiventi-vernazza.it, info@larosadeiventi-vernazza.it).

SCATTERED THROUGH TOWN AND THE HARBORSIDE

For the places not located on the map in this chapter, arrange a meeting time and/or ask for directions when you reserve.

$$$ La Malà is Vernazza's jet-setter pad. Four crisp, pristine white rooms boast fancy-hotel-type extras and a common seaview terrace. It's a climb—way up to the top of town—but they'll carry your bags to and from the station. Book early—this place fills up quickly (includes breakfast at a bar, family rooms, air-con, mobile 334-287-5718, www.lamala.it, info@lamala.it, charming Giamba and his mama, Armanda). They also rent the simpler **$ "Armanda's Room"** nearby—a great value, since you get Giamba's attention to detail and amenities without paying for a big view (includes simple breakfast, air-con).

$$$ Francamaria and her husband Andrea rent 10 sharp, comfortable, and creatively renovated rooms—all detailed on her website. Their reception desk is on the harbor square (on the ground floor at Piazza Marconi 30), but the rooms they manage are all over town (family rooms, some with air-con, spotty Wi-Fi, tel. 0187-812-002, mobile 328-711-9728, www.francamaria.com, info@francamaria.com).

$$$ Nicolina Rooms consists of seven units in three different buildings. Two cheaper rooms are in the center over the pharmacy, up a few steep steps; another, pricier studio with a terrace is on a twisty lane above the harbor; and four more rooms are in a building beyond the church, with great views and church bells (all include breakfast, Piazza Marconi 29—check in at Pizzeria Vulnetia, tel. 0187-821-193, mobile 333-842-6879, www.camerenicolina.it, camerenicolina.info@cdh.it).

$$ La Marina Rooms is run by hardworking Christian, who speaks English and happily meets guests at the station to carry bags. There are five well-tended (if slightly dated) units, most high above the main street: One single works as a (very) tight double, and three doubles share a fine oceanview terrace; they also have two **$$$** apartments—one with terrace and sea views, and the other on the harborfront square (mobile 338-476-7472, www.lamarinarooms.com, mapcri@yahoo.it).

$$ Martina Callo's four old-fashioned, spartan rooms overlook the harbor square; they're up plenty of steps near the silent-at-night church tower. While the rooms are simple, guests pay for and appreciate the views (family rooms, cheaper nonview room, air-con, ring bell at Piazza Marconi 26, tel. 0187-812-365, mobile 329-435-5344, www.roomartina.it, roomartina@roomartina.it).

$$ Rosa Vitali rents two four-person apartments across from the pharmacy overlooking the main street (and beyond the train noise). One has a terrace and fridge (top floor); the other has windows and a full kitchen (family rooms, ring bell at Via Visconti 10—just before the tobacco shop near Piazza Marconi, tel. 0187-821-181, mobile 340-267-5009, www.rosacamere.it, rosa.vitali@libero.it).

$ Memo Rooms rents three clean and spacious rooms overlooking the main street, in what feels like a miniature hotel. Enrica will meet you if you call upon arrival (Via Roma 15, try Enrica's mobile first at 338-285-2385, otherwise tel. 0187-812-360, www.memorooms.com, info@memorooms.com).

$ Monica Lercari rents several rooms with modern comforts, perched at the top of town (more for seaview terrace, includes breakfast, air-con, tel. 0187-812-296, mobile 320-025-4515, alcastellovernazza@yahoo.it). Monica and her husband, Massimo, run the Ristorante al Castello, in the old castle tower overlooking town.

CORNIGLIA

If you think of the Cinque Terre as the Beatles, Corniglia is Ringo. The only town of the Cinque Terre not on the water, Corniglia (pop. 240) is less visited and feels remote. It has cooler temperatures, a few restaurants, and a windy overlook on its promontory. Signs that say *al mare* or *Marina* lead from the town center steeply down to sunning rocks below the train station. The one-time beach has all been washed away.

According to legend, this tiny, sleepy town's ancient residents produced a wine so famous that vases found at Pompeii touted its virtues. Wine remains Corniglia's lifeblood today.

Orientation

Arrival in Corniglia: From the **train station,** located deep in a ravine, a footpath zigzags up 385 steps to town (allow at least 20 minutes). Thankfully, the shuttle bus—generally timed to meet arriving trains—connects the station with the hill town's Ciappà square (2/hour). **Drivers** can park on the main road into town, but check signs—spots closest to town are for residents only.

Rick's Tip: *To avoid the steep hike to Corniglia and the long descent to the train station,* **use the handy shuttle bus.** *Upon arrival in town (where a schedule is posted at the bus stop), jot down the departure times for the bus and plan your time accordingly.*

Tourist Information: A TI/park information office is down at the train station (likely daily 8:00-20:00, shorter hours off-season).

➲ Corniglia Walk

This self-guided walk might take up to 30 minutes...but only if you let yourself browse and lick a gelato cone.

• *Begin near the shuttle bus stop, located at the...*

Town Square: The gateway to this community is Ciappà square, with an ATM, phone booth, old wine press, and bus stop.

• *Look for the arrow pointing to the* centro. *Stroll the spine of the town—Via Fieschi. In the fall, the smell of grapes becoming wine wafts from busy cellars. Along this main street, you'll see...*

Enticing Shops: As you enter Via Fieschi, a trio of neighboring, fiercely competitive *gelaterie* jockey for your business. My favorite is **Alberto's Gelateria** (at #74).

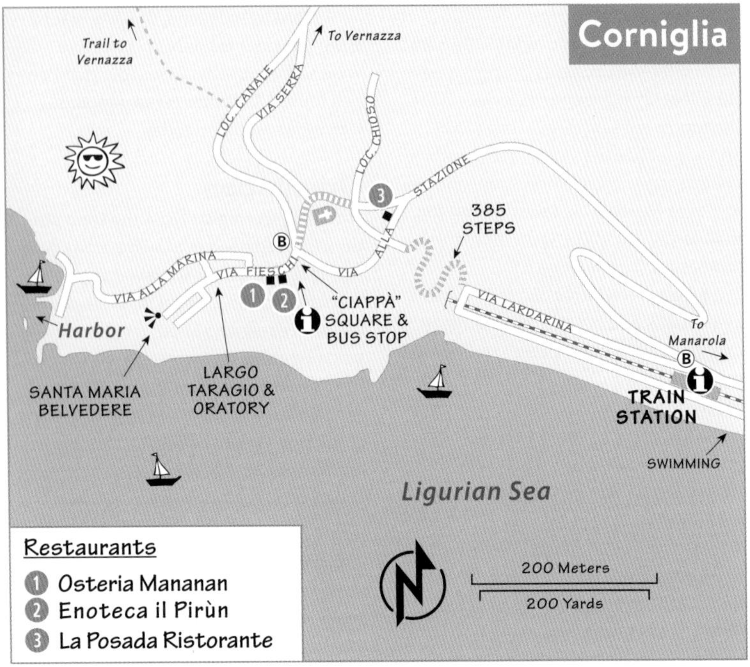

Corniglia

Trail to Vernazza
To Vernazza
LOC. CANALE
VIA SERRA
LOC. CHIOSO
STAZIONE
VIA ALLA
385 STEPS
VIA ALLA MARINA
VIA FIESCHI
VIA
"CIAPPÀ" SQUARE & BUS STOP
VIA LARDARINA
To Manarola
Harbor
SANTA MARIA BELVEDERE
LARGO TARAGIO & ORATORY
TRAIN STATION
SWIMMING
Ligurian Sea
200 Meters
200 Yards

Restaurants

1. Osteria Mananan
2. Enoteca il Pirùn
3. La Posada Ristorante

Before ordering, get a free taste of *miele di Corniglia,* made from local honey.

Farther along, on the left, **Enoteca il Pirùn**—named for an oddly shaped old-fashioned wine pitcher—is a cool cantina at Via Fieschi 115. Sample some local wines (small tastes generally free, or €3/glass). If you drink out of the *pirùn,* Mario will give you a bib. While this is a practical matter (rookies are known to dribble), it also makes a nice souvenir.

A bit farther along are two interesting shops—particularly for picnic shoppers. On the left (#151), Cinzia's shop **Kmo** ("kilometer zero") focuses on locally sourced wines, beers, meats, and cheeses (*panini,* smoothies; daily 10:00-22:00). Across the street, at **Butiega Gastromonia** (#142), Vincenzo and Veronica sell organic local specialties (€3 sandwiches and *antipasti misti* priced by the weight, daily 8:00-19:30). There are good places to picnic farther along on this walk.

• *Following Via Fieschi, you'll end up at the...*

Main Square: On Largo Taragio, tables from two bars and a trattoria spill around a WWI memorial and the town's old well. What looks like a church is the Oratory of Santa Caterina. Up the stairs behind the oratory, you'll find a clearing that children use as a soccer field. The stone benches and viewpoint make it a peaceful place for a picnic.

Hilltop Corniglia

• *From the square, continue up Via Fieschi to the...*

End-of-Town Viewpoint: The Santa Maria Belvedere, named for a church that once stood here, marks the scenic end of Corniglia and makes a super—but sometimes crowded—picnic spot. High to the west (right), the village and sanctuary of San Bernardino straddle a ridge. Below is the tortuous harbor, where locals hoist their boats onto the cruel rocks.

Eating

The typical array of pizzerias, *focaccerie,* and *alimentari* (grocery stores) line the narrow main drag. For a real meal, consider one of these options.

$$ Osteria Mananan—between the Ciappà bus stop and the main square—serves what many say is the best food in town in its stony, elegant interior (Tue-Sun 12:30-14:30 & 19:30-22:00, closed Mon, no outdoor seating, Via Fieschi 117, tel. 0187-821-166).

$$ Enoteca il Pirùn, next door on Via Fieschi, has a small restaurant above the wine bar that serves typical local fare (daily 12:00-16:00 & 19:30-23:30, tel. 0187-812-315).

$$ La Posada Ristorante offers dinner in a garden under trees, overlooking the Ligurian Sea. To get here, stroll out of town to the top of the stairs that lead down to the station (daily 12:00-16:00 & 19:00-23:00, closed Nov-March, tel. 0187-821-174, mobile 338-232-5734).

MANAROLA

Mellow Manarola feels just right. Its hillsides are blanketed with vineyards and it provides the easiest access to the Cinque Terre's remarkable dry-stone terraces. The trail ringing the town's cemetery peninsula provides some of the most accessible and most striking sea views anywhere.

The town fills a ravine, bookended by its harbor to the west and a hilltop church square to the east. The touristy zone squeezed between the train tracks and the harbor can be congested, but just a few steps uphill, you can breathe again. The higher you go, the less crowded it

Manarola

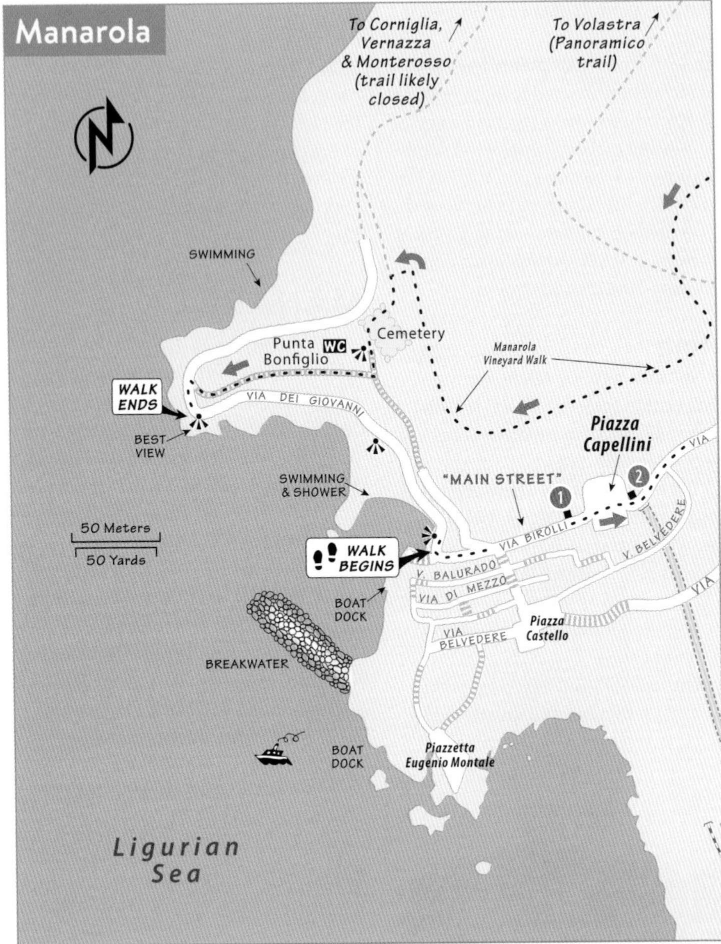

gets, culminating in the residential zone that clings to the ridge.

Orientation

Arrival in Manarola: The town is attached to its **train station** by a 200-yard-long tunnel. Walking through the tunnel, you'll reach Manarola's elevated square. To reach the hilltop church and vineyard strolls, turn right. Or, to reach the busy harbor, cross the square, then go down the other side. The **boat** docks near the base of the main street and the start of my self-guided walk.

Drivers can park in one of the two lots just before town (€2/hour), then walk down the road to the church; from there, the street twists down to the main piazza, train-station tunnel, and harbor.

Tourist Information: The TI/national park information office is in the train station (likely daily 7:30-19:30, shorter hours off-season).

Shuttle Bus: The ATC shuttle bus runs from near the post office (halfway up Manarola's main street), stopping first at the parking lots above town, and then going up to Volastra (about 2/hour).

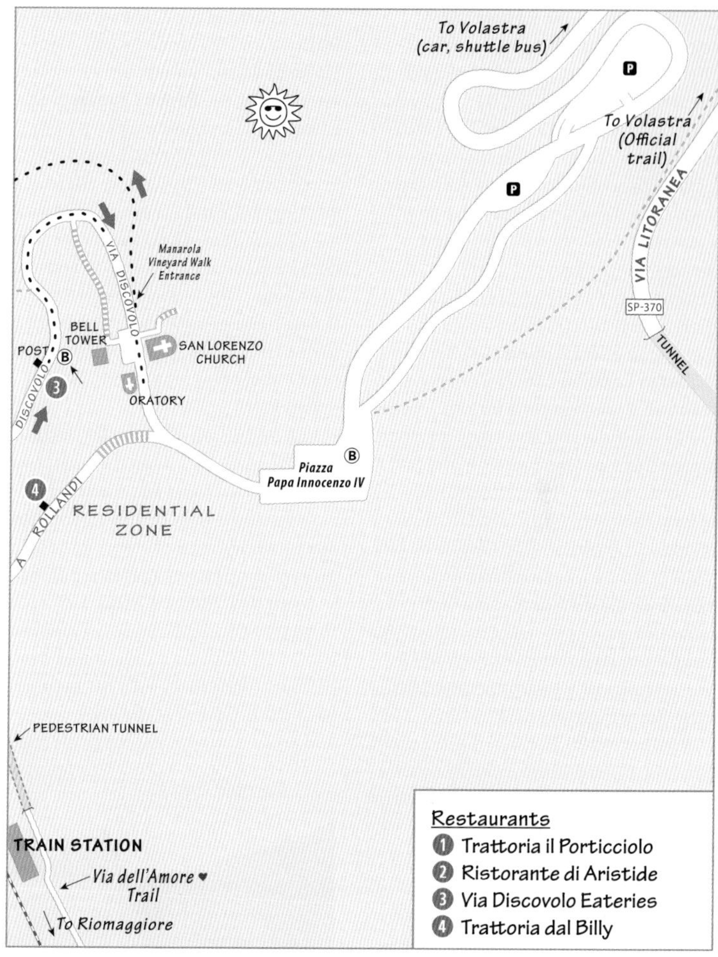

Hiking Gear and Tips: Cinque Terre Trekking, near the top of the main street (halfway up to the church), fills its shop with hiking gear (boots, clothes, walking sticks, and more); they also sell hiking maps and offer free advice (daily 10:00-13:00 & 14:00-19:00, shorter hours off-season, Via Discovolo 136, tel. 0187-920-834, www.cinqueterretrekking.com).

➲ Manarola Walk

From the harbor, this 45-minute, self-guided circular walk shows you the town and surrounding vineyards and ends at a fantastic viewpoint, perfect for a picnic.

• *Start down at the waterfront. Belly up to the wooden banister overlooking the rocky harbor, between the two restaurants.*

The Harbor: Manarola is a picturesque tumble of buildings bunny-hopping down its ravine to the fun-loving waterfront. The breakwater was built just over a decade ago.

Facing the water, look up to the right, at the hillside Punta Bonfiglio cemetery and park. The trail running around the base of the point—where this walk ends—offers magnificent views.

The town's swimming hole is just below you. Manarola has no sand, but offers the best deep-water swimming in the area. The first "beach" has a shower, ladder, and wonderful rocks. The second has tougher access and no shower, but feels more pristine (follow the paved path toward Corniglia, just around the point). For many, the tricky access makes this "beach" dangerous.

• *Hiking inland up the town's main drag, climb a steep ramp to reach Manarola's "new" square, which covers the train tracks.*

Piazza Capellini: This square gives the town a safe, fun zone for kids. Locals living near the tracks also enjoy less train noise. Check out the mosaic in the middle of the square, which depicts the varieties of local fish in colorful enamel. The recommended Ristorante di Aristide has an inviting terrace right out on the square.

• *Go down the stairs at the upper end of the square. On your right, notice the tunnel that leads to Manarola's train station (and the Via dell'Amore trailhead—though trail is likely closed). But for now, head up...*

Via Discovolo: The sleepy main street twists up through town, lined by modest shops. Just before the road bends sharply right, watch (on the right) for a waterwheel. Mills like this once powered the local olive oil industry. Manarola's stream was covered over by a modern sewage system after World War II. Before then, romantic bridges arched over its ravine. You can peek below the concrete street in several places to see the stream surging below your feet.

Across the street from the waterwheel and a bit farther up, notice the helpful **Cinque Terre Trekking** shop (on your left).

• *Keep switchbacking up until you come to the square at the...*

Top of Manarola: The square is faced by a church, an oratory, and a bell tower which once served as a watchtower. Behind the church is a hostel, originally the church's schoolhouse. To the right of the oratory, a stepped lane leads to Manarola's residential zone. The recommended Trattoria dal Billy is nearby (see map).

According to the white marble plaque in its facade, the **Parish Church of St. Lawrence** (San Lorenzo) dates from "MCCCXXXVIII" (1338). Step inside to see two late-15th-century altarpiece paintings from the unnamed Master of the Cinque Terre, the only painter of any note from this region (left wall and above main altar). The humble painted stone ceiling features Lawrence, the patron saint of the Cinque Terre, with his grill, the symbol of his martyrdom (he was roasted on it).

• *With the bell tower on your left, head about 20 yards back down the main street below the church and find a wooden railing on the right. It marks the start of a stroll around the high side of town, and back to the seafront. This is the beginning of the...*

Manarola Vineyard Walk: Don't miss this experience. Follow the wooden railing, enjoying lemon groves and wild red valerian. Along the mostly flat path, you'll get a close-up look at the dry-stone walls and finely crafted vineyards (with dried-

Church of St. Lawrence

Vineyards above Manarola

Manarola's cemetery

heather thatches to protect the grapes from the southwest winds). Smell the rosemary and pick out the remains of an old fort. Notice the S-shape of the main road, which was once a riverbed. The town's roofs are made of locally quarried slate, rather than tile, and are held down by rocks during windstorms.

Halfway along the lip of the ravine, a path marked *Panoramico Volastra (Corniglia)* leads steeply up into the vineyards on the right. This path passes a variety of simple wooden religious scenes, the work of local resident Mario Andreoli. Before his father died, Mario promised him he'd replace the old cross on the family's vineyard—he's been adding figures ever since.

High above, a recent fire burned off the tree cover, revealing ancient terraces that line the terrain. This path also marks the start of the scenic route to Volastra (on the hilltop above), and eventually to Corniglia (see page 145).

• *Continue on the level trail around the base of the hill. Soon the harbor comes into view. Keep looping around the hill for even better views of town. Once you're facing the sea (after passing the cemetery peninsula below you), the trail takes a sharp left and heads down toward the water on concrete steps. When you're almost back to town, you'll see the entrance (on your right) to...*

The Cemetery: Ever since Napoleon—who was king of Italy in the early 1800s—decreed that cemeteries were health risks, Cinque Terre's burial spots have been located outside the towns. The result: The dearly departed get first-class views. Each cemetery—with evocative yellowed photos and finely carved Carrara marble memorials—is worth a visit.

• *The Manarola cemetery is on...*

Punta Bonfiglio: This point offers commanding views of the entire region. For the best vantage point, take the stairs just below the cemetery (through the green gate), then walk farther out toward the water through a park. Your Manarola finale is the bench at the tip of the point. Pause and take in the view. The easiest way back to town is to take the stairs at the end of the point, which join the main walking path—offering more views on the way back to the harbor.

Eating

These restaurant options are listed from lowest to highest, in terms of elevation.

Touristy restaurants are concentrated in the tight zone between Piazza Capellini and the harbor. While these are mostly interchangeable, the Scorza family works hard at **$$ Trattoria il Porticciolo** (Thu-Tue 12:00-21:30, closed Wed, Via Birolli 92, tel. 0187-920-083).

$$ Ristorante di Aristide, right on Piazza Capellini, offers trendy atmosphere and a pleasant outdoor setting (Fri-Wed 12:00-22:30). Down the stairs, at the bottom of the main street, is their simpler **$ café** with indoor and streetside seating and breakfast options (Fri-Wed from 8:00, food served until restaurant opens for dinner, both closed Thu and Jan-Feb, Via Discovolo 290, tel. 0187-920-000).

Via Discovolo, the main street climbing up through town from Piazza Capellini to the church, is lined with simpler places, including some grocery stores and a *gelateria*.

Up at the top of town, in the residential zone above the church, **$$$ Trattoria dal Billy** offers both good food and impressive views over the valley. With black pasta with seafood and squid ink, mixed seafood starters, and homemade desserts, it's worth the climb. Across the street is an elegant dining room carved into the rock. Either setting is perfect for a romantic candlelight meal. Reservations are a must (Fri-Wed 12:00-15:00 & 18:00-22:00, closed Thu, Via Aldo Rollandi 122, tel. 0187-920-628, www.trattoriabilly.com).

RIOMAGGIORE

Riomaggiore is a laid-back, workaday town that feels more "real" than its touristy neighbors. The main drag through town, while traffic-free, feels more urban than "village," and surrounding the harbor is a fascinating tangle of pastel homes leaning on each other like drunken sailors.

Orientation

Arrival in Riomaggiore: The **train station** is separated from the town center by a steep hill. To easily get into town, take the pedestrian tunnel that begins at the south end of the train station (and parallels the rail tunnel). You'll exit at the bottom of Via Colombo, the main street. Other options: You can take my self-guided walk into town; catch the shuttle bus at the bottom of Via Colombo and ride it partway up; or ride the elevator up from the pedestrian tunnel (€1/person, daily 7:00-18:00). The **boat** docks near the base of Via Colombo. **Drivers** can park at one of two pay-and-display lots above town (€3.50/hour, €23/day, best to pay in cash).

Tourist Information: The TI is in the train station at the ticket desk (daily 8:00-20:00, shorter hours off-season). If it's

Jumping for joy in Riomaggiore

crowded, you can buy your park card at the Cinque Terre park info/shop office next door (daily 8:00-20:00, shorter hours off-season).

Baggage Storage: You can check your bag at the casually run bar that also functions as the ***deposito bagagli*** office, which is straight ahead as you exit the station (€5/bag, daily 8:30-19:00, closed in winter).

➲ Riomaggiore Walk

This partly uphill but easy self-guided loop takes the long way from the station into town. Enjoy some fine views before strolling down the main street to the harbor.

• *Start at the train station. (If you arrive by boat, cross beneath the tracks and take a left, then hike through the tunnel along the tracks to reach the station.)*

Stone Wall: With your back to the station, look at the long stone wall. The hilly Cinque Terre depends on walls. This one is made with mortar, but nearly 300 million cubic feet of the walls in the region are dry-stone—built entirely without mortar—giving the region its characteristic *muri a secco* terracing for vineyards and olive groves.

Looking left, notice the stairs climbing up just past the station building. These lead to the trail to Manarola, also known as the **Via dell'Amore** (likely closed for repairs).

• *Facing the wall, turn left, then go right up the wide street just before the station café. Head up this street for about 100 yards, and watch for the stairs leading through the garden on your right to the upper switchback. Then, once on high ground, turn right (back toward the sea). Soon you'll pass the top of the concrete elevator tower and, a bit farther, arrive at a fine viewpoint.*

Top o' the Town: Here you're treated to spectacular sea views. Hook left around the bluff; once you round the bend, ignore the steps marked *Marina Seacoast* (which lead to the harbor) and continue another five minutes along level ground to the church (follow *salita castello* signs). You'll go by the city hall, with murals celebrating the heroic grape-pickers and fishermen of

Riomaggiore's harbor

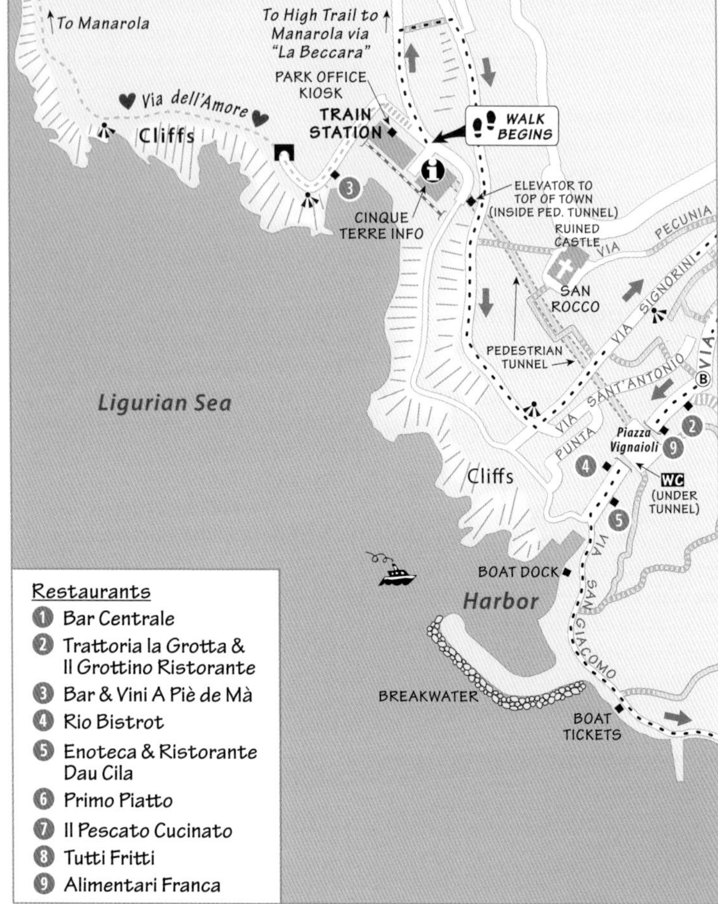

the region (also by Silvio Benedetto).

• *Before reaching the church, pause at the big terrace to enjoy the...*

Town View: The major river of this region once ran through this valley, as implied by the name Riomaggiore (local dialect for "river" and "major"). As in the other Cinque Terre towns, the river ravine is now paved over. The romantic arched bridges that once connected the two sides have been replaced by a practical modern road.

The church (established in 1340 and rebuilt in 1870) is dedicated to St. John the Baptist, the patron saint of Genoa, the maritime republic that once dominated the region.

• *Continue straight past the church and along the narrow lane, watching on the right for wide stairs leading down to Riomaggiore's main street...*

Via Colombo: Starting downhill, you'll pass (on the right, at #62) a good pizzeria/*focacceria,* facing the Co-op grocery store across the street (at #55). Below that is a delicious fresh pasta takeaway place (Primo Piatto, at #72). Farther along, the big covered terrace on the right belongs to Bar Centrale (at #144), the town's most popular hangout.

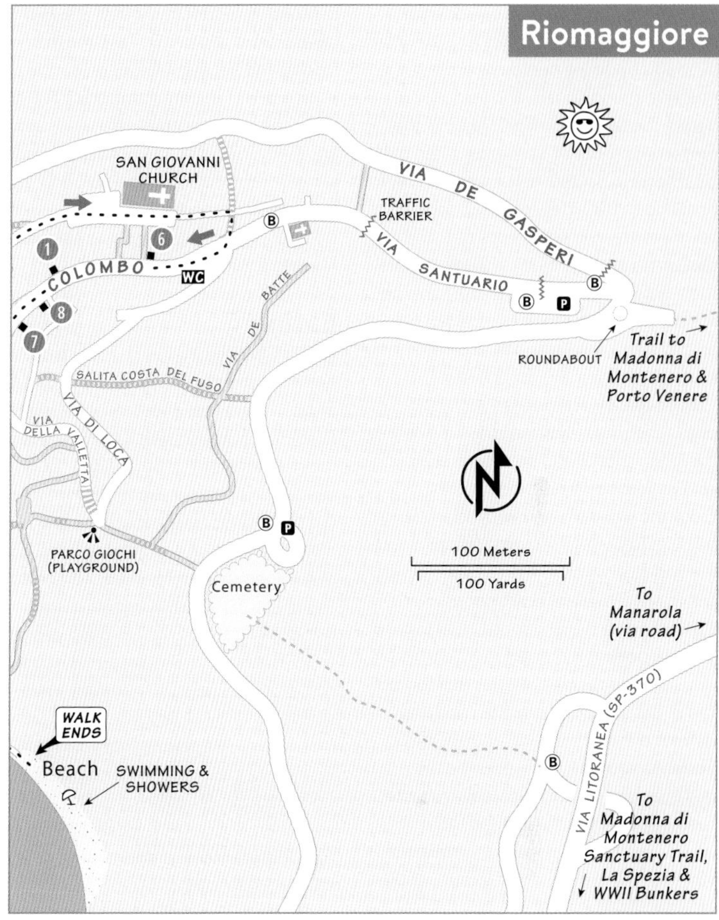

As you round the bend to the left, notice the old-time pharmacy just above (on the right). On your left, at #199, peek into the Il Pescato Cucinato shop, where Laura fries up her husband Edoardo's fresh catch; grab a paper cone of deep-fried seafood as a snack. Where the road bends sharply right, notice the bench on your left (just before La Zorza Café), probably occupied by the town's old-timers, who keep a running commentary on the steady flow of people. Straight ahead, you can already see where this street will dead-end. The last shop on the left, Alimentari Franca (at #251), is a well-stocked grocery where you can gather the makings for a picnic.

Where Via Colombo dead-ends, look right to see the tunnel leading back to the station. Look left to see two sets of stairs. The "up" stairs take you to a park-like square built over the train tracks, which provides the children of the town level land on which to kick their soccer balls. The murals above celebrate the great-grand-parents of these very children—the salt-of-the-earth locals who earned a humble living before the age of tourism.

• *The "down" stairs take you to a pay WC and the...*

Marina: This most picturesque corner of Riomaggiore features a cluster of buildings huddling nervously around a postage-stamp square and vest-pocket harbor. Because Riomaggiore lacks the protected harbor of Vernazza, when bad weather is expected, fishermen pull their boats up to the safety of the square. It's a team effort—the signal goes out, and anyone with a boat of their own helps move the whole fleet. Sometimes the fishermen are busy beaching their boats even on a bright, sunny day—an indication that they know something you don't know.

A couple of restaurants—with high prices and memorable seating—look down over the action. Head past them and up the walkway along the left side of the harbor. Enjoy the views of the town's colorful pastel buildings, with the craggy coastline just beyond. Below you, the breakwater curves out to sea. These rocks are popular with sunbathers by day and romantics at sunset.

For a peek at Riomaggiore's beach, continue around the bluff on this trail toward the Punta di Montenero, the cape that defines the southern end of the Cinque Terre. As you walk you'll pass the rugged boat landing and eventually run into Riomaggiore's beach *(spiaggia)*. Ponder how Europeans manage to look relaxed when lounging on football-sized "pebbles."

Experiences

Riomaggiore's rugged **beach** *(spiaggia)* is rocky, but still peaceful and inviting. There's a shower here in the summer, and another closer to town by the boat landing—where many enjoy sunning on and jumping from the rocks.

The town has a **diving center** that rents scuba, snorkeling, and kayaking gear (daily May-Sept 9:00-18:00, open in good weather only—likely weekends only in shoulder season, office down the stairs and under the tracks on Via San Giacomo, tel. 0187-920-011, www.5terrediving.it).

A **hiking trail** rises scenically from Riomaggiore to the 14th-century Madonna di Montenero sanctuary, high above the town (about one hour). Take the main road inland until you see signs, or ride the shuttle bus 12 minutes from the town center to the sanctuary trail, then walk uphill another 15 minutes. There's a great picnic spot up top. If the Via dell'Amore trail to Manarola is closed, consider the steep 1.5-hour hike on trail #531 over the bluff to Manarola, see page 147.

Eating

$$ Bar Centrale, run by sociable Ivo and Alberto, serves Italian specialties (pasta dishes, anchovies) and American comfort food (hamburgers) with San Franciscan rock music and a fun-loving vibe. During the day, this popular expat hangout feels like the village's living room. At night, it offers lively action and great mojitos. It's also a good spot for breakfast and gelato (open long hours daily, free Wi-Fi with drink, Via Colombo 144, tel. 0187-920-208).

$$ Trattoria la Grotta, also in the town center, serves reliable food with a passion for anchovies and mussels in a dramatic, cave-like setting (daily 12:00-14:30 & 17:30-22:30, closed Wed in winter, Via Colombo 247, tel. 0187-920-187). The same family runs the upscale **$$$ Il Grottino Ristorante** next door (same hours, tel. 0187-920-938).

$$ Bar & Vini A Piè de Mà, at the Via dell'Amore trailhead on the Manarola end of town, has piles of charm. A meal or cocktail on its terrace offers striking, memorable views (daily 10:00-20:00, June-Sept until 24:00, free Wi-Fi, tel. 0187-921-037).

$$$$ Rio Bistrot, small and intimate at the top of the harbor, tries to jazz up its Ligurian cuisine with international influences. You can order à la carte but they tend to push their €39 tasting menu (simpler and cheaper lunch menu, daily 12:00-16:00 & 18:00-22:00, Via San Giacomo 46, tel. 0187-920-616).

$$$$ Enoteca & Ristorante Dau Cila (pronounced "dow CHEE-lah") is a mel-

Kayakers flock to Riomaggiore.

The catch of the day

low hideaway in a centuries-old boat shed on the harbor, with extra tables on a rustic deck. It's cool for cocktails, with a jazz-and-Brazilian-lounge ambience (daily 12:00-24:00, closed Feb, Via San Giacomo 65, tel. 0187-760-032).

Various eateries along the main drag, which you'll encounter on my self-guided walk, offer good lunches or snacks. At the top of town, **$ Primo Piatto** offers take-away handmade pastas and sauces—it's cheap and delicious (Wed-Mon 10:30-19:30 or later, closed Tue, Via Colombo 72, tel. 0187-920-038). For deep-fried seafood in a paper cone, try **$ Il Pescato Cucinato,** where the chalkboard out front explains what's fresh (11:20-20:30, Via Colombo 199, mobile 339-262-4815), or **$ Tutti Fritti,** a few doors away (daily 10:00-21:00, Via Colombo 161, mobile 347-826-1729).

For picnic supplies, head to handy **Alimentari Franca,** at the bottom of the main street, conveniently located right by the train-station tunnel and stairs down to the marina (daily 8:00-20:00, Via Colombo 251).

TRANSPORTATION

Getting Around the Cinque Terre

The five towns are close together and have good public transportation connections by train and boat (as well as hiking trails). Little shuttle buses provide local transport per town.

By Train

By train, the five towns are just a few minutes apart. Along the coast here, trains go in only two directions: northbound toward Genoa; or southbound toward La Spezia.

A train ride of any length between Cinque Terre towns costs a hefty €4 during peak times—whether you're hopping one town or four. You must buy a new ticket for every train ride, and tickets are valid only on the day of purchase. Purchase tickets online (at www.trenitalia.com), at station windows, Cinque Terre park desks, or self-service machines. The €16 **Cinque Terre Treno Multi-Service Card** can be worthwhile (even if you don't hike), because it provides the easiest way to train-hop, allowing you to catch trains at the last minute without ticket concerns. It pays for itself if you take four rides in one day, but its value comes more from its convenience than its economy.

Validate your ticket or card before you board by stamping it in the green-and-white machines on platforms and in station passages, but note these exceptions: Printed online tickets and smartphone e-tickets are prevalidated. Conductors levy stiff fines for riding with a ticket that hasn't been validated.

Rick's Tip: *If you have a* **Eurail Pass,** *don't spend one of your valuable travel days on the relatively cheap Cinque Terre.*

Trains run about twice hourly in each direction, connecting several or all five towns. Shops, hotels, and restaurants often post the current schedule, and may also hand out copies. Check the key on the printed schedules carefully: certain departures listed are for only weekdays, only Sundays, etc.

In the **station,** real-time **monitors** are the best, most current source of information. They show the departure times and directions of the next trains (and if they're late—*in ritardo; SOPP* means "cancelled"). Northbound trains are marked for *(per)* Levanto, Genoa (Genova), or Sestri Levante; southbound trains are marked for La Spezia. To be sure you get on the right train, know your train's number and final destination.

Important: Trains from Levanto, Monterosso, Riomaggiore, or La Spezia sometimes skip lesser stations, and even the short milk-run trains may skip a station or two. Always confirm before boarding that the train will stop at the town you need.

Accept the unpredictability of Cinque Terre trains—they're often late. Relax while you wait—buy an ice cream or cup of coffee at a station bar. Scout the platform you need in advance, and then, when the train comes, hop on.

Know your stop. The train stations are small and the trains are long, so (especially in Vernazza and Monterosso) you might have to get off deep in a tunnel—if this happens to you, just head toward daylight. The door won't open automatically—push the green button, twist the black handle, or lift up the red one. If a door isn't working, go quickly to the next car to try another.

By Boat

From Easter through October, **daily boat service** connects Monterosso, Vernazza, Manarola, Riomaggiore, Porto Venere, and beyond. In peaceful weather, boats can be more reliable than trains, but if seas are rough, they don't run at all.

Boats depart Monterosso about hourly (10:30-18:00), stopping at the Cinque Terre towns (except for hilltop Corniglia) and ending up an hour later in nearby Porto Venere. (Porto Venere-Monterosso boats run 8:50-18:00.) The ticket price depends on the length of the boat ride (ranging from €6 for a short ride between towns, to €18 for a five-town, one-way ticket with stops; an all-day pass is €25, or €33 to include Porto Venere).

Buy **tickets** at stands at each town's harbor (tel. 0187-818-440). **Schedules** are posted at docks, harbor bars, Cinque Terre park offices, and hotels (www.navigazionegolfodeipoeti.it).

Rick's Tip: *In calm weather,* **boats connect the towns about as frequently as the trains,** *though at different times; if you're in a rush, take whichever form of transport is leaving first. In the unpredictable Cinque Terre, a departure now is worth two a little later.*

By Shuttle Bus

ATC shuttle buses (which locals call *pulmino*) connect each town with its closest parking lot and various points in the hills—but do not connect the towns with each other. The one you're most likely to use runs between Corniglia's sea-level train station and its hilltop town center. Most rides cost €1.50 one-way (€2.50 from driver, free with Cinque Terre park card). Ask about tickets and bus schedules at park info offices or TIs, or note the times posted at bus stops. Shuttle schedules change constantly; confirm the details carefully. Shuttles may not run from 12:30 to 15:00, when they break for lunch. As you board, tell the driver where you want to go. Departures often coordinate with train arrival times. Some shuttles go beyond the parking lots and high into the hills. To soak in the scenery, ride up and hike down, or just ride both ways (30-45 minutes covered by one ticket).

Arriving and Departing

By Train

Most big, fast trains from elsewhere in Italy speed right past the Cinque Terre, though some stop in Monterosso. Unless you're coming from a nearby town, you'll usually have to change trains at least once to reach Vernazza, Corniglia, or Manarola.

Generally, if you're coming from the north, you'll change trains at Genoa's Piazza Principe station, Sestri Levante, Levanto, or Monterosso. If you're coming from the south or east, you'll probably switch trains at La Spezia's Centrale station (not La Spezia Migliarina). Check your full schedule and route options in the train station before you leave (use the kiosks or ask at a ticket window).

TRAIN CONNECTIONS

The five towns of the Cinque Terre are on a milk-run line, with trains coming through about every 30 minutes (and connecting with La Spezia and Levanto). For points beyond the Cinque Terre (for example, Milan or Pisa), you'll usually have to change in La Spezia, Monterosso, Levanto, or Sestri Levante.

From Monterosso by Train to: Venice (5/day, 6 hours, change in Milan), **Milan** (8/day direct, otherwise hourly with change in Genoa, 3 hours), **Genoa** (hourly, 1.5 hours), **Pisa** (hourly, 1-1.5 hours), **Sestri Levante** (hourly, 30 minutes, most trains to Genoa stop here), **La Spezia** (2-3/hour, 15-30 minutes), **Levanto** (2-3/hour, 4 minutes), **Rome** (hourly, 4.5 hours, change in La Spezia).

From La Spezia Centrale by Train to: Rome (8/day direct, more with transfers in Pisa, 3-4.5 hours), **Pisa** (about hourly, 1 hour), **Florence** (5/day direct, 2.5 hours, otherwise nearly hourly with change in Pisa), **Milan** (about hourly, 3 hours direct or with change in Genoa), **Venice** (about hourly, 5-6 hours, 1-3 changes).

By Taxi

Cinqueterre Taxi covers all five towns, providing transport to the nearest port or airport (mobile 334-776-1946 or 347-652-0837, www.cinqueterretaxi.com). The pricey **5 Terre Transfer** service can connect the five towns or beyond (Luciana mobile 339-130-1183; Marzio mobile 340-356-5268).

By Car

Given the narrow roads and lack of parking, bringing a car to the Cinque Terre is a bad idea. Consider parking in **Levanto** or **La Spezia** and riding the train into town. Or for simplicity, stay at a Cinque Terre hotel with parking; for this, **Monterosso** is your best bet (and it has parking lots in town). Each Cinque Terre town has a parking lot (handy for day-trippers) on its outskirts, with a shuttle bus into town. Try to arrive between 9:00 and 11:00, when overnight visitors are usually departing. But don't drive to **Vernazza,** where parking is particularly tight.

It's smart to have your hotel confirmation in hand during busy times—holidays, summer, and weekends—when police at the top of town may deny entry to cars without a hotel reservation. The rare street parking in the towns is best left for locals. Wherever you park, leave nothing of value in your car.

Florence

Florence is the birthplace of the Renaissance and the modern world. It's geographically small but culturally rich—containing more artistic masterpieces per square mile than anyplace else. In a single day, you can look Michelangelo's *David* in the eyes, fall under the seductive sway of Botticelli's *Birth of Venus,* and climb the modern world's first dome, which still dominates the skyline.

A cosmopolitan vibe courses through the city's narrow lanes. You'll encounter children licking gelato, students riding Vespas, supermodels wearing Gucci fashions, and artisans sipping Chianti—Florence has long been perfecting the art of civilized living.

FLORENCE IN 2 DAYS

Compact Florence is packed with sights, but crowds and long lines can ruin your day's agenda. To maximize your time, either reserve the top two sights—Accademia (Michelangelo's *David*) and Uffizi Gallery (Renaissance paintings)—or get a pricey Firenze Card that allows you to skip the lines. Avoid both sights on Monday when they're closed, and on the first Sunday of the month, when they're free but impossibly crowded. Some sights such as the Bargello close early off-season and on Sundays or Mondays.

Day 1: In the cool of the morning, take my Renaissance Walk. Afterward, depending on your interests, choose among Florence's many sights: the Bargello (best statues), Medici Chapels (Michelangelo statues), Santa Maria Novella (Masaccio's 3-D painting), Palazzo Vecchio (Medici palace), Santa Croce Church (famous tombs), Galileo Science Museum, Pitti Palace (art), and Brancacci Chapel (more Masaccio). For lunch, grab a quick bite between sights; you have many options, including Mercato Centrale's upscale, upstairs food hall.

Around 16:30 when crowds die down, see the Uffizi Gallery's unforgettable paintings.

On any evening: Linger over dinner. Take a stroll, gelato in hand. Or take a taxi or bus to Piazzale Michelangelo for spectacular city views, and walk back into town for dinner. You can sightsee late at some sights, attend a concert at a church, or drop by a wine bar.

Day 2: See the Accademia *(David)* and visit the nearby Museum of San Marco (Fra Angelico's art). Then hit the street markets, wander, or do more museum-going. Stroll to the river and cross the historic bridge, Ponte Vecchio, to the Oltrarno neighborhood for dinner.

With extra time: Fit in a day trip to Pisa (book ahead to climb the famous tower) or Siena (just 1.5 hours away by bus—and magic after dark.

ORIENTATION

Florence (pop. 360,000) can be intense. Prepare for scorching summer heat, crowded lanes and sidewalks, slick pickpockets, few WCs, steep prices, and long lines. The best of the city lies on the north bank of the Arno River. The main sights cluster around the dome of the cathedral (Duomo). Everything is within a 20-minute walk of the train station, cathedral, or Ponte Vecchio (Old Bridge). The less famous but more characteristic Oltrarno area (south bank) is just over the bridge. Here's a neighborhood-by-neighborhood rundown:

Historic Core: The Duomo—with its iconic, towering dome—is the visual, geographical, and historical center of Florence. A 10-minute walk away is the Palazzo Vecchio (city hall), with its skyscraping medieval spire. Connecting these two landmarks is the north-south pedestrian street called Via de' Calzaiuoli. This central axis—Duomo to the Palazzo Vecchio to the Arno River—is the spine for Florentine sightseeing and the route of my self-guided Renaissance Walk. Via de' Calzaiuoli also links two central piazzas—Piazza della Repubblica and Piazza della Signoria (fronting the Uffizi Gallery). To the west of this axis is a glitzy shopping zone, and to the east is a characteristic web of narrow lanes.

Rick's Tip: **Don't drive into the city center.** *Don't even try it. Florence's traffic-reduction system is confusing even to locals. If you don't have a permit, you'll get a* **€100 traffic ticket** *in the mail. The no-go zone is confusing; several streets are classified ZTL ("limited traffic zone") at only certain times of day.*

Accademia/San Lorenzo (north of the Duomo): The area north of the Duomo is less atmospheric but has several crucial sights. From the Duomo, Via Cavour runs north, bisecting the neighborhood. To the east lies the Accademia (Michelangelo's *David*) and the Museum of San Marco. The western part clusters around the Basilica of San Lorenzo, with its Medici Chapels. The area near San Lorenzo teems with tourists: There are the vendor stalls of San Lorenzo Market, the lively Mercato Centrale, and many hotels and trattorias.

Train Station/Santa Maria Novella (west of the Duomo): The area near the train station and Church of Santa Maria Novella is somewhat urban and dreary, but has inexpensive hotels and characteristic eateries. Closer to the river (near Palazzo Strozzi) is a posh shopping zone, with a more affordable mix of shops lining Via del Parione and Borgo Ognissanti.

Santa Croce (east of the Duomo): A 10-minute walk east from the Palazzo Vecchio leads to the neighborhood's main landmark, the Church of Santa Croce. Along the way is the Bargello sculpture museum. The area stretching north and west from Santa Croce is increasingly authentic and workaday, offering a glimpse at untouristy Florence.

Oltrarno (south of the river): Literally the "Other Side of the Arno River," this neighborhood reveals a Florence from a time before tourism. Many artisans still have workshops here, and open their doors to passing visitors. The Oltrarno starts just across Ponte Vecchio (jammed with tourists and tackiness) and stretches south to the giant Pitti Palace and surrounding gardens (Boboli and Bardini). To the west is the rough-but-bohemian Piazza di Santo Spirito and the lavishly frescoed Brancacci Chapel. To the east of Pitti Palace, perched high on the hill, is Piazzale Michelangelo, with Florence's most popular viewpoint. Tucked between there and the river is the funky little San Niccolò neighborhood, with lively bars and eateries.

Tourist Information

The city TI has several branches. The crowded main branch is across the square

▲▲▲**Accademia** Michelangelo's *David* and powerful (unfinished) *Prisoners.* Reserve ahead or get a Firenze Card. **Hours:** Tue-Sun 8:15-18:50, possibly Tue until 22:00 June-Sept, closed Mon. See page 184.

▲▲▲**Uffizi Gallery** Greatest collection of Italian paintings anywhere. Reserve well in advance or get a Firenze Card. **Hours:** Tue-Sun 8:15-18:50, closed Mon. See page 186.

▲▲▲**Bargello** Underappreciated sculpture museum with Michelangelo, Donatello, and Medici treasures. **Hours:** Tue-Sat 8:15-17:00, until 13:50 Nov-March; also open second and fourth Mon and first, third, and fifth Sun of each month. See page 190.

▲▲▲**Duomo Museum** Underrated cathedral museum with sculptures. **Hours:** Daily 9:00-20:00, closed first Tue of each month. See page 181.

▲▲**Duomo** Gothic cathedral with colorful facade and the first dome built since ancient Roman times. **Hours:** Mon-Fri 10:00-17:00 (Thu until 16:30), Sat 10:00-16:45, Sun 13:30-16:45. See page 180.

▲▲**Museum of San Marco** Best collection anywhere of artwork by the early Renaissance master Fra Angelico. **Hours:** Tue-Fri 8:15-13:50, Sat 8:15-16:50; also open 8:15-13:50 on first, third, and fifth Mon and 8:15-16:50 on second and fourth Sun of each month. See page 185.

▲▲**Medici Chapels** Tombs of Florence's great ruling family, designed and carved by Michelangelo. **Hours:** Tue-Sat 8:15-17:00 except Nov-March until 13:50; also open second and fourth Mon and first, third, and fifth Sun of each month. See page 186.

▲▲**Palazzo Vecchio** Fortified palace, once the home of the Medici family, wallpapered with history. **Hours:** Museum and excavations open Fri-Wed 9:00 -23:00 (Oct-March until 19:00), Thu 9:00-14:00; shorter hours for tower. See page 189.

▲▲**Galileo Science Museum** Fascinating old clocks, telescopes, maps, and three of Galileo's fingers. **Hours:** Wed-Mon 9:30-18:00, Tue until 13:00. See page 190.

▲▲**Santa Croce Church** Precious art, tombs of famous Florentines, and Brunelleschi's Pazzi Chapel in 14th-century church. **Hours:** Mon-Sat 9:30-17:30, Sun 14:00-17:30. See page 191.

▲▲**Church of Santa Maria Novella** Thirteenth-century Dominican church with Masaccio's famous 3-D painting. **Hours:** Mon-Thu 9:00-19:00 (Oct-March until 17:30), Fri 11:00-19:00 (Oct-March until 17:30), Sat 9:00-17:30, Sun 13:00-17:30. See page 192.

▲▲**Pitti Palace** Several museums in lavish palace plus sprawling Boboli and Bardini Gardens. **Hours:** Palatine Gallery, Royal Apartments, and Gallery of Modern Art—Tue-Sun 8:15-18:50, closed Mon; Boboli and Bardini Gardens, Costume Gallery, Argenti/Silverworks Museum, and Porcelain Museum—daily June-Aug 8:15-19:30, April-May and Sept until 18:30, March and Oct until 17:30, Nov-Feb until 16:30, closed first and last Mon of each month. See page 192.

▲▲**Brancacci Chapel** Works of Masaccio, early Renaissance master who reinvented perspective. **Hours:** Mon and Wed-Sat 10:00-17:00, Sun 13:00-17:00, closed Tue. Reservations required (unless you have a Firenze Card), though often available on the spot. See page 193.

▲▲**San Miniato Church** Sumptuous Renaissance chapel and sacristy showing scenes of St. Benedict. **Hours:** Mon-Sat 9:30-13:00 & 15:30-20:00, until 19:00 off-season, Sun 9:30-20:00, closed sporadically for special occasions. See page 196.

▲**Mercato Centrale** Bustling covered market with picnic fare on the ground floor and an upscale foodie court upstairs. **Hours:** Produce—Mon-Fri 7:00-14:00, Sat 7:00-17:00, closed Sun; food court—daily 10:00-24:00. See page 186.

▲**Ponte Vecchio** Famous, touristy bridge lined with gold and silver shops. **Hours:** Bridge always open. See page 179.

▲**Climbing the Duomo's Dome** Grand view into the cathedral, close-up of dome architecture, and, after 463 steps, a glorious city vista; reservations required. **Hours:** Mon-Fri 8:30-20:00, Sat 8:30-17:40, Sun 13:00-16:00. See page 180.

▲**Baptistery** Bronze doors fit to be the gates of paradise. **Hours:** Doors always viewable; interior open Mon-Sat 8:15-20:00, Sun 8:30-14:00. See page 181.

▲**Piazzale Michelangelo** Hilltop square with stunning view of Duomo and Florence. See page 194.

from the **train station** (Mon-Sat 9:00-19:00, Sun until 14:00; at the back corner of the Church of Santa Maria Novella at Piazza della Stazione 4; tel. 055-212-245, www.firenzeturismo.it). For help you'll need to take a number from the touch-screen computer by the door. Upstairs, the "Experience Florence" visitors center has big touch screens to help you virtually explore the city, and a well-produced 3-D movie of the big landmarks (free, 13 minutes, English subtitles).

A smaller branch is centrally located **next to the Duomo,** at the west corner of Via de' Calzaiuoli (inside the loggia, same hours as train station branch, tel. 055-288-496). Another TI is at the **airport.**

The least crowded and most helpful TI, which covers both the city and the greater province of Florence, can be less crowded and more helpful. It's a couple of blocks **north of the Duomo** (Mon-Fri 9:00-13:00, closed Sat-Sun, Via Cavour 1 red, tel. 055-290-832).

Sightseeing Pass, Advance Reservations, and Combo-Tickets

Firenze Card

The **Firenze Card** is pricey (€72) but convenient. This three-day sightseeing pass gives you admission to many of Florence's sights, including the Uffizi Gallery and Accademia. Just as important, it lets you skip the ticket-buying lines without needing to make reservations (except for the Duomo dome climb). Simply go to the entrance, find the Firenze Card priority line, show the card, and you'll be let in.

But even with the card, security bottlenecks may delay your entry. At some sights, you must first present your card at the ticket booth or info desk to get a physical ticket before proceeding to the entrance. For the Duomo sights, this means going to the ticket office across from the Baptistery (at #7), though there's a priority queue for cardholders. Note that the Firenze Card does not let you skip the line for the Duomo dome climb—you must make a reservation for that—nor does it let you skip the line to enter the (free) Duomo.

Cost and Coverage: The Firenze Card costs €72 and is valid for 72 hours from when you validate it at your first museum (e.g., Tue at 15:00 until Fri at 15:00). Validate your card only when you're ready to tackle the covered sights on three consecutive days. Make sure the sights you want to visit will be open (some sights are closed Sun or Mon).

The Firenze Card covers the regular admission price as well as any special-exhibit surcharges, and is good for one visit per sight. (The €77 Firenze Card+ also includes free public transportation.)

To make the card pay for itself, you'd need to see all of these sights within three days: the Uffizi, Accademia, Bargello, Palazzo Vecchio, Medici Chapels, Duomo sights, and Pitti Palace's Palatine Gallery and Royal Apartments. But the real value of the card is that you can spend more time sightseeing rather than waiting in ticket-buying lines.

For a complete list of included sights, see www.firenzecard.it. Don't confuse this card with the lesser Firenze PASSport.

You can **buy the Firenze Card** at most TIs and most participating sights. The least-crowded sales point is the TI north of the Duomo (Via Cavour 1 red). The Palazzo Strozzi also has short lines and long hours. Other uncrowded, central sights covered by the card include the Bargello, the Bardini Museum, and the back ticket desk at the Church of Santa Maria Novella (on Piazza della Stazione, across from the train station). Buying the card at the Uffizi Gallery is surprisingly easy: Just enter door #2, passing to the left of the ticket-buying line.

You can also buy the card at more crowded places like the TI across from the train station and the airport TI, though not from the TI next to the Duomo. It's also sold at big sights like the Palazzo Vecchio and Pitti Palace.

Don't bother buying the card online, as you have to go to one of these desks to swap the voucher for the actual pass. The Firenze Card is not shareable, and there are no family or senior discounts.

If planning to climb the Duomo's dome, you must make a reservation in person when you present your Firenze Card at the Duomo ticket office—but in high season the chances of getting a time slot for the same day are slim (you're better off buying a Duomo combo-ticket online well in advance and booking your climb time then).

Children under 18 are allowed free into any state museum in Italy, and into any municipal museum in Florence. However, at the Uffizi and Accademia, if they want to skip the lines with their Firenze Card-holding parents, children still must (technically) pay the €4 "reservation fee." This can be paid on the spot—no need to reserve ahead. Enforcement of this policy varies.

Advance Reservations

If you only want to see the Accademia and Uffizi, you can skip the Firenze Card and instead make **reservations** for these two top sights, ideally as soon as you know when you'll be in town. Without a reservation at the Accademia and Uffizi, you can usually enter without significant lines from November through March after 16:00. But from April through October and on weekends, it can be crowded even late in the day. I'd reserve a spot any time of year. Reservations are not possible on the first Sunday of the month, when the museums are free and very busy.

Reservations are mandatory to climb the Duomo's dome. You can also make reservations for several other Florence sights—including the Bargello, Medici Chapels, and Pitti Palace—though they're unnecessary. The Brancacci Chapel officially requires a reservation (unless you have a Firenze Card, in which case you can walk right in), though it's usually possible to get a reservation on the spot at the chapel or in advance at the Palazzo Vecchio.

There are several ways to make reservations for the **Accademia** and **Uffizi:**

Online: Book and pay for your Accademia or Uffizi visit via the city's official site. You'll receive an order confirmation email, which is followed shortly by a voucher email. Bring your voucher to the ticket desk to swap for an actual ticket (€4/ticket reservation fee, www.firenzemusei.it—click on "B-ticket").

Pricey middleman sites—such as www.uffizi.com and www.tickitaly.com—are reliable and more user-friendly than the official site, but their booking fees run about €10 per ticket. (If ordering from a broker site, don't confuse Florence's Accademia with Venice's gallery of the same name.)

You can avoid waiting in line...

...if you make advance reservations.

By Phone: From a US phone, dial 011-39-055-294-883, or from an Italian phone call 055-294-883. When you get through, an English-speaking operator talks you through the process within a few minutes, and you'll end up with an entry time and a confirmation number. Present your confirmation number at the museum and pay for your ticket. You pay only for the tickets you pick up; for example, if you reserved two tickets but only use one, you'll pay for just one ticket (€4/ticket reservation fee; booking office open Mon-Fri 8:30-18:30, Sat until 12:30, closed Sun).

Through Your Hotel: Some hoteliers will make museum reservations (for a small fee) for guests who request this service when they book their room.

Private Tour: Various tour companies—including the ones listed in "Tours" in the next section—offer tours that include a reserved museum admission.

Last-Minute Strategies: If you arrive without a reservation, call the reservation number (tel. 055-294-883); ask your hotelier for help; or head to a booking window, either at Orsanmichele Church (daily 9:00-16:00, closed Sun off-season, along Via de' Calzaiuoli) or at Liberia My Accademia bookstore across from the Accademia's exit (Tue-Sun 8:15-17:30, closed Mon, Via Ricasoli 105 red). It's also possible to ask at the Uffizi's ticket office if they have any short-notice reservations available (ask the custodian at door #2 and ignore the long ticket-buying line). Any of these options will cost you the €4 reservation fee. Because both museums are closed on Mondays, the hardest day to snare last-minute, same-day reservations is Tuesday. If you've exhausted these options without success, remember you can buy a Firenze Card or take a private tour to see the sights.

Uffizi Combo-Ticket

Valid for three consecutive days, this combo-ticket offers a cost-saving, one-time priority (skip-the-line) admission to the Uffizi Gallery, Pitti Palace, and Boboli Gardens (€38 March-Oct, €18 Nov-Feb, not valid first Sun of the month when admission is free; www.uffizi.it).

Duomo Combo-Ticket

While the Duomo itself is free to enter, several related sights are all covered by a single €18 **combo-ticket** (valid for 48 hours): the Baptistery, dome climb (reservations required), Campanile, Duomo Museum, and Santa Reparata crypt. If you have a Firenze Card, you won't need the Duomo combo-ticket (both cover the same sights), unless you want to reserve your dome climb in advance (see page 180).

Tours

🎧 To sightsee on your own, download free audio tours via my free **Rick Steves Audio Europe** app (see page 28 for details).

Tour companies offer city tours as well as excursions in Tuscany (such as Siena, San Gimignano, Pisa, and the Chianti region for wine-tasting). Several offer Accademia and Uffizi tours, gaining you easy access to these popular sights. (And they often run cooking classes, too.)

Florencetown runs tours on foot or by bike. Their "Walk and Talk Florence" introductory tour includes the Oltrarno neighborhood (€25, 2.5 hours). My readers get a 10 percent discount, with an extra 10 percent off for second tours (if booking online, enter code "RICKSTEVES"; Via de Lamberti 1, facing Orsanmichele Church, tel. 055-281-103, www.florencetown.com).

Artviva offers a variety of tours (18 people maximum), including these popular overviews: "Original Florence" town walk (€29, 3 hours) and "Florence in One Glorious Day" (€104, 6 hours, adds Uffizi and Accademia tours). They offer a 10 percent discount at www.artviva.com/ricksteves (username "ricksteves," password "reader"; Via de' Sassetti 1, second floor, near Piazza della Repubblica, tel. 055-264-5033, www.artviva.com).

Good **private guides** for walking tours and countryside excursions include **Alessandra Marchetti,** a Florentine who has lived in the US (€60-75/hour, mobile 347-386-9839, www.tuscanydriverguide.com, alessandramarchettitours@gmail.com), and **Paola Migliorini** and her partners, who also offer cooking classes (€60/hour without car, €70/hour in a van for up to 8 people, mobile 347-657-2611, www.florencetour.com, info@florencetour.com).

Helpful Hints

Theft and Safety: Beware of the "slow count": Cashiers may count change back with odd pauses in hopes you'll gather up the money early and say *"Grazie."* Keep an eye out for slick pickpockets, especially near the train station, the station's underpass (particularly where the tunnel surfaces), and at major sights. Some thieves even dress like tourists to fool you. Any crowded bus likely holds at least one thief.

Medical Help: To reach a doctor who speaks English, call **Medical Service Firenze** at 055-475-411 (answered 24 hours a day); they can send a doctor to your hotel within an hour of your call, or you can go to their clinic when the doctor's in (Mon-Sat 11:00-12:00 & 13:00-15:00 plus Mon-Fri 17:00-18:00, closed Sun, no appointment necessary, Via Roma 4, between the Duomo and Piazza della Repubblica, www.medicalservice.firenze.it).

Visiting Churches: Modest dress is required at the Duomo, Santa Maria Novella, Santa Croce, Santa Maria del Carmine/Brancacci Chapel, and the Medici Chapels. Be respectful of worshippers and the paintings; don't use a flash. Churches usually close from 12:00 or 12:30 until 15:00 or 16:00.

Addresses: Florence has a ridiculously confusing system for street addresses. They use "red" numbers for businesses and "black" numbers for residences; in print, addresses are indicated with "r" (as in Via Cavour 2r) or "n" (for black—*nero,* as in Via Cavour 25n). Red and black numbers are interspersed on the same street; each set goes in roughly consecutive order, but their numbers bear no connection with each other.

Free Water: Carry a water bottle to refill at Florence's twist-the-handle public fountains (near the Duomo dome entrance, around the corner from the "Piglet" statue at Mercato Nuovo, or in front of Pitti Palace). Try the *fontanello* (dispenser of free cold water, *gassata* or *naturale*) on Piazza della Signoria, behind the statue of Neptune (on the left side of the Palazzo Vecchio).

Wi-Fi: The city's free Wi-Fi hotspot network ("Firenze WiFi," click on "Accedi") covers all of the main squares (no registration, good for two hours).

Useful App: For free audio versions of my Renaissance Walk and tours of the Uffizi, Bargello, Museum of San Marco, and Accademia Gallery, get the **Rick Steves Audio Europe** app (see page 28).

WCs: Public restrooms are scarce. Use them when you can, in any café or museum. Pay WCs are typically €1. Handy locations include one at the Baptistery ticket office (near the Duomo); just down the street from Piazza Santa Croce (at Borgo Santa Croce 29 red); up near Piazzale Michelangelo; and inside the train station (near track 5).

Laundry: The **Wash & Dry Lavarapido** chain offers long hours and efficient, self-service launderettes at several locations (generally daily 7:30-23:00). Locations are: near **David** (Via dei Servi 105 red); between the train station and river (Via del Sole 29 red and Via della Scala 52 red); near the Palazzo Vecchio (Via Ghibellina 143 red); and in the Oltrarno neighborhood (Via dei Serragli 87 red).

Getting Lost: The Duomo, the cathedral with the distinctive red dome, is the center of Florence. If you ever get lost, home's the dome.

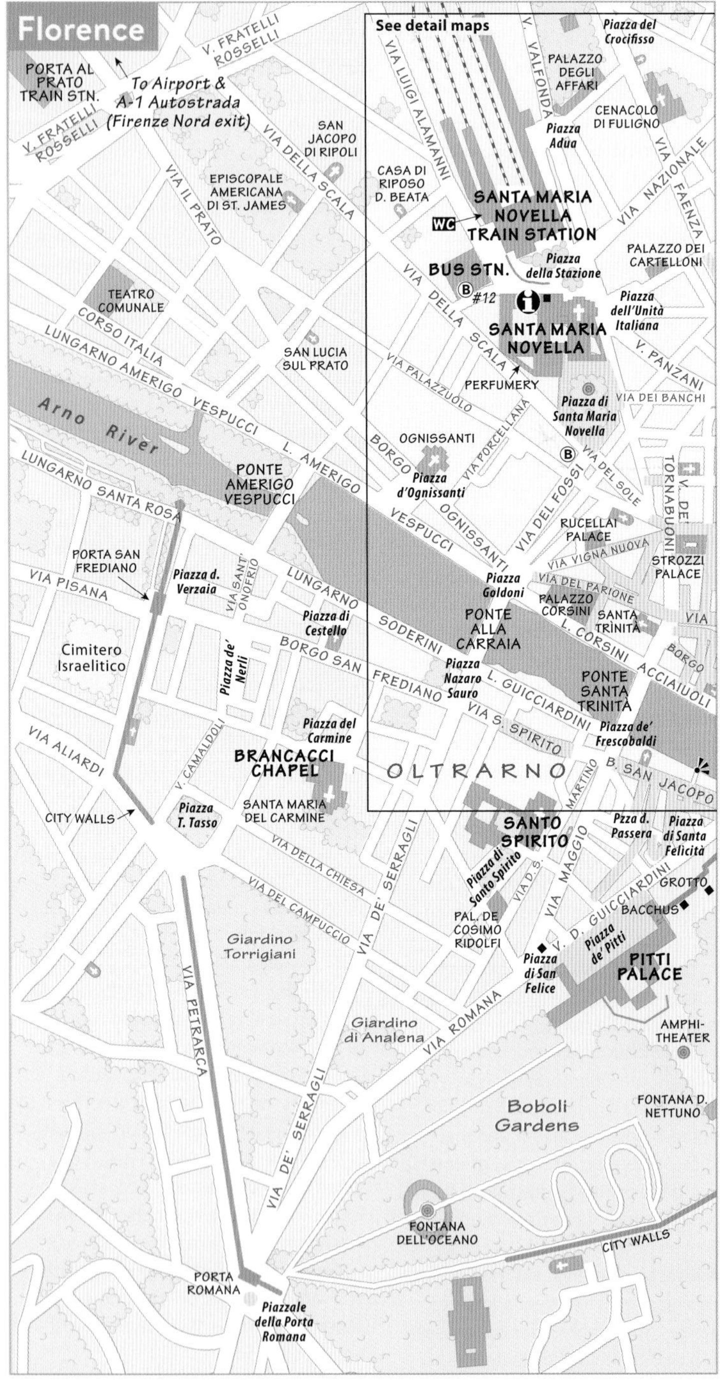
Florence
See detail maps
PORTA AL PRATO TRAIN STN.
To Airport & A-1 Autostrada (Firenze Nord exit)
V. FRATELLI ROSSELLI
SAN JACOPO DI RIPOLI
EPISCOPALE AMERICANA DI ST. JAMES
VIA DELLA SCALA
VIA IL PRATO
CASA DI RIPOSO D. BEATA
VIA LUIGI ALAMANNI
V. VALFONDA
PALAZZO DEGLI AFFARI
Piazza del Crocifisso
CENACOLO DI FULIGNO
Piazza Adua
SANTA MARIA NOVELLA TRAIN STATION
WC
VIA NAZIONALE
VIA FAENZA
BUS STN.
Piazza della Stazione
PALAZZO DEI CARTELLONI
#12
SANTA MARIA NOVELLA
Piazza dell'Unità Italiana
V. PANZANI
TEATRO COMUNALE
CORSO ITALIA
LUNGARNO AMERIGO VESPUCCI
SAN LUCIA SUL PRATO
VIA PALAZZUOLO
PERFUMERY
Piazza di Santa Maria Novella
VIA DEI BANCHI
Arno River
OGNISSANTI
VIA PORCELLANA
Piazza d'Ognissanti
BORGO OGNISSANTI
VIA DEL SOLE
V. DE' TORNABUONI
PONTE AMERIGO VESPUCCI
L. AMERIGO VESPUCCI
LUNGARNO SANTA ROSA
VIA DEL FOSSI
RUCELLAI PALACE
VIA VIGNA NUOVA
STROZZI PALACE
PORTA SAN FREDIANO
Piazza d. Verzaia
VIA SANT' ONOFRIO
LUNGARNO SODERINI
Piazza Goldoni
VIA DEL PARIONE
PALAZZO CORSINI
SANTA TRINITÀ
VIA PISANA
Piazza di Cestello
PONTE ALLA CARRAIA
L. CORSINI
BORGO SS. APOSTOLI
Cimitero Israelitico
BORGO SAN FREDIANO
Piazza de' Nerli
Piazza Nazaro Sauro
L. GUICCIARDINI
PONTE SANTA TRINITÀ
ACCIAIUOLI
VIA ALIARDI
V. CAMALDOLI
Piazza del Carmine
VIA S. SPIRITO
Piazza de' Frescobaldi
BRANCACCI CHAPEL
OLTRARNO
B. SAN JACOPO
V. S. MARTINO
CITY WALLS
Piazza T. Tasso
SANTA MARIA DEL CARMINE
SANTO SPIRITO
Pzza d. Passera
Piazza di Santa Felicità
VIA DELLA CHIESA
VIA DE' SERRAGLI
Piazza di Santo Spirito
VIA D. S.
VIA MAGGIO
V. D. GUICCIARDINI
GROTTO
VIA DEL CAMPUCCIO
BACCHUS
PAL. DE COSIMO RIDOLFI
Piazza de' Pitti
Giardino Torrigiani
Piazza di San Felice
PITTI PALACE
VIA PETRARCA
VIA ROMANA
Giardino di Analena
AMPHI-THEATER
Boboli Gardens
FONTANA D. NETTUNO
FONTANA DELL'OCEANO
CITY WALLS
PORTA ROMANA
Piazzale della Porta Romana

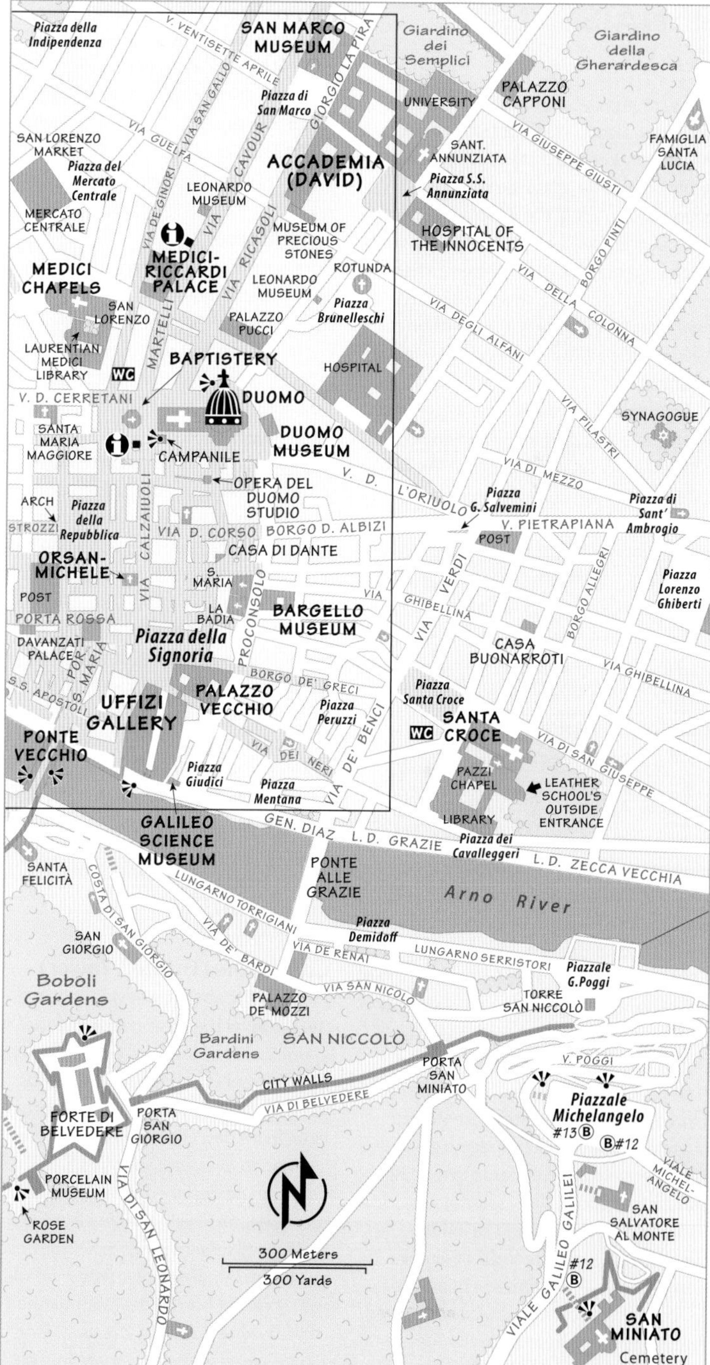

Piazza della Indipendenza
SAN MARCO MUSEUM
V. VENTISETTE APRILE
VIA SAN GALLO
GIORGIO LA PIRA
Piazza di San Marco
Giardino dei Semplici
Giardino della Gherardesca
UNIVERSITY
PALAZZO CAPPONI
VIA GUELFA
VIA CAVOUR
SAN LORENZO MARKET
Piazza del Mercato Centrale
MERCATO CENTRALE
ACCADEMIA (DAVID)
SANT. ANNUNZIATA
Piazza S.S. Annunziata
VIA GIUSEPPE GIUSTI
FAMIGLIA SANTA LUCIA
VIA DE' GINORI
LEONARDO MUSEUM
VIA RICASOLI
MUSEUM OF PRECIOUS STONES
HOSPITAL OF THE INNOCENTS
BORGO PINTI
MEDICI CHAPELS
MEDICI-RICCARDI PALACE
ROTUNDA
LEONARDO MUSEUM
Piazza Brunelleschi
VIA DELLA COLONNA
VIA DEGLI ALFANI
SAN LORENZO
MARTELLI
PALAZZO PUCCI
LAURENTIAN MEDICI LIBRARY
WC
BAPTISTERY
HOSPITAL
V. D. CERRETANI
DUOMO
VIA PILASTRI
SYNAGOGUE
SANTA MARIA MAGGIORE
CAMPANILE
DUOMO MUSEUM
VIA DI MEZZO
V. D. L'ORIUOLO
OPERA DEL DUOMO STUDIO
Piazza G. Salvemini
Piazza di Sant' Ambrogio
ARCH
Piazza della Repubblica
STROZZI
VIA CALZAIUOLI
VIA D. CORSO
BORGO D. ALBIZI
V. PIETRAPIANA
POST
CASA DI DANTE
ORSAN-MICHELE
S. MARIA
VIA VERDI
BORGO ALLEGRI
Piazza Lorenzo Ghiberti
POST
PORTA ROSSA
LA BADIA
PROCONSOLO
BARGELLO MUSEUM
VIA GHIBELLINA
DAVANZATI PALACE
Piazza della Signoria
POR S. MARIA
CASA BUONARROTI
VIA GHIBELLINA
S.S. APOSTOLI
BORGO DE' GRECI
PALAZZO VECCHIO
UFFIZI GALLERY
Piazza Santa Croce
Piazza Peruzzi
SANTA CROCE
WC
PONTE VECCHIO
VIA DEI NERI
VIA DE' BENCI
VIA DI SAN GIUSEPPE
Piazza Giudici
PAZZI CHAPEL
LEATHER SCHOOL'S OUTSIDE ENTRANCE
Piazza Mentana
LIBRARY
GALILEO SCIENCE MUSEUM
GEN. DIAZ
L. D. GRAZIE
Piazza dei Cavalleggeri
L. D. ZECCA VECCHIA
SANTA FELICITÀ
PONTE ALLE GRAZIE
COSTA DI SAN GIORGIO
LUNGARNO TORRIGIANI
Arno River
VIA DE' BARDI
Piazza Demidoff
SAN GIORGIO
VIA DE RENAI
LUNGARNO SERRISTORI
Piazzale G.Poggi
Boboli Gardens
PALAZZO DE' MOZZI
VIA SAN NICOLÒ
TORRE SAN NICCOLÒ
Bardini Gardens
SAN NICCOLÒ
V. POGGI
CITY WALLS
PORTA SAN MINIATO
Piazzale Michelangelo
VIA DI BELVEDERE
FORTE DI BELVEDERE
PORTA SAN GIORGIO
#13 B
B #12
VIALE MICHELANGELO
PORCELAIN MUSEUM
VIA DI SAN LEONARDO
SAN SALVATORE AL MONTE
ROSE GARDEN
300 Meters
300 Yards
VIALE GALILEO GALILEI
#12 B
SAN MINIATO
Cemetery

RENAISSANCE WALK

This walk gives you an overview of Florence's top sights. We'll start with the soaring church dome that stands as the proud symbol of the Renaissance spirit. Just opposite, you'll find the Baptistery doors that opened the Renaissance. Finally, we'll reach Florence's political center, dotted with monuments of that proud time. For more details on many of the sights on this walk, see the individual listings later in this chapter.

Length of This Walk: The walk is less than a mile long, but allow two hours if you add visits to the interiors of the Baptistery and Orsanmichele Church.

Tours: 🎧 Download my free Renaissance Walk audio tour.

Self-Guided Walk

• *Stand in front of the Duomo as you get your historical bearings.*

Florentine Renaissance

During the Dark Ages, it was obvious to the people of Italy—sitting on the rubble of the Roman Empire—that there had to be a brighter age on the horizon. The long-awaited rebirth, or Renaissance, began in Florence for good reasons: It was wealthy because of its cloth industry, trade, and banking, all powered by the Medici, the rich banking family who ruled Renaissance Florence. Locals were powered by a fierce city-state pride—they'd pee into the Arno with gusto, knowing rival city-state Pisa was downstream. And Florence was fertile with more than its share of artistic genius; imagine guys like Michelangelo and Leonardo attending the same high school.

The cultural explosion called the Renaissance—the "rebirth" of Greek and Roman culture that swept across Europe—started around 1400 and lasted about 150 years. In politics, the Renaissance meant democracy; in science, a renewed interest in exploring nature. Renaissance art was a return to the realism and balance of Greek and Roman sculpture. In architecture, domes and round arches replaced Gothic spires and pointed arches. The Duomo kicked off the architectural Renaissance in Florence.

The Duomo

Florence's massive cathedral is Florence's geographical and spiritual heart. Its dome, visible from all over the city, inspired Florentines to do great things. (Most recently, it inspired the city to make the area around the cathedral delightfully traffic-free.)

The church was begun in the 1296, in the Gothic style. After generations of work, it was still unfinished, lacking a roof. Its facade was little more than bare brick, and it stood that way until it was completed in 1870 in the "Neo"-Gothic style. Its "retro" look captures the feel of the original medieval facade, with green, white, and pink marble sheets that cover the brick construction. This over-the-top facade is adored by many, while others call it "the cathedral in pajamas."

We won't go inside the church on this tour. It has a cavernous, bare interior with a few noteworthy sights. Entry is free, but there's often a long wait (lines decrease late in the day).

Campanile (Giotto's Tower)

The 270-foot bell tower was begun in the 1300s by the great painter Giotto. As a forerunner of the Renaissance genius, Giotto excelled in many artistic fields, just as Michelangelo would do two centuries later. In his day, Giotto was called the ugliest man to ever walk the streets of Florence, but he designed what many call the most beautiful bell tower in all of Europe.

The bell tower served as a sculpture gallery for Renaissance artists. Find the four statues of prophets (about a third of the way up) done by the great Early Renaissance sculptor, Donatello. The most striking of them is bald-headed Habbakuk. Closer to ground level are several hexagonal panels that ring the Campanile. These reliefs depict Bible scenes. The realism of these groundbreaking works paved the way for Michelangelo and the High Renaissance generations later. (By the way, these are copies—the originals are at the excellent **Duomo Museum,** just behind the church.)

You can climb the Campanile for great views. It doesn't require a reservation, just a Duomo combo-ticket.

• *Now take in the Duomo's star attraction: the dome. The best viewing spot is just to the right of the facade, from the corner of the pedestrian-only Via de' Calzaiuoli.*

View of the Dome, by Brunelleschi

The dome rises 330 feet from ground level. It's made of red brick, held together

The Renaissance and Brunelleschi's dome live on in Florence.

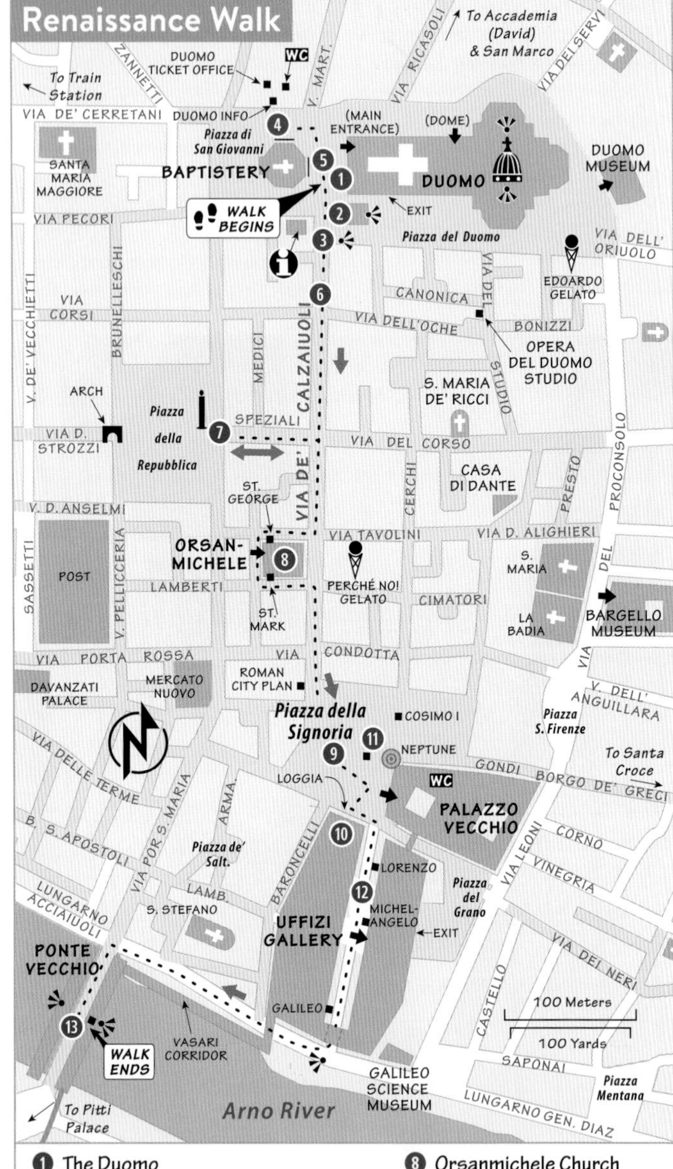

1. The Duomo
2. Campanile
3. View of the Dome
4. Baptistery – North Doors
5. Baptistery – East Doors (Gates of Paradise)
6. Via de' Calzaiuoli
7. Piazza della Repubblica
8. Orsanmichele Church
9. Piazza della Signoria
10. Loggia dei Lanzi
11. Savonarola Plaque
12. Uffizi Courtyard Statues
13. Ponte Vecchio

The Campanile

Ghiberti's bronze doors

with eight white ribs, and capped with a lantern.

Remember, although construction of the church had been begun in 1296, by the 1400s there still was no suitable roof. They'd intended to top it with a dome, but the technology to span the 140-foot-wide hole had yet to be invented. **Non c'è problema.** The brash Florentines knew that someday someone would come along who could handle the challenge. That man was Filippo Brunelleschi and he had a plan.

Brunelleschi built a dome within a dome. What you see is the outer shell, covered in terra-cotta tile. The inner dome is thicker and provides much of the structural support. The grand white skeletal ribs connect at the top, supporting each other in a way similar to a pointed arch. Hidden between them are interlocking bricks, laid in a herringbone pattern. Rather than being stacked horizontally, like traditional brickwork, the alternating vertical bricks act as "bookends." The dome grew upward like an igloo, supporting itself as it proceeded from the base. When the ribs reached the top, Brunelleschi arched them in and fixed them in place with the lantern at the top. His dome, built in only 14 years, was the largest since ancient Rome's Pantheon.

When completed in 1436, Brunelleschi's dome was the wonder of the age. It became the model for many domes to follow, from St. Peter's to the US Capitol.

You can climb the dome for Florence's best views, but it requires a reservation, usually in advance (for details, see page 180).

• *Next up, the Baptistery. Step into the zone between the Duomo and the Baptistery that local tour guides call the "Piazza of Paradise."*

Baptistery and Ghiberti's Bronze Doors

The Baptistery's bronze doors bring us out of the Middle Ages and into the Renaissance. (These are copies; the originals are in the Duomo Museum.) Lorenzo Ghiberti beat out heavyweights such as Brunelleschi to design the **north doors,** which show scenes from the New Testament. (The original entries of Brunelleschi and Ghiberti are in the Bargello.) About the time Ghiberti completed the first set of doors, the Baptistery needed another set of doors for the entrance that faces the church. Ghiberti's Old Testament bronze panels for the **east doors** added a new dimension to art: depth. Here we see how the Renaissance masters merged art and science. Realism was in, and Renaissance artists used math, illusion, and dissection to create it. Ghiberti spent 27 years (1425-1452) working on these panels. That's him in the center of the doorframe, atop the second row of panels—the head on the left with the shiny male-pattern baldness.

The Baptistery **interior** features a fine example of pre-Renaissance mosaic art (1200s-1300s) in the Byzantine style (more on page 181).

• *Head south toward the river, taking the main pedestrian drag...*

Via de' Calzaiuoli

This street, Via de' Calzaiuoli (kahlts-ay-WOH-lee), has always been the main axis of the city; it was part of the ancient Roman grid plan that became Florence. Around the year 1400, as the Renaissance was blooming, this street connected the religious center (where we are now) with the political center (where we're heading), a five-minute walk away. In recent years this historic core has been transformed into a pleasant place to stroll, window-shop, lick your gelato cone, and wonder why American cities can't be more pedestrian-friendly.

Two blocks down from the Baptistery, look right on Via degli Speziali to see a triumphal arch that marks **Piazza della Repubblica.** The arch celebrates the unification of Italy in 1870 and stands as a reminder that, in ancient Roman times, this piazza was the city center. (Today the square hosts a carousel and the Rinascente department store, with a bar that has a rooftop terrace.)

• *A block farther, at the intersection with Via Orsanmichele, is the...*

Orsanmichele Church

Originally, this was an open loggia (covered porch) with a huge grain warehouse upstairs. The arches of the loggia were artfully filled in (14th century), and the building gained a new purpose—as a church. The 14 niches in the exterior walls feature replicas of the remarkable-in-their-day statues paid for by the city's rising middle class of merchants and their 21 guilds. The interior has a glorious Gothic tabernacle (1359) and a painted wooden panel that depicts *Madonna delle Grazie* (1346).

Head up Via Orsanmichele (to the right of the church) and circle the church exterior counterclockwise to enjoy the statues (these are all copies; the originals are in the museum on the church's top floor—open Mon only, and the most famous of the statues—St. George—is in the Bargello).

In the third niche is **Nanni di Banco's Quattro Santi Coronati** (c. 1415-1417). These four early Christians were sculp-

Donatello, St. George

Donatello, St. Mark

tors martyred by Roman emperor Diocletian because they refused to sculpt pagan gods. They seem to be contemplating the consequences of the fatal decision they're about to make. While Banco's saints are deep in the church's niche, the next statue, just to the right, feels ready to step out.

Donatello's St. George is alert, perched on the edge of his niche, scanning the horizon for dragons. He's anxious, but he's also self-assured. Comparing this Renaissance-style *St. George* to *Quattro Santi Coronati,* you can psychoanalyze the heady changes underway. This is humanism.

Continue counterclockwise around the church (bypassing the entrance), all the way to the opposite side. The first niche you come to features **Donatello's St. Mark** (1411-1413). The evangelist cradles his gospel in his strong, veined hand and gazes out, resting his weight on the right leg while bending the left. Though subtle, St. Mark's twisting *contrapposto* pose was the first seen since antiquity. Eighty years after young Donatello carved this statue, a teenage Michelangelo Buonarroti stood here and marveled at it.

The church hosts evening **concerts;** same-day tickets are sold from the door facing Via de' Calzaiuoli; you can also book tickets here for the Uffizi and Accademia (ticket window open daily 9:00-16:00, closed Sun off-season).

• *Continue down Via de' Calzaiuoli 50 more yards, to the huge and historic square.*

Piazza della Signoria

What a view! This piazza—the main civic center of Florence—is dominated by the massive stone facade of the Palazzo Vecchio, with a tower that reaches for the sky. The square is dotted with statues. The stately Uffizi Gallery is nearby, and the marble greatness of old Florence litters the cobbles. Piazza della Signoria still vibrates with the echoes of the city's past—executions, riots, and celebrations. There's even Roman history: Look for the **chart** showing the ancient city (on a freestanding display to your right as you enter the square, in front of Chanel). Today, it's a tourist's world with pigeons, selfie sticks, horse buggies, and tired tourists. For a sugar jolt, stop in at the **Rivoire** café to enjoy its fine desserts, pudding-thick hot chocolate, and the best view seats in town.

Piazza della Signoria

Before you towers the **Palazzo Vecchio,** the palatial Town Hall of the Medici—a fortress designed to contain riches and survive the many riots that went with local politics. The windows are just beyond the reach of angry stones, and the tower was a handy lookout post. Justice was doled out sternly on this square. Until 1873, Michelangelo's *David* stood where you see the replica today. The original was damaged in a 1527 riot (when a bench thrown from a palace window knocked its left arm off), but it remained here for several centuries, vulnerable to erosion and pollution, before being moved indoors for protection.

Step past the fake *David* through the front door into the Palazzo Vecchio's courtyard (free). This palace was Florence's symbol of civic power. You're surrounded by art for art's sake—a cherub frivolously marks the courtyard's center, and ornate stuccoes and frescoes decorate the walls and columns. Such luxury represented a big change 500 years ago. (For more on the palazzo and climbing its tower, see page 189.)

• *Back outside, check out the statue-filled...*

Loggia dei Lanzi

The loggia, a.k.a. **Loggia della Signoria,** was once a forum for public debate, perfect for a city that prided itself on its democratic traditions. But later, when the Medici figured that good art was more desirable than free speech, it was turned into an outdoor sculpture gallery. Notice the squirming Florentine themes—conquest, domination, rape, and decapitation. The statues lining the back are Roman originals brought back to Florence by a Medici when his villa in Rome was sold. Two statues in the front deserve a closer look: Giambologna's ***The Rape of the Sabine Women*** (c. 1583)—with its pulse-quickening rhythm of muscles—is from the restless Mannerist period, which followed the stately and confident Renaissance; Benvenuto Cellini's ***Perseus*** (1545-1553), the loggia's most noteworthy piece, shows the Greek hero who decapitated the snake-headed Medusa.

• *Cross the square to the big* **fountain of Neptune** *by Bartolomeo Ammanati that Florentines (including Michelangelo) consider a huge waste of marble. The guy on the horse, to the left, is Cosimo I, one of the post-Renaissance Medici. Find the round marble plaque on the ground 10 steps in front of the fountain.*

Savonarola Plaque

The Medici family was briefly thrown from power by an austere monk named Savonarola, who made Florence a constitutional republic. He organized huge rallies lit by bonfires here on the square where he preached. While children sang hymns, the devout brought their rich "vanities" (such as paintings, musical instruments, and playing cards) and threw them into the flames. Encouraged by the pope, the Florentines fought back and arrested Savonarola. For two days, they tortured him, trying unsuccessfully to persuade him to see their side of things. Finally, on the very spot where Savonarola's followers had built bonfires of vanities, the monk was burned. The bronze plaque, engraved in Italian (*"Qui dove..."*), reads, "Here, Girolamo Savonarola and his Dominican brothers were hanged and burned" in the year "MCCCCXCVIII" (1498). Soon after, the Medici returned to power. The Renaissance picked up where it left off.

• *Stay cool, we have 200 yards to go. Follow the gaze of the fake David into the courtyard of the two-tone horseshoe-shaped building.*

Uffizi Courtyard Statues

The top floor of this building, known as the *uffizi* (offices) during Medici days, is filled with the greatest collection of Florentine painting anywhere. It's one of Europe's top art galleries (described on page 186). The courtyard, filled with souvenir stalls and hustling young artists, is watched over by 19th-century statues of the great figures of the Renaissance:

artists (Michelangelo, Giotto, Donatello, and Leonardo), philosophers (Niccolò Machiavelli), scientists (Galileo), writers (Dante), poets (Petrarch), cartographers (Amerigo Vespucci), and the great patron of so much Renaissance thinking, Lorenzo "the Magnificent" de' Medici. His support of Leonardo, Botticelli, and teenage Michelangelo helped Florence become Europe's most enlightened city.

After hours, talented street musicians take advantage of the space's superior acoustics.

• *Exiting at the far end of the courtyard, pause at the Arno River, overlooking...*

Ponte Vecchio

Ponte Vecchio (Old Bridge), rated ▲, has spanned this narrowest part of the Arno since Roman times. While Rome "fell," Florence never really did, remaining a bustling trade center along the river.

• *Hike to the center of the bridge.*

A famous goldsmith is honored with a fine bust at the central point of the bridge—the sculptor Cellini. This statue is a reminder that, in the 1500s, the Medici booted out the bridge's butchers and tanners and installed the gold- and silversmiths who still tempt visitors to this day.

During World War II, the local German commander was instructed to blow up all of Florence's bridges to cover the Nazi retreat. But even some Nazis appreciate history: He blew up the other bridges, and left the Ponte Vecchio impassable but intact. Look up to notice the protected and elevated passageway (called the Vasari Corridor) that led the Medici from the Palazzo Vecchio through the Uffizi, across Ponte Vecchio, and up to Pitti Palace, four blocks beyond the bridge.

• *Now that you've had a full meal of high culture, finish it off with a dessert of the world's finest gelato. Enjoy.*

Ponte Vecchio

SIGHTS

When you see a 🎧 in a listing, it means the sight is covered in an audio tour via my free **Rick Steves Audio Europe** app (see page 28).

The Duomo and Nearby Sights

A single **combo-ticket,** valid for 48 hours, covers all the paid Duomo sights: Baptistery, dome climb (which requires reservations), Campanile, Duomo Museum, and Santa Reparata crypt.

The main ticket office faces the Baptistery entrance (at #7 on the square) and has a staffed counter (credit cards or cash) as well as ticket machines (credit cards only, requires PIN); there's another office at the Duomo Museum. You can also buy tickets at the Santa Reparata crypt or at the Campanile, but they don't make reservations—which are mandatory—for the dome climb.

If you buy the €18 combo-ticket online in advance (**www.museumflorence.com**), you can make a dome-climb reservation at that time. Or you can reserve the climb in person at two of the Duomo ticket offices.

The **Firenze Card** also covers all the Duomo sights. Before entering any of the Duomo sights, you must present your Firenze Card at the ticket office opposite the Baptistery (look for a priority queue) to obtain a free combo-ticket and—with luck—reserve a time for the dome climb.

▲▲DUOMO

Florence's Gothic cathedral has the third-longest nave in Christendom. The church's noisy Neo-Gothic facade (from 1870) is covered with pink, green, and white Tuscan marble. The cathedral's claim to artistic fame is Brunelleschi's magnificent dome—the first Renaissance dome and the model for domes to follow. While viewing it from the outside is well worth ▲▲ (and it's described earlier on my Renaissance walk), the massive but empty-feeling interior is lucky to rate ▲—it doesn't justify the massive crowds that line up to get inside. Much of the church's great art is stored in the Duomo Museum behind the church.

Cost and Hours: Free; Mon-Fri 10:00-17:00 (Thu until 16:30); Sat 10:00-16:45, Sun 13:30-16:45; opening times sometimes change due to religious functions, modest dress code enforced, tel. 055-230-2885, www.operaduomo.firenze.it.

Tours: Themed tours (€30, which includes a combo-ticket you'll keep) cover the Duomo (daily at 10:30), Baptistery mosaics (Mon, Wed, and Fri at 16:30), and the still-active workshop where Michelangelo carved *David* (Mon, Wed, and Fri at 12:00). To reserve, call 055-282-226, email info@operaduomo.firenze.it, or go to the ticket office next to the Baptistery.

The Duomo is covered on my free Renaissance Walk audio tour.

Rick's Tip: *Dome climb time slots can fill up days in advance, so it's smart to reserve online well ahead. Otherwise, try to reserve a time at the main Duomo ticket office (facing Baptistery entrance) or in the Duomo Museum (also has ticket machines).*

▲CLIMBING THE DUOMO'S DOME

For a grand view into the cathedral from the base of the dome, a chance to see Brunelleschi's "dome-within-a-dome" construction, a glorious Florence view from the top, and the equivalent of 463 plunges on a StairMaster, climb the dome. The claustrophobic one-way route takes you up narrow, steep staircases and walkways to the top of the dome.

Rick's Tip: *If you're* **claustrophobic** *or* **acrophobic, skip climbing the dome.** *Once you start up the narrow staircase, there's no turning back until you reach the top. The slow climb to the top can feel like torture.*

As you're waiting in line, spend a few minutes studying the recently restored side entrance door, called the Porta della Mandorla ("Almond Door"): Just above the delicately carved door frame is a colorful Annunciation mosaic by Nanni di Banco, and above that, in a sculpted almond-shaped frame, the Madonna is borne heavenward by angels.

Cost: €18 combo-ticket covers all Duomo sights, covered by Firenze Card;

The Duomo with Brunelleschi's dome

with either, must reserve a dome-climb time when obtaining your ticket—to ensure a climb it's best to buy a combo-ticket and reserve a time well ahead at www.museumflorence.com.

Hours: Mon-Fri 8:30-20:00, Sat 8:30-17:40, Sun 13:00-16:00, enter from outside church on north side. The dome is closed during rain.

▲CAMPANILE

The 270-foot bell tower has 50-some fewer steps than the Duomo's dome (but that's still 414 steps—no elevator); offers a faster, relatively less-crowded climb (with typically shorter lines); and has a view of that magnificent dome to boot. On the way up, there are several intermediate levels where you can catch your breath and enjoy ever-higher views. The stairs narrow as you go up, creating a mosh-pit bottleneck near the top—but the views are worth the hassle. While the various viewpoints are enclosed by cage-like bars, the gaps are big enough to let you snap great photos. Still, acrophobes and claustrophobes should beware!

Cost and Hours: €18 combo-ticket covers all Duomo sights, covered by Firenze Card, daily 8:30-20:00, last entry 40 minutes before closing.

▲BAPTISTERY

This is the octagonal building next to the Duomo. Check out the gleaming copies of Lorenzo Ghiberti's bronze doors facing the Duomo's facade (the originals are in the Duomo Museum); Michelangelo said these doors were fit to be the gates of paradise. Making a breakthrough in perspective, Ghiberti used mathematical laws to create the illusion of receding distance on a basically flat surface. The doors on the north side of the building were designed by Ghiberti when he was young; he'd won the honor and opportunity by beating Brunelleschi in a competition (the rivals' original entries are in the Bargello).

Last Judgment *mosaic in the Baptistery*

Cost and Hours: €18 combo-ticket covers all Duomo sights, covered by Firenze Card, interior open Mon-Sat 8:15-20:00, Sun 8:30-14:00. The (facsimile) bronze doors are on the exterior, so they are always viewable and free.

Visiting the Baptistery: Workers from St. Mark's in Venice came here to make the remarkable ceiling mosaics (of Venetian glass) in the late 1200s. Sit and savor the ceiling, where it's always Judgment Day, giving us a glimpse of the medieval worldview. Life was a preparation for the afterlife, when you would be judged and saved, or judged and damned—with no in-between. Christ, peaceful and reassuring, blessed those at his right hand with heaven (thumbs-up) and sent those on his left to hell (the ultimate thumbs-down) to be tortured by demons.

The rest of the ceiling mosaics tell the history of the world, from Adam and Eve (over the north/entrance doors, top row) to Noah and the Flood (over south doors, top row), to the life of Christ (second row, all around), to the life, ministry, and eventual beheading of John the Baptist (bottom row, all around)—all bathed in the golden glow of pre-Renaissance heaven.

▲▲▲DUOMO MUSEUM

Brunelleschi's dome, Ghiberti's bronze doors, and Donatello's statues define the 1400s (the Quattrocento) in Florence, when the city blossomed and classical arts were reborn. While copies now decorate the exteriors of the cathedral, Baptistery, and Campanile, the originals are restored and displayed safely indoors, filling the Duomo Museum with some of

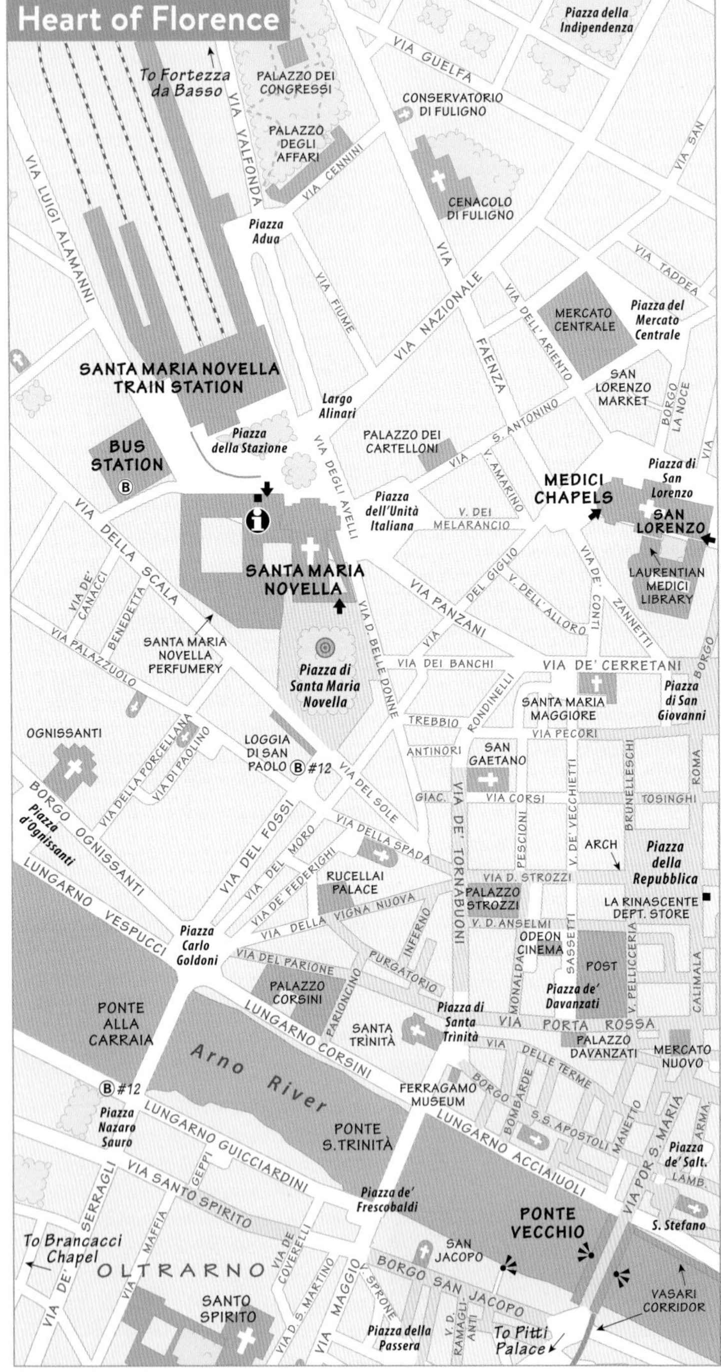
Heart of Florence
To Fortezza da Basso
PALAZZO DEI CONGRESSI
PALAZZO DEGLI AFFARI
CONSERVATORIO DI FULIGNO
CENACOLO DI FULIGNO
Piazza della Indipendenza
Piazza Adua
SANTA MARIA NOVELLA TRAIN STATION
BUS STATION
Largo Alinari
Piazza della Stazione
MERCATO CENTRALE
Piazza del Mercato Centrale
SAN LORENZO MARKET
PALAZZO DEI CARTELLONI
Piazza dell'Unità Italiana
MEDICI CHAPELS
Piazza di San Lorenzo
SAN LORENZO
LAURENTIAN MEDICI LIBRARY
SANTA MARIA NOVELLA
SANTA MARIA NOVELLA PERFUMERY
Piazza di Santa Maria Novella
SANTA MARIA MAGGIORE
Piazza di San Giovanni
OGNISSANTI
LOGGIA DI SAN PAOLO
#12
SAN GAETANO
Piazza d'Ognissanti
ARCH
Piazza della Repubblica
RUCELLAI PALACE
PALAZZO STROZZI
LA RINASCENTE DEPT. STORE
ODEON CINEMA
POST
Piazza Carlo Goldoni
PALAZZO CORSINI
Piazza de' Davanzati
PONTE ALLA CARRAIA
Piazza di Santa Trinità
SANTA TRÌNITÀ
PALAZZO DAVANZATI
MERCATO NUOVO
Arno River
FERRAGAMO MUSEUM
Piazza Nazaro Sauro
PONTE S.TRINITÀ
Piazza de' Salt.
Piazza de' Frescobaldi
PONTE VECCHIO
S. Stefano
To Brancacci Chapel
OLTRARNO
SAN JACOPO
VASARI CORRIDOR
SANTO SPIRITO
Piazza della Passera
To Pitti Palace
VIA GUELFA
VIA VALFONDA
VIA CENNINI
VIA LUIGI ALAMANNI
VIA FIUME
VIA NAZIONALE
VIA FAENZA
VIA DELL'ARIENTO
VIA TADDEA
VIA SAN
BORGO LA NOCE
VIA S. ANTONINO
V. AMARINO
VIA DEGLI AVELLI
V. DEI MELARANCIO
VIA DELLA SCALA
VIA DE' CANACCI
BENEDETTA
VIA PALAZZUOLO
VIA PANZANI
VIA DEL GIGLIO
V. DELL'ALLORO
VIA DE' CONTI
ZANNETTI
VIA D. BELLE DONNE
VIA DEI BANCHI
VIA DE' CERRETANI
BORGO
TREBBIO
RONDINELLI
VIA PECORI
ANTINORI
VIA DELLA PORCELLANA
VIA DI PAOLINO
VIA DEL SOLE
GIAC.
VIA CORSI
TOSINGHI
ROMA
BRUNELLESCHI
VIA DE' TORNABUONI
PESCIONI
V. DE' VECCHIETTI
BORGO OGNISSANTI
VIA DEL FOSSI
VIA DEL MORO
VIA DELLA SPADA
VIA DE' FEDERIGHI
VIA D. STROZZI
LUNGARNO VESPUCCI
VIA DELLA VIGNA NUOVA
V. D. ANSELMI
INFERNO
VIA DEL PARIONE
PURGATORIO
MONALDA
SASSETTI
V. PELLICCERIA
CALIMALA
PARIONCINO
LUNGARNO CORSINI
VIA PORTA ROSSA
VIA DELLE TERME
BORGO S.S. APOSTOLI
BOMBARDE
MANETTO
VIA POR S. MARIA
ARMA.
LAMB.
LUNGARNO GUICCIARDINI
LUNGARNO ACCIAIUOLI
VIA SANTO SPIRITO
GEPPI
VIA DE' SERRAGLI
VIA MAFFIA
VIA DE COVERELLI
VIA D. S. MARTINO
VIA MAGGIO
V. SPRONE
BORGO SAN JACOPO
V. D. RAMAGLIANTI

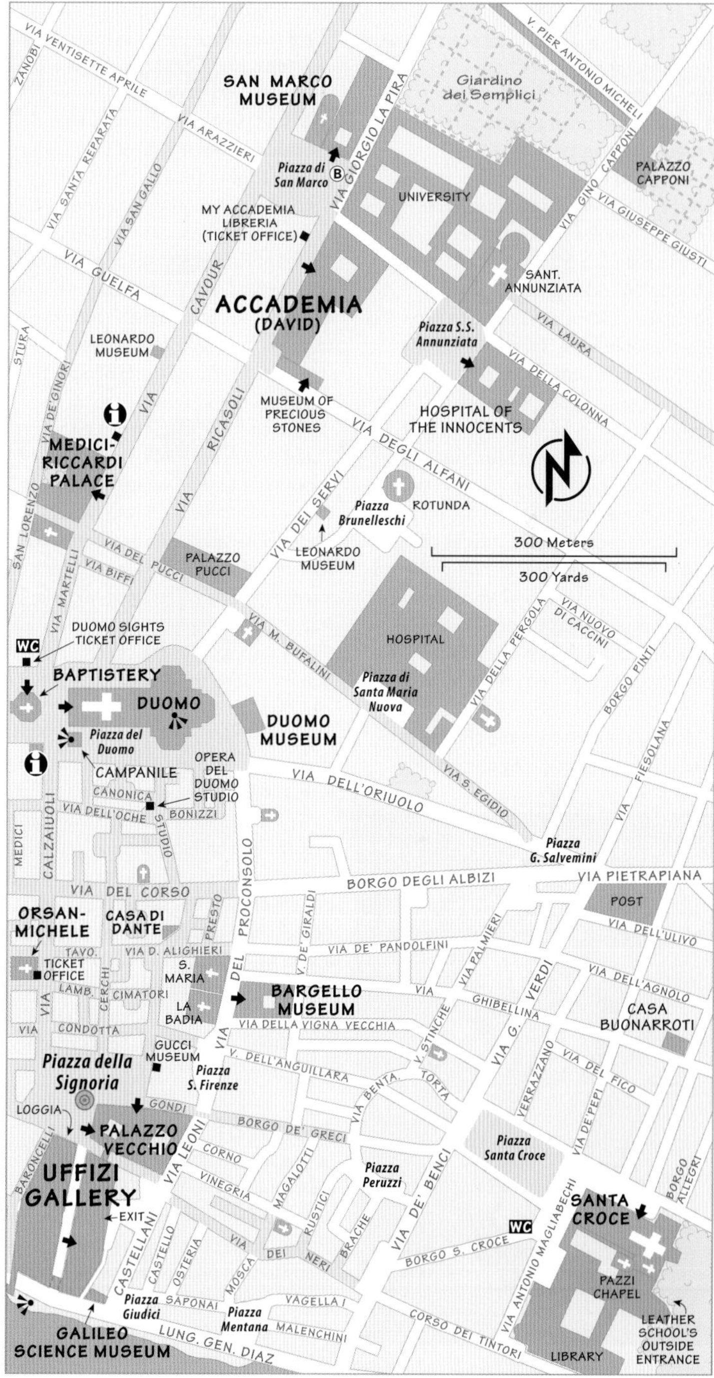
SAN MARCO MUSEUM
Giardino dei Semplici
PALAZZO CAPPONI
UNIVERSITY
Piazza di San Marco
MY ACCADEMIA LIBRERIA (TICKET OFFICE)
SANT. ANNUNZIATA
ACCADEMIA (DAVID)
Piazza S.S. Annunziata
LEONARDO MUSEUM
MUSEUM OF PRECIOUS STONES
HOSPITAL OF THE INNOCENTS
MEDICI-RICCARDI PALACE
ROTUNDA
Piazza Brunelleschi
LEONARDO MUSEUM
PALAZZO PUCCI
300 Meters
300 Yards
HOSPITAL
Piazza di Santa Maria Nuova
DUOMO SIGHTS TICKET OFFICE
BAPTISTERY
DUOMO
Piazza del Duomo
DUOMO MUSEUM
CAMPANILE
OPERA DEL DUOMO STUDIO
Piazza G. Salvemini
POST
ORSAN-MICHELE
CASA DI DANTE
TICKET OFFICE
S. MARIA
LA BADIA
BARGELLO MUSEUM
CASA BUONARROTI
GUCCI MUSEUM
Piazza della Signoria
Piazza S. Firenze
LOGGIA
PALAZZO VECCHIO
UFFIZI GALLERY
EXIT
Piazza Santa Croce
Piazza Peruzzi
SANTA CROCE
PAZZI CHAPEL
Piazza Giudici
Piazza Mentana
GALILEO SCIENCE MUSEUM
LIBRARY
LEATHER SCHOOL'S OUTSIDE ENTRANCE
WC
VIA VENTISETTE APRILE
ZANOBI
VIA ARAZZIERI
VIA GIORGIO LA PIRA
V. PIER ANTONIO MICHELI
VIA GINO CAPPONI
VIA GIUSEPPE GIUSTI
VIA SANTA REPARATA
VIA SAN GALLO
VIA GUELFA
CAVOUR
VIA LAURA
VIA DELLA COLONNA
STURA
VIA DE' GINORI
VIA RICASOLI
VIA DEGLI ALFANI
VIA DEI SERVI
SAN LORENZO
VIA DEL PUCCI
VIA BIFFI
VIA MARTELLI
VIA M. BUFALINI
VIA DELLA PERGOLA
VIA NUOVO DI CACCINI
BORGO PINTI
VIA FIESOLANA
VIA DELL'ORIUOLO
VIA S. EGIDIO
CANONICA
VIA DELL'OCHE
BONIZZI
STUDIO
MEDICI
CALZAIUOLI
VIA DEL PROCONSOLO
VIA DEL CORSO
BORGO DEGLI ALBIZI
VIA PIETRAPIANA
VIA DELL'ULIVO
PRESTO
V. DE' GIRALDI
VIA DE' PANDOLFINI
VIA PALMIERI
VIA G. VERDI
VIA DELL'AGNOLO
TAVO.
VIA D. ALIGHIERI
LAMB.
CERCHI
CIMATORI
VIA GHIBELLINA
VIA CONDOTTA
VIA DELLA VIGNA VECCHIA
V. STINCHE
V. DELL'ANGUILLARA
VIA BENTA.
TORTA
VERRAZZANO
VIA DEL FICO
VIA DE' PEPI
GONDI
BORGO DE' GRECI
VIA LEONI
CORNO
VINEGRIA
MAGALOTTI
RUSTICI
VIA DE' BENCI
BORGO ALLEGRI
BARONCELLI
CASTELLANI
CASTELLO
OSTERIA
VIA DEI NERI
MOSCA
BRACHE
BORGO S. CROCE
VIA ANTONIO MAGLIABECHI
SAPONAI
VAGELLAI
MALENCHINI
CORSO DEI TINTORI
LUNG. GEN. DIAZ

the best sculpture from the Renaissance. The museum also has two powerful statues by Florence's powerhouse sculptors—Donatello and Michelangelo. The museum has reopened after a remodel—expect changes.

Cost and Hours: €18 combo-ticket covers all Duomo sights, covered by Firenze Card. Daily 9:00-20:00, closed first Tue of each month, last entry one hour before closing, one of the few museums in Florence always open on Mon, free app available from iTunes and Google Play, Via del Proconsolo 9, tel. 055-282-226 or 055-230-7885, www.operaduomo.firenze.it.

Visiting the Duomo Museum: Start in Room 6, the big Sala del Paradiso (Hall of Paradise), which dominates the museum. This room recreates the facades of the Duomo and the Baptistery, which were a showcase of the greatest art of Florence from roughly 1300 to 1600. The original statues, doors, and reliefs face each other as they once did on the buildings for which they were designed.

Facing the facade of the church, as they did in the Middle Ages, are the famous **bronze doors** of the Baptistery. The Renaissance began in 1401 with a citywide competition to build new doors for the Baptistery. Lorenzo Ghiberti (c. 1378-1455) won the job and built the doors for the north side of the building. Everyone loved them, so he was then hired to make another set of doors for the east entrance, facing the Duomo. These "Gates of Paradise" revolutionized the way Renaissance people saw the world around them. Each panel is bronze with a layer of gold on top. They tell several stories in one frame using perspective and realism as never before.

Michelangelo, Pietà

Also on the ground floor are rooms dedicated to the museum's most famous and evocative statues. Donatello's ***Mary Magdalene*** *(Maddalena,* c. 1455), carved from white poplar and originally painted with realistic colors, is a Renaissance work of intense devotion. The aging Michelangelo (1475-1564) designed his own tomb, with a ***Pietà*** (1547-1555) as the centerpiece. Three mourners tend the broken body of the crucified Christ. We see Mary, his mother; Mary Magdalene (on the left); and Nicodemus, the converted Pharisee, whose face is that of Michelangelo himself.

Upstairs, the first floor displays original **statues and panels** from the bell tower's third story, where copies stand today, two marble **choir lofts** *(cantorie;* by Lucca della Robbia and Donatello) that once sat above the sacristy doors of the Duomo, an exquisite half-ton **silver altar** honoring John the Baptist that once stood in the Baptistery, and **Brunelleschi's model** of the dome.

North of the Duomo

▲▲▲ACCADEMIA

This museum houses Michelangelo's *David,* the consummate Renaissance statue of the buff, biblical shepherd boy ready to take on the giant. When you look into the eyes of this magnificent sculpture, you're looking into the eyes of Renaissance Man.

Rick's Tip: *On the first Sunday of the month, all state museums are free.* **Free admission makes the Accademia and Uffizi Gallery impossibly crowded.** *Avoid visiting these museums on that day.*

Cost and Hours: €12.50 (€8 if there's no special exhibit), additional €4 for reservation, free and crowded on first Sun of the month, covered by Firenze Card; Tue-Sun 8:15-18:50, possibly Tue until 22:00 June-Sept, closed Mon; audioguide-€6, Via Ricasoli 60, reservation tel. 055-294-883, www.galleriaaccademiafirenze.beniculturali.it. To bypass long lines in peak season, get the Firenze Card (see page 166) or make reservations (see page 167).

🎧 Download my free Accademia audio tour.

Visiting the Accademia: In 1501, Michelangelo Buonarroti, a 26-year-old Florentine, was commissioned to carve a large-scale work. The figure comes from a Bible story. The Israelites are surrounded by barbarian warriors, who are led by a brutish giant named Goliath. When the giant challenges the Israelites to send out someone to fight him, a young shepherd boy steps forward. Armed only with a sling, David defeats the giant. This 17-foot-tall symbol of divine victory over evil represents a new century and a whole new Renaissance outlook.

Originally, *David* was meant to stand on the roofline of the Duomo, but was placed more prominently at the entrance of the Palazzo Vecchio (where a copy stands today). In the 19th century, *David* was moved indoors for his own protection; he stands under a Renaissance-style dome designed just for him.

Nearby are some of the master's other works, including his powerful (unfinished) *Prisoners, St. Matthew,* and a *Pietà* (possibly by one of his disciples). Michelangelo Buonarroti believed that the sculptor was a tool of God, responsible only for chipping away at the stone until the intended sculpture emerged.

▲▲MUSEUM OF SAN MARCO (MUSEO DI SAN MARCO)

Located one block north of the Accademia, this 15th-century monastery houses the greatest collection of frescoes and paintings by Renaissance master Fra Angelico. Upstairs are 43 cells decorated by Fra Angelico and his assistants. Trained in the medieval style, he adopted Renaissance techniques to produce works that blended Christian symbols with realism. Be sure to see the cell of Savonarola, the charismatic monk who threw out the Medici, and sponsored "bonfires of the vanities."

Cost and Hours: €4, covered by Firenze Card, Tue-Fri 8:15-13:50, Sat 8:15-16:50; also open 8:15-13:50 on first, third, and fifth Mon and 8:15-16:50 on second and fourth Sun of each month; on Piazza San Marco, tel. 055-238-8608.

Michelangelo, David

Michelangelo sculptures, Medici Chapels

🎧 Download my free Museum of San Marco audio tour.

▲▲MEDICI CHAPELS

The burial site of the ruling Medici family in the Basilica of San Lorenzo includes the dusky crypt; the big, domed Chapel of Princes; and the magnificent New Sacristy, featuring architecture, tombs, and statues almost entirely by Michelangelo. The Medici made their money in textiles and banking, and patronized a dream team of Renaissance artists that put Florence on the cultural map. Michelangelo, who spent his teen years living with the Medici, was commissioned to create the family's final tribute.

Cost and Hours: €8, free and crowded on first Sun of month, covered by Firenze Card; Tue-Sat 8:15-17:00 (Nov-March until 13:50), last entry 40 minutes before closing; also open second and fourth Mon and first, third, and fifth Sun of each month; reservations possible but unnecessary (€3 fee), audioguide-€6, modest dress required, tel. 055-238-8602, www.bargellomusei.beniculturali.it.

▲MERCATO CENTRALE

Florence's giant iron-and-glass-covered central market is a wonderland of picturesque produce. While the San Lorenzo Market that fills the surrounding streets is only a step up from a flea market, Mercato Centrale retains its Florentine elegance.

Downstairs, you'll see parts of the cow (and bull) you'd never dream of eating (no, that's not a turkey neck), enjoy free samples, watch pasta being made, and have your pick of plenty of fun eateries sloshing out cheap and tasty pasta to locals (Mon-Fri 7:00-14:00, Sat until 17:00, closed Sun).

Upstairs, the meticulously restored glass roof and steel rafters soar over a sleek and modern food court, serving up a bounty of Tuscan cuisine (daily 10:00-24:00).

Mercato Centrale

On and near Piazza della Signoria

▲▲▲UFFIZI GALLERY

This greatest collection of Italian paintings anywhere features works by Giotto, Leonardo, Raphael, Caravaggio, Titian, and Michelangelo, and a roomful of Botticellis, including the *Birth of Venus.* Start with Giotto's early stabs at Renaissance-style realism, then move on through the 3-D experimentation of the early 1400s to the real thing, rendered by the likes of Botticelli and Leonardo. Finish off with Michelangelo and Titian. Because only 600 visitors are allowed inside the building at any one time, there's generally a very long wait. The good news: no Vatican-style mob scenes inside. The museum is nowhere near as big as it is great. Few tourists spend more than two hours inside.

Cost and Hours: €20 (€10 if no special exhibit), extra €4 for reservation, €38 combo-ticket with Pitti Palace and Boboli Gardens gives you priority entry, admission is cheaper in winter, free and extremely crowded on first Sun of the month—don't visit on this day, covered by Firenze Card, Tue-Sun 8:15-18:50, closed Mon, audioguide-€6, reservation tel. 055-294-883, www.uffizi.it. To avoid the long ticket lines, get a Firenze Card (see page 166) or make reservations (see page 167).

🎧 Download my free Uffizi Gallery audio tour.

Getting In: There are several entrances; which one you use depends on whether you have a Firenze Card, a reservation, or neither.

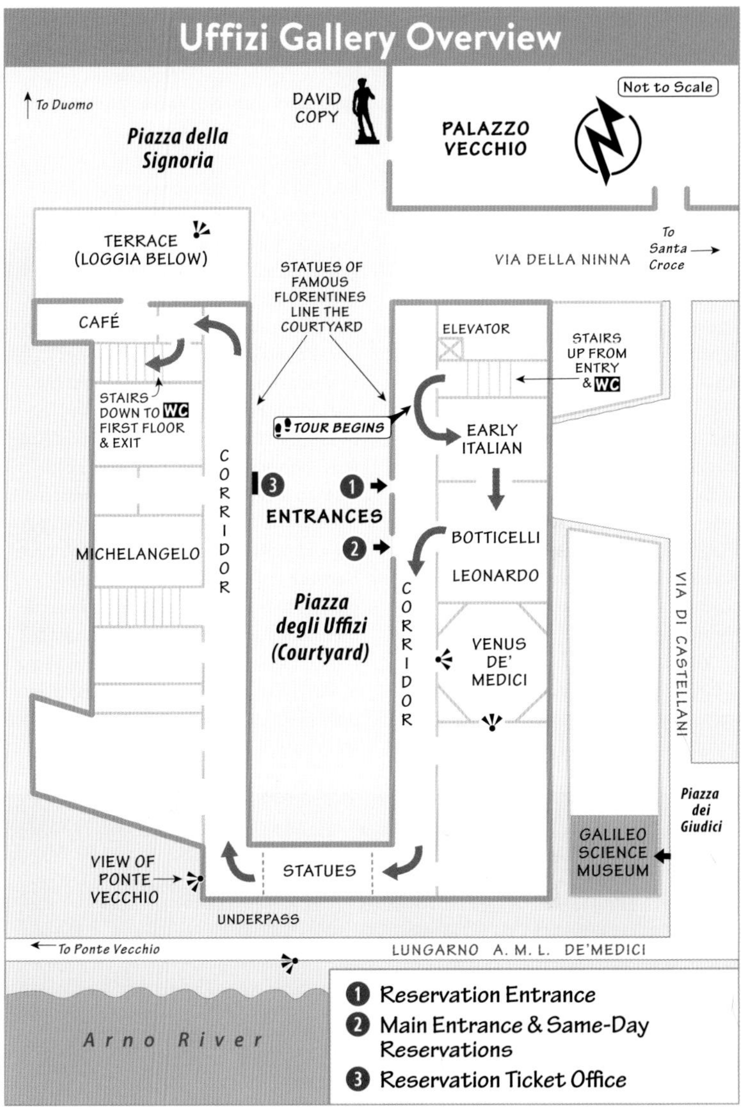

Firenze Card holders enter at door #1 (labeled *Reservation Entrance*). Read the signs carefully and get in the line for individuals—not groups—between door #1 and door #2.

People **buying a ticket on the spot** line up with everyone else at door #2, marked *Main Entrance.* An estimated wait time is posted.

To **buy a Firenze Card,** or to see if there are any same-day reservations available (€4 extra), enter door #2 to the left of the same-day ticket-buying line (marked *Booking Service and Today* or *Advance Sale*) to the left of the same-day ticket-buying line. Don't be shy: Ask the attendant to let you pass—and don't get into the long ticket-buying line. The doorway is kept open for same-day reservation buyers.

If you've **already made a reservation** and need to pick up your ticket, go to door #3 (labeled *Reservation Ticket Office,* across the courtyard from doors #1 and #2, under an archway and to the right). Tickets are available for pickup 10 minutes before your appointed time. If you booked online and have already prepaid, you'll exchange your voucher for a ticket. If you booked by phone, give them your confirmation number and pay for the ticket. Then walk briskly past the ticket-buying line. Get in the correct queue: groups to the left of door #1, individuals between doors #1 and #2.

Expect long waits even if you have a reservation or Firenze Card in hand. There may be a queue to pick up your reservation at door #3, another 30-minute wait to enter at door #1, and a slow shuffle through security.

Visiting the Uffizi: The Uffizi is U-shaped, running around the courtyard. The east wing contains Florentine paintings from medieval to Renaissance times. At the south end, you pass through a short hallway filled with sculpture. The west wing has later Florentine art (especially Michelangelo) and a café terrace facing the Duomo. Many more rooms of art are downstairs, showing how the Florentine Renaissance spread to Rome (Raphael) and Venice (Titian), and inspired the Baroque (Caravaggio). The gallery is nearing the end of a major, multiyear overhaul. Pieces frequently move, and new rooms open, so expect changes.

Medieval (1200-1400): Paintings by **Duccio, Cimabue,** and **Giotto** show the baby steps being made from the flat Byzantine style toward realism. In his *Madonna and Child with Angels,* Giotto created a "stage" and peopled it with real beings. The triumph here is Mary herself—big and monumental, like a Roman statue. Beneath her robe, she has knees and breasts that stick out at us. This three-dimensionality was revolutionary, a taste of the Renaissance a century before it began.

Early Renaissance (mid-1400s): Piero della Francesca's *Federico da Montefeltro and Battista Sforza* heralds the era of

Titian, Venus of Urbino

humanism and the new centrality of ordinary people in art. Fra Filippo Lippi's radiant Madonnas are light years away from the generic Marys of the medieval era.

Renaissance (1450-1500): The Botticelli room is filled with masterpieces and classical fleshiness (the famous *Birth of Venus* and *Spring*). Here is the Renaissance in its first bloom. This is a return to the pagan world of classical Greece, where things of the flesh are not sinful. Madonna is out; Venus is in.

Classical Sculpture: The foundation of the Renaissance was classical sculpture. Sculptors, painters, and poets turned for inspiration to ancient Greek and Roman works as the epitome of balance, 3-D perspective, human anatomy, and beauty.

In the Tribune Room, the highlight is the *Venus de' Medici,* a Roman copy of the lost original of the great Greek sculptor Praxiteles. Balanced, harmonious, and serene, this statue was considered the epitome of beauty and sexuality in Renaissance Florence.

The **sculpture hall** has 2,000-year-old copies of 2,500-year-old Greek originals... and the best view in Florence of the Arno River and Ponte Vecchio through the window, dreamy at sunset.

Palazzo Vecchio

High Renaissance (1500-1550): Don't miss Michelangelo's *Holy Family,* the only surviving completed easel painting by the greatest sculptor in history (in the Michelangelo Room).

After a break to enjoy Duomo views from the café terrace, head downstairs to find Raphael's *Madonna of the Goldfinch,* with Mary and the Baby Jesus brought down from heaven into the real world (Room 66), and Titian's voluptuous *Venus of Urbino* (Room 83).

More Art on the Lower Floor: On your way out, you'll see temporary exhibitions and works by foreign painters. It's worth pausing in Room 90 for works by Caravaggio.

Nearby: The statue-filled Uffizi courtyard and Loggia dei Lanzi are covered in the Renaissance Walk on page 178.

▲▲PALAZZO VECCHIO

This fortress with the 300-foot spire dominates Florence's main square. In Renaissance times, it was the Town Hall, where citizens pioneered the once-radical notion of self-rule. Its official name—Palazzo della Signoria—refers to the elected members of the city council. In 1540, the tyrant Cosimo I made the building his personal palace, redecorating the interior in lavish style. Today the building functions once again as the Town Hall.

Entry to the ground-floor courtyard is free, so even if you don't go upstairs to the museum, you can step inside and feel the essence of the Medici. Paying customers can see Cosimo's lavish royal apartments, decorated with paintings and statues by Michelangelo and Donatello. The highlight is the 13,000-square-foot Grand Hall (Salone dei Cinquecento), lined with frescoes and statues.

Underneath the Palazzo Vecchio are Roman-era excavations—the ruins of a 2,000-year-old theater from ancient Florentia. Other than heavily restored brickwork and an interesting 10-minute video about the city's evolution over 22 centuries, there's little to see.

Cost and Hours: Courtyard-free, museum-€10, tower climb-€10 (418 steps), museum plus tower-€14, excavations-€4, combo-ticket for all three-€18, covered by Firenze Card (first pick up ticket at ground-floor info desk before entering museum). Museum and excavations open Fri-Wed 9:00-23:00 (Oct-March until 19:00), Thu 9:00-14:00 year-round; tower keeps shorter hours (last entry one hour before closing); last tickets for all sights sold one hour before closing; videoguide-€5, English tours available, Piazza della Signoria, tel. 055-276-8224, www.musefirenze.it.

▲▲GALILEO SCIENCE MUSEUM

When we think of the Renaissance, we think of visual arts: painting, mosaics, architecture, and sculpture. But when the visual arts declined in the 1600s (abused and co-opted by political powers), music and science flourished. Florence hosted many scientific breakthroughs, as you'll see in this collection of clocks, telescopes, maps, and ingenious gadgets. Trace the technical innovations as modern science emerges from 1000 to 1900. Exhibits include various tools for gauging the world, from a compass and thermometer to Galileo's telescopes. Some of the most talked about bottles in Florence are the ones here that contain Galileo's fingers. The museum is friendly, comfortably cool, never crowded, and just a block east of the Uffizi on the Arno River.

Cost and Hours: €9, €22 family ticket, covered by Firenze Card, Wed-Mon 9:30-18:00, Tue until 13:00, guided tours available, Piazza dei Giudici 1, tel. 055-265-311, www.museogalileo.it.

East of Piazza della Signoria

▲▲▲BARGELLO

The Renaissance began with sculpture—the great Florentine painters were "sculptors with brushes." You can see the birth of this revolution of 3-D in the Bargello (bar-JEL-oh), which boasts the best collection of Florentine sculpture. Housed

Celestial globe at Galileo Science Museum

Donatello, David

in a former police station, this small, uncrowded museum is a pleasure to visit.

Highlights include Donatello's influential, painfully beautiful *David* (the first male nude to be sculpted in a thousand years), multiple works by Michelangelo, and rooms of Medici treasures. Moody Donatello, who embraced realism with his lifelike statues, set the personal and artistic style for many Renaissance artists to follow. The best pieces are in the ground-floor room at the foot of the outdoor staircase (with fine works by Michelangelo, Cellini, and Giambologna) and in the "Donatello room" directly above (including his two different *Davids*, plus Ghiberti and Brunelleschi's revolutionary dueling door panels and yet another *David* by Verrocchio).

Cost and Hours: €8, cash only, free and crowded on first Sun of the month, covered by Firenze Card; Tue-Sat 8:15-17:00 (later for special exhibits), Nov-March until 13:50; also open second and fourth Mon and the first, third, and fifth Sun of each month, last entry 40 minutes before closing; reservations possible but unnecessary, audioguide-€6 (€10/2 people), Via del Proconsolo 4, tel. 055-238-8606, www.bargellomusei.beniculturali.it.

🎧 Download my free Bargello audio tour.

▲▲SANTA CROCE CHURCH

This 14th-century Franciscan church, decorated with centuries of precious art, holds the tombs of great Florentines. The loud 19th-century Victorian Gothic facade faces a huge square ringed with tempting shops and littered with foot-sore tourists. Escape into the church and admire its sheer height and spaciousness.

Cost and Hours: €8, covered by Firenze Card, Mon-Sat 9:30-17:30, Sun 14:00-17:30, multimedia guide-€6 (€8/2 people), modest dress required, 10-minute walk east of the Palazzo Vecchio along Borgo de' Greci, tel. 055-246-6105, www.santacroceopera.it. The **leather school,** at the back of the church, is free and sells church tickets—handy when the church has a long line (daily 10:00-18:00, closed Sun Nov-March, has own entry behind church, plus an entry within church, www.scuoladelcuoio.com).

Santa Croce Church

Visiting the Church: On the left wall (as you face the altar) is the tomb of **Galileo Galilei** (1564-1642), the Pisan who lived his last years under house arrest near Florence. His crime? Defying the Church by saying that the earth revolved around the sun. His heretical remains were only allowed in the church long after his death.

Directly opposite (on the right wall) is the tomb of **Michelangelo Buonarroti** (1475-1564). Santa Croce was Michelangelo's childhood church, as he grew up a block west of here. Farther up the nave is the tomb of **Niccolò Machiavelli** (1469-1527), a champion of democratic Florence and author of *The Prince,* a how-to manual on hardball politics—which later Medici rulers found instructive.

The first chapel to the right of the main altar features the famous *Death of St. Francis* fresco by Giotto. With simple but eloquent gestures, Francis' brothers bid him a sad farewell. In the hallway near the bookstore, notice the photos of the devastating flood of 1966. Beyond that is the leather school (free entry).

Exit between the Rossini and Machiavelli tombs into the delightful cloister (peaceful open-air courtyard). On the left, enter Brunelleschi's Pazzi Chapel, which captures the Renaissance in miniature.

Near the Train Station

▲▲CHURCH OF SANTA MARIA NOVELLA

This 13th-century Dominican church is rich in art. Along with crucifixes by Giotto and Brunelleschi, it contains every textbook's example of the early Renaissance mastery of perspective: *The Trinity* by Masaccio. The exquisite chapels trace art in Florence from medieval times to early Baroque. The outside of the church features a dash of Romanesque (horizontal stripes), Gothic (pointed arches), Renaissance (geometric shapes), and Baroque (scrolls). Step in and look down the 330-foot nave for a 14th-century optical illusion.

Next to the church are the cloisters and the **museum,** located in the old Dominican convent of Santa Maria Novella. Its highlight is the breathtaking Spanish Chapel, with walls covered by a series of frescoes by Andrea di Bonaiuto.

Cost and Hours: Church and museum-€5, covered by Firenze Card; Mon-Thu 9:00-19:00 (Oct-March until 17:30), Fri 11:00-19:00 (Oct-March until 17:30), Sat 9:00-17:30, Sun 13:00-17:30, last entry 45 minutes before closing; multimedia guide-€3, modest dress required, main entrance on Piazza Santa Maria Novella, tel. 055-219-257, www.smn.it.

South of the Arno River

▲▲PITTI PALACE

Pitti Palace, several blocks southwest of Ponte Vecchio, offers many reasons for a visit: the palace itself, with its imposing exterior and lavish interior; the second-best collection of paintings in town; the statue-dotted Boboli Gardens; and a host of secondary museums. Focus on the highlights: the painting collection in the Palatine Gallery, plus the sumptuous rooms of the Royal Apartments. The paintings pick up where the Uffizi leaves off, at the High Renaissance. Lovers of Raphael's Madonnas and Titian's portraits will find some of the world's best here. If it's a nice day, take a stroll in the inviting Boboli Gardens, a rare patch of green space within old Florence.

Cost and Hours: The Palatine Gallery, Royal Apartments, and Gallery of Modern Art are covered by **ticket #1**—€16 (€8 if no special exhibits)—and are open Tue-Sun 8:15-18:50, closed Mon, last entry 45 minutes before closing. The Boboli and Bardini Gardens, Costume Gallery, Argenti/Silverworks Museum (the Medici treasures), and Porcelain Museum are covered by **ticket #2**—€10 (€7 if no special exhibits)—and are open daily June-Aug 8:15-19:30, April-May and Sept until 18:30, March and Oct until 17:30, Nov-Feb until 16:30, closed first and last

Pitti Palace

Mon of each month, last entry one hour before closing. Reservations are possible but unnecessary. All palace sights are covered by the Firenze Card. The place is free and crowded on the first Sun of the month. The €8 audioguide (€13/2 people) explains the sprawling palace. Tel. 055-238-8614, www.uffizi.it.

Visiting Pitti Palace: In the **Palatine Gallery** you'll walk through one palatial room after another, walls sagging with masterpieces by 16th- and 17th-century masters, including Rubens, Titian, and Rembrandt. The Pitti's Raphael collection is the second-biggest anywhere—the Vatican beats it by one. Each room has some descriptions in English, though the paintings themselves have limited English labels.

The collection is all on one floor. To see the highlights, walk straight down the spine through a dozen or so rooms. Before you exit, consider a visit to the Royal Apartments. These 14 rooms (of which only a few are open at any one time) are where the Pitti's rulers lived in the 18th and 19th centuries. Each room features a different color and time period. Here, you get a real feel for the splendor of the dukes' world.

The rest of Pitti Palace is skippable, unless the various sights match your interests: the **Gallery of Modern Art** (second floor; Romantic, Neoclassical, and Impressionist works by 19th- and 20th-century Tuscan painters), **Argenti/Silverworks Museum** (ground and mezzanine floors; Medici treasures from jeweled crucifixes to gilded ostrich eggs), **Costume Gallery, Porcelain Museum,** and **Boboli and Bardini gardens** (behind the palace; enter from Pitti Palace courtyard—be prepared to climb uphill).

▲▲BRANCACCI CHAPEL

For the best look at works by Masaccio (one of the early Renaissance pioneers of perspective in painting), see his restored frescoes here. Instead of medieval religious symbols, Masaccio's paintings feature simple, strong human figures with facial expressions that reflect their emotions. The accompanying works of Masolino and Filippino Lippi provide illuminating contrasts.

Your ticket includes a 20-minute film (English subtitles) on the chapel, the frescoes, and Renaissance Florence; find it in the room next to the bookstore. The film's computer animation brings the paintings to 3-D life, while narration describes the events depicted in the panels. The film takes liberties with the art, but it's the best way to see the frescoes close up.

Cost and Hours: €6, cash only, covered by Firenze Card (which allows you to enter without a reservation); without a

Masaccio, Expulsion from the Garden of Eden

Firenze Card, free and easy reservations are required, though it's usually possible to walk right in on weekdays and any day off-season, especially if you arrive before 15:30; Mon and Wed-Sat 10:00-17:00, Sun 13:00-17:00, closed Tue, last entry 45 minutes before closing; free 20-minute film, videoguide-€3, knees and shoulders must be covered; in Church of Santa Maria del Carmine, on Piazza del Carmine in Oltrarno neighborhood; reservations tel. 055-276-8224 or 055-276-8558, ticket desk tel. 055-284-361, www.musefirenze.it.

Reservations: To reserve in advance, stop by the information desk in the Palazzo Vecchio or call the chapel a day ahead (tel. 055-276-8224 or 055-276-8558, English spoken, call center open Mon-Sat 9:30-13:00 & 14:00-17:00, Sun 9:30-12:30). You can also try reserving via email (info.muse@comune.fi.it).

▲PIAZZALE MICHELANGELO

Overlooking the city from across the river (look for the huge bronze statue of

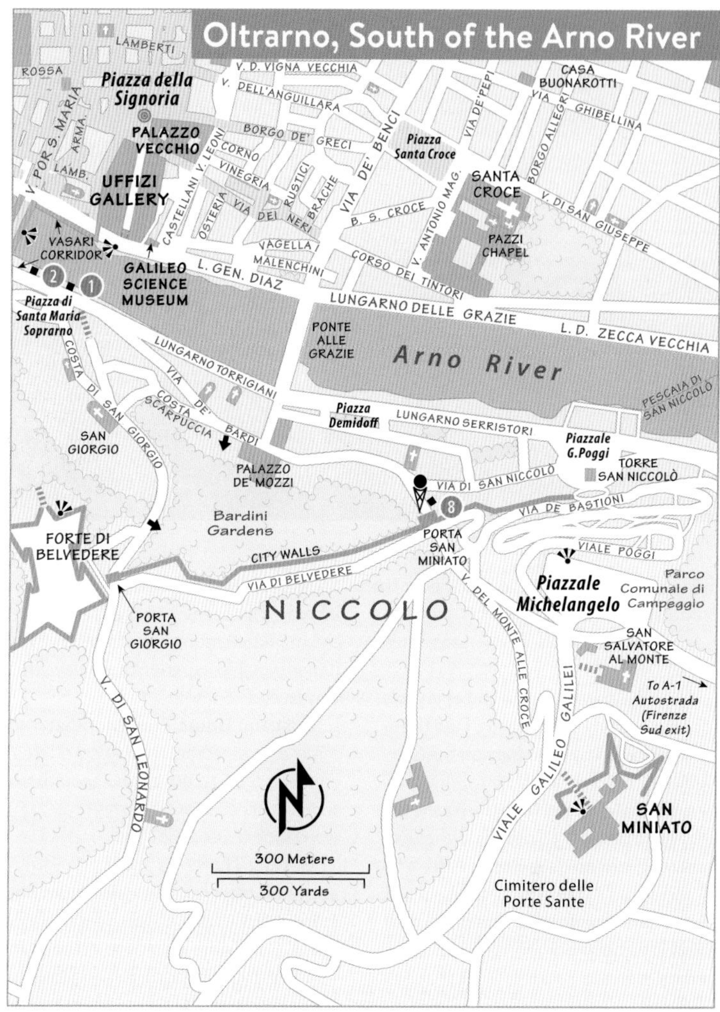

David), this square has a superb view of Florence and the stunning dome of the Duomo. It's worth the 25-minute hike, taxi, or bus ride. When you're there, you can also visit the stark, beautiful, crowd-free, Romanesque San Miniato Church, about 200 yards beyond the square (see next listing).

At the square, the best cityscape photos are taken from the street immediately below the overlook (go around to the right and down a few steps). Nearby is an inviting café (open seasonally) with great views. Off the west side of the piazza is a hidden terrace, excellent for a retreat from the mobs. After dark, the square is packed with school kids licking ice cream and each other. A WC is located just off the road, halfway between the two sights.

Getting There (and Back): It makes sense to take a taxi or ride the bus up and then enjoy the easy downhill walk back into town. Bus #12 takes you up (departs from train station, near Piazza

The view from Piazzale Michelangelo

di Santa Maria Novella, and just over the Ponte alla Carraia bridge on Oltrarno side of river; takes 20-30 minutes, longer in bad traffic).

The hike down is quick and enjoyable (or take bus #13 back down). Find the steps between the two bars on the San Miniato Church side of the parking lot (Via San Salvatore al Monte). At the first landing (marked #3), peek into the rose garden (Giardino delle Rose). After a few minutes, you'll walk through the old wall (Porta San Miniato) and emerge in the funky little neighborhood of San Niccolò in the Oltrarno.

▲▲SAN MINIATO CHURCH

According to legend, the martyred St. Minias—this church's namesake—was beheaded on the banks of the Arno in A.D. 250. He picked up his head and walked here (this was before the #12 bus), where he died and was buried in what became the first Christian cemetery in Florence. In the 11th century, this church was built to house Minias' remains. Imagine this fine church all alone—without any nearby buildings or fancy stairs—a quiet refuge where white-robed Benedictine monks could pray and work (their motto: ora et labora). The evening vesper service with the monks chanting in Latin offers a meditative worship experience—a peaceful way to end your visit.

Cost and Hours: Free, Mon-Sat 9:30-13:00 & 15:30-20:00, until 19:00 off-season, Sun 9:30-20:00, closed sporadically for special occasions, tel. 055-234-2731, www.sanminiatoalmonte.it.

Getting There: It's about 200 yards above Piazzale Michelangelo. From the station, bus #12 takes you right to the San Miniato al Monte stop (hop off and hike up the grand staircase); bus #13 takes you back down the hill.

San Miniato Church

EXPERIENCES

Shopping

One of Europe's best shopping towns, Florence has been known for its sense of style since the Medici days. Smaller stores are generally open about 9:00-13:00 and 15:30-19:30, usually closed on Sunday, often closed on Monday (or at least Monday morning), and sometimes closed for a couple of weeks around August 15. Bigger stores have similar hours, without the afternoon break.

Busy street scenes and markets abound. The vast open-air **San Lorenzo Market** sprawls in the streets ringing Mercato Centrale, between the Duomo and the train station (daily 9:00-19:00, closed Mon in winter). Originally a silk and straw market, **Mercato Nuovo** still functions as a rustic yet touristy market at the intersection of Via Calimala and Via Porta Rossa (daily 9:00-18:30). It's where you'll find *Il Porcellino* (a statue of a wild boar nicknamed "The Piglet"), which people rub and give coins to ensure their return to Florence. Other shopping areas can be found near Santa Croce and on Ponte Vecchio. At stalls or shops, prices are soft—don't be shy about bargaining, especially at San Lorenzo.

Leather jackets and handbags, perfume and cosmetics, edible goodies, and stationery are popular souvenirs. For authentic, locally produced wares, look for shops displaying the **Esercizi Storici Fiorentini** seal ("Historical Florentine Ventures"), with a picture of the Palazzo Vecchio's tower. You may pay a premium, but you can be assured of quality (for a list of shops, see www.esercizistorici.it).

The area between the Arno River and the cathedral is busy with fashion boutiques; browse along **Via della Vigna Nuova** (runs west from Via de' Tornabuoni) and **Via degli Strozzi** (runs east from Via de' Tornabuoni to Piazza della Repubblica). A tempting string of streets—**Borgo Santi Apostoli, Via del Parione,** and **Borgo Ognissanti**—runs parallel to the river one block inland, from near the Uffizi westward.

Across the river in the Oltrarno, known for its artisanal workshops, a short walk

San Lorenzo Market

Florence is a popular place to buy leather.

past the tourist crowds takes you to some less-discovered zones: near Pitti Palace, and the main street parallel to the river (**Borgo San Jacopo** to **Via di Santo Spirito**). Pick up the brochure "A Tour of Artisan Workshops" from the TI or at participating shops.

Nightlife

For me, nighttime is for dining, catching a concert, strolling through the old town with a gelato, or hitting one of the many pubs. Get the latest on nightlife from *The Florentine* magazine (free from TI, www.theflorentine.net) or *Firenze Spettacolo* (sold at newsstands, www.firenzespettacolo.it), or check www.firenzeturismo.it.

Strolling After Dark: Join the parade of locals on their evening *passegiata,* strolling from the Duomo to the Arno on Via de' Calzaiuoli, enjoying cafés, gelato shops, great people-watching, and street performers. Pop into a wine bar *(enoteca)* to sample regional wines by the glass or a plate of meats and cheeses. (Psst. Near the Duomo, find La Congrega Lounge Bar—a tiny retreat on a tiny lane just off the main pedestrian drag, at Via Tosinghi 3/4 red.) End at the Arno, to stand atop Ponte Vecchio and watch the sun set, the moon rise, and lovers kiss.

Lively squares include Piazzale Michelangelo's marvelous viewpoint, Piazza della Repubblica (with a carousel and street musicians), Piazza Santa Croce (with the popular, youthful Moyo bar nearby, at Via de' Benci 23 red), and Piazza di Santo Spirito (with trendy Volume and Pop Café on this Oltrarno square).

Live Music: Orsanmichele Church hosts chamber music under its Gothic arches (tickets sold on day of concert from door facing Via de' Calzaiuoli). **St. Mark's English Church** offers opera music several nights each week from February through October (Via Maggio 18, www.concertoclassico.info).

The recommended **Golden View Open Bar,** a river-view restaurant near Ponte Vecchio, has live jazz several nights a week at 21:00 (see page 202). **Boxoffice Toscana** sells tickets for rock concerts and more (Via delle Vecchie Carceri 1, tel. 055-210-804, www.boxofficetoscana.it).

Movies: Find English-language films at **Odeon Cinema** (near Piazza della Repubblica on Piazza Strozzi, tel. 055-214-068, www.odeonfirenze.com).

Ponte Vecchio after dark

EATING

Restaurants in Florence like to serve what's fresh. Seasonal ingredients are featured in the *piatti del giorno* (specials of the day) section on menus. Foodies should consider purchasing Elizabeth Minchilli's excellent app, Eat Florence (www.elizabethminchilliinrome.com).

Budget Eating: To save money and time, you can keep lunches fast and simple by eating at pizzerias, self-service cafeterias, or the countless sandwich shops and stands (though you may want to avoid the *trippa* carts selling tripe sandwiches—a prized local specialty).

Picnicking is easy. You can picnic your way through Mercato Centrale. You'll also find good *supermercati* throughout the city. I like the classy Sapori & Dintorni markets (run by Conad), which has branches near the Duomo (Borgo San Lorenzo 15 red) and just over Ponte Vecchio in the Oltrarno (Via de Bardi 45). Despar is another handy grocery chain (there's one around the corner from the Duomo Museum at Via dell'Oriuolo 66).

Mercato Centrale and Nearby

In Mercato Centrale

The Mercato Centrale (Central Market) is a foodie wonderland.

$ Ground Floor: The market zone, with lots of raw ingredients and a few humble food counters, is open only through lunchtime (Mon-Fri 7:00-14:00, Sat 7:00-17:00, closed Sun). Buy a picnic of fresh mozzarella cheese, olives, fruit, and crunchy bread to munch on the steps of the nearby Basilica of San Lorenzo. The fancy deli, Perini, is famous for its quality (pricey) products and enticing display. For a simple sit-down meal, head for the venerable Nerbone in the Market. Join the shoppers and workers who crowd up to the bar to grab their inexpensive plates, and then find a stool at the cramped shared tables nearby. Of the several cheap market diners, this feels the most authentic (lunch menu served Mon-Sat 12:00-14:00, sandwiches available from 8:00 until the bread runs out, cash only, on the side closest to the Basilica of San Lorenzo). Its less-famous sisters, nearby, have better seating and fewer crowds.

$$ Upstairs: Under the old glass roof, the upper floor features a dozen upscale food counters open for lunch and dinner (daily 10:00-24:00). Grab what you want—pizza, pasta, fish, meat, *salumi, lampredotto,* wine, and so on—and pull up a stool at one of the food-court tables. Before choosing, do a full circuit around the scene to get to know your options.

Near Mercato Centrale

If you can't find what you want in the market itself, consider one of these alternatives on the surrounding streets. These eateries skew to an especially touristy clientele.

$$ Trattoria Mario's has been serving hearty lunches to market-goers since 1953 (Fabio and Romeo are the latest generation). Their simple formula: no-frills, bustling service, old-fashioned good value, and shared tables. It's *cucina casalinga*—home cooking *con brio.* Their best dishes (*ribollita,* bean soup, *amatriciana*) often sell out first, so go early. If there's a line, put your name on the list (cash only, Mon-Sat 12:00-15:30, closed Sun and Aug, no reservations, Via Rosina 2, tel. 055-218-550).

Gelato

The best ice cream in Italy—maybe the world—is in Florence. But beware of scams at touristy joints that turn a simple request for a cone into a €10 rip-off. Survey the options and specify the size you want—for example, *un cono da tre euro* (a €3 cone).

All of these places, a cut above, are open daily for long hours:

Near the Accademia: Gelateria Carabè is famous for *granite* (Italian ices made with fresh fruit). Try a *cremolata*: a *granita* with a dollop of gelato (Via Ricasoli 60 red; from the Accademia, it's a block toward the Duomo).

In the City Center: A favorite, **Edoardo** features organic ingredients and tasty handmade cones (facing the southwest corner of the Duomo at Piazza del Duomo 45 red). Creative **Perchè No!** is near Orsanmichele Church, just off busy Via de' Calzaiuoli (Via dei Tavolini 19). Mod **Carapina,** near Ponte Vecchio, has unusual flavors and seasonal ingredients (Via Lambertesca 18 red).

Near the Church of Santa Croce: Gelateria de' Neri has a wide array of enticing flavors (Via dei Neri 9 red).

In the Oltrarno: Tiny **Il Gelato di Filo** boasts some of Florence's best gelato (Via San Miniato 5 red).

$$ Pepò, a colorful and charmingly unpretentious space, is tucked just around the corner from the touristy Trattoria Zà-Zà glitz on Piazza del Mercato Centrale. The chef offers a short menu of simple but well-prepared Florentine classics such as *ribollita* and *pollo alla cacciatora*—chicken cacciatore (daily 12:00-14:30 & 19:00-22:30, Via Rosina 4 red, tel. 055-283-259).

$$ Trattoria Sergio Gozzi is your classic neighborhood lunch-only place, serving hearty, traditional Florentine fare to market-goers since 1915. The handwritten menu is limited and changes daily, and the service can be hectic, but it remains a local favorite (Mon-Sat 12:00-15:00, closed Sun, reservations smart, Piazza di San Lorenzo 8, tel. 055-281-941).

Around the Duomo

At lunchtime, my first listing is more of a sit-down place; the others are better for a fast meal.

$$ Enoteca Coquinarius—hip and welcoming—has a slow food ethic and great €15 salads and €10 pastas (open daily, a couple blocks south of the Duomo at Via delle Oche 11 red, tel. 055-230-2153).

$ Self-Service Ristorante Leonardo is an inexpensive, air-conditioned, quick, and handy cafeteria. While it's no-frills and old-school, the food is better than many table-service eateries in this part of town. It's a block from the Duomo, southwest of the Baptistery (lots of veggies, daily 11:45-14:45 & 18:45-21:45, upstairs at Via Pecori 11, tel. 055-284-446).

$$ Paszkowski Café is a venerable place on Piazza della Repubblica. While famously expensive as a restaurant, it serves up inexpensive, quick lunches. At the display case, order a salad or plate of pasta or cooked veggies (or half-and-half), pay the cashier, and find a seat upstairs or at one of the tables reserved for self-serve diners on the square (lunch served 12:00-15:00, Piazza della Repubblica 35 red—northwest corner, tel. 055-210-236).

$$ EATaly, a slick, modern space a half-block from the Duomo, is an outpost of a chain of foodie mini-malls located in big Italian cities. Along with a world of gifty edibles, it offers several food options under one roof, including an espresso counter, a soft-serve gelato counter and tempting pastry shop, a grocery store for top-end Italian ingredients and kitchen gadgets, and a bright, modern dining area serving pastas, pizzas, salads, and *secondi,* including daily specials (food shop open daily 10:00-22:30, restaurants open 12:00-15:00 and from 19:00, Via de' Martelli 22 red, tel. 055-015-3601).

Near Piazza della Signoria

Piazza della Signoria, the scenic square facing the Palazzo Vecchio, is ringed by beautifully situated yet touristy eateries serving overpriced and probably microwaved food. The following places offer better values off the square.

Dining

$$ Osteria Vini e Vecchi Sapori is a colorful eatery—tight and tiny, and with attitude. They serve Tuscan food—like pappardelle with duck—from a fun, accessible menu of delicious pastas and secondi (Mon-Sat 12:30-14:30 & 19:30-22:30, closed Sun, reservations smart, Via dei Magazzini 3 red, tel. 055-293-045, run by Mario while wife Rosanna cooks and son Tommaso serves).

$$$$ Frescobaldi Ristorante and Wine Bar, the showcase of Italy's aristocratic wine family, serves sophisticated dishes by candlelight under high-vaulted ceilings. They offer the same seasonal menu in their cozy interior, tight wine bar, and at a few outside tables. If coming for dinner, make a reservation and dress up (lighter wine-bar and good-value set menus at lunch, daily 12:00-14:30 & 19:00-22:30, air-con, Via dei Magazzini 2 red, tel. 055-284-724, www.deifrescobaldi.it).

Cheap, Simple Fare

$$ Cantinetta dei Verrazzano, a long-established bakery/café/wine bar, serves delightful sandwich plates in an old-time setting. Their *selezione Verrazzano* is a plate of four little crostini featuring different breads, cheeses, and meats from the Chianti region. The *tagliere di focacce,* a sampler plate of mini-focaccia sandwiches, is also fun. Office workers pop in for a quick lunch, and it's traditional to share tables. They also have benches and tiny tables for eating at takeout prices (Mon-Sat 8:00-21:00, Sun 10:00-16:30, no reservations taken, just off Via de' Calzaiuoli, at Via dei Tavolini 18 red, tel. 055-268-590).

$ I Fratellini is a hole-in-the-wall serving more than 30 kinds of sandwiches and a fine selection of wine at great prices (see list on wall) since 1875. Join the local crowd to order, then sit on a nearby curb to eat, placing your glass on the wall rack before you leave. It's worth ordering the most expensive wine they're selling by the glass (daily 9:00-19:30 or until the bread runs out, 20 yards in front of Orsanmichele Church on Via dei Cimatori, tel. 055-239-6096).

Café with a View

$$ Caffè La Terrazza is on the rooftop of La Rinascente department store overlooking Piazza della Repubblica. While fairly plain, it comes with commanding views of the Duomo, which looms gloriously on the horizon (€6 coffee drinks, daily 9:00-20:30).

The Oltrarno

Dining in the Oltrarno, south of the Arno River, offers a more authentic experience. While it's just a few minutes' walk from Ponte Vecchio, it sees far fewer tourists.

Dining or Drinking with a Ponte Vecchio View

$$ Signorvino is an *enoteca* (wine shop) with a simple restaurant that has a rare terrace literally over the Arno River. Fun-loving and unpretentious, this place has a passion for quality Italian ingredients, offering regional dishes and plates of fine meats and cheeses to pair with just the right wine from a wonderful array. If you're up for a bottle rather than a glass, their huge selection is available for the same fair prices at a table as in their wine store (shop open daily 9:30-24:00, food served 11:30-23:00, Via dei Bardi 46 red, tel. 055-286-258, www.signorvino.com, call to reserve, especially for terrace seating).

Cooking Classes

At cooking classes, you'll typically spend a couple of hours cooking, then sit down to a hard-earned meal. The options listed below represent only a few of your many choices. As this is a fast-changing scene, it's worth doing some homework online and booking well ahead.

In Tavola is a dedicated cooking school in the Oltrarno, featuring Italian, English-speaking chefs who quickly demonstrate each step before setting you loose. You'll work in a kitchen, then eat in the cozy wine cellar (€53-73/person, between Pitti Palace and Brancacci Chapel at Via dei Velluti 18 red, tel. 055-217-672, www.intavola.org, info@intavola.org, Fabrizio).

Both **Artviva** and **Florencetown** (listed under "Tours" on page 168) offer cooking classes and a 10 percent discount to my readers (Artviva: €53-68/person; Florencetown: €89/person for 5-hour class that includes shopping for the food you'll cook; €49/person for 3-hour pizza- and gelato-making class).

$$$ Golden View Open Bar is a modern, noisy, and touristy bistro, good for a salad, pizza, or pasta with fine wine and a fine view of Ponte Vecchio. Reservations for window tables are essential. They have three seating areas: a riverside pizza place, a classier restaurant, and a jazzy lounge. In the afternoon (12:00-18:00), they offer wine tastings (€9-15) that include three pours. Later (18:30 to 21:30), the wine bar serves a buffet of appetizers free with your €10 drink (daily 12:00-24:00, café opens at 7:30, jazz usually Mon, Fri, and Sat nights at 21:00, 50 yards east of Ponte Vecchio at Via dei Bardi 58, tel. 055-214-502, www.goldenviewopenbar.com, run by Antonio, Paolo, and Tommaso).

On or near Piazza di Santo Spirito

Piazza di Santo Spirito is a thriving neighborhood square with a collection of lively eateries and bars. Several bars offer *aperitivo* buffets with their drinks during happy hour. Late in the evening the area becomes a clubbing scene.

$$ Gusta Osteria, just around the corner from the piazza, serves big salads and predictable Tuscan fare at fun, cozy indoor seating or at outdoor tables (Tue-Sun 12:00-23:00, closed Mon, Via de' Michelozzi 13 red, tel. 055-285-033). For cheaper bites, try its sister restaurant **$ Gusta Panino,** a sandwich bar directly on the square.

At **$$ Trattoria Casalinga,** an inexpensive standby, Florentines (who enjoy the tripe and tongue) and tourists (who opt for easier to swallow Tuscan favorites) alike pack the place and leave full and happy (Mon-Sat 12:00-14:30 & 19:00-22:00, after 20:00 reserve or wait, closed Sun and Aug, just off Piazza di Santo Spirito, near the church at Via de' Michelozzi 9 red, tel. 055-218-624, www.trattorialacasalinga.it, Andrea and Paolo).

Dining Well

These are my favorite restaurants in the Oltrarno. Make reservations for dinner or come early.

$$$ Il Santo Bevitore Ristorante, lit like a Rembrandt painting and unusually spacious, serves creative modern Tuscan cuisine at dressy tables. They're enthusiastic about matching quality produce from the area with the right wine. This is a good break from the big, sloppy plates of pasta you'll get at many Florence eateries (good wine list by the glass or bottle, daily 12:30-14:30 & 19:30-23:00, closed Sun or Mon for lunch, reservations smart, three tables on the sidewalk, acoustics can make it noisy inside, Via di Santo Spirito 64 red, tel. 055-211-264, www.ilsantobevitore.com).

$$ Enoteca Il Santino Gastronomia, Il Santo Bevitore's smaller wine bar next door, feels like the perfect after-work hangout for foodies who'd like a glass of wine and a light bite. Tight, cozy, and atmospheric, the place has a prominent bar, where you can assemble an €8-12 *tagliere* of locally sourced cheeses and *salumi.* They also have a few affordable hot dishes (daily 12:30-23:00, Via di Santo Spirito 60 red, no reservations, tel. 055-230-2820).

$$$ Trattoria 4 Leoni creates the quintessential Oltrarno dinner scene, and is understandably popular with tourists. The Tuscan-style food is made with an innovative twist and an appreciation for vegetables. You'll enjoy the fun energy and characteristic seating, both outside on the colorful square and inside, where you'll dine in exposed-stone sophistication. While the wines by the glass are pricey, the house wine is good (daily 12:00-24:00, dinner reservations smart; midway between Ponte Vecchio and Piazza di Santo Spirito, on Piazza della Passera at Via dei Vellutini 1; tel. 055-218-562, www.4leoni.com).

$$$$ Olio & Convivium is primarily a catering company for top-end events. Their three intimate rooms are surrounded by fine *prosciutti,* cheeses, and wine shelves. Their list of €14-25 *gastronomia* plates offers an array of taste treats and fine wines by the glass. They also have €35-49 tasting menus and stylish €18 lunches with wine (Tue-Sun 12:00-14:30 & 19:00-22:30, closed Mon, Via di Santo Spirito 4, tel. 055-265-8198, www.oliorestaurant.it, Tommaso is the chef and owner).

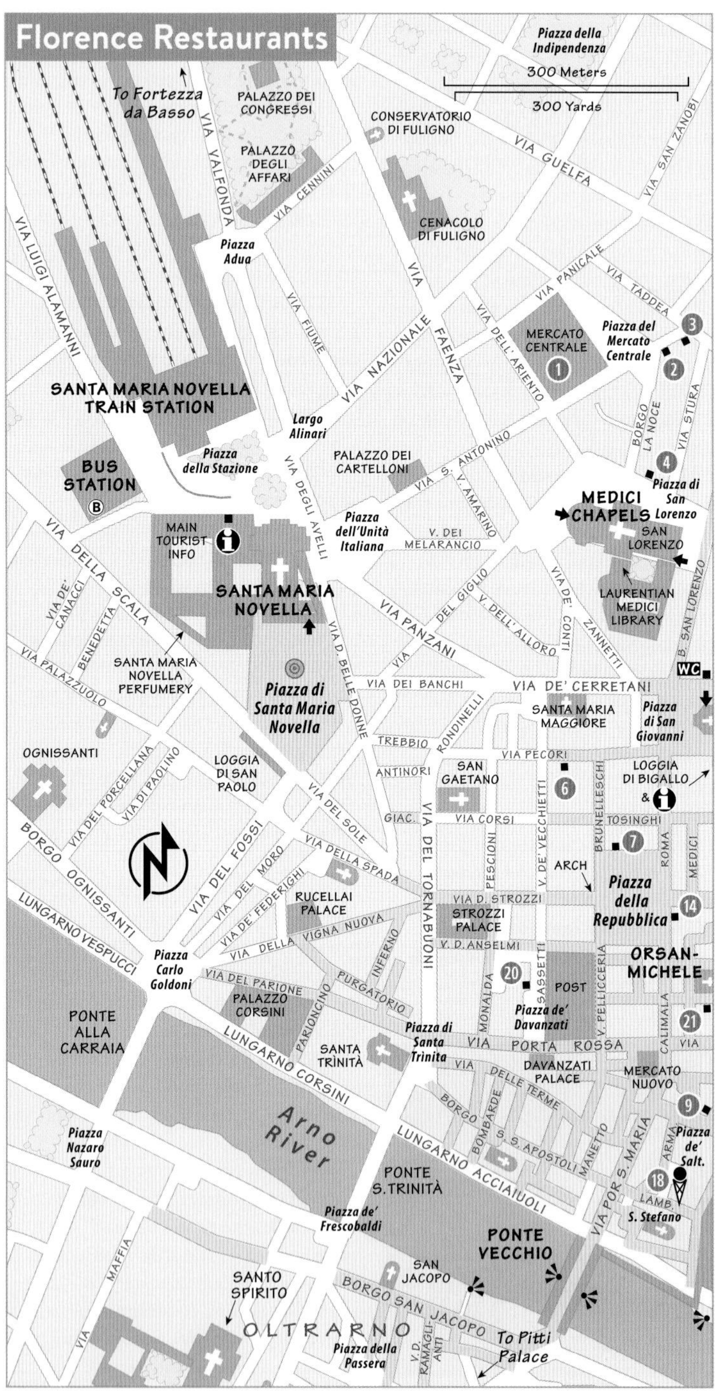
Florence Restaurants
Piazza della Indipendenza
300 Meters
300 Yards
To Fortezza da Basso
PALAZZO DEI CONGRESSI
PALAZZO DEGLI AFFARI
CONSERVATORIO DI FULIGNO
CENACOLO DI FULIGNO
VIA VALFONDA
VIA CENNINI
VIA GUELFA
VIA SAN ZANOBI
VIA LUIGI ALAMANNI
Piazza Adua
VIA FIUME
VIA FAENZA
VIA NAZIONALE
VIA PANICALE
VIA TADDEA
VIA DELL' ARIENTO
MERCATO CENTRALE
Piazza del Mercato Centrale
BORGO LA NOCE
VIA STURA
SANTA MARIA NOVELLA TRAIN STATION
Largo Alinari
Piazza della Stazione
BUS STATION
PALAZZO DEI CARTELLONI
VIA S. ANTONINO
V. AMARINO
VIA DEGLI AVELLI
Piazza dell'Unità Italiana
V. DEI MELARANCIO
MEDICI CHAPELS
SAN LORENZO
Piazza di San Lorenzo
MAIN TOURIST INFO
VIA DELLA SCALA
VIA DE' CANACCI
BENEDETTA
SANTA MARIA NOVELLA
LAURENTIAN MEDICI LIBRARY
VIA DEL GIGLIO
V. DELL' ALLORO
VIA DE' CONTI
ZANNETTI
B. SAN LORENZO
VIA PANZANI
SANTA MARIA NOVELLA PERFUMERY
VIA PALAZZUOLO
VIA D. BELLE DONNE
Piazza di Santa Maria Novella
VIA DEI BANCHI
VIA DE' CERRETANI
WC
SANTA MARIA MAGGIORE
Piazza di San Giovanni
RONDINELLI
TREBBIO
OGNISSANTI
VIA DEL PORCELLANA
VIA DI PAOLINO
LOGGIA DI SAN PAOLO
ANTINORI
SAN GAETANO
VIA PECORI
LOGGIA DI BIGALLO
VIA DEL SOLE
GIAC.
VIA CORSI
VIA DE' VECCHIETTI
BRUNELLESCHI
TOSINGHI
BORGO OGNISSANTI
VIA DEI FOSSI
VIA DEL MORO
VIA DELLA SPADA
VIA DEL TORNABUONI
PESCIONI
ARCH
ROMA
MEDICI
Piazza della Repubblica
VIA DE' FEDERIGHI
RUCELLAI PALACE
VIA D. STROZZI
STROZZI PALACE
LUNGARNO VESPUCCI
VIA DELLA VIGNA NUOVA
V. D. ANSELMI
INFERNO
ORSANMICHELE
Piazza Carlo Goldoni
VIA DEL PARIONE
PURGATORIO
PALAZZO CORSINI
MONALDA
SASSETTI
POST
V. PELLICCERIA
CALIMALA
PONTE ALLA CARRAIA
PARIONCINO
Piazza de' Davanzati
Piazza di Santa Trìnita
VIA PORTA ROSSA
LUNGARNO CORSINI
SANTA TRÌNITÀ
DAVANZATI PALACE
VIA DELLE TERME
MERCATO NUOVO
Arno River
BORGO
BOMBARDE
S. S. APOSTOLI
MANETTO
VIA POR S. MARIA
ARMA
Piazza de' Salt.
Piazza Nazaro Sauro
LUNGARNO ACCIAIUOLI
PONTE S. TRINITÀ
LAMB.
S. Stefano
Piazza de' Frescobaldi
PONTE VECCHIO
MAFFIA
SANTO SPIRITO
SAN JACOPO
BORGO SAN JACOPO
OLTRARNO
VIA
Piazza della Passera
V. D. RAMAGLIANTI
To Pitti Palace
1
2
3
4
6
7
9
14
18
20
21

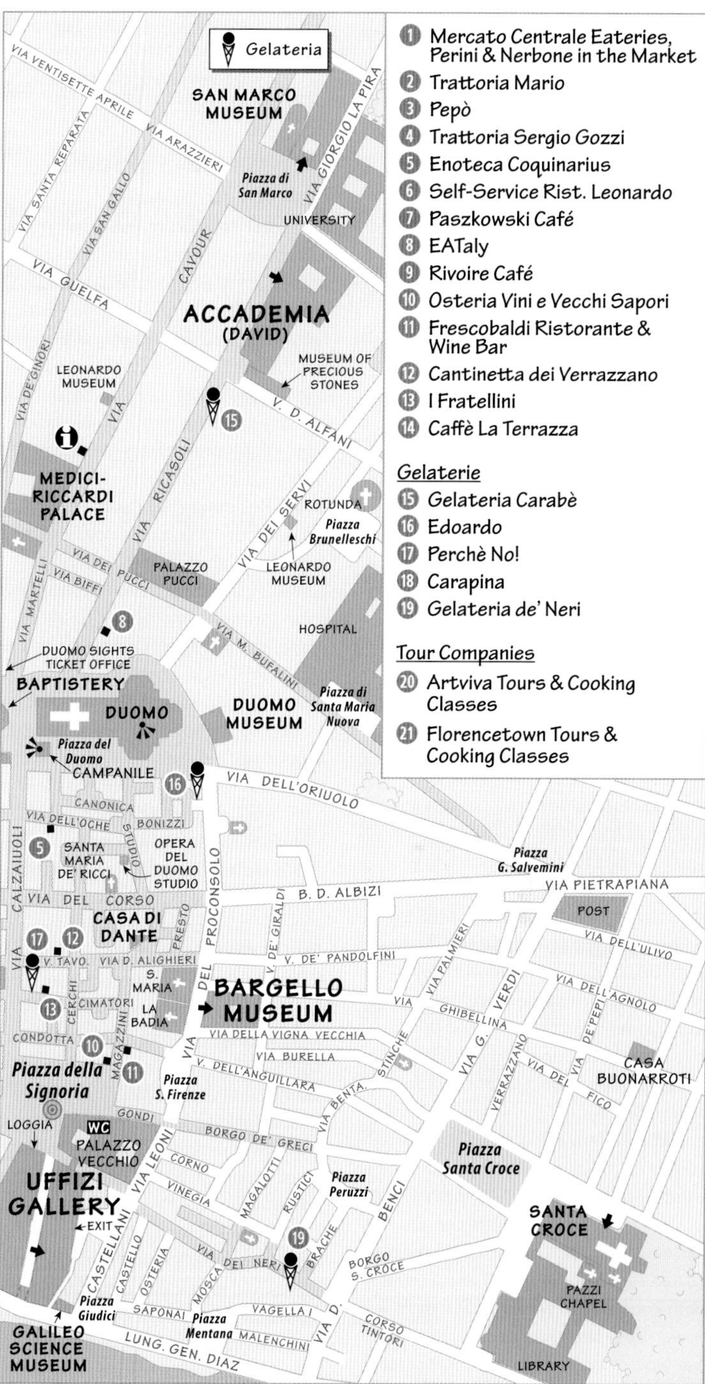
1 Mercato Centrale Eateries, Perini & Nerbone in the Market
2 Trattoria Mario
3 Pepò
4 Trattoria Sergio Gozzi
5 Enoteca Coquinarius
6 Self-Service Rist. Leonardo
7 Paszkowski Café
8 EATaly
9 Rivoire Café
10 Osteria Vini e Vecchi Sapori
11 Frescobaldi Ristorante & Wine Bar
12 Cantinetta dei Verrazzano
13 I Fratellini
14 Caffè La Terrazza
Gelaterie
15 Gelateria Carabè
16 Edoardo
17 Perchè No!
18 Carapina
19 Gelateria de' Neri
Tour Companies
20 Artviva Tours & Cooking Classes
21 Florencetown Tours & Cooking Classes
Gelateria
SAN MARCO MUSEUM
Piazza di San Marco
UNIVERSITY
ACCADEMIA (DAVID)
MUSEUM OF PRECIOUS STONES
LEONARDO MUSEUM
MEDICI-RICCARDI PALACE
ROTUNDA
Piazza Brunelleschi
PALAZZO PUCCI
LEONARDO MUSEUM
HOSPITAL
DUOMO SIGHTS TICKET OFFICE
BAPTISTERY
DUOMO
DUOMO MUSEUM
Piazza di Santa Maria Nuova
Piazza del Duomo
CAMPANILE
CANONICA
SANTA MARIA DE' RICCI
OPERA DEL DUOMO STUDIO
CASA DI DANTE
S. MARIA
LA BADIA
BARGELLO MUSEUM
Piazza G. Salvemini
POST
CASA BUONARROTI
Piazza della Signoria
Piazza S. Firenze
LOGGIA
WC
PALAZZO VECCHIO
UFFIZI GALLERY
EXIT
Piazza Santa Croce
Piazza Peruzzi
SANTA CROCE
PAZZI CHAPEL
LIBRARY
Piazza Giudici
Piazza Mentana
GALILEO SCIENCE MUSEUM
VIA VENTISETTE APRILE
VIA ARAZZIERI
VIA GIORGIO LA PIRA
VIA SANTA REPARATA
VIA SAN GALLO
CAVOUR
VIA GUELFA
VIA DE' GINORI
VIA RICASOLI
V. D. ALFANI
VIA DEI SERVI
VIA DEI PUCCI
VIA BIFFI
VIA MARTELLI
VIA M. BUFALINI
VIA DELL'ORIUOLO
VIA DELL'OCHE
BONIZZI
STUDIO
VIA CALZAIUOLI
VIA DEL CORSO
PRESTO
VIA DEL PROCONSOLO
B. D. ALBIZI
V. DE' GIRALDI
VIA PIETRAPIANA
V. DE' PANDOLFINI
VIA PALMIERI
VIA DELL'ULIVO
VIA DELL'AGNOLO
V. TAVO.
VIA D. ALIGHIERI
CERCHI
CIMATORI
MAGAZZINI
CONDOTTA
VIA GHIBELLINA
VIA G. VERDI
VIA DE' PEPI
VIA DELLA VIGNA VECCHIA
VIA BURELLA
V. DELL'ANGUILLARA
STINCHE
VIA BENTA.
VERRAZZANO
VIA DEL FICO
GONDI
BORGO DE' GRECI
VIA LEONI
CORNO
VINEGIA
MAGALOTTI
RUSTICI
BENCI
BRACHE
CASTELLANI
CASTELLO
OSTERIA
VIA DEI NERI
MOSCA
BORGO S. CROCE
SAPONAI
VAGELLAI
MALENCHINI
VIA D.
CORSO TINTORI
LUNG. GEN. DIAZ

SLEEPING

Most of my recommended hotels are grouped in central Florence, to either side of the River Arno. Around the big sights you'll find tourist-friendly options, just steps away from everything you came to Florence to see. And across the Arno in the Oltrarno area—between the Pitti Palace and Ponte Vecchio—good budget alternatives dot an area with a neighborly vibe. If arriving by train, you can either walk (usually around 10-20 minutes) or take a taxi (roughly €6-8) to reach most of my recommended accommodations.

Florence is notorious for its mosquitoes. If your hotel lacks air-conditioning, request a fan and don't open your windows, especially at night. Many hotels furnish a small plug-in bulb *(zanzariere)*—usually set in the ashtray—to keep the blood-suckers at bay. If not, you can purchase one cheaply at any pharmacy *(farmacia)*.

Near the Duomo

While touristy—and expensive—this location puts just about everything at your doorstep.

$$$$ Hotel Duomo's 24 rooms are modern and comfortable enough, but you're paying for the location and the views—the Duomo looms like a monster outside the hotel's windows. If staying here, you might as well spring the extra €20 for a "superior" room with a view (RS%, air-con, historic elevator, Piazza del Duomo 1, fourth floor, tel. 055-219-922, **www.hotelduomofirenze.it, info@hotelduomofirenze.it**; Paolo, Gilvaneide, and Federico).

$$$ Residenza Giotto B&B offers a well-priced chance to stay on Florence's upscale shopping drag, Via Roma. Occupying the top floor of a 19th-century building, this place has six bright rooms (three with Duomo views) and a terrace with knockout views of the Duomo's tower. Reception is generally open Mon-Sat 9:00-17:00 and Sun 9:00-13:00; let them know your arrival time in advance (RS%, air-con, elevator, Via Roma 6, tel. 055-214-593, www.residenzagiotto.it, info@residenzagiotto.it, Giorgio).

North of the Duomo

Near the Accademia

$$$ Hotel dei Macchiaioli offers 15 fresh and spacious rooms on one high-ceilinged, noble floor in a restored palazzo owned for generations by a well-to-do Florentine family. You'll eat breakfast under original frescoed ceilings while enjoying modern comforts (RS%, air-con, Via Cavour 21, tel. 055-213-154, www.hoteldeimacchiaioli.com, info@hoteldeimacchiaioli.com, helpful Francesca and Paolo).

$$$ Residenza dei Pucci rents 13 pleasant rooms (each one different) spread over three floors (with no elevator). The decor, a mix of soothing earth tones and aristocratic furniture, makes this place feel upscale for this price range (RS%—use code "RICK," family rooms, air-con, reception open 9:00-20:00, shorter hours off-season—let them know if you'll arrive late, Via dei Pucci 9, tel. 055-281-886, www.residenzadeipucci.com, info@residenzadeipucci.com, friendly Rossella and Marina).

$$$ Hotel Morandi alla Crocetta, a former convent, envelops you in a 16th-century cocoon. Located on a quiet street with 12 rooms, its period furnishings, squeaky clean parquet floors, and original frescoes take you back a few centuries and up a few social classes (family rooms, air-con, elevator, pay parking—reserve ahead, a block off Piazza S.S. Annunziata at Via Laura 50, tel. 055-234-4747, www.hotelmorandi.it, welcome@hotelmorandi.it, well-run by Maurizio, Rolando, and Cristiano).

$$$ Hotel Europa, family run since 1970, has a welcoming atmosphere fostered by cheery Miriam and Roberto. The breakfast room is large, and most of the 12 bright, simple rooms have views of the Duomo, including one with a terrace (RS%, family rooms, air-con, elevator, Via Cavour 14, tel. 055-239-6715, www.webhoteleuropa.com, firenze@webhoteleuropa.com).

Near the Medici Chapels

This touristy zone has lots of budget and midrange hotels, stacks of basic trattorias, and easy access to major sights. The mostly pedestrianized Via Faenza is the spine of this neighborhood, with lots of tourist services.

$$$$ Hotel Centrale is indeed central, just a short walk from the Duomo. The 35 spacious but overpriced rooms—with a tasteful mix of old and new decor—are over a businesslike conference center (RS%, air-con, elevator, Via dei Conti 3, check in at big front desk on ground floor, tel. 055-215-761, www.hotelcentralefirenze.it, info@hotelcentralefirenze.it, Margherita and Roberto).

$$$ Hotel Accademia has 21 newly renovated rooms in a well-located 14th-century mansion. Linger on its interior terrace or curl up with a book in its cozy reading room (air-con, nearby pay parking, Via Faenza 7, tel. 055-290-993, www.hotelaccademiafirenze.com, info@hotelaccademiafirenze).

East of the Duomo

While convenient to the sights and offering a good value, these places are located mostly along nondescript urban streets, lacking the grit, appeal, or glitz of other neighborhoods.

$$$ Residenza il Villino has 10 charming rooms and a picturesque, peaceful little courtyard. The owner, Neri, has turned part of the breakfast room into a museum-like tribute to his grandfather, a pioneer of early Italian fashion. As it's in a "little villa" (as the name implies) set back from the street, this is a quiet refuge from the bustle of Florence (RS%, family rooms, air-con, parking available, just north of Via degli Alfani at Via della Pergola 53, tel. 055-200-1116, www.ilvillino.it, info@ilvillino.it).

$$$ Panella's Residence, once a convent and today part of owner Graziella's extensive home, is a classy B&B, with five chic, romantic, and ample rooms, antique furnishings, and historic architectural touches (RS%, air-con, Via della Pergola 42, tel. 055-234-7202, mobile 345-972-1541, www.panellaresidence.com, panella_residence@yahoo.it).

$ Hotel Dalí has 10 cheery, worn rooms in a nice location for a great price.

Florence Hotels
To Fortezza da Basso
PALAZZO DEI CONGRESSI
PALAZZO DEGLI AFFARI
VIA VALFONDA
VIA CENNINI
CONSERVATORIO DI FULIGNO
CENACOLO DI FULIGNO
VIA GUELFA
Piazza della Indipendenza
300 Meters
300 Yards
VIA LUIGI ALAMANNI
Piazza Adua
VIA FIUME
VIA FAENZA
VIA NAZIONALE
VIA DELL' ARIENTO
MERCATO CENTRALE
Piazza del Mercato Centrale
SANTA MARIA NOVELLA TRAIN STATION
Largo Alinari
Piazza della Stazione
PALAZZO DEI CARTELLONI
VIA S. ANTONINO
V. AMARINO
BORGO LA NOCE
BUS STATION
VIA DEGLI AVELLI
Piazza dell'Unità Italiana
V. DEI MELARANCIO
SAN LORENZO
MEDICI CHAPELS
MAIN TOURIST INFO
VIA DELLA SCALA
SANTA MARIA NOVELLA
VIA PANZANI
DEL GIGLIO
V. DELL' ALLORO
VIA DE' CONTI
LAURENT. MEDICI LIBRARY
ZANNETTI
VIA DE' CANACCI
BENEDETTA
VIA PALAZZUOLO
SANTA MARIA NOVELLA PERFUMERY
Piazza di Santa Maria Novella
VIA D. BELLE DONNE
VIA DEI BANCHI
VIA DE' CERRETANI
RONDINELLI
SANTA MARIA MAGGIORE
TREBBIO
OGNISSANTI
BORGO OGNISSANTI
VIA DELLA PORCELLANA
VIA DI PAOLINO
LOGGIA DI SAN PAOLO
ANTINORI
SAN GAETANO
V. PESC.
VIA PECORI
VIA DE' TORN.
GIAC.
VIA CORSI
V. DE' VECCHIETTI
BRUNELLESCHI
Piazza d'Ognissanti
VIA DEL FOSSI
VIA DEL SOLE
VIA D. SPADA
VIA D. STROZZI
STROZZI PALACE
Piazza della Repubblica
ARCH
V. ANSELMI
INFERNO
PURGATORIO
MONALDA
SASSETTI
POST
V. PELLICCERIA
Piazza de' Davanzati
SANTA TRINITÀ
Piazza di Santa Trinità
V. PORTA ROSSA
MERCATO NUOVO
BORGO
BOMBARDE
V. DELLE TERME
S. S. APOSTOLI
VIA POR S. MARIA
PONTE S. TRINITÀ
L. ACCIAIUOLI
Arno River
Piazza de' Frescobaldi
SAN JACOPO
PONTE VECCHIO
BORGO SAN JACOPO
V. SPRONE
To Pitti Palace
1 Hotel Duomo
2 Residenza Giotto B&B
3 Hotel dei Macchiaioli
4 Residenza dei Pucci
5 Hotel Morandi alla Crocetta
6 Hotel Europa
7 Hotel Centrale
8 Hotel Accademia
9 Residenza il Villino
10 Panella's Residence
11 Hotel Dalí
12 Oblate Sisters of the Assumption
13 In Piazza della Signoria B&B
14 B&B Il Bargello
15 Hotel Maxim
16 Hotel Davanzati
17 Hotel Torre Guelfa
18 Relais Ufizzi

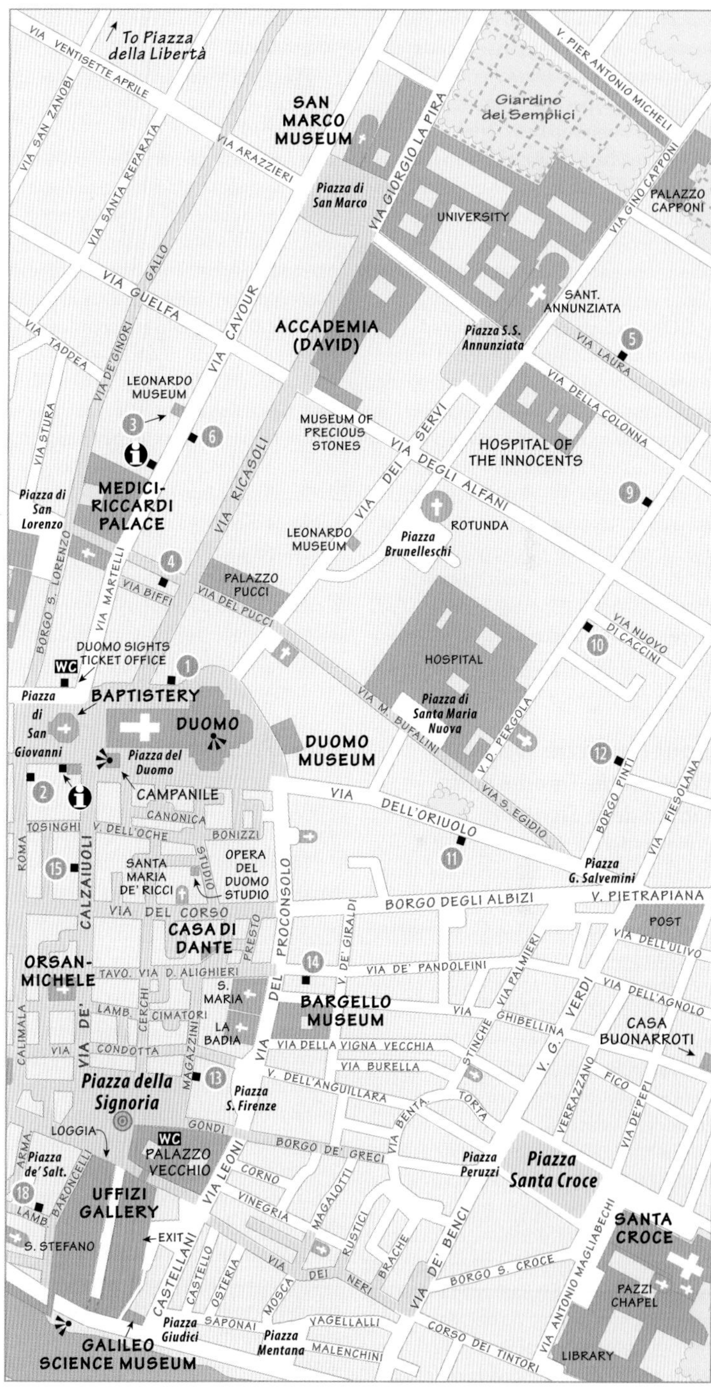
To Piazza della Libertà
VIA VENTISETTE APRILE
VIA SAN ZANOBI
VIA SANTA REPARATA
VIA ARAZZIERI
SAN MARCO MUSEUM
Piazza di San Marco
VIA GIORGIO LA PIRA
Giardino dei Semplici
V. PIER ANTONIO MICHELI
VIA GINO CAPPONI
PALAZZO CAPPONI
UNIVERSITY
VIA GUELFA
GALLO
VIA CAVOUR
ACCADEMIA (DAVID)
SANT. ANNUNZIATA
Piazza S.S. Annunziata
VIA LAURA
VIA TADDEA
VIA DE' GINORI
LEONARDO MUSEUM
VIA STURA
MUSEUM OF PRECIOUS STONES
VIA DELLA COLONNA
HOSPITAL OF THE INNOCENTS
VIA RICASOLI
VIA DEI SERVI
VIA DEGLI ALFANI
MEDICI-RICCARDI PALACE
Piazza di San Lorenzo
ROTUNDA
Piazza Brunelleschi
LEONARDO MUSEUM
BORGO S. LORENZO
VIA MARTELLI
VIA BIFFI
PALAZZO PUCCI
VIA DEL PUCCI
VIA NUOVO DI CACCINI
DUOMO SIGHTS TICKET OFFICE
WC
HOSPITAL
Piazza di San Giovanni
BAPTISTERY
DUOMO
Piazza di Santa Maria Nuova
VIA M. BUFALINI
V. D. PERGOLA
DUOMO MUSEUM
Piazza del Duomo
CAMPANILE
VIA DELL'ORIUOLO
VIA S. EGIDIO
BORGO PINTI
VIA FIESOLANA
CANONICA
TOSINGHI
V. DELL'OCHE
BONIZZI
ROMA
SANTA MARIA DE' RICCI
OPERA DEL DUOMO STUDIO
STUDIO
CALZAIUOLI
Piazza G. Salvemini
VIA DEL CORSO
PROCONSOLO
BORGO DEGLI ALBIZI
V. PIETRAPIANA
POST
CASA DI DANTE
PRESTO
VIA DE' GIRALDI
VIA DELL'ULIVO
ORSANMICHELE
TAVO.
VIA D. ALIGHIERI
VIA DE' PANDOLFINI
VIA PALMIERI
S. MARIA
LA BADIA
VIA DEL
BARGELLO MUSEUM
VIA DELL'AGNOLO
V. G. VERDI
CALIMALA
VIA DE'
LAMB.
CERCHI
CIMATORI
VIA GHIBELLINA
CASA BUONARROTI
VIA CONDOTTA
MAGAZZINI
VIA DELLA VIGNA VECCHIA
VIA BURELLA
STINCHE
Piazza della Signoria
Piazza S. Firenze
V. DELL'ANGUILLARA
VIA BENTA
TORTA
VERRAZZANO
FICO
VIA DE' PEPI
LOGGIA
GONDI
ARMA.
Piazza de' Salt.
PALAZZO VECCHIO
BORGO DE' GRECI
Piazza Peruzzi
Piazza Santa Croce
VIA LEONI
CORNO
BARONCELLI
UFFIZI GALLERY
VINEGRIA
MAGALOTTI
LAMB.
EXIT
S. STEFANO
RUSTICI
VIA DE' BENCI
SANTA CROCE
VIA ANTONIO MAGLIABECHI
CASTELLANI
CASTELLO
OSTERIA
VIA MOSCA
DEI NERI
BRACHE
BORGO S. CROCE
PAZZI CHAPEL
Piazza Giudici
SAPONAI
Piazza Mentana
VAGELLALLI
MALENCHINI
CORSO DEI TINTORI
GALILEO SCIENCE MUSEUM
LIBRARY

Samanta and Marco, who run this guest-house with a charming passion and idealism, are a delight to know (request one of the quiet and spacious rooms facing the courtyard when you book, cheaper rooms with shared bath available, nearby apartments sleep 2-6 people, no breakfast, fans but no air-con, elevator, free parking, 2 blocks behind the Duomo at Via dell'Oriuolo 17 on second floor, tel. 055-234-0706, www.hoteldali.com, hoteldali@tin.it).

$ Oblate Sisters of the Assumption run an institutional 30-room hotel in a Renaissance building with a dreamy garden, great public spaces, appropriately simple rooms, and a quiet, prayerful ambience (family rooms, single beds only, air-con, elevator, Wi-Fi with suggested donation, 23:30 curfew, limited pay parking—request when you book, Borgo Pinti 15, tel. 055-248-0582, www.bb-oblate.com, sroblateborgopinti@virgilio.it). As there's no night porter, it's best to time your arrival and departure to occur during typical business hours.

South of the Duomo

Between the Duomo and Piazza della Signoria

Buried in the narrow, characteristic lanes in the heart of town, these are the most central of my recommendations (and therefore a little overpriced). While this location can be worth the extra cost, nearly every hotel I recommend is conveniently located, given Florence's walkable, essentially traffic-free core.

$$$$ In Piazza della Signoria B&B, in a stellar location overlooking Piazza della Signoria, is peaceful, refined, and homey. The service is friendly, but the rates are high. The "partial view" rooms, while slightly larger, require craning your neck to see anything—not worth the extra euros. Guests enjoy socializing at the big, shared breakfast table (RS%, family apartments, air-con, tiny elevator, Via dei Magazzini 2, tel. 055-239-9546, mobile 348-321-0565, www.inpiazzadellasignoria.com, info@inpiazzadellasignoria.com, Sonia and Alessandro).

$$$ Hotel Maxim, run by the Maoli family since 1981, has 26 straightforward rooms in a good location on the main pedestrian drag. Its narrow, painting-lined halls and cozy lounge have old Florentine charm (RS%—use code "RICK," family rooms, air-con, elevator, Via de' Calzaiuoli 11, tel. 055-217-474, www.hotelmaximfirenze.it, reservation@hotelmaximfirenze.it, Chiara).

$$ B&B Il Bargello is a home away from home, run by friendly and helpful Canadian expat Gabriella. Hike up three long flights (no elevator) to reach six smart, relaxing rooms, a cozy living room, and a communal kitchenette, along with an inviting rooftop terrace with close-up views of Florence's towers (RS%, fully equipped apartment across the hall sleeps up to six; air-con, 20 yards off Via Proconsolo at Via de' Pandolfini 33 black, tel. 055-215-330, mobile 339-175-3110, www.firenze-bedandbreakfast.it, info@firenze-bedandbreakfast.it).

Near Ponte Vecchio

This sleepy zone is handy to several sights and some fine shopping streets, though it lacks a neighborhood feel of its own.

$$$$ Hotel Davanzati, bright and shiny with artistic touches, has 25 cheerful rooms with all the comforts. It's a family affair, thoughtfully run by friendly Tommaso and father Fabrizio, who offer drinks and snacks each evening at their candlelit happy hour, plus lots of other extras (RS%, family rooms, free tablets in every room, air-con, 20 steep steps to the elevator, handy room fridges, next to Piazza Davanzati at Via Porta Rossa 5—easy to miss so watch for low-profile sign above the door, tel. 055-286-666, www.hoteldavanzati.it, info@hoteldavanzati.it).

$$$$ Hotel Torre Guelfa has grand public spaces and is topped by a fun medieval tower with a panoramic rooftop terrace (72 stairs take you up—and back 720 years). Its 31 pricey rooms vary wildly in size and furnishings, but most come with the noise of the city center. Room 315, with a private terrace, is worth reserving several months in advance (RS%, family rooms, air-con, elevator, a couple of blocks northwest of Ponte Vecchio, Borgo S.S. Apostoli 8, tel. 055-239-6338, www.hoteltorreguelfa.com, info@hoteltorreguelfa.com, Niccolo and Barbara).

$$$$ Relais Uffizi is a peaceful little gem, offering a friendly welcome and a tight maze of 15 classy rooms tucked away down a tiny alley off Piazza della Signoria. The lounge has a huge window overlooking the action in the square below (family rooms, air-con, elevator; official address is Chiasso del Buco 16—from the square, go down tiny Chiasso de Baroncelli lane—right of the loggia—and after 50 yards turn right through the arch and look for entrance on your right; tel. 055-267-6239, www.relaisuffizi.it, info@relaisuffizi.it, charming Alessandro and Elizabetta).

TRANSPORTATION

Getting Around Florence

I organize my sightseeing geographically and do it all on foot. Think of Florence as a Renaissance treadmill—it requires a lot of walking.

By Bus

The city's full-size buses don't cover the old center well (the whole area around the Duomo is off-limits to motorized traffic). To visit outlying sights, pick up a map of transit routes at the ATAF windows at the train station (TIs do not have them); you'll also find routes online (www.ataf.net). Of the many bus lines, I find these the most helpful:

Bus **#12** goes from the train station over the Carraia bridge to Porta Romana, then up to San Miniato Church and Piazzale Michelangelo. Bus #13 makes the return trip down the hill.

The train station and Piazza San Marco are two major hubs near the city center; to get between these two, either walk (about 15 minutes) or take bus #1, #6, #14, #17, or #23.

Minibuses run every 10 minutes from 7:00 to 21:00 (less frequent on Sun), winding through the town center and up and down the river—just €1.20 gets you a 1.5-hour joyride. These buses also connect many major parking lots with the historic center (buy tickets from machines at lots).

Bus #C1 stops behind the Palazzo Vecchio and Piazza Santa Croce, then heads north, passing near the Accademia before ending up at Piazza Libertà.

Bus #C2 twists through the congested old center from the train station, passing near Piazza della Repubblica and Piazza della Signoria to Piazza Beccaria.

Bus #C3 goes up and down the Arno River, with stops near Piazza Santa Croce, Ponte Vecchio, the Carraia bridge to the Oltrarno (including Pitti Palace), and beyond.

Bus #D goes from the train station to Ponte Vecchio, cruises through the Oltrarno (passing Pitti Palace), and finishes in the San Niccolò neighborhood at Ponte San Niccolò.

Buying Bus Tickets: Buy bus tickets at tobacco shops *(tabacchi),* newsstands, or the ATAF ticket windows inside the train station. Validate your ticket in the machine on board (€1.20/90 minutes, €4.70/4 tickets, €5/24 hours, €12/3 days, €18/week, day passes aren't always available in tobacco shops, tel. 800-424-500, www.ataf.net). You can sometimes buy a ticket on board, but you'll pay more (€2) and you'll need exact change.

By Taxi

The minimum cost for a taxi ride is €5 (€8.30 after 22:00, €7 on Sun); rides in the center of town should be charged as tariff #1. A taxi ride from the train station to the Duomo costs about €8. Taxi fares and supplements (e.g., €2 extra to a cab rather than hail one) are clearly explained on signs in each taxi. Look for an official, regulated cab (white; marked with *Taxi/Comune di Firenze,* red fleur-de-lis, and one of the official phone numbers: 4390 or 4242). Before getting in a cab, mention your destination and ask for an approximate cost (*"Più o meno, quanto costa?"* pew oh MEH-noh, KWAHN-toh KOH-stah). If you can't get a straight answer or the price is outrageous, walk away. It can be hard to find a cab on the street; call 055-4390 or 055-4242 to summon one, or have your hotelier or restaurateur call for you. Uber does not operate in Florence.

Arriving and Departing

Florence is Tuscany's transportation hub, with fine train, bus, and plane connections to virtually anywhere in Italy.

By Train

Florence's main train station is called **Santa Maria Novella** (*Firenze S.M.N.* on schedules and signs). The city also has two suburban train stations: **Firenze Rifredi** and **Firenze Campo di Marte.** Note that some trains don't stop at the main station—before boarding, confirm that you're heading for S.M.N., or you may overshoot the city. (If this happens, don't panic; the other stations are a short taxi ride from the center.)

Rick's Tip: **Don't trust "porters"** *who want to help carry your bags (they're not official), and politely decline offers of help using the ticket machines by anyone other than uniformed staff.*

To orient yourself to Santa Maria Novella Station, stand with your back to the tracks. Look left to see the green cross of a 24-hour pharmacy (*farmacia*) and the exit to the taxi queue. **Baggage storage** (*deposito bagagli*) is also to the left, halfway down track 16 (long hours daily, passport required). **Fast-food outlets** and a **bank** are also along track 16. Directly ahead of you is the main hall (*salone biglietti*), where you can buy train and bus tickets. **Pay WCs** are to the right, near the head of track 5.

To reach the **TI,** walk away from the tracks and exit the station; it's straight across the square, 100 yards away, by the stone church.

To buy **ATAF city bus tickets,** stop at windows #8-9 in the main hall—and ask for a transit map while you're there (TIs don't have them).

Getting to the Duomo and City Center: Orienting yourself with your back to the tracks, the Duomo and town center are to your left. Out the doorway to the left, you'll find city buses and the taxi stand. Taxis cost about €6-8 to the Duomo. If you'd rather walk (10-15 minutes), exit the station straight ahead through the main hall, and head straight across the square outside, toward the Church of Santa Maria Novella (and the TI). On the far side of the square, keep left and head down the main Via dei Panzani, which leads directly to the Duomo.

TRAIN CONNECTIONS

For travel within Italy, there's no reason to stand in line at a ticket window. It's quickest and easiest to buy tickets online; with a smartphone app, you can even purchase them minutes before the train departs. If you decide to buy tickets at the station, take advantage of the ticket (*biglietto*)

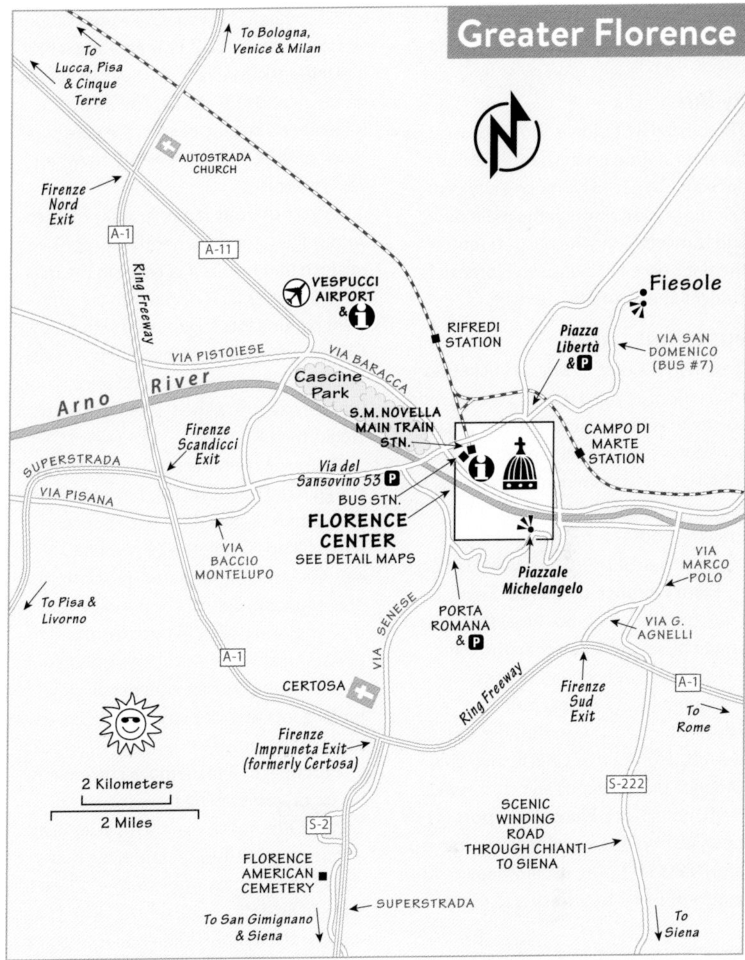

machines that display schedules, issue tickets, and make reservations for rail-pass holders.

There are two train companies: **Trenitalia,** with most connections (toll tel. 892-021, www.trenitalia.it) and **Italo,** with high-speed routes (no rail passes accepted, tel. 06-0708, www.italotreno.it). Both companies have bright red self-service machines, so be sure you use the right one. For Trenitalia information, use window #18 or #19 (take a number). For Italo information, use window #10 or #11, or visit their main office, opposite track 5, near the exit

From Florence by Train to: Pisa (2-3/hour, 45-75 minutes), **Lucca** (2/hour, 1.5 hours), **Siena** (direct trains hourly, 1.5-2 hours; bus is better because Siena's train station is far from the center), **Milan** (Trenitalia: hourly, 2 hours; Italo: 2/hour, 2 hours), **Venice** (Trenitalia: hourly, 2-3 hours, may transfer in Bologna; often crowded—reserve ahead; Italo: 4/day, 2 hours), **Assisi** (8/day direct, 2-3 hours), **Orvieto** (hourly, 2 hours, some with change in Campo di Marte or Rifredi Station), **Rome** (Trenitalia: 2-3/hour, 1.5 hours, most require seat reservations;

Italo: 2/hour, 1.5 hours), **Naples** (Trenitalia: hourly, 3 hours; Italo: hourly, 3 hours).

By Bus

The BusItalia Station is 100 yards west of the train station on Via Santa Caterina da Siena. To get to Florence's city center, exit the station through the main door, and turn left along the busy street toward the brick dome. Downtown Florence is straight ahead and to the right.

BUS CONNECTIONS

Generally it's best to buy bus tickets in the station, as you'll pay 30 percent more to buy tickets onboard. The bus posts schedules for regional trips, and video monitors show imminent departures. Bus service drops dramatically on Sunday. Bus info: tel. 800-373-760 (Mon-Fri 9:00-15:00, closed Sat-Sun), www.fsbusitalia.it.

From Florence by Bus to: Siena (roughly 2/hour, 1.5-hour *rapida/via superstrada* buses are faster than the train, avoid the slower *ordinaria* buses, www.sienamobilita.it), **Montepulciano** (1-2/day, 2 hours, change in Bettolle, LFI bus, www.lfi.it; or train to Chiusi, then Siena Mobilità bus to Montepulciano, www.sienamobilita.it), **Florence airport** (2/hour, 30 minutes, pay driver and immediately validate ticket, usually departs from platform 1, first bus departs at 5:30).

By Car

The autostrada has several exits for Florence. Get off at the Nord, Scandicci, Impruneta (formerly Certosa), or Sud exits and follow signs toward—but not into—the *Centro*.

Don't even attempt driving into the city center. Instead, park on the outskirts and take a bus, tram, or taxi in. Florence's traffic-reduction system is baffling even to locals. Every car passing into the "limited traffic zone" (*Zona Traffico Limitato,* or ZTL) is photographed; those who don't have a permit get a €100 ticket in the mail (with an "administrative" fee from the rental company). If you have a reservation at a hotel within the ZTL area—and it has parking—ask in advance if they can get you permission to enter town. The ZTL zone is Florence's historic center (the core plus much of the Oltrarno)—nearly anywhere you'd want to go.

Using **bus-only lanes** (usually marked with yellow stripes) is another expensive mistake that results in a ticket in the mail.

The city center is ringed with big, efficient **parking lots** (signposted with a big *P*). Check www.firenzeparcheggi.it for details on parking lots, availability, and prices. From the freeway, follow the signs to *Centro,* then *Stadio,* then *P.*

If arriving from the north, park at **Parcheggio del Parterre,** just beyond Piazza della Libertà. They have 600 spots and never fill up completely (€2/hour, €12/day, €70/week, automated, pay with cash or credit card, open 24 hours daily, tel. 055-500-1994). To get into town, find the taxi stand at the elevator exit, or ride one of the minibuses that connect all major parking lots with the city center (see www.ataf.net for routes).

Parcheggio Sansovino, a convenient lot for drivers coming from the south, is on the Oltrarno side of the river, right at a tram stop (€1/hour, €12/day, 24 hours daily, Via Sansovino 53—from A-1 take the Firenze Scandicci exit, tel. 055-363-362, www.scaf.fi.it). Park, then ride four quick stops to Santa Maria Novella Station.

By Plane

Amerigo Vespucci Airport, also called Peretola Airport, is about five miles northwest of the city (open 4:00-24:30, no overnighting allowed, has a TI, airport code: FLR, tel. 055-306-1830, www.aeroporto.firenze.it).

Shuttle buses (to the far right as you exit the arrivals hall) connect the airport with Florence's train and bus stations (2/hour until 22:00, then hourly until 00:30, 30 minutes, runs 5:00-00:30, €6—buy ticket on board and validate immediately).

If you're changing to a different intercity bus in Florence (for instance, one bound for Siena), stay on the bus through the first stop (at the train station); it will continue on to the bus station nearby. Allow about €25 and 30 minutes for a taxi.

The airport's **car rental** offices share one big parking lot just a three-minute drive away, but the streets around the airport are a dizzying maze, making it tricky to find the place to drop off your car. One option is to drive to the airport, wait for the rental-car shuttle bus to show up, then follow that bus to the lot.

By Private Car Service

For small groups with more money than time, hiring a private car service to zip comfortably to nearby towns can be a good value. Consider **Transfer Chauffeur Service** (tel. 338-862-3129, www.transfercs.com, marco.masala@transfercs.com, Marco) or **Prestige Rent** (office near Piazza della Signoria at Via Porta Rossa 6 red, tel. 055-398-6598, mobile 333-842-4047, www.prestigerent.com, usa@prestigerent.com, Saverio). Or you could simply hire a **taxi** after agreeing upon a rate (e.g., €120 from your Florence hotel to your Siena hotel).

BEST OF THE REST

PISA

For nearly three centuries (1000-1300), Pisa rivaled Venice and Genoa as a sea-trading power, exchanging European goods for luxury items in Muslim lands. The city used its sea-trading wealth to build the now-famous Leaning Tower. Many visitors are surprised to see that the iconic tower is only one part of a huge, gleaming white architectural complex, the "Campo dei Miracoli"—Field of Miracles.

Orientation

Pisa's three important sights—the Duomo, Baptistery, and Tower—float regally on the best lawn in Italy (no picnicking allowed). The style throughout is Pisa's very own Pisan Romanesque. Even as the church was being built in the 11th century, the area was nicknamed "the Field of Miracles" for the grandness of the undertaking.

Day Plan: Pisa is a touristic quickie. Seeing the famous Tower (reservations required), wandering through the Duomo, and visiting the other sights around "the Field of Miracles" can be done in a half-day.

Extend your visit with a leisurely one-hour stroll from the train station to the Tower and Field of Miracles. The two main streets for tourists and shoppers are Via Santa Maria (running south from the Tower) and Corso Italia/Borgo Stretto (running north from the station).

Getting There: Pisa is an easy day trip from Florence, whether coming by **train** (frequent departures, 45-75 minutes) or **car** (excellent highways). The city's close-in **Galileo Galilei Airport** handles both international and domestic flights (PSA, www.pisa-airport.com).

Arrival in Pisa: Most trains arrive at Pisa Centrale station, about a mile south of the Field of Miracles (baggage check—*deposito bagagli*—at far end of platform 1, after police station). To get to the Field of Miracles, you can **walk** for 30 minutes, take a **taxi** (€10), or go by **public bus** (LAM Rossa line, stops outside the main station entrance and to the right, buy a €1.20 bus ticket from the magazine kiosk in the station's main hall or any tobacco shop, or pay €2 on board). If your train stops at the smaller Pisa San Rossore Station, hop off; it's just a four-block walk from the Tower.

For a quick visit, **drivers** should park at the *Parcheggio di Piazza dei Miracoli* lot, just northwest of the tower (€2/hour, enter from Via Giovanni Battista Niccolini). From here, the tower is practically across the street. Otherwise, leave cars at the big parking lot on Via Pietrasantina—exit the autostrada at *Pisa Nord* and follow signs to *Pisa* (on the left), then *Bus Parking*; from the lot, catch the LAM Rossa bus to the Field of Miracles.

From the airport, take the Pisa Mover train to Pisa Centrale train station (then LAM Rossa bus to Tower), or hop in a taxi (€10).

Tourist Information: The main TI is located on the Field of Miracles, next to the Duomo's ticket office (daily 9:30-17:30, until 15:30 off-season, Piazza Duomo 7, tel. 050-550-100, www.turismo.pisa.it). The TI offers baggage storage (€3-4), helpful for day-trippers. The airport also has a TI.

Private Guides: Good guides with similar rates (about €140/3 hours) are **Vincenzo Riolo** (mobile 338-211-2939, www.pisatour.it) and **Martina Manfredi** (mobile 328-898-2927, www.tuscanyatheart.it).

Sights

▲▲▲FIELD OF MIRACLES (CAMPO DEI MIRACOLI)

Scattered across a golf-course green lawn are five grand buildings: the cathedral (or Duomo), its bell tower (the Leaning Tower), the Baptistery, the hospital (today's Museum of the Sinopias), and the Camposanto Cemetery.

Architecturally, the Campo is unique and exotic. Traditionally, these buildings marked the main events of every Pisan's life: christened in the Baptistery, married in the Duomo, honored in ceremonies at the Tower, healed in the hospital, and buried in the cemetery.

▲▲▲LEANING TOWER

A 15-foot lean from the vertical makes the Tower one of Europe's most recognizable images. See it from the outside for free, or pay to climb to the top.

Cost and Hours: €18, kids under age 8 not allowed, daily April-Sept 8:00-20:00 (until 22:00 mid-June-Aug), Oct 9:00-19:00, Nov-Feb 10:00-17:00, March 9:00-18:00, one ticket office is behind the Leaning Tower and the other is at the Museum of the Sinopias (near the TI)—ticket office opens 30 minutes early, reservations necessary, www.opapisa.it.

Reservations: Entry to the tower is by a timed ticket good for a 30-minute visit. Every 15 minutes, 45 people can clamber up the 294 tilting steps to the top. Children ages 8-18 must be accompanied by—and stay at all times with—an adult. Be at the Tower 15 minutes before your entry time or you may not be allowed in.

Reserve your timed entry online or in person at either ticket office. **Online bookings** are accepted no earlier than 20 days and no later than one day in advance. Choose your entry time and buy your ticket at www.opapisa.it. Print out the voucher and bring it to the Tower no less than 15 minutes before your entry time.

To reserve in person, go to the **ticket office,** behind the Tower on the left (in the yellow building), or to the Museum of the Sinopias ticket office. You'll clearly see

The Leaning Tower

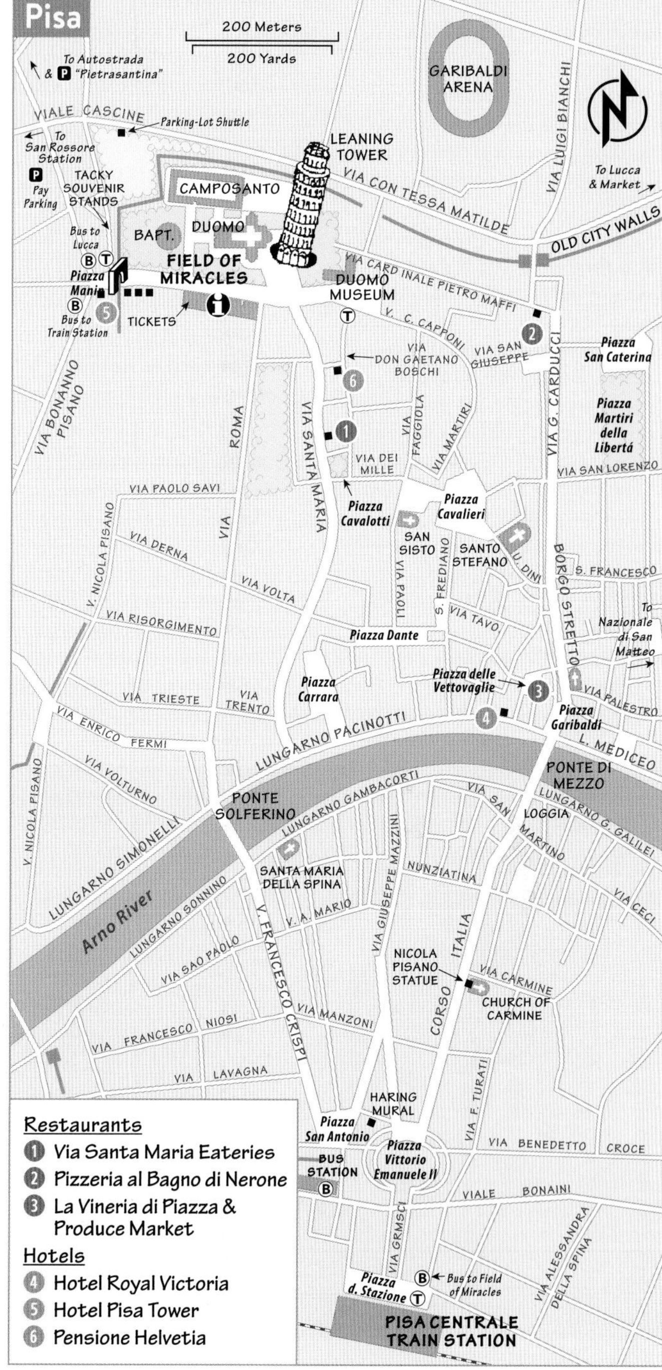
Pisa
200 Meters
200 Yards
To Autostrada & P "Pietrasantina"
VIALE CASCINE
Parking-Lot Shuttle
To San Rossore Station
P Pay Parking
TACKY SOUVENIR STANDS
Bus to Lucca
Piazza Manin
Bus to Train Station
TICKETS
CAMPOSANTO
BAPT.
DUOMO
FIELD OF MIRACLES
LEANING TOWER
GARIBALDI ARENA
VIA LUIGI BIANCHI
To Lucca & Market
VIA CON TESSA MATILDE
OLD CITY WALLS
VIA CARDINALE PIETRO MAFFI
DUOMO MUSEUM
V. C. CAPPONI
VIA SAN GIUSEPPE
VIA DON GAETANO BOSCHI
Piazza San Caterina
Piazza Martiri della Libertá
VIA G. CARDUCCI
VIA BONANNO PISANO
VIA ROMA
VIA SANTA MARIA
VIA FAGGIOLA
VIA MARTIRI
VIA DEI MILLE
VIA SAN LORENZO
VIA PAOLO SAVI
Piazza Cavalotti
Piazza Cavalieri
SAN SISTO
SANTO STEFANO
U. DINI
VIA DERNA
V. NICOLA PISANO
VIA VOLTA
VIA PAOLI
S. FREDIANO
VIA TAVO
BORGO STRETTO
S. FRANCESCO
To Nazionale di San Matteo
VIA RISORGIMENTO
Piazza Dante
Piazza delle Vettovaglie
Piazza Carrara
VIA TRIESTE
VIA TRENTO
VIA PALESTRO
Piazza Garibaldi
VIA ENRICO FERMI
LUNGARNO PACINOTTI
L. MEDICEO
PONTE DI MEZZO
VIA VOLTURNO
PONTE SOLFERINO
LUNGARNO GAMBACORTI
VIA SAN MARTINO
LOGGIA
LUNGARNO G. GALILEI
V. NICOLA PISANO
LUNGARNO SIMONELLI
SANTA MARIA DELLA SPINA
NUNZIATINA
VIA CECI
Arno River
LUNGARNO SONNINO
V. A. MARIO
VIA GIUSEPPE MAZZINI
V. FRANCESCO CRISPI
VIA SAO PAOLO
NICOLA PISANO STATUE
CORSO ITALIA
VIA CARMINE
CHURCH OF CARMINE
VIA MANZONI
VIA FRANCESCO NIOSI
VIA LAVAGNA
HARING MURAL
VIA F. TURATI
Piazza San Antonio
VIA BENEDETTO CROCE
BUS STATION
Piazza Vittorio Emanuele II
VIALE BONAINI
VIA GRMSCI
VIA ALESSANDRA DELLA SPINA
Piazza d. Stazione
Bus to Field of Miracles
PISA CENTRALE TRAIN STATION
Restaurants
1 Via Santa Maria Eateries
2 Pizzeria al Bagno di Nerone
3 La Vineria di Piazza & Produce Market
Hotels
4 Hotel Royal Victoria
5 Hotel Pisa Tower
6 Pensione Helvetia

(on reader boards above the ticket windows) when time slots are available.

Rick's Tip: **If you arrive without a reservation to climb the Tower,** *go straight to one of the ticket offices on the Field of Miracles to buy a ticket. Expect a 2-3-hour wait to ascend.*

Visiting the Tower: The Tower was built over two centuries by at least three different architects. It started to lean almost immediately after construction began in 1173. Just as the base and the first arcade were finished, someone said, "Is it just me, or does that look crooked?" The heavy Tower—resting on a shallow 13-foot foundation—was sinking on the south side into marshy, unstable soil. The builders carried on anyway. Several attempts were made over the centuries to stop its slow-motion fall, but it finally got so bad that in 1990 the Tower closed for 10 years of stabilizing repairs. Art historians figure it leans today as much as it did some 400 years ago, when Galileo reputedly conducted his gravity experiments here.

Even though your tower climb is technically a guided visit, the "guide" is a museum guard who makes sure you don't stay past your scheduled time. For your 30-minute time slot, figure about 10 minutes to climb, and 10 to descend. This leaves about 10 minutes for vertigo at the top.

When it's time for you to enter, gape up through the hollow Tower to the oculus at the top, and marvel at the acoustics. Then wind your way up along a spiraling ramp, climbing 294 stairs. At the top, you'll have fine views over the Duomo and the rest of the Field of Miracles.

▲▲DUOMO (CATHEDRAL)

Begun in 1063, the huge Pisan Romanesque Duomo is the centerpiece of the Field of Miracles' religious buildings. Budget some sightseeing time for the church's artistic and historic treasures, including Giovanni Pisano's early 14th-century marble pulpit, smothered with 400 intricately sculpted figures. A modest dress code is requested, but not really enforced.

Pisa's Duomo and the Field of Miracles

Cost and Hours: Free, but pick up an entry voucher at one of the nearby ticket offices (every 30 minutes, any combo-ticket or Tower ticket also acts as a Duomo voucher), daily April-Sept 10:00-20:00, shorter hours off-season.

MORE SIGHTS ON THE FIELD OF MIRACLES

The Baptistery, Camposanto Cemetery, Museum of the Sinopias, and Duomo Museum share the same pricing and schedule.

Cost and Hours: €5 for one sight, €7 for two sights, €8 includes all the sights; daily April-Sept 8:00-20:00, shorter hours off-season.

Visiting Field of Miracles Sights: The **Baptistery,** in front of the Duomo, is the biggest in Italy. It's interesting for its superb acoustics and another fine Pisano pulpit. The cloistered open-air courtyard of the **Camposanto Cemetery** (built in 1277), on the north side of the Field of Miracles, is surrounded by Gothic porticoes once decorated with frescoes; in the Middle Ages, important Pisans were buried here in ancient Roman sarcophagi. The **Museum of the Sinopias,** housed in a 13th-century hospital across from the Baptistery, features the preparatory sketches (sinopias) for the Camposanto's frescoes. The **Duomo Museum,** behind the Tower, is big on Pisan art, displaying treasures of the cathedral, paintings, silver, and sculptures (from the 12th to 14th centuries), as well as ancient Egyptian, Etruscan, and Roman artifacts. Note that this museum will likely be closed for renovation through 2018.

Eating

The **Via Santa Maria** tourist strip is pedestrianized and lined with touristy eateries, easy for grabbing a quick sandwich, pizza, or salad. **$$ Pizzeria al Bagno di Nerone** is a five-minute walk from the Tower (closed Tue, Largo Carlo Fedeli 26). If you're walking between the train station and the Tower, you could lunch at Piazza delle Vettovaglie, Pisa's historic market square, either at **$$ La Vineria di Piazza** trattoria (under the arcades) or by assembling a picnic from the sandwich shops and fruit-and-veggie stalls ringing the square.

Sleeping

If staying the night, consider the romantic **$$ Hotel Royal Victoria** (Lungarno Pacinotti 12, www.royalvictoria.it), the stately **$$ Hotel Pisa Tower** (Via Andrea Pisano 3, www.hotelpisatower.com), or the no-frills **$ Pensione Helvetia** (Via Don G. Boschi 31, www.pensionehelvetiapisa.com).

The Hill Towns of Central Italy

The sun-soaked hill towns of central Italy offer the quintessential Italian experience. Wispy cypress-lined driveways lead to fortified 16th-century farmhouses set in rolling fields, atmospheric *enoteche* serve famous wines alongside homemade pasta, and dusty old-timers warm the same bench day after day while soccer balls buzz around them like innocuous flies. Hill towns are best enjoyed by adapting to the pace of the countryside. Slow...down...and savor the delights that this region offers.

How in Dante's name does a traveler choose from Italy's hundreds of hill towns? I've listed my favorites. If you linger longer to explore, you're sure to find a favorite of your own. When sampling hill towns, spend the night if you can, as many towns can get mobbed by day-trippers.

THE HILL TOWNS IN 3 DAYS

Italy's best hill towns are Siena, Assisi, and Orvieto. They're each worth at least one full day and an overnight, and are accessible by train or bus.

Siena's main sight is the city itself. Its elegant Il Campo main square is a people-magnet, marked by a tall City Tower you can climb. The cathedral's eye-catching colorful facade draws you inside. The Duomo Museum and Pinacoteca gracefully exhibit graceful art for the pleasure of art lovers. Enjoy a sleepy medieval evening on the main square. Although you could day-trip from Florence, it's worth staying over: Evenings are magical here.

Assisi's old town has a half-day of sightseeing and another half-day of wonder. The essential sight is the Basilica of St. Francis. My self-guided Assisi Town Walk leads downhill to the basilica, where you can follow my self-guided tour.

The town of **Orvieto,** conveniently close to Rome, can be seen in a few hours. It's famous for its cathedral and Classico wine (tastings, anyone?). A 45-minute bus ride away, the tiny, neighboring hill village of **Civita** is nearly huggable.

With extra time (and a car): Visit the wineries of Montepulciano and Montalcino.

GETTING AROUND THE HILL TOWNS

The towns I recommend can all be connected by public transportation, though you can get around easier and quicker by car. If you want to explore this area further and be able to stop at any hill town that appeals to you along the way, a car is the better choice.

By Public Transit: Buses are often the best option. While trains link some towns, hills don't quite fit in the railroad plan. Train stations are likely to be in the valley

HILL TOWNS AT A GLANCE

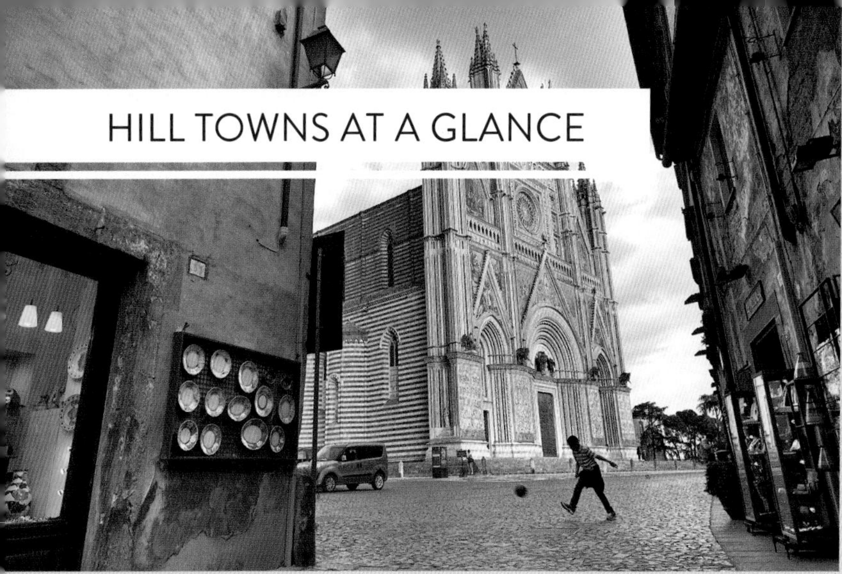

▲▲▲**Siena** Florence's smaller and (some say) more appealing rival, with its grand Il Campo square and striking striped cathedral. See page 225.

▲▲**Assisi** St. Francis' hometown, perched on a hillside, with a divinely Giotto-decorated basilica. See page 259.

▲▲**Orvieto and Civita** More hill-town adventures, featuring Orvieto's classic views and ornate cathedral, plus the adorable pocket-sized village of Civita di Bagnoregio. See pages 285 and 300.

▲**Montepulciano and Montalcino** Picturesque, wine-soaked villages of Italy's heartland. See page 251.

Hill Towns: Public Transportation

30 Kilometers
30 Miles

Rail
High Speed Rail
Bus

a couple of miles from the town center, connected by a local bus. If you're using public transit and are pinched for time, you may need to narrow your focus to just one town.

By Car: Pick up your rental car in the last sizable town you visit (Florence or Siena are good options) or at the nearest airport (to avoid big-city traffic). Carry a good, detailed road map in addition to any digital navigation systems. Superhighways (such as the toll autostrada and the non-toll *superstrada*) are the fastest way to connect two points, but smaller roads, including scenic S-222, which connects Florence and Siena, are more rewarding.

Parking can be challenging. Some towns don't allow visitors to park or even drive in the center. Signs reading *ZTL (Zona Traffico Limitato)*—often above a red circle—indicate no driving or parking allowed. Use a parking lot; identified by blue *P* signs, these are usually plentiful outside city walls (and sometimes linked to the town center by elevators or escalators). To minimize theft, avoid street parking. Your hotelier can also recommend parking options.

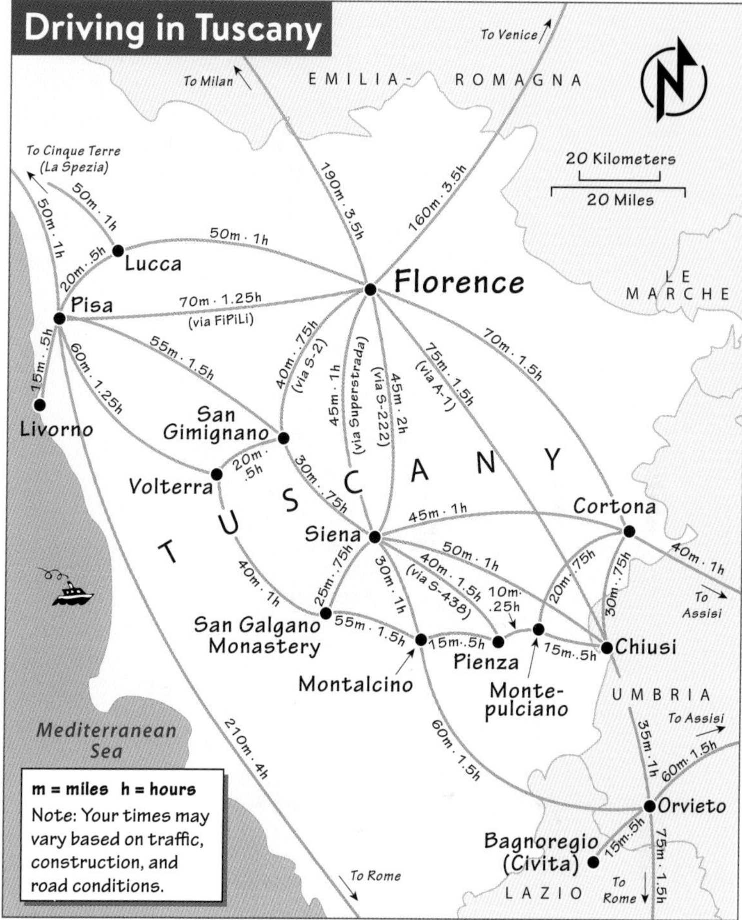

SIENA

Siena was medieval Florence's archrival. And while Florence ultimately won the battle for political and economic superiority, Siena still competes for the tourists. Florence has the heavyweight sights, but Siena seems to be every Italy connoisseur's favorite town.

From 1260-1348, Siena was a major trade center and military power in a class with Florence and Venice. In 1348, the Black Death—an epidemic of bubonic plague—hit Siena and cut the population by more than a third. The city never recovered. In the 1550s, Florence conquered the flailing city-state, forever rendering it a backwater. Siena's loss became our gain, as its political irrelevance pickled the city in a medieval brine.

Today, Siena is known for its thrilling Palio horse race and for its hometown saint, Catherine, but above all, for its ambience. Red-brick lanes cascade every which way, courtyards sport flower-decked wells, alleys dead-end at rooftop views, and the sky is a rich blue dome. Relax at a café on the main square. Wander narrow streets lined with colorful flags and studded with iron rings to

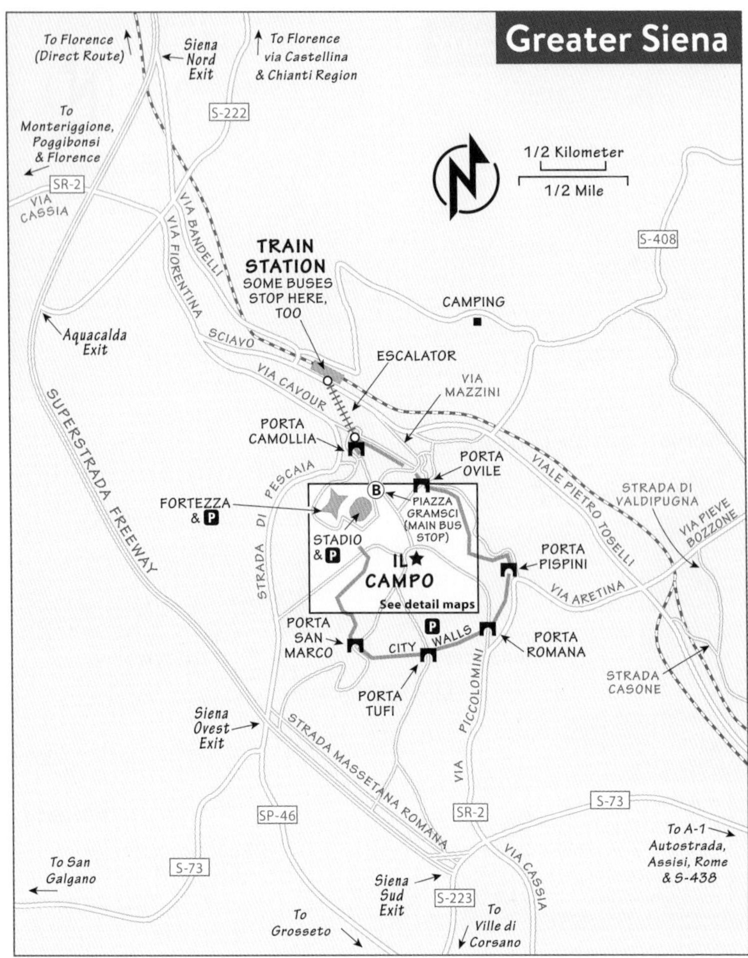

tether horses. While it may not have the blockbuster museums of Florence, Siena has soul.

Orientation

Siena lounges atop a hill, stretching its three legs out from Il Campo, the main square and historic meeting point of Siena's neighborhoods. Pedestrians rule here, as the only drivers allowed are residents and cabbies.

Just about everything worth seeing is within a 15-minute walk of the square. Navigate by three major landmarks—Il Campo, Duomo (cathedral), and Church of San Domenico—following the excellent system of street-corner signs. Most visitors stick to the Il Campo-San Domenico axis, but make it a point to stray from this main artery to explore. Sienese streets go in anything but a straight line, so it's easy to get lost—but just as easy to get found.

Siena's attractions come in two clusters: the square (Civic Museum and City Tower) and the Duomo (Baptistery and Duomo Museum, with its art and surprise viewpoint), plus the Pinacoteca for more art. Check off these sights, and you're free to wander.

Rick's Tip: Don't drive in Siena's city center. *If you drive or park anywhere marked Zona Traffico Limitato (ZTL), expect a* **hefty ticket** *in the mail back home.*

Sightseeing Passes: Siena always seems to be experimenting with different combo-tickets, but only a couple are worth considering:

The **€13 Opa Si Pass** includes the Duomo, Duomo Museum, Crypt, and Baptistery; the €20 **Opa Si Pass + Porta del Cielo** upgrade adds an escorted visit to the Duomo's dome and rooftop (valid three days; sold only at ticket office next to Santa Maria Della Scala).

A **€13 combo-ticket** covers the Civic Museum and Santa Maria della Scala; the €20 version adds the City Tower (valid two days).

Tourist Information: The TI is just across from the Duomo (daily 9:00-18:00, until 17:30 off-season; Piazza del Duomo 1, tel. 0577-280-551, www.enjoysiena.it). They hand out a few pretty booklets (including the regional *Terre di Siena* guide) and a free map. The bookshop next to the info desk sells more detailed Siena maps.

Laundry: Lavanderia Barbara is in the historic center (Mon-Fri 8:30-12:30 & 16:00-19:30, morning hours only Sat, closed Sun, near Porta Romana at Via Pantaneto 129, tel. 0577-289-501).

Travel Agency: Carroccio Viaggi sells train, plane, and some bus tickets for a small fee (Mon-Fri 9:00-12:30 & 15:30-19:00, Sat 9:30-12:00, closed Sun, Via Montanini 20, tel. 0577-226-964, www.carroccioviaggi.com, info@carroccioviaggi.com).

Tours: The **TI** offers walking tours of the old town. Guides usually conduct their walks in both English and Italian (€20, pay guide directly, daily April-Oct at 11:00, 2 hours, no interiors except for the Duomo, depart from TI, Piazza del Duomo 1, tel. 0577-280-551).

Tours by Roberto offers off-the-beaten-path minibus tours of the surrounding countryside (up to eight passengers, convenient pickup at hotel), arranges city walks, and offers multiday tours. Roberto's passions are Sienese culture, Tuscan history, and local cuisine (tour options explained on website, special Rick Steves discount prices: full-day minibus tours-€90/person, 4-hour off-season tours-€60/

Siena's main square, Il Campo

person, entry fees extra; booking mobile 320-147-6590, Roberto's mobile 328-425-5648, www.toursbyroberto.com, toursbyroberto@gmail.com).

➲ Siena City Walk

This short self-guided walk serves as a quick orientation, or can be used to lace together the most important sights. You could break the narration to tour City Hall, the Duomo, the Duomo Museum, and Santa Maria della Scala—all described in more detail later. If you don't plan on entering the sights, the walk works great at night when the city is peaceful.

🎧 Download my free Siena City Walk audio tour.

• *Start in the center of the main square, Il Campo, standing just below the fountain.*

IL CAMPO

This square is the geographic and metaphoric heart of Siena. It fans out from City Hall as if to create an amphitheater. Twice each summer, all eyes are on Il Campo when it hosts the famous Palio horse races (see page 243).

Originally, this area was just a field *(campo)* located outside the city walls, which encircled the Duomo. In the 1200s, with the advent of the Sienese republic, the city expanded. Il Campo became its marketplace and the historic junction of Siena's various competing *contrade* (neighborhood districts). The square and its buildings are the color of the soil upon which they stand—a color known to artists and Crayola users as "Burnt Sienna."

City Hall (Palazzo Pubblico), with its looming tower, dominates the square. In medieval Siena, this was the center of the city, and the whole focus of Il Campo still flows down to it.

The **City Tower** was built around 1340. At 330 feet, it's one of Italy's tallest secular towers. Medieval Siena was a proud republic, and this tower stands like an exclamation point—an architectural declaration of independence from papacy and empire. The open **chapel** located at the base of the tower was built in 1348 as thanks to God for ending the Black Death (after it killed more than a third of the population). These days, the chapel is used to bless Palio contestants (and to provide an open space for EMTs who stand by during the race).

You can visit the Civic Museum inside City Hall and climb the tower (see page 235).

• *Now turn around and take a closer look at the fountain in the top center of the square.*

FOUNTAIN OF JOY (FONTE GAIA)

This fountain—a copy of an early 15th-century work by Jacopo della Quercia—marks the square's high point. The joy is all about how the Sienese republic blessed its people with water. Find Lady Justice with her scales and sword (right of center), overseeing the free distribution of water to all. Imagine residents gathering here in the 1400s to fill their jugs. The Fountain of Joy still reminds locals that life in Siena is good. Notice the pigeons

City Hall and its tower

politely waiting their turn to tightrope gingerly down slippery spouts to slurp a drink from wolves' snouts. The relief panel on the left shows God creating Adam by helping him to his feet. It's said that this reclining Adam (carved a century before Michelangelo's day) influenced Michelangelo when he painted his Sistine Chapel ceiling. The original fountain is exhibited indoors at Santa Maria della Scala, opposite the Duomo.

• *Leave Il Campo uphill on the widest ramp. With your back to the tower, using an imaginary clock as a directional guide, it's at 10:00. After a few steps you reach Via di Città. Turn left and walk 100 yards uphill toward the imposing white palace.*

Halfway there, at the first corner, notice small plaques on the first level of the building facades—these mark the neighborhood, or **contrada**. *You are stepping from the* **contrada** *of the Forest (Selva) into the Eagle (Aquila). Notice also the once mighty and foreboding medieval tower house. Towers once soared all around town, but they're now truncated and no longer add to the skyline—look for their bases as you walk the city.*

On the left, you reach the big...

CHIGI-SARACINI PALACE (PALAZZO CHIGI-SARACINI)

This old fortified noble palace is today home to a prestigious music academy, the Accademia Musicale Chigiana. If it's open, step into the courtyard with its photogenic well. The walls of the loggia are decorated with the busts of Chigi-Saracini patriarchs, and the vaults are painted in the "grotesque" style popular during the Renaissance. The palace hosts a festival each July and August with popular concerts almost nightly, international talent, and affordable tickets (one-hour tours of the palace's library, art, and musical instruments cost €7 and run 2/day; box office just off courtyard, Via di Città 89, www.chigiana.it).

• *Continue up the hill on Via di Città to the next big intersection. As you walk, notice how strict rules protect the look of exteriors. Many families live in each building, but all shutters are the same color. Inside, apartments can be modern, and expensive—some of the priciest in Italy.*

QUATTRO CANTONI

The intersection known as Quattro Cantoni (the Four Corners) offers a fine perch

Fountain of Joy

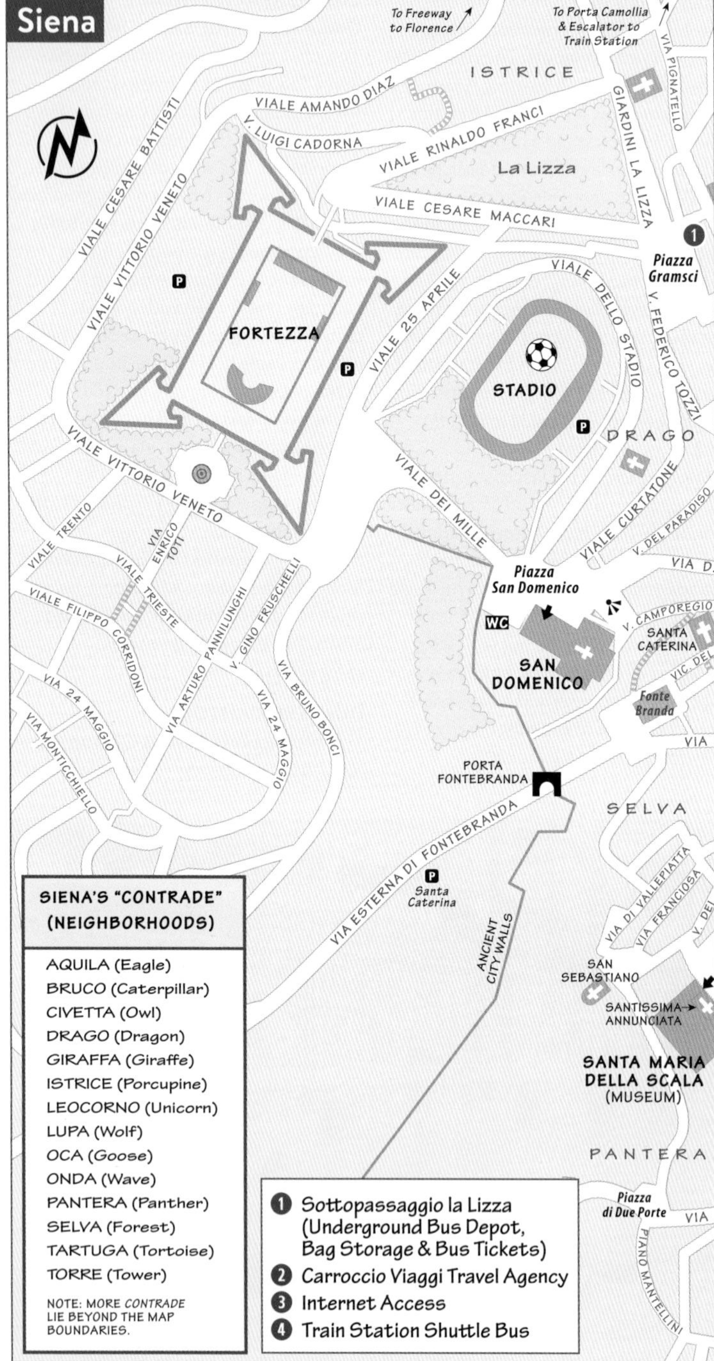
Siena
To Freeway to Florence
To Porta Camollia & Escalator to Train Station
ISTRICE
VIALE AMANDO DIAZ
V. LUIGI CADORNA
VIALE RINALDO FRANCI
La Lizza
GIARDINI LA LIZZA
VIA PIGNATELLO
VIALE CESARE MACCARI
VIALE CESARE BATTISTI
VIALE VITTORIO VENETO
FORTEZZA
VIALE 25 APRILE
Piazza Gramsci
VIALE DELLO STADIO
V. FEDERICO TOZZI
STADIO
DRAGO
VIALE DEI MILLE
VIALE CURTATONE
V. DEL PARADISO
VIA D.
Piazza San Domenico
WC
V. CAMPOREGIO
SANTA CATERINA
SAN DOMENICO
VIC. DEL
Fonte Branda
VIA
VIALE TRENTO
VIA ENRICO TOTI
VIALE TRIESTE
VIALE FILIPPO CORRIDONI
VIA ARTURO PANNILUNGHI
V. GINO FRUSCHELLI
VIA BRUNO BONCI
VIA 24 MAGGIO
VIA MONTICCHIELLO
PORTA FONTEBRANDA
SELVA
VIA ESTERNA DI FONTEBRANDA
Santa Caterina
ANCIENT CITY WALLS
VIA DI VALLEPIATTA
VIA FRANCIOSA
V. DEI
SAN SEBASTIANO
SANTISSIMA ANNUNCIATA
SANTA MARIA DELLA SCALA (MUSEUM)
PANTERA
Piazza di Due Porte
VIA
PIANO MANTELLINI
SIENA'S "CONTRADE" (NEIGHBORHOODS)
AQUILA (Eagle)
BRUCO (Caterpillar)
CIVETTA (Owl)
DRAGO (Dragon)
GIRAFFA (Giraffe)
ISTRICE (Porcupine)
LEOCORNO (Unicorn)
LUPA (Wolf)
OCA (Goose)
ONDA (Wave)
PANTERA (Panther)
SELVA (Forest)
TARTUGA (Tortoise)
TORRE (Tower)
NOTE: MORE CONTRADE LIE BEYOND THE MAP BOUNDARIES.
1 Sottopassaggio la Lizza (Underground Bus Depot, Bag Storage & Bus Tickets)
2 Carroccio Viaggi Travel Agency
3 Internet Access
4 Train Station Shuttle Bus

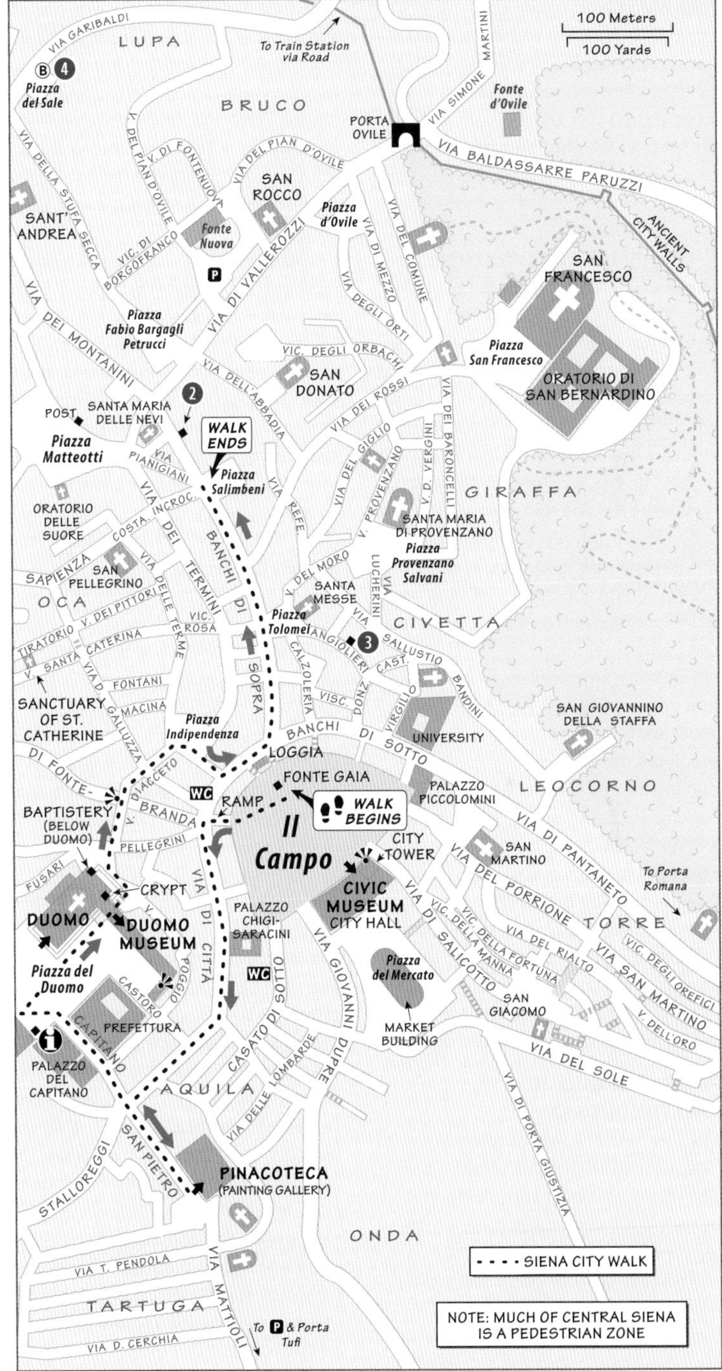
100 Meters
100 Yards
LUPA
BRUCO
To Train Station via Road
Piazza del Sale
PORTA OVILE
Fonte d'Ovile
SAN ROCCO
Piazza d'Ovile
SANT' ANDREA
Fonte Nuova
SAN FRANCESCO
ANCIENT CITY WALLS
Piazza Fabio Bargagli Petrucci
Piazza San Francesco
ORATORIO DI SAN BERNARDINO
SAN DONATO
POST
SANTA MARIA DELLE NEVI
WALK ENDS
Piazza Matteotti
Piazza Salimbeni
GIRAFFA
ORATORIO DELLE SUORE
SANTA MARIA DI PROVENZANO
Piazza Provenzano Salvani
SAN PELLEGRINO
OCA
SANTA MESSE
Piazza Tolomei
CIVETTA
SANCTUARY OF ST. CATHERINE
Piazza Indipendenza
LOGGIA
UNIVERSITY
SAN GIOVANNINO DELLA STAFFA
FONTE GAIA
PALAZZO PICCOLOMINI
LEOCORNO
WC
RAMP
WALK BEGINS
BAPTISTERY (BELOW DUOMO)
Il Campo
CITY TOWER
SAN MARTINO
To Porta Romana
CRYPT
DUOMO
DUOMO MUSEUM
PALAZZO CHIGI-SARACINI
CIVIC MUSEUM
CITY HALL
TORRE
Piazza del Duomo
Piazza del Mercato
PREFETTURA
MARKET BUILDING
SAN GIACOMO
PALAZZO DEL CAPITANO
AQUILA
PINACOTECA (PAINTING GALLERY)
ONDA
SIENA CITY WALK
TARTUGA
To P & Porta Tufi
NOTE: MUCH OF CENTRAL SIENA IS A PEDESTRIAN ZONE

from which to study the city. The modern column (from 1996) with a Carrara marble she-wolf on top functions as a flag holder for the *contrada.* You are still in the Eagle district (see the fountain and the corner plaque)—but beware. Just one block up the street, a ready-to-pounce panther—from the rival neighboring district—awaits.

Only the rich could afford stone residences. The fancy buildings here hide their economical brick construction behind a stucco veneer. The stone tower on this corner had only one door—30 feet above street level and reached by ladder, which could be pulled up as necessary. Within a few doors, you'll find a classy bar, an upscale grocery store, and a *gelateria.*

Take a little side-trip, venturing up Via di San Pietro. Interesting stops include the window with Palio video clips playing (at #1), Simon and Paula's art shop with delightful Palio and *contrade* knickknacks (#5), a weaver's shop (#7), a gelato purveyor (#10), an art gallery (#11), and four enticing little *osterias.* After a block, you'll reach the best art museum in town, the **Pinacoteca.** From there to the former town gate (Porta all'Arco), the street becomes more workaday, with local shops and no tourists.

• *Back at the Four Corners, head up Via del Capitano, passing another massive Chigi family palace (bankers sure know how to get their hands on people's money) to the Duomo and Piazza del Duomo. Find a shady seat on the stone bench against the wall of the old hospital opposite the church.*

PIAZZA DEL DUOMO AND THE DUOMO

The pair of she-wolves atop columns flanking the Duomo's facade says it all: The church was built and paid for not by the pope but by the people and the republic of Siena.

This 13th-century Gothic cathedral, with its six-story striped bell tower—Siena's ultimate tribute to the Virgin Mary—is heaped with statues, plastered with frescoes, and paved with art. Study the richly ornamented facade. The interior is a riot of striped columns, intricate inlaid-marble floors, a Michelangelo statue, Bernini sculptures, and the Piccolomini Library. (If you want to enter now, you'll need a ticket from the booth around to the right; for a self-guided tour, see page 237).

Facing the Duomo is Santa Maria della Scala, a huge building that housed pilgrims and, until the 1990s, was used as a hospital. Its labyrinthine 12th-century cellars—carved out of volcanic tuff and finished with brick—go down several floors, and during medieval times were used to store supplies for the hospital upstairs. Today, the exhibit-filled hospital and cellars can be a welcome refuge from the hot streets.

As massive as Siena's Duomo is, it's actually the rump of a failed vision. After rival republic Florence began its grand Duomo (1296), proud Siena planned to build an even bigger one, the biggest in all Christendom. But Siena is so hilly that there wasn't enough flat ground upon which to build a church of that size. What to do? Build a big church anyway, and prop up the overhanging edge with the Baptistery (which we'll pass shortly).

Walk around to the right of the church and find the unfinished wall with see-through windows (circa 1330). From here you can envision the audacity of this vision—today's cathedral would have been just a transept. But the plan underestimated the complexity of constructing such a building without enough land. That, coupled with the devastating effects of the 1348 plague, killed the project. Many Sienese saw the Black Death as a sign from God, punishing them for their pride. They canceled their plans and humbly faded into the background of history.

• *Walk to the rear of the church (past the Duomo Museum) and pause at the top of the marble stairs leading down. The Duomo Museum (to your right) houses the church's art (see page 240).*

SUPPORTING AN OVERSIZED CHURCH

From here, look down the stairs leading behind the church and see the architect's quandary. The church sticks out high above the lower street level. Partway down the stairs is the Crypt, and below that is the Baptistery. Each is an integral part of the foundation for the oversized structure. (Both the Crypt and the Baptistery are worth entering; see page 241).

• *Descend the stairs, nicknamed "The Steps of St. Catherine," as the hometown saint would have climbed them each day on her walk from home to the hospital. Below the Baptistery, jog right, then left, and through a tunnel down Via di Diacceto. Pause for a beautiful view of the towering brick Dominican church in the distance on the left. Then continue straight up the lane until you reach the next big square.*

PIAZZA INDIPENDENZA

This square celebrates the creation of a unified Italy (1860) with a 19th-century loggia sporting busts of the first two Italian kings. The neo-Renaissance loggia is backed by a Gothic palace and an older medieval tower.

• *Head right downhill one block (on Via delle Terme), back to the grand Via di Città, and take a few steps to the left to see another fancier loggia.*

LOGGIA DELLA MERCANZIA

This Gothic-Renaissance loggia was built around 1420 as a headquarters for the union of merchants (it's just above Il Campo). Siena's nobility purchased it, and eventually it became the clubhouse of the local elites. To this day, it's a private, ritzy, and notoriously out-of-touch men's club. The *Gli Uniti* above the door is a "let's stick together" declaration.

• *From here, steep steps lead down to Il Campo, but we'll go left and uphill on Via Banchi di Sopra. Pause at the intersection of...*

VIA BANCHI DI SOPRA AND VIA BANCHI DI SOTTO

These main drags are named "upper row of banks" and "lower row of banks." They were once lined with market tables (*banchi*), and vendors paid rent to the city for a table's position along the street. If the owner of a *banco* neglected to pay up, thugs came along and literally broke (*rotto*) his table. It is from this practice—*banco rotto,* broken table—that we get the English word "bankrupt."

In medieval times, these streets were part of Via Francigena, the main thoroughfare linking Rome with northern Europe. Today, strollers—out each evening for their *passeggiata*—fill Via Banchi di Sopra. Join the crowd, strolling past Siena's finest shops. You could nip into Nannini, a venerable café and *pasticceria* famous for its local sweets. The traditional Sienese taste treats—such as *ricciarelli* (macaroon and almond cookies) and *panforte* (fruity, nutty cake)—are around the far end of the counter in the back (sold by weight, small amounts are fine, a little slice of *panforte* costs about €3).

A block or so farther up the street, Piazza Tolomei faces the imposing Tolomei family palace (now an imposing bank). This is a center for the Owl *contrada.* The column in the square, topped by the she-wolf, is for *contrada* announcements of births, deaths, parties, and festivals.

• *Continue on Via Banchi di Sopra to Piazza Salimbeni; this gets my vote for Siena's finest stretch of palaces.*

PIAZZA SALIMBENI

The next square, Piazza Salimbeni, is dominated by Monte dei Paschi, the head office of a bank founded in 1472—still in business on this square after more than 500 years. Notice the Fort Knox-style base of the building. The statue in the center honors Sallustio Antonio Bandini. His claim to fame: He invented the concept of collateral.

Directly across from Piazza Salimbeni, the steep little lane called Costa dell'Incrociata leads straight (down and then up) to the Church of San Domenico (see page 242). Also nearby (behind the cute green newsstand) is the most elegant grocery store in town, Consorzio Agrario di Siena.

• *With this walk under your belt, you've got the lay of the land. The city is ready for further exploration—the sights associated with City Hall and the Duomo are all just a few minutes away. Enjoy delving deeper into Siena.*

Sights

Il Campo and Nearby

The gorgeous red-brick square known as Il Campo was first laid out in the 12th century. At the flat end of its clam-shell shape is City Hall, where you can tour the Civic Museum and climb the City Tower.

▲▲CIVIC MUSEUM (MUSEO CIVICO)

Siena's City Hall is the spot where secular government got its start in Renaissance Europe. Stroll the halls to see fascinating frescoes and portraits extolling Siena's greats, saints, and the city-as-utopia.

Cost and Hours: Museum-€9, €13 combo-ticket with Santa Maria della Scala, €20 combo-ticket includes City Tower and Santa Maria della Scala (valid two days), ticket office is straight ahead as you enter City Hall courtyard, open daily 10:00-19:00, Nov-mid March until 18:00, last entry 45 minutes before closing, audioguide-€5, tel. 0577-292-232, www.comune.siena.it.

Visiting the Museum: Start in the Sala del Risorgimento, with dramatic scenes of Victor Emmanuel II's unification of Italy (surrounded by statues that don't seem to care).

Passing through the chapel, enter the Sala del Mappamondo. On opposite walls are two large frescoes. The beautiful *Maestà (Enthroned Virgin,* 1315), by Siena's great Simone Martini (c. 1280-1344), is groundbreaking as the city's first fresco showing a Madonna not in a faraway, gold-leaf heaven but under the blue sky of a real space that we inhabit. Facing the *Maestà* is the famous *Equestrian Portrait of Guidoriccio da Fogliano* (1330), which depicts a mercenary general surveying the imposing castle that his armies have jut conquered.

Next is the Sala della Pace—where the city's fat cats met. Looking down on the oligarchy was a fresco series showing the *Effects of Good and Bad Government,*

Siena's Civic Museum

Ambrogio Lorenzetti, Effects of Good and Bad Government

by Sienese painter Ambrogio Lorenzetti. Compare the whistle-while-you-work happiness of the utopian community (in the better-preserved fresco) against the crime, devastation, and societal mayhem of a community ruled by politicians with more typical values. The message: Without justice, there can be no prosperity.

On your way out, climb up to the loggia (using the stairs just before the Sala del Risorgimento) for a sweeping view of the city and its surroundings.

▲CITY TOWER

The tower's nearly 400 steps get pretty skinny at the top, but the reward is one of Italy's best views (for more on the tower, see page 228).

Cost and Hours: €10, €20 combo-ticket with Civic Museum and Santa Maria della Scala, daily March-mid-Oct 10:00-19:00, mid-Oct-Feb until 16:00, last entry 45 minutes before closing, closed in rain, free and mandatory bag check.

Crowd Alert: Admission is limited to 50 people at a time. Wait at the bottom of the stairs for the green *Avanti* light. Try to avoid midday crowds (up to an hour wait at peak times).

▲PINACOTECA

This quiet, uncrowded museum walks you through Siena's art chronologically, from the 12th through the 16th centuries, when a revolution in realism was percolating in Tuscany.

Cost and Hours: €4, Tue-Sat 8:15-19:15, Sun-Mon 9:00-13:00, free and mandatory bag check. From Il Campo, walk out Via di Città and go left on Via San Pietro to #29; tel. 0577-281-161, www.pinacotecanazionale.siena.it.

Visiting the Museum: The collection lets you follow the evolution of painting styles from Byzantine to Gothic, then

City Tower on Il Campo

to International Gothic, and finally to Renaissance.

Long after Florentine art went realistic, the Sienese embraced a timeless, otherworldly style glittering with gold. In this city of proud craftsmen, the gilding and carpentry of the frames compete with the actual paintings. The exquisite attention to detail gives a glimpse into the wealth of the 13th and 14th centuries, Siena's Golden Age. The woven silk and gold clothing you'll see was worn by the very people who once walked these halls (appreciate the colonnaded courtyard).

The core of the collection is on the second floor, in Rooms 1-19. Works by Duccio di Buoninsegna (the artist of the *Maestà* in the Duomo Museum) feature groundbreaking but subtle innovations: less gold-leaf background, fewer gold creases in robes, translucent garments, inlaid-marble thrones, and a more human Mary and Jesus. Notice that the Madonna-and-Bambino pose is eerily identical in each version. *St. Augustine of Siena,* by Duccio's assistant, Simone Martini (who did the *Maestà* and possibly the Guidoriccio frescoes in the Civic Museum), sets the saint's life in realistic Sienese streets, buildings, and landscapes. In each panel, the saint pops out at the oddest angles to save the day.

Also look for religious works by the hometown Lorenzetti brothers (Ambrogio is best known for the secular masterpiece, the *Effects of Good and Bad Government,* in the Civic Museum). *Città sul Mare (City by the Sea)* and *Castello in Riva al Lago (Castle on the Lakeshore)* feature a strange, medieval landscape Cubism. Notice the weird, melancholy light that captures the Dark Ages.

Several colorful rooms on the first floor are dedicated to Domenico Beccafumi (1486-1551), who designed many of the Duomo's inlaid pavement panels (including *Slaughter of the Innocents*). With strong bodies, twisting poses, and dramatic gestures, Beccafumi's works epitomize the Mannerist style.

Cathedral Area

The cathedral-related sights—the Duomo, Duomo Museum, Crypt, and Baptistery—are clustered together on the hill. Across the street from the Duomo is Santa Maria della Scala, a former hospital (requiring a separate admission).

▲▲▲DUOMO

Siena's 13th-century cathedral and striped bell tower are an illustrious example of Romanesque-Gothic style in Italy. The interior showcases the work of the greatest sculptors of every era—Pisano, Donatello, Michelangelo, and Bernini—and the Piccolomini Library features a series of 15th-century frescoes chronicling the adventures of Siena's philanderer-turned-pope, Aeneas Piccolomini.

Cost: €4, €5 mid-Aug-Oct, includes Duomo and Piccolomini Library, buy ticket at Duomo ticket office (facing the cathedral entry, the ticket office is behind you to the right).

Consider the **Opa Si Pass** to add the Duomo Museum, Crypt, and Baptistery; to also add an escorted visit into the dome and rooftop, get the **Opa Si Pass + Porta del Cielo.**

Rick's Tip: *Check the line for the* **Duomo** *before buying tickets—if there's a long wait, you can pay* **an extra €1 for a "reservation"** *that lets you* **skip the line** *(available at the "reserved/fast entrance" queue).*

Hours: Mon-Sat 10:30-19:00, Sun 13:30-18:00; Nov-Feb closes daily at 17:30.

Dress Code: Modest dress is required, but stylish paper ponchos are provided for the inappropriately clothed.

Information: Tel. 0577-286-300, www.operaduomo.siena.it.

Tours: The **videoguide** is informative but dry (€8).

Duomo Roof Visit: The Opa Si Pass + Porta del Cielo includes all of the cathedral sights plus a 30-minute accompanied Porta del Cielo ("Heaven's Gate") visit to the dome's cupola and roof (timed-entry ticket, escorted visits of 18 people go each half-hour, March-Oct Mon-Sat 10:30-18:00, Sun 13:30-17:00, less frequent off-season, tel. 0577-286-300 for advance reservations).

➲ SELF-GUIDED TOUR

Grab a spot on a stone bench opposite the Duomo entry.

Facade: Survey this architectural festival of green, white, pink, and gold. Like a medieval altarpiece, the facade is divided into sections, each frame filled with patriarchs and prophets, studded with gargoyles, and topped with pinnacles.

The current structure dates back to 1215, with the major decoration done during Siena's heyday (1250-1350). The lower story, by Giovanni Pisano, features remnants of the fading Romanesque style (round arches over the doors), topped with the pointed arches of the new Gothic style that was seeping in from France. The upper half, in full-blown frilly Gothic, was designed and built a century later.

• *Step inside, putting yourself in the mindset of a pilgrim as you take in this trove of religious art.*

Nave: The heads of 172 popes—who reigned from the time of St. Peter to the 12th century—peer down from above, looking over the fine inlaid art on the floor. With a forest of striped columns, a coffered dome, a large stained-glass window at the far end, and a museum's worth of early Renaissance art, this is one busy interior. Look closely at the popes; you'll see the same four faces repeated over and over.

For almost two centuries (1373-1547), 40 artists paved the marble floor. The series starts near the entrance with historical allegories; the larger, more elaborate scenes surrounding the altar are mostly stories from the Old Testament. Many of the floor panels are roped off and covered to prevent further wear and tear. But from mid-August through October, the cathedral uncovers them and holds Mass in another church. The following two panels are always visible. The **She-Wolf Pavement Panel** (the second from the entrance) depicts Siena at the center of the Italian universe, orbited by such lesser lights as Roma, Florentia (Florence), and

Siena's Duomo

Pisa. The fourth panel from the entrance is the **Fortune Pavement Panel,** with Lady Luck (lower right) parachuting down to earth, where she teeters back and forth on a ball and a tipsy boat. The lesson? Fortune is an unstable foundation for life. On the right wall hangs a dim **painting of St. Catherine** (fourth from entrance), Siena's homegrown saint who had a vision in which she mystically married Christ.

Look for the marble altarpiece decorated with statues. **Piccolomini Altar:** This was commissioned by the Sienese-born Pope Pius III (born Francesco Piccolomini) as a memorial honoring his uncle Pius II. As the cardinal of Siena at the time, Piccolomini expected this fancy tomb to be his own final resting place, but because he later became pope, he was buried in the Vatican instead. The altar is most interesting for its statues: one by Michelangelo and three by his students. Michelangelo was originally contracted for 15 statues, but another sculptor had started the marble blocks, and Michelangelo's heart was never in the project. He personally finished only one—the figure of St. Paul (lower right, clearly more interesting than the bland, bored popes above him).

• *Now grab a seat under the...*

She-wolf pavement panel

Dome: The dome sits on a 12-sided base, but its "coffered" ceiling is actually a painted illusion. Get oriented to the array of sights we'll see by thinking of the church floor as a big 12-hour clock. You're in the middle, and the altar is high noon: You'll find the *Slaughter of the Innocents* roped off on the floor at 10 o'clock; Pisano's pulpit between two pillars at 11 o'clock; a copy of Duccio's round stained-glass window at 12 o'clock; Bernini's chapel at 3 o'clock; the Piccolomini Altar at 7 o'clock; the Piccolomini Library at 8 o'clock; and a Donatello statue at 9 o'clock.

Pisano's Pulpit: The octagonal Carrara marble pulpit (1268) rests on the backs of lions, symbols of Christianity triumphant. Like the lions, the Church eats its catch (devouring paganism) and nurses its cubs. The seven relief panels tell the life of Christ in rich detail. The pulpit is the work of Nicola Pisano (c. 1220-1278), the "Giotto of sculpture," whose revival of classical forms (columns, sarcophagus-like relief panels) signaled the coming Renaissance. His son Giovanni (c. 1240-1319) carved many of the panels, mixing his dad's classicism and realism with the decorative detail and curvy lines of French Gothic.

Duccio's Stained-Glass Rose Window: This is a copy of the original, famous window now preserved in the Duomo Museum.

Slaughter of the Innocents: This pavement panel shows Herod (left), sitting enthroned amid Renaissance arches, as he orders the massacre of all babies to prevent the coming of the promised Messiah. It's a chaotic scene of angry soldiers, grieving mothers, and dead babies, reminding locals that a republic ruled by a tyrant will experience misery.

• *Step into the chapel just behind you (next to the Piccolomini Library) to see the...*

St. John the Baptist Statue: The statue of the rugged saint in his famous rags was created by Donatello. The aging Florentine sculptor, whose style was now considered passé in Florence, came here to build bronze doors for the church (similar to Ghiberti's in Florence). He didn't complete the door project, but he did finish this bronze statue (1457). Notice the cherubs high above it, playfully dangling their feet.

• *Cross the church. Directly opposite find the Chigi Chapel, also known as the...*

Chapel of the Madonna del Voto: To understand why Gian Lorenzo Bernini (1598-1680) is considered the greatest Baroque sculptor, step into this sumptuous chapel (designed in the early 1660s for Fabio Chigi, a.k.a. Pope Alexander VII). Move up to the altar and look back at the two Bernini statues: Mary Magdalene in a state of spiritual ecstasy and St. Jerome playing the crucifix like a violinist lost in beautiful music.

The painting over the altar is the *Madonna del Voto,* a Madonna and Child adorned with a real crown of gold and jewels (painted by a Sienese master in the mid-13th century). In typical medieval fashion, the scene is set in the golden light of heaven. Mary has the almond eyes, long fingers, and golden folds in her robe that are found in orthodox icons of the time. Still, this Mary tilts her head and looks out sympathetically, ready to listen to the prayers of the faithful. This is the Mary to whom the Palio is dedicated, dear to the hearts of the Sienese. In thanks, they give **offerings** of silver hearts and medallions, many of which hang on the wall just to the left as you exit the chapel.

Pisano's marble pulpit

• *Cross back to the other side of the church to find the...*

Piccolomini Library: Brilliantly frescoed, the library captures the exuberant, optimistic spirit of the 1400s, when humanism and the Renaissance were born. The never-restored frescoes look nearly as vivid now as the day they were finished 550 years ago. The painter Pinturicchio (c. 1454-1513) was hired to celebrate the life of one of Siena's hometown boys, a man many call "the first humanist," Aeneas Piccolomini (1405-1464), who became Pope Pius II. Each of the 10 scenes is framed with an arch, as if Pinturicchio were opening a window onto the spacious 3-D world we inhabit.

The library also contains intricately decorated, illuminated music scores and a statue (a Roman copy of a Greek original) of the Three Graces, who almost seem to dance to the beat. The huge sheepskin sheets of music are from the days before individual hymnals—they had to be big so that many singers could read the music from a distance. Appreciate the fine painted decorations on the music—the gold-leaf highlights, the blue tones from ultramarine (made from precious lapis lazuli), and the miniature figures. All of this detail was lovingly crafted by Benedictine monks for the glory of God.

• *Exit the Duomo and make a U-turn to the left, walking alongside the church to Piazza Jacopo della Quercia.*

Unfinished Church: Construction began in the 1330s on an extension off the right side of the existing Duomo (today's cathedral would have been used as a transept). The nave of the Duomo was supposed to be where the piazza is today. Worshippers would have entered the church from the far end of the piazza through the unfinished wall. (Look up at the highest part of the wall. That viewpoint is accessible from inside the Duomo Museum.) Some of the nave's green-and-white-striped columns were built, but are now filled in with a brick wall. White stones in the pavement mark where a row of pillars would have been.

The vision was grand, but reality—and the plague—intervened. Look through the unfinished entrance facade, note blue sky where the stained-glass windows would have been, and ponder the struggles of the human spirit.

▲▲DUOMO MUSEUM AND VIEWPOINT (MUSEO DELL'OPERA E PANORAMA)

Located in a corner of the Duomo's grand but unfinished extension (to the right as you face the main facade), Siena's most enjoyable museum was built to house the Duomo's art. Here you stand eye-to-eye with the saints and angels who once languished, unknown, in the church's upper reaches (where copies are found today).

Cost and Hours: €8, daily 10:30-19:00, Nov-Feb until 17:30, next to the Duomo, in the skeleton of the unfinished part of the church on the Il Campo side, tel. 0577-286-300, www.operaduomo.siena.it.

Tours: You can rent a videoguide for €4.

➲ SELF-GUIDED TOUR

Start your tour at the bottom and work your way up.

Ground Floor: This floor is filled with the Duomo's original Gothic sculptures by Giovanni Pisano, who spent 10 years in the late 1200s carving and orchestrating the decoration of the Duomo with saints, prophets, sibyls, animals, and the original she-wolf with Romulus and Remus.

On the ground floor you'll also find Donatello's fine, round *Madonna and Child* carved relief. A slender, tender Mary gazes down at her chubby-cheeked baby; her sad eyes show that she knows the eventual fate of her son.

On the opposite side of the room is Duccio's original stained-glass window, which was originally located above and behind the Duomo's altar. Now the church has a copy, and art lovers can enjoy a close-up look at this masterpiece. The rose window—20 feet across, made in 1288—is dedicated to the Virgin Mary. The work is by Siena's most famous artist, Duccio di Buoninsegna (c. 1255-1319) and combines elements from rigid Byzantine icons (Mary's almond-shaped bubble, called a *mandorla,* and the full-frontal saints that flank her) with a budding sense of 3-D realism (the throne turned at a three-quarter angle to simulate depth, with angels behind).

Duccio's *Maestà*: Upstairs awaits the *Maestà (Enthroned Virgin,* 1311), whose panels were once part of the Duomo's main altarpiece. Although the former altarpiece was disassembled (and the frame was lost), most of the pieces are

Duccio, Christ's Entry into Jerusalem, *from the* Maestà

displayed here, with the front side (*Maestà*, with Mary and saints) at one end of the room, and the backside (26 Passion panels) at the other.

The *Maestà* was revolutionary for the time in its sheer size and opulence, and in Duccio's increasing sense of realism. Duccio, at the height of his powers, used every innovative arrow in his quiver. He replaced the standard gold-leaf background (symbolizing heaven) with a gold, intricately patterned curtain draped over the throne. Mary's blue robe opens to reveal her body; the curve of her knee suggests real anatomy. Baby Jesus wears a delicately transparent garment. Their faces are modeled with light—a patchwork of bright flesh and shadowy valleys, as if lit from the left (a technique learned from his contemporary Giotto during a visit to Florence).

The flip side of the *Maestà* featured 26 smaller panels—the medieval equivalent of pages—showing colorful scenes from the Passion of Christ.

Panorama dal Facciatone: About 40 claustrophobic spiral stairs take you to the first viewpoint. You can continue up another 100 steps of a similar spiral staircase to reach the top. Standing on the wall from this high point in the city, you're rewarded with a stunning view of Siena... and an interesting perspective. Look toward the Duomo and consider this: If Siena's grandiose plans to expand the cathedral had come to fruition, you'd be looking straight down the nave toward the altar.

▲BAPTISTERY (BATTISTERO)

This richly adorned and quietly tucked-away cave is worth a look for its cool tranquility and exquisite art, including an ornately painted vaulted ceiling. The highlight is the baptismal font designed by Jacopo della Quercia and adorned with bronze panels and angels by Quercia, Ghiberti, and Donatello. It dates from the 1420s, the start of the Renaissance.

Cost and Hours: €4, daily 10:30-19:00, Nov-Feb until 17:30.

CRYPT (CRIPTA)

The Duomo's crypt is archaeologically important. The site of a small 12th-century Romanesque church, it was filled in with dirt a century after its creation to provide a foundation for the huge church that sits atop it today. After being excavated, the rooms exhibit what are likely the oldest frescoes in town.

Cost and Hours: €8, daily 10:30-19:00, Nov-Feb until 17:30, entrance near the top of the stairs between the Baptistery and Duomo Museum.

▲SANTA MARIA DELLA SCALA

This museum, opposite the Duomo, operated for centuries as a hospital, foundling home, and pilgrim lodging. Many of those activities are visible in the 15th-century frescoes of its main hall, the Pellegrinaio. Today, the hospital and its cellars are filled with fascinating exhibits.

Cost and Hours: €9, €13 combo-ticket with Civic Museum, €20 combo-ticket includes the Civic Museum and Tower (valid two days); daily 10:00-19:00, Fri until 22:00; closes earlier mid-Oct-mid-March; tel. 0577-534-571, www.santamariadellascala.com.

Visiting the Museum: It's easy to get lost in this gigantic complex, so stay focused on the main attractions—the fancily frescoed Pellegrinaio Hall (ground floor), most of the original *Fountain of Joy* and some of the most ancient Byzantine reliquaries in existence (first basement), and the Etruscan collection in the Archaeological Museum (second basement), where the Sienese took refuge during WWII bombing.

From the entrance, follow signs to **Pellegrinaio**—the long hall with sumptuously frescoed walls (by Sienese painters, c. 1442, wonderfully described in English). This was originally a reception hall for visiting pilgrims, then a hospital. Starting in the 11th century, the hospital nursed the sick and cared for abandoned children, as is vividly portrayed in these frescoes. The good works paid off, as bequests and donations poured in, creating the wealth that's evident throughout this building.

Head down the stairs, then continue straight into the darkened rooms that contain pieces of Siena's landmark fountain—follow signs to La Fonte Gaia.

An engaging exhibit explains Jacopo della Quercia's early 15th-century **Fountain of Joy** *(Fonte Gaia)*—and displays the disassembled pieces of the original fountain itself. In the 19th century, after serious deterioration, the ornate fountain was dismantled and plaster casts were made. (These casts formed the replica that graces Il Campo today.) Here you'll see the eroded original panels paired with their restored casts, along with the actual statues that once stood on the edges of the fountain.

To visit the reliquaries, retrace your steps and follow the signs for *Il Tesoro.* Many of these **Byzantine reliquaries** are made of gold, silver, and precious stones. Legend has it that some were owned by Helen, Constantine's mother. They were "donated" to the hospital around 1350, shortly after the plague that decimated the city, since the sale of reliquaries was forbidden.

Now, descend into the cavernous second basement. Under the vaults of the **Archaeological Museum,** you're alone with piles of ancient Etruscan stuff excavated from tombs dating centuries before Christ (displayed in another labyrinthine exhibit). You'll see terra-cotta funeral urns for ashes (the design was often a standard body with the heads personalized) and many domestic artifacts from the 8th to the 5th century B.C.

San Domenico Area

CHURCH OF SAN DOMENICO

This huge brick church is worth a quick look. Spacious and plain (except for the colorful flags of the city's 17 *contrade*), the Gothic interior fits the austere philosophy of the Dominicans and invites meditation on the thoughts and deeds of St. Catherine (1347-1380). Walk up the steps in the rear to see paintings from her life. Halfway up the church on the right, find a copper bust of St. Catherine (for four centuries it contained her skull), a small case housing her thumb (on the right), and a page from her personal devotional book (12th century, on the left). In the chapel (15 feet to the left) surrounded with candles, you'll see Catherine's head (a clay mask around her skull with her actual teeth showing through) atop the altar. Through the door just beyond are the sacristy and the bookstore.

Cost and Hours: Free, daily 7:00-18:30, shorter hours off-season, www.basilicacateriniana.com.

SANCTUARY OF ST. CATHERINE

Step into the cool, peaceful site of Catherine's home. Siena remembers its favorite hometown gal, a simple, unschooled, but mystically devout soul who helped convince the pope to return from France to Rome. She's one of Italy's two patron saints (the other is St. Francis). Pilgrims have visited her home since 1464. Architects and artists have embellished what was once a humble dwelling (her family worked as wool dyers). Paintings throughout show scenes from her life.

Enter through the courtyard, and walk down the stairs at the far end. The church on your right contains the wooden crucifix upon which Catherine was meditating when she received the stigmata (the wounds of Christ) in 1375. Back outside, the oratory across the courtyard stands where the kitchen once was. Go down the stairs (left of the gift shop) to reach the saint's room. Catherine's bare cell is behind wrought-iron doors.

Cost and Hours: Free, daily 9:00-18:00, Chapel of the Crucifixion closed from 12:30-15:00 but church stays open, a few downhill blocks toward the center from San Domenico—follow signs to *Santuario di Santa Caterina*—at Costa di Sant'-Antonio 6.

Experiences

The Palio

Siena's 17 historic neighborhoods, or *contrade,* compete in the city's world-famous horse race, the **Palio di Siena,** held twice a year on July 2 and August 16. Ten of the 17 neighborhoods participate (chosen by rotation and lot), hurling themselves with medieval abandon into several days of trial races and traditional revelry. Jockeys—usually from out of town—are considered hired guns, no better than paid mercenaries. Bets are placed on which *contrada* will win...and lose. Despite the shady behind-the-scenes dealing, on the big day, the horses are taken into their *contrada*'s church to be blessed. ("Go and return victorious," says the priest.) It's considered a sign of luck if a horse leaves droppings in the church.

On the evening of the race, Il Campo is stuffed to the brim with locals and tourists. Dirt is brought in and packed down to create the track's surface, while mattresses pad the walls of surrounding buildings. The most treacherous spots are the sharp corners.

Ten snorting horses and their nervous riders line up near the pharmacy (on the west side of the square) to await the starting signal. Then they race like crazy while spectators wave the scarves of their neighborhoods. One lap around the course is about a third of a mile (350 meters); three laps make a full circuit. In this no-holds-barred race—which lasts just over a minute—a horse can win even without its rider.

When the winner crosses the line, 1/17th of Siena—the prevailing neighborhood—goes berserk. Winners receive a *palio* (banner), typically painted by a local artist and always featuring the Virgin Mary (the race is dedicated to her). But the true prize is proving that your *contrada* is *numero uno,* and mocking your losing rivals.

Bleacher and balcony seats are expensive, but it's free to join the masses in the square. If you're packed in with 60,000 people, you may not see much, but you'll feel the excitement. Go with an empty bladder as there are no WCs, and be prepared to surrender any sense of personal space.

You can more easily see the horse-race trials—called *prove*—on any of the three days before the main event (usually at 9:00 and after 19:00, free seats in bleachers). For

Palio pageantry

more info, visit www.ilpalio.org and www.comitatoamicidelpalio.it.

Eating

You can enjoy ordering high on the menu here without going broke. For pasta, a good option is *pici* (PEE-chee), a thick Sienese spaghetti that seems to be at the top of every menu.

In the Old Town

FINE DINING

$$$$ Antica Osteria Da Divo is a great splurge. The kitchen is inventive, the ambience is flowery and candlelit, some of the seating fills old Etruscan tombs, and the food is delicate and top-notch. Fanatical for fresh ingredients and giving traditional dishes a creative spin, Claudia will make you feel at home (wine by the glass on request, Wed-Mon 12:00-14:30 & 19:00-22:30, closed Tue; facing Baptistery door, take the far right street to Via Franciosa 29; tel. 0577-284-381, www.osteriadadivo.it). Show this book to finish with a complimentary biscotti and vin santo or coffee.

$$$$ Osteria le Logge caters to a fancy crowd and offers Tuscan favorites with a gourmet twist, made with seasonal local ingredients. Inside you'll enjoy a gorgeous living-room setting, and outside there's fine seating on a pedestrian street (Mon-Sat 12:00-15:00 & 19:00-23:00, closed Sun, two blocks off Il Campo at Via del Porrione 33, tel. 0577-48013, www.giannibrunelli.it).

$$$ Enoteca I Terzi is dressy and modern under medieval vaults, with a simple yet enticing menu of creative dishes. They have a few tables on a quiet square out front and an elegant main dining area, but avoid the back room (daily 12:30-15:00 & 19:30-23:00, Via dei Termini 7, tel. 0577-44329, www.enotecaiterzi.it).

MORE DINING OPTIONS

$$ Ristorante Guidoriccio, just a few steps below Il Campo, feels warm and welcoming. You'll get smiling service from Ercole and Flora, especially if you let gentle Ercole explore the menu and follow his suggestions (Mon-Sat 12:30-14:30 & 19:00-22:30, closed Sun, air-con, Via Giovanni Dupre 2, tel. 0577-44350).

$$$$ Ristorante Tar-Tufo is the only place in the old center offering a gourmet meal on a countryside view terrace. Tucked in the basement of a former school, the restaurant specializes in modern Tuscan cuisine garnished with truffles (daily 12:00-14:30 & 16:30-22:00, Via del Sole 6, tel. 0577-284-031).

$$$ Compagnia dei Vinattieri serves modern Tuscan dishes with a creative touch. In this elegant space, you can enjoy a romantic meal under graceful brick arches. Owners Marco and Gianfranco are happy to take you down to the marvelous wine cellar (beef is big here, leave this book on the table for a complimentary *aperitivo* or *digestivo,* daily 12:30-15:00 & 19:30-23:00, enter at Via dei Pittori 1 or Via delle Terme 79, tel. 0577-236-568).

$$ Osteria Il Carroccio, artsy and convivial, seats guests in a characteristic but tight dining room. They serve traditional "slow food" recipes with innovative flair at affordable prices (€30 tasting *menu*—minimum two people, reservations wise, Thu-Tue 12:30-15:00 & 19:30-22:00, closed Wed, Casato di Sotto 32, tel. 0577-41165).

TRADITIONAL AND RUSTIC PLACES

$$ Trattoria Papei has a casual, rollicking family atmosphere and friendly servers dishing out generous portions of rib-stickin' Tuscan specialties and grilled meats. This big, sprawling place is often jammed—so call to reserve (daily 12:00-15:00 & 19:00-22:30, on the market square behind City Hall at Piazza del Mercato 6, tel. 0577-280-894, **www.anticatrattoriapapei.com**; Amedeo and Eduardo speak English).

$$ La Taverna Di Cecco is a simple, comfortable little eatery on an uncrowded back lane where grandma Olga cooks and earnest Luca and Gianni serve. They offer a simple menu of traditional Sienese favorites made with fresh ingredients, along with hearty salads (daily 12:00-16:00 & 19:00-23:00, Via Cecco Angiolieri 19, tel. 0577-288-518).

$$ Trattoria La Torre is an unfussy family-run *casalinga* (home-cooking) place, popular for its homemade pasta. Its open kitchen and 10 tables are packed under one medieval brick arch. Service is brisk and casual—even with its priceless position below the namesake tower, it feels more like a local hangout than a tourist trap (Fri-Wed 12:00-15:00 & 19:00-22:00, closed Thu, just steps below Il Campo at Via di Salicotto 7, tel. 0577-287-548).

$ Il Pomodorino is a lively restaurant serving meal-size salads and some of the best pizza in town, and a wide selection of beer—unusual in wine-crazy Tuscany. The intimate modern interior is covered by brick vaulting, but the real appeal is the outdoor terrace with a great view of the Duomo (daily 12:00-late, a few steps above the recommended Alma Domus hotel at Via Camporegio 13, tel. 0577-286-811).

On Il Campo

If you choose to eat on perhaps the finest town square in Italy, you'll pay a premium and get mediocre food. Yet I highly recommend it. Survey the scene during the day and reserve an evening table at the place that suits you.

$$$ Ristorante Alla Speranza has primo views and is a decent option for dining on the square (daily 9:00-late, Piazza Il Campo 32, tel. 0577-280-190, www.allasperanza.it).

$$$ Il Bandierino is another option for drinks or food, with an angled view of City Hall (no cover but a 20 percent service charge, daily 11:00-23:00, Piazza Il Campo 64, tel. 0577-275-894).

$$$ Bar Il Palio is the best bar on Il Campo for a before- or after-dinner drink: It has straightforward prices, no cover, and a fantastic perspective out over the square (daily 8:30-late, Piazza Il Campo 47, tel. 0577-282-055).

Sleeping

Finding a room in Siena is tough during Easter or the Palio (July 2 and Aug 16). Many hotels won't take reservations until the end of May for the Palio, and even then they may require a four-night stay. Day-trippers pack the town in midsummer, but Siena is basically yours in the evenings and off-season.

Part of Siena's charm is its lively, festive character—this means that all hotels can be plagued with noise, especially in the pedestrian-only zone. If tranquility is important, ask for a room off the street.

Bigger Hotels near Il Campo

These well-run places are a 10-minute walk from Il Campo. If driving, get parking instructions from your hotel in advance and make sure that you don't violate the Zona Traffico Limitato (ZTL) restrictions.

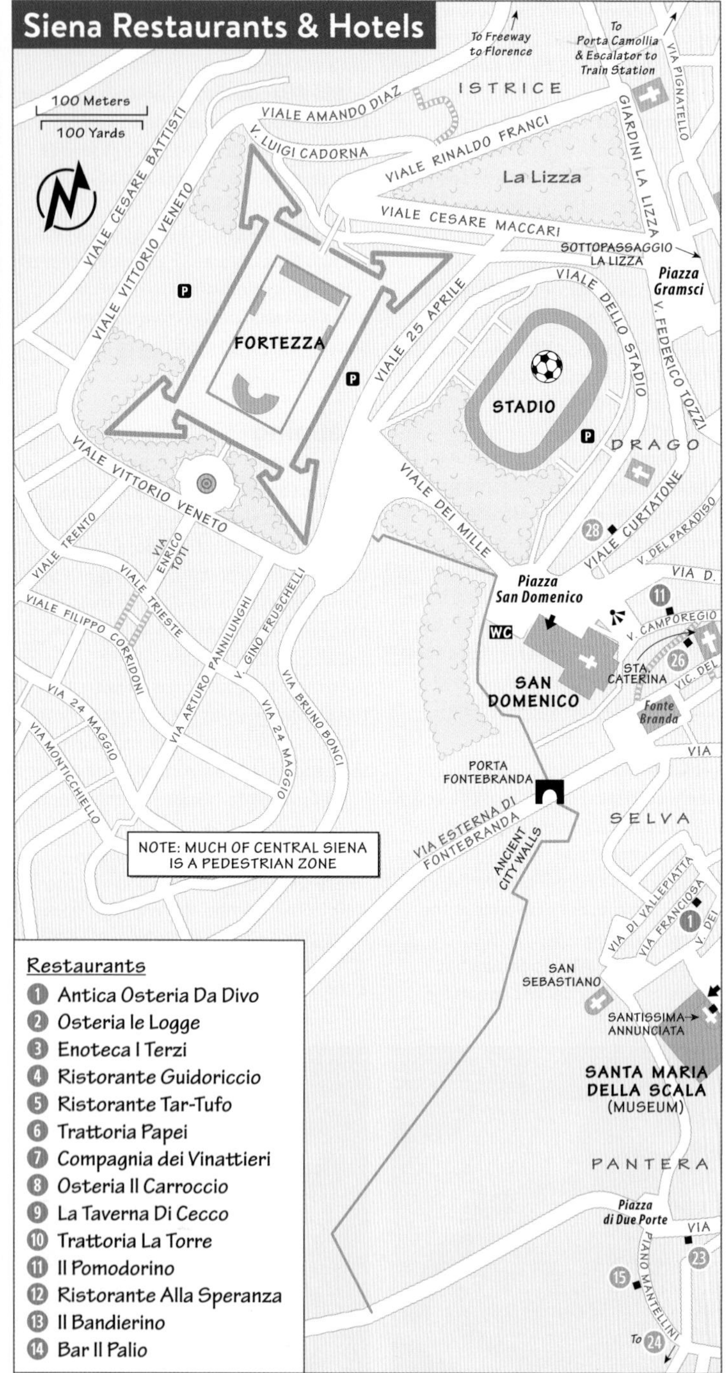
Siena Restaurants & Hotels
To Freeway to Florence
To Porta Camollia & Escalator to Train Station
ISTRICE
100 Meters
100 Yards
VIALE AMANDO DIAZ
V. LUIGI CADORNA
VIALE RINALDO FRANCI
La Lizza
GIARDINI LA LIZZA
VIA PIGNATELLO
VIALE CESARE MACCARI
SOTTOPASSAGGIO LA LIZZA
Piazza Gramsci
VIALE CESARE BATTISTI
VIALE VITTORIO VENETO
FORTEZZA
VIALE 25 APRILE
VIALE DELLO STADIO
V. FEDERICO TOZZI
STADIO
DRAGO
VIALE DEI MILLE
VIALE CURTATONE
V. DEL PARADISO
VIA D.
VIA TRENTO
VIA ENRICO TOTI
VIALE TRIESTE
VIALE FILIPPO CORRIDONI
VIA ARTURO PANNILUNGHI
V. GINO FRUSCHELLI
VIA BRUNO BONCI
VIA 24 MAGGIO
VIA MONTICCHIELLO
Piazza San Domenico
WC
V. CAMPOREGIO
STA. CATERINA
VIC. DEL
SAN DOMENICO
Fonte Branda
VIA
PORTA FONTEBRANDA
VIA ESTERNA DI FONTEBRANDA
ANCIENT CITY WALLS
SELVA
NOTE: MUCH OF CENTRAL SIENA IS A PEDESTRIAN ZONE
VIA DI VALLEPIATTA
VIA FRANCIOSA
V. DEI
SAN SEBASTIANO
SANTISSIMA ANNUNCIATA
SANTA MARIA DELLA SCALA (MUSEUM)
PANTERA
Piazza di Due Porte
VIA
PIANO MANTELLINI
To 24
Restaurants
1 Antica Osteria Da Divo
2 Osteria le Logge
3 Enoteca I Terzi
4 Ristorante Guidoriccio
5 Ristorante Tar-Tufo
6 Trattoria Papei
7 Compagnia dei Vinattieri
8 Osteria Il Carroccio
9 La Taverna Di Cecco
10 Trattoria La Torre
11 Il Pomodorino
12 Ristorante Alla Speranza
13 Il Bandierino
14 Bar Il Palio

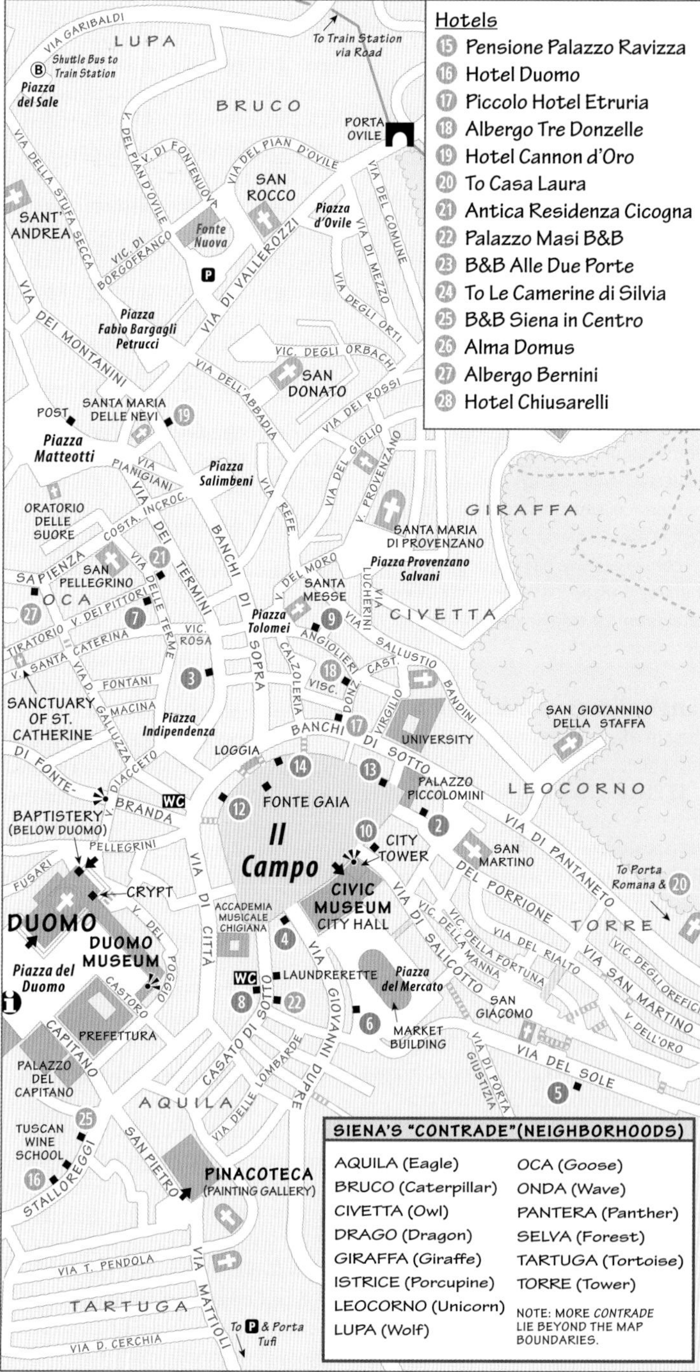
Hotels
15 Pensione Palazzo Ravizza
16 Hotel Duomo
17 Piccolo Hotel Etruria
18 Albergo Tre Donzelle
19 Hotel Cannon d'Oro
20 To Casa Laura
21 Antica Residenza Cicogna
22 Palazzo Masi B&B
23 B&B Alle Due Porte
24 To Le Camerine di Silvia
25 B&B Siena in Centro
26 Alma Domus
27 Albergo Bernini
28 Hotel Chiusarelli
SIENA'S "CONTRADE" (NEIGHBORHOODS)
AQUILA (Eagle)
BRUCO (Caterpillar)
CIVETTA (Owl)
DRAGO (Dragon)
GIRAFFA (Giraffe)
ISTRICE (Porcupine)
LEOCORNO (Unicorn)
LUPA (Wolf)
OCA (Goose)
ONDA (Wave)
PANTERA (Panther)
SELVA (Forest)
TARTUGA (Tortoise)
TORRE (Tower)
NOTE: MORE CONTRADE LIE BEYOND THE MAP BOUNDARIES.
To Train Station via Road
Shuttle Bus to Train Station
Piazza del Sale
LUPA
BRUCO
PORTA OVILE
SAN ROCCO
Fonte Nuova
Piazza d'Ovile
SANT' ANDREA
Piazza Fabio Bargagli Petrucci
SAN DONATO
POST
SANTA MARIA DELLE NEVI
Piazza Matteotti
Piazza Salimbeni
ORATORIO DELLE SUORE
GIRAFFA
SANTA MARIA DI PROVENZANO
Piazza Provenzano Salvani
SAN PELLEGRINO
OCA
SANTA MESSE
CIVETTA
Piazza Tolomei
SANCTUARY OF ST. CATHERINE
Piazza Indipendenza
UNIVERSITY
SAN GIOVANNINO DELLA STAFFA
LOGGIA
FONTE GAIA
PALAZZO PICCOLOMINI
LEOCORNO
BAPTISTERY (BELOW DUOMO)
Il Campo
CITY TOWER
SAN MARTINO
To Porta Romana & 20
CRYPT
CIVIC MUSEUM CITY HALL
ACCADEMIA MUSICALE CHIGIANA
TORRE
DUOMO
DUOMO MUSEUM
Piazza del Duomo
LAUNDRERETTE
Piazza del Mercato
PREFETTURA
SAN GIACOMO
MARKET BUILDING
PALAZZO DEL CAPITANO
AQUILA
TUSCAN WINE SCHOOL
PINACOTECA (PAINTING GALLERY)
TARTUGA
To P & Porta Tufi

Go through Porta San Marco, turn right, and follow signs to your hotel—drop your bags, then park as they instruct.

$$$$ Pensione Palazzo Ravizza is elegant, friendly, and well-run, with 40 rooms and an aristocratic feel. Guests enjoy a peaceful garden set on a dramatic bluff, along with a Steinway in the upper lounge (RS%, family rooms, air-con, elevator, Via Piano dei Mantellini 34, tel. 0577-280-462, www.palazzoravizza.it, bureau@palazzo ravizza.it). As parking here is free and the hotel is easily walkable from the center, this is a particularly good value for drivers.

$$$ Hotel Duomo is dreary but well located, with20 spacious but overpriced rooms (some with Duomo views—request when booking), a picnic-friendly roof terrace, and a bizarre floor plan (family rooms, elevator with some stairs, air-con, expensive pay parking; Via di Stalloreggi 38, tel. 0577-289-088, www.hotelduomo.it, booking@hotelduomo.it, Alessandro and Tony).

Simple Places near Il Campo

Most of these listings are forgettable but well-priced.

$$ Piccolo Hotel Etruria, with 20 simple, recently redecorated rooms, is well-located, restful, and a fine value (RS%—use code "RSITA," family rooms, breakfast extra, air-con May-Oct only, elevator, at Via delle Donzelle 3, tel. 0577-288-088, www.hoteletruria.com, info@hoteletruria.com, friendly Leopoldo and Lucrezia).

$ Albergo Tre Donzelle is a fine budget value with welcoming hosts and 20 homey rooms—these may be the best-value rooms in the center. Il Campo, a block away, is your terrace (RS%—use code "RSITA," cheaper rooms with shared bath, family rooms, breakfast extra, fans, no elevator; with your back to the tower, head away from Il Campo toward 2 o'clock to Via delle Donzelle 5; tel. 0577-270-390, www.tredonzelle.com, info@tredonzelle.com).

$ Hotel Cannon d'Oro, a few blocks up Banchi di Sopra, is a labyrinthine slumbermill renting 30 institutional, overpriced rooms (RS%, family rooms, fans, Via dei Montanini 28, tel. 0577-44321, www.cannondoro.com, info@cannondoro.com; Maurizio, Tommaso, and Rodrigo).

$ Casa Laura has eight clean, charming, well-maintained rooms, some of which have brick-and-beam ceilings (RS%, more expensive rooms with air-con, no elevator, Via Roma 3, about a 10-minute walk from Il Campo toward Porta Romana, mobile 392-811-0364, www.casalaurasiena.com, info@casalaurasiena.com).

B&Bs in the Old Center

$$ Antica Residenza Cicogna is a seven-room guesthouse with a homey elegance and an ideal location. It's warmly run by the young and charming Elisa and her friend Ilaria. With artfully frescoed walls and ceilings, this is remarkably genteel for the price (air-con, no elevator, Via delle Terme 76, tel. 0577-285-613, mobile 347-007-2888, www.anticaresidenzacicogna.it, info@anticaresidenzacicogna.it).

$$ Palazzo Masi B&B, run by friendly Alizzardo and Daniela, has rent six spacious, antique-furnished rooms on the second and third floors of a restored 13th-century building (RS%—use code "RICK," cheaper rooms with shared bath, no elevator; from City Hall, walk 50 yards down Casato di Sotto to #29; mobile 349-600-9155, www.palazzomasi.com, info@palazzomasi.it). The place is sometimes unstaffed, so confirm your arrival time in advance.

$$ B&B Alle Due Porte is a charming little establishment renting three big rooms under medieval beams. The breakfast room is delightful. The manager, Egisto, is a phone call and 10-minute scooter ride away (3 rooms have air-con, Via di Stalloreggi 51, mobile 368-352-3530, www.sienatur.it, soldatini@interfree.it).

$ Le Camerine di Silvia, a romantic hideaway perched near a sweeping, grassy olive grove, rents five simple rooms in a converted 16th-century building. A small breakfast terrace with fruit trees and a private hedged garden lends itself to contemplation (cash only, view room on request, no breakfast, fans, free parking nearby, Via Ettore Bastianini 1, just below recommended Pensione Palazzo Ravizza, mobile 338-761-5052 or 339-123-7687, www.lecamerinedisilvia.com, info@lecamerinedisilvia.com, Conti family).

$ B&B Siena in Centro is a clearinghouse managing 15 rooms and five apartments. Their handy office functions as a reception area; stop by here to pick up your key and be escorted, or meet the owners at your room. The rooms are generally spacious, quiet, and comfortable. Their website lets you visualize your options (RS%, some with air-con and others with fans, family rooms, reception open 9:00-13:30 & 15:00-22:00, Via di Stalloreggi 16, tel. 0577-48111, mobile 331-281-0136 or 347-465-9753, www.bbsienaincentro.com, info@bbsienaincentro.com, Gioia or Michela).

Near San Domenico Church

These hotels are within a 10- to 15-minute walk northwest of Il Campo.

$$$ Hotel Chiusarelli, with 48 classy rooms in a beautiful, frescoed Neoclassical villa, is just outside the medieval town center on a busy street. Expect traffic noise at night—ask for a quieter room in the back, which can be guaranteed with reservation (RS%, family rooms, air-con, several free parking spots, nearby pay parking, across from San Domenico at Viale Curtatone 15, tel. 0577-280-562, www.chiusarelli.com, info@chiusarelli.com).

$$ Albergo Bernini makes you part of a Sienese family in a modest, clean home with 10 traditional rooms. Giovanni, charming wife Daniela, and their daughters welcome you to their spectacular view terrace—a great spot for a glass of wine or a picnic (cheaper rooms with shared bath, family rooms, breakfast extra, fans, on the main Il Campo-San Domenico drag at Via della Sapienza 15, tel. 0577-289-047, www.albergobernini.com, info@albergobernini.com).

$ Alma Domus is a church-run hotel featuring 28 tidy rooms with quaint balconies, some fantastic views (ask for a room con vista), stately public rooms, and a pleasant atmosphere. However, the thin doors, echoey halls, and nearby church bells can be drawbacks, particularly on upper floors. Consider upgrading to a snazzy superior room for slightly more (RS%, family rooms, air-con, elevator; from San Domenico, walk downhill toward the view with the church on your right, turn left down Via Camporegio, make a U-turn down the brick steps to Via Camporegio 37; tel. 0577-44177, www.hotelalmadomus.it, info@hotelalmadomus.it, Louis).

Transportation

Arriving and Departing

Siena is a great hub for buses to the hill towns, though frequency drops on Sundays and holidays. For most, Florence is the gateway to Siena. Even if you're a rail-pass user, connect these two cities by bus—it's faster than the train, and Siena's bus station is more convenient and central than its train station on the edge of town.

BY BUS

Most buses arrive in Siena at Piazza Gramsci, a few blocks north of the city center. Some buses only go to the train station; others go first to the train station, then continue to Piazza Gramsci—to find out if yours does, ask your driver, "pee-aht-sah GRAHM-shee?" From Piazza Gramsci, it's an easy walk into the town center—just head in the opposite direction of the tree-filled park.

The main bus companies, which cover the region and beyond, are Tiemme/Siena Mobilità and Sena/Baltour. Their offices, with posted bus schedules, are in an underground passageway called **Sottopassaggio la Lizza,** underneath

Piazza Gramsci (look for the stairwells in front of NH Excelsior Hotel). You can buy bus tickets at these offices, or from the driver when you board, but it costs €3-5 extra.

Tiemme/Siena Mobilità covers mainly regional destinations (cash only, Mon-Fri 6:30-19:30, Sat-Sun 7:00-19:30, tel. 0577-204-111, www.sienamobilita.it) and also offers **luggage storage** for day-trippers (daily 7:00-19:00, carry-on-sized luggage no more than 33 pounds, no overnight storage).

Sena/Baltour buses operate mainly long-distance connections (accepts credit cards, Mon-Fri 7:30-20:00, Sat 7:30-12:30 & 13:45-16:15, Sun 10:15-13:15 & 14:00-18:45, tel. 0861-199-1900, www.baltour.it and www.sena.it).

Tiemme/Siena Mobilità Bus Connections to: Florence (roughly 2/hour, 1.5-hour *rapida/via superstrada* buses are faster than the train, avoid the 2-hour *ordinaria* buses unless you have time to enjoy the beautiful scenery en route; tickets also available at tobacco shops/*tabacchi*; generally leaves from Piazza Gramsci as well as train station), **Montepulciano** (6-8/day, none on Sun, 1.5 hours, from train station), **Montalcino** (6/day Mon-Sat, 4/day Sun, 1.5 hours, from train station or Piazza del Sale), **Pisa's Galileo Galilei Airport** (3/day, 2 hours, one direct, two via Poggibonsi), **Rome's Fiumicino Airport** (3/day, 3.5 hours, from Piazza Gramsci).

Sena/Baltour Bus Connections to: Rome (9/day, 3 hours, from Piazza Gramsci, arrives at Rome's Tiburtina station on Metro line B with easy connections to the central Termini train station), **Naples** (2/day, 6.5 hours, one at 17:00 and an overnight bus that departs at 00:20), **Milan** (2/day direct, 4.5 hours, more with change in Bologna, departs from Piazza Gramsci, arrives at Milan's Cadorna Station with Metro access and direct trains to Malpensa Airport), **Assisi** (daily at 17:30, 2 hours, departs from Siena train station, arrives at Assisi Santa Maria degli Angeli; from there it's a 10-minute taxi/bus ride uphill to city center). To reach the town center of **Pisa,** the train is better.

BY TRAIN

The small train station at the base of the hill, on the edge of Siena, has a bar/tobacco shop, a bus office (Mon-Fri 7:15-19:30, Sat until 17:45, Sun 7:15-12:00 & 15:15-18:30, opens later in winter), and a newsstand (which sells local bus tickets—buy one if you're taking the city bus into town), but no baggage check or lockers (stow bags at Piazza Gramsci). A shopping mall with a Pam supermarket is across the plaza right in front of the station. WCs are at the far north on track 1, past the pharmacy to the left.

To reach central Siena, you can hop aboard the city bus, ride a long series of escalators, or take a taxi.

To ride the **city bus,** go through the shopping mall's right-hand door at the corner entrance and take the elevator down to the subterranean bus stop. If you didn't buy bus tickets in the train station, you can get them from the blue machine or buy them onboard. Buses leave frequently (6/hour, fewer on Sun and after 22:00, €1.20, exact change required, about a 10-minute ride into town). Smaller shuttle buses go up to Piazza del Sale, while bigger city buses head to nearby Piazza Gramsci (both at the north end of town, walkable to most of my recommended hotels). Before boarding, double-check the destination with the driver by asking *"Centro?"* Validate your ticket in the machine onboard.

Riding the **escalator** into town takes a few minutes longer and requires more walking than the bus. Head for the shopping mall across the square. From the tracks, go down the stairs into the tunnel that connects the platforms; this leads (with escalators) right up into the mall. Alternatively, you can exit the station out the front door, bear left across the square, and use the corner entrance marked *Galleria Porta Siena* (near the Pam supermarket). Once inside, go straight ahead and ride the escalators up two floors to the food court. Continue directly through the glass doors to another escalator (marked *Porta Camollia/Centro*) that takes you gradually up into town. Exiting the escalator, turn left down the big street, bear left at the fork, then continue straight through the town gate. From here, landmarks are well-signed (go up Via Camollia).

The **taxi stand** is to your left as you exit the train station, but getting one can take a while (about €10 to Il Campo, taxi tel. 0577-49222).

If **leaving Siena by train,** here's how to get from the city center to the station: Ride a small shuttle bus from Piazza del Sale, or catch an orange or red-and-silver city bus from Piazza Gramsci (which may take a more roundabout route). Multiple bus routes make this trip—look for *Ferrovia* or *Stazione* on schedules and marked on the bus, and confirm with the driver that the bus is going to the *stazione* (staht-see-OH-nay).

Train Connections from Siena to: Florence (direct trains hourly, 1.5-2 hours; bus is better), **Pisa** (2/hour, 2 hours, change at Empoli), **Assisi** (10/day, about 4 hours, most involve 2 changes, bus is faster), **Rome** (1-2/hour, 3-4 hours, change in Florence or Chiusi), **Orvieto** (12/day, 2.5 hours, change in Chiusi). For more info, visit www.trenitalia.com.

BY CAR

Driving within Siena's city center is restricted to local cars and is policed by automatic cameras. Plan on parking in a big lot or garage and walking into town. Check with your hotel in advance if you plan to drop off your bags before parking.

Drivers coming from the autostrada take the **Siena Ovest exit** and follow signs for *Centro,* then *Stadio* (stadium). The soccer-ball signs take you to the **stadium lot** (Parcheggio Stadio, €2/hour, pay when you leave) near Piazza Gramsci and the huge, bare-brick Church of San Domenico. The nearby **Fortezza lot** charges the same amount.

Another good option is the underground **Santa Caterina garage** (you'll see signs on the way to the stadium lot, same price). From the garage, hike 150 yards uphill through a gate to an escalator on the right, which carries you up into the city. If you're staying in the south end of town, try the **Il Campo lot,** near Porta Tufi.

MONTEPULCIANO AND MONTALCINO

Wine aficionados head for Montepulciano and Montalcino—each a happy gauntlet of wine shops and art galleries. Montepulciano is the more all-around engaging town; it's the better choice for those without a car (though connections can still be tricky), and also works well for drivers. With its easy access to the vineyards, Montalcino makes sense for wine pilgrims.

Montepulciano

Curving its way along a ridge, Montepulciano (mohn-teh-pull-chee-AH-noh) delights visitors with *vino* and views.

Orientation

Commercial action centers in the lower town, mostly along Via di Gracciano nel Corso, which begins at the town gate called Porta al Prato and winds up through town to the main square, Piazza Grande, at the top.

Getting There: Montepulciano has good bus connections with **Siena** (6-8/day, none on Sun, 1.5 hours), as well as **Florence** (1-2/day, 2 hours, change in Bettolle, LFI bus, www.lfi.it; or catch the hourly train to Chiusi for the 50-minute trip, then the bus to Montepulciano). Connecting Montepulciano and **Montalcino** by bus requires a transfer (3-4/daily except Sun, 1 hour). Or consider hiring a **taxi** to Montalcino or other destinations nearby (about €70, tel. 348-702-4124, www.strollingintuscany.com). For bus schedules, check www.sienamobilita.it

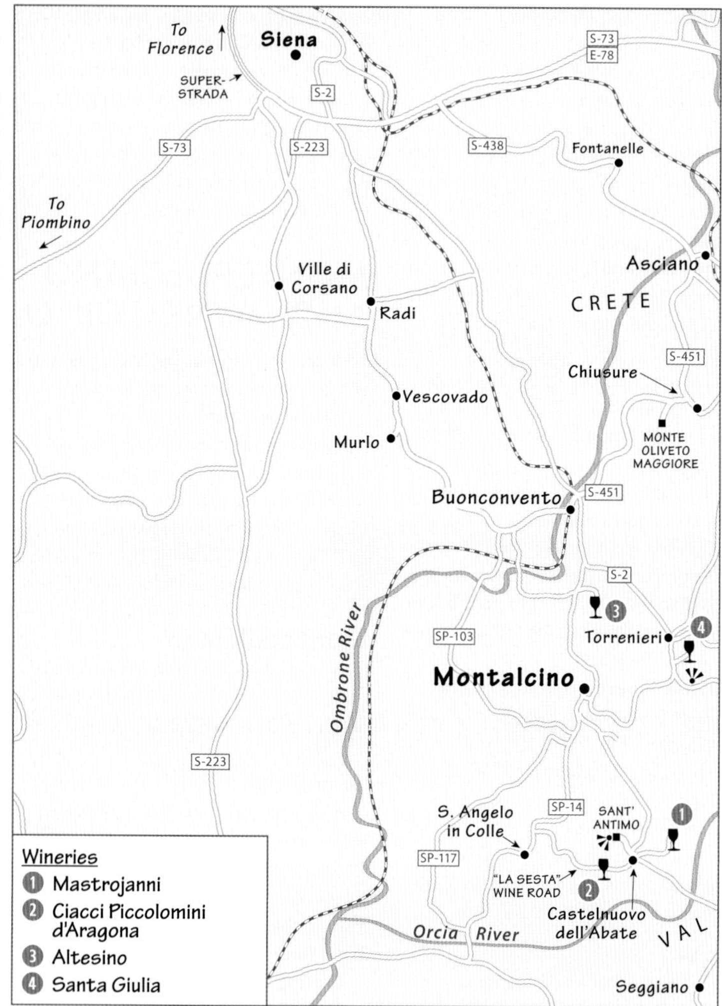

or www.tiemmespa.it. The nearest train station is five miles away on a minor train line, but can be useful on Sundays when few buses run.

Arrival in Montepulciano: Buses stop at the bus station on Piazza Nenni; across the street inside the modern orange-brick structure is a series of two elevators. Ride the first to level 1, walk straight down the corridor (following signs for *centro storico*), and ride a second elevator up to the main gate. There's no official **luggage storage** in town, but the TI might let you leave bags with them if they have space.

Drivers will find pay parking lots ringing the city center; try to park at the north end of town, near the Porta al Prato gate. A twice-hourly **shuttle bus** travels from the parking lot near the bus station and from the lane leading to the Porta al Prato gate, just above the TI, to the main square (€1.10, buy tickets at TI, bars, or tobacco shops). Avoid the "ZTL" no-traffic zone (marked with a red circle).

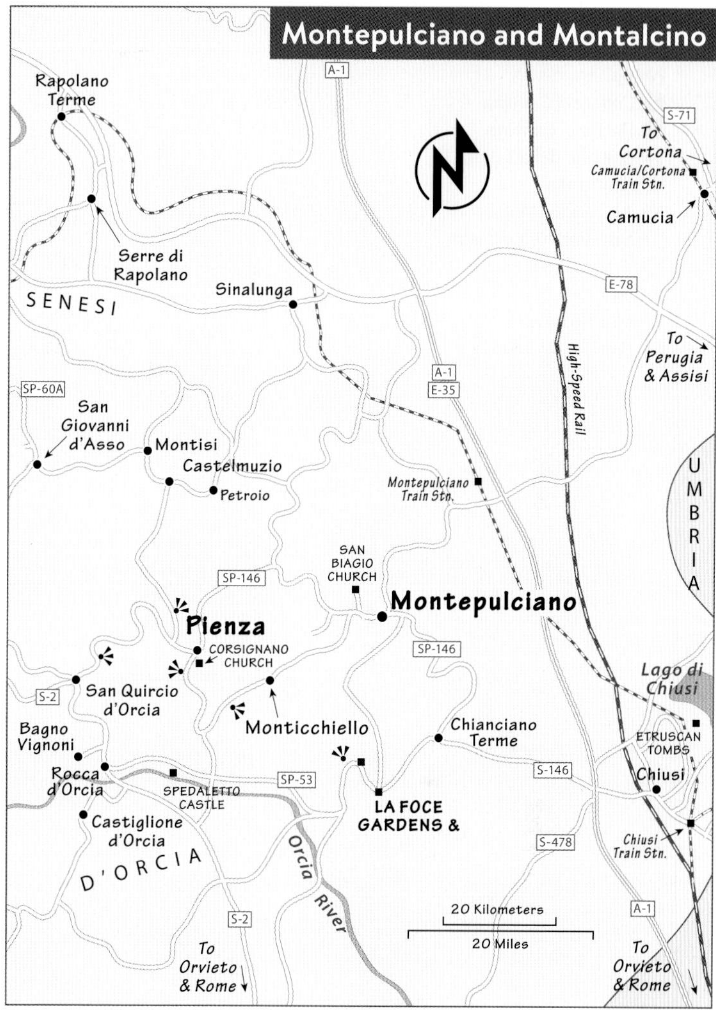

Tourist Information: The TI is just outside the Porta al Prato city gate, in the small P1 parking lot (Mon-Sat 9:00-13:00 & 15:00-19:00, Sun 9:00-13:00, daily until 20:00 in July-Aug, Piazza Don Minzoni, tel. 0578-757-341, www.prolocomontepulciano.it).

The private **"Strada del Vino" office** on the main square provides wine-road maps, and tours (Mon-Fri 10:00-13:00 & 15:00-18:00, Piazza Grande 7, tel. 0578-717-484, www.stradavinonobile.it).

Experiences

Montepulciano's famous wine, Vino Nobile, can be tasted in any of the cantinas lining Via Ricci and Via di Gracciano nel Corso.

▲▲CONTUCCI CANTINA

The cantina in the basement of Palazzo Contucci is both historic and fun. Skip the palace's formal wine-tasting showroom facing the square, and instead head down the lane on the right to the actual cellars.

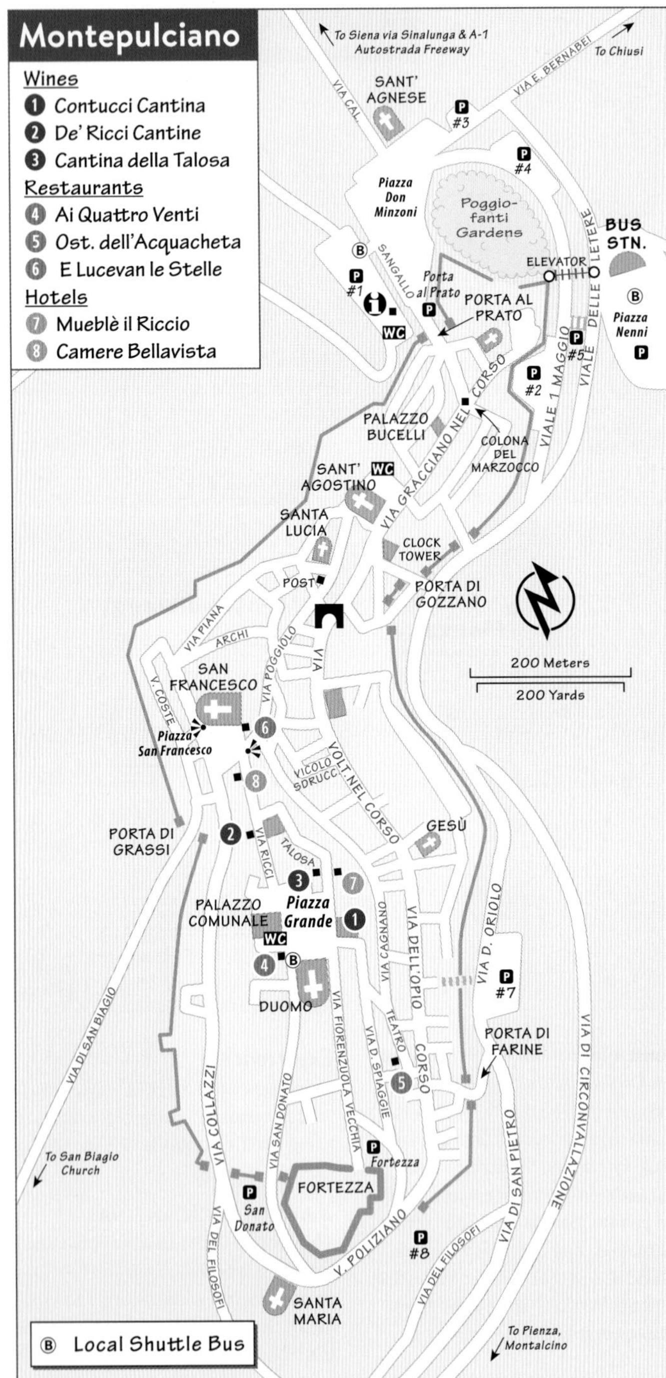
Montepulciano
Wines
1 Contucci Cantina
2 De' Ricci Cantine
3 Cantina della Talosa
Restaurants
4 Ai Quattro Venti
5 Ost. dell'Acquacheta
6 E Lucevan le Stelle
Hotels
7 Mueblè il Riccio
8 Camere Bellavista
To Siena via Sinalunga & A-1 Autostrada Freeway
To Chiusi
VIA E. BERNABEI
VIA CAL.
SANT' AGNESE
#3
#4
Piazza Don Minzoni
Poggio-fanti Gardens
BUS STN.
ELEVATOR
VIALE DELLE LETERE
Piazza Nenni
SANGALLO
#1
WC
Porta al Prato
PORTA AL PRATO
#5
#2
VIALE 1 MAGGIO
VIA GRACCIANO NEL CORSO
PALAZZO BUCELLI
COLONA DEL MARZOCCO
SANT' AGOSTINO
SANTA LUCIA
CLOCK TOWER
POST
PORTA DI GOZZANO
VIA PIANA
ARCHI
VIA POGGIOLO
VIA
200 Meters
200 Yards
SAN FRANCESCO
V. COSTE
Piazza San Francesco
VICOLO SDRUCC.
VOLT. NEL CORSO
GESÙ
PORTA DI GRASSI
VIA RICCI
TALOSA
PALAZZO COMUNALE
Piazza Grande
VIA CAGNANO
VIA DELL'OPIO
VIA D. ORIOLO
#7
DUOMO
VIA DI SAN BIAGIO
VIA FIORENZUOLA VECCHIA
VIA D. SPIAGGIE
TEATRO
CORSO
PORTA DI FARINE
VIA DI CIRCONVALLAZIONE
VIA COLLAZZI
VIA SAN DONATO
To San Biagio Church
Fortezza
FORTEZZA
San Donato
VIA DI SAN PIETRO
V. POLIZIANO
#8
VIA DEL FILOSOFI
VIA DEL FILOSOFI
SANTA MARIA
To Pienza, Montalcino
Local Shuttle Bus

The Contucci family has lived here since the 11th century; they usually have a half-dozen bottles open for tastings. After sipping a little wine, explore the palace basement, with its 13th-century vaults that have been filled with huge wine barrels since the 1500s.

Cost and Hours: Free drop-in tasting, daily 9:30—19:00, Piazza Grande 13, tel. 0578-757-006, www.contucci.it.

▲DE' RICCI CANTINE

The most impressive wine cellars in Montepulciano sit below Palazzo Ricci, just a few steps off the main square (toward the Church of San Francesco). Enter through the unassuming door and make your way down the spiral staircase to the dramatic cellars, with gigantic vaults several stories high. At the deepest point, you can peer into the atmospheric Etruscan cave. Finally you wind up in the shop, where you can taste a few wines; their sweet vin santo is good.

Cost and Hours: Tasting €3, free with this book; €12-20 bottles, affordable shipping, daily 11:00-19:00; enter Palazzo Ricci at Via Ricci 11, look for signs for *Cantine de' Ricci*; tel. 0578-757-166, www.cantinadericci.it.

CANTINA DELLA TALOSA

This historic cellar, which goes down and down to an Etruscan tomb at the bottom, ages a well-respected wine. With a passion and love of their craft, Cristian Pepi and Andrea give enthusiastic tours and tastings. While you can drop by for a free tasting, call ahead to book a tour, which includes five wines to taste.

Cost and Hours: Free tasting, €10 tour, daily March-Oct 10:00-19:30, shorter hours off-season, a block off Piazza Grande at Via Talosa 8, tel. 0578-757-929, www.talosa.it.

Eating

$$ Ai Quattro Venti is flavorful, fun, and convenient, right on Piazza Grande (closed Thu, tel. 0578-717-231). **$$$ Osteria dell'Acquacheta** is a carnivore's dream come true. Reserve for dinner (closed Tue, Via del Teatro 22, tel. 0578-717-086, www.acquacheta.eu). **$ E Lucevan le Stelle** has a terrace on a tranquil square, perfect for nursing a glass of local wine (daily 12:00-24:00, closed Nov-Easter, Piazza San Francesco 5, tel. 0578-758-725).

Sleeping

Try medieval-elegant **$$ Mueblè il Riccio** (a block below the main square at Via Talosa 21, tel. 0578-757-713, www.ilriccio.net) or tidy **$ Camere Bellavista** (Via Ricci 25, mobile 347-823-2314, www.camerebellavista.it).

Montalcino

On a hill overlooking vineyards and valleys, Montalcino is famous for its delicious, pricey Brunello di Montalcino red wines. The surrounding countryside is littered with upscale wineries, some of which offer tastings.

Montepulciano

Wine tasting at Contucci Cantina

Orientation

Sitting atop a hill amidst a sea of vineyards, Montalcino is surrounded by walls and dominated by the Fortezza (a.k.a. "La Rocca"). From here, roads lead down into the two main squares: Piazza Garibaldi and Piazza del Popolo.

Getting There: Montalcino is well-connected to **Siena** by bus (6/day Mon-Sat, 4/day Sun, 1.5 hours). Montalcino and **Montepulciano** bus connections require a transfer (3-4/daily except Sun, 1 hour). Check schedules locally or online (www.sienamobilita.it or www.tiemmespa.it), but since the Montepulciano bus connection is sporadic, consider hiring a taxi (about €70 one-way). The nearest train station is a 30-minute bus ride away, in Buonconvento.

Arrival in Montalcino: The **bus** station is on Piazza Cavour, within the town walls and about 300 yards from the town center. From here, simply follow Via Mazzini straight up into town. A few shops offer limited, short-term **luggage storage;** ask at the TI.

Drivers should skirt around the fortress (Fortezza), take the first right, and follow signs to *parking* and *Fortezza* (€1.50/hour, free 20:00-8:00). Or, if you don't mind a climb, park for free below the fortress: At the roundabout, take the small downhill lane into the big lower parking lot. If these lots are full, follow the town's western wall toward the Madonna del Soccorso church and a long pay lot.

Tourist Information: The helpful TI, just off Piazza Garibaldi in City Hall, offers a list of more than 150 regional wineries and books visits for a small fee (daily 10:00-13:00 & 14:00-17:50, tel. 0577-849-331, www.prolocomontalcino.com).

Regional Wines

Montepulciano is known for its Vino Nobile, while Montalcino is famous for its Brunello. In each wine, the predominant grape is a clone of sangiovese (Tuscany's red wine grape).

The oldest red wine in Tuscany, **Vino Nobile di Montepulciano** ("noble wine of Montepulciano") has been produced since the late 1500s. It's a dry ruby red, made mostly with the Prugnolo Gentile variety of sangiovese (70 percent). Aged two years—one year of which must be in oak casks—it's more full-bodied than a typical Chianti and less tannic than a Brunello. It pairs well with meat and local cheeses.

First created by the Biondi Santi clan in the late 19th century, **Brunello di Montalcino** ("the little brown one of Montalcino"—named for the color of the grapes before harvest) ranks among Italy's finest and most expensive wines. Made from 100 percent Sangiovese Grosso (a.k.a. Brunello) grapes, it's smooth, dry, and aged for a minimum of two years in wood casks, plus an additional four months in the bottle. It's designed to cellar for 10 years or longer—but who can wait? It pairs well with the local cuisine; the perfect match is Chianina beef. You'll also see Rosso di Montalcino (a younger version of Brunello), which is aged for one year. This "poor man's Brunello" is good, at half the price.

Wine Tasting

As Brunello is the poshest of Italian wines, these wineries feel a bit upscale, and most require an advance reservation. Tours generally last 45-60 minutes, cost €10-15 per person, and conclude with a tasting. The **Brunello Wine Bus** laces together visits to four wineries, with a lunch break in the middle (€90, May-Oct Tue and Thu-Sat, departs at 10:00, returns at 19:00, tel. 0577-846-021, www.winetravelsforyou.com). If you have a car, these wineries are easy to visit (see map on page 253):

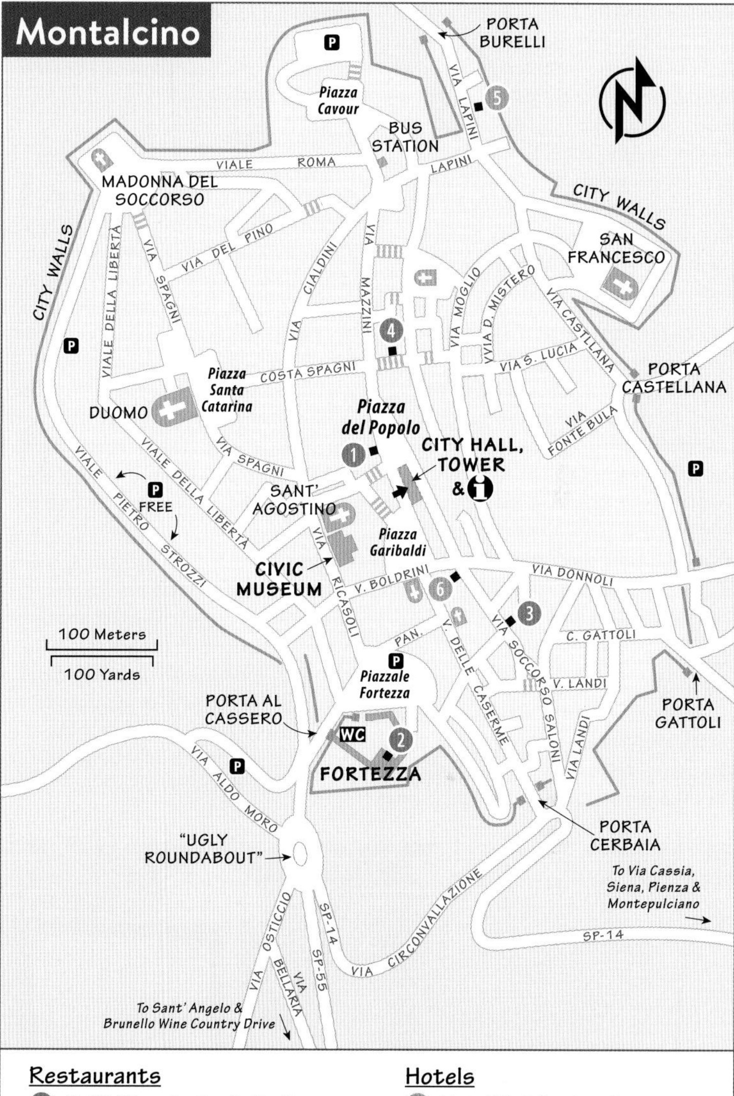

Restaurants

1. Caffè Fiaschetteria Italiana
2. Enoteca la Fortezza di Montalcino
3. Re di Macchia
4. Taverna del Grappolo Blu

Hotels

5. Hotel Dei Capitani
6. Palazzina Cesira

MASTROJANNI

This big, glitzy winery is perched high above the Romanesque Sant'Antimo Abbey, overlooking sprawling vineyards (€17-36 bottles, Podere Loreto e San Pio, tel. 0577-835-681, www.mastrojanni.com). To reach it, head up into the town of Castelnuovo dell'Abate (just above Sant'Antimo Abbey), bear left at the Bassomondo restaurant, and continue up along the gravel road (enjoying vineyard and abbey views).

CIACCI PICCOLOMINI D'ARAGONA

This family-run vineyard offers two or three free tastes or formal tastings and tours in a classy *enoteca* with an outdoor view terrace (€10-25 tours, Mon-Fri 9:00-19:00, Sat 10:30-18:30, closed Sun, head toward Castelnuovo dell'Abate but go right before entering that town, following signs toward Sant'Angelo in Colle, tel. 0577-835-616, www.ciaccipiccolomini.com, visite@ciaccipiccolomini.com).

ALTESINO

Elegant Altesino is in a stunning location, just off a back road that winds up cypress-lined gravel lanes to expansive vineyard views (€15 for tour and basic tasting, daily, Loc. Altesino 54, tel. 0577-806-208, www.altesino.it). You'll find the turnoff for Altesino along the back road (SP-45) between Montalcino and Buonconvento (not the main SR-2 highway).

SANTA GIULIA

This family winery emphasizes quality over quantity, with a rustic tasting room on a working farm. Call ahead for a farm-fresh tasting (€15 for tasting and tour, 2-person minimum, €13-30 bottles, closed Sun, Loc. Santa Giulia 48, tel. 0577-834-270, www.santagiuliamontalcino.it). From Torrenieri's main intersection, follow the brown *Via Francigena* signs. After crossing the train tracks and a bridge, watch on the left to follow signs for *Sasso di Sole*, then *Sta. Giulia*; you'll take gravel roads through farm fields to the winery.

Eating

Caffè Fiaschetteria Italiana is a grand café serving wine, light lunches, and the best espresso in town (daily 7:30-23:00, Piazza del Popolo 6, tel. 0577-849-043).

Enoteca la Fortezza di Montalcino serves top-end wines and light snacks by the glass in a medieval setting inside Montalcino's fort (daily 9:00-20:00,

Wine tasting near Montalcino

closes at 18:00 Nov-March, inside Fortezza, tel. 0577-849-211).

Intimate **$$$ Re di Macchia** serves a seasonal menu alongside a fine wine list (Fri-Wed 12:00-14:00 & 19:00-21:00, closed Thu, Via Soccorso Saloni 21, tel. 0577-846-116).

$$ Taverna del Grappolo Blu is unpretentious but serious about its wine, game, and homemade pasta (Sat-Thu 12:00-15:00 & 19:00-22:00, closed Fri, Scale di Via Moglio 1, tel. 0577-847-150, www.grappoloblu.it).

Sleeping

Consider plush **$$$ Hotel Dei Capitani** (RS%, request a view room, Via Lapini 6, tel. 0577-847-227, www.deicapitani.it) or refined and tranquil **$$ Palazzina Cesira** (RS%, 2-night minimum, Via Soccorso Saloni 2, tel. 0577-846-055, www.montalcinoitaly.com).

ASSISI

Assisi is famous for its hometown boy, St. Francis, who made very, very good. While Francis the saint is interesting, Francesco Bernardone the man is even more so. Mementos of his days here are everywhere—where he was baptized, a shirt he wore, a hill he prayed on, and a church where a vision changed his life.

About the year 1200, this simple friar from Assisi countered the decadence of society with a powerful message of non-materialism and a "slow down and smell God's roses" lifestyle. Christianity's most popular saint and its purest example of simplicity is now glorified in beautiful churches, along with his female counterpart, St. Clare.

Francis' message of love has timeless appeal, inspiring the current "people's pope" to take his name. But every pilgrimage site is inevitably commercialized: Today, this Umbrian town bursts with Franciscan knickknacks. Look past the glow-in-the-dark rosaries and bobblehead friars. Even a block or two off the congested main drag, it's possible to find pockets of the serenity Francis knew. While it's crowded with tourists by day, Assisi after dark is closer to a place Francis could call home.

Orientation

The city stretches across a ridge that rises from a flat plain. The Basilica of St. Francis sits at the low end of town; Piazza Matteotti (bus stop and parking lot) is at the high end; and the main square, Piazza del Comune, lies in between. The main drag (called Via San Francesco for most of its course) runs from Piazza del Comune to the basilica. Capping the hill above the town is a ruined castle, called Rocca Maggiore. Walking uphill from the basilica to Piazza Matteotti takes 30 minutes, while the downhill journey takes about 15 minutes.

Some Francis sights lie outside the city walls, in the valley beneath the ridge; this modern part of town is called Santa Maria degli Angeli.

Tourist Information: The TI is in the center of the old town on Piazza del Comune (Mon-Fri 8:30-18:30, Sat-Sun 9:00-18:00, tel. 075-813-8680, www.visit-assisi.it). From April to October, there's also a branch down in the valley in Santa Maria degli Angeli, across the street from the big piazza in front of the Basilica of St. Mary of the Angels.

Laundry: 3 Elle Blu' Lavanderia will do your laundry at a reasonable price on the same day (closed Sun, Via Borgo Aretino 6a, tel. 075-816-084).

Travel Agencies: You can purchase train, bus, and plane tickets at **Agenzia Viaggi Stoppini,** which also offers day trips to nearby towns, between Piazza del Comune and the Basilica of St. Clare (Mon-Fri 9:00-12:30 & 15:30-19:00, Sat 9:00-12:30, closed Sun, Corso Mazzini 31, tel. 075-812-597, www.viaggistoppiniassisi.it).

Private Guides: Giuseppe Karabotis is a good, licensed guide (€130/3 hours, €260/6 hours, mobile 328-867-0567, iokarabot@libero.it). **Daniela Moretti** knows both

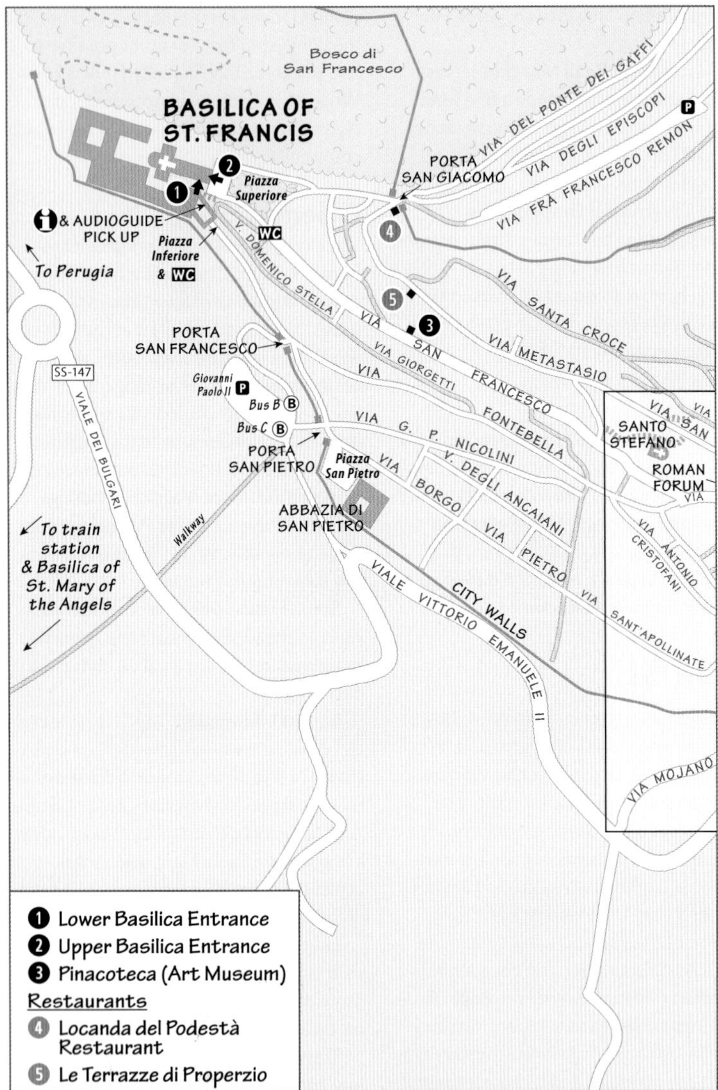

Assisi and all of Umbria (€120/half-day, €240/day, mobile 335-829-9984, www.danyguide.com, danyguide@hotmail.com).

Rick's Tip: *Tacky knickknacks line the streets leading to the Basilica of St. Francis. For* **better shops,** *head to* **Via San Rufino** *and* **Corso Mazzini** *(both just off Piazza del Comune).*

Assisi Town Walk

This self-guided walk covers the town from top to bottom. To get to Piazza Matteotti, you have several options: Ride the bus from the train station (or from Piazza Giovanni Paolo II) to the last stop; drive up (and park in the underground lot); or hike five minutes uphill from Piazza del Comune.

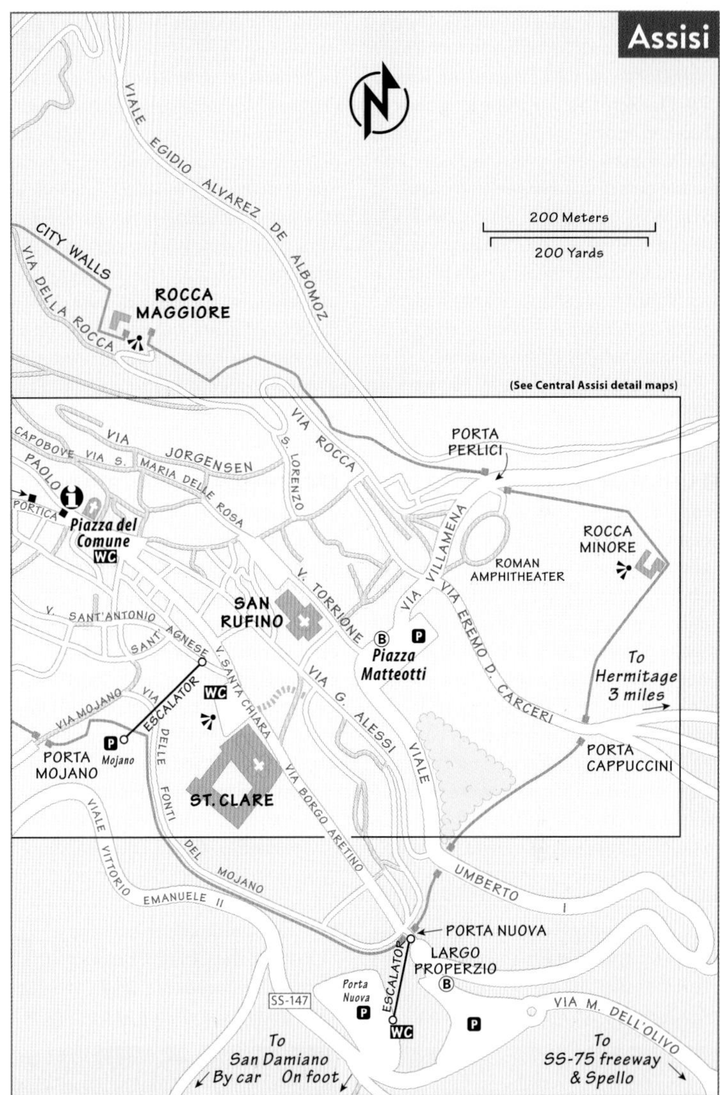

Download my free Assisi Town Walk audio tour.

• *Start 50 yards beyond Piazza Matteotti (down the small lane between two stone houses, away from city center).*

❶ THE ROMAN AMPHITHEATER

A lane named Via Anfiteatro Romano skirts the cozy neighborhood built around the site of a long-ago Roman amphitheater—a reminder that Assisi was once an important Roman town. Circle to the right along the curved lane that marks the amphitheater's footprint. Imagine how colorful the town laundry basin (on the right) must have been when the women of Assisi gathered here to do their wash. Just beyond, above another small rectangular basin, are the coats of arms of Assisi's leading families. A few steps farther, leave the amphitheater, hiking up the stairs on the right to the top of the hill for an overhead view of the ancient oval. The Roman stones have long been absorbed into the medieval architecture. It was Roman tradition to locate the amphitheater outside of town, which this used to be. While the amphitheater dates from the first century A.D., the buildings filling it today were built in the 13th and 14th centuries. Notice how carefully maintained the town's complexion is—when re-shingling a roof, locals will mix old and new tiles.

• *Continue on, enjoying the grand view of the fortress in the distance. The lane leads down to a city gate on the right and an...*

❷ UMBRIAN VIEW

Step outside of Assisi at the Porta Perlici gate for a commanding view. Umbria, called the "green heart of Italy," is the country's geographical center and only landlocked region. Enjoy the various shades of green: silver green on the valley floor (olives), emerald green (grapevines), and deep green on the hillsides (oak trees). The valleys are dotted by small family farms, many of which rent rooms. Also notice the Rocca Maggiore ("big fortress"), which provided townsfolk a refuge in times of attack, and, behind you, atop the nearer hill, Rocca Minore ("little fortress"), which gives the town's young lovers a little privacy. The quarry (under the Rocca Maggiore) was a source for Assisi's characteristic pink limestone.

• *Go back through the gate and follow Via Porta Perlici—immediately on your right—downhill into town (toward Hotel La Rocca). Enjoy the higgledy-piggledy architecture (this neighborhood has some of the most photogenic back lanes in town). Fifty yards down, to the left of the arched gate, find the wall containing an aqueduct that dates back to Roman times. It still brings water from a mountain spring into the city (push the brass tap for a taste). After another 50 yards, turn left through a medieval town gate (with Hotel La Rocca on your right). Just after the hotel, you'll pass a second gate dating from Roman times. Follow Via Porta Perlici downhill until you hit a fine square facing a big church.*

❸ CATHEDRAL OF SAN RUFINO

Trick question: Who's Assisi's patron saint? While Francis is one of Italy's patron saints, Rufino (the town's first bishop, martyred and buried here in the third century) is Assisi's. This 11th-century Romanesque cathedral (with a Neoclassical interior) is dedicated to Rufino. Although it has one of the best and purest Romanesque facades in all of Umbria, the big triangular top was added in Gothic times.

Cost and Hours: Cathedral—free, daily 7:00-19:00, Nov-mid-March closed midday; museum—€3.50, Thu-Tue 10:00-13:00 & 15:00-18:00, closed Wed, shorter hours off-season and Sun, tel. 075-812-283, www.assisimuseodiocesano.it.

Visiting the Church: Before going in, study the facade—a jungle of beasts emphasizing the church as a refuge in a

Assisi

The outline of the Roman amphitheater

St. Francis of Assisi (1181-1226)

In 1202, young Francesco Bernardone donned armor and rode out to battle the Perugians (residents of Umbria's capital city). After being captured and imprisoned for a year, Francis returned a changed man. He avoided friends and his father's lucrative business and spent more and more time outside the city walls fasting and praying. In 1206, he had a vision and declared his loyalty to God alone.

Francis became a cult figure, attracting huge crowds who'd never seen anything like him. He preached sermons outdoors and in the local language (not Church Latin), making God accessible to all. Idealistic young men followed Francis, wandering Italy to spread the Gospel to rich and poor. Francis' new order of monks extolled poverty and simplicity. Despite its radicalism, the order eventually gained the pope's approval and spread throughout the world. Francis, who died in Assisi at the age of 45, left a legacy of humanism, equality, and love of nature.

scary world. Notice the lions at the base of the facade, flanking each door. One is eating a Christian martyr, reminding worshippers of the courage of early Christians.

Enter the church. While the front of the church is an unremarkable mix of 17th- and 18th-century Baroque and Neoclassical, the rear (near your entrance) has several points of interest. Notice first the two fine statues: *St. Francis* and *St. Clare* (by Giovanni Dupré, 1888). To your right is an old baptismal font (in the corner with the semicircular black iron grate). In about 1181, a baby boy was baptized in this font. His parents were well-to-do Francophiles who called him Francesco ("Frenchy"). In 1194, a nobleman baptized his daughter Clare here. Eighteen years later, their paths crossed in this same church, when Clare attended a class and became mesmerized by the teacher—Francis. The children of Assisi are still baptized here.

The striking glass panels in the floor reveal foundations preserved from the ninth-century church that once stood here. After the 1997 earthquake, structural inspectors checked the church from ceiling to floor. When they looked under the paving stones, they discovered graves (it was common practice to bury people in churches until Napoleon decreed otherwise). Underneath that level, they found Roman foundations and some animal bones (suggesting the possibility of animal sacrifice). There might have been a Roman temple here; churches were often built upon temple ruins. Stand at the back of the church facing the altar, and look left to the Roman cistern that collected rainwater (just beyond the great stone archway, next to where you entered). Take the three steps down (to trigger the light) and marvel at the fine stonework and Roman engineering. In the Middle Ages, this was the town's emergency water source.

Diocesan Museum: Underneath the

Cathedral of San Rufino

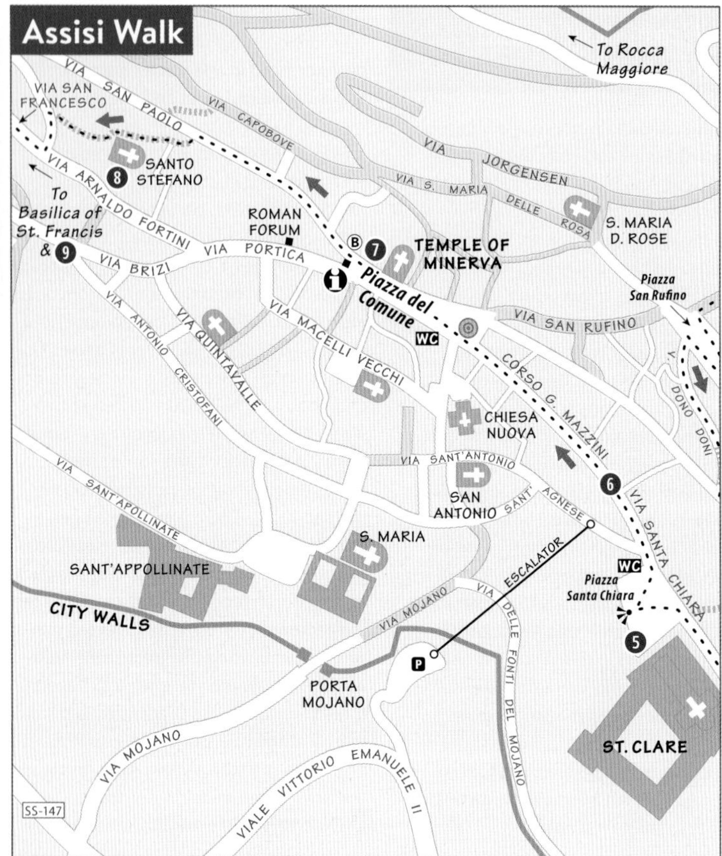

church, incorporated into the Roman ruins and columns, are the foundations of an earlier Church of San Rufino, now the crypt and a small museum. When it's open, you can go below to see the saint's third-century sarcophagus and art from centuries past (down the stairs, near the baptismal font, well-described in English).

• *Leaving the church, take a sharp left (at the pizza joint, on Via Dono Doni). After 20 yards, take a right and go all the way down the stairway to see some...*

❹ MEDIEVAL ARCHITECTURE

At the bottom of the stairs, notice the pink limestone pavement, part of the surviving medieval town. The arches built over doorways indicate that the buildings date from the 12th through the 14th centuries, when Assisi was booming. Italian cities at the time were inventing free-market capitalism, dabbling in democratic self-rule, and creating the modern urban lifestyle. The vaults you see that turn lanes into tunnels are reminders of medieval urban expansion—creating more living space (mostly 15th century). While the population grew, people wanted to live within the town's protective walls. Medieval Assisi had several times the population density of modern Assisi. Notice the blooming balconies; Assisi holds a flower competition each June.

• *From the bottom of the stairs, head to the left and continue downhill. When you arrive at a street, turn left, going slightly uphill for a*

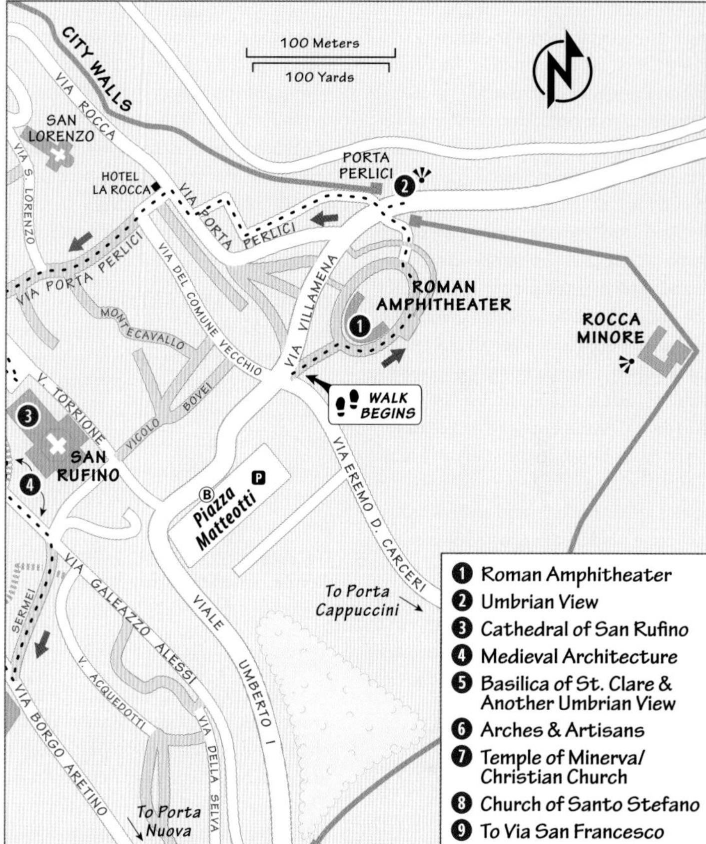

long block, then take the low road (right) at the Y, and head down Via Sermei. Continue down to the big church. Walk right, under the three massive buttresses, to Piazza Santa Chiara and the front of the church.

❺ BASILICA OF ST. CLARE (BASILICA DI SANTA CHIARA)

Dedicated to the founder of the Order of the Poor Clares, this Umbrian Gothic church is simple, in keeping with the nuns' dedication to a life of contemplation. At age 18, Clare (1194-1253) became a nun after listening to Francis' teaching, and spent the rest of her life following a regimen of prayer, meditation, and simple manual labor. Her order was originally located in the humble Church of San Damiano, in the valley below, but after Clare's death, a bigger and more glorious building was built in 1265; the huge buttresses were added in the next century.

Cost and Hours: Free, daily 6:30-12:00 & 14:00-19:00, until 18:00 in winter, Mon-Fri crypt opens at 9:00.

Visiting the Basilica: The interior's fine frescoes were whitewashed in Baroque times. The battered remains of one on the left show how the fresco surface was hacked up so whitewash would stick. Imagine all the pristine frescoes hiding behind the whitewash.

The Chapel of the Crucifix of San Damiano, on the right, has the wooden crucifix that changed Francis' life. In 1206, an emaciated, soul-searching, stark-raving Francis knelt before this crucifix of a living Christ (then located in the Church of San Damiano) and asked for guidance. According to legend, the crucifix spoke: "Go and rebuild my Church, which you can see has fallen into ruin." Francis followed the call.

Stairs lead from the nave down to the tomb of St. Clare. Her tomb—discovered in about 1850—is at the far right end of the ornamented neo-Gothic crypt (the image is fiberglass; her actual bones lie underneath). The paintings on the walls depict spiritual lessons from Clare's life and death. At the opposite end of the crypt (back between the stairs, in a large glassed-in area) are important relics: the saint's robes, her hair, and an enormous tunic she made—along with relics of St. Francis (including a blood-stained stocking he wore after receiving the stigmata). The attached cloistered community of the Poor Clares has flourished for 700 years.

• *Leave the church and belly up to the viewpoint at the edge of the square for...*

Another Umbrian View: On the left is the convent of St. Clare. Below you lies the olive grove of the Poor Clares, which has been there since the 13th century. In the distance is a grand view. Assisi overlooks the richest and biggest valley in otherwise mountainous Umbria. Across the valley to the far right (and over the Tiber River), the rival town Perugia, where Francis was imprisoned, sits on its own hill. The municipality of Assisi has a population of 25,000, but only 3,500 people live in the old town. The lower town, called Santa Maria degli Angeli, grew up with the coming of the railway in the 19th century. In the haze, the church with the grayish-blue dome is St. Mary of the Angels, the cradle of the Franciscan order and a popular pilgrimage site today.

• *From the church square, step out into Via Santa Chiara.*

6 ARCHES AND ARTISANS

Notice the three medieval town gates (two behind the church, and one uphill toward the town center). The gate over the road behind the church dates from 1265. Farther on, you can just see the Porta Nuova, which marks the final medieval expansion of Assisi in 1316. Toward the city center (on Via Santa Chiara, the high road), an arch marks the site of the Roman wall. These three gates represent the town's three walls, illustrating how much the city has grown since ancient times.

Walk uphill along Via Santa Chiara (which becomes Corso Mazzini) to the city's main square. As you pass under the arch you enter what was Roman Assisi. The street is lined with interesting shops selling traditional embroidery, religious souvenirs, and local edibles. The shops on Corso Mazzini, on the stretch between the gate and Piazza del Comune, showcase handicrafts. **Galleria d'Arte Perna** (on the left, #20b) sells the medieval fantasy townscapes of Paolo Grimaldi, a local painter. The recommended travel agency,

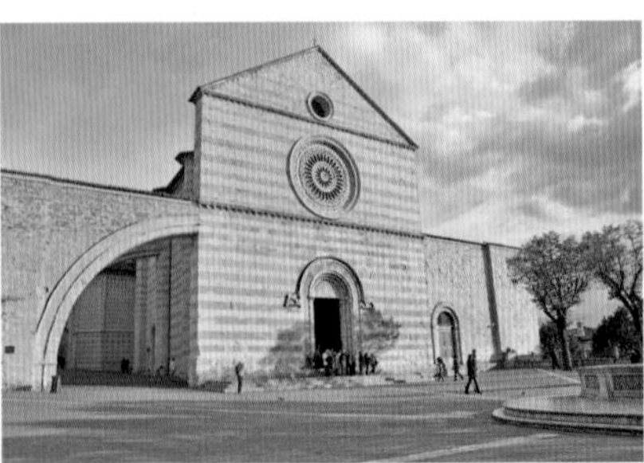

Basilica of St. Clare

Porta Nuova Gate

Agenzia Viaggi Stoppini, is across the street and a few steps up, at #31.

Next, the aptly named **Assisi Olive Wood** (on the left at #14E) sells carvings, as does **d'Olivo** (across the street at #23). It's said that St. Francis made the first Nativity scene to help humanize the Christmas message. That's why you'll see so many crèches in Assisi. (Even today, Italians everywhere set up elaborate crèches for Christmas.) Further along at #14A is a bakery, **Bar Sensi,** selling traditional raisin-and-apple strudel called *rocciata* (roh-CHAH-tah, splittable and served warm). Farther along on the left is **Antichita Il Duomo** (on the corner at #2b), selling religious art. Across the street, on the right, is **Galleria del Corso,** selling embroidered linens. And on the square, **La Bottega dei Sapori** (at #34, opposite the flags) is worth a visit if you're hungry or thirsty.

You've walked up what was, in ancient times, the main drag into town. Ahead of you, the six fluted Corinthian columns of the Temple of Minerva marked the forum (today's Piazza del Comune). Sit at the fountain on the piazza for a few minutes of people-watching. Within a few hundred yards of this square were the medieval walls. Imagine the commotion of 5,000 people confined within these walls. No wonder St. Francis needed some peace and quiet.

• *Now, head over to the temple on the square.*

❼ TEMPLE OF MINERVA/ CHRISTIAN CHURCH

The Romans went to great lengths to make this Temple of Minerva, which dates from the first century B.C., a centerpiece of their city. Notice the columns that cut into the stairway. It was a tight fit here on the hilltop. In ancient times, the stairs went down—about twice as far as they do now—to the main drag, which has gradually been filled in over time. The Church of Santa Maria sopra ("over") Minerva was added in the ninth century.

Pop inside the temple/church. Today's interior is 17th-century Baroque. Flanking the altar are the original Roman temple floor stones. You can even see the drains for the bloody sacrifices that took place here. Behind the statues of Peter and Paul, the original Roman embankment peeks through.

Cost and Hours: Free, daily 7:15-19:30, in winter closes for a lunch break and at sunset.

• *Across the square next to #11, step into the 16th-century frescoed vaults of the...*

Loggia of Palazzo del Comune: Notice the Italian flair for design. Even this little loggia was once finely decorated. The art style is called "Grotesque," named for the Renaissance-era discovery of Roman paintings featuring bizarre creatures on the walls of Nero's Golden House in Rome (the lower levels, still largely unexcavated, appeared cave-like: grottoesque). This scene was indisputably painted after 1492. How do they know? Because it features turkeys—first seen in Europe after Columbus returned from the Americas. The turkeys painted here may have been that bird's European debut.

Temple of Minerva

• *From the main square, hike past the temple up the high road, Via San Paolo. After 200 yards (across from #24), a sign directs you down a stepped lane to the...*

❽ CHURCH OF SANTO STEFANO
Surrounded by cypress, fig, and walnut trees, Santo Stefano—which used to be outside the town walls in the days of St. Francis—is an interesting bit of off-beat Assisi (free, daily 8:30-20:00, shorter hours off-season). Legend has it that its bells miraculously rang on October 3, 1226, the day St. Francis died. This is a typical rural Romanesque church—no architect, just built by simple stonemasons who put together the most basic design. Hundreds of years later, it still stands.

• *The lane zigzags down to Via San Francesco. Turn right and walk under the arch toward the Basilica of St. Francis.*

❾ VIA SAN FRANCESCO
This main drag leads from the town to the basilica holding the body of St. Francis. He was made a saint in 1228—the same year that the basilica's foundations were laid—and his body was moved here by 1230. Assisi was a big-time pilgrimage center, and this street was its booming hub. The arch marks the end of what was Assisi in St. Francis' day. Notice the fine medieval balcony immediately past the arch (on the left). About 30 yards farther down (on the left), cool yourself at the fountain, as medieval pilgrims might have. The hospice next door was built in 1237 to house pilgrims. Notice the three surviving faces of its fresco: Jesus, Francis, and Clare. Farther down on the left, across from #12A (on the left), is Oratorio dei Pellegrini, dating from the 1450s. A brotherhood ran a hostel here for travelers passing through to pay homage to St. Francis. The chapel offers a richly frescoed 14th-century space designed to inspire—perfect for any traveler to pause and contemplate the saint's message.

• *Continuing on, you'll eventually reach*

Church of Santo Stefano

Assisi's main sight, the Basilica of St. Francis. For the start of my self-guided tour, walk downhill to the basilica's lower courtyard.

Sights

▲▲▲BASILICA OF ST. FRANCIS
The Basilica of St. Francis (Basilica di San Francesco) is one of the artistic and religious highlights of Europe. It rises where, in 1226, St. Francis was buried outside of his town on the "Hill of the Damned"—now called the "Hill of Paradise." The basilica is frescoed from top to bottom with scenes by the leading artists of the day: Cimabue, Giotto, Simone Martini, and Pietro Lorenzetti. A 13th-century historian wrote, "No more exquisite monument to the Lord has been built."

From a distance, you see the huge arcades "supporting" the basilica. These were 15th-century quarters for the monks. The arcades that line the square and lead to the church housed medieval pilgrims.

ORIENTATION

Cost and Hours: Free entry; lower basilica and tomb—daily 6:00-18:50, Nov-March until 18:00; reliquary chapel in lower basilica—generally open Mon-Fri

The Franciscan Message

Not only did Francis follow Christ's teachings, he followed Christ's lifestyle, living as a poor, wandering preacher. He traded a life of power and riches for one of obedience, poverty, and chastity. He was never ordained as a priest, but his influence on Christianity was monumental.

The Franciscan realm (Brother Sun, Sister Moon, and so on) is a space where God, man, and the natural world frolic harmoniously. Francis treated every creature—animal, peasant, pope—with equal respect. He and his "brothers" (*fratelli*, or friars) slept in fields, begged for food, and exuded the joy of non-materialism. Franciscan friars were known as the "Jugglers of God," who roved the countryside singing, telling stories, and cracking jokes.

In an Italy torn by conflict, Francis promoted peace. While the Church was waging bloody Crusades, Francis pushed ecumenism and understanding. In 1288, just 62 years after Francis died, a Franciscan became pope (Nicholas IV). Francis' message also led to Church reforms that many believe delayed the Protestant Reformation by a century.

Assisi's richly decorated basilica seems to contradict the teachings of the poor monk it honors, but it was built as an act of religious and civic pride. It was also designed as a pilgrimage center and a splendid classroom. Though monks in robes may not give off an "easy-to-approach" vibe, the Franciscans of today are still God's jugglers (and many of them speak English).

Here is Francis' message, in his own words:

The Canticle of the Sun

Good Lord, all your creations bring praise to you!
Praise for Brother Sun, who brings the day. His radiance reminds us of you!
Praise for Sister Moon and the stars, precious and beautiful.
Praise for Brother Wind, and for clouds and storms and rain that sustain us.
Praise for Sister Water. She is useful and humble, precious and pure.
Praise for Brother Fire who cheers us at night.
Praise for our sister, Mother Earth, who feeds us and rules us.
Praise for all those who forgive because you have forgiven them.
Praise for our sister, Bodily Death, from whose embrace none can escape.
Praise and bless the Lord, and give thanks, and, with humility, serve him.

9:00-18:00, often closed Sat-Sun and occasionally at other times for religious services; upper basilica—daily 8:30-18:55, Nov-March until 18:00; treasury—free but donation requested, daily 10:00-13:00 & 14:00-17:30.

Information: The church courtyard at the entrance of the lower basilica has an info office (Mon-Sat 9:15-17:30, closed Sun year-round, tel. 075-819-001, www.sanfrancescoassisi.org). Call or check the website to find out about upcoming **events** at the basilica.

Dress Code: Modest dress is required to enter the church—no above-the-knee skirts or shorts and no sleeveless tops for men, women, or children.

Tours: Videoguides loaded with a one-hour tour are available at the information office under the arcade in the courtyard of the lower basilica (€6, €10/2 people) or download the €2 "Basilica San Francesco Assisi" **app** to your own device.

🎧 Download my free Basilica of St. Francis **audio tour.**

Church Services: On summer Sundays (Easter-Oct), a Mass is held in English in the lower basilica at 9:00. The basilica choir sings the Mass on many Sundays at 10:30. Or join one of the many Masses in *Italiano* (Sun at 7:30, 9:00, 10:30, 12:00, 17:00, and 18:30; Nov-March at 7:15, 11:00, and 17:00). Additional English and sung Masses don't follow a set schedule. Call the basilica to find out when English-speaking pilgrimage groups or choirs have reserved Masses, and attend with them—although groups change their plans fairly often (tel. 075-819-001).

Bookstore: The church bookshop is in the inner courtyard behind the upper and lower basilica. It sells an excellent guidebook, *The Basilica of Saint Francis: A Spiritual Pilgrimage* (€3, by Goulet, McInally, and Wood). I used this book, and a tour with Brother Michael, as sources for this self-guided tour.

Visitor Services: Two different pay WCs are within a half-block of the lower entrance—up the road in a squat building, and halfway down the big piazza on the left. There aren't any WCs inside the basilica.

OVERVIEW

Since the basilica is the reason that most people visit Assisi, I've designed this self-guided tour with an emphasis on the place's theology (rather than art history).

A disclaimer: Just as Francis used many biblical legends to help teach the Christian message, legends from the life of Francis were told in later ages to teach the same message. Are they true? Probably not. Are they in keeping with Francis' message? Yes. Do I share legends here as if they are historic? Sure.

The church has three parts: the upper basilica, the lower basilica, and the saint's tomb. To get oriented, stand at the lower entrance in the courtyard. While empty today, centuries ago this main plaza was cluttered with pilgrim services and medieval souvenir shops.

On Via San Francesco

➲ SELF-GUIDED TOUR

Enter through the grand doorway of the lower basilica. Just inside, decorating the top of the first arch, look up and see St. Francis, who greets you with a Latin inscription. Sounding a bit like John Wayne, he says the equivalent of, "Slow down and be joyful, pilgrim. You've reached the Hill of Paradise. If you're observant and thoughtful, this church will knock your spiritual socks off."

• *Start with the tomb. To get there, turn left into the nave. Midway down, follow the signs and go right, to the tomb downstairs.*

The Tomb: The saint's remains are above the altar in the stone box with the iron ties. Holy relics were the "ruby slippers" of medieval Europe. Relics gave you power—they answered your prayers and won your wars—and ultimately helped you get back to your eternal Kansas. Assisi made no bones about promoting the saint's relics, but hid his tomb for security. His body was buried secretly while the basilica was under construction, and over the next 600 years, the exact location was forgotten. When the tomb was opened to the public in 1818, it took more than a month to find his actual remains.

Francis' four closest friends and first followers are memorialized in the corners of the room. Opposite the altar, up four steps between the entrance and exit, notice the small copper box behind the metal grill, which contains the remains of Francis' rich Roman patron, Jacopa dei Settesoli. She traveled to see him on his deathbed but was turned away because she was female. Francis waived the rule and welcomed "Brother Jacopa" to his side. These five tombs—in the Franciscan spirit of being with your friends—were added in the 19th century.

The candles you see are the only real candles in the church (others are electric). Pilgrims pay a coin, pick up a candle, and place it in the small box on the side. Franciscans will light it later.

• *Climb back up to the lower nave.*

Lower Basilica: Subdued and Romanesque, this nave is frescoed with parallel scenes from the lives of Christ (right) and Francis (left), connected by a ceiling of stars. The Passion of Christ and the Compassion of Francis lead to the altar built over Francis' tomb. After the church was built and decorated, side chapels were erected to provide mausoleums for the rich families that patronized the work of the order. Unfortunately, in the process, huge arches were cut out of some frescoed scenes, but others survive. In the fresco directly above the entry to the tomb, Christ is being taken down from the cross (just the bottom half of his body can be seen, on the left), and it looks like the story is over. Defeat. But in the opposite fresco (above the tomb's exit), we see Francis preaching to the birds, reminding the faithful that the message of the Gospel survives.

These stories directed the attention of the medieval pilgrim to the altar, where he could meet God through the sacraments. The church was thought of as a community of believers sailing toward God. The prayers coming out of the nave (*navis,* or ship) fill the triangular sections of the ceiling—called *vele,* or sails—with spiritual wind. With a priest for a navigator and the altar for a helm, faith propels the ship.

Walk around and stand behind the altar (toes to the bottom step, facing the entrance) and look up. The three scenes above you represent the creed of the

Basilica of St. Francis

Franciscans: Directly above the tomb of St. Francis, to the right, **Obedience** (Francis appears twice, wearing a rope harness and kneeling in front of Lady Obedience); to the left, **Chastity** (in her tower of purity held up by two angels); and straight ahead, **Poverty.** Here Jesus blesses the marriage as Francis slips a ring on Lady Poverty. In the foreground, two pint-size merchants (the new rich of a thriving northern Italy) are throwing sticks and stones at the bride. But Poverty, in her patched wedding dress, is fertile and strong, and even bare brambles blossom into a rosebush crown.

The three knots in the rope that ties the Franciscan robe symbolize the monks' vows of obedience, chastity, and poverty, serving as a constant reminder of their vows. The jeweled belt of a rich person was all about material wealth, hung with a bag of coins, along with a weapon to protect that person's wealth. St. Francis called money the "devil's dung."

Now turn around and put your heels to the altar and—bending back like a drum major—look up for a peek at the reward for a life of obedience, chastity, and poverty: **Francis on a heavenly throne** in a rich, golden robe. He traded a life of earthly simplicity for glory in heaven.

• *Turn to the right and march to the corner, where steps lead down into the...*

Reliquary Chapel: This chapel is filled with fascinating relics (which a €0.50 flier explains in detailed English; often closed Sat-Sun). Step in and circle the room clockwise. You'll see the silver chalice and plate that Francis used for the bread and wine of the Eucharist (in a small, dark, windowed case set into the wall, marked *Calice e Patena*). Francis believed that his personal possessions should be simple, but the items used for worship should be made of the finest materials. Next, the Veli di Lino is a cloth Jacopa used to wipe her friend's brow on his deathbed. In the corner display case is a small section of the itchy haircloth *(cilizio)*—made from scratchy horse or goat hair—worn by Francis as penance (the cloth he chose was the opposite of the fine fabric his father sold). In the next corner are the tunic and slippers that Francis donned during his last days. Next, find a prayer (in a fancy silver stand) that St. Francis wrote for Brother Leo and signed with a T-shaped character—his tau cross. The last letter in the Hebrew alphabet, tav ("tau" in Greek) is symbolic of faithfulness to the end, and Francis adopted it for his signature. Next is a papal document (1223) legitimizing the Franciscan order and assuring his followers that they were not risking a (deadly) heresy charge. Finally, just past the altar, see the tunic that was lovingly patched and stitched by followers of the five-foot, four-inch-tall St. Francis.

Before leaving the chapel, notice the modern paintings by local artists. Over the entrance, Francis is shown being born in a stable like Jesus (by Capitini).

• *Return up the stairs, stepping into the...*

Lower Basilica's Transept: The decoration of this church brought together the greatest Sienese (Lorenzetti and Simone Martini) and Florentine (Cimabue and Giotto) artists of the day. Look around at the painted scenes. In 1300, this was radical art—homespun scenes, landscapes, trees, real people. Directly opposite the reliquary chapel, study **Giotto's painting of the Crucifixion,** with the eight sparrow-like angels. For the first time, holy people express emotion: One angel turns her head sadly at the sight of Jesus; another scratches her cheeks, drawing blood. Mary (lower left) has fainted in despair. The Franciscans, with the goal of bringing God to the people, found a natural partner in Europe's first naturalist (and therefore modern) painter, Giotto.

To grasp Giotto's artistic leap, compare his work with the painting to the right, by Cimabue. It's Gothic, without the 3-D architecture, natural backdrop, and slice-of-life reality of Giotto's work. **Cimabue's St. Francis** (far right) shows the saint with

Basilica of St. Francis—Lower Level

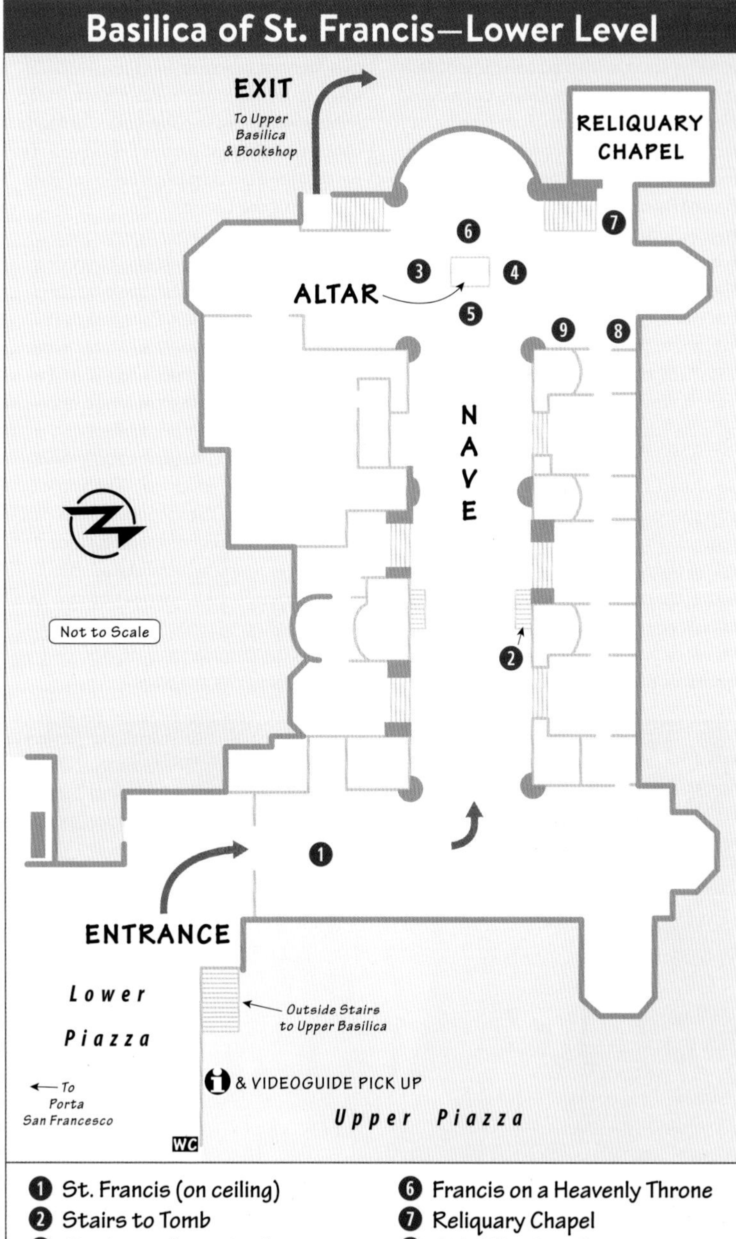

1. St. Francis (on ceiling)
2. Stairs to Tomb
3. Obedience (on ceiling)
4. Chastity (on ceiling)
5. Poverty (on ceiling)
6. Francis on a Heavenly Throne
7. Reliquary Chapel
8. GIOTTO – Crucifixion
9. CIMABUE – St. Francis

the stigmata—Christ's marks of the Crucifixion. Contemporaries described Francis as being short, with a graceful build, dark hair, and sparse beard. This is considered the most accurate portrait of Francis, according to the description of one who knew him. To the left, at eye level under the angels, are paintings of saints and their exquisite halos (by Simone Martini or his school). To the right of the door at the same level, see five of Francis' closest followers—just simple folk.

Francis' friend, "Sister Bodily Death," was really not all that terrible. In fact, Francis would like to introduce you to her now (above and to the right of the door leading into the reliquary chapel). Go ahead, block the light from the door with this book and meet her. Before his death, Francis added a line to *The Canticle of the Sun:* "Praise for our sister, Bodily Death, from whose embrace none can escape."

• *Now cross the transept to the other side of the altar (enjoying some of the oldest surviving bits of the inlaid local-limestone flooring—c. 13th century), and find the staircase going up. Immediately above the stairs is Pietro Lorenzetti's Francis Receiving the Stigmata. Francis is considered the first person ever to earn the marks of the cross through his great faith and love of the Church.*

Make your way up the stairs to the...

Courtyard: The courtyard overlooks the 15th-century cloister, the heart of this monastic complex. Pope Sixtus IV (of Sistine Chapel fame) had it built as a secure retreat for himself. Balanced and peaceful by design, the courtyard also functioned as a cistern to collect rainwater, supplying enough for 200 monks (today, there are about 40). The Franciscan order emphasizes teaching. This place functioned as a kind of theological center of higher learning, which rotated monks in for a six-month stint, then sent them back home inspired to preach effectively. That explains the complex narrative of the frescoes wallpapering the walls.

Giotto, Crucifixion

The **treasury** *(Museo del Tesoro)* to the left of the bookstore features ornately decorated chalices, reliquaries, vestments, and altarpieces.

• *From the courtyard, climb the stairs (next to the bookshop) to the...*

Upper Basilica: Built later than its counterpart below, the brighter upper basilica (started in 1228) is considered the first Gothic church in Italy. You've followed the pilgrims' route, entering the lower church and finishing here. Notice how the pulpit (embedded in the corner pillar) can be seen and heard from every spot in the packed church. The spirit of the order was to fill the church and preach. See also the design in the round window in the west end (high above the entry). The tiny centerpiece reads "IHS" (the first three letters of Jesus' name in Greek). And, as you can see, this kaleidoscope seems to declare that all light radiates from Jesus.

The windows here are treasures from the 13th and 14th centuries. Those behind the apse are among the oldest and most precious in Italy. Imagine illiterate medieval peasants entranced by these windows, so full of meaning that they were nicknamed "Bibles of the Poor." But for art lovers, the basilica's draw is that Giotto and his assistants practically wallpapered it circa 1297-1300 (scholars debate it—perhaps the job was subcontracted to other artists). Whatever the case, the anatomy, architectural depth, and drama of these frescoes helped kick off the Renaissance. The gallery of frescoes shows 28 scenes from the life of St. Francis. The events are a mix of documented history and folk legend.

• *Working clockwise, start on the north wall (to the left, if you just climbed the stairs from the bookstore) and follow along with the help of the numbered map key. The subtitles in the faded black strip below the frescoes describe each scene in clear Latin—and affirm my interpretation.*

❶ A common man spreads his cape before Francis in front of the Temple of Minerva on Piazza del Comune. Before his conversion, young Francis was handsome and well-dressed, befitting the son of a wealthy cloth dealer. He was a natural charmer who led his fellow teens in nights of wine, women, and song. Medieval pilgrims understood the deeper meaning of this scene: The "eye" of God (symbolized

Upper Basilica

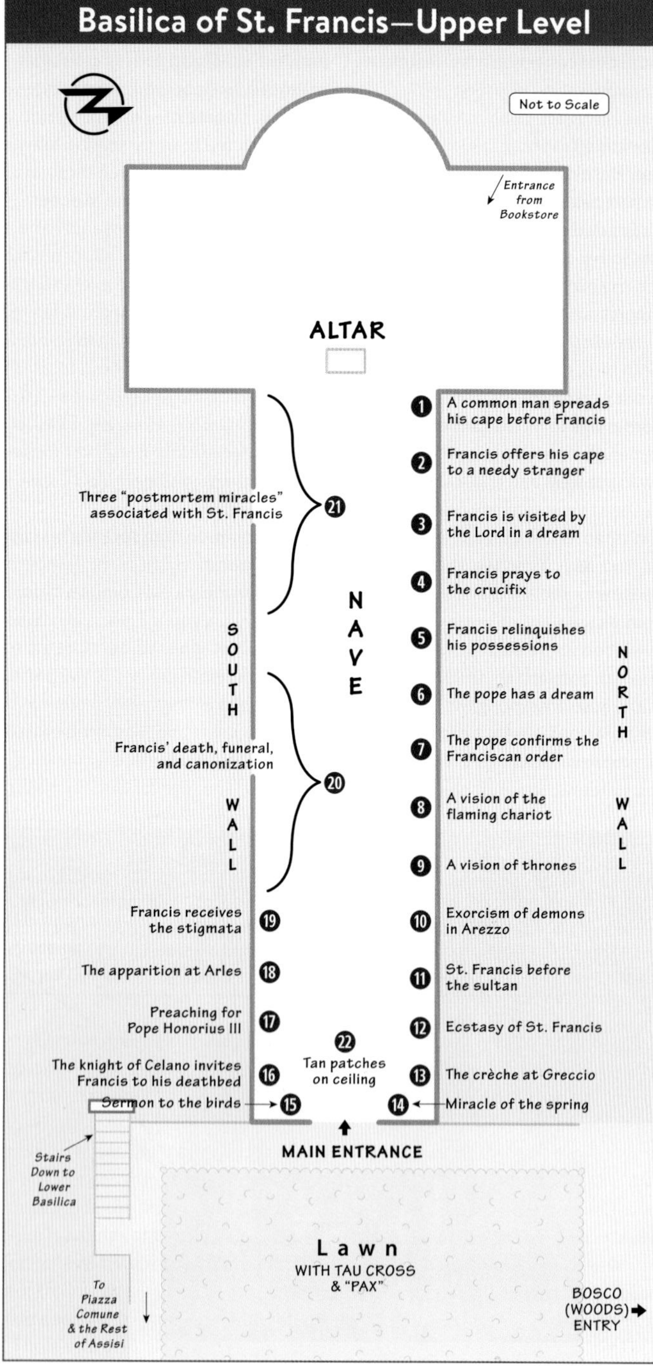
Basilica of St. Francis—Upper Level
Not to Scale
Entrance from Bookstore
ALTAR
NAVE
SOUTH WALL
NORTH WALL
1 A common man spreads his cape before Francis
2 Francis offers his cape to a needy stranger
3 Francis is visited by the Lord in a dream
4 Francis prays to the crucifix
5 Francis relinquishes his possessions
6 The pope has a dream
7 The pope confirms the Franciscan order
8 A vision of the flaming chariot
9 A vision of thrones
10 Exorcism of demons in Arezzo
11 St. Francis before the sultan
12 Ecstasy of St. Francis
13 The crèche at Greccio
14 Miracle of the spring
15 Sermon to the birds
16 The knight of Celano invites Francis to his deathbed
17 Preaching for Pope Honorius III
18 The apparition at Arles
19 Francis receives the stigmata
20 Francis' death, funeral, and canonization
21 Three "postmortem miracles" associated with St. Francis
22 Tan patches on ceiling
MAIN ENTRANCE
Stairs Down to Lower Basilica
To Piazza Comune & the Rest of Assisi
Lawn
WITH TAU CROSS & "PAX"
BOSCO (WOODS) ENTRY

by the rose window in the Temple of Minerva) looks over the young Francis, a dandy "imprisoned" in his own selfishness (the Temple—with barred windows—was once a prison).

❷ **Francis offers his cape to a needy stranger.** Francis was always generous of spirit. He became more so after being captured in battle and held for a year as a prisoner of war, then suffering from illness. Charity was a Franciscan forte.

❸ **Francis is visited by the Lord in a dream.** Still unsure of his calling, Francis rode off to the Crusades. One night, he dreams of a palace filled with armor marked with crosses. Christ tells him to leave the army—to become the first "conscientious objector"—and go home to wait for a non-military assignment in a new kind of knighthood. He returned to Assisi and, though reviled as a coward, would end up fighting for spiritual wealth, not earthly riches.

❹ **Francis prays to the crucifix** in the Church of San Damiano. After months of living in a cave, fasting, and meditating, Francis kneels in the run-down church and prays. The crucifix speaks, telling him: "Go and rebuild my Church, which you can see has fallen into ruin." Francis hurried home and sold his father's cloth to pay for God's work. His furious father dragged him before the bishop.

❺ **Francis relinquishes his possessions.** In front of the bishop and the whole town, Francis strips naked and gives his dad his clothes, credit cards, and a timeshare on Capri. Francis raises his hand and says, "Until now, I called you father. From now on, my only father is my Father in Heaven." Notice God's hand blessing the action from above. Francis then ran off into the hills, naked and singing. In this version, Francis is covered by the bishop, symbolizing his transition from a man of the world to a man of the Church. Notice the disbelief and concern on the bishop's advisors' faces; subtle expressions like these wouldn't have made it into other medieval frescoes of the day.

❻ **The pope has a dream.** Francis headed to Rome, seeking the pope's blessing on his fledgling movement. Initially rebuffing Francis, the pope then dreams of a simple, barefooted man propping up his teetering Church, and then...

❼ **The pope confirms the Franciscan order,** handing Francis and his gang the 1223 document now displayed in the reliquary chapel.

Francis' life was peppered with visions and miracles, shown in three panels in a row: ❽ **vision of the flaming chariot,** ❾ **vision of thrones,** and ❿ **exorcism of demons in Arezzo.**

• *Next see...*

⓫ **St. Francis before the sultan.** Francis' wandering ministry took him to Egypt during the Crusades (1219). He walked unarmed into the Muslim army camp. They captured him, but the sultan was impressed with Francis' manner and let him go, reportedly whispering, "I'd convert to your faith, but they'd kill us both." Here the sultan gestures from his throne.

⓬ **Ecstasy of St. Francis.** This oft-painted scene shows the mystic communing with Christ.

⓭ **The crèche at Greccio.** A creative teacher, Francis invents the tradition of manger scenes.

• *Around the corner, see the...*

⓮ **Miracle of the spring.** Shown here getting water out of a rock to quench a stranger's thirst, Francis felt closest to God when in the hills around Assisi, seeing the Creator in the creation.

• *Cross over to the far side of the entrance door.*

⓯ **Sermon to the birds.** In his best-known miracle, Francis is surrounded by birds as they listen to him teach. Francis embraces all levels of creation. One interpretation of this scene is that the birds, which are of different species, represent the diverse flock of humanity and nature, all created and beloved by God and worthy of one another's love.

This image of well-fed birds is an appropriate one to take with you. It's designed to remind pilgrims that, like the birds, God gave us life, plenty of food, wings, and a world to explore. Francis, patron saint of the environment and animals, taught his followers to count their blessings. A monk here reminded me that even a student backpacker today eats as well as the wealthiest nobleman in the days of Francis.

• *Continue to the south wall for the rest of the panels.*

Despite the hierarchical society of his day, Francis was welcomed by all classes, shown in these three panels: ⑯ **the knight of Celano invites Francis to his deathbed;** ⑰ **preaching for Pope Honorius III,** who listens intently; and ⑱ **the apparition at Arles,** which illustrates how Francis could be in two places at once (something only Jesus and saints can pull off). The proponents of Francis, who believed he was destined for sainthood, show him performing the necessary miracles.

⑲ **Francis receives the stigmata.** It's September 17, 1224, and Francis is fasting and praying on nearby Mount Alverna when a six-winged angel (called a seraph) appears with laser-like powers to burn in the marks of the Crucifixion, the stigmata. For the strength of his faith, Francis is given the marks of his master, the "battle scars of love." These five wounds suffered by Christ (nails in palms and feet, lance in side) marked Francis' body for the rest of his life.

Giotto, St. Francis' Sermon to the Birds

The next panels deal with ⑳ **Francis' death, funeral, and canonization.** The last panels show ㉑ **miracles** associated with the saint after his death, proving that he's in heaven and bolstering his eligibility for sainthood.

Francis died thanking God and singing his *Canticle of the Sun.* Just as he referred to the sun as his brother and the moon as his sister, Francis called his body "brother." On his deathbed he conceded, "Maybe I was a bit tough on brother ass." Ravaged by an asceticism extreme enough to earn him both the stigmata and tuberculosis, Francis died in 1226.

Before leaving through the front entrance, look up at the ceiling and the walls near the rose window to see ㉒ **large tan patches.** In 1997, when a 5.5-magnitude quake hit Assisi, it shattered the upper basilica's frescoes into 300,000 fragments. Shortly after the quake, an aftershock shook the ceiling frescoes down, killing two monks and two art scholars standing here. Later, the fragments were meticulously picked up and pieced back together. The tan parts couldn't be fixed.

Outside, on the lawn, the Latin word *pax* (peace) and the Franciscan tau cross are sculpted from shrubbery. For a drink or snack, the Bar San Francesco (facing the upper basilica) is handy. For *pax,* take the high lane back to town, up to the castle, or into the countryside.

▲ROMAN FORUM (FORO ROMANO)

For a look at Assisi's Roman roots, tour the Roman Forum, underneath Piazza del Comune. The floor plan is clearly explained in English, as are the surviving odd bits and obscure pieces. During your visit, you'll walk on an ancient Roman road.

Cost and Hours: €4, €8 combo-ticket with Rocca Maggiore, daily June-Aug

10:00-13:00 & 14:30-19:00, shorter hours off-season; from Piazza del Comune, go a half-block to Via Portica 2—it's on your right; tel. 075-815-5077.

▲ROCCA MAGGIORE

The "big castle" offers a few restored medieval rooms, a good look at a 14th-century fortification, and a fine view of Assisi and the Umbrian countryside. If you're pinching your euros, skip it—the view is just as good from outside the castle.

Cost and Hours: €5.50, €8 combo-ticket with Roman Forum, daily from 10:00 until an hour before sunset—about 19:15 in summer, Via della Rocca, tel. 075-815-5077.

In Santa Maria Degli Angeli

▲▲BASILICA OF ST. MARY OF THE ANGELS

The huge basilica, towering above the buildings of Santa Maria degli Angeli—the modern part of Assisi in the flat valley below the hill town—marks the spot where Francis lived, worked, and died. It's a grandiose church built around a humble chapel—reflecting the monumental impact of this simple saint on his town and the world.

Cost and Hours: Free, Mon-Sat 6:15-12:50 & 14:30-19:30, Sun from 6:45, tel. 075-805-11. A little TI is across the street from the souvenir stands (generally daily 10:00-13:00 & 15:00-18:30, tel. 075-804-4554). As you face the church, the best pay WC is behind the bushes on your right.

Dress Code: Modest dress is required (no shorts or tank tops).

Getting There: Whether you're traveling by car or by train, it's practical to visit this sight on the way into or out of town. From Assisi's train station, it's a five-minute walk to the basilica (exit station left, after 50 yards take the underground pedestrian walkway—*sottopassaggio*—on your left, then walk straight ahead, passing several handy eateries). There's ample well-marked parking next to the train station.

If you're coming from the old town, you can reach the basilica on the same Busitalia bus (line #C) that runs down to the train station (stay on one more stop to reach the basilica; confirm with driver). In the opposite direction, buses from the basilica up to the old town run twice hourly, usually at :14 and :44 after the hour. Leaving the church, the stop is on your right, by the side of the building.

Visiting the Basilica: The grand Basilica di Santa Maria degli Angeli was built in the 16th century around the tiny but historic **Porziuncola Chapel** (now directly under the dome), after the chapel became too small to accommodate the many pilgrims wanting to pay homage to St. Francis. Some local monks had given Francis this *porziuncola,* or "small portion," after his conversion—a little land with a fixer-upper chapel. Francis lived here after he founded the Franciscan Order; this was where he consecrated St. Clare as a Bride of Christ. What would humble Francis think of the huge church—Christianity's 10th largest—built over his tiny chapel?

Behind the Porziuncola Chapel on the right, find the **Cappella del Transito,** which marks the site of Francis' death on October 3, 1226. Francis died as he'd lived—simply, in a small hut located here. On his last night on earth, he invited some friars to join him in breaking bread. Then he undressed, lay down on the bare

Basilica of St. Mary of the Angels

ground, and began to recite Psalm 141: "Lord, I cry unto thee." He spoke the last line, "Let the wicked fall into their own traps, while I escape"...and he passed on.

From the right transept, follow *Roseto* signs to the rose garden. You'll walk down a passage with gardens on either side (viewable through the windows)—on the left, a tranquil park with a statue of Francis petting a sheep, and on the right, the **rose garden.** Francis, fighting a temptation that he never named, once threw himself onto the roses. As the story goes, the thorns immediately dropped off. Thornless roses have grown here ever since.

Exiting the passage, turn right to find the **Rose Chapel** (Cappella delle Rose), built over the place where Francis lived.

In the autumn, a room in the next **hallway** displays a giant animated Nativity scene (a reminder to pilgrims that Francis first established the tradition of manger scenes as a teaching aid). The bookshop has some works in English and an "old pharmacy" selling herbal cures.

Continuing on, you'll pass the **Porziuncola Museum,** featuring early depictions of St. Francis by 13th-century artists, a model of Assisi during Francis' lifetime, and religious art and objects from the basilica. On the museum's upper floor are some monks' cells, which provide intriguing insight into the spartan lifestyles of the pious and tonsured (€3, Thu-Tue 9:30-12:30 & 15:00-18:30, closed Wed, tel. 075-805-1419, www.porziuncola.org).

Eating

Assisi's food is heavy and rustic. Locals brag about their sausage and love to grate truffles on pasta. Consider a glass or bottle of the favorite homegrown red wine, Sagrantino de Montefalco.

Fine Dining

$$$ Trattoria Pallotta is a local favorite with white tablecloths and a living-room ambience. It's run by a friendly and hardworking family and offers delicious, well-presented regional specialties. And they enjoy serving split courses *(bis)* featuring the two local pastas. Reservations are smart (always a vegetarian menu, €28 fixed-price meal showcases local specialties; Wed-Mon 12:00-14:30 & 19:00-21:30, closed Tue, a few steps off Piazza del Comune across from temple/church at Vicolo della Volta Pinta 2, tel. 075-815-5273, www.pallottaassisi.it).

$$$ Ristorante Medioevo is a venerable splurge. William Ventura's restaurant features traditional cuisine with a modern twist. Beef and game dishes are the specialties, and the wonderful Sagrantino wine is served by the glass. (€40 tasting menu with matching wines, Tue-Sun 12:30-15:00 & 19:00-22:00, closed Mon, in winter open weekends only; Via Arco dei Priori 4; tel. 075-813-068, www.ristorantemedioevoassisi.it).

Casual Eateries

$$ Osteria Piazzetta dell'Erba is an inviting, trendy restaurant under medieval vaulted ceilings. Dishes are beautifully presented and inspired by local cuisine (Tue-Sun 12:30-14:30 & 19:30-22:30, closed Mon, reservations smart, just off the main piazza towards the Cathedral of San Rufino at Via S. Gabriele dell'Addolorata 15a, tel. 075-815-352, www.osterialapiazzetta.it, chef Matteo).

$$ Trattoria degli Umbri is your best bet for a meal overlooking Assisi's main square, with a few nice tables just above the fountain. They serve delightful Umbrian dishes and top-notch wines by the glass (closed Thu, Piazza del Comune 40, tel. 075-812-455).

$$ Hostaria Terra Chiama is a bright, modern little place run by Diego and his family, who serve traditional dishes with seasonal specials (daily, lunch from 12:30, dinner from 19:00, Via San Rufino 16, tel. 075-819-9051).

$$ Locanda del Podestà is where chef Stelvio cooks up tasty grilled Umbrian sausages, *gnocchi della locanda,* and all manner of truffles. Try the tasty *scottadito* lamb chops (Thu-Tue 12:00-14:30 & 19:00-21:30, closed Wed and Feb, 5-minute walk uphill along Via Cardinale Merry del Val from basilica, Via San Giacomo 6C—see map on page 260, tel. 075-816-553).

$$ Le Terrazze di Properzio, just up the street from Podestà, offers seasonal specials, a traditional menu, and Assisi's best view terrace for dining (daily 12:00-14:30 & 19:00-21:30, except closed Wed for dinner, terrace closed in bad weather, Via Metastasio 9, tel. 075-816-868).

$$ Trattoria da Erminio has peaceful tables on a tiny square and indoor seating. Run by Federico and his family for three generations, it specializes in local meat cooked on an open-fire grill. They have good Umbrian wines—before you order, ask Federico or Giuliana for a taste of their specialties (Fri-Wed 12:00-14:30 & 19:00-21:00, closed Thu; from Piazza San Rufino, go a block up Via Porta Perlici and turn right to Via Montecavallo 19a; tel. 075-812-506).

$ Pizza al Taglio da Andrea, facing the Church of San Rufino, has perhaps the best pizza by the slice in town. Locals also like their *torta al testo,* the Umbrian flatbread sandwich (daily, Via San Rufino 26, tel. 075-815-325).

Sleeping

Assisi accommodates large numbers of pilgrims on religious holidays. Finding a room at any other time should be easy. Expect slightly lower rates in midsummer and winter.

Rick's Tip: *Most* **Assisi hotels are not air-conditioned.** *Keep your windows and blinds closed through the middle of the day so that your room will be as cool as possible in the evening.*

$$$ Hotel Ideale, on a ridge overlooking the valley, offers 13 bright and airy remodeled rooms (all with views and balconies), a tranquil garden setting, and free (but tight) private parking (RS%, two apartments with fully equipped kitchens available, air-con, Piazza Matteotti 1, tel. 075-813-570, www.hotelideale.it, info@hotelideale.it, friendly sisters Lara and Ilaria). The hotel is across the street from the parking lot at Piazza Matteotti, at the top end of town.

$$ Hotel Umbra, a quiet villa in the middle of town, has 24 spacious but overpriced rooms with great view terraces. While well-worn, it's friendly and beautifully located. Stepping into the breakfast room is like entering a time warp (RS%, family rooms, air-con, elevator, peaceful garden, and view sun terrace, most rooms have views, closed Dec-March, just off Piazza del Comune under the arch at Via degli Archi 6, tel. 075-812-240, www.hotelumbra.it, info@hotelumbra.it, family Laudenzi).

$ Hotel Belvedere, a great value, is a modern building with 12 spacious, classic-feeling rooms; eight come with sweeping views (breakfast extra, elevator, large communal view terrace, 2 blocks past Basilica of St. Clare at Via Borgo Aretino 13, tel. 075-812-460, www.assisihotelbelvedere.it, hotelbelvedereassisi@yahoo.it, thoughtful Enrico speaks fluent New Jerseyan). Coming by bus from the train station, get off at Porta Nuova; the hotel is steps away.

$ Hotel Pallotta offers seven fresh, bright, small rooms and a shared top-floor lounge with view. Friendly and helpful, the owners provide guests with loads of extra niceties including a loaner Assisi guidebook, free use of washer and drying rack, and free hot drinks and cake at teatime (RS%, a block off Piazza del Comune at Via San Rufino 6; tel. 075-812-307, www.pallottaassisi.it, pallotta@pallottaassisi.it; Stefano, Serena, and family).

$ Hotel San Rufino offers a great locale, solid stone quality, and 11 comfortable rooms (breakfast extra, elevator, air-con, family rooms; from Cathedral of San Rufino, follow sign to Via Porta Perlici 7a; tel. 075-812-803, www.hotelsanrufino.it, info@hotelsanrufino.it).

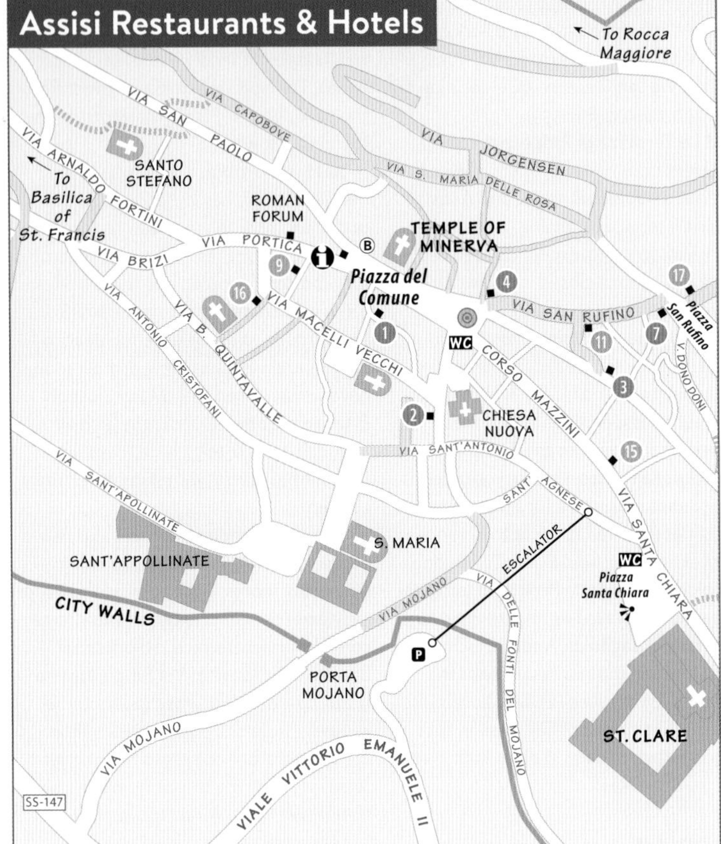

$ Albergo Il Duomo, Hotel San Rufino's nine-room annex a block away, is tidy and *tranquillo.* Located on a stair-stepped lane, it's more atmospheric and has nicer bathrooms than its parent hotel, but more steps and no elevator (breakfast extra, Vicolo San Lorenzo 2 but check in at Hotel San Rufino—see earlier, tel. 075-812-742, www.hotelsanrufino.it, info@hotelsanrufino.it).

$ Hotel La Rocca, on the peaceful top end of town, has 32 solid and basic, business-like rooms in a medieval shell (breakfast extra, family rooms, air-con, elevator, pay parking, sunny rooftop terrace, decent restaurant upstairs, 3-minute walk from Piazza Matteotti at Via Porta Perlici 27, tel. 075-812-284, www.hotelarocca.it, info@hotelarocca.it, Carlo and Christian).

$ Hotel Sole, renting 38 rooms in a 15th-century building, is low-energy, well-worn, and forgettable, but the location is central. Half of its rooms are in a newer annex across the street (RS%, family rooms, air-con extra, elevator in annex only, pay parking nearby, 100 yards before Basilica of St. Clare at Corso Mazzini 35, tel. 075-812-373, www.assisihotelsole.com, info@assisihotelsole.com).

¢ Camere Annalisa Martini is a cheery home amid vines and roses in the town's medieval core. This is a good budget choice with a picnic garden, communal

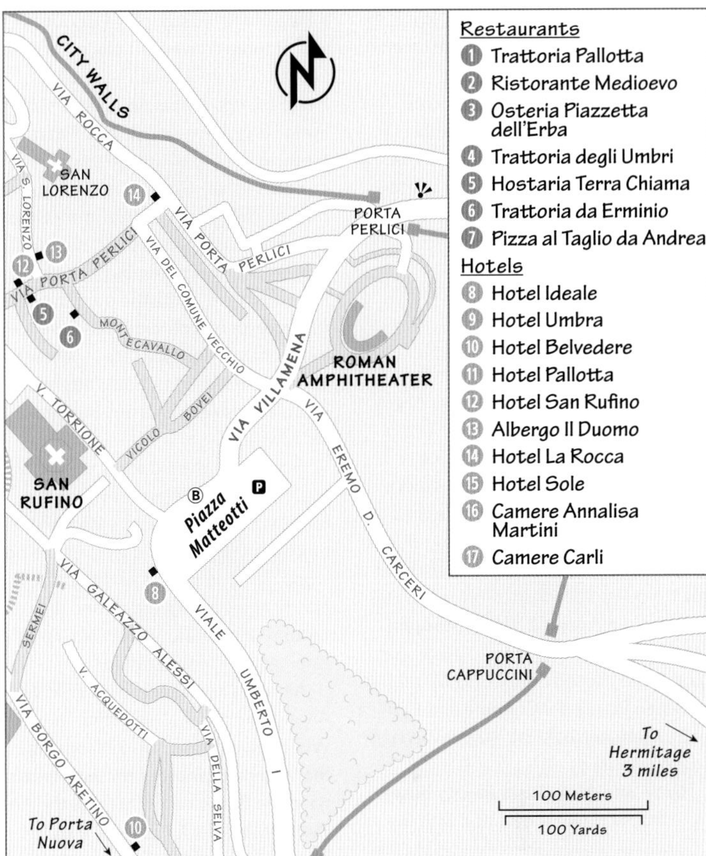

refrigerator, and six homey rooms with cheerful peeling wallpaper and flea market furniture (cash only, 3 rooms share 2 bathrooms, no breakfast; one block from Piazza del Comune—go downhill toward basilica, turn left on Via San Gregorio to #6; tel. 075-813-536, cameremartini@libero.it, Mamma Rosignoli doesn't speak English, but Annalisa does).

¢ Camere Carli has six spacious rooms with bizarre floor plans in a solid, minimalist place above an art gallery. The loft rooms are a great value for families (RS%, no breakfast, family rooms, lots of stairs and no elevator, free parking 150 yards away, just off Piazza San Rufino at Via Porta Perlici 1, tel. 075-812-490, mobile 339-531-1366, www.camerecarli.it, carliarte@live.it, pleasant Franco, who runs the pottery shop below and speaks limited English).

Transportation

Getting Around Assisi

Within the old town, orange **minibuses #A and #B** run every 20-40 minutes, linking the lower end (near the Basilica of St. Francis) with the middle (Piazza del Comune) and the top (Piazza Matteotti).

If you're exhausted after your basilica visit and need a sweat-free five-minute return to the top of the old town (and my recommended hotels), hop on a bus marked *Piazza Matteotti.* Catch the bus below the Basilica of St. Francis, just outside Porta San Francesco. Before boarding, confirm the destination.

You can buy a bus ticket (good on any city bus) at a newsstand or tobacco shop for €1.30, or get a ticket from the driver for €2 (exact change only). After you've stamped your ticket on board the bus, it's valid for 90 minutes.

Arriving and Departing

BY TRAIN

The **train station** is about two miles below Assisi, in Santa Maria degli Angeli. There is no bagage storage.

The train station's **ticket office** is often open only Mon-Fri 12:30-20:00, closed Sat-Sun; when the office is closed, use the ticket machine (newsstand sells only regional tickets). Up in Assisi's old town, you can get train information and tickets from **Agenzia Viaggi Stoppini** (Mon-Fri 9:00-12:30 & 15:30-19:00, Sat 9:00-12:30, closed Sun, Corso Mazzini 31, between Piazza del Comune and Basilica of St. Clare, tel. 075-812-597, www.viaggistoppiniassisi.it).

Gray-and-blue Busitalia city buses (line #C) connect the station with the

hilltop old town, stopping just outside the wall at three convenient places: at Piazza Giovanni Paolo II, near the Basilica of St. Francis; Largo Properzio, just outside the Porta Nuova city gate; and at Piazza Matteotti, at the top of the old town.

Buses usually leave at :16 and :46 past the hour from the bus stop immediately to your left as you exit the station (daily 5:30-23:00, 15 minutes; buy tickets at the newsstand inside the train station for €1.30, or on board the bus for €2—exact change only, validate in yellow box as you board, valid 1.5 hours after being stamped, also good for any bus within the old town).

Going from the old town to the train station, the orange buses reverse the route, starting at the top at Piazza Matteotti (usually at :10 and :40 past the hour), stopping in the middle next (outside Porta Nuova at Largo Properzio), and then at the bottom (Piazza Giovanni Paolo II), before zipping down to the station.

All buses are marked either *SM degli Angeli/Stazione* or *Matteotti/S. Francesco.* While you may find yourself looping into the hinterland, most of these buses also go to the Basilica of St. Mary of the Angels (Santa Maria degli Angeli, one stop beyond the station, confirm with driver).

Taxis from the train station to the old town cost about €15. You can be charged extra for luggage, night service, additional people (four is customary)...and sometimes just for being a tourist. When departing the old town, you'll find taxi stands at Piazza del Comune, the Basilica of St. Clare, the Basilica of St. Francis, and Piazza Giovanni Paolo II (or have your hotel call for you, tel. 075-812-600). Expect to pay a minimum of €10 for any ride.

Train Connections to: Rome (nearly hourly, 2-3.5 hours, 5 direct, most others change in Foligno), **Florence** (8/day direct, 2-3 hours), **Orvieto** (roughly hourly, 2-3 hours, with transfer in Terontola or Orte), **Siena** (10/day, about 4 hours, most involve 2 changes; bus is faster).

BY BUS

Most intercity buses arrive at the base of the old town near the Basilica of St. Francis, but buses from Siena may arrive at the stop next to the Basilica of St. Mary of the Angels (Santa Maria degli Angeli), near the train station (see above for directions from the station up to the old town).

Bus Connections: Service to **Rome** is operated by the Sulga bus company (2/day, 3 hours, pay driver, departs from Piazza San Pietro, arrives at Rome's Tiburtina station, where you can connect with the regional train to Fiumicino Airport, tel. 800-099-661, www.sulga.it).

A bus for **Siena** departs from the stop next to the Basilica of St. Mary of the Angels, near the train station (daily at 10:20, 2 hours, search on "Santa Maria degli Angeli" for timetable, www.baltour.it). You usually can't buy Siena tickets from the driver—buy them at **Agenzia Viaggi Stoppini** in Assisi's old town (Mon-Fri 9:00-12:30 & 15:30-19:00, Sat 9:00-12:30, closed Sun, Corso Mazzini 31, between Piazza del Comune and Basilica of St. Clare, tel. 075-812-597, www.viaggistoppiniassisi.it).

Don't take the bus to **Florence;** the train is better.

BY CAR

Drivers visiting for the day can follow the signs to several handy **parking lots** *(parcheggi)*. **Piazza Matteotti**'s wonderful underground parking garage is at the top of the town and comes with bits of ancient Rome in the walls. Another big lot, **Parcheggio Giovanni Paolo II,** is at the bottom end of town, 200 yards below the Basilica of St. Francis. At **Parcheggio Porta Nuova,** an escalator delivers you to Porta Nuova near St. Clare's. Prices are similar (about €1.50/hour, most are €20/day). For day-trippers, the best plan is to park at **Piazza Matteotti,** follow my self-guided town walk, tour the basilica, and then either catch a bus back to Piazza Matteotti or simply wander back up through town to your car.

BY PLANE

Perugia/Assisi Airport, about 10 miles from Assisi, has daily connections to London, Brussels, Barcelona, and a few Mediterranean destinations (airport code: PEG, tel. 075-592-141, www.airport.umbria.it). Bus service between Assisi and the airport is so sporadic that you should plan on taking a taxi (about €30).

ORVIETO

Just off the freeway and the main train line, Umbria's grand hill town sits majestically a thousand feet above the valley floor, enticing those heading to and from Rome. While no secret, it's well worth a visit. Orvieto became a regional power in the Middle Ages, and even earlier, a few centuries before Christ, it was one of a dozen major Etruscan cities. Some historians believe Orvieto may have been a religious center—a kind of Etruscan Mecca.

Orvieto has three claims to fame: cathedral, Classico wine, and ceramics. Drinking a shot of the local white wine in a ceramic cup as you gaze up at the cathedral lets you experience Orvieto's three C's all at once. Though crowded by day, Orvieto is quiet by night, and comes with a wonderful bonus: close proximity to the unforgettable and tiny hill town of Civita di Bagnoregio (covered later in this chapter).

Orientation

Orvieto has two distinct parts: the old-town hilltop and the plain new town below (called Orvieto Scalo). Whether coming by train or car, you first arrive in the nondescript, modern, lower part of town. From there you can drive or take the funicular, elevator, or escalator up to the medieval upper town, an atmospheric labyrinth of streets and squares.

Tourist Information: The TI is on the cathedral square at Piazza del Duomo 24 (Mon-Fri 8:15-13:50 & 16:00-19:00, Sat-Sun 10:00-13:00 & 15:00-18:00, tel. 0763-341-772). The ticket office next to the

Orvieto outdoor market

main TI sells combo-tickets and books reservations for Underground Orvieto Tours (tel. 0763-340-688).

Sightseeing Passes: The €20 **Carta Unica** combo-ticket covers Orvieto's top sights and one round-trip on the bus and/or funicular. To cover your funicular ride, you can buy the combo-ticket on your arrival in the lower town—either at the bar or newsstand at the train station, or at a summer-only ticket office in the parking lot below the station. The combo-ticket is also available at the ticket office next to the TI on Piazza del Duomo, as well as at most of the sights it covers.

Laundry: The coin launderette in the lower town, a 10-minute walk from the train station, has instructions in Italian only, but it's workable if you're desperate (daily 7:00-22:00, Piazza del Commercio, off via Monte Nibbio, mobile 393-758-6120).

Car Service: Giuliotaxi offers excursions by car and minibus to Civita and beyond; for details, see page 307.

Car Rental: Hertz has an office 100 yards to the left of the funicular station (Via Sette Martiri 32f, tel. 0763-301-303).

Private Guides: David Tordi organizes custom tours focused on food and culture (€250/half-day, €350/day, tel. 0763-300-491, www.teseotur.com, info@teseotur.com). **Manuela del Turco** is also good (€120 for a small group 2.5-hour tour, mobile 333-221-9879, manueladel@virgilio.it).

➲ Orvieto Walk

Piazza del Duomo: Face the cathedral and admire its attention-grabbing facade. The papal palace (now hosting various museums) is to your right, and the TI and shuttle bus to the funicular are over your right shoulder. A nice gelato shop is around the church to the left.

• *Head left a few steps to the...*

Clock Tower and Via del Duomo: Also known as the Maurizio Tower, this was built in the 14th century and equipped with an early mechanized clock. The tower marks the start of Via del Duomo, lined with shops selling ceramics. The tradition of fine ceramics in Orvieto goes way back—the clay from the banks of the nearby Tiber is ideal for pottery.

• *Stroll down Via del Duomo.*

At the second left, The Wizard of Oz (Il Mago di Oz) awaits a few steps down Via dei Magoni (at #3). The shop is a wondrous toy land created by eccentric Giuseppe Rosella. Have Giuseppe push a few buttons, and you're far from Kansas.

Back on Via del Duomo, about 30 yards before the next tower is Emilio's meat-and-cheese shop (at #11). Pop in for a fragrant reminder that wild boar is an Umbrian specialty.

• *Follow Via del Duomo to where it meets Corso Cavour. Here you'll find the tall, stark, 11th-century...*

Tower of the Moor (Torre del Moro): Eighty such towers, each the pride and security of a powerful noble family, once decorated the town's skyline. An elevator leaves you with 173 steps still to go to earn a commanding view (€3, daily March-Oct 10:00-19:00, May-Aug until 20:00, shorter hours off-season).

• *Side-trip a block farther ahead, behind the tower, for a look at the striking...*

Palazzo del Popolo: This is a textbook example of a fortified medieval public palace: a fortress designed to house the city's leadership and military (built atop an Etruscan temple), with a market at its base, fancy meeting rooms upstairs, and aristocratic living quarters on the top level. A lively market still bustles here every Thursday and Saturday mornings, selling food, clothes, and household goods.

Via dei Magoni

• *Return to the tower, turn right, and head down Corso Cavour past classic storefronts to...*

Piazza della Repubblica and Church of Sant'Andrea: The original vision—though it never came to fruition—was for the City Hall to have five arches flanking the central arch (marked by the flags today). The Church of Sant'Andrea (left of City Hall) sits atop an Etruscan temple that was likely the birthplace of Orvieto centuries before Christ. Inside is an interesting architectural progression: 11th-century Romanesque (with few frescoes surviving), Gothic (the pointy vaults over the altar), and a Renaissance barrel vault in the apse (behind the altar)—all dimly lit by alabaster windows.

• *From Piazza Repubblica, continue straight downhill for 100 yards on Via Filippeschi until you reach a fork (with a friendly, traditional bakery on the right). Walk downhill along Via della Cava about 50 yards to a restaurant with a green sign to find the...*

Well of the Quarry (Pozzo della Cava): While renovating their trattoria here in the oldest part of town, an Orvieto family discovered a vast underground network of Etruscan-era caves, wells, and tunnels. The excavation started in 1984 and continues to this day. A visit to the well makes for a fun subterranean wander (see page 296 for details).

• *Climb back up to the fork (with the bakery), then take a hard left up Via Malabranca. After about 80 yards, at #22, you'll reach...*

Palazzo Filippeschi and Viewpoint: The friendly, noble Filippeschi family leaves their big, green door open so visitors can peek into their classic medieval courtyard, with black travertine columns scavenged from nearby ancient Roman villas. Enjoy a moment of exquisite medieval tranquility.

Immediately across from the palazzo,

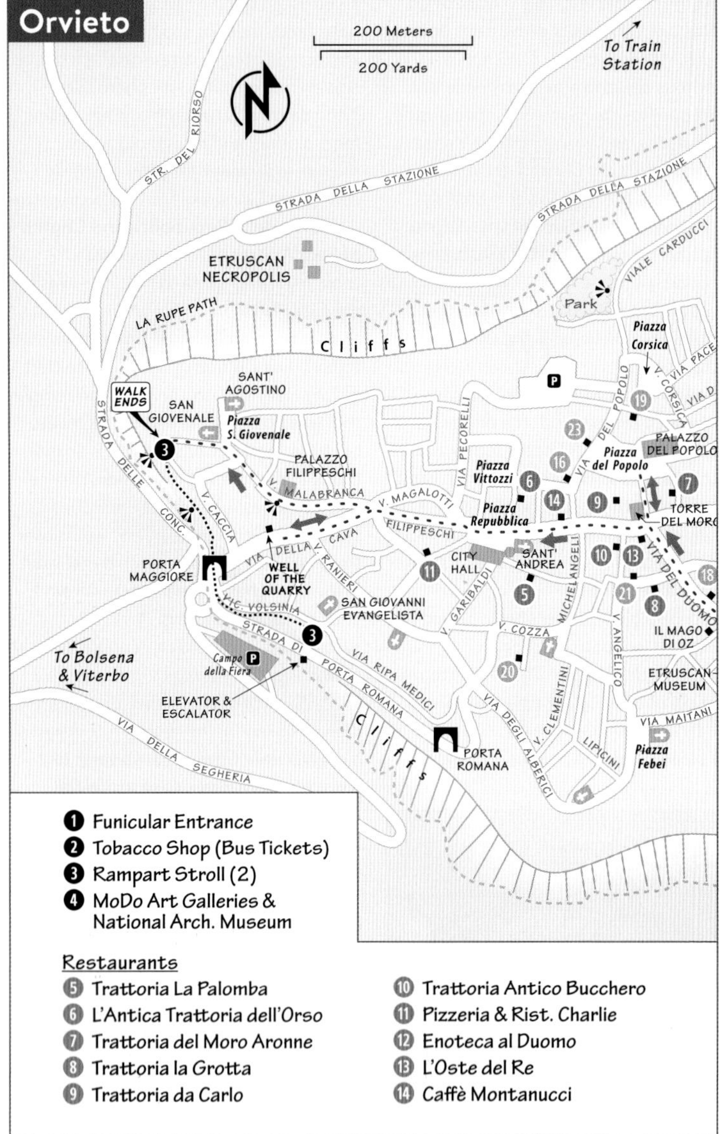

belly up to the viewpoint overlooking a commotion of red-tile roofs. This tradition goes back to Etruscan times, when such tiles were molded on a seated tile-maker's thigh—wide to narrow. They nest so that water flows without leaking—handy for both rooftops and plumbing. Originally scavenged from Etruscan ruins and reused as watertight roofing, this tradition survives.

• *Continue on, downhill now, to a square with the Church of Sant'Agostino, and then on to the Church of San Giovenale, the oldest in town, with 11th-century frescoes, and finally reach a commanding...*

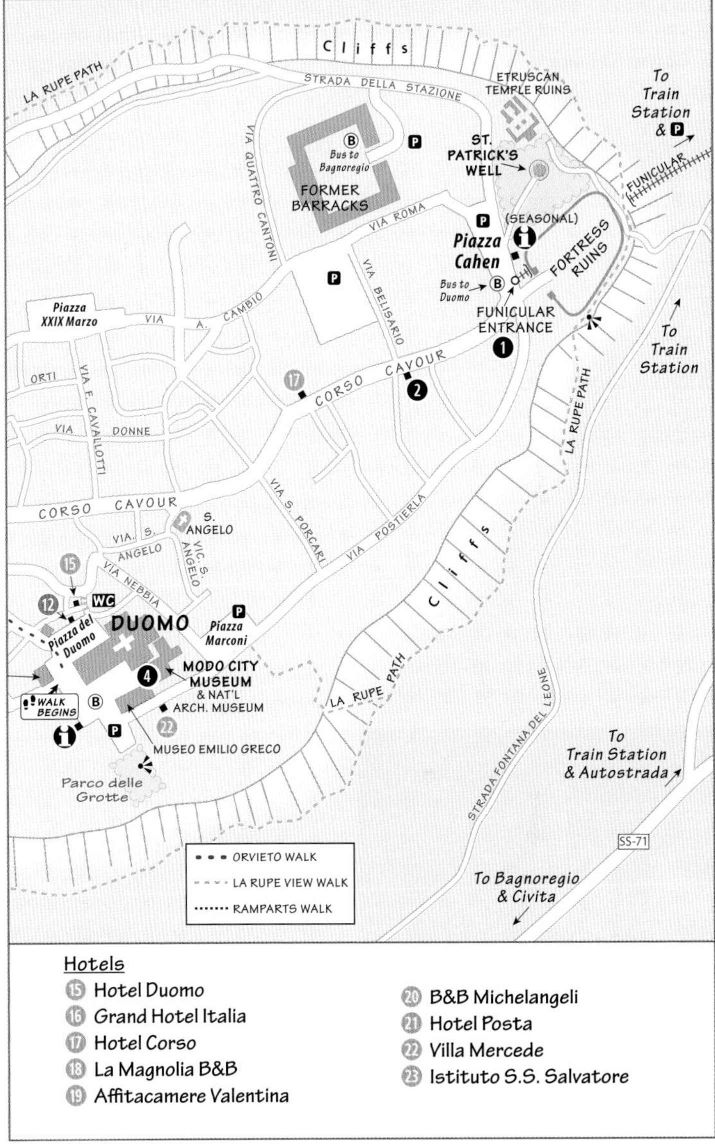

Rampart View: You're at the end of Orvieto. The fertility of the land (with its olives, vines, and fruit orchards) is clear. The manicured little forest of cypress trees straight ahead marks the Orvieto cemetery. In the distance to the right is Mount Cetona, guarding the south end of Tuscany.

Sights

▲▲▲DUOMO

Orvieto's cathedral has Italy's liveliest facade. This colorful, prickly Gothic facade, divided by four pillars, has been compared to a medieval altarpiece. The optical-illusion interior features some fine art, including

Luca Signorelli's lavishly frescoed Chapel of San Brizio.

Cost and Hours: €4; April-Sept Mon-Sat 9:30-19:00 (March and Oct until 18:00), Sun 13:00-17:30 (July-Sept until 18:30); shorter hours Nov-Feb; sometimes closes for religious services. A €5 combo-ticket includes the Duomo, the chapel, and the Museo dell'Opera del Duomo, called the "MoDo" (available at the chapel; MoDo alone costs €4). Admission is also covered by the Carta Unica combo-ticket.

➲ SELF-GUIDED TOUR

Begin by viewing the **exterior facade,** a gleaming mass of mosaics, stained glass, and sculpture (c. 1300, by Lorenzo Maitani and others).

At the base of the cathedral, the four broad **marble pillars** carved with biblical scenes tell the history of the world in four acts, from left to right. The relief on the far left shows the ❶ **Creation** (see God creating Eve from Adam's rib, and the snake tempting Eve). Next is the ❷ **Tree of Jesse** (Jesus' family tree—with Mary, then Jesus on top) flanked by Old Testament stories, then the ❸ **New Testament** (look for the manger scene and other events from the life of Christ). On the far right is the ❹ **Last Judgment** (Christ judging on top, with all hell breaking loose at the bottom).

Orvieto's Duomo

Each pillar is topped by a bronze symbol of one of the Evangelists (left to right): angel (Matthew), lion (Mark), eagle (John), and ox (Luke). The bronze doors are modern, by the Sicilian sculptor Emilio Greco. (A gallery devoted to Greco's work is to the immediate right of the church.) In the mosaic below the rose window, Mary is transported to heaven. In the uppermost mosaic, Mary is crowned.

• *Now step inside.*

The **nave** feels less cluttered than most Italian churches. Until 1877, it was busier, with statues of the apostles at each column and fancy chapels. Then the people decided they wanted to "un-Baroque" their church. (The original statues are now on display in the Church of Sant'Agostino, at the west end of town.)

The interior is lit by **alabaster windows,** highlighting the black-and-white striped stonework. Why such a big and impressive church in such a little town? Its historic importance and wealth is due to a miracle that happened nearby in 1263. According to the story, a skeptical priest, named Peter of Prague, passed through Bolsena (12 miles from Orvieto) while on a pilgrimage to Rome. He had doubts that the bread used in communion could really be transformed into the body of Christ. But during Mass, as he held the host aloft and blessed it, the bread began to bleed, running down his arms and dripping onto a linen cloth (a "corporal") on the altar. That miraculously blood-stained cloth is now kept here, in the Chapel of the Corporal.

• *We'll tour the church's interior. First, find the chapel in the north transept, left of the altar.*

Chapel of the Corporal: The ❺ **bloody cloth** from the miracle is displayed in

Orvieto's Duomo

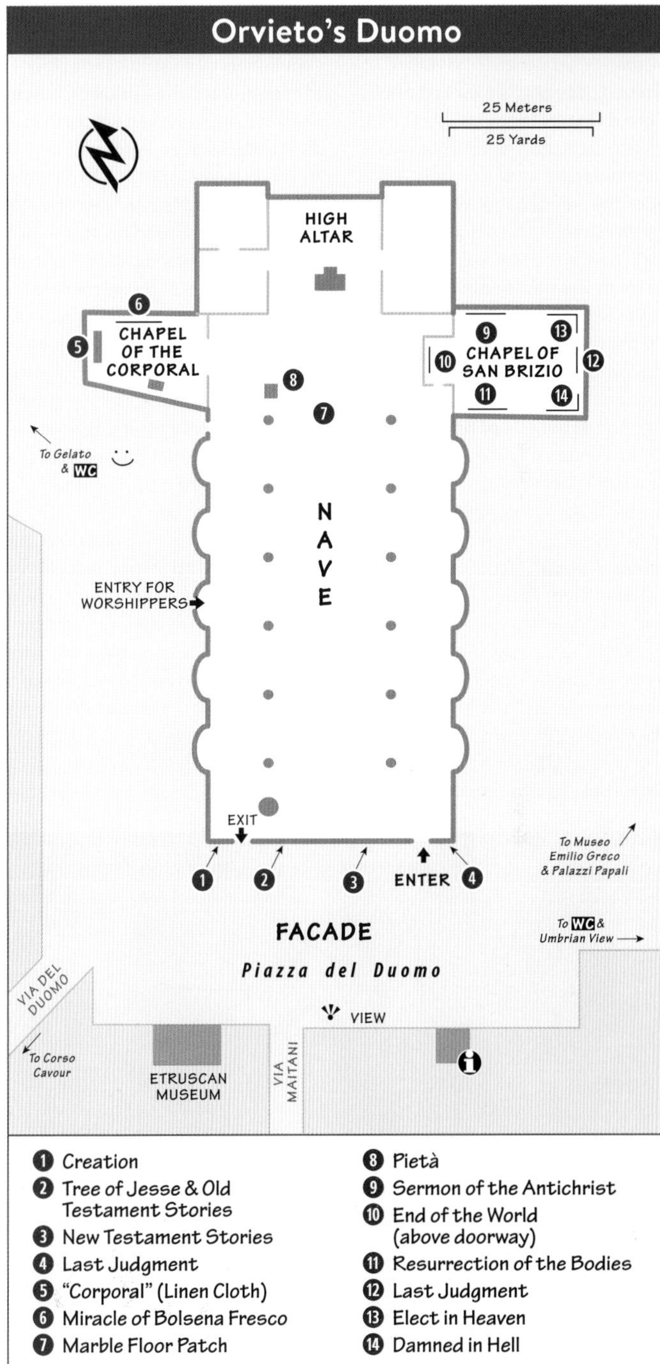

1. Creation
2. Tree of Jesse & Old Testament Stories
3. New Testament Stories
4. Last Judgment
5. "Corporal" (Linen Cloth)
6. Miracle of Bolsena Fresco
7. Marble Floor Patch
8. Pietà
9. Sermon of the Antichrist
10. End of the World (above doorway)
11. Resurrection of the Bodies
12. Last Judgment
13. Elect in Heaven
14. Damned in Hell

the turquoise frame atop the altar. It was brought from Bolsena to Orvieto, where Pope Urban IV happened to be visiting. The amazed pope proclaimed a new holiday, Corpus Domini (Body of Christ), and the Orvieto cathedral was built (begun in 1290) to display the miraculous relic. For centuries, the precious linen was paraded through the streets of Orvieto in an ornate reliquary (now in the MoDo City Museum).

The room was frescoed in the 14th century with scenes attesting to Christ's presence in the communion wafer (for example, the panel above the glass case to the left illustrates how the wafer bleeds if you cook it). The ❻ **miracle of Bolsena** (here set in 13th-century Orvieto) is depicted on the chapel's right wall.

• *Now walk to the middle front of the church, where you'll see a decorative area in the floor the size of a Turkish carpet.*

❼ **Marble Floor Patch:** This patch in the marble floor marks where the altar stood before the Counter-Reformation. It's a reminder that as the Roman Catholic Church countered the Reformation, it made reforms of its own. For instance, altars were moved back so that the congregation could sit closer to the spectacular frescoes and stained glass. (These decorations were designed to impress commoners by illustrating the glory of heaven—and the Catholic Church needed that propaganda more than ever during the Counter-Reformation.)

This cathedral put Orvieto on the map; with lots of pilgrims came lots of wealth. Two future popes used the town—perched on its easy-to-defend hilltop—as a refuge when their enemies forced them to flee Rome. The sparkling stained glass is the restored original, from the 14th century. The fine organ, high on the left, has more than 5,000 pipes. Look high up in the right transept at the alabaster rose window.

• *A few steps to your left as you face the altar, near the first pillar, is a beautiful white-marble statue.*

❽ **Pietà:** The marble **pietà** was carved in 1579 by local artist Ippolito Scalza. Clearly inspired by Michelangelo's *Pietà,* this exceptional work, with four figures, was sculpted from one piece of marble. Walk around it to notice the texture that Scalza achieved, and how the light plays on the sculpture from every angle.

• *Now face the main altar. To the right is Orvieto's one must-see artistic sight, the...*

Duomo interior

Chapel of San Brizio: This chapel features Luca Signorelli's brilliantly lit frescoes of the Day of Judgment and Life after Death (painted 1499-1504). Step into the chapel and you're surrounded by vivid scenes crammed with figures. Although the frescoes refer to themes of resurrection and salvation, they also reflect the turbulent political and religious atmosphere of late 15th-century Italy.

The chapel is decorated in one cohesive story. Start with the wall to your left as you enter, and slowly turn counterclockwise to follow the plot:

In the ❾ **Sermon of the Antichrist** (left wall), a crowd gathers around a man preaching from a pedestal. It's the Antichrist, who poses as Jesus to mislead the faithful. This befuddled Antichrist forgets his lines mid-speech, but the Devil is on hand to whisper what to say next. His words sow wickedness through the world, including executions (upper right). The worried woman in red and white (foreground, left of pedestal) gets money from a man for something she's not proud of (perhaps receiving funds from a Jewish moneylender—notice the Stars of David on his purse).

Most likely, the Antichrist himself is a veiled reference to Savonarola (1452-1498), the charismatic Florentine monk who defied the pope, drove the Medici family from power, and riled the populace with apocalyptic sermons. Many Italians—including the painter Signorelli—viewed Savonarola as a tyrant and heretic, the Antichrist who was ushering in the Last Days.

In the upper left, notice the hardworking angel. He looks as if he's at batting practice, hitting followers of the Antichrist back to earth as they try to get through the pearly gates. In the bottom left is a self-portrait of the artist, **Luca Signorelli** (c. 1450-1523), dressed in black with long golden hair. Signorelli, from nearby Cortona, was at the peak of his powers, and this chapel was his masterpiece. He looks out proudly as if to say, "I did all this in just five years, on time and on budget." Next to him (also in black) is the artist Fra Angelico, who started the chapel decoration five decades earlier but completed only a small part of it.

Signorelli, Resurrection of the Bodies

Around the arch, opposite the windows, are signs of the ⑩ **end of the world:** eclipse, tsunami, falling stars, earthquakes, violence in the streets, and a laser-wielding gray angel.

On the right wall (opposite the Antichrist) is the ⑪ **Resurrection of the Bodies.** Trumpeting angels blow a wake-up call and the dead climb dreamily out of the earth to be clothed with new bodies. On the same wall (below the action, at eye level) is a gripping pietà. Also by Signorelli, this pietà gives an insight into the artist's genius and personality. Look at the emotion in the faces of the two Marys and consider that Signorelli's own son had just died. The Deposition scene (behind Jesus' leg) seems inspired by ancient Greek scenes of a pre-Christian hero's death. In the confident spirit of the Renaissance, the artist incorporates a pagan scene to support a Christian story. This 3-D realism in a 2-D sketch shows the work of a talented master.

The altar wall (with the windows) features the ⑫ **Last Judgment.** To the left of the altar (and continuing around the corner, filling half the left wall) are the ⑬ **Elect in Heaven.** They spend eternity posing like bodybuilders while listening to celestial Muzak. To the right (and continuing around the corner on the right wall) are the ⑭ **Damned in Hell,** in the scariest mosh pit ever. Devils torment sinners in graphic detail, while winged demons control the airspace overhead. In the center, one lusty demon turns to tell the frightened woman on his back exactly what he's got planned for their date. (According to legend, this was Signorelli's lover, who betrayed him...and ended up here.) Signorelli's ability to tell a story through human actions and gestures, rather than symbols, inspired his younger contemporary, Michelangelo, who meticulously studied the elder artist's nudes.

In this chapel, Christian theology sits physically and figuratively upon a foundation of classical logic. Below everything are Greek and Latin philosophers, plus Dante, struggling to reconcile Classical truth with Church doctrine.

• *Our tour is finished. Leaving the church, turn left (passing a small parking lot and WC) to reach a park that affords a fine Umbrian view. Turn left twice, and you'll circle behind the church to reach the cathedral's art collections (part of MoDo, described next).*

Near the Duomo

▲▲MODO CITY MUSEUM (MUSEO DELL'OPERA DEL DUOMO)

This museum is an ensemble of three different sights scattered around town: the cathedral art collection behind the cathedral; the Emilio Greco collection next to the cathedral; and, at the far end of town, the Church of Sant'Agostino, which has the 12 apostle statues that were originally in the Duomo.

Cost and Hours: €4 MoDo ticket covers all MoDo sights (or get the €5 combo-ticket that includes the Duomo); April-Sept daily 9:30-19:00; March and Oct Wed-Mon 10:00-17:00, closed Tue; midday closure Nov-Feb; Piazza Duomo, tel. 0763-343-592, www.opsm.it.

Cathedral Art Collections: Behind the Duomo, a complex of medieval palaces called Palazzi Papali shows off the city's best devotional art. It comes in two parts: the skippable collection of frescoes on the ground floor and a delightful collection up the metal staircase. The highlight is just inside the upstairs entrance: a marble Mary and Child who sit beneath a bronze canopy, attended by exquisite angels. This proto-Renaissance ensemble, dating from around 1300, once filled the niche in the center of the cathedral's facade (where a replica sits today). In several rooms on this floor, you'll find a *Madonna and Child* from 1322 by the Sienese great Simone Martini, who worked in Orvieto; saintly wooden statues and fine inlaid woodwork from the original choir; a carved 14th-century Crucifixion that shows the dead

Christ in gripping detail; and Luca Signorelli's *Mary Magdalene* (1504).

Museo Emilio Greco: This collection shows off the work of Emilio Greco (1913-1995), a Sicilian artist who designed the modern doors of Orvieto's cathedral. His sketches and about 30 of his bronze statues are on display here, showing his absorption with gently twisting and turning nudes. The artful installation of his work in this palazzo, with walkways and a spiral staircase up to the ceiling, is designed to let you view his sculptures from different angles.

NATIONAL ARCHAEOLOGICAL MUSEUM OF ORVIETO

This small, five-room collection, immediately behind the cathedral in the ground floor of Palazzi Papali (under MoDo), shows off a trove of well-preserved Etruscan bronzes, terra-cotta objects, and ceramics—many from the necropolis at the base of Orvieto, and some with painted colors surviving from 500 B.C. To see the treasure of this museum, ask an attendant for the Golini tombs (named after the man who discovered them in 1836). She'll escort you to the reconstructed, fourth-century B.C. tombs, frescoed with scenes from an Etruscan banquet in the afterlife.

Cost and Hours: €4, daily 8:30-19:30, tel. 0763-341-039, www.archeopg.arti.beniculturali.it.

▲ETRUSCAN MUSEUM (MUSEO CLAUDIO FAINA E MUSEO CIVICO)

This 19th-century, Neoclassical nobleman's palace stands on the main square facing the cathedral. Its elegantly frescoed rooms hold an impressive Etruscan collection. The ground floor features the "Museo Civico," with fragments of Etruscan sculpture. On the first floor is the "Collezione Conti Faina," with Etruscan jewelry and an array of Roman coins (push the brass buttons and the coins rotate so you can see both sides). The top floor features the best of the Etruscan vases and bronzes, and lots of votives found buried in nearby tombs.

Cost and Hours: €4.50; April-Sept daily 9:30-18:00; Oct-March Tue-Sun 10:00-17:00, closed Mon; tel. 0763-341-511, www.museofaina.it.

Underground Orvieto

▲▲ST. PATRICK'S WELL (POZZO DI SAN PATRIZIO)

Modern engineers are impressed by this deep well—175 feet deep and 45 feet wide—designed in the 16th century with a double-helix pattern. The two spiral stairways allow an efficient one-way traffic flow: intriguing now, but critical then. Imagine if donkeys and people, balancing jugs of water, had to go up and down the same stairway. At the bottom is a bridge that people could walk on to scoop up water.

The well was built because a pope got nervous. After Rome was sacked in 1527 by renegade troops of the Holy Roman Empire, the pope (Clement VII) fled to Orvieto. He feared that even this little town (with no water source on top) would be besieged. He commissioned a well, which was started in 1527 and finished 10 years later. It was a huge project. (As it turned out, the town was never besieged, but supporters believed that the well was worth the cost and labor because of its deterrence value—attackers would think twice about besieging a town with a reliable water source.) It's a total of 496 steps up and down—allow about 20 minutes

St. Patrick's Well

total—lots of exercise and not much to see other than some amazing 16th-century engineering. Bring a sweater.

Cost and Hours: €5, daily May-Aug 9:00-19:45, shorter hours off-season, interesting €1 audioguide, to your right as you exit the funicular, Viale Sangallo, tel. 0763-343-768.

▲WELL OF THE QUARRY (POZZO DELLA CAVA)

This complex of Etruscan-era caves, wells, and tunnels leads down to a fat, cylindrical, beautifully carved 2,500-year-old well. Go ahead, spit (or drop a coin 100 feet down—coins are collected each Christmas for a local charity). Your visit is capped with a review of local pottery-making.

Cost and Hours: €3, €2 with this book, Tue-Sun 9:00-20:00, closed Mon, Via della Cava 28).

UNDERGROUND ORVIETO TOURS (PARCO DELLE GROTTE)

Guides weave archaeological history into a good look at 100 yards of Etruscan and medieval caves. You'll see the remains of an old olive press, a 130-foot-deep Etruscan well shaft, what's left of a primitive cement quarry, and an extensive dovecote (pigeon coop) where the birds were reared for roasting (pigeon dishes are still featured on many Orvieto menus; look for—or avoid—*piccione*).

Cost and Hours: €6; 45-minute English tours depart at 11:15, 12:30, 16:15, and 17:30; more often with demand, book tour and depart from ticket office at Piazza Duomo 23 (next to main TI); confirm times at TI or by calling 0763-340-688, www.orvietounderground.it.

View Walks

▲HIKE AROUND THE CITY ON THE RUPE

Orvieto's Rupe is a peaceful path that circles the town at the base of the cliff upon which it sits. The TI's **Anello della Rupe** map shows five access points from the town for the three-mile walk, which includes a series of sightseeing stops (allow two hours round-trip). From the access points, you'll walk or take stairs down to the trail. It's wide, easy to follow (marked with **Anello della Rupe** signs when needed), and partially paved, though it has some steep, gravelly descents—wear good shoes and be prepared for a climb. On one side is the cliff, with the town high above, and on the other side are Umbrian views. You'll share this peaceful path with only a few other people and the sound of the wind and birds. It's a delightful evening walk (but not after dark—it's not lit).

I'd leave Orvieto at Piazza Marconi and walk left (counterclockwise) three-quarters of the way around the town (see the fine view down onto the Etruscan Necropolis midway), and ride the escalator and elevator back up to the town from the big Campo della Fiera parking lot.

▲SHORTER ROMANTIC RAMPART STROLL

Thanks to its dramatic hilltop setting, several fine little walks wind around the edges of Orvieto. My favorite after dark, when it's lamp-lit and romantic, is along the ramparts at the far west end of town. Start at the Church of Sant'Agostino (near the end of my self-guided Orvieto Walk). With your back to the church, go a block to the right to the end of town. Then head left along the ramparts, with cypress-dotted Umbria to your right, and follow Vicolo Volsinia to the Church of San Giovanni Evangelista, where you can reenter the old town center near several recommended restaurants.

Experiences

Wine Tasting

Orvieto Classico wine is justly famous. Two inviting wineries sit just outside Orvieto on the scenic Canale route to Bagnoregio (see map on page 301). For drivers en route to

Civita, it's easy to stop at either or both for a tasting (but call ahead for a reservation).

For a short tour of a winery with Etruscan cellars, make an appointment to visit **Tenuta Le Velette** (€8-24 for tour and tasting, price varies depending on wines, number of people, and if food is requested, no drop-ins, Mon-Fri 8:30-12:00 & 14:00-17:00, Sat 8:30-12:00, closed Sun, tel. 0763-29090, mobile 348-300-2002, www.levelette.it). From their sign (5-minute drive past Orvieto at top of switchbacks just before Canale, on road to Bagnoregio), cruise down a long tree-lined drive, then park at the striped gate.

Custodi is another respected family-run winery that produces Orvieto Classico, grappa, and olive oil on a 140-acre estate. Reserve ahead for a tour and a tasting (€7/person for wines only, €16/person with light lunch, daily 8:30-12:30 & 15:30-18:30 except closed Sun afternoons, Viale Venere S.N.C. Loc. Canale; on the road from Orvieto to Civita, a half-mile after Le Velette, it's the first building before Canale; tel. 0763-29053, mobile 392-161-9334, www.cantinacustodi.com).

Eating

Trattorias

$$$ Trattoria La Palomba features excellent game and truffle specialties in a wood-paneled dining room. Truffles are shaved right at your table—try the *umbricelli al tartufo* (homemade pasta with truffles) or *spaghetti dell'Ascaro* (with truffles). Their *filetto alla cardinale* and mixed-cheese plates are popular, and they use organic and locally sourced ingredients (Thu-Tue 12:30-14:15 & 19:30-22:00, closed Wed and July, reservations smart, Via Cipriano Manente 16, tel. 0763-343-395).

$$$ L'Antica Trattoria dell'Orso offers well-prepared Umbrian cuisine paired with fine wines in a homey, bohemian-chic, peaceful atmosphere. Owner Stefano and chef Hania offer a good deal for my readers: €30 for two people, including their house wine and water—my vote for the best dining value in town (Wed-Mon 12:00-14:30 & 19:30-22:00, closed Tue and Feb, just off Piazza della Repubblica at Via della Misericordia 18, tel. 0763-341-642).

$ Trattoria del Moro Aronne is a long-established family bistro run by Cristian and his mother, Rolanda, who lovingly prepare homemade pasta and market-fresh Umbrian specialties. Consider their **nidi**—folds of fresh pasta enveloping warm, gooey pecorino cheese sweetened with honey. Three small and separate dining areas make the interior feel intimate. While touristy and not particularly atmospheric, this place is known locally as an excellent value (Wed-Mon 12:30-14:30 & 19:30-22:00, closed Tue, Via San Leonardo 7, tel. 0763-342-763).

$$$ Trattoria la Grotta prides itself on serving only the freshest food and finest wine. Owner-chef Franco has been at it for 52 years, and promises diners a free coffee, *grappa, limoncello,* or vin santo with this book (Wed-Mon opens at 12:00 for lunch and at 19:00 for dinner, closed Tue, Via Luca Signorelli 5, tel. 0763-341-348).

$$ Trattoria da Carlo, between Via Corso Cavour and Piazza del Popolo, is a cozy spot with a bright, white-tiled interior and inviting tables outside. Animated and opinionated Carlo's slogan is "simple food for simple people." He puts an unpretentious modern twist on

traditional dishes such as pasta with *guanciale* (pork cheeks—like bacon), fennel fronds, and pecorino cheese (daily 12:00-15:00 & 19:00-24:00, Vicolo del Popolo 1, tel. 0763-343-916).

$$$ Trattoria Antico Bucchero makes for a nice memory with its candlelit ambience and delicious food—especially game and wild boar (daily 12:00-15:00 & 19:00-23:00 except closed Wed Nov-March, seating indoors and on a peaceful square in summer, air-con, between Torre del Moro and Piazza della Repubblica at Via de Cartari 4, tel. 0763-341-725).

$$ Pizzeria Charlie is a local favorite, popular with families and students for casual dinners of wood-fired gourmet pizzas. They also have a small menu of big salads. In a quiet courtyard guarded by a medieval tower, it's a block southwest of Piazza della Repubblica (Wed-Mon 12:30-14:30 & 19:00-23:00, no midday closure in summer, closed Tue year-round, Via Loggia dei Mercanti 14, tel. 0763-344-766).

$$ Enoteca al Duomo is to the left of the Duomo and has pleasant outdoor seating. They serve a small variety of rustic *panini* (cheaper to go), wines by the glass and a vast selection of Italian wines by the bottle, and a full menu of local dishes in a wine-bar atmosphere (daily 10:00-24:00, closed Feb, Piazza del Duomo 13, tel. 0763-344-607).

Fast and Cheap Eats

$ L'Oste del Re is a simple osteria on Corso Cavour, where Maria Grazia and Claudio offer pasta, bruschetta, enticing meat-and-cheese plates, and hearty, made-to-order sandwiches to eat in or take out (good gluten-free options, daily 11:00-15:30 & 19:00-22:00, Corso Cavour 58, tel. 0763-343-846).

$ Caffè Montanucci lays out an appetizing display of pastas and main courses behind the counter. Choose one (or two—called a *bis*), find a seat in the modern interior or sunny courtyard, and they'll bring it out on a tray. They also serve dinner with regular table service (good Wi-Fi, daily 7:00-24:00, Corso Cavour 21, tel. 0763-341-261).

Sleeping

The hotels are located in or near the town center.

$$$ Hotel Duomo is centrally located and modern, with splashy art in 17 rooms and a friendly welcome. Double-paned windows keep the sound of the church bells well-muffled (RS%, family rooms, air-con, elevator, private pay parking, sunny terrace, a block from the Duomo at Vicolo di Maurizio 7, tel. 0763-341-887, www.orvietohotelduomo.com, info@orvietohotelduomo.com, Gianni and Maura Massaccesi don't speak English, daughter Elisa and son-in-law Diego do). They also own a three-room B&B 50 yards from the hotel (lower prices, breakfast at the main hotel).

$$$ Grand Hotel Italia is impersonal and businesslike, bringing predictable modern amenities to this small town. The 46 rooms are well-located in the heart of Orvieto, near the market square (RS%, air-con, elevator, stay-awhile lobby and terrace, pay parking—reserve ahead, Via di Piazza del Popolo 13, tel. 0763-342-065, www.grandhotelitalia.it, hotelita@libero.it).

$$ Hotel Corso is friendly, with 18 frilly and flowery rooms—a few with balconies and views. Their sunlit little terrace is enjoyable, but the location—halfway between the center of town and the funicular—is less convenient than others (RS%, family rooms, ask for quieter room off street, air-con, elevator, reserved pay parking, Corso Cavour 339, tel. 0763-342-020, www.hotelcorso.net, info@hotelcorso.net, Carla).

$ La Magnolia B&B has lots of fancy terra-cotta tiles, terraces, and other welcoming touches. Its seven unique rooms, some like mini-apartments with kitchens, are on the town's main drag. The three units facing the busy street are air-conditioned and have double-paned windows (RS%, family rooms, no elevator, washing machine; Via Duomo 29, tel. 0763-342-808, mobile 349-462-0733, www.bblamagnolia.it, info@bblamagnolia.it, Serena and Loredana).

$$ Affittacamere Valentina rents six clean, airy, well-appointed rooms, all with big beds and antique furniture. Her place is located in the heart of Orvieto, on a quiet street behind the palace on Piazza del Popolo (RS%, family rooms, pay parking, Via Vivaria 7, tel. 0763-341-607, mobile 393-970-5868, www.bandbvalentina.com, camerevalentina@gmail.com). Welcoming Valentina also rents three lower-priced rooms across the square (shared bath and kitchen, no air-con) and three offsite apartments.

$ B&B Michelangeli offers two comfortable and well-appointed apartments a few blocks from the tourist scene. It's run by eager-to-please Francesca, who speaks limited English but provides homey touches and free tea, coffee, and breakfast supplies. From the Corso, follow Via Michelangeli, a street full of wood sculptures made by her famous artistic family (family rooms, fully equipped kitchen, washing machine, private pay parking, Via dei Saracinelli 20—ring bell labeled M. Michelangeli, tel. 0763-393-862, mobile 347-089-0349, www.bbmichelangeli.com).

$ Hotel Posta is a central, long-ago-elegant palazzo renting 20 quirky, clean rooms with chipped plaster and vintage furniture. It feels a little institutional, but the rooms without private bath are among the cheapest in town (breakfast extra, elevator, Via Luca Signorelli 18, tel. 0763-341-909, www.orvietohotels.it, hotelposta@orvietohotels.it).

$ Villa Mercede, a good value and excellent location, is owned by a religious institution and offers 23 cheap, simple, mostly twin-bedded rooms, each with a big modern bathroom and many with glorious Umbrian views (elevator, free parking, a half-block from Duomo at Via Soliana 2, reception upstairs, tel. 0763-341-766, www.villamercede.it, info@villamercede.it).

$ Istituto S.S. Salvatore rents nine spotless twin rooms and five singles in their convent, which comes with a peaceful terrace and garden, great views, and a 23:00 curfew. Though the nuns don't speak English, they have mastered Google Translate, and will happily use it to answer your questions (cash only, no breakfast, elevator, Wi-Fi in common areas only, free parking, just off Piazza del Popolo at Via del Popolo 1, tel. 0763-342-910).

Transportation

Arriving and Departing

BY TRAIN

The train station is at the foot of the hill the old town sits on. There's no baggage storage at the train station, but Info Point, just below and behind the train station at the tour bus depot, has a secure bag check—the only one in town (9:00-18:00 daily). Check at the station for the train schedule to your next destination (schedule is also available at the TI or online at www.trenitalia.com).

From the station, the easiest way to get to the top of Orvieto (including the cathedral and my recommended hotels) is by **funicular:** Buy your ticket at the entrance to the *funiculare;* look for the *biglietteria* sign (€1.30, good for 1.5 hours, includes minibus from Piazza Cahen to Piazza del Duomo, Mon-Sat 7:15-20:30, Sun 8:00-20:30, about every 10 minutes). Or buy a Carta Unica combo-ticket (described earlier) to cover your funicular ride and the top sights.

As you exit the funicular at the top, you're in Piazza Cahen, located at the east end of the upper town. To your left is a ruined fortress with a garden and a commanding view. To your right, down a steep path, is St. Patrick's Well. Farther to the right is a park with Etruscan ruins and another sweeping view.

Just in front of you is the small **shuttle bus** (usually white or orange), waiting to take you to Piazza del Duomo at no extra charge (included in your funicular ticket; 3-6/hour). The bus fills up fast, but the views from the ruined fortress are worth pausing for—if you miss the bus, you can wait for the next one, or just walk to the cathedral (head uphill on Corso Cavour; after about 10 minutes, take a left onto Via del Duomo). The bus drops you in Piazza del Duomo, just steps from the main TI and within easy walking distance of most of my recommended sights and hotels.

If you arrive outside the funicular's operating hours, you can reach the upper part of town by **bus** to Piazza della Repubblica (buses run roughly 2/hour until midnight, buy €1.30 ticket at bar inside station). **Taxis** line up in front of the train station and charge about €15 for a ride to the cathedral (mobile 360-433-057).

Train Connections from Orvieto to: Rome (every 1-2 hours, 1.5 hours), **Florence** (6/day, 2.5 hours, use Firenze S.M.N. train station), **Siena** (12/day, 2.5 hours, change in Chiusi, all Florence-bound trains stop in Chiusi), **Assisi** (roughly hourly, 2-3 hours, 1 or 2 transfers), **Milan** (2/day direct, 5.5 hours; otherwise about hourly with a transfer in Florence, Bologna, or Rome, 4.5-5 hours). The train station's Buffet della Stazione is surprisingly good if you need a quick focaccia sandwich or pizza picnic for the train ride.

BY CAR

For **free parking,** use the huge lot below the train station (5 minutes off the autostrada; turn right immediately after the autostrada underpass and follow the **Tour Bus Parking** signs). Walk through the station and ride the funicular up the hill.

Rick's Tip: *If you're considering* **driving to Rome, stash your car in Orvieto** *instead. You can easily park the car, safe and free, in the big lot below the Orvieto train station (for up to a week or more), and zip effortlessly into Rome by train (1.5 hours).*

It's also possible to park in the old town. While little free parking is available, there are several pay options: blue-lined spots on Piazza Cahen; a parking lot on Via Roma northwest of Piazza Cahen; and the Campo della Fiera lot just below the west end of town (from the lot's top level, walk up into town or ride the escalator—7:00-21:00—or elevator—7:00-24:00; both are free). The private, tree-lined lot with an attendant just beyond Piazza Marconi, next to the cathedral, is best for overnight stays (€12/day). While white lines generally indicate free parking, much of it is marked for residents only. Blue lines require you to buy a "pay and display" slip from a nearby machine.

While you can drive up Via Postierla and Via Roma to get to central parking lots, **Corso Cavour** and other streets in the old center are **closed to traffic** and monitored by cameras (look for red lights, and avoid streets marked by a red circle).

CIVITA DI BAGNOREGIO

Perched on a pinnacle in a grand canyon, the 2,500-year-old, traffic-free village of Civita di Bagnoregio is my favorite Italian hill town. Its only connection to the world is a long pedestrian bridge—with the town of Bagnoregio at the other end. While Bagnoregio lacks the romance of Civita, it's a healthy, vibrant community.

Civita's history goes back to Etruscan and ancient Roman times. In the early Middle Ages, Bagnoregio was a suburb of Civita, which had a population of about 4,000. Later, Bagnoregio surpassed Civita in size—especially following a 1695 earthquake (residents fled Civita's hilltop to live in Bagnoregio, fearing their houses would be shaken off into the valley below). You'll notice Bagnoregio is dominated by Renaissance-style buildings while, architecturally, Civita remains stuck in the Middle Ages.

Civita Walk

Begin at the base of the pedestrian bridge leading up to Civita (you'll have arrived here either by car or by an Orvieto-Bagnoregio bus, then a walk; follow the directions at the end of this chapter).

Pay the €1.50 admission fee at the brown kiosk on your left, just before you start walking up the pedestrian bridge. The fee (waived for overnight guests) helps with the town's extensive maintenance expenses.

Civita was once connected to Bagnoregio, before the saddle between the separate towns eroded away. Photographs around town show the old donkey path, the original bridge. It was bombed in World War II and replaced in 1966 with the footbridge that you're climbing today.

• *Entering the town, you'll pass through Porta Santa Maria, a 12th-century Romanesque arch. This stone passageway was cut by the Etruscans 2,500 years ago, when this town was a stop on an ancient trading route. Inside the archway, you enter a garden of stones. Stand in the little square—the town's antechamber—facing the Bar La Piazzetta. To your right are the remains of a...*

RENAISSANCE PALACE

The wooden door and windows (above the door) lead only to thin air. They were part of the facade of one of five palaces that once graced Civita. Much of the palace fell into the valley, riding a chunk of the ever-eroding rock pinnacle. Today, the door leads to a remaining section of the palace—complete with Civita's first hot tub. It was once owned by the "Marchesa," a countess who married into Italy's biggest industrialist family.

• *A few steps uphill, farther into town (on your left, beyond the Bottega souvenir store), notice the two shed-like buildings.*

OLD WC AND LAUNDRY

In the nearer building (covered with ivy), you'll see the town's old laundry, which dates from just after World War II, when water was finally piped into the town. Until a few years ago, this was a lively village gossip center. Now, locals park their mopeds here. Just behind that is another stone shed, which houses a poorly marked and less-than-pristine WC.

• *The main square is just a few steps farther along, but we'll take the scenic circular route to get there, detouring around to the right. Belly up to the...*

CANYON VIEWPOINT

Lean over the banister and listen to the sounds of the birds and the bees. Survey old family farms, noticing how evenly they're spaced. Historically, each one owned just enough land to stay in business. Turn left along the belvedere and walk a few steps to the site of the long-gone home of Civita's one famous son, St. Bonaventure, known as the "second founder of the Franciscans" (look for the small plaque on the wall).

• *From here, a lane leads past picturesque old homes and gardens, and then to...*

CIVITA'S MAIN SQUARE

The town church faces Civita's main piazza. Grab a stone seat along the biggest building fronting the square (or a drink at Peppone's bar) and observe the scene. They say that in a big city you can see a lot, but in a small town like this you can feel a lot. The generous bench is built into the long side of the square, reminding me of how, when I first discovered Civita back in the 1970s and 1980s, the town's old folks would gather here every night. Piazzas have been integral to Italian culture

Civita di Bagnoregio

since ancient Roman times. While Civita is humble today, imagine the town's former wealth, when mansions of the leading families faced this square, along with the former city hall (opposite the church, to your left). The town's history includes a devastating earthquake in 1695. Notice how stone walls were reinforced with thick bases, and how old stones and marble slabs were recycled and built into walls.

Here in the town square, you'll find Bar Da Peppone, with local wines and microbrews, and an inviting fire in the winter (open daily), and two restaurants. There are wild donkey races on the first Sunday of June and the second Sunday of September. At Christmastime, a living Nativity scene is enacted in this square, and if you're visiting at the end of July or beginning of August, you might catch a play here. The pillars that stand like giants' bar stools are ancient Etruscan. The church, with its Campanile (bell tower), marks the spot where an Etruscan temple, and then a Roman temple, once stood. Across from Peppone's, on the side of the former city hall, is a small, square, stone counter. Old-timers remember when this was a meat shop, and how one day a week the counter was stacked with fish for sale.

Renaissance Palace facade

The humble **Geological Museum,** next to Peppone's, tells the story of how erosion is constantly shaping the surrounding "Bad Lands" valley, how landslides have shaped (and continue to threaten) Civita, and how the town plans to stabilize things (€3, June-Sept Tue-Sun 9:30-13:30 & 14:00-18:30, closed Mon, Fri-Sun only off-season, closed Jan-Feb, mobile 328-665-7205, www.museogeologicoedellefrane.it).

• *Now step inside...*

CIVITA'S CHURCH

A cathedral until 1699, the church houses records of about 60 bishops that date back to the seventh century (church open daily 10:00-13:00 & 15:00-17:00, often closed Feb). Inside you'll see Romanesque columns and arches with faint Renaissance frescoes peeking through Baroque-era whitewash. The central altar is built upon the relics of the Roman martyr St. Victoria, who once was the patron saint of the town. St. Marlonbrando served as a bishop here in the ninth century; an altar dedicated to him is on the right. The fine crucifix over this altar, carved out of pear wood in the 15th century, is from the school of Donatello. It's remarkably expressive and greatly venerated by locals. Jesus' gaze is almost haunting. Some say his appearance changes based on what angle you view him from: looking alive from the front, in agony from the left, and dead from the right. On Good Friday, this crucifix goes out and is the focus of the midnight procession.

On the left side, midway up the nave above an altar, is an intimate fresco of the *Madonna of the Earthquake,* given this name because—in the great shake of 1695—the whitewash fell off and revealed this tender fresco of Mary and her child. (During the Baroque era, a white-and-bright interior was in vogue, and churches such as these—which were covered with precious and historic frescoes—were simply whitewashed over. Look around to see examples.) On the same wall—just toward the front from the *Madonna*—find the faded portrait of Santa Apollonia, the patron saint of your teeth; notice the scary-looking pincers.

• *From the square, you can follow the...*

MAIN STREET

A short walk takes you from the church to the end of the town. Along the way, you'll pass a couple of little eateries, olive presses, gardens, a rustic town museum, and valley views. The rock below Civita is honeycombed with ancient tunnels, caverns (housing olive presses), cellars (for keeping wine at a constant temperature all year), and cisterns (for collecting rainwater, since there was no well in town). Many date from Etruscan times.

Civita's main square and church

Wherever you choose to eat (or just grab a bruschetta snack), be sure to take advantage of the opportunity to poke around. At the trendy **Alma Civita,** notice the damaged house facing the main street—broken since the 1695 earthquake and scarred to this day. Just beyond, the rustic **Antico Frantoio Bruschetteria** serves bruschetta in an amazing old space. Whether or not you buy food, venture into their back room to see an interesting collection of old olive presses (if you're not eating here, a €1 donation is requested). The huge olive press in the entry is about 1,500 years old. Until the 1960s, blindfolded donkeys trudged in the circle here, crushing olives and creating paste that filled the circular filters and was put into a second press. Notice the 2,500-year-old sarcophagus niche. The hole in the floor (with the glass top) was a garbage hole. In ancient times, residents would toss their jewels down when under attack; excavations uncovered a windfall of treasures.

In front is the well head of an ancient cistern—designed to collect rainwater from neighboring rooftops—carved out of the volcanic rock and covered with clay to be waterproof.

• *Across the street and down a tiny lane, find...*

ANTICA CIVITA

This is the closest thing the town has to a history museum. The humble collection is the brainchild of Felice, the old farmer who's hung black-and-white photos, farm tools, olive presses, and local artifacts in a series of old caves. Climb down to the "warm blood machine" (another donkey-powered grinding wheel) and a viewpoint. You'll see rooms where a mill worker lived until the 1930s. Felice wants to give visitors a feeling for life in Civita when its traditional economy was strong (€1, daily 10:00-19:00, until 17:00 in winter, some English explanations).

• *Another few steps along the main street take you to...*

THE END OF CIVITA

Here the road is literally cut out of the stone, with a dramatic view of the Bad Lands valley opening up. Pop in to the cute "Garden of Poets" (immediately on the left just outside town, with the tiny local crafts shop) to savor the view. Then, look back up at the end of town and ponder the precarious future of Civita. There's a certain stillness here, far from the modern world and high above the valley.

Continue along the path a few steps toward the valley below the town, and you come to some shallow caves used as stables until a few years ago. The third cave, cut deeper into the rock, with a barred door, is the **Chapel of the Incarcerated** (Cappella del Carcere). In Etruscan times, the chapel—with a painted tile depicting the Madonna and child—may have been a tomb, and in medieval times, it was used as a jail (which collapsed in 1695).

• *Hike back into town. Make a point to take some time to explore the peaceful back lanes before returning to the modern world.*

Eating

$$ Osteria Al Forno di Agnese is a delightful spot where Manuela and her friends serve visitors simple yet delicious meals, including good salads, on a covered patio just off Civita's main square or in a little dining room in gloomy weather (gluten-free options, good selection of local wines, opens daily at 12:00 for lunch, June-Sept also at 19:00 for dinner, closed sometimes in bad weather, tel. 0761-792-571, mobile 340-1259-721).

$$ Trattoria Antico Forno serves up rustic dishes, homemade pasta, and salads at affordable prices. Try their homemade pasta with truffles (daily for lunch 12:30-15:30 and dinner 19:00-22:00, on main square, also rents rooms—see Civita B&B listing earlier, tel. 076-176-0016, Franco, daughter Elisabetta, and assistant Nina).

$$ Trattoria La Cantina de Arianna is a family affair, with a busy open fire specializing in grilled meat and wonderful bruschetta. After eating, wander down to their cellar, where you'll see winemaking gear and provisions for rolling huge kegs up the stairs. Tap on the kegs in the bottom level to see which are full (daily 11:00-16:30, tel. 0761-793-270).

$$ Alma Civita feels like a fresh, new take on old Civita. Choose from one of three seating areas: outside on a stony lane, in the modern and trendy-feeling main-floor dining room, or in the equally modern but atmospheric cellar (May-Oct lunch Wed-Mon 12:00-16:00, dinner Fri-Sat only 19:00-21:30, closed Tue; Nov-April Fri-Sun only for lunch, tel. 0761-792-415).

$ Antico Frantoio Bruschetteria, the last place in town, is a rustic, super-atmospheric spot for a bite to eat. The specialty here: bruschetta toasted over hot coals. Peruse the menu, choose your toppings (chopped tomato is super), and get a glass of wine for a fun, affordable snack or meal (roughly 10:00-18:00, mobile 328-689-9375, Fabrizio).

$$$ Hostaria del Ponte, at the parking lot at the base of Civita's bridge, recently closed due to erosion problems but may reopen soon. A more serious restaurant than anything in Civita itself, it offers creative and traditional cuisine. Big space heaters make it comfortable to enjoy the wonderful view of Civita as you dine from the rooftop terrace, even in spring and fall (tel. 076-179-3565, www.hostariadelponte.it, Lorena).

Sleeping

Off-season, when Civita and Bagnoregio are deadly quiet—and cold—I'd side-trip in from Orvieto rather than spend the night. Those staying overnight in Civita don't pay the admission charge.

$$$ Alma Civita is a classic old stone house that was recently renovated by a sister-and-brother team, Alessandra and Maurizio (hence the name: Al-Ma). These are Civita's two most comfortable, modern, and warmly run rooms (Wi-Fi in restaurant, tel. 0761-792-415, mobile 347-449-8892, www.almacivita.com, prenotazione@almacivita.com).

$$ Civita B&B has three little rooms above Trattoria Antico Forno. Two are doubles with private bath. The third is a triple, which has its own bathroom across the hall (RS%, family rooms, continental breakfast, Piazza del Duomo Vecchio, tel. 076-176-0016, mobile 347-611-5426, www.civitadibagnoregio.it, fsala@pelagus.it). Franco also rents two apartments.

Transportation

Getting from Orvieto to Civita

BY BUS

From Orvieto, you'll catch a bus to Bagnoregio, then walk to Civita.

To Bagnoregio by Bus: The trip takes about 45 minutes (€2.20 one-way if bought in advance, €7 one-way if purchased from driver). In Orvieto, buy tickets at the tobacco shop at Corso Cavour 306, a block up from the funicular (daily 8:00-13:00 & 16:00-20:00). If you're returning to Orvieto by bus, it's smart to get a return ticket here rather than in Bagnoregio.

Here are likely departure times (confirm at TI) from Orvieto (Mon-Sat only, no buses on Sun or holidays): 6:20, 7:25, 7:50, 12:45, 13:55, 14:00, 15:45, 17:40, and 18:20. If you take the 12:45 bus for a day trip, you can make the last (17:20) bus back, but your time in Civita will feel a little rushed.

The **blue Cotral bus** to Bagnoregio departs from a courtyard within the former military barracks (see map on page 288), marked **Ex Caserma Piave** on maps. With your back to the funicular, walk to the right. At the end of Piazza Cahen, you'll see a large building across the street on the left. Follow **Parking** signs to find the buses waiting between yellow lines in the parking lot at the center of the building. The bus you want says *Bagnoregio* in the window.

Buses departing the barracks stop five minutes later at Orvieto's train station—to catch the bus there, wait to the left of the funicular station (as you're facing it); schedule and tickets are available in the tobacco shop/bar in the train station. For more info, call 06-7205-7205 or 800-174-471 or see www.cotralspa.it.

From Bagnoregio, it's a 30-minute walk to the base of Civita's pedestrian bridge. Then you'll have a fairly steep 10-minute walk up to Civita.

From the Bagnoregio bus stop in Piazzale Battaglini, take the road going uphill, Via Garibaldi (overlooking the big parking lot). Once on the road, take the first right, and then an immediate left, to cut over onto the main drag, Via Roma. Follow this straight out to the belvedere for a superb viewpoint. From there, backtrack a few steps (staircase at end of viewpoint is a dead end), and take the stairs down to the road leading to the pedestrian bridge up to Civita.

To shorten the walk from Bagnoregio to Civita, take the **shuttle bus** that runs to the belvedere from a stop just 20 yards from the Piazzale Battaglini bus stop. Look for white minibuses labeled **EPF Tours** (usually 1-2/hour, 5 minutes, 7:30-18:15 but few buses 13:15-15:30 or on Sun Oct-March, €0.70 one-way, €1 round-trip, pay driver).

BY SHUTTLE OR TAXI

The **Teseotur** travel agency in Orvieto offers a shuttle to Civita on Saturdays and Sundays during the summer (€15, includes onboard audiotour of region, tel. 0763-300-491, www.teseotur.com, info@teseotur.com).

If you can share the cost, a 30-minute taxi ride from Orvieto to the base of Civita can be a good deal. **Giuliotaxi** can take groups by car (€90 for up to 4) and minibus (€120 for up to 8) from Orvieto to Civita for a one-hour visit. For a longer trip, book a two-hour visit to Civita, then explore Lake Bolsena (5 hours total, €160/car, €200/minibus). They cover other destinations as well (mobile 349-690-6547, giuliotaxi@libero.it).

BY CAR

Driving from Orvieto to Civita takes about 30 minutes. Orvieto overlooks the autostrada (and has its own exit). From the Orvieto exit, the shortest way to Civita is to turn left (below Orvieto), and then simply follow the signs to *Lubriano* and *Bagnoregio.*

Rick's Tip: *Just before Bagnoregio, follow the signs left to Lubriano, head into that village, turn right as you enter town, and pull into the first little square by the yellow church (on the left) for a* **breathtaking view of Civita.**

Drive through the town of Bagnoregio (following yellow *Civita* signs), park in the pay-and-display lot just before the belvedere, and take the stairs down to the bridge. If that small lot is full, there are often spots along the road leading up to it.

Rome

Rome is magnificent and brutal at the same time. It's a showcase of Western civilization, with truly ancient sights and a modern vibrance. But with the wrong attitude, you'll be frustrated by the kind of chaos that only an Italian can understand. On my last visit, a cabbie struggling with the traffic said, *"Roma chaos."* I responded, *"Bella chaos."* He agreed.

Over 2,000 years ago the word "Rome" meant civilization itself. Today, Rome is Italy's political capital, the capital of Catholicism, and the center of its ancient empire, littered with evocative remains. As you peel through its fascinating and jumbled layers, you'll find Rome's buildings, cats, laundry, traffic, and 2.8 million people endlessly entertaining.

Despite Rome's rough edges, you'll fall in love with it...if you pace yourself, if you're well-organized, if you protect yourself and your valuables with extra caution, if your hotel provides a comfortable refuge, and if you embrace the siesta. Rome is much easier to love if you can avoid the midsummer heat.

ROME IN 3 DAYS

Rome wasn't built in a day, and you can't hope to see it all in three. Pace yourself; never regret a siesta. If you miss something, add it to your list of excuses to return.

Day 1: The Colosseum is the best place to begin your tour of ancient Rome. Then continue to the Arch of Constantine, Roman Forum, Trajan's Column, and Pantheon. Have dinner on the atmospheric Campo de' Fiori. Then take this book's Heart of Rome Walk to the Trevi Fountain and Spanish Steps.

Day 2: See St. Peter's Basilica and climb its dome, then tour the Vatican Museums, featuring the divine Sistine Chapel (closed Sun, except first Sun of month; smart to reserve a museum entry time in advance).

With any remaining stamina, choose among these sights (or save for tomorrow afternoon): the Church of San Giovanni in Laterano (Holy Stairs), St. Peter-in-Chains (Michelangelo's *Moses*), and Capuchin Crypt (bone chapel).

Evening options: Do as the Romans do—join the Dolce Vita Stroll along the Via del Corso. Explore the Monti neighborhood; linger over dinner, or stop by an *enoteca* (wine bar) for a drink. Enjoy a classical concert or jazz.

Day 3: See the Borghese Gallery (reservations required, closed Mon; stroll through the park afterwards) and the Capitoline Museums. Zip up to the top of the nearby Victor Emmanuel Monument for a grand view of the Eternal City.

With extra time: Take a day trip to Ostia Antica (the remains of an ancient Roman town; closed Mon) or to the hill

town of Orvieto. Or visit Naples and Pompeii in a blitz day trip from Rome; take the early Rome-Naples express train (usually daily 7:35-8:45), see Naples, then Pompeii, and you'll be back in Rome before bedtime (but avoid this trip on Tue, when Naples' archaeological museum is closed).

Rick's Tip: *The* **siesta is the key to survival** *in summertime Rome. Lie down and contemplate the extraordinary power of gravity in the Eternal City. Drink lots of cold, refreshing water from Rome's many drinking fountains.*

ORIENTATION

Sprawling Rome actually feels manageable once you get to know it. The old core, with most of the tourist sights, sits in a diamond formed by Termini train station (in the east), the Vatican (west), Villa Borghese Gardens (north), and the Colosseum (south). The Tiber River runs through the diamond from north to south. In the center of the diamond sits Piazza Venezia, a busy square and traffic hub. It takes about an hour to walk from Termini Station to the Vatican. Think of Rome as a series of neighborhoods, huddling around major landmarks.

ROME AT A GLANCE

▲▲▲**Heart of Rome Walk** A stroll lacing the narrow lanes, intimate piazzas, fanciful fountains, and lively scenes of Rome's most colorful neighborhood. **Hours:** Any time, but best in evening. See page 319.

▲▲▲**Colosseum** Huge stadium where gladiators fought. **Hours:** Daily 8:30 until one hour before sunset: April-Aug until 19:15, Sept until 19:00, Oct until 18:30, off-season closes as early as 16:30. See page 330.

▲▲▲**Roman Forum** Ancient Rome's main square, with ruins and grand arches. **Hours:** Same hours as Colosseum. See page 335.

▲▲▲**Capitoline Museums** Ancient statues, mosaics, and expansive view of Forum. **Hours:** Daily 9:30-19:30. See page 345.

▲▲▲**Pantheon** The defining domed temple—2,000 years old. **Hours:** Mon-Sat 8:30-19:30, Sun 9:00-18:00, holidays 9:00-13:00, closed for Mass Sat at 17:00 and Sun at 10:30. See page 349.

▲▲▲**St. Peter's Basilica** Most impressive church on earth, with Michelangelo's *Pietà* and dome. **Hours:** Church—daily April-Sept 7:00-19:00, Oct-March 7:00-18:30, often closed Wed mornings; dome—daily April-Sept 8:00-18:00, Oct-March 8:00-17:00. See page 351.

▲▲▲**Vatican Museums** Four miles of the finest art of Western civilization, culminating in Michelangelo's glorious Sistine Chapel. **Hours:** Mon-Sat 9:00-18:00. Closed on religious holidays and Sun, except last Sun of the month (open 9:00-14:00). Open some Fri nights by online reservation only. See page 359.

▲▲▲**Borghese Gallery** Bernini sculptures and paintings by Caravaggio, Raphael, and Titian in a Baroque palazzo. Reservations mandatory. **Hours:** Tue-Sun 9:00-19:00, closed Mon. See page 365.

▲▲▲**National Museum of Rome** Greatest collection of Roman sculpture anywhere. **Hours:** Tue-Sun 9:00-19:45, closed Mon. See page 368.

▲▲**Palatine Hill** Ruins of emperors' palaces, Circus Maximus view, and museum. **Hours:** Same as Colosseum. See page 343.

▲▲**Trajan's Column** Tall ancient Roman column with narrative relief. See page 347.

▲▲**Museo dell'Ara Pacis** Shrine marking the beginning of Rome's Golden Age. **Hours:** Daily 9:30-19:30. See page 367.

▲▲**Dolce Vita Stroll** Evening *passeggiata,* where Romans strut their stuff. **Hours:** Roughly Mon-Sat 17:00-19:00 and Sun afternoons. See page 327.

▲▲**Church of San Giovanni in Laterano** Grandiose and historic "home church of the popes," with one-of-a-kind Holy Stairs across the street. **Hours:** Church—daily 7:00-18:30; Holy Stairs—generally same hours. See page 370.

▲**Arch of Constantine** Honors the emperor who legalized Christianity. See page 334.

▲**Monti Neighborhood** Lively fun-to-explore neighborhood with trendy eateries, workaday shops, and inviting lanes. See page 347.

▲**St. Peter-in-Chains Church** with Michelangelo's *Moses*. **Hours:** Daily 8:00-12:30 & 15:00-19:00, Oct-March until 18:00. See page 348.

▲**Piazza del Campidoglio** Square atop Capitoline Hill, designed by Michelangelo, with a museum, grand stairway, and Forum overlooks. See page 343.

▲**Victor Emmanuel Monument** Gigantic edifice celebrating Italian unity, with Rome from the Sky elevator ride up to 360-degree city view. **Hours:** Monument—daily 9:00-19:00 (shorter in winter); elevator—until 19:30. See page 346.

▲**Spanish Steps** Popular hangout by day and night, particularly atmospheric when floodlit at night. See page 367.

▲**Trevi Fountain** Baroque hot spot into which tourists throw coins to ensure a return trip to Rome. See page 351.

▲**Baths of Diocletian/Basilica S. Maria degli Angeli** Once ancient Rome's immense public baths, now a Michelangelo church. **Hours:** Daily 7:30-18:30, closes later May-Sept and Sun year-round. See page 369.

Ancient Rome: In ancient times, this was home to the grandest buildings of a city of a million people. Today, the best of the classical sights stand in a line from the Colosseum to the Forum to the Pantheon. Just north of this area, between Via Nazionale and Via Cavour, is the atmospheric and trendy Monti district.

Pantheon Neighborhood: The Pantheon anchors the neighborhood I like to call the "Heart of Rome." It stretches eastward from the Tiber River through Campo de' Fiori and Piazza Navona, past the Pantheon to the Trevi Fountain.

Vatican City: Located west of the Tiber, it's a compact world of its own, with two great sights: St. Peter's Basilica and the Vatican Museums.

North Rome: With the Spanish Steps, Villa Borghese Gardens, and trendy shopping streets (Via Veneto and the "shopping triangle"—the area along Via del Corso and between the Spanish Steps, Piazza Venezia, and Piazza del Popolo), this is a more modern, classy area.

East Rome: This includes the area around Termini Station and Piazza della Repubblica, with many public-transportation connections.

South Rome: South of Vatican City is Trastevere, the colorful, wrong-side-of-the-river neighborhood that provides a look at village Rome. It's the city at its crustiest—and perhaps most "Roman."

Tourist Information

Rome has about a dozen small city-run tourist information offices scattered around town. The largest TIs are at Fiumicino Airport (daily 8:00-21:00, Terminal 3) and Termini train station (daily 8:00-18:45, exit by track 24 and walk 100 yards down along Via Giovanni Giolitti). Other TIs are directly across from the Forum entrance (on Via dei Fori Imperiali), at the Tiburtina train station, and at Ciampino Airport.

Info kiosks (generally open daily 9:30-19:00) are on Via Nazionale (at Palazzo delle Esposizioni), between the Trevi Fountain and Pantheon (at the corner of Via del Corso and Via Minghetti), near Piazza Navona (at Piazza delle Cinque Lune), and in Trastevere (at Piazza Sidney Sonnino).

The TI's website is www.turismoroma.it, but a better site for practical information is www.060608.it. That's also the number for Rome's **call center**—the best source of up-to-date tourist information, with English speakers on staff (answered daily 9:00-19:00, just dial 06-0608, and press 2 for English).

Two English-oriented **websites** provide insight into events and daily life in the city: www.inromenow.com (light tourist info on lots of topics); www.wantedinrome.com (events and accommodations).

Advance Tickets and Sightseeing Passes

Roma Pass: Rome offers several sightseeing passes. The Roma Pass is the clear winner (www.romapass.it). Two versions are available: three-day and 48-hour.

The **three-day Roma Pass** costs €38.50, includes free admission to your first two sights, discounts on subsequent sights, and unlimited use of public transit for 72 hours (buses, trams, and Metro, plus the suburban train to Ostia, but not the airport train). Using the pass at the Colosseum/Roman Forum/Palatine Hill (considered a single sight) lets you go directly to the front of the regular line (be aggressive as you wave your pass to get there). Other covered sights include: Borghese Gallery (though a reservation is still required), Capitoline Museums, Ara Pacis, and Trajan's Market. The pass also covers the National Museum of Rome. The pass does not cover the Vatican Museums (which contain the Sistine Chapel).

If you'll be using public transit and visiting any two of the major sights in a three-day period, get the full pass. They are sold at participating sights, TIs, and many tobacco shops and newsstands all over town (look for a *Roma Pass* sign; all should charge the same price). Don't wait to buy it at a crowded sight like the Colosseum. There's no advantage in ordering a pass online—you still have to pick it up in Rome.

The pass is activated when you use it for the first time at a sight or on public transport. Once the pass is validated you can hop on any bus without showing it, but you'll need to swipe it to get through Metro turnstiles. At other sights, show it at the ticket office to get about 30 percent off.

Rick's Tip: *To get the most out of your* **Roma Pass, visit the two most expensive sights first**—*for example, the Colosseum/Roman Forum/Palatine Hill (€12) and the Capitoline Museums (up to €15 with temporary exhibits).*

The **48-hour Roma Pass** costs €28 and includes free entry to one sight, discounts on additional ones, and unlimited use of public transit (for 48 hours after validation).

For families, only adults will need a Roma Pass. Since children under age 18 get into national museums and sights for free, and kids under 6 get into city museums (including Museo dell'Ara Pacis) for free, they can skip the lines alongside their pass-holding parents. Kids 10 and over need their own transit tickets or passes; those 9 and under ride free.

Colosseum, Forum, and Palatine Hill: These are covered by the Roma Pass and also two different tickets: The €12 combo-ticket allows one entry for the Colosseum (after 14:00) and one entry for the Forum/Palatine Hill complex. With a €18 SUPER ticket, you can enter the Colosseum anytime and visit the Forum/Palatine separately. To avoid lines, buy online (www.coopculture.it) or at the lesser-used Forum entrance near Palatine Hill.

Museum Reservations: The Borghese Gallery requires reservations in advance (see page 365). You can also reserve online to avoid long lines at the Vatican Museums (see page 359).

Opening Hours: Rome's sights have notoriously variable hours from season to season. It's smart to check each sight's website in advance. On holidays, expect shorter hours or closures.

Churches: Many churches, which have divine art and free entry, open early (around 7:00-7:30), close for lunch (roughly 12:00-15:30), and close late (about 19:00). Visit churches before 9:00 or late in the day; if you're not resting during the siesta, see major sights that stay open all day (St. Peter's, Colosseum, Forum, Capitoline Museums, Pantheon, and National Museum of Rome). Dress modestly for church visits.

Tours

🎧 To sightsee on your own, download my **free audio tours** that illuminate some of Rome's top sights and neighborhoods, including tours of the Pantheon, Colosseum, Roman Forum, St. Peter's Basilica,

Spiral staircase at the Vatican Museums

Backstreet Rome

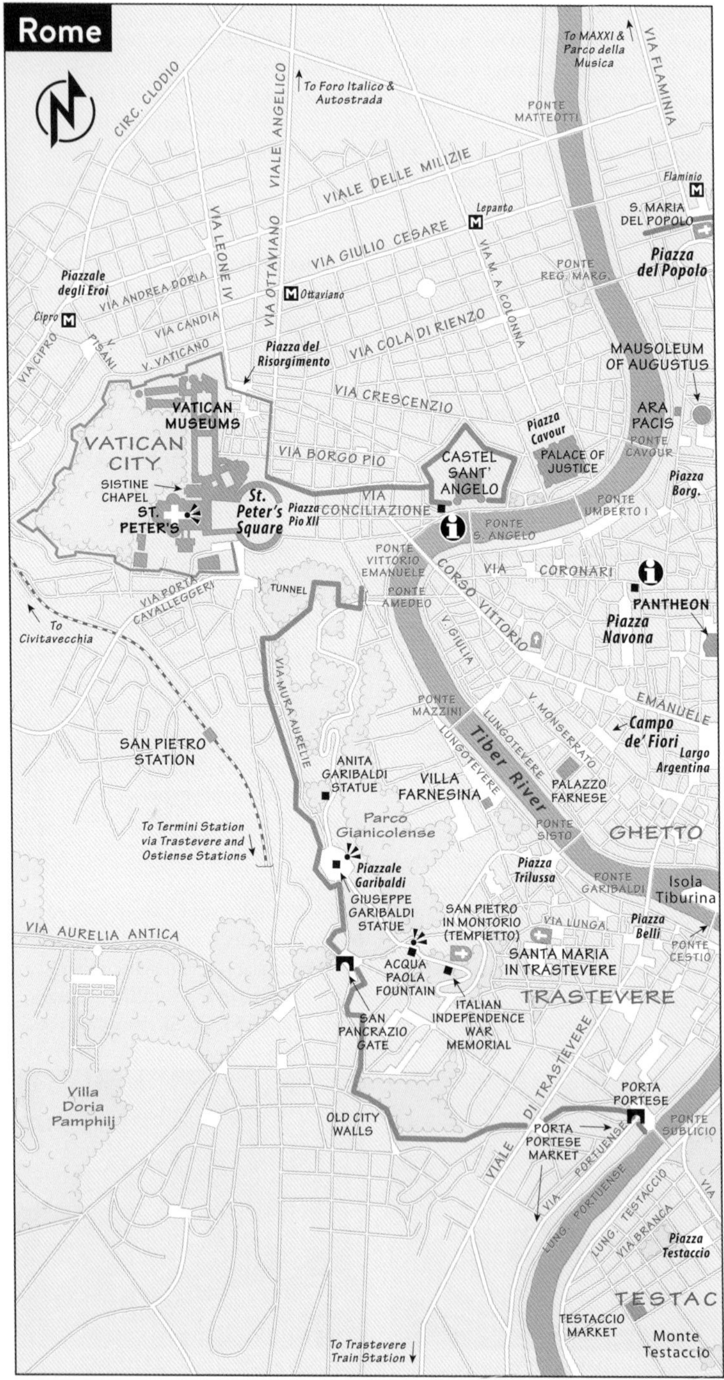
Rome
VATICAN CITY
VATICAN MUSEUMS
SISTINE CHAPEL
ST. PETER'S
St. Peter's Square
Piazza Pio XII
CASTEL SANT' ANGELO
PALACE OF JUSTICE
Piazza Cavour
MAUSOLEUM OF AUGUSTUS
ARA PACIS
Piazza del Popolo
S. MARIA DEL POPOLO
PANTHEON
Piazza Navona
Campo de' Fiori
Largo Argentina
PALAZZO FARNESE
GHETTO
Isola Tiburina
Tiber River
VILLA FARNESINA
Parco Gianicolense
ANITA GARIBALDI STATUE
Piazzale Garibaldi
GIUSEPPE GARIBALDI STATUE
SAN PIETRO IN MONTORIO (TEMPIETTO)
ACQUA PAOLA FOUNTAIN
ITALIAN INDEPENDENCE WAR MEMORIAL
SAN PANCRAZIO GATE
SANTA MARIA IN TRASTEVERE
TRASTEVERE
OLD CITY WALLS
PORTA PORTESE
PORTA PORTESE MARKET
TESTAC
TESTACCIO MARKET
Monte Testaccio
Piazza Testaccio
Piazza Trilussa
Piazza Belli
Piazza Borg.
SAN PIETRO STATION
Villa Doria Pamphilj
To MAXXI & Parco della Musica
To Foro Italico & Autostrada
To Civitavecchia
To Termini Station via Trastevere and Ostiense Stations
To Trastevere Train Station
Piazzale degli Eroi
Piazza del Risorgimento
Cipro
Ottaviano
Lepanto
Flaminio
VIA FLAMINIA
CIRC. CLODIO
VIALE ANGELICO
VIALE DELLE MILIZIE
VIA LEONE IV
VIA OTTAVIANO
VIA GIULIO CESARE
VIA ANDREA DORIA
VIA CANDIA
V. VATICANO
V. PISANI
VIA CIPRO
VIA COLA DI RIENZO
VIA M. A. COLONNA
VIA CRESCENZIO
VIA BORGO PIO
VIA CONCILIAZIONE
VIA CORONARI
CORSO VITTORIO EMANUELE
V. GIULIA
V. MONSERRATO
LUNGOTEVERE
VIA PORTA CAVALLEGGERI
TUNNEL
VIA MURA AURELIE
VIA AURELIA ANTICA
VIA LUNGA.
VIALE DI TRASTEVERE
VIA PORTUENSE
LUNG. PORTUENSE
LUNG. TESTACCIO
VIA BRANCA
VIA
PONTE MATTEOTTI
PONTE REG. MARG.
PONTE CAVOUR
PONTE UMBERTO I
PONTE S. ANGELO
PONTE VITTORIO EMANUELE
PONTE AMEDEO
PONTE MAZZINI
PONTE SISTO
PONTE GARIBALDI
PONTE CESTIO
PONTE SUBLICIO

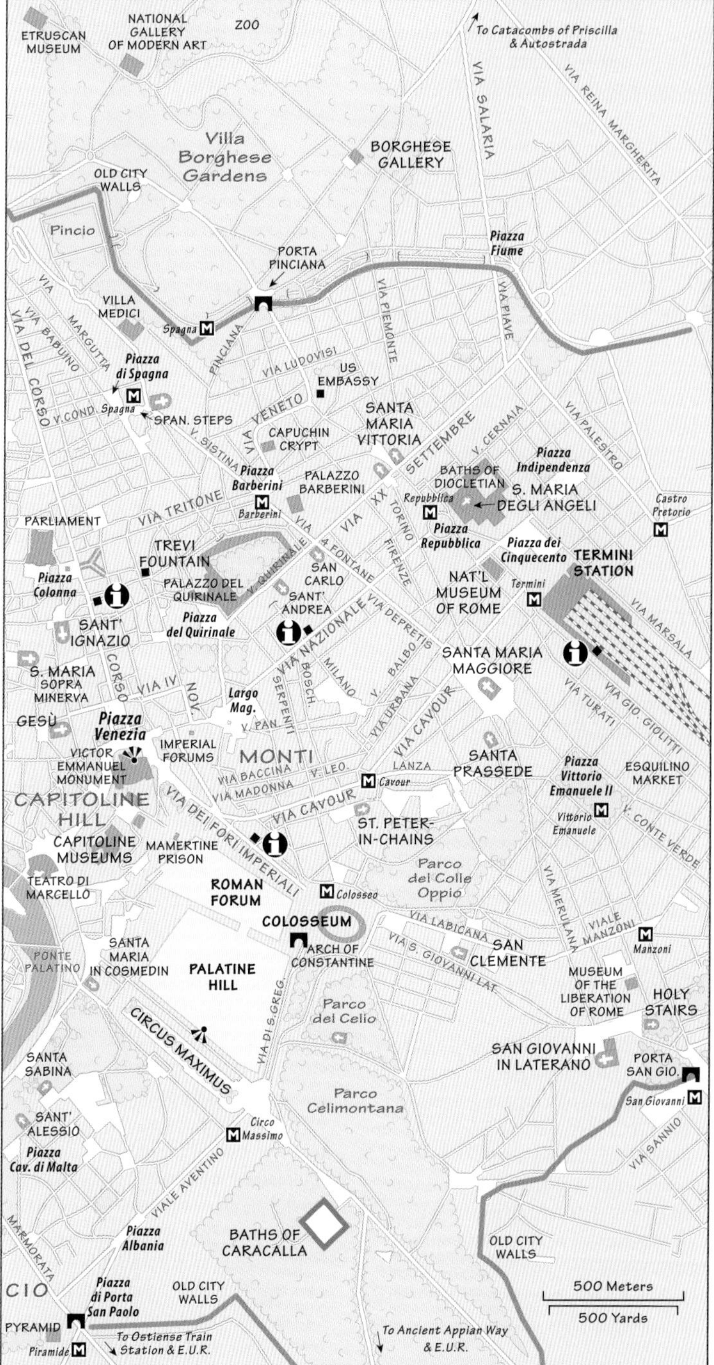
ETRUSCAN MUSEUM
NATIONAL GALLERY OF MODERN ART
ZOO
To Catacombs of Priscilla & Autostrada
VIA SALARIA
VIA REINA MARGHERITA
Villa Borghese Gardens
BORGHESE GALLERY
OLD CITY WALLS
Pincio
PORTA PINCIANA
Piazza Fiume
VILLA MEDICI
Spagna
VIA PIEMONTE
VIA PIAVE
VIA BABUINO
VIA MARGUTTA
VIA DEL CORSO
PINCIANA
VIA LUDOVISI
US EMBASSY
Piazza di Spagna
V. COND.
SPAN. STEPS
VIA VENETO
SANTA MARIA VITTORIA
V. CERNAIA
VIA PALESTRO
V. SISTINA
CAPUCHIN CRYPT
VIA XX SETTEMBRE
Piazza Indipendenza
Piazza Barberini
PALAZZO BARBERINI
BATHS OF DIOCLETIAN
S. MARIA DEGLI ANGELI
Castro Pretorio
Barberini
VIA TRITONE
Repubblica
TORINO
PARLIAMENT
Piazza Repubblica
TREVI FOUNTAIN
VIA 4 FONTANE
Piazza dei Cinquecento
TERMINI STATION
SAN CARLO
PALAZZO DEL QUIRINALE
V. QUIRINALE
FIRENZE
NAT'L MUSEUM OF ROME
Termini
Piazza Colonna
SANT' ANDREA
VIA DEPRETIS
SANT' IGNAZIO
Piazza del Quirinale
VIA NAZIONALE
VIA MARSALA
SANTA MARIA MAGGIORE
S. MARIA SOPRA MINERVA
CORSO
VIA IV NOV.
SERPENTI
BOSCH.
MILANO
V. BALBO
VIA URBANA
VIA CAVOUR
VIA TURATI
VIA GIO. GIOLITTI
Largo Mag.
V. PAN.
GESÙ
Piazza Venezia
IMPERIAL FORUMS
MONTI
SANTA PRASSEDE
VICTOR EMMANUEL MONUMENT
LANZA
Piazza Vittorio Emanuele II
ESQUILINO MARKET
VIA BACCINA
V. LEO.
VIA MADONNA
Cavour
CAPITOLINE HILL
VIA DEI FORI IMPERIALI
ST. PETER-IN-CHAINS
Vittorio Emanuele
V. CONTE VERDE
CAPITOLINE MUSEUMS
MAMERTINE PRISON
Parco del Colle Oppio
TEATRO DI MARCELLO
ROMAN FORUM
Colosseo
VIA MERULANA
COLOSSEUM
VIA LABICANA
VIALE MANZONI
Manzoni
SANTA MARIA IN COSMEDIN
PONTE PALATINO
ARCH OF CONSTANTINE
VIA S. GIOVANNI LAT.
SAN CLEMENTE
PALATINE HILL
MUSEUM OF THE LIBERATION OF ROME
HOLY STAIRS
VIA DI S. GREG.
Parco del Celio
CIRCUS MAXIMUS
SAN GIOVANNI IN LATERANO
SANTA SABINA
PORTA SAN GIO.
Parco Celimontana
San Giovanni
SANT' ALESSIO
Circo Massimo
VIA SANNIO
Piazza Cav. di Malta
VIALE AVENTINO
MARMORATA
Piazza Albania
BATHS OF CARACALLA
OLD CITY WALLS
CIO
Piazza di Porta San Paolo
OLD CITY WALLS
500 Meters
500 Yards
PYRAMID
Piramide
To Ostiense Train Station & E.U.R.
To Ancient Appian Way & E.U.R.

Vatican Museums, Sistine Chapel, and Ostia Antica, and walks through the Heart of Rome, Jewish Ghetto, and Trastevere (for more on the audio tours, see page 28).

Rome's tour companies are highly competitive; I've listed several that are creative and well-established. Check their websites to learn about their various tours—there's always an introductory tour. Three-hour guided walks (always in English) generally cost €25-30 per person. It's sometimes required, and always smart, to book a spot in advance (easy to do online). Scheduling mishaps can occur. Make sure you know what you're booking, and when and where to meet.

Each of these companies offers a 10 percent discount with online bookings for Rick Steves travelers:

Enjoy Rome—Tel. 06-445-1843, www.enjoyrome.com, info@enjoyrome.com.

Europe Odyssey—Tel. 06-8854-2416, mobile 328-912-3720, www.europeodyssey.com, run by Rahul.

Through Eternity—For discount look for "Group Tours Rome" and enter "RICKSTEVES"; tel. 06-700-9336, www.througheternity.com, office@througheternity.com, run by Rob.

Walks of Italy—For discount enter "10ricksteves"; US tel. 888/683-8670, tel. 06-9480-4888, www.walksofitaly.com, info@walksofitaly.com.

Helpful Hints

Sightseeing Tips: Those planning at least a couple of days of sightseeing can save money by buying the Roma Pass, available at TIs and participating sights. For the crowded Colosseum and Roman Forum/Palatine Hill, use the Roma Pass or buy a combo-ticket online to shorten your wait in line. To sidestep the long Vatican Museums line, reserve an entry time online (see page 359). Reservations are required for the Borghese Gallery—make them at least a few days in advance (see page 365).

Theft and Safety: While violent crime is rare in the city center, petty theft is rampant. Pickpockets troll through the tourist crowds around the Colosseum, Forum, Vatican, and all train and Metro stations. Always use your money belt. Keep nothing important in your pockets. If you carry a backpack, never leave it unattended and try to keep it attached to your body in some way (even when you're seated for a meal). To report lost or stolen items, file a police report (at Termini Station, with polizia at track 11 or with Carabinieri at track 20; offices are also at Piazza Venezia and at the corner of Via Nazionale and Via Genova).

Medical Help: Embassies and hotels can recommend English-speaking doctors. Consider MEDline, a 24-hour home-medical service; doctors speak English and make calls at hotels for about €150 (tel. 06-808-0995, www.soccorso-medico.com). Anyone is entitled to emergency treatment at public hospitals. The hospital closest to Termini Station is Policlinico Umberto 1 (entrance for emergency treatment on Via Lancisi, Metro: Policlinico, translators available).

Emergency Numbers: Police—tel. 113. Ambulance—tel. 118.

Beggars: Throughout Rome, you may encounter downtrodden people asking for money. Know that social services are available to them, and give at your own discretion.

Traffic Safety: Use caution when crossing streets. Some streets have pedestrian-crossing signals (red means stop—or jaywalk carefully; green means go...also carefully; and yellow means go... extremely carefully, as cars may be whipping around the corner). Just as often, multilane streets have crosswalks with no signals at all. And even when there are traffic lights, they are provisional: Scooters don't need to stop at red lights, and even cars exercise what drivers call the "logical option" of not stopping if they see no oncoming traffic. As noisy, gasoline-powered scooters are replaced by electric ones, the streets get quieter (hooray) but more dangerous for pedestrians.

Follow locals like a shadow when you cross a street. Find a gap in the traffic and walk with confidence while making eye contact with approaching drivers—they won't hit you if they can tell where you intend to go.

Wi-Fi: All hotels in this book have Wi-Fi, but if yours doesn't, your hotelier can point you to a café that does.

Free Water: Carry a **water bottle** and refill it at Rome's many public drinking spouts.

WCs: Public restrooms are scarce. Use them when you can at museums, restaurants, and bars.

Laundry: Coin launderettes are common in Rome; ask your hotelier. The Wash & Dry Lavarapido chain has a branch near Piazza Barberini (Mon-Sat 9:00-21:00, closed Sun, Via degli Avignonesi 17, tel. 06-4201-3158).

Travel Agencies: You can get train tickets and rail-pass-related reservations and supplements at travel agencies (at little or no additional cost), instead of making a trip to a train station or purchasing online. Your hotelier will know of an agency nearby.

ROME WALKS

These two self-guided walks give you a moving picture of this ancient yet modern city.

➲ Heart of Rome Walk

Rated ▲▲▲, this walk through Rome's most colorful neighborhood takes you through squares lively with locals, small lanes sporting shops or chunks of Roman ruins, and playful fountains that are people-magnets. During the day, this walk shows off the Campo de' Fiori market and trendy fashion boutiques as it meanders past major monuments such as the Pantheon and the Spanish Steps.

But the sunset brings unexpected magic. A stroll in the cool of the evening offers the romance of the Eternal City at its best. Sit so close to a bubbling fountain that traffic noise evaporates. Jostle with kids to see the gelato flavors. Watch lovers straddling more than the bench. And marvel at the ramshackle elegance that softens this brutal city. These are the flavors of Rome, best enjoyed after dark.

This walk is equally pleasant in reverse order. You could ride the Metro to the Spanish Steps and finish at Campo de' Fiori, near my recommended restaurants.

🎧 Download my free Heart of Rome Walk audio tour via my Rick Steves Audio Europe app—see page 28.

• *Start this walk at Campo de' Fiori, my favorite outdoor dining room (see page 385). It's a few blocks west of Largo Argentina, a major transportation hub. Buses #40, #64, and #492 stop at Largo Argentina and along Corso Vittorio Emanuele II (a long block northwest of Campo de' Fiori).*

❶ CAMPO DE' FIORI

This picturesque, bohemian piazza hosts a fruit and vegetable **market** in the morning, cafés in the evening, and pub-crawlers at night. In ancient times, the "Field of Flowers" was an open meadow. Later, Christian pilgrims passed through on their way to the Vatican, and a thriving market developed.

The square is watched over by a brooding statue of **Giordano Bruno,** an intellectual heretic who was burned on this spot in 1600. The pedestal shows scenes from Bruno's trial and execution, and reads, "And the flames rose up." When this statue honoring a heretic was erected in 1889, the Vatican protested, but they were overruled by angry Campo locals. The neighborhood is still known for its free spirit and anti-authoritarian demonstrations.

Campo de' Fiori is the product of centuries of unplanned urban development. At the east end of the square (behind Bruno), ramshackle apartments are built right into the outer wall of ancient Rome's mammoth Theater of Pompey. Julius Caesar was assassinated in the theater complex, where the Senate was renting space.

The square is surrounded by fun eateries, and is great for people-watching. Bruno faces the bustling **Forno** (in a corner of the square), where takeout *pizza bianca* ("white pizza," without red sauce) is sold hot from the oven. On weekend nights, when the Campo is packed with beer-drinking kids, the medieval square is transformed into a vast street party.

• *If Bruno did a hop, step, and jump forward, then turned left, in a block he'd reach...*

❷ PIAZZA FARNESE

While Campo de' Fiori feels free and easy, the 16th-century Renaissance Piazza Farnese, named for the family whose palace dominates it, stresses order. The nouveau riche Farnese family hired Michelangelo to help design their palace—which today houses the French embassy. The twin Roman tubs in the fountains decorating the square date from the third century and are from the Baths of Caracalla. They ended up here because the Farneses excavated the baths, giving them first dibs on the choicest finds.

• *Walk back to Campo de' Fiori, cross the square, and continue a couple of blocks down...*

❸ VIA DEI BAULLARI AND CORSO VITTORIO EMANUELE II

With a crush of cheap cafés, bars, and restaurants, the center of medieval Rome is now a playground for tourists, students, and suburban locals. High rents are driving families out and changing the character of this district. That's why the Campo de' Fiori market increasingly sells more gifty edibles than basic fruits and vegetables.

After a couple of blocks, you reach busy Corso Vittorio Emanuele II. In Rome, any road big enough to have city buses like this is post-unification: constructed after 1870. Look left and right down the street—the facades are mostly 19th century Neo-Renaissance, built after this main thoroughfare sliced through the city. Traffic in much of central Rome is limited to city buses, taxis, motorbikes, "dark cars" (limos and town cars of VIPs), delivery vans, residents, and disabled people with permits (a.k.a. friends of politicians). This is one of the rare streets where any vehicle is welcome.

Campo de' Fiori

• *Cross Corso Vittorio Emanuele II, and enter a square with a statue of Marco Minghetti, an early Italian prime minister. Angle left at the statue, walking along the left side of the Museum of Rome, down Via di San Pantaleo. A block down, at the corner, you'll find a beat-up old statue.*

❹ PASQUINO

A third-century B.C. statue that was discovered near here, Pasquino is one of Rome's "talking statues." For 500 years, this statue has served as a kind of community billboard, allowing people to complain anonymously when it might be dangerous to speak up. To this day, you'll see old Pasquino strewn with political posters, strike announcements, and grumbling graffiti. The statue looks literally worn down by centuries of complaining about bad government.

• *Facing Pasquino, veer to the left and head up Via di Pasquino to...*

❺ PIAZZA NAVONA

Piazza Navona has been a center of Roman life since ancient times. By its shape you might guess that it started out as a racetrack, part of the training grounds built here by Emperor Domitian around A.D. 80. But much of what we see today came in the 1600s, when the whole place got a major renovation. At the time, the popes were trying to put some big scandals behind them, and beautification projects like this were a peace offering to the public.

Three Baroque fountains decorate the piazza. The first fountain, at the southern end, features a Moor wrestling with a dolphin. In the fountain at the northern end, Neptune slays a giant octopus.

The most famous fountain is in the center: the **Four Rivers Fountain** by Gian Lorenzo Bernini. Four burly river gods (representing the four quarters of the known world) support an Egyptian-style obelisk made in Rome.

Stroll around the fountain counterclockwise and admire the gods: The good-looking figure represents the Danube (for Europe). Next comes the Ganges (for Asia), holding an oar. After an exotic palm tree, you find the Nile (for Africa) with his head covered, since the river's source was unknown back then. Uruguay's Rio de la Plata, representing the Americas, tumbles backward in shock, wondering how he even made the top four. The

Piazza Navona with Bernini's Four Rivers fountain

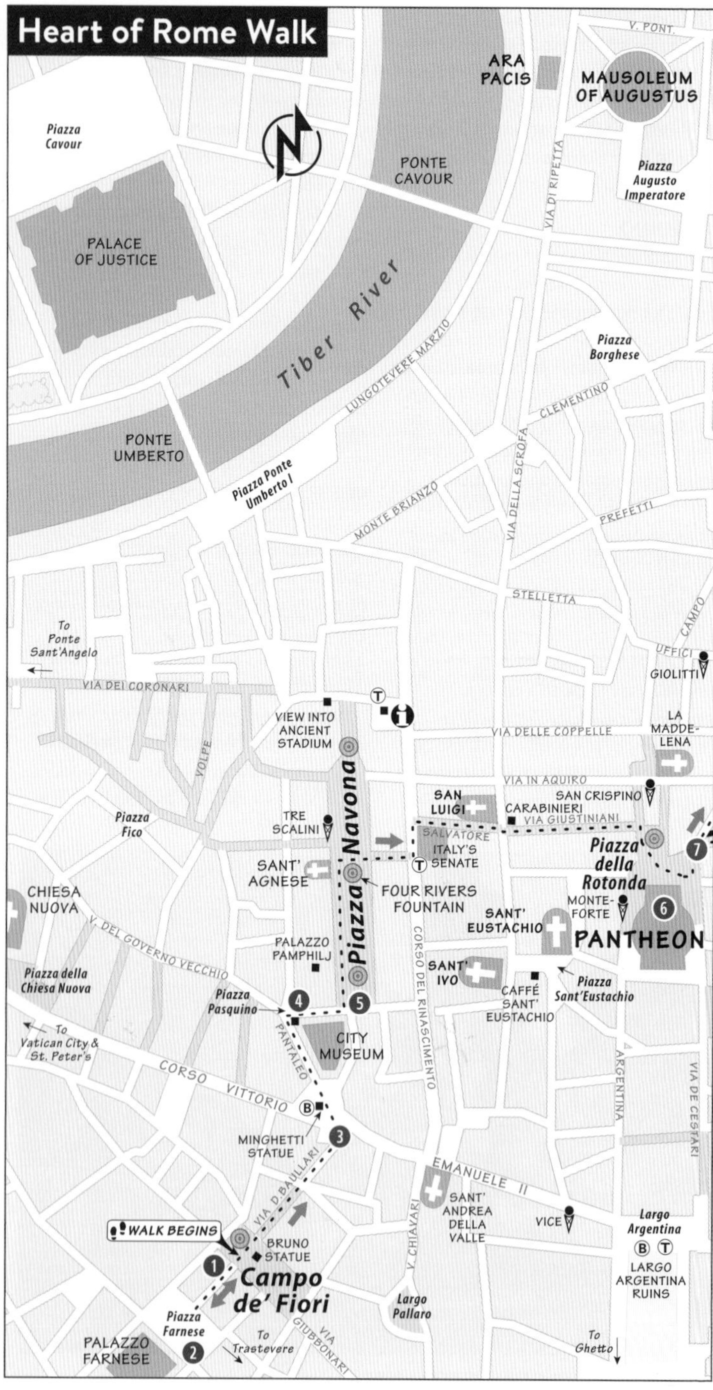
Heart of Rome Walk
V. PONT.
ARA PACIS
MAUSOLEUM OF AUGUSTUS
Piazza Cavour
PONTE CAVOUR
Piazza Augusto Imperatore
VIA DI RIPETTA
PALACE OF JUSTICE
Tiber River
LUNGOTEVERE MARZIO
Piazza Borghese
CLEMENTINO
PONTE UMBERTO
Piazza Ponte Umberto I
VIA DELLA SCROFA
MONTE BRIANZO
PREFETTI
STELLETTA
CAMPO
To Ponte Sant'Angelo
UFFICI
GIOLITTI
VIA DEI CORONARI
VIEW INTO ANCIENT STADIUM
LA MADDE-LENA
VIA DELLE COPPELLE
VOLPE
VIA IN AQUIRO
SAN LUIGI
SAN CRISPINO
CARABINIERI
VIA GIUSTINIANI
Piazza Fico
TRE SCALINI
SALVATORE
ITALY'S SENATE
Piazza della Rotonda
SANT' AGNESE
FOUR RIVERS FOUNTAIN
CHIESA NUOVA
MONTE-FORTE
SANT' EUSTACHIO
PANTHEON
V. DEL GOVERNO VECCHIO
PALAZZO PAMPHILJ
Piazza Navona
CORSO DEL RINASCIMENTO
SANT' IVO
Piazza della Chiesa Nuova
CAFFÈ SANT' EUSTACHIO
Piazza Sant'Eustachio
Piazza Pasquino
PANTALEO
CITY MUSEUM
To Vatican City & St. Peter's
ARGENTINA
VIA DE CESTARI
CORSO VITTORIO
MINGHETTI STATUE
EMANUELE II
VIA D. BAULLARI
V. CHIAVARI
SANT' ANDREA DELLA VALLE
VICE
Largo Argentina
WALK BEGINS
BRUNO STATUE
LARGO ARGENTINA RUINS
Campo de' Fiori
Largo Pallaro
Piazza Farnese
To Trastevere
GIUBBONARI
VIA
To Ghetto
PALAZZO FARNESE

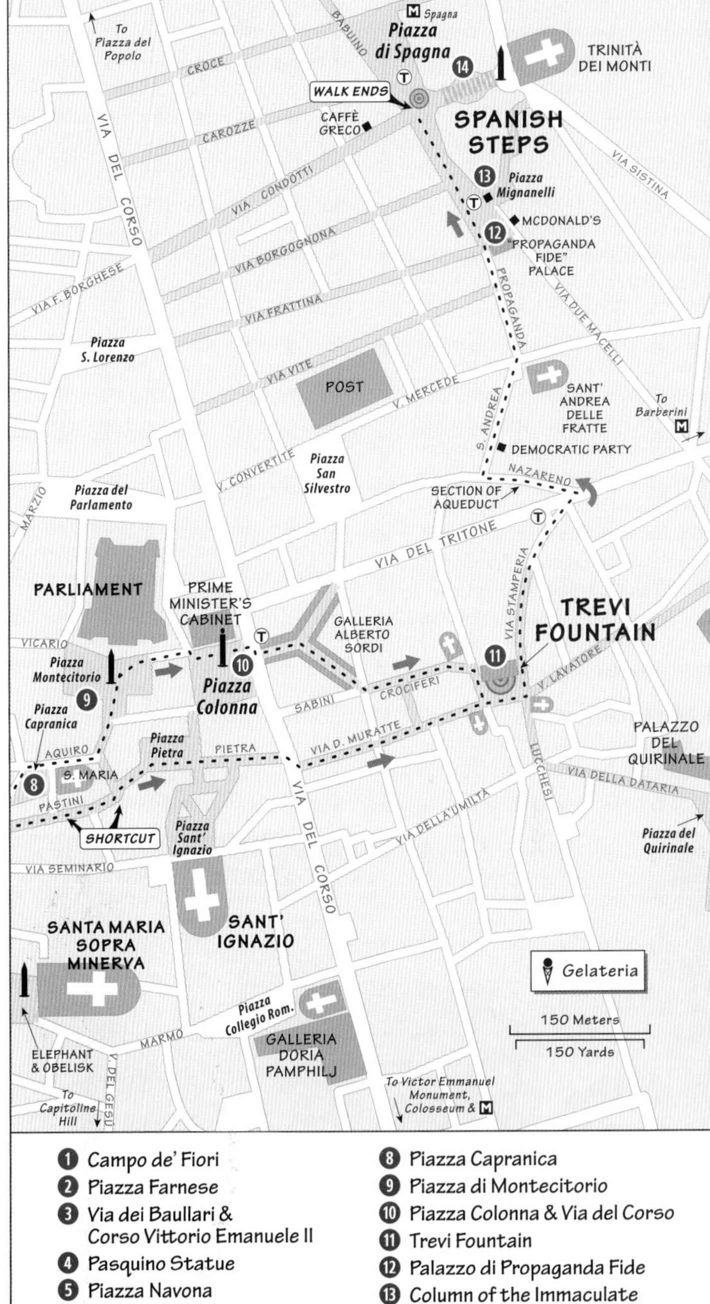
To Piazza del Popolo
Spagna
Piazza di Spagna
TRINITÀ DEI MONTI
BABUINO
CROCE
WALK ENDS
CAFFÈ GRECO
SPANISH STEPS
CAROZZE
VIA CONDOTTI
VIA DEL CORSO
Piazza Mignanelli
MCDONALD'S
"PROPAGANDA FIDE" PALACE
VIA SISTINA
VIA BORGOGNONA
VIA F. BORGHESE
VIA FRATTINA
PROPAGANDA
VIA DUE MACELLI
Piazza S. Lorenzo
VIA VITE
POST
V. MERCEDE
SANT' ANDREA DELLE FRATTE
To Barberini
S. ANDREA
DEMOCRATIC PARTY
V. CONVERTITE
Piazza San Silvestro
Piazza del Parlamento
MARZIO
NAZARENO
SECTION OF AQUEDUCT
VIA DEL TRITONE
PARLIAMENT
PRIME MINISTER'S CABINET
GALLERIA ALBERTO SORDI
VIA STAMPERIA
TREVI FOUNTAIN
VICARIO
Piazza Montecitorio
Piazza Colonna
SABINI
CROCIFERI
V. LAVATORE
Piazza Capranica
AQUIRO
Piazza Pietra
PIETRA
VIA D. MURATTE
PALAZZO DEL QUIRINALE
S. MARIA
LUCCHESI
VIA DELLA DATARIA
PASTINI
SHORTCUT
Piazza Sant' Ignazio
VIA DELL'UMILTÀ
Piazza del Quirinale
VIA SEMINARIO
SANTA MARIA SOPRA MINERVA
SANT' IGNAZIO
Gelateria
Piazza Collegio Rom.
150 Meters
150 Yards
MARMO
GALLERIA DORIA PAMPHILJ
ELEPHANT & OBELISK
V. DEL GESÙ
To Capitoline Hill
To Victor Emmanuel Monument, Colosseum &
1 Campo de' Fiori
2 Piazza Farnese
3 Via dei Baullari & Corso Vittorio Emanuele II
4 Pasquino Statue
5 Piazza Navona
6 Pantheon
7 Caffè Tazza d'Oro
8 Piazza Capranica
9 Piazza di Montecitorio
10 Piazza Colonna & Via del Corso
11 Trevi Fountain
12 Palazzo di Propaganda Fide
13 Column of the Immaculate Conception
14 Spanish Steps

spilled coins represent the wealth of the New World. Bernini enlivens the fountain with horses plunging through rocks and the exotic flora and fauna of faraway lands.

Piazza Navona is Rome's most interesting night scene, with street music, artists, fire-eaters, local Casanovas, ice cream, and outdoor cafés worth the splurge for their front-row seats for people-watching.

• *Leave Piazza Navona directly across from* **Tre Scalini** *(famous for its rich chocolate gelato), and go east down Corsia Agonale, past rose peddlers and palm readers. Ahead of you (across the busy street) stands the stately Palazzo Madama, where the Italian Senate meets and the security is high. Jog left around this building, and follow the brown sign to the Pantheon, straight down Via del Salvatore.*

After a block, you'll pass (on your left) the **Church of San Luigi dei Francesi,** *with its* très *French decor and precious Caravaggio paintings. If it's open, pop in. Otherwise, continue along, following the crowd, as everyone seems to be heading for the...*

6 PANTHEON

Sit for a while under the floodlit and moonlit portico of the Pantheon. The 40-foot, single-piece granite columns of the entrance show the scale of ancient Roman building. The columns support a triangular Greek-style roof with an inscription that says "M. Agrippa built this." In fact, the present structure was built *(fecit)* by Emperor Hadrian (A.D. 120), who gave credit to the builder of an earlier temple. This impressive entranceway gives no clue that the greatest wonder of the building is inside—a domed room that inspired later domes, including Michelangelo's St. Peter's and Brunelleschi's Duomo in Florence.

• *With your back to the Pantheon, veer to the right, uphill toward the yellow sign on Via Orfani that reads Casa del Caffè—you've reached the...*

7 CAFFÈ TAZZA D'ORO

This is one of Rome's top coffee shops, dating back to the days when this area was licensed to roast coffee beans. Locals come here for *granita di caffè con panna* (coffee and crushed ice with whipped cream).

• *From here, our walk continues past some interesting landmarks to the Trevi Fountain. But if you'd like to get to the fountain directly, take a* **shortcut** *by bearing right at the coffee shop onto Via de' Pastini, which leads through Piazza di Pietra, then across*

Pantheon

busy Via del Corso, where it becomes the pedestrianized Via delle Muratte and heads straight for the fountain.

To stick with me for the slightly longer version, bear left at the coffee shop and continue up Via degli Orfani to the next square...

❽ PIAZZA CAPRANICA

This square is home to the big, plain Florentine-Renaissance-style Palazzo Capranica (directly opposite as you enter the square). The six-story building to the left was once an apartment building for 17th-century Rome's middle class. Like so many of Rome's churches, Santa Maria in Aquiro, the church on the square, is older than the facade it was given during the Baroque period. Notice the little circular shrine on the street corner (between the palace and the apartment building).

• *Leave the piazza to the right of the palace, heading down Via in Aquiro. The street jogs to the left and into a square.*

❾ PIAZZA DI MONTECITORIO

The square is marked by a sixth-century B.C. **Egyptian obelisk,** taken as a trophy by Augustus after his victory in Egypt over Mark Antony and Cleopatra. The obelisk was originally set up as a sundial. Follow the zodiac markings to the well-guarded front door of Italy's **parliament building.**

• *One block to your right is Piazza Colonna, where we're heading next—unless you like gelato. A one-block detour to the left (past Albergo Nazionale) brings you a famous Roman* gelateria, **Giolitti** *(open daily until past midnight, Via Uffici del Vicario 40).*

❿ PIAZZA COLONNA AND VIA DEL CORSO

The centerpiece of **Piazza Colonna** is a huge second-century column. Its relief depicts the victories of Emperor Marcus Aurelius over the barbarians. Marcus once capped the column, but he was replaced by Paul, one of Rome's patron saints.

Beyond Piazza Colonna runs noisy **Via del Corso,** Rome's main north-south boulevard. It's named for the riderless horse races that took place here during Carnevale. Every evening, the pedestrian-only stretch of the Corso is packed with people on parade, taking to the streets for their *passeggiata.* It's an ideal venue for Romans to show off what they might have purchased from those classy shops (see the next walk, "Dolce Vita Stroll"). Before crossing the street, look left (to the obelisk marking Piazza del Popolo—the ancient north gate of the city) and right (to the Victor Emmanuel Monument).

• *Cross Via del Corso to enter a big palatial building with columns, the* **Galleria Alberto Sordi** *shopping mall. To the left are convenient toilets and ahead is Feltrinelli, the biggest Italian bookstore chain.*

Go to the right and exit out the back (if you're here after 21:00, when the mall is closed, circle around the right side of the Galleria on Via dei Sabini). At any time, be on guard for pickpockets, who thrive in the nearby Trevi Fountain crowds. Once out the back, the tourist kitsch builds as you head up Via de Crociferi to the roar of the water, lights, and people at the...

⓫ TREVI FOUNTAIN

This watery avalanche celebrates the abundance of pure water, which has been brought into the city since the days of ancient aqueducts. Oceanus rides across the waves in his chariot, pulled by horses and horn-blowing tritons, as he commands the flow of water. The illustrious Bernini sketched out the first designs. Nicola Salvi continued the project (c. 1740), using the palace behind the fountain as a theatrical backdrop.

The magic of the square is enhanced by the fact that no vehicular streets directly approach it. You can hear the excitement as you draw near, and then—*bam!*—you're there. The scene is always lively, with lucky Romeos clutching dates while unlucky ones clutch beers. Romantics toss a coin over their shoulder, thinking it will give them a wish and assure their return to Rome. It sounds silly, but every year I go through this tourist ritual...and so far it's working.

• *Facing the Trevi Fountain, walk along its right side up Via della Stamperia. Cross busy Via del Tritone. Continue about 30 yards up Via del Nazareno to #9, where you'll pass a fence on the left, with an exposed bit of the ancient Acqua Vergine aqueduct. Continue on to the T-intersection ahead, and turn right on Via Sant'Andrea delle Fratte. The street becomes Via di Propaganda. You'll pass alongside the...*

⓬ PALAZZO DI PROPAGANDA FIDE

At #1, on the right, the white-and-yellow entrance marks the palace from which the Catholic Church "propagated," or spread, its message to the world. Back in the 1600s, this "Propaganda Palace" was the headquarters of the Catholic Church's P.R. department—a priority after the Reformation. The building was designed by that dynamic Baroque duo, Bernini and Borromini (with his concave lines). It flies the yellow-and-white flag signifying that it is still owned by the Vatican.

Trevi Fountain

• *The street opens up into a long piazza. You're approaching the Spanish Steps. But first, pause at the...*

⓭ COLUMN OF THE IMMACULATE CONCEPTION

Atop a tall column stands a bronze statue of Mary. She wears a diadem of stars for a halo, and stands on a crescent moon atop a globe of the earth, which is crushing a satanic serpent.

The monument celebrates the Catholic doctrine of Immaculate Conception. This was the idea that, not only was Jesus born pure, but his mother Mary also was conceived without sin. The concept had been around since medieval times, but in 1854, Pope Pius IX finally proclaimed it official dogma and erected this statue in celebration. Every year on December 8, the feast day of the Immaculate Conception, this spot is the scene of a special celebration. The pope attends, the fire department places flowers on Mary's statue, and the Christmas season begins.

To Mary's immediate left stands the Spanish embassy to the Vatican. Rome has double the embassies of a normal capital because here countries need two: one to Italy and one to the Vatican. And because of this 300-year-old embassy, the square and its famous steps are called "Spanish."

• *Just 100 yards past Mary, you reach the climax of our walk, the...*

⓮ SPANISH STEPS

Piazza di Spagna, with the popular Spanish Steps, has been the hangout of many Romantics over the years (Keats, Wagner, Openshaw, Goethe, and others).

The British poet John Keats pondered his mortality, then died of tuberculosis at age 25 in the orange building on the right side of the steps. Fellow Romantic Lord Byron lived across the square at #66.

The 138 steps lead sharply up from Piazza di Spagna, forming a butterfly shape as they fan out around a central terrace. The design culminates in an obelisk framed between two Baroque church towers.

The **Sinking Boat Fountain** at the foot of the steps, built by Gian Lorenzo Bernini or his father, Pietro, is powered by an aqueduct (like all of Rome's fountains).

The main sight here is not the steps but the people who gather around them. By day, shoppers swarm the high-fashion boutiques at the base of the steps, along Via Condotti. At night, the area is alive with people enjoying—and creating—the ambience of Rome's piazzas.

• *Our walk is finished. To reach the top of the steps sweat-free, take the free elevator just inside the Spagna Metro stop (to the left, as you face the steps; elevator closes at 21:00). A pay WC is underground in the piazza near the Metro entrance, by the middle palm tree (10:00-19:30). A huge McDonald's (with a WC) is a block to the right of the steps. When you're ready to leave, zip home on the Metro or grab a taxi at either end of the piazza.*

➲ Dolce Vita Stroll

This chic evening stroll, rated ▲▲, moves from Piazza del Popolo (Metro: Flaminio) down a traffic-free section of Via del Corso, and up Via Condotti to the Spanish Steps. You'll see people-watchers, flirts on the prowl, and shoppers browsing Rome's most fashionable stores (some are open roughly 16:00-19:30, after the siesta).

Although it's busy at any hour, crowds really come out from 17:00 to 19:00 (Fri and Sat are best), except on Sunday, when the stroll begins earlier in the afternoon. Leave before 18:00 if you plan to visit the Ara Pacis (Altar of Peace), which closes at 19:30 (last entry at 18:30). If you get hungry, see page 375 for a couple of restaurant listings.

To reach **Piazza del Popolo,** take Metro line A to Flaminio and walk south to the square. The car-free piazza is marked by an obelisk that was brought to Rome by Augustus after he conquered Egypt. It used to stand in the Circus Maximus.

If you're starting your stroll early enough, visit the Baroque church of **Santa Maria del Popolo,** next to the gate in the old wall on the north side of the square (Mon-Sat until 19:00, Sun until 19:30); look for Raphael's Chigi Chapel

Piazza del Popolo

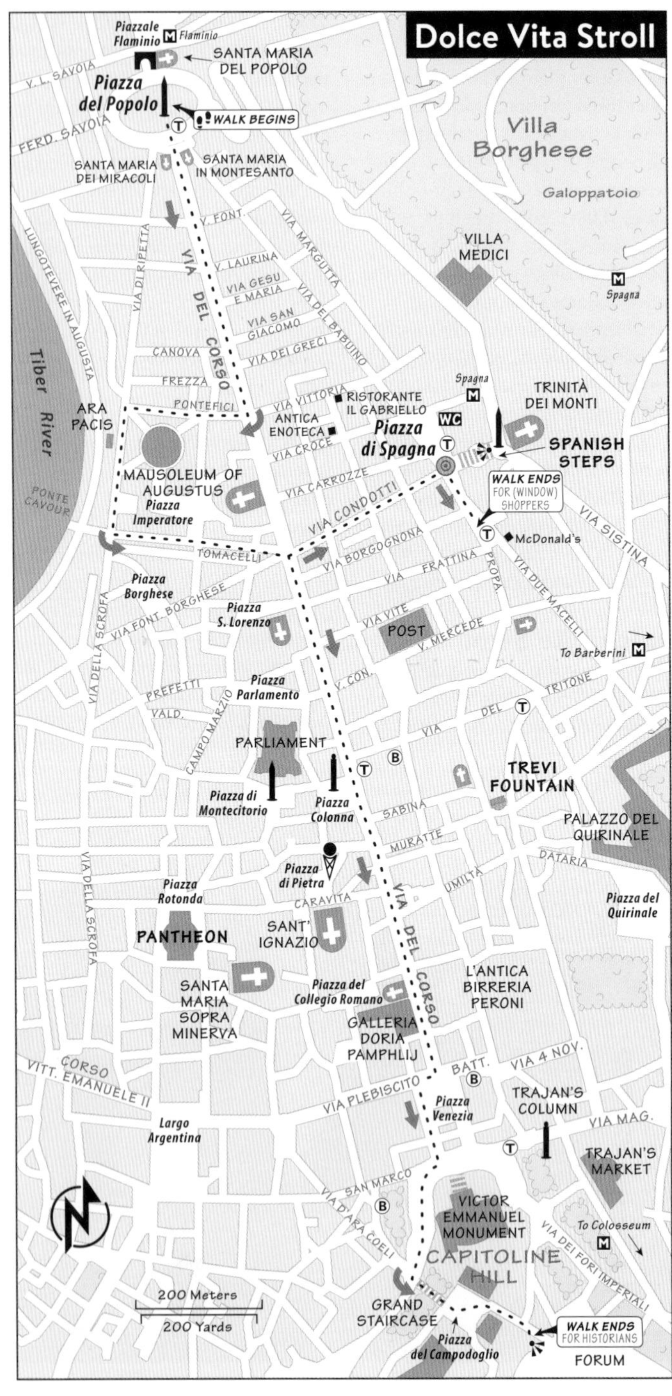
Dolce Vita Stroll
Piazzale Flaminio
Flaminio
SANTA MARIA DEL POPOLO
Piazza del Popolo
WALK BEGINS
V. L. SAVOIA
FERD. SAVOIA
SANTA MARIA DEI MIRACOLI
SANTA MARIA IN MONTESANTO
Villa Borghese
Galoppatoio
VILLA MEDICI
Spagna
V. FONT.
VIA MARGUTTA
V. LAURINA
VIA GESU E MARIA
VIA SAN GIACOMO
VIA DEI GRECI
VIA DEL BABUINO
VIA DI RIPETTA
VIA DEL CORSO
LUNGOTEVERE IN AUGUSTA
Tiber River
CANOVA
FREZZA
PONTEFICI
ARA PACIS
VIA VITTORIA
RISTORANTE IL GABRIELLO
ANTICA ENOTECA
VIA CROCE
Piazza di Spagna
WC
TRINITÀ DEI MONTI
SPANISH STEPS
WALK ENDS FOR (WINDOW) SHOPPERS
MAUSOLEUM OF AUGUSTUS
Piazza Imperatore
PONTE CAVOUR
VIA CARROZZE
VIA CONDOTTI
VIA SISTINA
McDonald's
TOMACELLI
VIA BORGOGNONA
VIA FRATTINA
PROPA.
VIA DUE MACELLI
Piazza Borghese
VIA FONT. BORGHESE
Piazza S. Lorenzo
VIA VITE
POST
V. MERCEDE
To Barberini
VIA DELLA SCROFA
PREFETTI
VALD.
CAMPO MARZIO
Piazza Parlamento
V. CON.
VIA DEL TRITONE
PARLIAMENT
TREVI FOUNTAIN
Piazza di Montecitorio
Piazza Colonna
SABINA
MURATTE
PALAZZO DEL QUIRINALE
DATARIA
Piazza di Pietra
UMILTÀ
Piazza Rotonda
CARAVITA
Piazza del Quirinale
PANTHEON
SANT' IGNAZIO
SANTA MARIA SOPRA MINERVA
Piazza del Collegio Romano
GALLERIA DORIA PAMPHLIJ
L'ANTICA BIRRERIA PERONI
CORSO VITT. EMANUELE II
BATT.
VIA 4 NOV.
VIA PLEBISCITO
Piazza Venezia
TRAJAN'S COLUMN
VIA MAG.
Largo Argentina
TRAJAN'S MARKET
SAN MARCO
VIA D'ARA COELI
VICTOR EMMANUEL MONUMENT
To Colosseum
CAPITOLINE HILL
VIA DEI FORI IMPERIALI
200 Meters
200 Yards
GRAND STAIRCASE
Piazza del Campidoglio
WALK ENDS FOR HISTORIANS
FORUM

(second on left as you face main altar) and two paintings by Caravaggio (in Cerasi Chapel, left of altar).

From Piazza del Popolo, browse your way down **Via del Corso.** With the proliferation of shopping malls, many chain stores lining Via del Corso are losing customers and facing hard times. Still, this remains a fine place to feel the pulse of Rome at twilight.

History buffs should turn right down **Via Pontefici** to see the massive, round-brick **Mausoleum of Augustus,** topped with overgrown cypress trees. This neglected sight, honoring Rome's first emperor, is slated for restoration and redevelopment. Beyond it, next to the river, is Augustus' **Ara Pacis,** enclosed within a protective glass-walled museum (see page 367). From the mausoleum, walk down Via Tomacelli to return to Via del Corso and the 21st century.

From Via del Corso, window shoppers should take a left down **Via Condotti** to join the parade to the **Spanish Steps,** passing big-name boutiques. The streets that parallel Via Condotti to the south (Borgognona and Frattina) are also filled with high-end shops. A few streets to the north hides the narrow Via Margutta, where Gregory Peck's *Roman Holiday* character lived (at #51). Today it's filled with pricey artisan and antique shops.

Historians should ignore Via Condotti and forget the Spanish Steps. Stay on Via del Corso and walk a half-mile down to the **Victor Emmanuel Monument.** Climb Michelangelo's stairway to his glorious square atop Capitoline Hill, floodlit at night. The mayor's palace is straight ahead. Stand on the balcony (to the right of the palace) overlooking the Forum. Enjoy one of the finest views in the city as the horizon reddens and cats prowl the unclaimed rubble of ancient Rome.

SIGHTS

I've clustered Rome's sights into walkable neighborhoods, some close together.

When you see a 🎧 in a listing, it means the sight is covered on a free audio tour (via my Rick Steves Audio Europe app—see page 28).

Spanish Steps

The best website for current opening hours is www.060608.it.

Rick's Tip: *Especially in this large city, make it a point to* **visit sights in a logical order.** *Needless backtracking wastes precious time and energy.*

Ancient Rome

The core of ancient Rome, where the grandest monuments were built, is between the Colosseum and Capitoline Hill. You can tour these sights in one great day: Start at the Colosseum, then it's a few minutes' walk to the Forum, then Capitoline Hill. From there, it's another 15-minute walk to the Pantheon. As a pleasant conclusion to your busy day, walk back south along the broad, parklike Via dei Fori Imperiali.

Ancient Core

▲▲▲COLOSSEUM (COLOSSEO)

This 2,000-year-old stadium is one of Europe's most recognizable landmarks—and a classic example of Roman engineering. Whether you're playing gladiator or simply marveling at the ancient design and construction, the Colosseum gets a unanimous thumbs-up.

Cost and Hours: €12 combo-ticket with Roman Forum/Palatine Hill (you must see both the Forum and Palatine on the same visit) and allows separate entry to the Colosseum after 14:00 only; the €18 SUPER ticket allows you to see all three sights on separate visits and you can enter the Colosseum anytime; also covered by Roma Pass; Colosseum free for children 17 and under but must present proof of age; free—and crowded—for everyone on the first Sun of the month, open daily 8:30 until one hour before sunset, last entry one hour before closing, audioguide-€5.50, Metro: Colosseo, tel. 06-3996-7700, www.coopculture.it.

Avoiding Lines: A line typically has already formed at 8:30 when the Colosseum opens. Crowds are thinner and lines shorter in the afternoon (especially after 16:00 in summer).

You'll save time if you...

1. Buy tickets online at www.coopculture.it (€2 booking fee; must pay fee even to obtain "free" youth ticket).

2. Buy a Roma Pass (see page 314), which you can use to cover your Colosseum and Forum admissions—and lets you skip the line and use the group entrance. The pass is sold at TIs, many

Colosseum

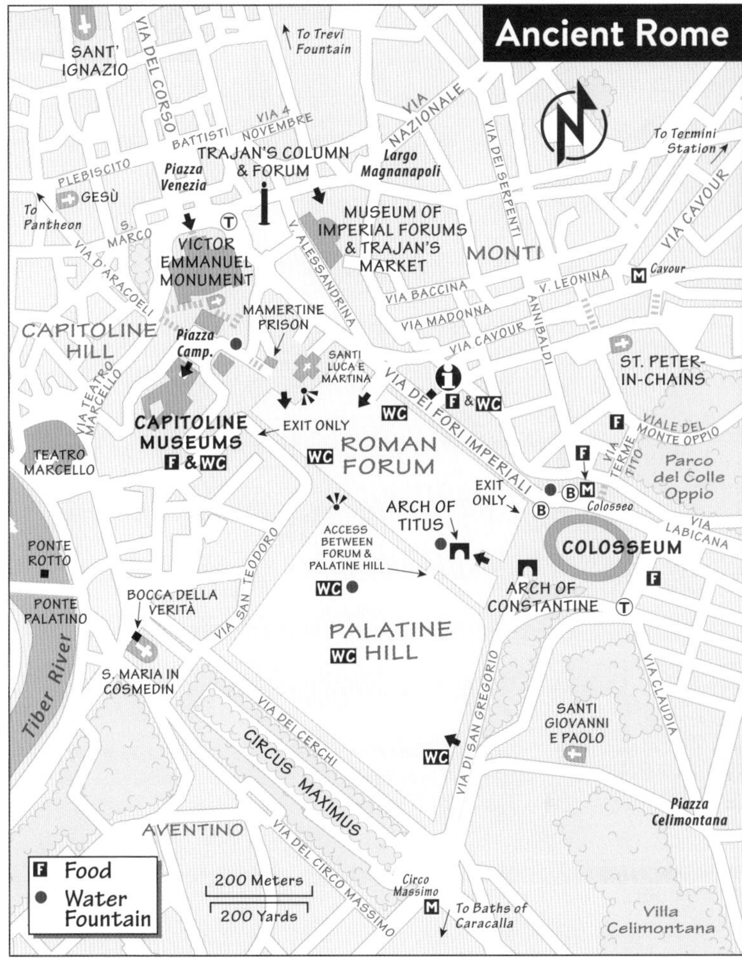

tobacco shops and newsstands, at the green kiosk in front of the Colosseo Metro station, and at the Roman Forum information center on Via dei Fori Imperiali.

3. Buy tickets at a less-crowded place than the Colosseum. First check the Forum/Palatine Hill entrance facing the Colosseum (a 5-minute walk away). If that's crowded, try the Forum/Palatine Hill entrance 150 yards away, on Via di San Gregorio (facing the Forum, with the Colosseum at your back, go left).

4. Pay to join an official guided tour, or rent an audioguide or videoguide (see "Tours," later). If the guard asks, say that you want to sign up for a tour, and they'll let you march right up to the guided visits (*Visite didattiche*) desk.

5. Hire a private guide. Guides linger outside the Colosseum, offering tours that allow you to bypass the line. Be aware that these private guides may try to mislead you into thinking the Colosseum lines are longer than they really are.

Getting There: The Colosseo Metro stop on line B is just across the street from the monument. Buses #51, #75, #85,

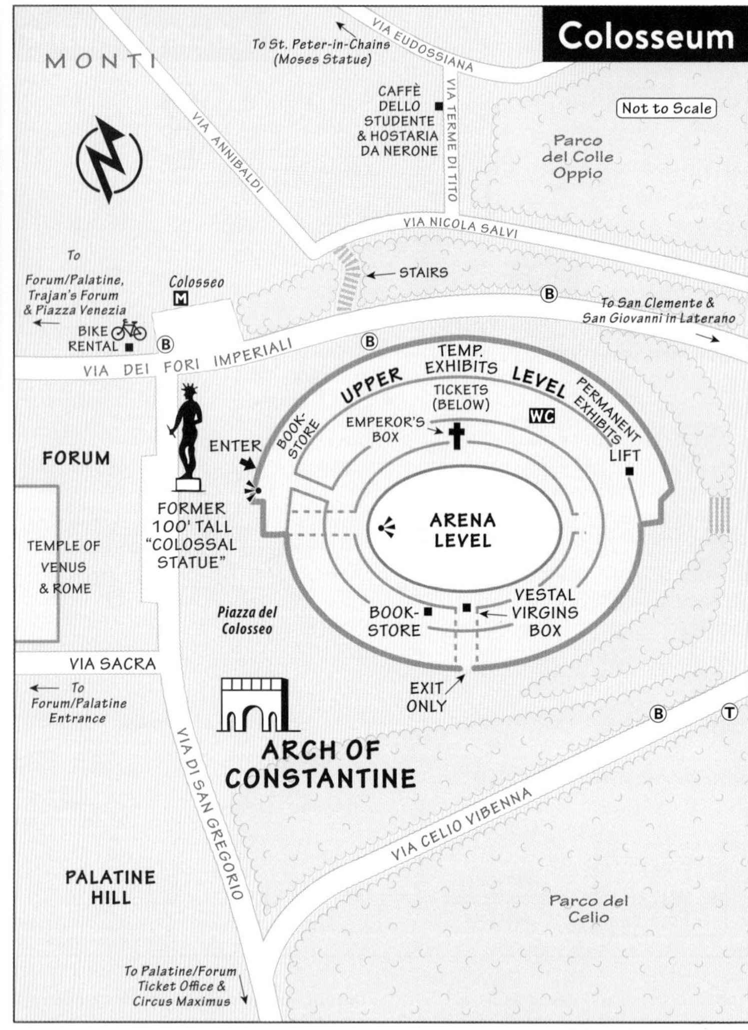

and #87, stop along Via dei Fori Imperiali near the Colosseum entrance, one of the Forum/Palatine Hill entrances, and Piazza Venezia. Tram #3 stops behind the Colosseum.

Getting In: Several lines lead to the turnstiles and into the Colosseum. Follow the signs to get into your correct line: 1) for ticket buyers; 2) for ticket holders (combo-ticket, SUPER ticket, Roma Pass, or those signing up for a tour); 3) for ticket pick-up (for those who've reserved but don't yet have a physical ticket). Farther beyond these lines, there's a group entrance (with a Roma Pass, you can likely use the group line—I did).

Tours: A fact-filled **audioguide** is available just past the turnstiles (€5.50). A handheld **videoguide** senses where you are in the site and plays related clips (€6).

🎧 Download my free Colosseum **audio tour.**

Official guided tours in English depart nearly hourly between 10:15 and 15:00, and last 45-60 minutes (€5 plus Colosseum ticket, purchase inside the Colosseum near the ticket booth marked *Visite didattiche*). A longer, interesting, but not essential 1.5-hour guided tour takes you through areas that are otherwise off-limits, including the top floor and underground passageways. Advance reservations are strongly advised, either by phone or online (no same-day reservations).

Private guides stand outside the Colosseum looking for business (€25-30/2-hour tour of the Colosseum, Forum, and Palatine Hill). Make sure that your tour will start right away and covers all three sights: the Colosseum, Forum, and Palatine Hill.

Services: A WC is inside the Colosseum.

Background: Built when the Roman Empire was at its peak in A.D. 80, the Colosseum represents Rome at its grandest. Known as the Flavian Amphitheater, it was an arena for gladiator contests and public spectacles. When killing became a spectator sport, the Romans wanted to share the fun with as many people as possible, so they stuck two semicircular theaters together to create a freestanding amphitheater. Towering 150 feet high, it could accommodate 50,000 roaring fans (100,000 thumbs). The outside (where slender cypress trees stand today) was decorated with a 100-foot-tall bronze statue of Nero that gleamed in the sunlight. In a later age, the colossal structure was nicknamed a "coloss-eum."

Rick's Tip: *Beware of the* **greedy, modern-day gladiators.** *They pose for photos with tourists and then attempt to intimidate them for lots of money. Don't be swindled. Also, look out for* **pickpockets.**

Exterior: The Romans were great engineers, not artists; the building is more functional than beautiful. (Ancient Romans visiting the US today might send home postcards of our greatest works of art—freeways.) While the essential structure is Roman, the four-story facade is decorated with mostly Greek columns—Tuscan columns on the ground level, Ionic on the second story, Corinthian on the next level, and at the top, half-columns with a mix of all three. Copies of Greek statues once stood in the arches of the middle two stories, adding sophistication to this arena of death.

Colosseum interior

Only a third of the original Colosseum remains. Earthquakes destroyed some of it, but most was carted off to build other buildings during the Middle Ages and Renaissance.

Interior: The games took place in the oval-shaped arena, 280 feet long by 165 feet wide. When you look down into the arena, you're seeing the underground passages beneath the playing surface (which can only be visited on a private tour). The arena was originally covered with a wooden floor, then sprinkled with sand (*arena* in Latin). The bit of reconstructed floor gives you a sense of the original arena level and the subterranean warren where animals and prisoners were held. The spectators ringed the playing area in bleacher seats that slanted up from the arena floor. Around you are the big brick masses that supported the tiers of seats.

The games began with a few warm-up acts—dogs bloodying themselves attacking porcupines, female gladiators fighting each other, or a one-legged man battling a dwarf. Then came the main event—the gladiators.

"Hail, Caesar! *(Ave, Caesar!)* We who are about to die salute you!" The gladiators would enter the arena from the west end, parade around to the sound of trumpets, acknowledge the Vestal Virgins (on the south side), then stop at the emperor's box (marked today by the cross that stands at the "50-yard line" on the north side—although no one knows for sure where it was). They would then raise their weapons, shout, and salute—and begin fighting. The fights pitted men against men, men against beasts, and beasts against beasts. Picture 50,000 screaming people around you (did gladiators get stage fright?), and imagine that they want to see you die.

▲ARCH OF CONSTANTINE

This well-preserved arch, which stands between the Colosseum and the Forum, commemorates a military coup and, more important, the acceptance of Christianity by the Roman Empire. The ambitious Emperor Constantine (who had a vision that he'd win under the sign of the cross) defeated his rival Maxentius in A.D. 312 to become sole emperor of the Roman Empire. He legalized Christianity soon after. The arch is free and always open.

🎧 It's covered in my free Colosseum audio tour.

Arch of Constantine

▲▲▲ROMAN FORUM (FORO ROMANO)

This is ancient Rome's birthplace and civic center, and the common ground between Rome's famous seven hills. As just about anything important that happened in ancient Rome happened here, it's arguably the most important piece of real estate in Western civilization. While only fragments of that glorious past remain, you'll find plenty to ignite your imagination amid the half-broken columns and arches.

Cost: €12 combo-ticket includes Palatine Hill on same visit, plus Colosseum (after 14:00 only); €18 SUPER ticket allows separate visits to Forum and Palatine, with no time restriction for Colosseum. Also covered by Roma Pass. Forum is free and crowded the first Sun of month.

Hours: The Roman Forum, Palatine Hill, and Colosseum are open daily 8:30 until one hour before sunset: April-Aug until 19:15, Sept until 19:00, Oct until 18:30, Nov-mid-Feb until 16:30, mid-Feb-mid-March until 17:00, mid-March-late March until 17:30; last entry one hour before closing.

Avoiding Lines: Buy your combo-ticket (or Roma Pass) at a less-crowded place or get a combo-ticket online; for specifics, see page 314. Or visit later in the day when crowds diminish.

Getting There: The closest Metro stop is Colosseo. Except on Sundays, buses #51, #75, #85, and #87 stop along Via dei Fori Imperiali near the Colosseum, the Forum, and Piazza Venezia.

Getting In: There are three main entrances to the Forum/Palatine Hill sight: 1) from the Colosseum—nearest the Arch of Titus, where this chapter's guided walk starts; 2) from Via dei Fori Imperiali; and 3) from Via di San Gregorio—at the south end of Palatine Hill, which is least crowded. A fourth entry for those who already have their tickets is from the north (below Capitoline Hill).

Information: The free info center, located across from the Via dei Fori Imperiali entrance can sell you a Roma Pass and has a bookshop, small café, and WCs (daily 9:30-19:00). Vendors outside sell a variety of colorful books with plastic overlays that restore the ruins (official price in bookstore for larger version with DVD is €20 and for smaller version is €10—don't pay more than these prices). Ticket info: Tel. 06-3996-7700, www.coopculture.it. General info: www.archeoroma.beniculturali.it/en.

Tours: An **audioguide** helps decipher the rubble (€5/2 hours, €7 version includes Palatine Hill and lasts 3 hours, must leave ID), but you have to return it to where you rented it.

🎧 Download my free Roman Forum **audio tour.**

Length of This Walk: Allow 1.5 hours. If you have less time, end the walk at the Arch of Septimius Severus. And don't miss the Basilica of Constantine hiding behind the trees.

Services: WCs are at the ticket entrances at Palatine Hill and at Via dei Fori Imperiali. Within the Forum itself, there's one near the Arch of Titus (in the "Soprintendenza" office), and another in the middle, near #7 on the map. Others are atop Palatine Hill.

Plan Ahead: The ancient paving at the Forum is uneven; wear sturdy shoes. I carry a water bottle and refill it at the Forum's public drinking fountains.

Improvise: Because of ongoing restoration, paths through the Forum are often rerouted. Use this tour as a starting point, but be prepared for a few detours and backtracking.

Nearby: Nighttime sound-and-light shows illuminate Caesar's Forum and the Forum of Augustus (part of the Imperial Forums). For details, see page 347.

➲ SELF-GUIDED TOUR

• Start at the Arch of Titus (Arco di Tito). It's the white triumphal arch that rises above the rubble on the east end of the Forum (closest to the Colosseum). Stand at the viewpoint alongside the arch and gaze over the valley known as the Forum.

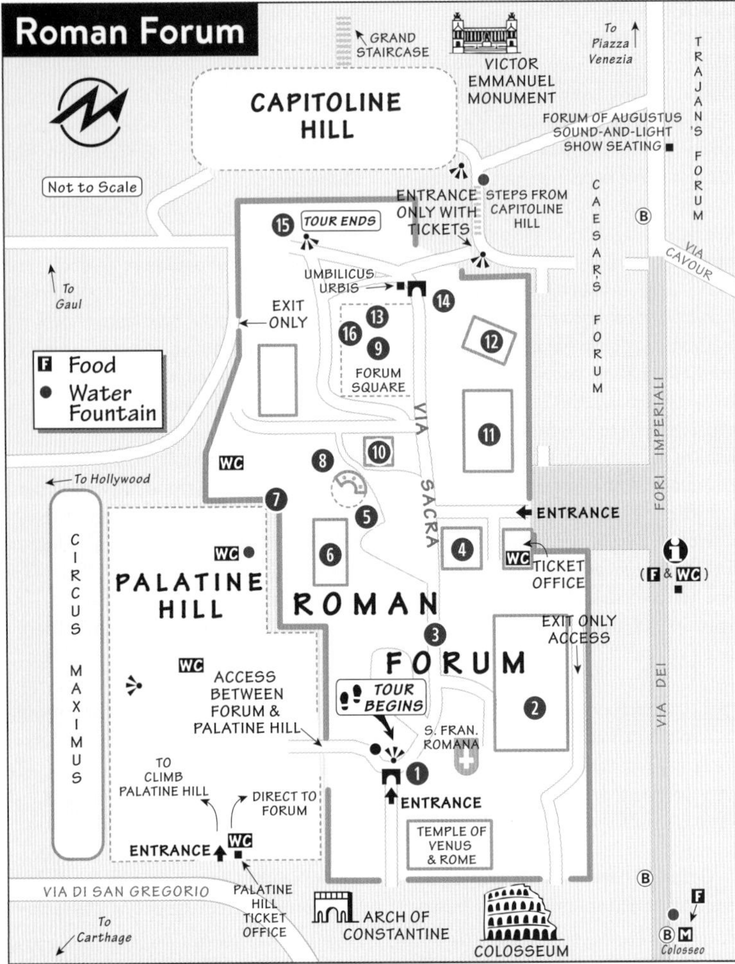

1. Arch of Titus
2. Basilica of Constantine
3. Via Sacra
4. Temple of Antoninus Pius & Faustina
5. Temple of Vesta
6. House of the Vestal Virgins
7. Caligula's Palace
8. Temple of Castor & Pollux
9. The Forum's Main Square
10. Temple of Julius Caesar
11. Basilica Aemilia
12. The Curia
13. Rostrum
14. Arch of Septimius Severus
15. Temple of Saturn
16. Column of Phocas

Viewing the Ruins: Try to see the Forum with "period eyes." We imagine the structures in ancient Rome as mostly white, but ornate buildings and monuments were originally more colorful. Through the ages, builders scavenged stone from the Forum; the colored marble was cannibalized first. The white stone is generally what was left. Statues were vividly painted, but the organic paint rotted away as they lay buried for centuries. Lettering was inset bronze and eyes were inset ivory. Even seemingly intact structures, like the Arch of Titus, have been reassembled. The columns are half smooth and half fluted. The fluted halves are original; the smooth parts are reconstructions.

❶ **Arch of Titus (Arco di Tito):** The Arch of Titus commemorated the Roman victory over the province of Judaea (Israel) in A.D. 70. The Romans had a reputation as benevolent conquerors who tolerated local customs and rulers. All they required was allegiance to the empire, shown by worshipping the emperor as a god. No problem for most conquered people, who already had half a dozen gods on their prayer lists anyway. But Israelites believed in only one god, and it wasn't the emperor. Israel revolted. After a short but bitter war, the Romans defeated the rebels, took Jerusalem, destroyed their temple (leaving only a fragment of one wall's foundation—today's revered "Wailing Wall"), and brought home 50,000 Jewish slaves...who were forced to build the Colosseum (and this arch).

Roman propaganda decorates the inside of the arch. A relief shows the emperor Titus in a chariot being crowned by the goddess Victory. The other side shows booty from the sacking of the temple in Jerusalem. Carved after Titus' death, the relief at the top of the ceiling shows him riding an eagle to heaven, where he'll become one of the gods.

• *Walk down Via Sacra into the Forum. The original basalt stones under your feet were walked on by Caesar Augustus 2,000 years ago. After about 50 yards, turn right and follow a path uphill to the three huge arches of the...*

❷ **Basilica of Constantine (Basilica Maxentius):** These arches represent only one-third of the original Basilica of Constantine, a mammoth hall of justice. There was a similar set along the Via Sacra side

Roman Forum

Rome's Rise and Fall (500 B.C.-A.D. 500)

Ancient Rome lasted for 1,000 years, from about 500 B.C. to A.D. 500. During that time, Rome expanded from a small tribe of barbarians to a vast empire, then dwindled slowly to city size again. For the first 500 years, when Rome's armies made her ruler of the Italian peninsula and beyond, Rome was a republic governed by elected senators. Over the next 500 years, a time of world conquest and eventual decline, Rome was an empire ruled by a military-backed dictator.

Julius Caesar bridged the gap between republic and empire. This ambitious, charismatic general and politician, popular because of his military victories, suspended the Roman constitution and assumed dictatorial powers in about 50 B.C. A few years later, he was assassinated by a conspiracy of senators. His adopted son, Augustus, succeeded him, and soon "Caesar" was not just a name but a title.

Emperor Augustus ushered in the Pax Romana, or Roman peace (A.D. 1-200), a time when Rome reached its peak, controlling an empire that stretched from England to Egypt, from Turkey to Morocco.

Then Rome fell into 300 years of gradual decay. Its fall had many causes, among them the barbarians who pecked away at Rome's borders. Christians blamed the fall on moral decay. Pagans blamed it on Christians. Socialists blamed it on a shallow economy based on the spoils of war. (Republicans blamed it on Democrats.) Whatever the reasons, the far-flung empire could no longer keep its grip on conquered lands. Barbarian tribes from Germany and Asia attacked the Italian peninsula, looting Rome itself in A.D. 410. In 476, when the last emperor checked out and switched off the lights, Europe plunged into centuries of ignorance and poverty—the Dark Ages.

But Rome lived on in the Catholic Church. Christianity was the state religion of Rome's last generations. Emperors became popes (both called themselves "Pontifex Maximus"), senators became bishops, orators became priests, and basilicas became churches. The glory of Rome remains eternal.

(only a few brick piers remain). Between them ran the central hall, spanned by a roof 130 feet high—about 55 feet higher than the side arches you see. (The stub of brick you see sticking up began an arch that once spanned the central hall.) The hall itself was as long as a football field, lavishly furnished with inlaid marble, a bronze ceiling, and statues. At the far (west) end was an enormous marble statue of Emperor Constantine on a throne. Pieces of this statue, including a hand the size of a man, are on display in Rome's Capitoline Museums.

• *Now stroll deeper into the Forum, downhill along the...*

❸ **Via Sacra:** Stroll through the trees, down this main drag of the ancient city. Imagine being an out-of-town visitor during Rome's heyday; nothing would have prepared you for the bustle of Rome—a city of a million people—by far the biggest city in Europe. This street would be swarming with tribunes, slaves, and courtesans. Chariots whizzed by. Wooden stalls lined the roads, where merchants peddled their goods.

On your right, you'll pass a building with a green door still swinging on its 17th-century hinges—the original bronze door to a temple that survived because it became a church shortly after the fall of

Rome. This ancient temple is still in use, sometimes hosting modern exhibits. No wonder they call Rome the Eternal City.

• *Just past the ancient temple, 10 huge columns stand in front of a much newer church. The colonnade was part of the...*

❹ **Temple of Antoninus Pius and Faustina:** This temple honors Emperor Antoninus Pius (A.D. 138-161) and his deified wife, Faustina. The 50-foot-tall Corinthian (leafy) columns were awe-inspiring to out-of-towners who grew up in thatched huts. Although the temple has been inhabited by a church, you can still see the basic layout—a staircase led to a shaded porch (the columns), which admitted you to the main building (now a church), where the statue of the god sat. Originally, these columns supported a triangular pediment decorated with sculptures.

Picture these columns supporting brightly painted statues in the pediment, with the whole building capped by a bronze roof. Today's gray rubble is a faded black-and-white photograph of a 3-D Technicolor era.

• *With your back to the colonnade, walk straight ahead—jogging a bit to the right to stay on the path—and head for the three short columns, all that's left of the...*

❺ **Temple of Vesta:** This was perhaps Rome's most sacred spot. Rome considered itself one big family, and this temple represented a circular hut, like the kind that Rome's first families lived in. Inside, a fire burned, just as in a Roman home. As long as the sacred flame burned, Rome would stand. The flame was tended by priestesses known as Vestal Virgins.

Temple of Antoninus Pius and Faustina

• *Backtrack a few steps up the path, behind the Temple of Vesta. You'll find a few stairs that lead up to a big, enclosed field with two rectangular brick pools (just below the hill). This was the courtyard of the...*

❻ **House of the Vestal Virgins:** The Vestal Virgins lived in a two-story building surrounding a long central courtyard with two pools at one end. This place was the model—both architecturally and sexually—for medieval convents and monasteries.

Chosen from noble families before they reached the age of 10, the six Vestal Virgins served a 30-year term. Honored and revered, the Vestals even had their own box opposite the emperor in the Colosseum. The statues that line the courtyard honor dutiful Vestals.

A Vestal took a vow of chastity. If she served her term faithfully—abstaining for 30 years—she was given a huge dowry and allowed to marry. But if they found any Virgin who wasn't, she was strapped to a funeral car, paraded through the streets of the Forum, taken to a crypt...and buried alive. Many suffered the latter fate.

• *Looming just beyond this field is Palatine Hill—the corner of which may have been...*

❼ **Caligula's Palace (Palace of Tiberius):** Emperor Caligula (ruled A.D. 37-41) had a huge palace on Palatine Hill overlooking the Forum. It actually sprawled down the hill into the Forum (some supporting arches remain in the hillside). Caligula tortured enemies, stole senators' wives, and parked his chariot in handicap spaces. He was not a nice person. But Rome's luxury-loving emperors only added to the glory of the Forum, with each one trying to make his mark on history.

• *Continue downhill, passing the three short columns of the Temple of Vesta, where you'll get a view of three very tall columns just beyond.*

❽ **Temple of Castor and Pollux:** These three columns are all that remain of a prestigious temple—one of the city's oldest, built in the fifth century B.C. It commemorated the Roman victory over the Tarquin, the notorious, oppressive Etruscan king. After the battle, the legendary twin brothers Castor and Pollux watered their horses here, at the Sacred Spring of Juturna (which was recently excavated nearby). As a symbol of Rome's self-governing republic, the temple was often used as a meeting place of senators; its front steps served as a podium for free speech.

• *The path spills into a flat, open area that stretches before you. This was the center of the ancient Forum.*

❾ **Forum's Main Square:** The original Forum, or main square, was this flat patch about the size of a football field, stretching to the foot of Capitoline Hill. Surrounding it were temples, law courts, government buildings, and triumphal arches.

Rome was born here. According to legend, twin brothers Romulus and Remus were orphaned in infancy and raised by a she-wolf on top of Palatine Hill. Growing up, they found it hard to get dates. So they and their cohorts attacked the nearby Sabine tribe and kidnapped their women. After they made peace, this marshy valley became the meeting place and then the trading center for the scattered tribes on the surrounding hillsides.

Temple of Castor and Pollux

The square was the busiest—and often the seediest—section of town. Besides the senators, politicians, and currency exchangers, there were souvenir hawkers, pickpockets, fortune-tellers, gamblers, slave marketers, drunks, hookers, lawyers, and tour guides.

Ancient Rome's population exceeded one million, more than any city until London and Paris in the 19th century. All those Roman masses lived in tiny apartments as we would live in tents at a campsite, basically just to sleep. The Forum—today's piazza—is where they did their living. To this day, urban Italians spend a major part of their time outside, in the streets and squares.

The Forum is now rubble, but imagine it in its prime: brilliant marble buildings with 40-foot-high columns and shining metal roofs; rows of statues painted in realistic colors; processional chariots rattling down Via Sacra. Mentally replace tourists in T-shirts with tribunes in togas. Imagine people buzzing around you while an orator gives a rabble-rousing speech. If you still only see a pile of rocks, at least tell yourself, "Julius Caesar once leaned against these rocks."

• *At the near end of the main square (the end closest to the Colosseum) find the foundations of a temple now capped with a peaked wood-and-metal roof.*

❿ **Temple of Julius Caesar (Tempio del Divo Giulio, or Ara di Cesare):** On March 15, in 44 B.C., Julius Caesar was stabbed 23 times by political conspirators. After his assassination, Caesar's body was cremated on this spot (under the metal roof). Afterward, this temple was built to honor him. Peek behind the wall into the small apse area, where a mound of dirt usually has fresh flowers—given to remember the man who personified the greatness of Rome.

Caesar (100-44 B.C.) changed Rome—and the Forum—dramatically. He cleared out many of the wooden market stalls and began to ring the square with even grander buildings. Caesar's house was located behind the temple, near that clump of trees. He walked by here on the day he was assassinated ("Beware the Ides of March!" warned a street-corner Etruscan preacher).

Although he was popular with the masses, not everyone liked Caesar's urban design or his politics. When he assumed dictatorial powers, he was ambushed and stabbed to death by a conspiracy of senators, including his adopted son, Brutus *("Et tu, Brute?")*.

The funeral was held here, facing the main square. Mark Antony stood up to say (in Shakespeare's words), "Friends, Romans, countrymen, lend me your ears. I come to bury Caesar, not to praise him." When Caesar's body was burned, his adoring fans threw anything at hand on the fire, requiring the fire department to come put it out. Later, Emperor Augustus dedicated this temple in his name, making Caesar the first Roman to become a god.

• *Continue past the Temple of Julius Caesar, to the open area between the columns of the Temple of Antoninus Pius and Faustina (which we passed earlier) and the boxy brick building (the Curia). You can view these ruins of the Basilica Aemilia from a ramp next to the Temple of Antoninus Pius and Faustina, or (if the path is open) walk among them.*

⓫ **Basilica Aemilia:** A basilica was a covered public forum, often serving as a hall of justice. In a society that was as legal-minded as America is today, you needed a lot of lawyers—and a big place to put them. Citizens came here to work out inheritances, file building permits, and sue each other.

It was a long, rectangular building. The row of stubby columns forms one long, central hall flanked by two side aisles. Medieval Christians required a larger meeting hall for their worship services than Roman temples provided, so they used the spacious Roman basilica as the model for their churches. Cathedrals from France to Spain to England, from Romanesque to Gothic to Renaissance, all have this same basic floor plan.

• *Now head for the big, well-preserved brick building with the triangular roof—the Curia. It's just to the right of the big triumphal arch at the foot of Capitoline Hill. While generally closed, the building is impressive even from outside.*

⓬ **Curia (Senate House):** The Curia was the most important political building in the Forum. While the present building dates from A.D. 283, this was the site of Rome's official center of government since the birth of the republic. Three hundred senators, elected by the citizens of Rome, met here to debate and create the laws of the land. Their wooden seats once circled the building in three tiers; the Senate president's podium sat at the far end. The marble floor is from ancient times. Listen to the echoes in this vast room—the acoustics are great.

Rome prided itself on being a republic. Early in the city's history, its people threw out the king and established rule by elected representatives. Each Roman citizen was free to speak his mind and have a say in public policy. Even when emperors became the supreme authority, the Senate was a power to be reckoned with. The Curia building is well preserved, having been used as a church since early Christian times. In the 1930s, it was restored and opened to the public as a historic site. (Although Julius Caesar was assassinated in "the Senate," it wasn't here—the Senate was temporarily meeting across town.)

• *Go back down the Senate steps and find the 10-foot-high wall just to the left of the big arch, marked...*

⓭ **Rostrum:** Nowhere was Roman freedom of speech more apparent than at this "Speaker's Corner." The Rostrum was a raised platform, 10 feet high and 80 feet long, decorated with statues, columns, and the prows of ships.

On a stage like this, Rome's orators, great and small, tried to draw a crowd and sway public opinion. Mark Antony rose to offer Caesar the laurel-leaf crown of kingship, which Caesar publicly refused—while privately becoming a dictator. Men such as Cicero—a contemporary of Julius Caesar—railed against the corruption and decadence that came with the city's newfound wealth. (Cicero paid the price: he was executed, and his head and hands were nailed to the Rostrum.)

In front of the Rostrum are trees bearing fruits that were sacred to the ancient Romans: olives (provided food, oil for light, and preservatives), figs (tasty), and wine grapes (made a popular export product).

• *The big arch to the right of the Rostrum is the...*

⓮ **Arch of Septimius Severus:** In imperial times, the Rostrum's voices of democracy would have been dwarfed by images of the empire, such as the huge six-story-high Arch of Septimius Severus (A.D. 203). The reliefs commemorate the African-born emperor's battles in Mesopotamia. Near ground level, see soldiers marching captured barbarians back to Rome for the victory parade.

• *Our next stop is the Temple of Saturn. You can see it from here—it's the eight big columns just up the slope of Capitol Hill. Or you could make your way to it for a closer look.*

⓯ **Temple of Saturn:** These columns framed the entrance to the Forum's oldest temple (497 B.C.). Inside was a humble wooden statue of the god Saturn. But the statue's pedestal held the gold bars, coins, and jewels of Rome's state treasury, the booty collected by conquering generals.

Even older than the Temple of Saturn is the Umbilicus Urbis, which stands nearby (next to the Arch of Septimius Severus). A humble brick ruin marks this historic "Navel of the City." The spot was considered the center of the cosmos, and all distances in the empire were measured from here.

• *Now turn your attention from the Temple of Saturn, one of the Forum's first buildings, to one of its last monuments. Find a lone, tall column standing in the Forum in front of the Rostrum. It's fluted and topped with a leafy Corinthian capital. This is the...*

⓰ **Column of Phocas:** The Forum's last monument (A.D. 608) was a gift from the powerful Byzantine Empire to a fallen empire—Rome. Given to commemorate the pagan Pantheon's becoming a Christian church, it's like a symbolic last nail in ancient Rome's coffin. After Rome's 1,000-year reign, the city was looted by Vandals, the population of a million-plus shrank to about 10,000, and the once-grand Forum was abandoned, slowly covered by centuries of silt and dirt. In the 1700s, English historian Edward Gib-

Arch of Septimius Severus

Temple of Saturn

bon overlooked this spot from Capitoline Hill, pondered the decline and fall of the Roman Empire, and thought, "Hmm, that's a catchy title..."

• *Your tour is over. If you want to see Palatine Hill, don't leave the Forum complex; you won't be allowed back in without a new ticket. To enter Palatine Hill, return to the Arch of Titus. If you'd rather exit the Forum, be aware that the exact ways in and out change from year to year. Refer to your map for possible exits.*

▲PALATINE HILL (MONTE PALATINO)

The hill overlooking the Forum is jam-packed with history—"the huts of Romulus," the huge Imperial Palace, a view of the Circus Maximus—but there's only the barest skeleton of rubble left to tell the story.

We get our word "palace" from this hill, where the emperors chose to live. It was once so filled with palaces that later emperors had to build out. (Looking up at it from the Forum, you see the substructure that supported these long-gone palaces.) The Palatine Museum contains statues and frescoes that help you imagine the luxury of the imperial Palatine. From the pleasant garden, you'll get an overview of the Forum. On the far side, unless excavations are blocking the viewpoint, look down into an emperor's private stadium and then beyond at the grassy Circus Maximus, once a chariot course.

While many tourists consider Palatine Hill extra credit after the Forum, it offers insight into the greatness of Rome. If you're visiting the Colosseum or Forum, you've already got a ticket.

Cost and Hours: €12 combo-ticket covers Forum on same visit, plus Colosseum (after 14:00 only); €18 SUPER ticket allows separate visits to all three sights, without time restriction for Colosseum. Also covered by Roma Pass. All three sights open daily 8:30 until one hour before sunset, last entry one hour before closing.

Getting In: The closest Metro stop is Colosseo. There are three entrances to the combined Palatine/Forum sight; see the map on page 336. The easiest for our tour is the entrance on Via di San Gregorio, 150 yards from the Colosseum. Upon entering, follow the path to the left as it winds to the top. Alternatively, if you sightsee the Forum first, to get to Palatine Hill you must walk up from the Arch of Titus.

Wherever you enter, our tour begins on the top of the hill at the one big building still standing—the museum. Remember, be sure to combine your visit with the Roman Forum; if you leave the complex, your ticket doesn't cover re-entry.

Services: WCs are at the ticket office when you enter, at the museum in the center of the site, and hiding among the orange trees in the Farnese Gardens.

Capitoline Hill

Of Rome's famous seven hills, this is the smallest, tallest, and most famous—home of the ancient Temple of Jupiter and the center of city government for 2,500 years. There are several ways to get to the top of Capitoline Hill. If you're coming from the north (from Piazza Venezia), take Michelangelo's impressive stairway to the right of the big, white Victor Emmanuel Monument. Coming from the southeast (the Forum), take the steep staircase near the Arch of Septimius Severus. From near Trajan's Forum along Via dei Fori Imperiali, take the winding road. All three converge at the top, in the square called Campidoglio (kahm-pee-DOHL-yoh).

▲PIAZZA DEL CAMPIDOGLIO

This square atop the hill, once the religious and political center of ancient Rome, is still the home of the city's government. In the 1530s, the pope called on Michelangelo to reestablish this square as a grand center. Michelangelo placed the ancient equestrian statue of Marcus Aurelius as its focal point. (The original statue is now in the adjacent museum.) The twin buildings on either side are the Capitoline Museums. Behind the replica of the statue is the mayor's palace (Palazzo Senatorio).

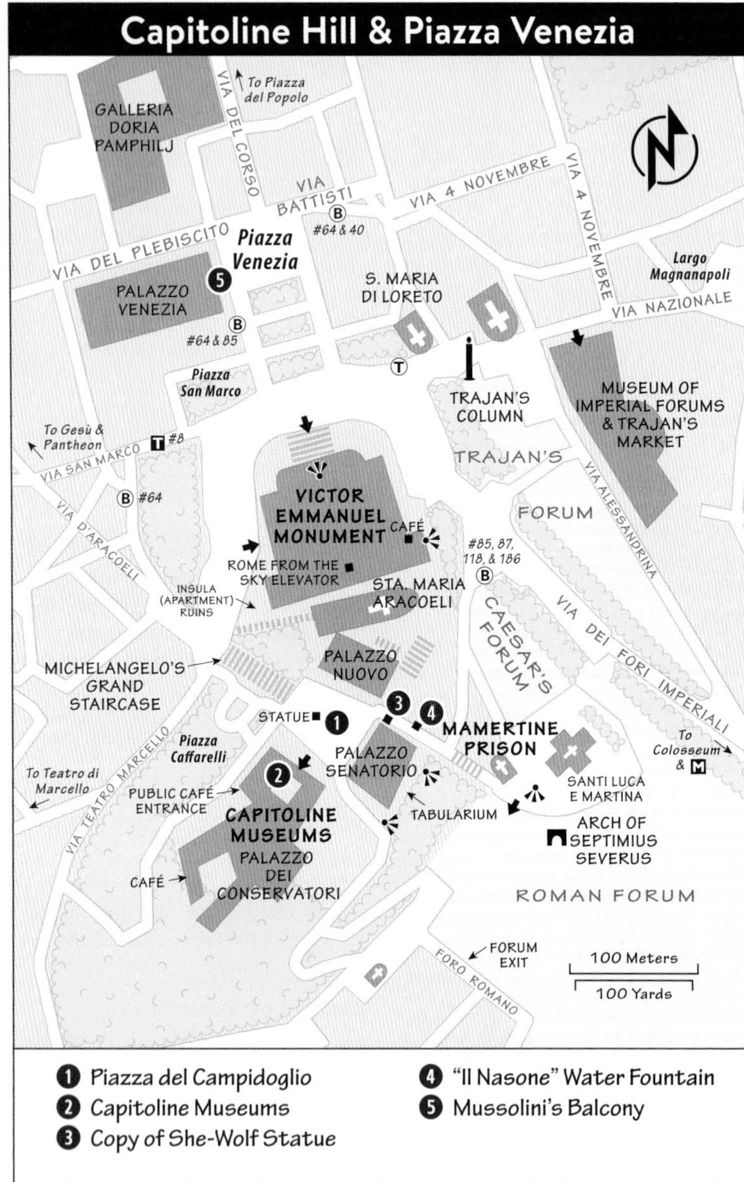

Michelangelo intended that people approach the square from his grand stairway off Piazza Venezia. From the top of the stairway, you see the new Renaissance face of Rome, with its back to the Forum. Michelangelo gave the buildings the "giant order"—huge pilasters make the existing two-story buildings feel one-storied and more harmonious with the new square. The statues atop these buildings welcome you and then draw you in.

The terraces just downhill (past either

side of the mayor's palace) offer grand views of the Forum. To the left of the mayor's palace is a copy of the famous **she-wolf statue** on a column. Farther down is ***Il Nasone*** ("the big nose"), a refreshing water fountain. Block the spout with your fingers, and water spurts up for drinking. Romans joke that a cheap Roman boy takes his date out for a drink at *Il Nasone.*

▲▲▲CAPITOLINE MUSEUMS

Some of ancient Rome's most famous statues and art are housed in the two palaces (Palazzo dei Conservatori and Palazzo Nuovo) that flank the equestrian statue in the Campidoglio. They're connected by an underground passage that leads to the Tabularium, an ancient building with panoramic views of the Roman Forum.

Cost and Hours: €15, €11.50 if no special exhibits, daily 9:30-19:30, last entry one hour before closing, videoguide-€6, tel. 06-0608, www.museicapitolini.org.

Visiting the Museums: You'll enter at Palazzo dei Conservatori (on your right as you face the equestrian statue), then walk through a passageway underneath the square—stopping for a look at the Tabularium—to Palazzo Nuovo (on your left), where you'll exit.

With lavish rooms and several great statues, the worthwhile **Palazzo dei Conservatori** was founded in 1471 when a pope gave ancient statues to the citizens of Rome. Many of the museum's statues have become recognizable cultural icons, including the 13th-century *Capitoline She-Wolf* (the statues of Romulus and Remus were added in the Renaissance). Don't miss the *Boy Extracting a Thorn* and the *Commodus as Hercules.* Behind Commodus is a statue of his dad, Marcus Aurelius, on a horse. The greatest surviving equestrian statue of antiquity, it was the original centerpiece of the square (where a copy stands today). Christians in the Dark Ages thought that the statue's hand was raised in blessing, which probably led to their misidentifying him as Constantine, the first Christian emperor. While most pagan statues were destroyed by Christians, "Constantine" was spared.

The museum's second-floor café, **Caffè Capitolino,** has a patio offering city views—lovely at sunset (public entrance

Piazza del Campidoglio

for those without a museum ticket off Piazzale Caffarelli and through door #4).

The **Tabularium,** built in the first century B.C., once held the archives of ancient Rome. Its name comes from "tablet," on which Romans wrote their laws. You won't see any tablets, but you will see a stunning head-on view of the Forum from the windows. **Palazzo Nuovo** houses two must-see statues: the *Dying Gaul* and the *Capitoline Venus* (both on the first floor up).

Piazza Venezia

This vast square, dominated by the Victor Emmanuel Monument, is the focal point of modern Rome. With your back to the monument (you'll get the best views from the terrace by the guards and eternal flame), look down Via del Corso, the city's axis, surrounded by Rome's classiest shopping district. In the 1930s, fascist dictator Benito Mussolini whipped up Italy's nationalistic fervor from a balcony above the square (it's the less-grand building on the left) and created the boulevard Via dei Fori Imperiali (to your right, capped by Trajan's Column) to open up views of the Colosseum in the distance.

With your back still to the monument, circle around the left side. At the back end of the monument, look down into the ditch on your left to see the ruins of an ancient apartment building from the first century A.D.; part of it was transformed into a tiny church (faded frescoes and bell tower). Rome was built in layers—almost everywhere you go, there's an earlier version beneath your feet.

▲VICTOR EMMANUEL MONUMENT

This oversize monument to Italy's first king, built to celebrate the 50th anniversary of the country's initial unification in 1861, was part of Italy's attempt to create a national identity. The over-the-top monument is 200 feet high and 500 feet wide. The 43-foot-long statue of the king on his high horse is one of the biggest equestrian statues in the world. The king's moustache forms an arc five feet long. A person could sit within the horse's hoof. At the base of this statue, Italy's Tomb of the Unknown Soldier is watched over by the goddess Roma (with the gold mosaic background).

Cost and Hours: Monument—free, daily 9:00-17:30, shorter in winter, a few scattered WCs, tel. 06-6920-2049. **Rome from the Sky elevator**—€7, daily until 19:30, ticket office closes 45 minutes earlier, WC at entrance, tel. 06-0608; follow *ascensori panoramici* signs inside the Victor Emmanuel Monument (no elevator access from street level).

Visiting the Monument: The "Vittoriano" (as locals call it) is open and free to the public. You can simply climb the front stairs, or go inside from one of several entrances: midway up the monument through doorways flanking the central statue, on either side at street level, and at the base of the colonnade (two-thirds of the way up). The little-visited **Museum of the Risorgimento** fills several floors with displays on the movement and war that led to the unification of Italy (€5 to enter museum, temporary exhibits around €14, tel. 06-679-3598, www.risorgimento.it).

Climb the stairs to the midway point for a decent view, keep climbing to the base of the colonnade for a better view, or, for the best view, ride the **Rome from the Sky** (Roma dal Cielo) **elevator,** which zips you from the top of the stair climb (at the back of the monument) to the roof-

Victor Emmanuel Monument

top for a 360-degree view of Rome that is even better than from the top of St. Peter's dome. Once on top, you stand on a terrace between the monument's two chariots. Look north up Via del Corso to Piazza del Popolo, west to the dome of St. Peter's Basilica, and south to the Roman Forum and Colosseum. Panoramic diagrams describe the skyline, with powerful binoculars available for zooming in. It's best in late afternoon, when it's beginning to cool off and Rome glows.

▲▲TRAJAN'S COLUMN

This 140-foot column is decorated with a spiral relief of 2,500 figures trumpeting the emperor's exploits. It has stood for centuries as a symbol of a cosmopolitan civilization. At one point, the ashes of Trajan and his wife were held in the base, and the sun glinted off a polished bronze statue of Trajan at the top. (Today, it's been replaced with St. Peter.) Built as a stack of 17 marble doughnuts, the column is hollow (note the small window slots) with a spiral staircase inside, leading up to the balcony.

The **relief** unfolds like a scroll, telling the story of Rome's last and greatest foreign conquest, Trajan's defeat of Dacia (modern-day Romania). Originally, the entire story was painted in bright colors. If you were to unwind the scroll, it would stretch over two football fields.

The column, just off Piazza Venezia, is free to see and always viewable.

SOUND-AND-LIGHT SHOWS

The Imperial Forums area hosts two atmospheric and inspirational sound-and-light shows that give you a chance to fantasize about the world of the Caesars—the Caesar's Forum Stroll and the Forum of Augustus Show. Consider one or both of the similar and adjacent evening experiences. During each of these "nighttime journeys through ancient Rome," you spend about an hour with a headphone dialed to English, listening to an artfully crafted narration synced with projections on ancient walls, columns, and porticos. The final effect is worth the price tag (€15, both for €25, they run nightly mid-April–mid-Nov, bring your warmest coat, tickets sold online and at the gate, shows can sell out on busy weekends, tel. 06-0608, www.viaggioneifori.it).

If you plan to see both, do Caesar first (runs every 20 minutes, last an hour, starting at Trajan's Column) and allow 80 minutes between starting times (Augustus showings offered on the hour, enter on Via dei Fori Imperiali just before Via Cavour—you'll see the bleachers).

North of Via dei Fori Imperiali

▲MONTI NEIGHBORHOOD: VILLAGE ROME

This quintessentially Roman district called Monti is one of the oldest corners of Rome...and newly trendy. Tucked behind Via dei Fori Imperiali, and squeezed between Via Nazionale and Via Cavour, this hilly tangle of lanes shows why Romans see their hometown not as a sprawling metropolis, but as a collection of villages. Neighbors hang out on the square and chat. Funky boutiques

Trajan's Column

share narrow streets with hole-in-the-wall hardware shops and grocery shops; and wisteria-strewn cobbled lanes beckon photographers.

To explore the Monti, head for its main square, **Piazza della Madonna dei Monti** (three blocks west of the Cavour Metro stop). To get oriented, face uphill, with the big fountain to your right.

From this hub, interesting streets branch off in every direction. I recommend strolling one long street with three names: **Via della Madonna dei Monti,** which leads from the ancient wall on the downhill side of the ancient forums, then to the central Piazza Madonna dei Monti, before continuing uphill as **Via Leonina** and then **Via Urbana.** Monti is an ideal place for a quick lunch or early dinner (see page 372).

▲St. Peter-in-Chains Church (San Pietro in Vincoli)

Built in the fifth century to house the chains that held St. Peter, this church is most famous for its Michelangelo statue of Moses, intended for the tomb of Pope Julius II (which was never built). Note that this church is not the famous St. Peter's Basilica, which is in Vatican City.

After viewing the much-venerated chains under the high altar, focus on mighty Moses. Pope Julius II commissioned Michelangelo to build a massive tomb, with 48 huge statues, topped with a grand statue of the egomaniacal pope himself. The pope had planned for his tomb to be in the center of St. Peter's Basilica. When Julius died, the work had barely started; no one had the money or necessary commitment to finish the project.

In 1542, remnants of the project were brought to St. Peter-in-Chains and pieced together by Michelangelo's assistants. Some of the best statues ended up elsewhere (*Prisoners* is in Florence and the *Slaves* is in the Louvre). *Moses* and the *Slaves* are the only statues Michelangelo personally completed for the project.

The statue of Moses is powerful. As he holds the Ten Commandments, his eyes show a man determined to win salvation for the people of Israel. Why the horns? Centuries ago, the Hebrew word for "rays" was mistranslated as "horns." Flanking *Moses* are the Old Testament sister-wives of Jacob, Leah (to our right) and Rachel, both begun by Michelangelo but probably finished by pupils.

Cost and Hours: Free, daily April-Sept

Michelangelo, Moses

8:00-12:20 & 15:00-19:00, until 18:00 in winter, modest dress required; the church is a 10-minute uphill walk from the Colosseum, or a shorter, simpler walk (but with more uphill steps) from the Cavour Metro stop; tel. 06-9784-4950.

Pantheon Neighborhood

The Pantheon area, despite its ancient sites and historic churches, has an urban-village feel. Exploring this neighborhood is especially good in the evening, when the restaurants bustle and the streets teem with pedestrians. Gather with the locals in squares marked by bubbling fountains.

Getting There: The Pantheon neighborhood is a 15-minute walk from Capitoline Hill. Taxis and buses stop at a chaotic square called Largo Argentina, a few blocks south of the Pantheon—from here you can walk north on either Via dei Cestari or Via di Torre Argentina to the Pantheon. Buses #40 and #64 run frequently between the Termini train station and Vatican City (#492 serves the same areas via a different route). Buses #85 and #87 connect to the Colosseum (stop: Corso/Minghetti).

▲▲▲PANTHEON

Built two millennia ago, this influential domed temple is perhaps the most influential building in art history, serving as the model for the Florence cathedral dome, which launched the Renaissance, and for Michelangelo's dome of St. Peter's, which capped it off. Its preserved interior offers the greatest look at the splendor of Rome.

Cost and Hours: Free, Mon-Sat 8:30-19:30, Sun 9:00-18:00, holidays 9:00-13:00, www.pantheonroma.com.

When to Go: Don't go at midday, when it's packed. To have it all to yourself, visit before 9:00.

Dress Code: No skimpy shorts or bare shoulders.

Tours: The Pantheon has a €6 audioguide that lasts 30 minutes.

🎧 Download my free Pantheon audio tour.

Visiting the Pantheon: The Pantheon was a Roman temple dedicated to all *(pan)* of the gods *(theos)*. The original temple was built in 27 B.C. by Augustus' son-in-law, Marcus Agrippa. The inscription below the triangular **pediment** proclaims in Latin, "Marcus Agrippa, son of Lucio, three times consul made this." But after two fires, the structure we see today was completely rebuilt by Emperor Hadrian around A.D. 120. After the fall of Rome, the Pantheon became a Christian church (from "all the gods" to "all the martyrs"), which saved it from architectural plunder and ensured its upkeep through the Dark Ages.

The **portico** is Greek in style, a visual reminder of the debt Roman culture owed to the Greeks. You cross this Greek space to enter a purely Roman space, the rotunda. The columns are huge and unadorned, made from 40-foot-high single pieces of red-gray granite. They were quarried in Egypt, then shipped down the Nile and across the Mediterranean to Rome.

The **dome,** which was the largest made until the Renaissance, is set on a circular base. The mathematical perfection of this design is a testament to Roman engineering. The dome is as high as it is wide—142 feet from floor to rooftop and from side to side. To picture it, imagine a basketball wedged inside a wastebasket so that it just touches bottom. It is made from concrete that gets lighter and thinner as it reaches the top. The base of the dome is 23 feet thick and made from heavy con-

Inside the Pantheon

crete mixed with travertine, while near the top, it's less than five feet thick and made with a lighter volcanic rock (pumice) mixed in.

At the top, the **oculus,** or eye-in-the-sky, is the building's only light source. It's completely open and almost 30 feet across. The 1,800-year-old floor—with 80 percent of its original stones surviving—has holes in it and slants toward the edges to let the rainwater drain. Though some of the floor's marble has been replaced, the design—alternating circles and squares—is original.

While its ancient statuary is long gone, the interior holds decorative statues and the tombs of famous people from more recent centuries. The artist **Raphael** lies to the left of the main altar. Facing each other across the base of the dome are the tombs of modern Italy's first two kings.

▲TREVI FOUNTAIN

The bubbly Baroque fountain is a minor sight to art scholars...but a major nighttime gathering spot for teens on the make and tourists tossing coins. For more on the fountain, see page 325.

Vatican City

Vatican City, the world's smallest country, contains St. Peter's Basilica (with Michelangelo's exquisite *Pietà*) and the Vatican Museums (with the Sistine Chapel). The entrances to St. Peter's and the Vatican Museums are a 15-minute walk apart (follow the outside of the Vatican wall, which links the two sights). The nearest Metro stop—Ottaviano—still involves a 10-minute walk to either sight.

▲▲▲ST. PETER'S BASILICA (BASILICA SAN PIETRO)

This is the richest and grandest church on earth. To call it vast is like calling Einstein smart. Plaques on the floor show you where other, smaller churches would end if they were placed inside. The ornamental cherubs would dwarf a large man. Birds roost inside, and thousands of people wander about, heads craned heavenward. Bernini's altar work and twisting, towering canopy are brilliant. Don't miss Michelangelo's *Pietà* (behind bulletproof glass) to the right of the entrance. The huge square in front of the church is marked by an obelisk and bordered by Bernini's colonnade.

St. Peter's Square and Basilica

Hello from Vatican City

The Vatican is the religious capital of 1.2 billion Roman Catholics. If you're not a Catholic, become one for your visit. The pope is both the religious and secular leader of Vatican City. For centuries, the Vatican was the capital of the Papal States, and locals referred to the pontiff as "King Pope." Because of the Vatican's territorial ambitions, it didn't always have good relations with Italy. Even though modern Italy was created in 1870, the Holy See didn't recognize it as a country until 1929.

The tiny independent country of Vatican City is contained entirely within Rome. The Vatican has its own postal system, armed guards, a helipad, mini train station, and radio station (KPOP). Like every European country, Vatican City has its own versions of the euro coin (with a portrait of the pope). You're unlikely to find one in your pocket, though, as they're snatched up by collectors before falling into circulation.

Post Offices: The Vatican postal service is famous for its stamps, which you can get from offices on St. Peter's Square (one next to the TI, another between the columns just before the security checkpoint), in the Vatican Museums (closed Sun), or from a "post bus" that's often parked on St. Peter's Square (open Sun). To get a Vatican postmark, mail your cards from postboxes at the Vatican itself (although the stamps are good throughout Rome).

Cost: Free entry to basilica and crypt. Dome climb—€6 if you take the stairs all the way up, or €8 to ride an elevator part way (to the roof), then climb to the top of the dome (cash only). Treasury Museum—€7 (€3 audioguide).

Hours: The **church** is open daily April-Sept 7:00-19:00, Oct-March 7:00-18:30. It closes on Wednesday mornings during papal audiences, until roughly 13:00. The **dome** *(cupola)* is open to climbers daily from 8:00; if you're climbing the stairs all the way up, the last entry time is 17:00 (16:00 Oct-March); if you're riding the elevator, you can enter until 18:00 (17:00 Oct-March). The **Treasury Museum** is open daily 8:00-18:50, Oct-March until 17:50. The **crypt** *(grotte)* is open daily 9:00-16:00.

Information: Tel. 06-6988-3731, www.vaticanstate.va.

Avoiding Lines: To avoid the worst crowds, visit before 10:00. Going after 16:00 works, too, but the crypt will be closed, and the area around the altar is often roped off to prepare for Mass. There's no surefire way to avoid the long security lines; the checkpoint is typically on the right (north) side of the huge square in front of the church, but is sometimes closer to the church or tucked under the south colonnade.

St. Peter's is often accessible directly from the Sistine Chapel inside the Vatican Museums—a great time-saving trick, but unfortunately not a reliable one (for details, see page 360).

Dress Code: No shorts, above-the-knee skirts, or bare shoulders (this applies to men, women, and children). Attendants enforce this dress code, even in hot weather. Carry a cover-up, if necessary.

Getting There: Take the Metro to Ottaviano, then walk 10 minutes south on Via Ottaviano. The #40 express bus drops off at Piazza Pio, next to Castel Sant'Angelo (Hadrian's Tomb)—a 10-minute walk from St. Peter's. The more crowded bus

#64 stops just outside St. Peter's Square to the south (get off the bus after it crosses the Tiber, at the first stop past the tunnel; backtrack toward the tunnel and turn left when you see the rows of columns; the return bus stop is adjacent to the tunnel). Bus #492 heads through the center of town, stopping at Largo Argentina, and gets you near Piazza Risorgimento (get off when you see the Vatican walls). Be alert for pickpockets on all public transit. A taxi from Termini train station to St. Peter's costs about €15.

Visitor Information: The Vatican TI, up close to the church on the left (south) side of the square is excellent (Mon-Sat 8:30-18:15, closed Sun, tel. 06-6988-1662).

Church Services: Mass is said daily, generally in Italian, usually in one of these three places: in the south (left) transept, the Blessed Sacrament Chapel (on the right side of the nave), or the apse. Typical schedule: Mon-Sat at 8:30, 10:00, 11:00, 12:00, 16:30, and 17:00 (in Latin, in the apse); and on Sun and holidays at 9:00, 10:30 (in Latin), 11:30, 12:15, 13:00, 16:00, 16:45 (vespers), and 17:30.

Tours: The Vatican TI conducts free 1.5-hour **tours of St. Peter's** (depart from TI Mon-Fri at 14:15, confirm schedule at TI). **Audioguides** can be rented near the checkroom (€5 plus ID, for church only, daily 9:00-17:00).

🎧 Download my free St. Peter's Basilica **audio tour.**

To see St. Peter's original grave, you can take a *Scavi* (excavations) tour into the **Necropolis** under the basilica (€13, 1.5 hours, ages 15 and older only). Book at least two months in advance by email (scavi@fsp.va) or fax (06-6987-3017), following the detailed instructions at www.vatican.va (search for "Excavations Office"); no response means they're booked.

Dome Climb: You can take the elevator (€8) or stairs (€6) to the roof (231 steps), then climb another 323 steps to the top of the dome. The entry to the elevator is just outside the north side of the basilica—look for signs to the *cupola.*

Length of This Tour: Allow one hour, plus another hour if you climb the dome (or a half-hour to the roof). With less time, you could stroll the nave, glance up at the dome, down at St. Peter's resting place, and adore the *Pietà* on your way out.

Vatican Museums Tickets: The Vatican TI at St. Peter's often has museum tickets (with same-day entry timed reservations) on sale for €20. There may also be a table for ticket sales in the narthex (portico) of St. Peter's (with a €5 service fee). See page 359 for other Vatican Museums ticketing options.

Baggage Check: The free bag check (mandatory for bags larger than a purse or daypack) is outside the basilica (to the right as you face the entrance), just inside the security checkpoint.

Services: WCs are to the right and left on St. Peter's Square (next to the Vatican post offices, with another near the baggage storage down the steps on the right side of the entrance) and on the roof.

➲ SELF-GUIDED TOUR

To sample the basilica's highlights, follow these points:

❶ **The narthex** (portico) is itself bigger than most churches. The huge white columns on the portico date from the first church (fourth century). Five famous bronze doors lead into the church. The central door, made from the melted-down bronze of the original door of Old St. Peter's, was the first Renaissance work in Rome (c. 1450). It's only opened on special occasions. The far-right entrance is the **Holy Door,** opened only during Holy Years (and Jubilee years, designated by the pope). On Christmas Eve every 25 years, the pope knocks three times with a silver hammer and the door opens, welcoming pilgrims to pass through.

• *Enter the nave. On the floor near the central doorway, look for the round maroon pavement stone.*

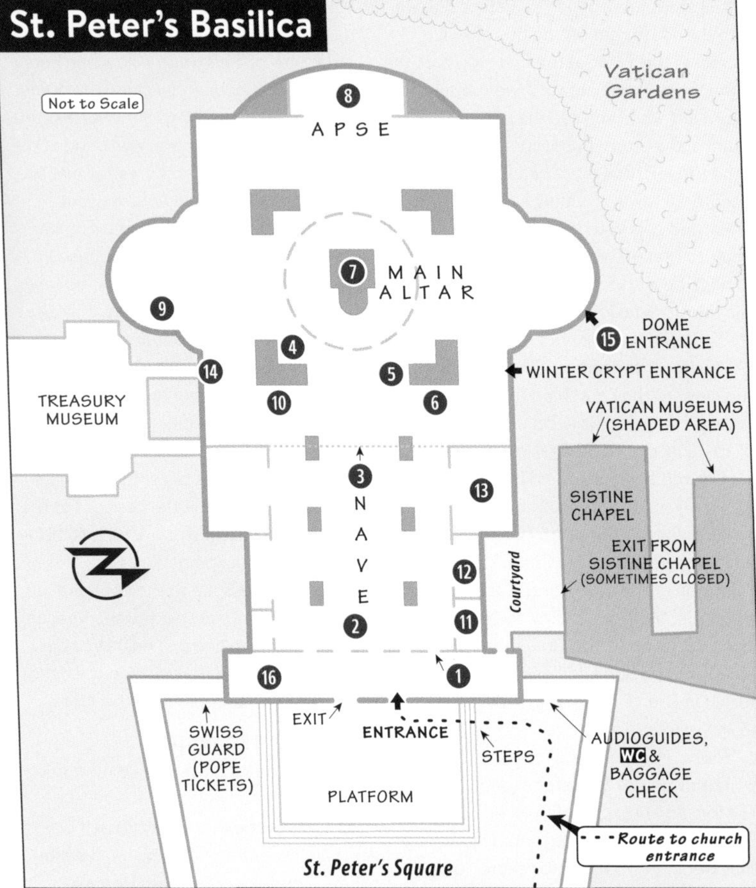

1. Holy Door
2. Charlemagne's Coronation Site
3. Extent of Original "Greek Cross" Plan
4. St. Andrew Statue; View of Dome; Crypt Entrance
5. St. Peter Statue (with Kissable Toe)
6. Pope John XXIII
7. Main Altar (under Bernini's Canopy & over Peter's Tomb)
8. BERNINI – Dove Window & Throne of St. Peter
9. St. Peter's Crucifixion Site
10. RAPHAEL – Mosaic Copy of The Transfiguration
11. MICHELANGELO – Pietà
12. Tomb of St. Pope John Paul II
13. Blessed Sacrament Chapel
14. Treasury Museum
15. Dome Entrance
16. Vatican Museums Tickets

❷ This is the spot where in A.D. 800 the king of the Franks, **Charlemagne,** was crowned Holy Roman Emperor. Look down the main hall—the golden window at the far end is two football fields away. The dove in the window has the wingspan of a 747 (OK, not quite, but it *is* big). The church covers six acres. The babies at the base of the pillars along the main hall are adult-size. The lettering in the gold band along the top of the pillars is seven feet high. The church has a capacity of 60,000 standing worshippers (or 1,200 tour groups).

• *Walk toward the altar.*

❸ Michelangelo was 71 years old when he took over the church project. He intended to put the dome over Donato Bramante's original **Greek-Cross** floor plan, with four equal arms. In the Renaissance, this symmetrical arrangement symbolized perfection—the orderliness of the created world and the goodness of man (created in God's image). But the Church, struggling against Protestants and its own corruption, opted for a plan designed to impress the world with its grandeur—the Latin cross of the Crucifixion, with its nave extended to accommodate the grand religious spectacles of the Baroque period.

❹ Park yourself in front of the **statue of St. Andrew** to the left of the altar, the guy holding an X-shaped cross. (The **crypt entrance,** described later, is usually here; in winter, it's by the dome entrance.) Like Andrew, gaze up into the dome and gasp. The dome soars higher than a football field on end, 448 feet from the floor of the cathedral to the top of the lantern. It glows with light from its windows, the blue-and-gold mosaics creating a cool, solemn atmosphere. In this majestic vision of heaven (not painted by Michelangelo), we see (above the windows) Jesus, Mary, and a ring of saints, rings of more angels above them, and, way up in the ozone, God the Father (a blur of blue and red, unless you have binoculars).

❺ Back in the nave sits a bronze **statue of Peter** under a canopy. This is one of a handful of pieces of art that were in the earlier church. In one hand he holds keys, the symbol of the authority given him by Christ, while with the other hand he blesses us. His big right **toe** has been worn smooth by the lips of pilgrims and foot fetishists. Stand in line to kiss it, or, to avoid foot-and-mouth disease, touch your hand to your lips, and then rub the toe. This is an act of reverence with no legend attached.

• *Circle to the right around the statue of Peter to find the lighted glass niche.*

The nave of St. Peter's Basilica

❻ The red-robed body was **Pope John XXIII,** whose papacy lasted from 1958 to 1963. He is best known for initiating the landmark Vatican II Council (1962–1965), bringing the Church into the modern age. In 2000, during the beatification process (a stop on the way to sainthood), Church authorities checked his body, and it was surprisingly fresh. So they moved it upstairs, put it behind glass, and now older Catholics who remember him fondly enjoy another stop on their St. Peter's visit. Pope John was canonized in 2014.

❼ Sitting over St. Peter's tomb, the **main altar** (the white marble slab with cross and candlesticks) is used only when the pope himself says Mass. He sometimes conducts the Sunday morning service when he's in town. The tiny altar would be lost in this enormous church if it weren't for Gian Lorenzo Bernini's seven-story **bronze canopy,** which "extends" the altar upward and reduces the perceived distance between floor and ceiling. The corkscrew columns echo the marble ones that surrounded the altar in Old St. Peter's.

❽ Bernini's **dove window** shines above the smaller front altar used for everyday services. The Holy Spirit, in the form of a six-foot-high dove, pours sunlight onto the faithful through the alabaster windows, turning into artificial rays of gold and reflecting off swirling gold clouds, angels, and winged babies. During a service, real sunlight passes through real clouds of incense, mingling with Bernini's sculpture. Beneath the dove is the centerpiece of this structure, the **Throne of St. Peter,** an oak chair built in medieval times for a king. Subsequently, it was encrusted with tradition and encased in bronze by Bernini as a symbol of papal authority.

• *In the south transept (left of main altar), find the dark "painting" of St. Peter crucified upside-down (far end, left side).*

❾ According to tradition, this is the exact spot of **Peter's crucifixion** 1,900 years ago. During the reign of Emperor Nero, he was arrested and brought to Nero's Circus so all of Rome could witness his execution. When the authorities told Peter he was to be crucified just like his Lord, Peter said, "I'm not worthy" and insisted they nail him on the cross upside down.

❿ Around the corner (heading back toward the central nave), pause at the mosaic copy of Raphael's epic painting of ***The Transfiguration.*** The original is now in the Pinacoteca of the Vatican Museums.

Michelangelo, Pietà

This and all the other "paintings" in the church are actually mosaic copies made from thousands of colored chips the size of a fingernail. Because smoke and humidity would damage real paintings, since about 1600 church officials have replaced the paintings with mosaics produced by the Vatican Mosaic Studio.

• *Back near the entrance of the church, in the far corner, behind bulletproof glass, is the sculpture everyone has come to see.*

⓫ Michelangelo was 24 years old when he completed this **pietà**—a representation of Mary with the body of Christ taken from the cross. It was his first major commission, for Holy Year 1500. Michelangelo, with his total mastery of the real world, captures the sadness of the moment. Mary cradles her crucified son in her lap. Christ's lifeless right arm drooping down lets us know how heavy this corpse is. Mary looks at her dead son with tenderness; her left hand turns upward, asking, "How could they do this to you?"

• *In the chapel to the left is a revered tomb.*

⓬ **John Paul II** (1920-2005) was one of the most beloved popes of recent times. During his papacy (1978-2005), he was the face of the Catholic Church. The first non-Italian pope in four centuries, he oversaw the fall of communism in his native Poland, survived an assassination attempt, and stoicly endured Parkinson's disease. When he died in 2005, hundreds of thousands lined up outside, waiting up to 24 hours to pay their respects. He was sainted in April 2014, just nine years after his death. St. John Paul II lies beneath a painting of the steadfast St. Sebastian, his favorite saint.

⓭ Step into the next chapel through the metalwork gates. It's the **Blessed Sacrament Chapel,** an oasis of peace reserved for prayer and meditation.

⓮ The skippable **Treasury Museum,** located on the left side of the nave near the altar, contains the room-size tomb of Sixtus IV by Antonio Pollaiuolo, a big pair of Roman pincers used to torture Christians, an original corkscrew column from Old St. Peter's, and assorted jewels, papal robes, and golden reliquaries.

• *When you're finished viewing the church's interior, go down to the foundations of Old St. Peter's, to the* **crypt** (**grotte** *or* **tombe**) *containing tombs of popes and memorial chapels. Save the crypt for last because it exits outside the basilica.*

In summer, the **crypt entrance** is usually beside the ❹ statue of St. Andrew, to the left of the main altar; in winter, it's by the dome entrance. Stairs lead you down to the floor level of the previous church, where you'll pass the sepulcher of Peter. This lighted niche with an icon is not Peter's actual tomb, but part of a shrine that stands atop Peter's tomb. Next are the tombs of past popes. Finally, you can see a few column fragments from Old St. Peter's (a.k.a. "Basilica Costantiniana"). Continue your one-way visit until it spills you out, usually near the checkroom.

⓯ For one of the best views of Rome, go up to the **dome.** The entrance is along the right (north) side of the church, but the line begins to form out front, at the church's right door (as you face the church). Look for *cupola* signs. There are

The view from atop St. Peter's

Seeing the Pope

Your best chances for a sighting are on Sunday or Wednesday. Most Sundays (though not always, especially in July or August), the pope gives a **blessing** at noon from the papal balcony (to the right as you face the basilica) on St. Peter's Square. You don't need a ticket—just show up. On most Wednesdays, the pope holds a **general audience** at 10:00 (tickets get you a closer-up spot but are not required; anyone can enjoy a look behind the fences via jumbo-screens). That's when he arrives in his Popemobile and gives a short sermon from a platform on the square. (In winter, it's sometimes held indoors at the Paolo VI Auditorium, next to St. Peter's Basilica, though Pope Francis prefers the square, even in cold weather.) Whenever the pope appears on the square, the basilica closes and crowds are substantial—so avoid these times if you just want to sightsee.

General Audience Tickets: For the Wednesday audience, a (free) ticket gets you closer to the papal action. You have several options:

- Reserve tickets a month or two in advance by sending a request by mail or fax (access the form at www.vatican.va, under "Prefecture of the Papal Household"—this path also shows his schedule). Pick up the tickets at St. Peter's Square before the audience (available Tue 15:00-19:00 and Wed 7:00-9:00; usually under Bernini's colonnade, to the left of the church).
- You can book tickets online through St. Patrick's Church, the American Catholic Church in Rome (free, but donations appreciated). Pick up your reserved tickets or check for last-minute availability at the church office the Tuesday before the audience between 16:30 and 18:30—some stay for the 18:00 English Mass (Via Boncompagni 31, Metro: Barberini, tel. 06-4201-4554, www.stpatricksamericanrome.org).
- Starting the Monday before the audience, Swiss Guards hand out tickets from their station near the basilica exit. There's no need to go through security—just march up, ask nicely, and say "*danke*." While this is perhaps the easiest way, it's best to reserve in advance.

Without a Ticket: If you just want to see the pope, get a long-distance photo, and don't mind standing, show up for the Wednesday audience at least by 9:30, and take your place behind the fences in the back of the square.

General Audience Tips: Dress appropriately (shoulders covered, no short shorts or tank tops; long pants or knee-length skirts are safest) and clear security (no big bags; lines move more quickly on the side of the square farthest from the Metro stop). To get a seat, get there a couple of hours early; there are far fewer seats than ticketholders. The service gets under way around 9:30 when the names of attending pilgrim groups are announced. Shortly thereafter, the Popemobile appears, winding through the adoring crowd (the best views are near the cloth-covered wooden fences that line the Popemobile route). Around 10:00, the Pope's multilingual message begins and lasts for about an hour (you can leave at any time).

two levels: the rooftop of the church and the top of the dome. Climb (for €6) or take an elevator (€8) to the first level, on the church roof just above the facade. From the roof, you can also go inside the gallery ringing the interior of the dome and look down inside the church. To get to the top of the dome, you'll take a staircase that winds between the outer shell and the inner one. It's a sweaty, crowded, claustrophobic, 15-minute, 323-step climb, but the view from the summit is great, and the fresh air is even better. Admire the arms of Bernini's colonnade encircling St. Peter's Square. Find the Victor Emmanuel Monument and the Pantheon. The large rectangular building to the left of the obelisk is the Vatican Museums complex, stuffed with art. And down in the square are tiny pilgrims buzzing like electrons around the nucleus of Catholicism.

Rick's Tip: *If you're* **claustrophobic** *or* **acrophobic, skip climbing the dome.**

▲▲▲VATICAN MUSEUMS (MUSEI VATICANI)

The four miles of displays in this immense museum complex culminate in the Raphael Rooms and Michelangelo's glorious Sistine Chapel. This is one of Europe's top three or four houses of art. It can be exhausting, so plan your visit carefully, focusing on a few themes. Allow two hours for a quick visit, three or four hours for enough time to enjoy it.

Cost and Hours: €16, €4 online reservation fee, Mon-Sat 9:00-18:00, last entry at 16:00 (though the official closing time is 18:00, the staff starts ushering you out at 17:30), closed on religious holidays and Sun except last Sun of the month (when it's free, more crowded, and open 9:00-14:00, last entry at 12:30); also open Fri nights mid-April-Oct 19:00-23:00 (last entry at 21:30) by online reservation only—check the website. Hours are subject to constant change.

The museum closes frequently for holidays, including: Jan 1 (New Year's), Jan 6 (Epiphany), Feb 11 (Vatican City established), March 19 (St. Joseph's Day), Easter Sunday and Monday, May 1 (Labor Day), June 29 (Sts. Peter and Paul), Aug 15 (Assumption of the Virgin), Nov 1 (All Saints' Day), Dec 8 (Immaculate Conception), and Dec 25 and 26 (Christmas). Before you visit, check the current hours, holiday closures, and calendar at www.museivaticani.va. Info tel. 06-6988-4676.

Reservations: Expect waits of up to two hours to buy tickets. You're crazy to come without a reservation. Bypass the long ticket lines by reserving an entry time at http://mv.vatican.va for €20 (€16 ticket plus €4 booking fee). Select the ticket called "Vatican Museums and Sistine Chapel," choose your day and time, then check your email for your confirmation and print out the voucher. At the Vatican Museums, you'll see three lines. Show your voucher to the guard and enter via the middle line. Inside, after the security check, go to any window on the left to show your voucher and pick up your ticket. With the actual ticket in hand, go up the steps and enter the museum.

When to Go: The museum is generally hot and crowded, except in winter. The worst days are Saturdays, the last Sunday of the month (when it's free), Mondays, rainy days, and any day before or after a holiday closure. Mornings are most crowded. It's best to visit on a weekday after 14:00—the later the better. Another good time is during the papal audience on Wednesday morning, when many tourists are at St. Peter's Square (the only drawback is that St. Peter's Basilica is closed until roughly 13:00, as is the exit to it from the Sistine Chapel—described later, under "Exit Strategies").

Avoiding Lines: Booking a **guided tour** (see "Tours," later) gets you right in—just show the guard your voucher. You can often buy **same-day timed-entry reservations** (for the same €20 online price) through the TI in St. Peter's Square (to the left, as you face the basilica). Also, the Opera Romana Pellegrinaggi (a.k.a., Roma Cristiana), a private pilgrimage tour company, sells same-day tickets for €30 (entrances almost hourly, office in front of St. Peter's Square, Piazza Pio XII 9, tel. 06-6980-6380, www.operaromanapellegrinaggi.org). If you're going to St. Peter's Basilica first, you can sometimes buy same-day Vatican Museums tickets in the narthex for €5 extra. Hawkers peddling skip-the-line access swarm the Vatican area, offering guided tours—but museum staff advise against accepting their offers (while legitimate, the tour caliber is often low).

Dress Code: Modest dress is required (no shorts, above-knee skirts, or bare shoulders).

Getting There: The Ottaviano Metro stop is a 10-minute walk from the entrance. Bus #49 from Piazza Cavour/Castel Sant'Angelo stops at Piazza Risorgimento and continues right to the entrance. Bus #492 heads from the city center past Piazza Risorgimento and the Vatican walls, and also stops on Via Leone IV. Bus #64 stops on the other side of St. Peter's Square, a 15- to 20-minute walk (facing the church from the obelisk, take a right through the colonnade and follow the Vatican Wall). A few other handy buses (see page 352) can get you close enough to snag a taxi for the final stretch. Or take a taxi from the city center—they are reasonable (hop in and say, "moo-ZAY-ee vah-tee-KAH-nee").

Getting In: Approaching the exterior entrance, you'll see three lines: individuals without reservations (far left), individuals with reservations (much shorter and faster, in the middle), and groups (on the right). Make sure you get in the correct entry line. All visitors must pass through a metal detector (no pocketknives allowed).

Tours: A €7 **audioguide** is available at the top of the spiral ramp/escalator, and can be prepaid when you book tickets online. A security ID is not required to rent an audioguide, and you can drop it off either where you rented it or after leaving the Sistine Chapel if taking the shortcut to St. Peter's (described later, under "Exit Strategies"). Confirm the drop-off location when renting.

🎧 Download my free Vatican Museums and Sistine Chapel **audio tours.**

The Vatican offers **guided tours** in English that are easy to book on their website (€32, includes admission). As with individual ticket reservations, present your confirmation voucher to a guard to the right of the entrance; then, once inside, go to the Guided Tours desk (in the lobby, up a few stairs).

For a list of **private tour** companies and guides, see page 318.

Length of This Tour: Until you expire, the museum closes, or 2.5 hours pass, whichever comes first. If you're short on time, see the octagonal courtyard *(Laocoön)*, then follow the crowd flow directly to the Sistine Chapel, sightseeing along the way. From the Sistine Chapel, head straight to St. Peter's (see "Exit Strategies," next).

Exit Strategies: The museum has two exits. The **main exit** is near the entrance. Use this one if you're asked to return an audioguide there or if you plan on following this self-guided tour exactly as laid out, visiting the Pinacoteca at the end.

The other exit is a handy (but sometimes closed) **shortcut** that leads from the Sistine Chapel directly to St. Peter's Basilica (spilling out alongside the church). The shortcut saves you a 30-minute walk backtracking to the basilica's main entrance and lets you avoid the long security line for others entering the basilica. Officially, this exit is for Vatican guides and their groups only. However, it's often open to anyone (depending on how crowded the chapel is and how the guards feel). It's worth a shot (try blending in with a group that's leaving), but be

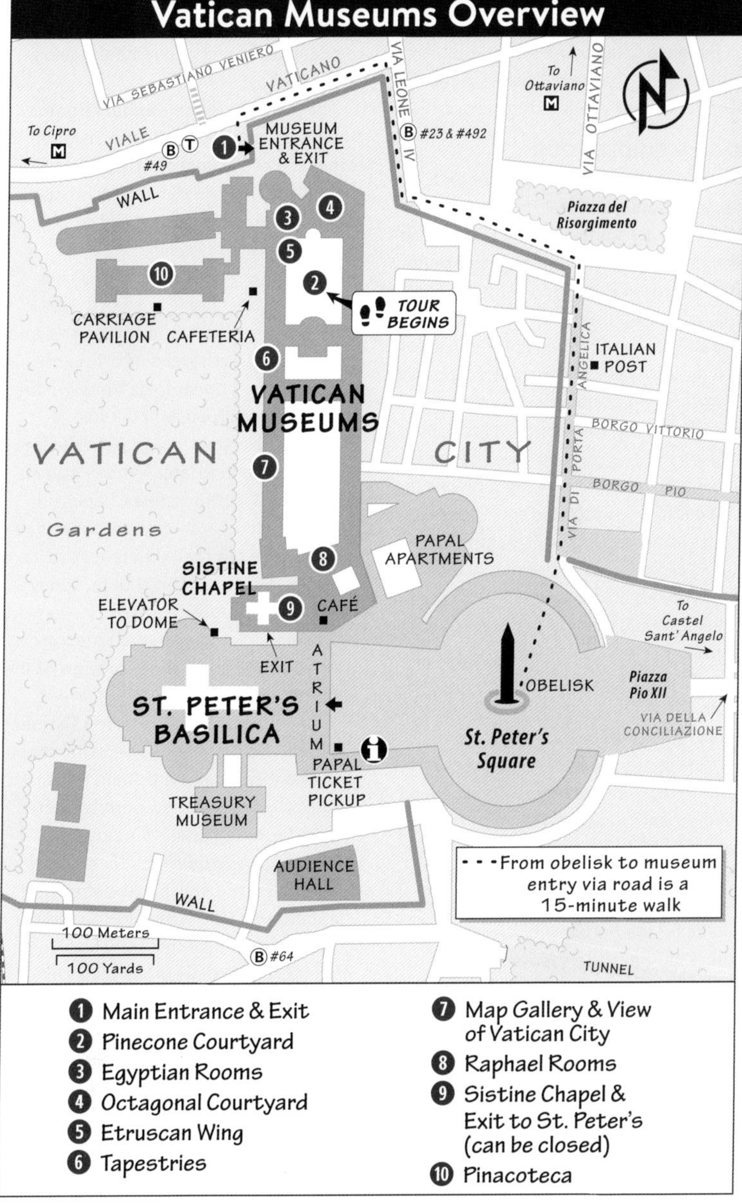
Vatican Museums Overview
VIA SEBASTIANO VENIERO
VIALE VATICANO
VIA LEONE IV
VIA OTTAVIANO
To Ottaviano M
To Cipro M
B T #49
MUSEUM ENTRANCE & EXIT
B #23 & #492
WALL
Piazza del Risorgimento
TOUR BEGINS
CARRIAGE PAVILION
CAFETERIA
VATICAN MUSEUMS
VIA DI PORTA ANGELICA
ITALIAN POST
BORGO VITTORIO
BORGO PIO
VATICAN CITY
Gardens
PAPAL APARTMENTS
SISTINE CHAPEL
ELEVATOR TO DOME
CAFÉ
EXIT
ATRIUM
To Castel Sant' Angelo
OBELISK
Piazza Pio XII
VIA DELLA CONCILIAZIONE
ST. PETER'S BASILICA
St. Peter's Square
PAPAL TICKET PICKUP
TREASURY MUSEUM
AUDIENCE HALL
From obelisk to museum entry via road is a 15-minute walk
WALL
100 Meters
100 Yards
B #64
TUNNEL
1 Main Entrance & Exit
2 Pinecone Courtyard
3 Egyptian Rooms
4 Octagonal Courtyard
5 Etruscan Wing
6 Tapestries
7 Map Gallery & View of Vatican City
8 Raphael Rooms
9 Sistine Chapel & Exit to St. Peter's (can be closed)
10 Pinacoteca

prepared for the possibility that you won't get through.

Baggage Check: The museum's "checkroom" (to the right after security) takes only bigger bags, not day bags.

➲ SELF-GUIDED TOUR

Start, as civilization did, in **Egypt and Mesopotamia.** Decorating the museum's courtyard are some of the best **Greek and Roman statues** in captivity. The **Apollo Belvedere** is a Roman copy (4th century B.C.) of a Hellenistic original that followed the style of the Greek sculptor Praxiteles. It fully captures the beauty of the human form. Instead of standing at attention, face-forward with his arms at his sides (Egyptian-style), Apollo is on the move, coming to rest with his weight on one leg.

Laocoön was sculpted some four centuries after the Golden Age (5th-4th century B.C.), after the scales of "balance" had been tipped. *Apollo* is serene and graceful, while *Laocoön* is emotional and gritty. The figures (carved from four blocks of marble pieced together seamlessly) are powerful, with twisted poses that accentuate each rippling muscle and bulging vein.

The centerpiece of the next hall is the 2,000-year-old **Belvedere Torso,** which had a great impact on the art of Michelangelo. Finishing off the classical statuary are two fine fourth-century porphyry sarcophagi. These royal purple tombs were made for the Roman emperor Constantine's mother and daughter.

After long halls of tapestries, old maps, broken penises, and fig leaves, you'll come to what most people are looking for: the Raphael Rooms and Michelangelo's Sistine Chapel.

The highlight of the **Raphael Rooms,** frescoed by Raphael and his assistants, is the restored ***School of Athens.*** It is remarkable for its blatant pre-Christian classical orientation, especially considering it originally wallpapered the apartments of Pope Julius II. Raphael honors the great pre-Christian thinkers—Aristotle, Plato, and company—who are portrayed as the leading artists of Raphael's day. Leonardo da Vinci, whom Raphael worshipped, is in the role of Plato. Michelangelo, brooding in the foreground, was added later. When Raphael snuck a peek at the Sistine Chapel, he decided that his arch-competitor was so good that he put their differences aside and included him in this tribute. Today's St. Peter's was under construction as Raphael was working. In the *School of Athens,* he gives us a sneak preview of the unfinished church.

Next is the brilliantly restored **Sistine Chapel.** This is the pope's personal chapel and also the place where, upon the death of the ruling pope, a new pope is elected.

The Sistine Chapel is famous for Michelangelo's pictorial culmination of the Renaissance, showing the story of creation, with God weaving in and out of each scene through that busy first week. It's a stirring example of the artistic and theological maturity of the 33-year-old

Laocoön

Raphael, School of Athens

Sistine Chapel

Michelangelo, who spent four years on this work.

The ceiling shows the history of the world before the birth of Jesus. We see God creating the world, creating man and woman, destroying the earth by flood, and so on. God himself, in his purple robe, actually appears in the first five scenes. Along the sides (where the ceiling starts to curve), we see the Old Testament prophets and pagan Greek prophetesses who foretold the coming of Christ. Dividing these scenes and figures are fake niches (a painted 3-D illusion) decorated with nude figures with symbolic meaning.

In the central panel of the **Creation of Adam,** God and man take center stage in this Renaissance version of creation. Adam, newly formed in the image of God, lounges dreamily in perfect naked innocence. God, with his entourage, swoops in with a swirl of activity (which—with a little imagination—looks like a cross-section of a human brain...quite a strong humanist statement). Their reaching hands are the center of this work. Adam's is passive; God's is forceful, his finger twitching upward with energy. Here is the very moment of creation, as God passes the spark of life to man, the crowning work of his creation.

This is the spirit of the Renaissance. God is not reaching down to puny man from way on high. They are on an equal plane, divided only by the diagonal bit of sky. God's billowing robe and the patch of green that holds Adam balance each other. They are like the yin and yang symbols finally coming together—uniting, complementing each other, creating wholeness. God and man work together in the divine process of creation.

When the ceiling was finished and revealed to the public, it blew 'em away. It both caps the Renaissance and turns it in a new direction. The style is more dramatic and emotional than the balanced Renaissance works before it. This is a personal work—the Gospel according to Michelangelo—but its themes and subject matter are universal. Many art scholars contend that the Sistine ceiling is the single greatest work of art by any one human being.

Later, after the Reformation wars had begun and after the Catholic army of Spain had sacked the Vatican, the reeling Church began to fight back. As part of its Counter-Reformation, a much older Michelangelo was commissioned to paint the ***Last Judgment*** (behind the altar).

It's Judgment Day, and Christ—the powerful figure in the center, raising his arm to spank the wicked—has come to find out who's naughty and who's nice. Beneath him, a band of angels blows its trumpets Dizzy Gillespie-style: a wake-up call to the sleeping dead. The dead at lower left leave their graves and prepare to be judged. The righteous, on Christ's right hand (the left side of the picture), are carried up to heaven. The wicked on the other side are hurled into hell. Charon, from the underworld of Greek mythology, waits below to ferry the souls of the damned to hell.

When *The Last Judgment* was unveiled to the public in 1541, it caused a sensation. The pope dropped to his knees and cried, "Lord, charge me not with my sins when thou shalt come on the Day of Judgment."

And it changed the course of art. The complex composition, with more than 300 figures swirling around the figure of Christ, went far beyond traditional Renaissance balance. The twisted figures shown from every imaginable angle challenged other painters to try and top this master of 3-D illusion. The sheer terror and drama of the scene was a striking contrast to the placid optimism of, say, Raphael's *School of Athens*. Michelangelo had Baroque-en all the rules of the Renaissance, signaling a new era of art.

If you take the long march back, you'll find, along with the Pinacoteca, a cafeteria (long lines, uninspired food), the underrated early-Christian art section, and the exit via the souvenir shop.

Rick's Tip: *A handy (but sometimes closed)* **shortcut leads from the Sistine Chapel directly to St. Peter's Basilica,** *saving a 30-minute walk backtracking to the basilica's main entrance and avoiding the security line there. Exit through the corner door labeled "for authorized guides and tour groups only." Try blending in, or pretend that your group has left you behind.*

North Rome

▲▲▲BORGHESE GALLERY (GALLERIA BORGHESE)

This plush museum, filling a cardinal's mansion in Rome's semiscruffy three-square-mile "Central Park," offers one of Europe's most sumptuous art experiences. Enjoy a collection of world-class Baroque sculpture, including Bernini's *David* and his excited statue of Apollo chasing Daphne, as well as paintings by Caravaggio, Raphael, Titian, and Rubens. The museum's mandatory reservation system keeps crowds to a manageable size.

Cost and Hours: €13, free and crowded first Sun of the month, Tue-Sun 9:00-19:00, closed Mon. Reservations are mandatory.

Information: Tel. 06-32810 (ticket service) or 06-841-3979 (museum), www.galleriaborghese.it.

Reservations: Reservations are mandatory and simple to get. Every two hours, 360 people are allowed to enter the museum. Entry times are 9:00, 11:00, 13:00, 15:00, and 17:00 (you'll get exactly two hours for your visit). The sooner you reserve, the better—at least several days in advance for a weekday visit, and at least a week ahead for weekends. (In winter, you may be able to get tickets on shorter notice.)

It's easiest to book online at www.tosc.it (€4/person booking fee; choose to pick up tickets at venue). You can also reserve with a real person over the telephone (€2/person booking fee, tel. 06-32810, press 2 for English, phones answered Mon-Fri 9:00-18:00, Sat 9:00-13:00, closed Sat in Aug and Sun year-round).

The museum recommends that you arrive at the gallery 30 minutes before your appointed time to pick up your ticket in the lobby on the lower level. Don't cut it close—arriving late can mean forfeiting your reservation.

You can use a Roma Pass for free or discounted entry, but you're still required to make a reservation (by phone only—not online; specify that you have the Roma Pass).

Getting There: The museum, at Piazzale del Museo Borghese 5, is set idyllically but inconveniently in the vast Villa Borghese Gardens. Bus #910 goes from Termini train station (and Piazza Repubblica) to the Via Pinciana stop, 100 yards from the museum. By Metro, from the Barberini Metro stop, walk 10 minutes up Via Veneto, enter the park, and turn right, following signs another 10 minutes to the Borghese Gallery.

Tours: Guided English tours are offered every day at 9:00 and 11:00, and occasionally on Thursdays at 13:00 (€6.50; reserve tours either online or by phone). The superb 1.5-hour audioguide tour (€5) covers more than my description.

Planning Your Time: Two hours is all you get...and you'll want every minute. Budget most of your time for the more interesting ground floor, but set aside 30 minutes for the paintings of the Pinacoteca upstairs (highlights are marked by the audioguide icons).

Services: Baggage check is free, mandatory, and strictly enforced.

Visiting the Museum: It's hard to believe that a family of cardinals and popes would display so many works with secular and sensual—even erotic—themes. But the Borgheses felt that all forms of human expression, including pagan myths and physical passion, glorified God.

Borghese Gallery—Ground Floor

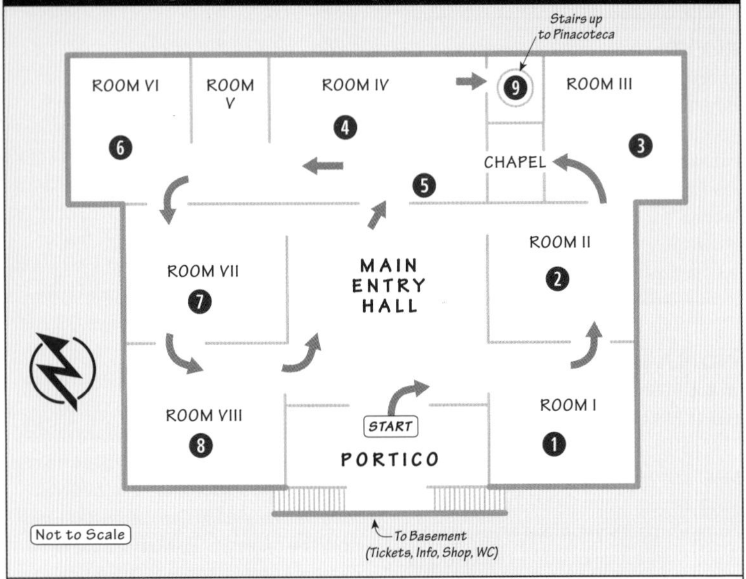

1. CANOVA – *Pauline Borghese as Venus*
2. BERNINI – *David*
3. BERNINI – *Apollo and Daphne*
4. BERNINI – *The Rape of Proserpina*
5. UNKNOWN – *Diana the Hunter; other marbles*
6. BERNINI – *Aeneas and Anchises*
7. *"Theater of the Universe"*
8. CARAVAGGIO – *Various*
9. *Stairs up to Pinacoteca*

The essence of the collection is the connection of the Renaissance with the classical world. As you enter, notice the second-century Roman reliefs with Michelangelo-designed panels above either end of the portico. The villa was built in the early 17th century by art collector Cardinal Scipione Borghese, to prove that the glories of ancient Rome were matched by the Renaissance.

In the main entry hall, high up on the wall, is a thrilling first-century Greek sculpture of a horse falling. The Renaissance-era rider was added by Pietro Bernini, father of the famous Gian Lorenzo Bernini.

Each room seems to feature a Baroque masterpiece. In Room I is ***Pauline Borghese as Venus,*** for which Napoleon's sister went the full monty for the sculptor Antonio Canova, scandalizing Europe. ("How could you have done such a thing?!" she was asked. She replied, "The room wasn't cold.") With the famous nose of her conqueror brother, she strikes the pose of Venus as conqueror of men's hearts. Her relaxed afterglow says she's already had her man.

In Room II, Gian Lorenzo Bernini's ***David*** twists around to put a big rock in his sling. He purses his lips, knits his brow, and winds his body like a spring as his eyes lock onto the target: Goliath, who's somewhere behind us, putting us right in the line of fire. Compared with Michelangelo's *David,* this is unvarnished realism—an unbalanced pose, bulging veins, unflattering face, and armpit hair. Michelangelo's *David* thinks, whereas Bernini's acts. Bernini slays the pretty-boy *David*s of the Renaissance and prepares to invent Baroque.

In Room III, Bernini's ***Apollo and Daphne*** is the perfect Baroque subject. Apollo—made stupid by Cupid's arrow of love—chases after Daphne, who has been turned off by the "arrow of disgust." Just as he's about to catch her, she calls to her father to save her. Magically, she transforms into a tree. Frustrated Apollo will end up with a handful of leaves.

In Room IV, Bernini's ***The Rape of Proserpina*** proves that even at the age of 24 the sculptor was the master of marble.

In Room VI, Bernini's ***Aeneas and Anchises*** reveals the then 20-year-old sculptor's astonishing aptitude for portraying human flesh. In the same room,

Bernini, Apollo and Daphne

Diana the Hunter is a rare Greek original (second century B.C., sculptor unknown).

In Room VIII is a fabulous collection of paintings by **Caravaggio,** who brought Christian saints down to earth with gritty realism.

Upstairs, in the Pinacoteca (Painting Gallery), are busts and paintings by Bernini, as well as works by Raphael, Titian, Correggio, and Domenichino.

CAPUCHIN CRYPT

If you want to see artistically arranged bones, this is the place. The crypt is below the Church of Santa Maria della Immacolata Concezione on the tree-lined Via Veneto, just up from Piazza Barberini. The bones of about 4,000 friars who died in the 1700s are in the basement, all lined up in a series of six crypts to instruct wide-eyed visitors of the inevitability of mortality. Its macabre motto (in the first chapel) is: "What you are now, we used to be."

Cost and Hours: €8.50, daily 9:00-19:00, modest dress required, Via Veneto 27, Metro: Barberini, tel. 06-8880-3695.

▲SPANISH STEPS

The wide, curving staircase, culminating with an obelisk between two Baroque church towers, is one of Rome's iconic sights. Beyond that, it's a people-gathering place. By day, the area hosts shoppers looking for high-end fashions; on balmy evenings, it attracts young and old alike. For more about the steps, see page 326.

▲▲MUSEO DELL'ARA PACIS (MUSEUM OF THE ALTAR OF PEACE)

On January 30, 9 B.C., soon-to-be-emperor Augustus led a procession of priests up the steps and into this newly built "Altar of Peace." They sacrificed an animal on the altar and poured an offering of wine, thanking the gods for helping Augustus pacify barbarians abroad and rivals at home. This marked the dawn of the Pax Romana (c. A.D. 1-200), a Golden Age of good living, stability, dominance, and peace *(pax)*. The Ara Pacis (AH-rah

PAH-chees) hosted annual sacrifices by the emperor until the area was flooded by the Tiber River. For an idea of how high the water could get, find the measure *(idrometro)* scaling the right side of the church closest to the entrance. Buried under silt, it was abandoned and forgotten until the 16th century, when various parts were discovered and excavated. Mussolini had the altar's scattered parts reconstructed in a building here in 1938. Today, the Altar of Peace stands in a striking pavilion designed by American architect Richard Meier (opened 2006). It's about the only entirely new structure permitted in the old center of Rome since Mussolini's day. To see what the altar looked like in its day, consider the virtual reality show—a colorful 3D reconstruction of the altar.

Cost and Hours: €10.50 when no special exhibits, daily 9:30-19:30, last entry one hour before closing, videoguide-€6; virtual reality show-€12, daily April-Oct from 20:45, 45 minutes, reserve online; a long block west of Via del Corso on Via di Ara Pacis, on the east bank of the Tiber near Ponte Cavour, Metro: Spagna plus a 10-minute walk down Via dei Condotti; tel. 06-0608, www.arapacis.it.

Visiting the Museum: Start with the model in the museum's lobby. The Altar of Peace was originally located east of here, along today's Via del Corso. The model shows where it stood in relation to the Mausoleum of Augustus (now next door) and the Pantheon. Approach the Ara Pacis and look through the doorway to see the raised altar. This simple structure has just the basics of a Roman temple: an altar for sacrifices surrounded by cubicle walls that enclose a consecrated space. Climb the 10 steps and go inside. From here, the priest would climb the 8 altar steps to make sacrifices. The walls of the enclosure are decorated with the offerings to the gods: animals, garlands of fruit, and ceremonial platters. The reliefs on the north and south sides depict the parade of dignitaries who consecrated the altar, while the reliefs on the west side (near the altar's back door) celebrate peace (goddess Roma as a conquering Amazon, right side) and prosperity (fertility goddess surrounded by children, plants, and animals, left side).

East Rome

▲▲▲NATIONAL MUSEUM OF ROME

The National Museum's main branch houses the greatest collection of ancient Roman art anywhere, including busts of emperors and a Roman copy of the Greek *Discus Thrower*.

Ara Pacis (Altar of Peace)

Cost and Hours: €7 combo-ticket valid for three days, also includes three other branches—all skippable, free and crowded first Sun of the month, Tue-Sun 9:00-19:45, closed Mon, last entry 45 minutes before closing, audioguide-€5.

Information: Tel. 06-3996-7700, www.museonazionaleromano.beniculturali.it.

Getting There: The museum is in Palazzo Massimo, situated between Piazza della Repubblica (Metro: Repubblica) and Termini Station (Metro: Termini). It's a few minutes' walk from either Metro stop. As you leave Termini, it's the sandstone-brick building on your left. Enter at the far end, at Largo di Villa Peretti.

Visiting the Museum: The museum is rectangular, with rooms and hallways built around a central courtyard. The ground-floor displays follow Rome's history as it changes from a republic to a dictatorial empire. The first-floor exhibits take Rome from its peak through its slow decline. The second floor houses rare frescoes and fine mosaics, and the basement presents coins and everyday objects.

On the first floor, along with statues and busts showing such emperors as Trajan and Hadrian, you'll see the best-preserved Roman copy of the Greek *Discus Thrower*. Statues of athletes like this commonly stood in the baths, where Romans cultivated healthy bodies, minds, and social skills, hoping to lead well-rounded lives. Other statues on this floor originally stood in the pleasure gardens of the Roman rich—surrounded by greenery with the splashing sound of fountains, all painted in bright, lifelike colors. Though created by Romans, the themes are mostly Greek, with godlike humans and human-looking gods.

The second floor contains frescoes and mosaics that once decorated the walls and floors of Roman villas. They feature everyday people, animals, flowery patterns, and geometrical designs. The Villa Farnesina frescoes—in black, red, yellow, and blue—are mostly architectural designs, with fake columns, friezes, and garlands. The Villa di Livia frescoes, owned by the wily wife of Augustus, immerse you in a leafy green garden full of birds and fruit trees, symbolizing the gods.

Finally, descend into the basement to see fine gold jewelry, an eight-year-old girl's mummy, and vault doors leading into the best coin collection in Europe, with fancy magnifying glasses maneuvering you through cases of coins from ancient Rome to modern times.

▲BATHS OF DIOCLETIAN/CHURCH OF SANTA MARIA DEGLI ANGELI

Of all the marvelous structures built by the Romans, their public baths were arguably the grandest, and the Baths of Diocletian were the granddaddy of them all. Built by Emperor Diocletian around A.D. 300 and sprawling over 30 acres—roughly five times the size of the Colosseum—these baths could cleanse 3,000 Romans at once. They functioned until A.D. 537, when barbarians attacked and the city's aqueducts fell into disuse, plunging Rome into a thousand years of poverty, darkness, and BO. Today, tourists can visit one

Baths of Diocletian

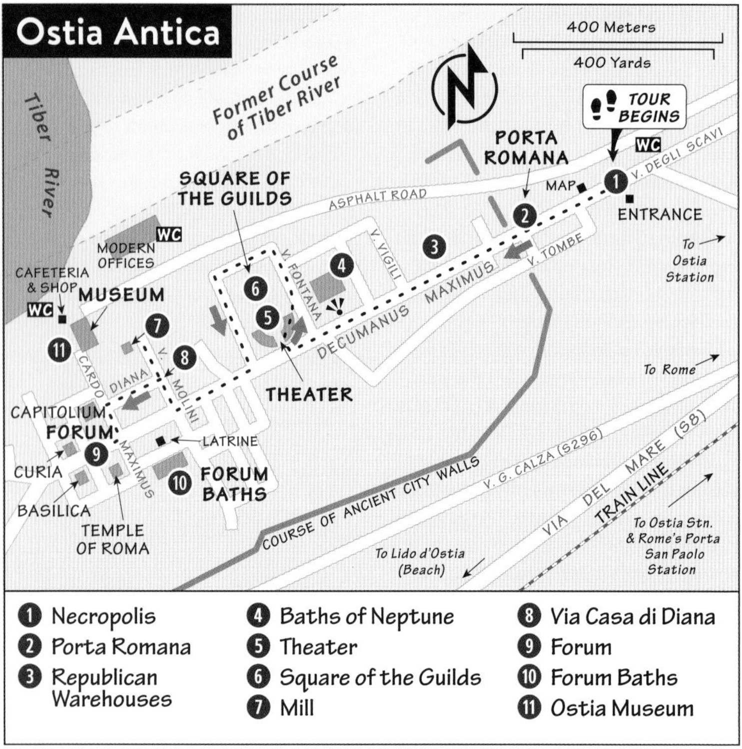

Ostia Antica

1. Necropolis
2. Porta Romana
3. Republican Warehouses
4. Baths of Neptune
5. Theater
6. Square of the Guilds
7. Mill
8. Via Casa di Diana
9. Forum
10. Forum Baths
11. Ostia Museum

grand section of the baths, the former main hall. This impressive remnant of the ancient complex was later transformed (with help from Michelangelo) into the Church of Santa Maria degli Angeli.

Cost and Hours: Free, daily 7:30-18:30, closes slightly later May-Sept and Sun year-round, entrance on Piazza della Repubblica (Metro: Repubblica), www.santamariadegliangeliroma.it.

▲▲CHURCH OF SAN GIOVANNI IN LATERANO

Built by Constantine, the first Christian emperor, this was Rome's most important church through medieval times. A building alongside the church houses the **Holy Stairs** (Scala Santa) said to have been walked up by Jesus, which today are ascended by pilgrims on their knees. You can join them.

Boxer at Rest *(National Museum of Rome)*

Pilgrims climbing the Holy Stairs

Cost and Hours: Church and Holy Stairs—free, cloister—€5, chapel at Holy Stairs—€3.50 (€10 combo-ticket covers cloister, chapel, and audioguide); church open daily 7:00-18:30; Holy Stairs open Mon-Sat 6:30-19:00, Sun 7:00-19:00, Oct-March closes daily at 18:30. The church is on Piazza di San Giovanni in Laterano (east of the Colosseum and south of Termini train station, Metro: San Giovanni, or bus #87). Tel. 06-772-6641, www.vatican.va (search for "San Giovanni in Laterano"); for Holy Stairs, visit www.scala-santa.it.

Near Rome: Ostia Antica

For an exciting day trip, pop down to the Roman port of Ostia, which is similar to Pompeii but a lot closer and, in some ways, more interesting. Because Ostia was a working port town, it offers a more complete and gritty look at Roman life than wealthier Pompeii. Wandering around today, you'll see warehouses, apartment flats, mansions, shopping arcades, and baths that served a once-thriving port of 60,000 people. At its peak, Ostia was vital to the Roman Empire. Most of what the city of Rome consumed—and that was a lot by historical standards—came in through this port.

Today, with more than 70 peaceful acres to explore and relatively few crowds, it's a welcome break from the bustle of Rome. You can buy a map or follow the map on page 370 (which lists the major stops) and explore the town, including the 2,000-year-old theater. Finish with the fine little museum.

Ostia Antica Theater

Cost and Hours: €8 for the site and museum, €11 with special exhibits, April-Aug Tue-Sun 8:30-19:15, Sept until 19:00, Oct until 18:30, Nov-mid-Feb 8:30-16:30, shorter hours mid-Feb-March, closed Mon year-round, last entry one hour before closing. The small museum closes one hour before the site does.

Getting There: Getting from Rome to Ostia Antica is a 45-minute combination Metro/train ride (costs only one Metro ticket each way): Take Metro line B to the Piramide stop, which is part of the Roma Porta San Paolo train station. Exiting the Metro, follow signs to *Lido*—go up the escalator, turn left, and go down the steps into the Roma-Lido train station. All trains depart for the Lido, leave every 15 minutes, and stop at Ostia Antica. Hop on the next train, ride for about 30 minutes (no need to stamp your Metro ticket again, but keep it handy in case it's checked), and get off at Ostia Antica. Leaving the train station, walk over the blue skybridge, then head straight down Via della Stazione di Ostia Antica, continuing straight (through a small parking lot) to the large parking lot for the site (entrance on your left).

Information: A map of the site with suggested itineraries is available for €2 from the ticket office. Tel. 06-5635-0215. Helpful websites include www.ostiaantica.beniculturali.it and www.ostia-antica.org.

Tours: Audioguide-€5; choose between a short version (lasts 3 hours) or a longer one (7 hours). Or you can 🎧 download my free Ostia Antica audio tour.

EXPERIENCES

Nightlife

The best after-dark activity is to grab a gelato and stroll the medieval lanes that connect the romantic, floodlit squares and fountains. Head for Piazza Navona, the Pantheon, Campo de' Fiori, Trevi Fountain, and the Spanish Steps; these marvelous sights are linked together in my self-guided

"Heart of Rome" walk (page 319). Another great evening activity is my "Dolce Vita Stroll" along Via del Corso (page 327).

A fun neighborhood to explore at night is **Monti,** which is more like a lively village. Hang out at the fountain on Piazza della Madonna dei Monti, a popular gathering spot. Stop at the shop on the uphill side of the square, which sells cheap bottles of wine with plastic glasses, beer, fruit, and munchies. Or head to an actual bar, like **Fafiuché** (Via della Madonna dei Monti 28) or **Enoteca Cavour 313** (Via Cavour 313).

Performances

Get a copy of the entertainment guide *Evento* (free at TIs and many hotels) and check the listings of concerts, operas, dance, and films. For the most up-to-date events calendar, check these English-language websites: www.inromenow.com, www.wantedinrome.com, and www.angloinfo.com/rome.

The **Teatro dell'Opera** has an active schedule of opera and classical concerts. You'll see locals in all their finery, so pull your fanciest outfit from your backpack (Via Firenze 72, a block off Via Nazionale, Metro: Repubblica; box office takes phone reservations beginning 5 days prior at tel. 06-4816-0255, www.operaroma.it).

The Episcopal **Church of St. Paul's Within the Walls** offers musical events ranging from orchestral concerts (usually Tue and Fri at 20:30) to operatic performances (usually Sat at 20:30). Some Sunday evenings at 18:30, the church hosts hour-long candlelit "Luminaria" concerts. Check the church website (under "Music") to see what's on (€10-30, same-day tickets usually available, arrive 30-45 minutes early for best seat, Via Napoli 58 at corner of Via Nazionale, Metro: Repubblica, tel. 06-482-6296, www.stpaulsrome.it).

The venerable **Alexanderplatz** hosts **jazz performances** most evenings (Sun-Thu concerts at 21:45, Fri-Sat at 22:30, closed in summer, Via Ostia 9, Metro: Ottaviano, tel. 06-3972-1867, www.alexanderplatzjazzclub.it).

EATING

Romans take great pleasure in dining well, treating it as a lengthy social occasion. Embrace this passion over a multi-course meal at an outdoor table, watching a parade of passersby while you sip wine with loved ones.

Rome's fabled squares (most notably Piazza Navona, near the Pantheon, and Campo de' Fiori) are lined with the outdoor tables of touristy restaurants with enticing menus and formal-vested waiters. The atmosphere is super romantic. I, too, like the idea of dining under floodlit monuments, amid a constantly flowing parade of people. But you'll likely be surrounded by tourists and hawkers, and awkward interactions can kill the ambience...leaving you with just a forgettable and overpriced meal. Restaurants in these areas are notorious for surprise charges, bad service, and mediocre, microwaved food.

I enjoy the view by savoring just a drink or dessert on a famous square, but I dine with locals on nearby low-rent streets, where the proprietor needs to serve a good-value meal and nurture a local following to stay in business. If you're set on eating—or just drinking and snacking—on a famous piazza, you don't need a guidebook listing to choose a spot; enjoy the ritual of slowly circling the square, observing both the food and the people eating it,

and sit where the view and menu appeal to you. (And pizza is probably your best value and least risky bet.)

I'm impressed by how small the price difference can be between a mediocre Roman restaurant and a fine one. You can pay about 20 percent more for double the quality. If I had $100 for three meals in Rome, I'd spend $50 for one and $25 each for the other two, rather than $33 on all three. For splurge meals, I'd consider Gabriello and Fortunato, in that order (details listed later).

Budget Eating: For a light budget meal, consider an *aperitivo* buffet. Bars all over town—especially in Monti—serve up an enticing buffet of small dishes, from about 18:00 to 21:00, and anyone buying a drink (generally €8-12) gets to eat "for free." Some places limit you to one plate; others allow refills.

For the cheapest meal, assemble a picnic and dine with Rome as your backdrop. Buy ingredients for your picnic at one of Rome's open-air produce markets (mornings only), an *alimentari* (corner grocery store), a *rosticcerie* (cheap food to go), or a *supermercato,* such as Conad or Coop. You'll find handy late-night supermarkets near the Pantheon (on Via Giustiniani), Spanish Steps (Via Vittoria), Trevi Fountain (Via del Bufalo), and Campo de' Fiori (Via di Monte della Farina).

Rome discourages people from picnicking or drinking at historic monuments (such as on the Spanish Steps) in the old center. Violators can be fined, though it rarely happens. You'll be OK if you eat *with* a view rather than *on* the view.

Pantheon Neighborhood

I've listed restaurants in this central area based on which landmark they're closest to: Piazza Navona, the Trevi Fountain, or the Pantheon.

Near Piazza Navona

Piazza Navona and the streets just to the west are jammed with an amazing array of restaurants. The places lining the piazza itself are traditional and touristy. Instead, survey the scene on the two streets heading west from the square.

$$ Ristorante and Bar del Fico is a sprawling, rustic-chic place with a split personality: The restaurant is a spacious, family-friendly, pizza-and-pasta type eatery, while the bar feels like a huge Italian saloon filled with young locals (3 blocks west of Piazza Navona at Via della Pace 34, tel. 06-688-91373).

$$ Ristorante Pizzeria "da Francesco," bustling and authentic, has a 50-year-old tradition, great indoor seating, and a few tables stretching along the quiet street. Their blackboard explains the daily specials (daily 12:00-15:30 & 19:00-24:00, requires reservations for evening seatings, Piazza del Fico 29, tel. 06-686-4009, www.dafrancesco.it).

$$ Vivi Bistrot is in the Museum of Rome building at the south end of Piazza Navona, with two delightful window tables overlooking the square. This cheery and modern little restaurant serves salads, pastas, and burger plates with a focus on organic ingredients (Tue-Sun 10:00-24:00, closed Mon, Piazza Navona 2, tel. 06-683-3779, www.vivibistrot.com).

$$ L'Insalata Ricca, specializing in filling salads alongside pastas and main courses, is handy and central (daily 12:00-24:00). They have a branch at Piazza Pasquino 72 (tel. 06-6830-7881) and a larger location a few blocks away, on a bigger square next to busy Corso Vittorio Emanuele (Largo dei Chiavari 85, tel. 06-6880-3656).

Near the Trevi Fountain

The streets surrounding the Trevi Fountain are littered with mediocre restaurants catering to tourists—try one of these instead.

$$$ Hostaria Romana is a busy bistro with a hustling, fun-loving gang of waiters. The upstairs is a glassed-in terrace, while the cellar has noisy walls graffitied by happy eaters. Try the traditional *saltimbocca alla romana* (veal) or the pasta dish, *bucatini*

Roman Cuisine

Simple, fresh, seasonal ingredients dominate Roman cuisine. It's robust, strongly flavored, and unpretentious—much like the people who've created it. Roman cooking didn't come out of emperors' or popes' kitchens, but from the *cucina povera*—the home cooking of the common people. That could explain why Romans have a fondness for meats known as the *quinto quarto* ("fifth quarter"), such as tripe *(trippa)*, tail, brain, and pigs' feet.

Appetizers *(Antipasti)*: Popular choices are *prosciutto e melone* (thin slices of ham wrapped around cantaloupe), *bruschetta* (toasted bread topped with chopped tomatoes), and *antipasto misto* (a plate of marinated or grilled vegetables, cheeses, cured meats, or seafood). *Fritti* are fried snacks that have been either battered or breaded, such as stuffed olives, potato croquettes, rice balls, and stuffed squash blossoms.

First Courses *(Primi)*: A pasta dish born in Rome is *spaghetti alla carbonara,* with eggs, pancetta (Italian bacon), cheese, and pepper. Another traditional pasta is *bucatini all'amatriciana,* with tomato sauce, onions, pancetta, and cheese. *Gnocchi alla romana* are small, flattened dumplings from semolina (not potatoes), and baked with butter and cheese. If you like spaghetti with clams, try *spaghetti alle vongole veraci.*

Second Courses *(Secondi)*: A very Roman dish is *saltimbocca alla romana* (thinly sliced, lightly fried veal layered with prosciutto). *Filetti di baccalà* is fried salt cod, like fish-and-chips minus the chips. Other choices are baby lamb chops *(abbacchio alla scottadito),* stewed baby eels *(anguillette in umid),* and braised oxtails *(coda alla vaccinara)*. *Trippa alla romana* is braised tripe with onions and carrots.

Desserts *(Dolci)*: Dessert can be a seasonal fruit, such as strawberries, peaches, or even cheese. *Bignè* are cream puff-like pastries filled with *zabaione* (egg yolks, sugar, and Marsala wine). *Tartufo* is a rich dark-chocolate gelato ball with a cherry inside, sometimes served *con panna* (with whipped cream). When you're out and about on a hot day, try a *grattachecca* (flavored, sweetened shaved ice) from a vendor's stand.

Local Wines *(Vini)*: Frascati, probably the best-known wine of the region, is an inexpensive dry white. Others are Castelli Romani, Marino, Colli Albani, and Velletri. Torre Ercolana is a medium-bodied red made from the regional cesanese grape, as well as cabernet and merlot (known as the region's best-quality red, aged at least five years).

all'amatriciana (Mon-Sat 12:30-15:00 & 19:15-23:00, closed Sun and Aug, reservations smart, a block past the entrance to the big tunnel near the Trevi Fountain, corner of Via Rasella and Via del Boccaccio, tel. 06-474-5284, www.hostariaromana.it).

$$ L'Antica Birreria Peroni is Rome's answer to a German beer hall. Serving hearty mugs of Peroni beer and lots of beerhall food and Italian classics, the place is a hit with Romans for a cheap night out (Mon-Sat 12:00-24:00, closed Sun, midway between Trevi Fountain and Capitoline Hill, a block off Via del Corso at Via di San Marcello 19, tel. 06-679-5310).

Close to the Pantheon

Eating on the square facing the Pantheon is a temptation worth considering, but a block or two away, you'll get fewer views and better value.

$$$$ Ristorante da Fortunato is an Italian classic, with fresh flowers on the tables and white-coated waiters serving good meat and fish to dignitaries and tourists with good taste. On the walls, everyone from Muammar Gaddafi and Prince Charles to Bill Clinton are pictured with the late Signore Fortunato, who started this restaurant in 1975. For a dressy night out, this is a worthwhile splurge—reserve ahead (figure €50 per person, daily 12:30-23:30, a block in front of the Pantheon at Via del Pantheon 55, tel. 06-679-2788, www.ristorantefortunato.it).

$$ Enoteca Corsi is a wine shop that grew into a thriving lunch spot, serving traditional cuisine to an appreciative crowd of office workers. Kids do their homework at the family table in back. Enjoy pastas, main dishes, and fine wine at a third of the price of most restaurants—buy from their shop and pay a corking fee (Mon-Sat 12:00-15:30, Thu-Fri also 19:00-22:30, closed Sun, no reservations, a block toward the Pantheon from Gesù Church at Via del Gesù 87, tel. 06-679-0821).

$$$ Ristorante la Campana is an authentic slice of old Rome, claiming a history dating to 1518. It still serves appreciative locals typical Roman dishes and daily specials, plus a good self-service *antipasti* buffet (Tue-Sun 12:30-15:00 & 19:30-23:00, closed Mon, inside seating only, reserve for dinner, just off Via della Scrofa and Piazza Nicosia at Vicolo della Campana 18, tel. 06-687-5273, www.ristorantelacampana.com).

$$ Osteria delle Coppelle, a slapdash, trendy place, serves traditional dishes to a local crowd. It has a rustic interior, jumbled exterior seating, and a fun selection of €3 *cicchetti*. They also have a much classier dining section in the back (12:30-16:00 & 19:00-late, Piazza delle Coppelle 54, tel. 06-4550-2826).

$$ Miscellanea is run by much-loved Mikki, who's on a mission to keep foreign students well-fed with inexpensive, hearty food. It's a good value in a convenient location (daily 10:00-24:00, just behind the Pantheon at Via della Palombella 37, tel. 06-6813-5318).

North Rome

Near the Spanish Steps and Ara Pacis

These restaurants are located near the route of the "Dolce Vita Stroll" (see map on page 328).

$$$ Ristorante il Gabriello is inviting and small—modern under medieval arches—serving creative Roman cuisine using farm-fresh, organic products. Trust your waiter and say, "Bring it on." The atmosphere is fun and convivial. Invest €55—not including wine—in "Claudio's Extravaganza," created especially for my readers—it's not on the menu (dinner only, Mon-Sat 19:00-23:00, closed Sun, reservations smart, air-con, dress respectfully—no shorts, 3 blocks from Spanish Steps at Via Vittoria 51, tel. 06-6994-0810, www.ilgabriello.com).

$$ Antica Enoteca is an upbeat, atmospheric 200-plus-year-old *enoteca*. For a light lunch, enjoy a glass of their best wine at the bar (listed on a big blackboard) and

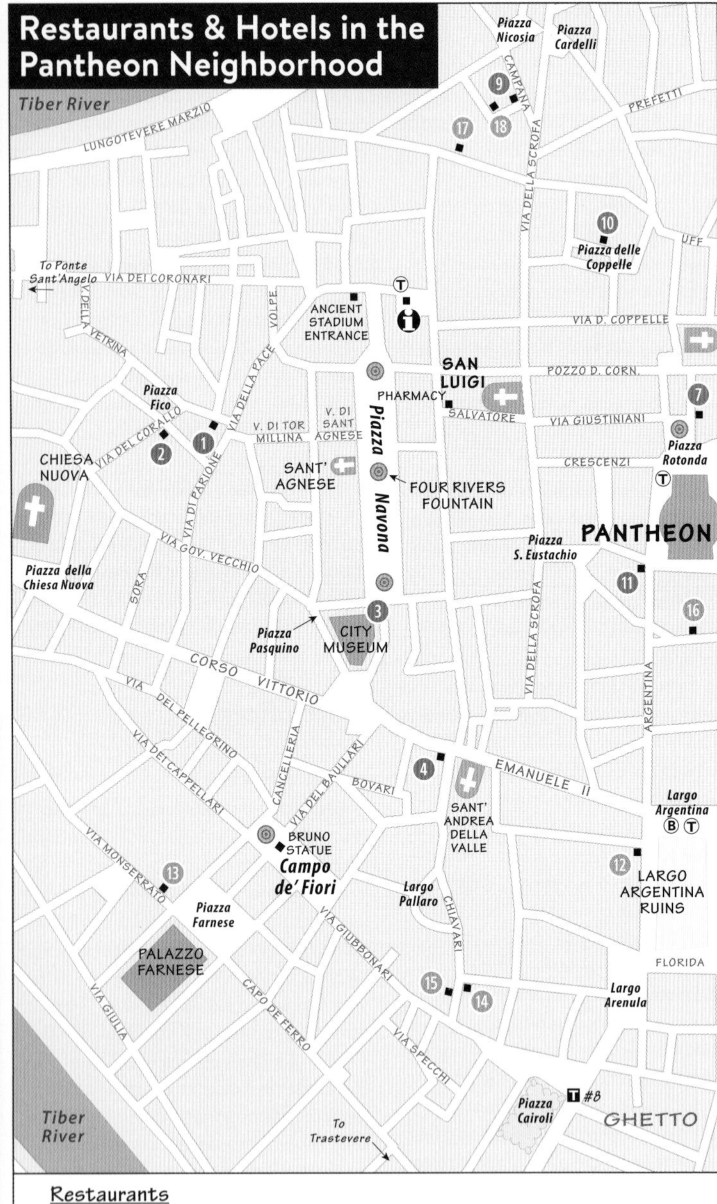

Restaurants

1. Ristorante & Bar del Fico
2. Rist. Pizzeria "da Francesco"
3. Vivi Bistrot
4. L'Insalata Ricca
5. To Hostaria Romana
6. L'Antica Birreria Peroni
7. Ristorante da Fortunato
8. Enoteca Corsi
9. Ristorante la Campana
10. Osteria delle Coppelle
11. Miscellanea

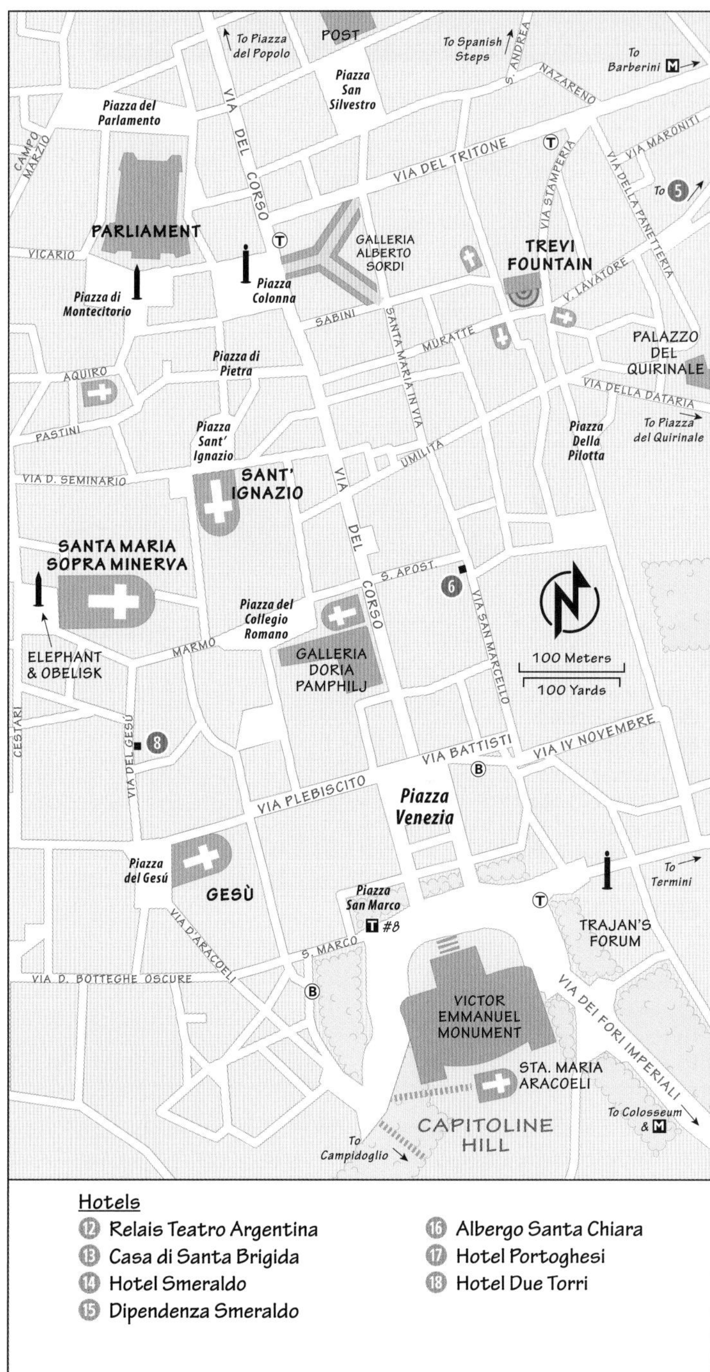
To Piazza del Popolo
POST
To Spanish Steps
To Barberini
Piazza San Silvestro
Piazza del Parlamento
CAMPO MARZIO
VIA DEL CORSO
S. ANDREA
NAZARENO
VIA DEL TRITONE
VIA STAMPERIA
VIA MARONITI
VIA DELLA PANETTERIA
To 5
PARLIAMENT
VICARIO
GALLERIA ALBERTO SORDI
TREVI FOUNTAIN
Piazza di Montecitorio
Piazza Colonna
V. LAVATORE
SABINI
SANTA MARIA IN VIA
MURATTE
PALAZZO DEL QUIRINALE
Piazza di Pietra
AQUIRO
VIA DELLA DATARIA
To Piazza del Quirinale
PASTINI
Piazza Sant' Ignazio
Piazza Della Pilotta
UMILTÀ
VIA D. SEMINARIO
SANT' IGNAZIO
SANTA MARIA SOPRA MINERVA
S. APOST.
6
VIA SAN MARCELLO
Piazza del Collegio Romano
ELEPHANT & OBELISK
MARMO
GALLERIA DORIA PAMPHILJ
100 Meters
100 Yards
CESTARI
VIA DEL GESÙ
8
VIA BATTISTI
VIA IV NOVEMBRE
VIA PLEBISCITO
Piazza Venezia
Piazza del Gesú
GESÙ
Piazza San Marco
#8
To Termini
TRAJAN'S FORUM
VIA D'ARACOELI
S. MARCO
VIA D. BOTTEGHE OSCURE
VIA DEI FORI IMPERIALI
VICTOR EMMANUEL MONUMENT
STA. MARIA ARACOELI
CAPITOLINE HILL
To Colosseum &
To Campidoglio
Hotels
12 Relais Teatro Argentina
13 Casa di Santa Brigida
14 Hotel Smeraldo
15 Dipendenza Smeraldo
16 Albergo Santa Chiara
17 Hotel Portoghesi
18 Hotel Due Torri

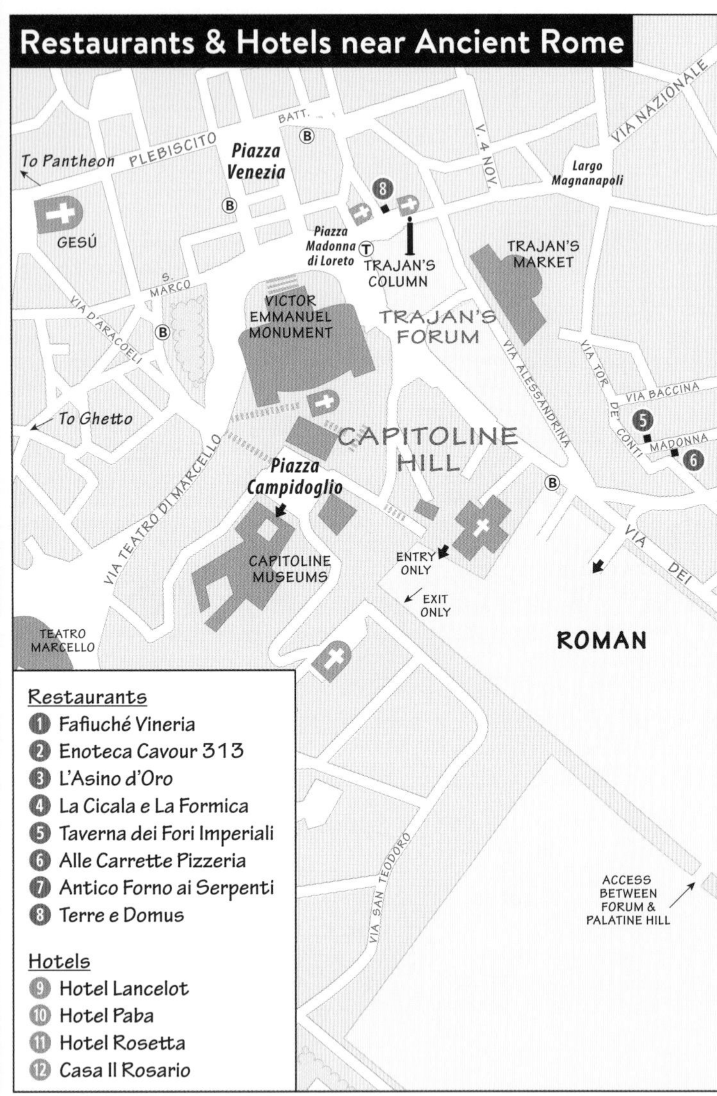

split their €22 *antipasti* plate of veggies, *salumi,* and cheese (daily 12:00-24:00, reserve for outdoor seating, Via della Croce 76B, tel. 06-679-0896).

Ancient Rome

Near the Colosseum and Forum

Within a block of the Colosseum and Forum, eateries cater to weary sightseers, offering neither memorable food nor good value. To get your money's worth, head to the Monti neighborhood. From the Forum, head up Via Cavour and then left on Via dei Serpenti; the action centers on Piazza della Madonna dei Monti and nearby lanes.

$$$ L'Asino d'Oro ("The Golden Donkey"), a top choice for foodies, serves Umbrian cuisine with a creative twist—

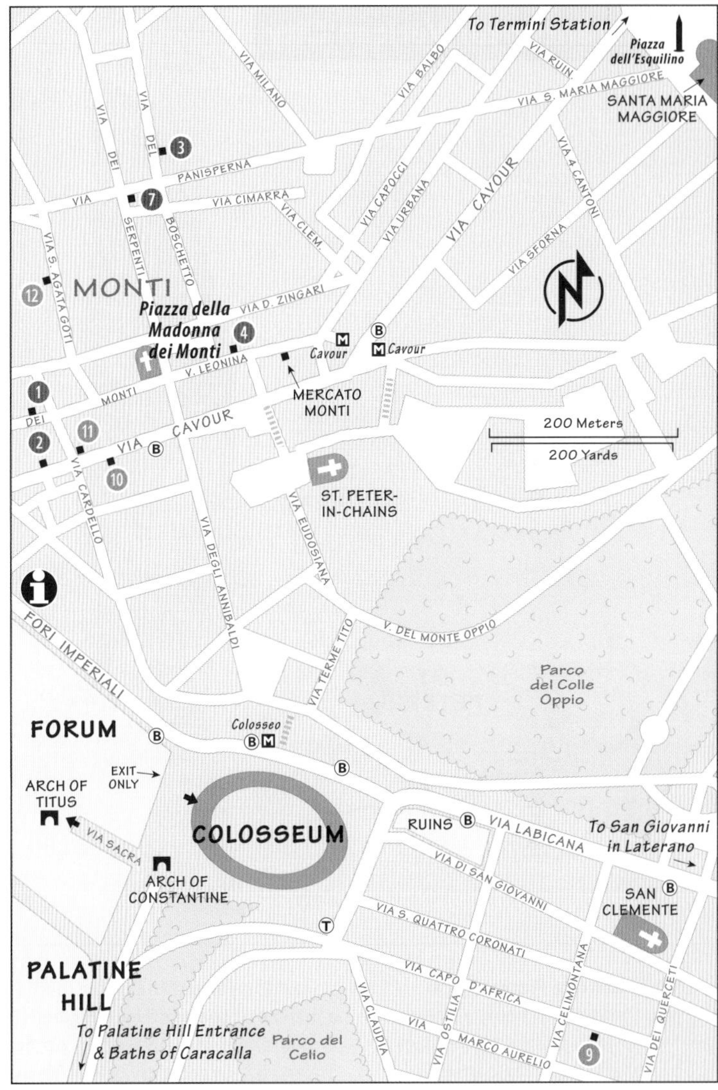

mingling savory and sweet. The modern space is filled with savvy diners (Tue-Sat 12:30-14:30 & 19:30-23:00, closed Sun-Mon, reserve for dinner, Via del Boschetto 73, tel. 06-4891-3832).

$$ La Cicala e La Formica has its own nook on Via Leonina. While a bit tired, with a forgettable menu, it has an old-school coziness, and a terrace good for people-watching (daily 12:00-16:00 & 18:30-22:30, Via Leonina 17, tel. 06-481-7490).

$$ Taverna dei Fori Imperiali serves typical Roman cuisine in a snug interior that bustles with energy (Wed-Mon 12:30-15:00 & 19:30-23:00, closed Tue, reserve for dinner, Via della Madonna dei Monti 9, tel. 06-679-8643, www.latavernadeiforiimperiali.com).

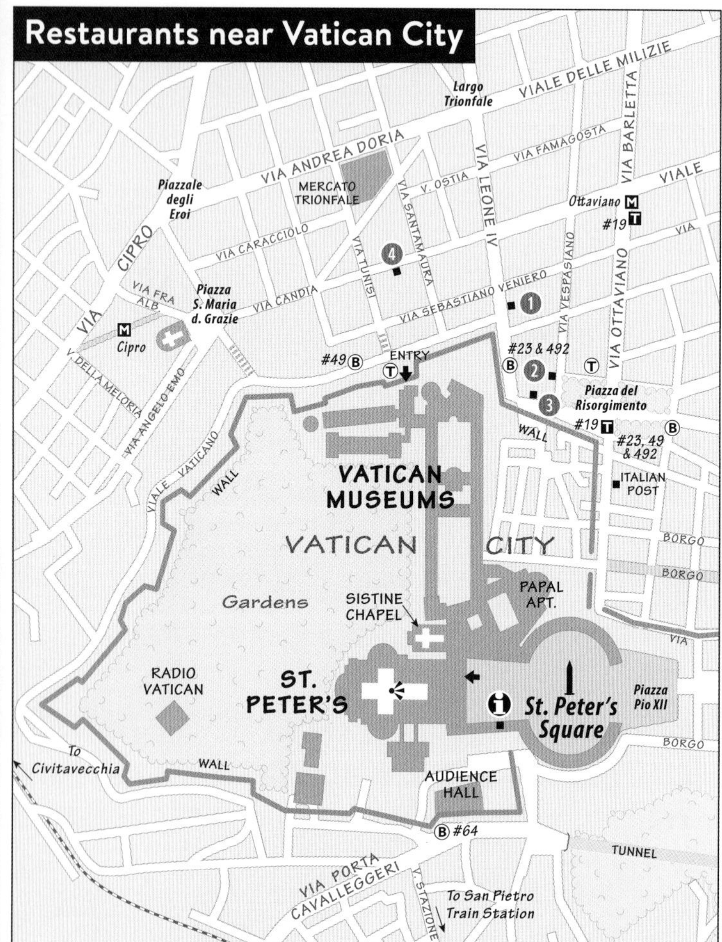

$$ Alle Carrette Pizzeria—simple, rustic, and family-friendly—serves great wood-fired pizza in Monti (daily 19:00-24:00, Vicolo delle Carrette 14, tel. 06-679-2770).

$ Antico Forno ai Serpenti, a hip bakery with a few simple tables, puts out a small selection of *panini,* baked potatoes, and lasagna. They also bake good bread and pastries and do breakfasts (order at the counter, daily 8:00-20:00, Via dei Serpenti 122, tel. 06-4542-7920).

$$ Terre e Domus, a modern eatery on the otherwise unwelcoming Piazza Venezia, has a peaceful dining room and a menu that shows off local ingredients and cuisine (daily 9:00-23:00, Foro Traiano 82, immediately below Trajan's Column, tel. 06-6994-0273).

Near Vatican City

Eateries near the Vatican cater to exhausted tourists. Avoid the restaurant pushers handing out fliers: Their venues have bad food and expensive menu tricks. Tide yourself over with a slice of pizza or at any of these eateries and save your splurges for elsewhere.

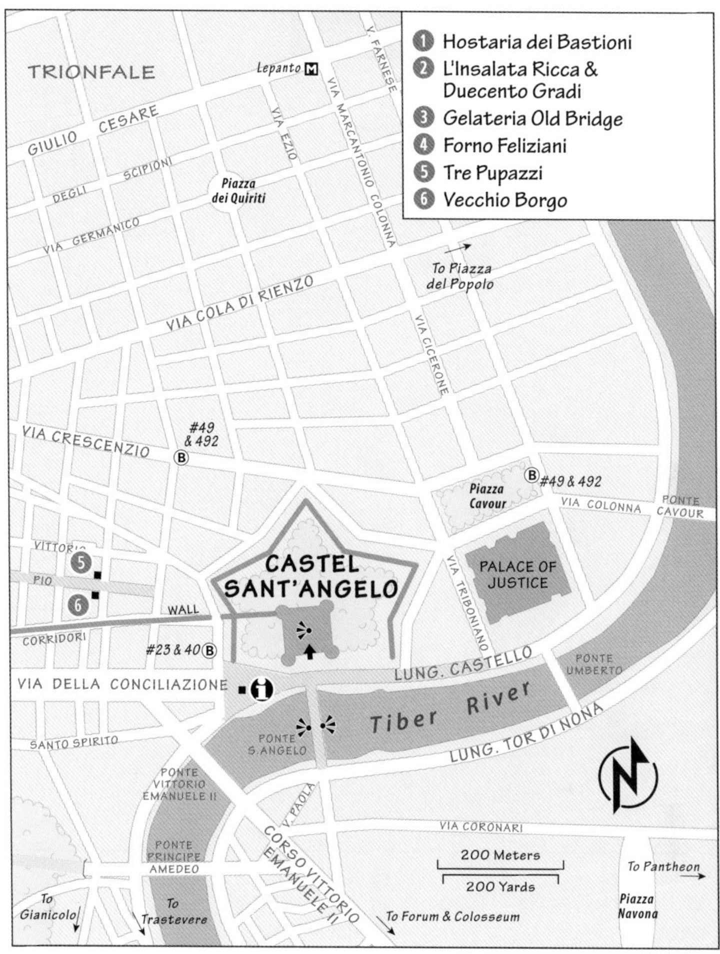

These listings are mostly fast and cheap, a stone's throw from the Vatican wall, near Piazza Risorgimento: **$$ Hostaria dei Bastioni** has noisy streetside seating and a quiet interior (Mon-Sat 12:00-15:00 & 18:00-23:00, closed Sun, at corner of Vatican wall at Via Leone IV 29, tel. 06-3972-3034); **$ L'Insalata Ricca** serves hearty salads and pastas (daily 12:00-23:30, across from Vatican walls at Piazza Risorgimento 5, tel. 06-3973-0387); and **$ Duecento Gradi** is a good bet for fresh and creative, though a bit pricey, €5-8 sandwiches (daily 10:30-24:00, Piazza Risorgimento 3, tel. 06-3975-4239). For a treat, try **Gelateria Old Bridge,** which scoops up hearty portions of fresh gelato for tourists and nuns alike (just off Piazza Risorgimento across from Vatican walls at Viale dei Bastioni di Michelangelo 3).

$ Forno Feliziani serves nicely presented pizza by the slice and simple cafeteria-style dishes that you can eat in or take out (closed Sun, Via Candia 61).

The pedestrians-only **Borgo Pio**—a block from Piazza San Pietro near St. Peter's Basilica—has restaurants worth a

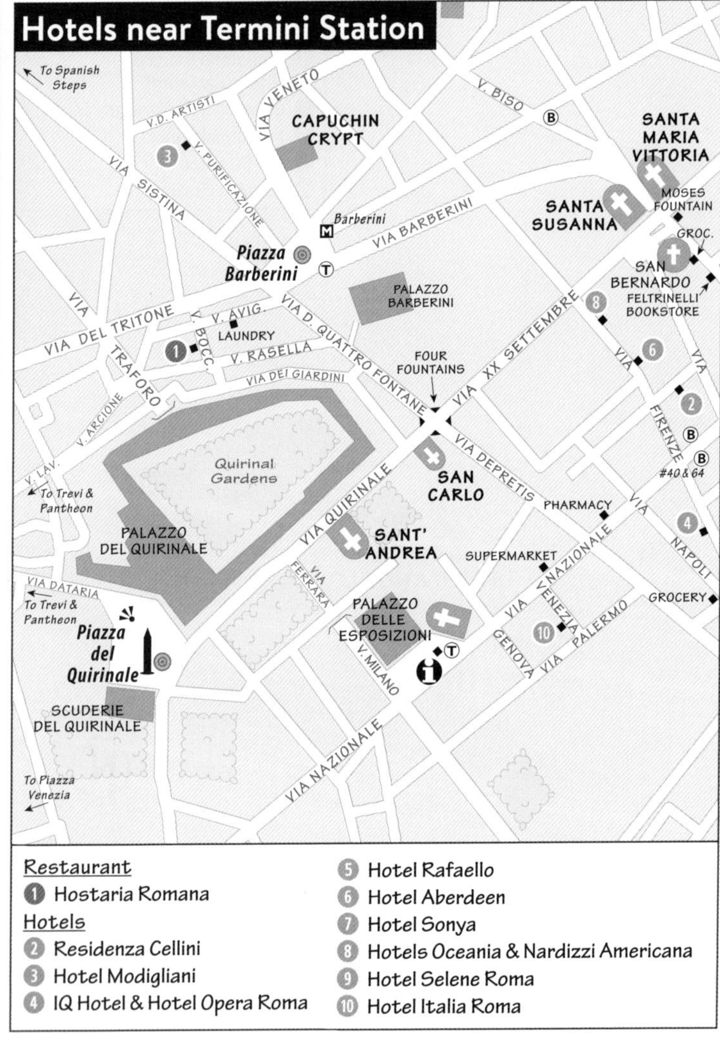

look. Consider **$$ Tre Pupazzi** (Mon-Sat 12:00-15:00 & 19:00-23:00, closed Sun, at the corner of Via Tre Pupazzi and Borgo Pio) or **$ Vecchio Borgo,** across the street (daily 9:30-22:30, Borgo Pio 27a).

SLEEPING

Choosing the right neighborhood in Rome is as important as choosing the right hotel. All of my recommended accommodations are in safe, pleasant areas convenient to sightseeing.

Near Termini Train Station

The Termini train station neighborhood is handy for public transit and services. While not as charming as other areas of Rome, the hotels near Termini train station are less expensive. The city's two main Metro lines intersect at the station, and most buses leave from here. Most of these hotels are a

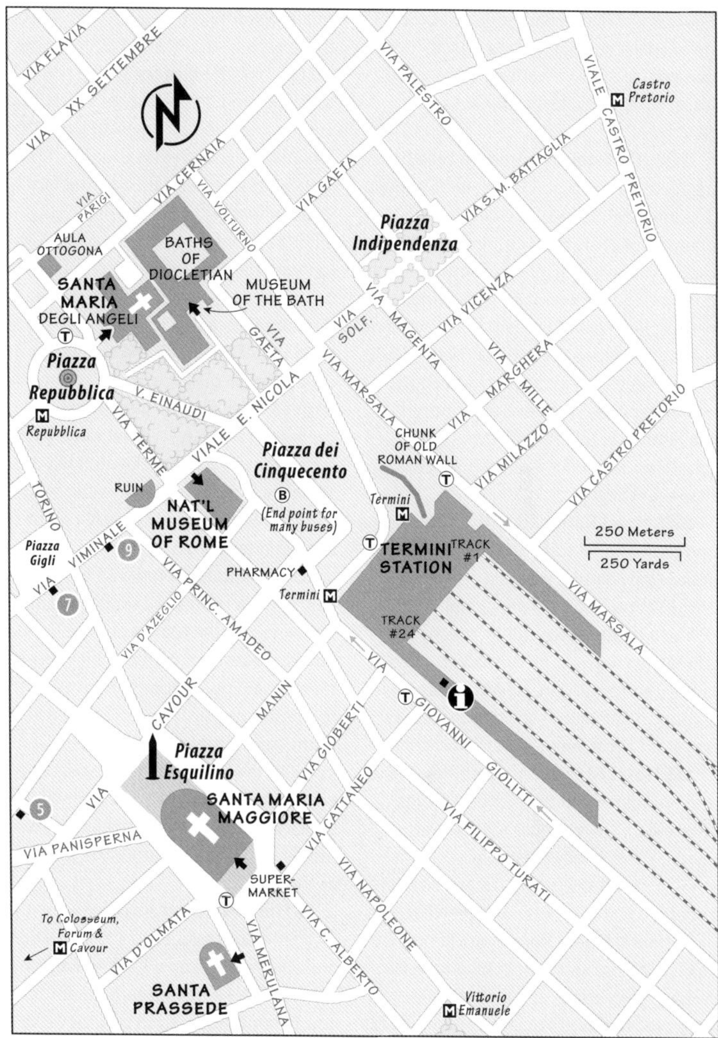

10-minute walk west of the station, on or near Via Firenze, a safe, handy, central, and relatively quiet street. The Defense Ministry is nearby, so you've got heavily armed guards watching over you all night.

$$$$ Residenza Cellini feels like the guest wing of a gorgeous Neoclassical palace. It offers 11 rooms, "ortho/anti-allergy beds," four-star comforts and service, and a small, breezy terrace (RS%, air-con, elevator, Via Modena 5, third floor, tel. 06-4782-5204, www.residenzacellini.it, info@residenzacellini.it; Barbara, Gaetano, and Donato).

$$$$ Hotel Modigliani, a delightful 23-room place, is energetically run in a clean, bright, minimalist yet in-love-with-life style that its artist namesake would appreciate. It has a vast and plush lounge, a garden, and a newsletter introducing you to each of the staff (RS%, air-con, elevator; northwest of Via Firenze—from Tritone

Fountain on Piazza Barberini, go 2 blocks up Via della Purificazione to #42; tel. 06-4281-5226, www.hotelmodigliani.com, info@hotelmodigliani.com, Giulia and Marco).

$$$$ IQ Hotel, in a modern blue building facing the Opera House, feels almost Scandinavian in its efficiency. It lacks charm, but more than compensates with modern amenities. Its 88 rooms are fresh and spacious, the roof garden comes with a play area and foosball, and vending machines dispense bottles of wine (RS%, family rooms, breakfast extra, air-con, elevator, cheap self-service laundry, gym, Via Firenze 8, tel. 06-488-0465, www.iqhotelroma.it, info@iqhotelroma.it, manager Diego).

$$$$ Hotel Raffaello, with its courteous and professional staff, offers 41 rooms in a grand 19th-century building on the edge of the Monti district. This formal hotel comes with generous public spaces and a breakfast room fit for aristocrats (RS%, family rooms, air-con, elevator, Via Urbana 3, Metro: Cavour, tel. 06-488-4342, www.hotelraffaello.it, info@hotelraffaello.it).

$$$ Hotel Aberdeen, combines quality and friendliness, with 36 comfy rooms (RS%—use "Rick Steves reader reservations" link, family rooms, air-con, Via Firenze 48, tel. 06-482-3920, www.hotelaberdeen.it, info@hotelaberdeen.it).

$$$ Hotel Opera Roma, with contemporary furnishings and marble accents, boasts 15 spacious, modern, and thoughtfully appointed rooms. It's quiet and just a stone's throw from the Opera House (air-con, elevator, Via Firenze 11, tel. 06-487-1787, www.hoteloperaroma.com, info@hoteloperaroma.com, Reza, Litu, and Federica).

$$$ Hotel Sonya offers 40 well-equipped if small rooms, a hearty breakfast, and decent prices (family rooms, air-con, elevator, faces the Opera House at Via Viminale 58, tel. 06-481-9911, www.hotelsonya.it, info@hotelsonya.it, Francesca and Ivan).

$$ Hotel Oceania is a peaceful slice of air-conditioned heaven. The 24 rooms are spacious, quiet, and tastefully decorated, and the elegant sitting room has a manor-house feel. Stefano runs a fine staff, serves wonderful coffee, provides lots of thoughtful extra touches, and works hard to maintain a caring family atmosphere (RS%—use code "RICKSTEVES," family rooms, elevator, TV lounge, Via Firenze 38, third floor, tel. 06-482-4696, www.hoteloceania.it, info@hoteloceania.it).

$$ Hotel Selene Roma spreads its 40 stylish rooms out on a few floors of a big palazzo. With elegant furnishings and room to breathe, it's a good value (RS%, family rooms, air-con, elevator, Via del Viminale 8, reception at #10, tel. 06-474-4781, www.hotelseleneroma.it, reception@hotelseleneroma.it).

$$ Hotel Italia Roma, in a busy and handy locale, is located safely on a quiet street next to the Ministry of the Interior. It has 35 modest but comfortable rooms plus four newer, more expensive "residenza" rooms on the third floor (RS%, family rooms, air-con, elevator, Via Venezia 18, just off Via Nazionale, tel. 06-482-8355, www.hotelitaliaroma.it, info@hotelitaliaroma.it). They offer eight similar annex rooms across the street for the same price as the main hotel.

$$ Hotel Nardizzi Americana, with a small rooftop terrace, 40 standard rooms, and a laidback atmosphere, is a decent value (RS%—email reservation for discount, family rooms, air-con, elevator, Via Firenze 38, fourth floor, tel. 06-488-0035, www.hotelnardizzi.it, info@hotelnardizzi.it; friendly Stefano, Fabrizio, Mario, and Giancarlo).

Near Ancient Rome

Stretching from the Colosseum to Piazza Venezia, this area is central. Sightseers are a short walk from the Colosseum, Roman Forum, and Trajan's Column—as well as restaurants and shopping in the Monti district. All except Hotel Lancelot are within a 10-minute walk of the Cavour Metro stop.

$$$$ Hotel Lancelot is a comfortable refuge—a 60-room hotel with an elegant feel, fair price, and located in a pleasant residential neighborhood a 10-minute stroll from the Colosseum. It's quiet and safe, with a shady courtyard, restaurant, bar, and tiny communal sixth-floor terrace (family rooms, some view rooms, air-con, elevator, good €25 dinner, wheelchair-accessible, cheap parking, near San Clemente Church at Via Capo d'Africa 47, tel. 06-7045-0615, www.lancelothotel.com, info@lancelothotel.com). Faris and Lubna speak the Queen's English.

$$ Hotel Paba is cozy, with fresh, chocolate-box-tidy rooms. It's just two blocks from the Forum. Even though some rooms overlook busy Via Cavour, it's quiet enough (RS%, email reservations preferred, big beds, breakfast served in room, air-con, elevator, Via Cavour 266, second floor, tel. 06-4782-4902, www.hotelpaba.com, info@hotelpaba.com).

$$ Casa Il Rosario is a peaceful, well-run Dominican convent renting 40 rooms with monastic simplicity to both pilgrims and tourists in a steep but pleasant corner of the Monti neighborhood. Doubles have two single beds that can be pushed together (cheaper single rooms with shared bath, reserve several months in advance, some rooms with air-con and others with fans, elevator, small garden and rooftop terrace, 23:00 curfew, near bottom of Via Nazionale at Via Sant'Agata dei Goti 10, bus #40 or #170 from Termini, tel. 06-679-2346, www.casailrosarioroma.it, irodopre@tin.it).

$ Hotel Rosetta, a homey and family-run *pensione,* rents 15 simple rooms. It's pretty minimal, with no lounge and no breakfast, but its great location makes it a fine budget option (air-con, up one flight of stairs, Via Cavour 295, tel. 06-4782-3069, www.rosettahotel.com, info@rosettahotel.com, Antonietta and Francesca).

Pantheon Neighborhood

The most romantic ambience is in neighborhoods near the Pantheon. Winding, narrow lanes are filled with foot traffic and lined with boutique shops and tiny trattorias...Rome at its best. Buses and taxis are the only practical way to connect with other destinations. The atmosphere doesn't come cheap, but this is where you want to be—especially at night.

This neighborhood has two main transportation hubs: Piazza delle Cinque Lune (just north of Piazza Navona) has a TI, a taxi stand, and (just around the corner) handy buses #81 and #87; Largo Argentina has buses to almost everywhere and a taxi stand.

Near Campo de' Fiori

You'll pay a premium (and endure a little extra night noise), but these places are set deep in the tangled back streets near idyllic Campo de' Fiori.

$$$$ Relais Teatro Argentina, a six-room gem, is steeped in tasteful old-Rome elegance, but has all the modern comforts. It's cozy and quiet like a B&B and couldn't be more centrally located (air-con, 3 flights of stairs, breakfast in room or on balcony, Via del Sudario 35, tel. 06-9893-1617, www.relaisteatroargentina.com, info@relaisteatroargentina.com, kind Paolo).

$$$$ Casa di Santa Brigida overlooks the elegant Piazza Farnese. With soft-spoken sisters gliding down polished hallways and pearly gates instead of doors, this lavish 20-room convent makes exhaust-stained Roman tourists feel like they've died and gone to heaven. If you don't need a double bed or a TV in your room, it's worth the splurge—especially if you luxuriate in its ample public spaces or on its lovely roof terrace (book well in advance, air-con, elevator, tasty €25 dinners, roof garden, plush library, Via di Monserrato 54, tel. 06-6889-2596, www.brigidine.org, piazzafarnese@brigidine.org).

$$$ Hotel Smeraldo, with 66 rooms, is clean and a reasonable deal in a good location. Sixteen of the rooms are in an annex across the street, but everyone has breakfast in the main building (RS%—use code "ricksteves," air-con, elevator, flowery roof terrace, midway between Campo de' Fiori and Largo Argentina at Via dei Chiavari 20, tel. 06-687-5929, www.smeraldoroma.com, info@smeraldoroma.com; Massimo and Walter).

Close to the Pantheon

These places are buried in the pedestrian-friendly heart of ancient Rome, about a five-minute walk from the Pantheon. They're an easy walk from many sights, but are a bit distant from the major public transportation arteries.

$$$$ Albergo Santa Chiara, in the old center, is big and solid, with marbled elegance (but basic furniture) and all the hotel services. Its ample public lounges are dressy and professional, and its 97 rooms are quiet and spacious (RS%, family rooms, air-con, elevator, behind the Pantheon at Via di Santa Chiara 21, tel. 06-687-2979, www.albergosantachiara.com, info@albergosantachiara.com).

$$$$ Hotel Portoghesi is a classic hotel with 27 colorful rooms in the medieval heart of Rome. It's peaceful, quiet, and calmly run, and comes with a delightful roof terrace—though you pay for the location (family rooms, breakfast on roof, air-con, elevator, Via dei Portoghesi 1, tel. 06-686-4231, www.hotelportoghesiroma.it, info@hotelportoghesiroma.it).

$$$$ Hotel Due Torri, hiding out on a tiny quiet street, is beautifully located. It feels professional yet homey, with an accommodating staff, generous public spaces, and 26 rooms (the ones on upper floors are smaller but have views). While the location is great, the rooms are overpriced unless you score a discount (family rooms, air-con, elevator, a block off Via della Scrofa at Vicolo del Leonetto 23, tel. 06-6880-6956, www.hotelduetorriroma.com, info@hotelduetorriroma.com, Cinzia).

TRANSPORTATION

Getting Around Rome

The cheap, efficient public transportation system consists primarily of buses, a few trams, and three Metro lines. For information, visit www.atac.roma.it, which has a useful route planner in English, or call 06-57003. If you have a smartphone and an international data plan, consider downloading the free apps "Roma Bus" (by Movenda) or "Muoversi a Roma."

Buying Tickets

All public transportation uses the same ticket (€1.50), valid for one Metro ride—including transfers underground—plus unlimited city buses and trams during a 100-minute period. Passes good on buses and the Metro are sold in increments of 24 hours (€7), 48 hours (€12.50), 72 hours (€18), one week (€24, about the cost of three taxi rides), and one month (€35, plus €3 for the rechargeable card, valid for a calendar month).

You can purchase tickets and passes from machines at Metro stations and a few major bus stops (cash only), and from some newsstands and tobacco shops (*tabacchi,* marked by a black-and-white T sign). Tickets are not sold on board.

Validate your ticket at the Metro turnstile (magnetic-strip-side up, arrow-side first) or in the machine when you board the bus (magnetic-strip-side down, arrow-side first). It'll return with your expiration time printed on it. To get through a Metro turnstile with a transit pass or Roma Pass, press the card to the turnstile's electronic sensor pad. On buses and trams, you need to validate your pass only on your first time using it.

Rick's Tip: Stock up on Metro tickets early *(or buy a Roma Pass) to avoid wasting time searching for an open tobacco shop that sells tickets.*

By Metro

The Roman subway system ("Metro") is simple, clean, cheap, and fast. The two lines you need to know—A and B—intersect at Termini Station. The Metro runs from 5:30 to 23:30 (Fri-Sat until 1:30 in the morning). The partly finished C line serves only a suburb of little use to tourists.

Rick's Tip: Beware of pickpockets *when boarding, while on board, and when leaving buses and subways. To experience less crowding and commotion—and less risk—***wait for the end cars** *of a subway rather than boarding the middle cars.*

By Bus

The Metro is handy, but it won't get you everywhere—take the bus (or tram). Bus routes are listed at each stop. Route and system maps aren't posted, but with some knowledge of major stops, you can wing it without one. (The ATAC website has a PDF bus map that you can download, bookstores sell paper transport maps, and the various ATAC journey planners are helpful.) Rome's few tram lines function nearly identically to buses.

Regular bus lines start running about 5:30, and during the day run every 10-15 minutes or so. After 23:30 (and sometimes earlier) and on Sundays, buses are less frequent. Night buses are marked with an *N* and an owl symbol on the bus-stop signs. The exact frequency of various bus routes is difficult to predict (and not printed at bus stops). At major stops, an electronic board shows the number of minutes until the next buses arrive.

Bus #64: Links Termini Station with the Vatican, stopping at Piazza della Repubblica (sights), Via Nazionale (recommended hotels), Piazza Venezia (near Forum), Largo Argentina (near Pantheon and Campo de' Fiori), St. Peter's Basilica (get off just past the tunnel), and San Pietro Station.

Bus #40: This express bus mostly follows the #64 route but has fewer stops and fewer crowds. It ends near Castel Sant'Angelo (Hadrian's Tomb, a 10-minute walk from St. Peter's) on the Vatican side of the river.

Rick's Tip: Buses #64 and #40 *are popular with tourists and* **pickpockets.** *If one bus is packed, there's likely a second one on its tail with fewer crowds and thieves.*

Other useful routes include:

Bus #16: Termini Station, Santa Maria Maggiore, and San Giovanni in Laterano.

Bus #49: Piazza Cavour/Castel Sant'Angelo, Piazza Risorgimento (Vatican), and Vatican Museums.

Bus #62: Tiburtina, Piazza Barberini, Piazza Venezia, Piazza Pia (near Castel Sant'Angelo).

Bus #81: San Giovanni in Laterano, Largo Argentina, and Piazza Risorgimento (Vatican).

Buses #85 and #87: Piazza Navona (#87 only), Pantheon, Via del Corso (#85 only), Piazza Venezia, Forum, Colosseum, San Clemente, and San Giovanni in Laterano.

Bus #492: Travels east-west across the city, connecting Tiburtina (train and bus stations), Largo Santa Susanna (near Piazza della Repubblica), Piazza Barberini, Piazza Venezia, Largo Argentina (near Pantheon and Campo de' Fiori), Piazza Cavour (Castel Sant'Angelo), and Piazza Risorgimento (St. Peter's Basilica and Vatican).

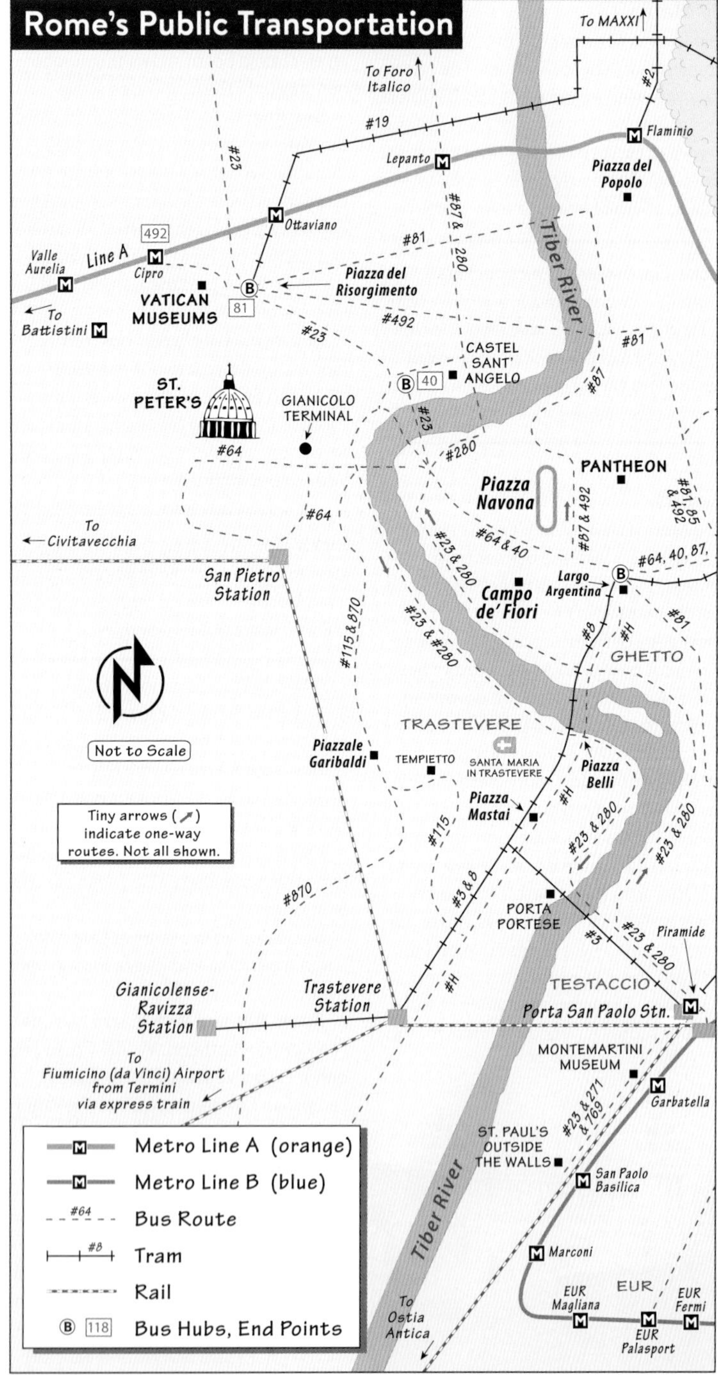
Rome's Public Transportation
To MAXXI
To Foro Italico
#19
#2
Flaminio
Lepanto
Piazza del Popolo
#23
#87 & 280
Ottaviano
Tiber River
#81
492
Line A
Valle Aurelia
Cipro
VATICAN MUSEUMS
Piazza del Risorgimento
81
To Battistini
#492
#23
#81
CASTEL SANT' ANGELO
40
#87
ST. PETER'S
GIANICOLO TERMINAL
#23
#280
#64
PANTHEON
Piazza Navona
#81, 85 & 492
#64
#87 & 492
To Civitavecchia
#23 & 280
#64 & 40
#64, 40, 87,
San Pietro Station
Largo Argentina
Campo de' Fiori
#115 & 870
#23 & #280
#8
#H
#81
GHETTO
Not to Scale
TRASTEVERE
Piazzale Garibaldi
TEMPIETTO
SANTA MARIA IN TRASTEVERE
Piazza Belli
Piazza Mastai
#H
Tiny arrows ( ) indicate one-way routes. Not all shown.
#115
#23 & 280
#23 & 280
#870
#3 & 8
PORTA PORTESE
#3
#23 & 280
Piramide
TESTACCIO
#H
Gianicolense-Ravizza Station
Trastevere Station
Porta San Paolo Stn.
MONTEMARTINI MUSEUM
To Fiumicino (da Vinci) Airport from Termini via express train
Garbatella
#23 & 271 & 769
Metro Line A (orange)
ST. PAUL'S OUTSIDE THE WALLS
Metro Line B (blue)
San Paolo Basilica
#64
Bus Route
Tiber River
#8
Tram
Marconi
Rail
EUR
EUR Magliana
EUR Fermi
118
Bus Hubs, End Points
To Ostia Antica
EUR Palasport

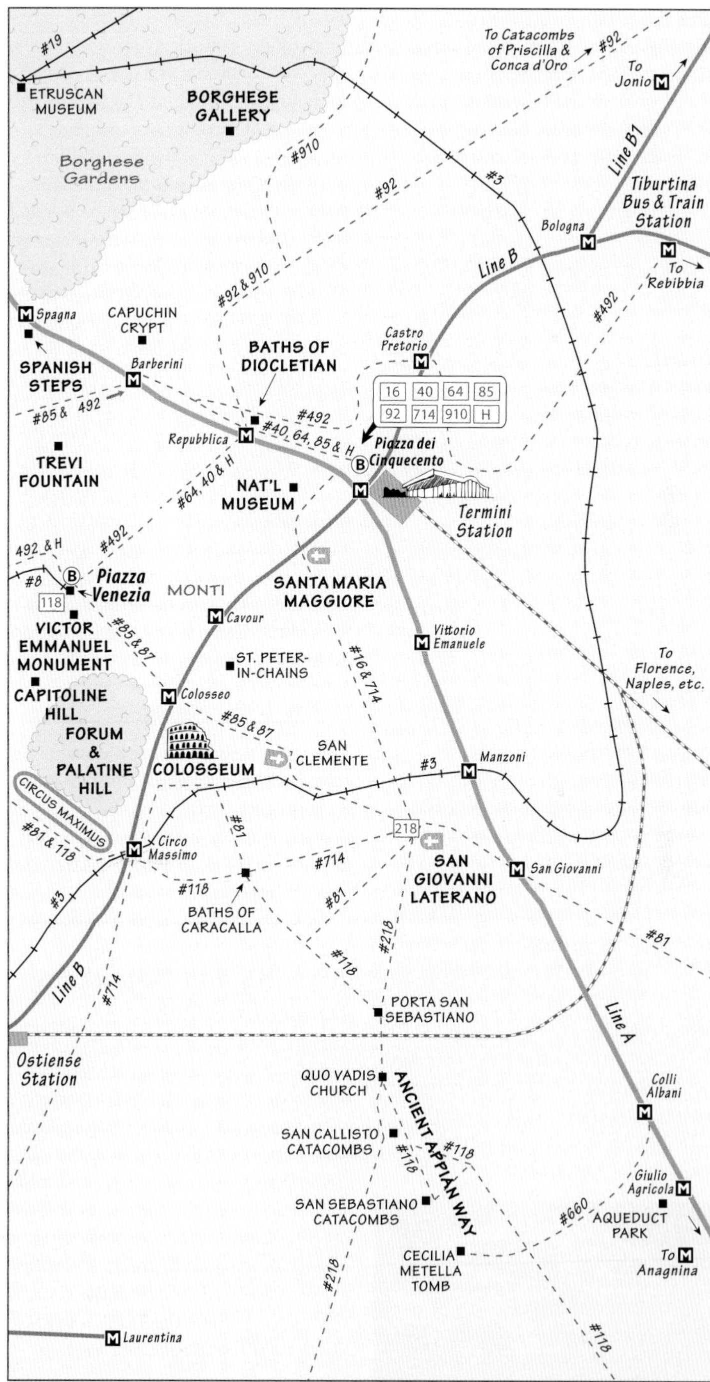
#19
ETRUSCAN MUSEUM
BORGHESE GALLERY
Borghese Gardens
To Catacombs of Priscilla & Conca d'Oro
#92
To Jonio
Line B1
#910
#92
#3
Tiburtina Bus & Train Station
Bologna
Line B
To Rebibbia
#92 & 910
#492
Spagna
CAPUCHIN CRYPT
SPANISH STEPS
Barberini
BATHS OF DIOCLETIAN
Castro Pretorio
16 40 64 85
92 714 910 H
#85 & 492
#492
Repubblica
#40, 64, 85 & H
Piazza dei Cinquecento
TREVI FOUNTAIN
NAT'L MUSEUM
#64, 40 & H
Termini Station
492 & H
#492
#8
Piazza Venezia
118
MONTI
SANTA MARIA MAGGIORE
VICTOR EMMANUEL MONUMENT
Cavour
#85 & 87
Vittorio Emanuele
ST. PETER-IN-CHAINS
#16 & 714
To Florence, Naples, etc.
CAPITOLINE HILL
Colosseo
FORUM & PALATINE HILL
#85 & 87
COLOSSEUM
SAN CLEMENTE
#3
Manzoni
CIRCUS MAXIMUS
#81
218
#81 & 118
Circo Massimo
#714
SAN GIOVANNI LATERANO
San Giovanni
#118
BATHS OF CARACALLA
#81
#3
#118
#218
#81
Line B
#714
PORTA SAN SEBASTIANO
Line A
Ostiense Station
QUO VADIS CHURCH
ANCIENT APPIAN WAY
Colli Albani
SAN CALLISTO CATACOMBS
#118
#118
Giulio Agricola
SAN SEBASTIANO CATACOMBS
#660
AQUEDUCT PARK
CECILIA METELLA TOMB
To Anagnina
#218
#118
Laurentina

Bus #714: Termini Station, Santa Maria Maggiore, and San Giovanni in Laterano.

Tram #3: Zips from the Colosseum to San Giovanni (and onward to Valle Giulia) in one direction, and to Piramide/Testaccio (and onward to Trastevere) in the other.

Tram #19: Connects Piazza del Risorgimento and the Ottaviano Metro stop (by the Vatican Museums) to the Etruscan Museum and Villa Borghese.

By Taxi

Taxis in Rome are reasonable and useful for efficient sightseeing. Three or four companions with more money than time should taxi almost everywhere. Taxis start at €3, then charge about €1.50 per kilometer (surcharges: €1.50 on Sun, €3.50 for nighttime hours of 22:00-6:00, one regular suitcase or bag rides free, tip by rounding up—€1 or so). Sample fares: Termini area to Vatican-€15; Termini area to Colosseum-€7; Termini area to the Borghese Gallery-€9 (or look up your route at www.worldtaximeter.com).

You can always just hail a cab on the street. But Romans generally walk to the nearest taxi stand (many are marked on this book's maps) or ask a passerby or a clerk in a shop, *"Dov'è una fermata dei taxi?"* (doh-VEH OO-nah fehr-MAH-tah DEH-ee TAHK-see). Easiest of all, have your hotelier or restaurateur call a taxi for you. The meter starts when the call is received. To call a cab on your own, dial 06-3570, 06-4994, or 06-6645, or use the official city taxi line, 06-0609; they'll ask for an Italian phone number (give them your mobile number or your hotel's).

The free MyTaxi app (www.mytaxi.com), popular with younger and tech-savvy Romans, lets you summon and pay for an official taxi using your smartphone. Uber works in Rome as it does in the US, but has been the focus of legal challenges.

Beware of corrupt taxis, including rip-off "express taxis" at the train station or airport. Only use official Rome taxis. They're white, with a taxi sign on the roof and a maroon logo on the door that reads *Roma Capitale.* When you get in, make sure the meter *(tassametro)* is turned on. If the meter isn't on, get out and hail another cab. Check that the meter is reset to the basic drop charge (should be around €3, or around €5 if you phoned for the taxi). You'll rarely pay more than €12 for a ride in town. Keep an eye on the fare on the meter as you near your destination; some cabbies turn the meter off instantly when they stop and tell you a higher price.

By law, every cab must display a multilingual official price chart—usually on the back of the seat in front of you. If the fare doesn't seem right, point to the chart and ask the cabbie to explain it.

Rick's Tip: *A* **common cabbie scam** *is to take your €20 note, drop it, and pick up a €5 note (similar color), claiming that's what you gave him. Pay in small bills; if you only have a large bill, show it to the cabbie as you state its face value.*

Arriving and Departing

Termini Train Station

Termini, Rome's main train station, is a buffet of tourist services. For security, entry to the train platforms themselves is restricted to ticketholders. Entrances are from the inner atrium and from the halls to the sides of the tracks. You may need to show your ticket, but there are no metal detectors and lines are generally short. In the hall along Via Giovanni Giolitti, on the southwest side of the station (near track 24), you'll find the **TI** (daily 8:00-18:45), a **car rental** desk, and **baggage**

storage *(deposito bagagli)*. A snack bar and a good selfservice **cafeteria** are perched one floor above the ticket windows in the outer atrium, accessible from the side closest to track 24.

Termini is a major transit hub. Local **Metro lines A and B** intersect downstairs at Termini Metro station. **Buses** leave from the square directly in front of the outer atrium. Buses to the airport leave from the streets on both sides of the station. The **Leonardo Express train** to Fiumicino Airport runs from track 23 or 24. **Taxis** queue in front and outside exits on both the north and south sides; if there's a long taxi line in front, try a side exit instead.

Rick's Tip: Shady characters *linger around the station, especially* **near ticket machines.** *Some offer help for a "tip"; others have official-looking business cards.* **Avoid anybody selling anything** *unless they're in a legitimate shop at the station. There are no official porters;* **carry your own bags.**

The banks of Trenitalia's user-friendly ticket machines (new ones are red, old ones are green-and-white; marked *Trenitalia/Biglietti*) are handy, but cover Italian destinations only. They take euros and credit cards (you may need to enter your PIN), display schedules, issue tickets, and even make reservations for railpass holders (found under the "Global Pass" ticket type).

TRAIN CONNECTIONS FROM TERMINI STATION

The customer service and ticket windows (in the outer, glassed-in atrium) can be jammed with travelers—find the small red kiosk, take a number, and wait. Whenever possible, use the ticket machines. Though most trains departing from Termini are operated by Italy's state rail company, Trenitalia, although a few Italo trains also use the station (for more on the privately run Italo, see page 498 and www.italotreno.it).

Rick's Tip: *Minimize your time in a train station—if you're not near a station,* **it's quicker to get tickets and train info from travel agencies or online.**

From Rome by Train to: Venice (Trenitalia: hourly, 4 hours, 1 direct night train, 7 hours; Italo: 4/day, 3-3.5 hours), **Florence** (Trenitalia: 2-3/hour, 1.5 hours; Italo: 2/hour, 1.5 hours), **Siena** (1-2/hour, 1 change, 3-4 hours), **Orvieto** (every 1-2 hours, 1.5 hours; regional trains are half the price and only slightly slower than Intercity trains), **Assisi** (4/day direct, 2 hours; more with change in Foligno), **Pisa** (1-2/hour, 3 hours, some change in Florence), **Milan** (Trenitalia: 1-3/hour, 3-3.5 hours; Italo: 11/day nonstop, 3 hours, more with stops), **Naples** (Trenitalia: 1-4/hour, 1 hour on Frecciarossa, 2 hours on Intercity, 2.5 hours and much cheaper on regional trains; Italo: hourly, 70 minutes).

Tiburtina Train Station

The smaller Tiburtina station is next to the Tiburtina Metro station in the city's northeast corner, and across the road from Rome's bus station. It's a pass-through station: Fast trains along the Milan-Naples line stop here and continue on quickly. A few of these fast trains now stop only at Tiburtina, but most stop at both Tiburtina and Termini. Use the station that's most convenient for you.

Autostazione Tiburtina, 200 yards from the Tiburtina train and Metro station, is a hub for bus service all across Italy. To reach the bus station from either Tiburtina station, don't follow the **Bus** signs, which lead to the city bus stop. Instead, exit the station, cross the street under the elevated freeway, and look for the fenced-in area with bus platforms. Ticket-window lines can be slow, so buy your ticket online in advance if possible.

Tiburtina is on **Metro line B,** with easy connections to Termini (a straight shot, four stops away) and the entire Metro system (when going to Tiburtina, Metro line B splits—you want a train signed *Rebibbia*). Or take **bus #492** from Tiburtina to various city-center stops (such as Piazza Barberini, Piazza Venezia, and Piazza Navona) and the Vatican neighborhood (as you emerge from the station, the city bus stop is to the left).

BUS CONNECTIONS FROM TRIBUTINA STATION

From Rome by Bus to: Assisi (2/day, 3 hours—the train makes more sense), **Siena** (9/day, 3 hours), **Sorrento** (1-2/day, 4 hours; this is a cheap and easy way to go straight to Sorrento, buy tickets at www.marozzivt.it—in Italian only, the Tiburtina ticket office, travel agencies, or on board for a €3.50 surcharge; tel. 080-579-0111).

By Plane

Rome has two airports: Fiumicino and the smaller Ciampino.

FIUMICINO AIRPORT

Rome's major airport, **Fiumicino** is manageable (a.k.a. Leonardo da Vinci, airport code: FCO, www.adr.it). Terminals T1, T2, and T3 are all under one roof—walkable end to end in 20 minutes. T5 is a separate building requiring a short shuttle trip. (T4 is still being built.) The T1-2-3 complex has a TI (daily 8:00-19:30, in T3), ATMs, banks, luggage storage, shops, and bars. For airport info, call 06-65951.

To get from the airport to downtown, take the direct **Leonardo Express train** to **Termini train station** (32 minutes for €14). Trains run twice hourly in both directions from roughly 6:00 to 23:00. From the airport's arrival gate, follow signs to the train icon or *Stazione/Railway Station*. Buy your ticket from a Trenitalia machine, a ticket office *(biglietteria)*, or a newsstand near the platform. Machines sell open tickets that can be used on any train. Board the train going to the central "Roma Termini" station, not "Roma Orte" or others.

Trains from Termini train station to the airport depart at about :05 and :35 past each hour, usually from track 23 or 24. Check the departure boards for "Fiumicino Aeroporto" and confirm with an official on the platform that the train is indeed going to the airport.

You can access most of the airport's terminals from the airport train station. If your flight leaves from terminal T5 (where most American air carriers flying direct to the US depart), catch the T5 shuttle bus *(navetta)* on the sidewalk in front of T3—it's too far to walk with luggage. Allow lots of time going to and from the airport; there's a fair amount of transportation involved. Flying to the US involves an extra level of security—plan on getting to the airport even earlier than normal (2.5 hours ahead of your flight).

Buses, including Terravision (www.terravision.eu), SIT (www.sitbusshuttle.com), Schiaffini (www.romeairportbus.com), and T.A.M. (www.tambus.it), connect Fiumicino and Termini train station, departing roughly every 40 minutes. While cheaper than the train (about €6 one-way), buses take twice as long (about an hour). The SIT bus also stops near the Vatican. At the airport, the companies' desks line up in T3, near the entrance to the train station.

Airport Shuttle vans can be economical for one or two people. Consider Rome Airport Shuttle (€25/1 person, extra people-€6 each, by reservation only, tel. 06-4201-4507, www.airportshuttle.it).

Your hotelier can arrange a taxi or private car service to the airport at any hour. A **taxi** between Fiumicino and downtown Rome takes 45 minutes in normal traffic and costs €48. (Add a €2-5 tip for good service.) Cabbies based in Fiumicino are allowed to charge €60. It's best to use a white Rome city cab (with a maroon *Roma Capitale* logo on the door); the airport fare should be posted on the door. Confirm the price before you get in. If your Roman cabbie tries to overcharge you, state the correct price and say, *"È la legge"* (ay lah LEJ-jay; which means, "It's the law"), and they should back off.

CIAMPINO AIRPORT

Rome's smaller airport (airport code: CIA; tel. 06-6595-9515) handles charter flights and some budget airlines (including most Ryanair flights).

Various **bus** companies—including Cotral, Terravision, Schiaffini, and SIT—will take you to Rome's Termini train station (about €5 and 2/hour for each company, 45 minutes). Cotral also runs a quicker route (25 minutes) from the airport to the Anagnina Metro stop, where you can connect by Metro to the stop nearest your hotel (departs every 40 minutes).

The fixed price for any official **taxi** (with the maroon *"Roma Capitale"* logo on the door) is €30 to downtown (within the old city walls, including most of my recommended hotels).

Rick's Tip: *A car is a worthless headache in Rome. To save money and a pile of stress,* **park in the hill town of Orvieto** *at the huge, easy, and relatively safe lot behind the train station (follow P signs from autostrada) and catch the train to Rome (roughly hourly, 1.5 hours). Or, if Rome is the first stop of your trip,* **enjoy the city car-free,** *then take the train to Orvieto and rent a car there.*

By Car

I don't advise driving into or within Rome, but if you need to, here's how: Rome's ring road, the Grande Raccordo Anulare, encircles the city, with spokes that lead into the center. Entering from the north, leave the autostrada at the Settebagni exit. Following Via Salaria and black-and-white *Centro* signs, work your way doggedly into the Roman thick of things. This will take you along the Villa Borghese Gardens and dump you right on Via Veneto in downtown Rome. Avoid rush hour and drive defensively: Roman cars stay in their lanes like rocks in an avalanche.

Park your car in a safe place during your stay. Get advice from your hotelier or use Villa Borghese's handy underground garage (€18/day, Viale del Galoppatoio 33, www.sabait.it).

During most of the week, you need a special permit to drive in the old center of Rome. The restricted zone is roughly bounded by Piazza del Popolo, Termini Station, the Colosseum, and the river (for details, go to www.agenziamobilita.roma.it and search for "LTZ" in English). Without a permit, you'll be photographed and fined. Your hotel can help you get a permit if you absolutely must drive or park downtown.

Naples, Sorrento, and the Amalfi Coast

Italy intensifies as you plunge deeper. If you like Italy as far south as Rome, keep going—it gets better. If Italy is getting on your nerves, don't go farther. Naples is Italy in the extreme—its best (the birthplace of pizza and Sophia Loren) and its worst (home of the Camorra, Naples' "family" of organized crime).

Naples is also the springboard for a region full of varied, fascinating sights. Just beyond Naples are the ancient Roman ruins of Pompeii, in the shadow of the brooding volcano, Mount Vesuvius. A few more miles down the road is the pleasant resort town of Sorrento and the island of Capri. And plunging farther south, you'll reach the dramatic scenery of the Amalfi Coast.

NAPLES, SORRENTO, AND THE AMALFI COAST IN 3 DAYS

Naples, with its incomparable Archaeological Museum (closed Tue), makes a memorable half-day stop between Rome and Sorrento. The resort town of Sorrento is a pleasant home base with easy transit connections to the surrounding sights: Pompeii, Capri, and the Amalfi Coast.

The following plan assumes you're heading south to Naples (from Rome, Orvieto, or Florence), but it also works if you fly into Naples to start your trip.

Day 1: For a quick stop in Naples, visit the Archaeological Museum, follow my self-guided Naples walk, and eat a pizza. Then head to Sorrento, your home base.

Day 2: Choose between busing along the Amalfi Coast or boating to Capri. Or add another day to fit in both.

Day 3: See the unforgettable ruins of Pompeii as a day trip from Sorrento, or en route heading north (to Rome or beyond).

Shared Tours

This chapter provides you with the necessary information to see any of the sights on your own. But if you want to take a tour of all or part of this region, consider Naples-based **Mondo Guide**'s shared tours for my readers, which give you the luxury of a private guide at a fraction of the usual cost because you're sharing the expense. I don't receive a cut from the tours; I set this up with Mondo Guide to help my readers have the most economical experience in this region, where transportation, particularly along the Amalfi Coast, can be challenging and time-consuming.

Mondo Guide offers these tours daily from April through October: a walking tour of **Naples** (€25, 3 hours), a walking tour of **Pompeii** (€15, admission extra, 2 hours), and two all-day excursions from Sorrento: an **Amalfi Coast** van tour (€50) and a boat trip to **Capri** (€90; tel. 081-751-3290,

NAPLES, SORRENTO, AND THE AMALFI COAST AT A GLANCE

▲▲ **Naples** Lively, gritty port city featuring vibrant street life and a top archaeological museum with treasures from Pompeii. See page 398.

▲▲▲ **Pompeii** Famous ruins of the ancient Roman town, stopped in its tracks by the eruption of Mount Vesuvius. See page 422.

▲▲ **Sorrento** Seaside resort port and transit hub, serving as a good home base for the region. See page 434.

▲▲ **Capri** Island getaway boasting the Blue Grotto, a short cruise from Sorrento. See page 448.

▲▲▲**The Amalfi Coast** String of seafront villages linked by a scenic, cliff-hanging road, overlooking the shimmering Mediterranean. See page 456.

mobile 340-460-5254, www.mondoguide.com, info@mondoguide.com).

Reservations are required. For specifics, see their website, www.sharedtours.com. Use your credit-card number to reserve a spot, though you'll pay cash for the tour. If you must cancel, email them more than three days in advance or you'll be billed.

Each tour requires a minimum of six participants. You'll receive email confirmation if your tour will or will not run. Confirmed departures are continually updated on their website.

NAPLES

Neapolis ("New City") was a thriving Greek commercial center 2,500 years ago. Today, it remains Italy's third-largest city with more than one million people. Naples impresses visitors with one of Europe's top archaeological museums and, of course, the best pizza anywhere.

The pulse of Italy throbs in Naples. It's appalling and captivating at the same time. While in many ways it feels like an urban jungle, Naples surprises the observant traveler with its impressive knack for living, eating, and raising children with good humor and decency. This tangled community manages to breathe, laugh, and sing—with a joyful Italian accent.

For some, a little Naples goes a long way. If you're not comfortable in chaotic and congested cities, think twice before spending the night here. Those intrigued by the city's street life will enjoy staying over. The city is cheap by Italian standards: Splurging on a sane and comfortable hotel is a worthwhile investment. On summer afternoons, life slows and churches, museums, and shops close as the temperature soars. The city comes back to life early in the evening.

Orientation

Naples is set deep inside a large, curving bay, with Mount Vesuvius looming just five miles away. Although Naples is a sprawling city, its fairly compact core contains the most interesting sights. The tourist's Naples is a triangle, with its points at the Centrale train station in the east, the Archaeological Museum to the west, and Piazza del Plebiscito and the port to the south. Steep hills rise above this historic core, including San Martino, capped with a mighty fortress.

Tourist Information: Central Naples has multiple, small TIs, none of them particularly helpful—just grab a map and browse the brochures (www.inaples.it). The handiest one is in **Centrale train station** (daily 9:00-18:00, near track 23, tel. 081-268-779). Others are by the entrance to the **Galleria Umberto I** shopping mall (Mon-Sat 9:00-17:00, Sun until 13:00, tel. 081-402-394) and on Spaccanapoli, across from the **Church of Gesù Nuovo** (Mon-Sat 9:00-17:00, Sun until 13:00, tel. 081-551-2701).

Theft and Safety: Don't venture into neighborhoods that make you uncomfortable. While the train station has been nicely spruced up, its glow only extends for a block or so. The areas a little farther away are especially seedy. Touristy Spaccanapoli and the posh Via Toledo shopping boulevard are more upscale, but you'll still see rowdy kids and panhandlers. Assume able-bodied beggars are thieves. Any jostle or commotion is probably a thief-team smokescreen. To keep bags safe, it's best to leave them at the left-luggage office in Centrale station or at your hotel. Always carry your bag on the side away from the street—thieves on scooters have been known to snatch bags as they swoop by. Keep valuables buttoned up.

For tips on avoiding scams and pickpockets if you take the Circumvesuviana commuter train, see page 420.

Sightseeing Pass: The **Campania ArteCard** regional passes could save you a few euros when visiting major sights (such as the Naples Archaeological Museum and Pompeii). Their €32 **three-day Tutta la Regione** version is good if you're visiting

Naples and Sorrento; it covers two sights (plus a 50 percent discount on others) and transportation within Naples and on the Circumvesuviana train and Amalfi Coast buses. The €34 **seven-day Tutta la Regione** option covers five sights (and discounts on others) but no transportation. For those lingering in Naples, the €21 **three-day Napoli-only** version covers transportation within Naples and three city sights, plus discounts on others. You can buy the cards at some Naples TIs and at participating sights (cards activate on first use, expire 3 days later at midnight, www.campaniartecard.it).

Traffic: In Naples, red lights are discretionary; be wary, particularly of motor scooters. Keep children close. Smart tourists jaywalk in the shadow of bold locals, who generally ignore crosswalks. Wait for a break in traffic, cross with confidence, and make eye contact with approaching drivers. The traffic will stop.

Tours: Pina Esposito offers fine walking and driving tours of Naples and the region as well as tours of the Archaeological Museum (€60/hour, 2-hour minimum, 10 percent off with this book, mobile 338-763-4224, annamariaesposito1@virgilio.it).

Mondo Guide offers private tours of the Archaeological Museum (€120/2 hours), the city (€240/4 hours), and the region (www.mondoguide.com). Reserve in advance at www.sharedtours.com if you want to take their shared walking tour of Naples (€25, daily at 15:00, 3 hours, meet at the steps of the Archaeological Museum—you can do the museum on your own before joining your guide).

CitySightseeing Napoli tour buses make three different hop-on, hop-off loops through the city, each lasting about one hour. The best is the **red line**, which loops around the historical center and stops at the Archaeological Museum (€22, ticket valid 24 hours, runs roughly hourly, buy from driver, tel. 081-551-7279, www.napoli.city-sightseeing.it).

🎧 To sightsee on your own, download free audio tours via my free **Rick Steves Audio Europe** app (see page 28 for details).

Sights

▲▲▲ARCHAEOLOGICAL MUSEUM

Naples' Archaeological Museum (Museo Archeologico) is one of the world's great museums of ancient art. It offers the best look at artifacts from Pompeii, an ancient town buried in ash by the eruption of Mount Vesuvius in A.D. 79. When Pompeii was excavated in the late 1700s, Naples' Bourbon king bellowed, "Bring me the best of what you find!" The finest art and artifacts ended up here, leaving the ancient sites themselves barren (though still impressive).

Cost and Hours: €8, sometimes more for temporary exhibits, free first Sun of the month, Wed-Mon 9:00-19:30, closed Tue. Early and temporary closures are noted on a board near the ticket office. In July and August, expect some rooms to be closed due to lack of staff.

Information: Tel. 081-442-2149, www.museoarcheologiconapoli.it.

Getting There: To take the **Metro** (Metropolitana) from Centrale station, first buy a single €1.20 transit ticket at a newsstand or tobacco shop. Then follow the signs for *Metro Linea 2* (down the stairs in front of track 13). Validate your ticket in the small yellow or blue boxes near the escalator going down to the tracks. You're looking for line 2 trains heading in the direction of Pozzuoli (they generally depart from track 4, but sometimes from track 2). Ride one stop to Piazza Cavour, and follow the *Museo* signs through the underground passage. Or exit and walk five minutes uphill through the park along the busy street. Look for a grand old red building located up a flight of stairs at the top of the block. You can also take the Metro's cheaper line 1 five stops from Centrale station to Museo—it's only a little slower.

A **taxi** from the train station to the museum should cost about €11 (though cabbies are infamous for overcharging).

Visitor Information: The shop sells a worthwhile *National Archaeological Museum of Naples* guidebook for €12.

Tours: The decent audioguide costs €5 (at ticket desk). Or 🎧 download my free Archaeological Museum audio tour.

Baggage Check: Bag check is obligatory and free.

Eating: The museum has no café, but vending machines sell drinks and snacks at reasonable prices. There are several good places nearby to grab a meal, such as La Stanza del Gusto, two blocks away (see "Eating," later).

➲ SELF-GUIDED TOUR

Enter the museum and stand at the base of the grand staircase. To your right, on the ground floor, are the larger-than-life statues of the Farnese Collection, starring the *Toro Farnese* and the *Farnese Hercules*. Up the stairs on the mezzanine level are mosaics and frescoes from Pompeii, including the Secret Room of erotic art. On the top floor are more artifacts from Pompeii, a scale model of the city, and bronze statues from Herculaneum. WCs are behind the staircase.

• *From the base of the* ❶ ***grand staircase,*** *turn right through the door marked Collezione Farnese and head for the far end—walking through a rich collection of idealistic and realistic ancient portrait* ❷ ***busts****—and jog right, then left, to reach the farthest room (Room 13).*

GROUND FLOOR: THE FARNESE COLLECTION

The Farnese Collection statues are not from Pompeii, but from Rome. Today they're displayed in this grand hall of huge, bright, and wonderfully restored statues excavated from Rome's Baths of Caracalla. The statues were dug up in the 1540s at the behest of Alessandro Farnese (by then Pope Paul III) while he was building the family palace on Campo dei Fiori in Rome. His main purpose in excavating the baths was to scavenge high-quality building stone. The sculptures were a nice extra and helped the palace come in under budget. In the 1700s, the collection ended up in the hands of Charles, the Bourbon king of Naples (whose mother was a Farnese). His son, the next king, had it brought to Naples.

• *Quick—look down to the left end of the hall. There's a woman being tied to a snorting bull.*

The tangled ❸ ***Toro Farnese*** tells a thrilling Greek myth. At 13 feet, it's the tallest ancient marble group ever found, and the largest intact statue from antiquity. A third-century A.D. copy of a lost bronze Hellenistic original, it was carved out of one piece of marble. Michelangelo and others "restored" it at the pope's request—meaning that they integrated surviving bits into a new work. Panels on the wall show which pieces were actually carved by Michelangelo (in blue on the chart): the head of the woman in back, the torso of the aunt under the bull, and the dog.

Here's the tragic story behind the statue: Once upon an ancient Greek time, King Lycus was bewitched by Dirce. He abandoned his pregnant wife, Antiope

Toro Farnese

Naples Archaeological Museum

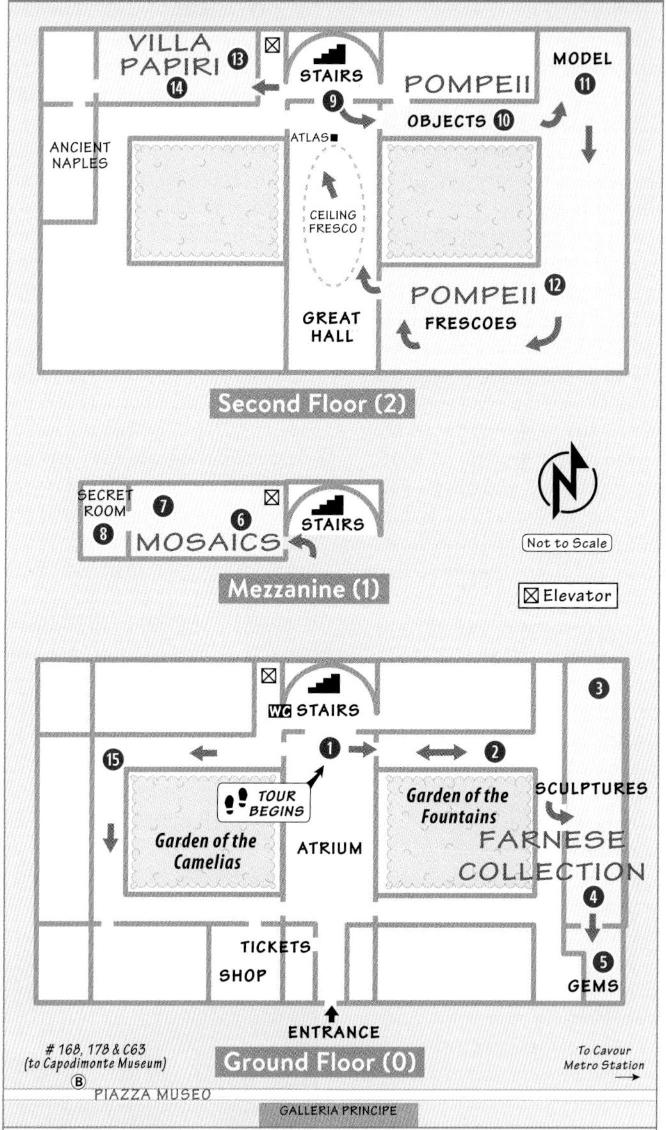

1. Grand Staircase
2. Hall of the Busts
3. Toro Farnese
4. Farnese Hercules
5. Farnese Cup
6. Various Mosaics
7. Dancing Faun & Battle of Alexander
8. Secret Room
9. Great Hall
10. Metal, Ivory & Glass Objects
11. Model of Pompeii
12. Frescoes
13. Papyrus Scrolls
14. Bronze Statues
15. Doriforo

(standing regally in the background), who later gave birth to twin boys. When they grew up, they killed their deadbeat dad and tied Dirce to the horns of a bull to be bashed against a mountain. Captured in marble, the action is exciting: cape flailing, dog snarling, hooves in the air. You can almost hear the bull snorting. In the back, Antiope oversees this harsh ancient justice with satisfaction.

At the opposite end of the hall stands the ❹ ***Farnese Hercules.*** The great Greek hero is exhausted. He leans wearily on his club (draped with his lion skin) and bows his head. He's just finished the daunting Eleventh Labor, having traveled the world, freed Prometheus from his rock, and carried Atlas' weight of the world on his shoulders. Now he's returned with the prize: the golden apples of the gods, which he cups behind his back. But, after all that, he's just been told he has to return the apples and do one final labor: descend into hell itself. Oh, man.

The 10-foot colossus is a third-century A.D. Roman marble copy (signed by "Glykon") of a fourth-century B.C. Greek bronze original (probably by Lysippos). The statue was famous in its day. Dozens of copies have been found in Roman villas and baths.

The *Farnese Hercules* was equally famous in the 16th-18th centuries. Tourists flocked to Rome to admire it, art students studied it from afar in prints, Louis XIV made a copy for Versailles, and petty nobles everywhere put small-scale knockoffs in their gardens. This curly-haired version of Hercules became the modern world's image of the Greek hero.

• *Behind Hercules is the door to the Farnese gem collection (Rooms 9 and 10), featuring the ancient cereal-bowl-shaped* ❺ ***Farnese Cup,*** *thought to bear a portrait of Cleopatra. Now backtrack to the main entry hall, then head up to the mezzanine level (turn left at the lion and go under the* Mosaici *sign), and enter Room 57.*

MEZZANINE: POMPEIIAN MOSAICS AND THE SECRET ROOM

These ❻ **mosaics**—mostly of animals, battle scenes, and geometric designs—were excavated from the walls and floors of Pompeii's ritzy villas. ***The Chained Dog*** once graced a home's entryway. The colorful mosaic columns (to your right in adjoining Room 58) shaded a courtyard, part of an ensemble of wall mosaics and bubbling fountains. In Room 59, admire the realism of the tambourine-playing musicians, the drinking doves, and the skull—a reminder of impending death.

Continue a few steps into Room 60, with objects taken from one of Pompeii's greatest villas, the House of the Faun (see page 431). The 20-inch-high statue in a freestanding glass case was the house's delightful centerpiece, the ❼ ***Dancing Faun.*** This rare surviving Greek bronze statue (from the fourth century B.C.) is surrounded by some of the best mosaics of that age.

A museum highlight, just beyond the statue, is the grand ***Battle of Alexander,*** a second-century B.C. copy of the now-lost original Greek fresco from a century earlier. It decorated a floor in the House of the Faun and was found intact; the damage you see occurred as this treasure was moved from Pompeii to the king's collection here. Alexander (left side of the scene, with curly hair and sideburns) is about to defeat the Persians under Darius (central figure, in chariot with turban

Battle of Alexander mosaic (detail)

and beard). This pivotal victory allowed Alexander to quickly overrun much of Asia (331 B.C.). Alexander is the only one without a helmet...a confident master of the battlefield while everyone else is fighting for their lives, their eyes bulging with fear. The horses, already in retreat, add to the scene's propaganda value. Notice the shading and perspective, which Renaissance artists would later work so hard to accomplish. (A modern reproduction of the mosaic is now back in Pompeii, at the House of the Faun.)

Farther on, the ❽ **Secret Room** (Gabinetto Segreto, Room 65) contains a sizable assortment of erotic frescoes, well-hung pottery, and perky statues that once decorated bedrooms, meeting rooms, brothels, and even shops at Pompeii. These bawdy statues and frescoes were once displayed in Pompeii's grandest houses as entertainment for guests. Roman nobles commissioned the wildest scenes imaginable. Think of them as ancient dirty jokes.

At the entrance, you're enthusiastically greeted by big stone penises that once projected over Pompeii's doorways. A massive phallus was not necessarily a sexual symbol, but a magical amulet used as protection against the "evil eye." It symbolized fertility, good luck, riches, straight A's, and general well-being.

Circulating counterclockwise through this section, look for the following: a faun playfully pulling the sheet off a beautiful woman, only to be shocked by a hermaphrodite's plumbing (#12); horny pygmies from Africa in action (#27); a toga with an embarrassing bulge (#34); a statue of a goat and a satyr illustrating an act of sodomy (#36); and, watching over it all with remarkable aplomb, Venus, the patron goddess of Pompeii (#39).

The back room is furnished and decorated the way an ancient brothel might have been. The 10 frescoes on the wall functioned as both a menu of services and a *Kama Sutra* of sex positions.

• *So, now that your travel buddy is finally showing a little interest in art...finish up your visit by climbing the stairs to the top floor.*

At the top of the stairs, pause and get oriented to our final sights. Directly ahead

Farnese Hercules

Dancing Faun

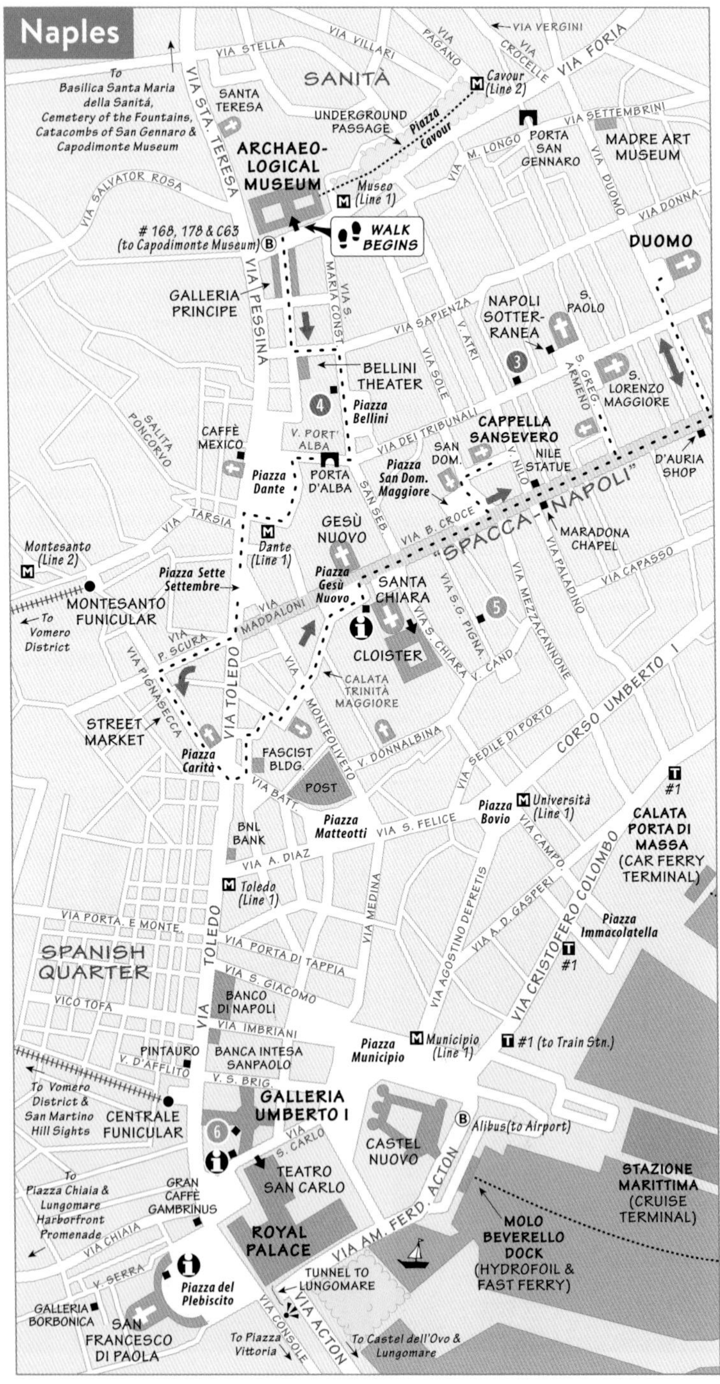
Naples
SANITÀ
VIA STELLA
VIA VILLARI
VIA PAGANO
VIA VERGINI
VIA CROCELLE
VIA FORIA
Cavour (Line 2)
To Basilica Santa Maria della Sanitá, Cemetery of the Fountains, Catacombs of San Gennaro & Capodimonte Museum
VIA STA. TERESA
SANTA TERESA
UNDERGROUND PASSAGE
Piazza Cavour
VIA SETTEMBRINI
PORTA SAN GENNARO
MADRE ART MUSEUM
ARCHAEO-LOGICAL MUSEUM
VIA M. LONGO
VIA DUOMO
VIA SALVATOR ROSA
Museo (Line 1)
VIA DONNA-
168, 178 & C63 (to Capodimonte Museum)
WALK BEGINS
DUOMO
VIA PESSINA
GALLERIA PRINCIPE
VIA S. MARIA CONST.
NAPOLI SOTTER-RANEA
S. PAOLO
VIA SAPIENZA
V. ATRI
VIA SOLE
BELLINI THEATER
S. GREG. ARMENO
S. LORENZO MAGGIORE
Piazza Bellini
SALITA PONCORVO
CAFFÈ MEXICO
V. PORT' ALBA
VIA DEI TRIBUNALI
CAPPELLA SANSEVERO
SAN DOM.
NILE STATUE
D'AURIA SHOP
Piazza Dante
PORTA D'ALBA
SAN SEB.
Piazza San Dom. Maggiore
V. NILO
"SPACCA-NAPOLI"
VIA TARSIA
Dante (Line 1)
GESÙ NUOVO
VIA B. CROCE
MARADONA CHAPEL
VIA PALADINO
Montesanto (Line 2)
Piazza Sette Settembre
Piazza Gesù Nuovo
SANTA CHIARA
VIA CAPASSO
MONTESANTO FUNICULAR
To Vomero District
VIA MADDALONI
VIA S. CHIARA
VIA S.G. PIGNA
VIA MEZZACANNONE
VIA P. SCURA
CLOISTER
V. CAND.
VIA PIGNASECCA
VIA TOLEDO
VIA MONTEOLIVETO
CALATA TRINITÀ MAGGIORE
CORSO UMBERTO I
STREET MARKET
VIA SEDILE DI PORTO
Piazza Carità
FASCIST BLDG.
V. DONNALBINA
POST
VIA BATT.
Piazza Bovio
Università (Line 1)
#1
CALATA PORTA DI MASSA (CAR FERRY TERMINAL)
BNL BANK
Piazza Matteotti
VIA S. FELICE
VIA CAMPO.
VIA CRISTOFERO COLOMBO
VIA A. DIAZ
Toledo (Line 1)
VIA MEDINA
VIA AGOSTINO DEPRETIS
VIA A. D. GASPERI
Piazza Immacolatella
VIA PORTA. E MONTE.
VIA PORTA DI TAPPIA
SPANISH QUARTER
VIA S. GIACOMO
BANCO DI NAPOLI
VICO TOFA
VIA IMBRIANI
Piazza Municipio
Municipio (Line 1)
#1 (to Train Stn.)
PINTAURO
BANCA INTESA SANPAOLO
V. D'AFFLITO
V. S. BRIG.
To Vomero District & San Martino Hill Sights
CENTRALE FUNICULAR
GALLERIA UMBERTO I
Alibus (to Airport)
CASTEL NUOVO
VIA S. CARLO
TEATRO SAN CARLO
VIA AM. FERD. ACTON
STAZIONE MARITTIMA (CRUISE TERMINAL)
To Piazza Chiaia & Lungomare Harborfront Promenade
GRAN CAFFÈ GAMBRINUS
VIA CHIAIA
ROYAL PALACE
MOLO BEVERELLO DOCK (HYDROFOIL & FAST FERRY)
V. SERRA
Piazza del Plebiscito
TUNNEL TO LUNGOMARE
GALLERIA BORBONICA
SAN FRANCESCO DI PAOLA
VIA CONSOLE
VIA ACTON
To Piazza Vittoria
To Castel dell'Ovo & Lungomare

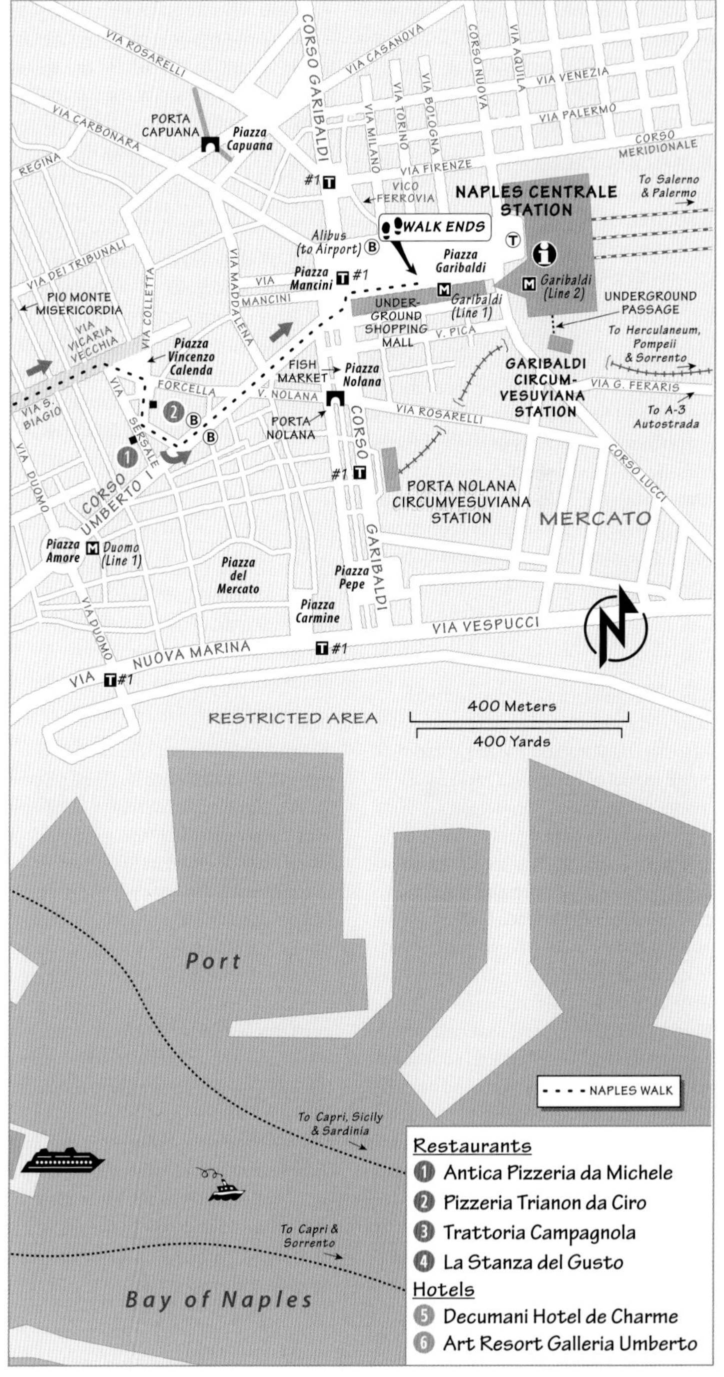
VIA ROSARELLI
VIA CARBONARA
REGINA
PORTA CAPUANA
Piazza Capuana
CORSO GARIBALDI
VIA CASANOVA
VIA MILANO
VIA TORINO
VIA BOLOGNA
CORSO NUOVA
VIA AQUILA
VIA VENEZIA
VIA PALERMO
CORSO MERIDIONALE
VIA FIRENZE
VICO FERROVIA
NAPLES CENTRALE STATION
To Salerno & Palermo
WALK ENDS
Alibus (to Airport)
Piazza Garibaldi
VIA DEI TRIBUNALI
VIA MADDALENA
VIA MANCINI
Piazza Mancini
#1
Garibaldi (Line 2)
PIO MONTE MISERICORDIA
VIA COLLETTA
UNDER-GROUND SHOPPING MALL
Garibaldi (Line 1)
UNDERGROUND PASSAGE
VIA VICARIA VECCHIA
V. PICA
To Herculaneum, Pompeii & Sorrento
Piazza Vincenzo Calenda
FISH MARKET
Piazza Nolana
GARIBALDI CIRCUM-VESUVIANA STATION
FORCELLA
VIA G. FERARIS
VIA S. BIAGIO
V. NOLANA
VIA ROSARELLI
To A-3 Autostrada
PORTA NOLANA
VIA SERSALE
CORSO LUCCI
VIA DUOMO
CORSO UMBERTO I
PORTA NOLANA CIRCUMVESUVIANA STATION
MERCATO
Piazza Amore
Duomo (Line 1)
Piazza del Mercato
Piazza Pepe
Piazza Carmine
VIA VESPUCCI
VIA NUOVA MARINA
RESTRICTED AREA
400 Meters
400 Yards
Port
NAPLES WALK
To Capri, Sicily & Sardinia
To Capri & Sorrento
Bay of Naples
Restaurants
1 Antica Pizzeria da Michele
2 Pizzeria Trianon da Ciro
3 Trattoria Campagnola
4 La Stanza del Gusto
Hotels
5 Decumani Hotel de Charme
6 Art Resort Galleria Umberto

is a doorway (marked Salone Meridiana) *that leads into a big, empty, hall. To the left of this grand hall is a series of rooms with more artifacts from Pompeii. To the right are rooms of statues from Herculaneum.*

TOP FLOOR: FRESCOES, STATUES, ARTIFACTS, AND A MODEL OF POMPEII

First, step into the Salone Meridiana. This was the ❾ **great hall** of the university (17th and 18th centuries) until the building became the royal museum in 1777. Walk to the center. The sundial (from 1791) still works. Look up to the far-right corner of the hall and find the tiny pinhole. At noon (13:00 in summer), a ray of sun enters the hall and strikes the sundial, showing the time of the year...if you know your zodiac.

Now enter the series of rooms to the left of the grand hall, with ❿ ***Metal, Ivory, and Glass Objects*** found in Pompeii. You enter through a doorway marked *Vetri e Avori,* which leads into Room 89. Browse your way to the far end, with the stunning *Blue Vase* (Room 85), decorated with cameo Bacchuses harvesting grapes. Turn left, then right, to find the huge, room-filling ⓫ ***model of Pompeii,*** a 1:100 scale model of the ruins (Room 96).

Continue on (through Rooms 83-80) and enter Room 75 (marked *affreschi*) to see the museum's impressive collection of (nonerotic) ⓬ **frescoes** taken from the walls of Pompeii villas. Pompeiians loved to decorate their homes with scenes from mythology (Hercules' labors, Venus and Mars in love), landscapes, everyday market scenes, and faux architecture. Look for the scene featuring Bacchus dressed in a robe of grapes standing alongside Mt. Vesuvius—a rare depiction of the volcano before it blew its top. To the left (in Room 78), find the famous dual portrait of baker Terentius Neo and his wife—possibly two of the 2,000 victims when Vesuvius erupted.

• *Eventually you'll end up back near the great hall. From here (facing the hall entrance), turn right and find the entrance to the wing labeled* La Villa dei Papiri.

These artifacts came from the Herculaneum holiday home of Julius Caesar's father-in-law. To the right of the entrance, in Room 114, find two of the 2,000 ⓭ **papyrus scrolls** that gave the villa its name. Displays explain how the half-burned scrolls were unrolled and (with luck) read after excavation in the 1750s. Continuing into Room 116, enjoy some of the villa's ⓮ **bronze statues.** Look into the lifelike blue eyes of the intense *Corridore* (athletes), bent on doing their best. The *Five Dancers,* with their inlaid-ivory eyes and graceful poses, decorated a portico. The next room has more fine works: *Resting Hermes* (with his tired little heel wings) is taking a break. Nearby, the *Drunken Faun* (singing and snapping his fingers to the beat, a wineskin at his side) is clearly living for today—true to the *carpe diem* lifestyle of the Epicurean philosophy.

• *Return to the ground floor. To reach the exit, circle around the museum courtyard to the gift shop. But for extra credit, stop at one more sight on your way out.*

DORIFORO

As you circle the courtyard toward the exit, find ⓯ ***Doriforo.*** (If he's been moved, ask a guard, *"Dov'è il Doriforo?"*) This seven-foot-tall "spear-carrier" (the literal translation of *doriforo*) just stands there. What's the big deal about this statue? It's a marble replica made by the Romans of one of the most-copied statues of antiquity, a fifth-century B.C. bronze Greek original by Polyclitus. This copy once stood in a Pompeii gym, where it inspired ancient athletes by showing the ideal proportions of Greek beauty. So full of motion, and so realistic in its *contrapposto* pose (weight on one foot), the *Doriforo* would later inspire Donatello and Michelangelo, helping to trigger the Renaissance. And so the glories of ancient Pompeii, once buried and forgotten, live on today.

➔ Naples Walk

This self-guided walk, worth ▲▲▲, takes you from the Archaeological Museum through the heart of town and back to Centrale Station. Allow at least two hours, plus time for pizza and sightseeing stops. (If you have the time and interest, you can make a side-trip to the Royal Palace/Piazza del Plebiscito area—covered in "Sights in Naples," later—halfway through this walk.) 🎧 Download my free Naples Walk audio tour.

PART 1: FROM THE ARCHAEOLOGICAL MUSEUM TO PIAZZA GESÙ NUOVO

Start at the Archaeological Museum (at the top of Piazza Cavour, Metro: Cavour or Museo). As you stroll, remember that here in Naples red traffic lights are considered "decorations." When crossing a street, try to draft behind a native.

• *From the door of the Archaeological Museum, cross the street, veer right, and enter the arched doorway of the beige-colored Galleria Principe di Napoli mall. (If the entrance is blocked, simply loop around the block to another entrance or pick up our walk behind the Galleria.)*

Galleria Principe di Napoli: There's no better example of Naples' grandeur—and decline—than this elegant 19th-century shopping mall. You'll enjoy a soaring skylight, carved woodwork, ironwork lanterns, playful cupids, an elegant atmosphere... and empty shops. This is "Liberty Style," Italy's version of Art Nouveau (named for a British department store) that was in vogue at a time when Naples was nicknamed the "Paris of the South." But despite its grandeur, the mall has suffered from the economic stagnation that began in the late-1800s. Even ambitious renovations in recent years have failed to attract much business.

• *Leaving the gallery through the opposite end, walk one block downhill. At Via Conte di Ruvo, turn left, passing the fine Bellini Theater (also in the Liberty Style). After one block, turn right on Via Santa Maria di Costantinopoli. Walking between two grand churches, continue directly downhill to a small park with a statue in the center called...*

Piazza Bellini: Suddenly you're in neighborhood Napoli. The statue honors the opera composer Vincenzo Bellini, whose career was launched in Naples in the early 1800s, when opera itself was being born. Just past the statue, peer down into the sunken area to see Naples' ancient origins as a fifth-century B.C. Greek colony called Neapolis— "the new city." You can see how the street level has risen from the rubble of centuries.

• *Walk 30 yards downhill. Stop at the horseshoe-shaped Port'Alba gate (on the right). Spin slowly 360 degrees and take in the scene. The proud tile across the street (upstairs, between the two balconies) shows Piazza Bellini circa 1890. Pass through the gate, down Via Port'Alba, and stroll through this pleasant passage lined with book stalls. You emerge into a big square called...*

Archaeological Museum

Piazza Bellini

Piazza Dante: This square is marked by a statue of Dante, the medieval poet. Fittingly, half the square is devoted to bookstores. Old Dante looks out over an urban area that was once grand, then chaotic, and is now slowly becoming grand again.

• *Before moving on, note the red "M" that Dante seems to be gesturing to. This marks the* ***Dante Metro station****, the best of Napoli's art-splashed Metro stations. (To take a look, go down three flights of escalators and then back up; you'll need a ticket, unless you can sweet-talk a guard.) Then, exit Piazza Dante at the far end, walking downhill on...*

Via Toledo: The long, straight street heading downhill from Piazza Dante is Naples' principal shopping drag. It originated as a military road built under Spanish rule in the 16th century. Via Toledo skirted the old town wall to connect the Spanish military headquarters (now the museum where you started this walk) with the Royal Palace (down by the bay, where you're heading).

After a couple hundred yards, you'll reach **Piazza Sette Settembre.** This square represents the event that precipitated Naples' swift decline. On September 7, 1860, from the white marble balcony of the Neoclassical building overlooking the square, the famous revolutionary Giuseppe Garibaldi declared Italy united and Victor Emmanuel II its first king. And a decade later, that declaration became reality when Rome also fell to unification forces. It was the start of a glorious new era for Italy, Rome, and the Italian people. But not for Naples.

Naples' treasury was confiscated to subsidize the industrial expansion of the north, and its bureaucrats were transferred to the new capital in Rome. Within a few decades, Naples went from being a thriving cultural and political capital to a provincial town, with its economy in shambles and its dialect considered backward.

• *Continue straight on Via Toledo. About three blocks below Piazza Dante and a block past Piazza Sette Settembre, you'll come to Via Maddaloni, which marks the start of the long, straight, narrow street nicknamed...*

Spaccanapoli: Via Maddaloni is the modern name for this thin street that,

Galleria Principe di Napoli

Piazza Dante

since ancient times, has bisected the city. The name Spaccanapoli translates as "split Naples." Look left down the street (toward the train station), and right (toward San Martino hill), and you get a sense of how Spaccanapoli divides this urban jungle of buildings.

• *At this point in our walk, take a moment to plan your next move. From here, our walk loops to the right, through the edge of the intense residential Spanish Quarter neighborhood to Piazza Carità before cutting over to the Spaccanapoli district. (If you were to side-trip to the Royal Palace and Piazza del Plebiscito-area sights—described later in "Sights in Naples"—you'd do that from here...but that makes this walk pretty long.)*

At the Spaccanapoli intersection, go right (toward the church facade on the hill), heading up Via Pasquale Scura. After about 100 yards, you hit a busy intersection. Stop. You're on one of Naples' most colorful open-air market streets.

Via Pignasecca Market: Snoop around from here if you're so inclined. Then, turn left down colorful Via Pignasecca. You'll pass meat and fish stalls, produce stands, street-food vendors, and much more. This is a taste of Naples' crowded, characteristic **Spanish Quarter** (its center is farther down Via Toledo—see map—but this area provides a good sampling).

• *Turn left and follow Via Pignasecca as it leads back to Via Toledo at the square called...*

Piazza Carità: Built for an official visit by Hitler to Mussolini in 1938, the square has fascist architecture full of stern, straight, obedient lines. The modern memorial statue in the center of the square celebrates **Salvo d'Acquisto,** a rare hometown hero. In 1943, he was executed after falsely confessing to sabotage...in order to save 22 fellow Italian soldiers from a Nazi revenge massacre.

• *From Piazza Carità, veer northwest (past more fascist-style architecture) on Via Morgantini through Piazza Monteoliveto. Cross the busy street, then angle up Calata Trinità Maggiore to the fancy column in the piazza at the top of the hill.*

PART 2: FROM PIAZZA GESÙ NUOVO TO CENTRALE STATION

• *You're in Piazza Gesù Nuovo, and you're back on the straight-as-a-Greek-arrow Spaccanapoli, formerly the main thoroughfare of the Greek city of Neapolis. (Spaccanapoli changes names several times: Via Maddaloni, Via B. Croce, Via S. Biagio dei Librai, and Via Vicaria Vecchia.) Stop at...*

Piazza Gesù Nuovo: This square is marked by a towering 18th-century Baroque monument to the Counter-Reformation. Although the Jesuit order was powerful in Naples because of its Spanish heritage, locals never attacked Protestants here with the full fury of the Spanish Inquisition.

If you'd like, you can visit two old churches, the **Church of Gesù Nuovo** and **Church of Santa Chiara** (described later, under "More Sights").

• *Continue along the main drag for another 200 yards. Since this is a university district, you'll see lots of students and bookstores. This neighborhood is also famously superstitious.*

"Spaccanapoli" street

Via Pignasecca Market

Fascist architecture

Piazza Gesù Nuovo

Look for incense-burning women with carts full of good-luck charms for sale.

Passing Palazzo Venezia—the embassy of Venice to Naples when both were independent powers—you'll emerge into the next square.

Piazza San Domenico Maggiore: It's marked by an ornate 17th-century monument built to thank God for ending the plague. From this square, detour left along the right side of the castle-like church, then follow yellow signs, taking the first right and walking one short block to **Cappella Sansevero,** worth a visit for its statuary (see page 412).

• *Return to Via B. Croce (a.k.a. Spaccanapoli), turn left, and continue your cultural scavenger hunt. At the intersection of Via Nilo, find the...*

Statue of the Nile (on the left): A reminder of the multiethnic makeup of Greek Neapolis, this statue is in what was the Egyptian quarter. Locals like to call this statue *The Body of Naples,* with the overflowing cornucopia symbolizing the abundance of their fine city. (I once asked a Neapolitan man to describe the local women, who are famous for their beauty. He replied simply, "Abundant.") This intersection is considered the center of old Naples.

• *Directly opposite the statue, inside of Bar Nilo, is the...*

"Chapel of Maradona": The small "chapel" on the right wall is dedicated to Diego Maradona, a soccer star who played for Naples in the 1980s. Locals consider soccer almost a religion, and this guy was practically a deity. You can even see a "hair of Diego" and a teardrop from the city when he went to another team for more money. Unfortunately, his reputation has since been sullied by problems with organized crime, drugs, and police. To take a photo, buy coffee first.

• *Continue to a tiny square at the intersection with Via San Gregorio Armeno.*

Via San Gregorio Armeno: Stroll up this tiny lane toward the fanciful tower that arches over the street. The street is lined with stalls selling lots of souvenir kitsch, as well as some of Naples' most distinctive local crafts. Among the many figurines on sale, find items relating to ***presepi*** (Nativity scenes). Just as many Americans keep an eye out year-round for Christmas-tree ornaments, Italians regularly add pieces to the family ***presepe***, the centerpiece of their holiday decorations. You'll see elaborate manger scenes made of bark and moss, with niches to hold Baby Jesus or mother Mary. You'll also see lots of jokey figurines caricaturing local politicians, soccer stars, and other celebrities. (Some of the highest-quality ***presepi*** pieces are sold at the D'Auria shop, a little farther down Spaccanapoli, on the right at #87. They even sell the classy ***campane*** version, under a glass bell.)

Another popular Naples souvenir is the ***corno,*** a skinny, twisted, red horn that resembles a chili pepper. The *corno* comes with a double symbolism for fertility: It's a horn of plenty, and it's also a phallic sym-

Presepi *nativity scenes*

bol turned upside-down. Neapolitans explain that fertility isn't sexual; it provides the greatest gift a person can give—life.

• *Continue down Spaccanapoli another 100 yards until you hit busy Via Duomo. Consider detouring five minutes north (left) up Via Duomo to visit Naples'* **Duomo;** *just around the corner is the* **Pio Monte della Misericordia Church,** *with a fine Caravaggio painting. But for now, continue straight, crossing Via Duomo. Here, Spaccanapoli is named...*

Via Vicaria Vecchia: Along this stretch, the street scenes intensify. The area is said to be a center of the Camorra (the Naples-based version of the Sicilian Mafia), but as a tourist, you won't notice.

Naples has the most intact street plan of any surviving ancient Greek or Roman city. Imagine this city during those times (and retain these images as you visit Pompeii), with streetside shop fronts that close up after dark, and private homes on upper floors. What you see today is just one more page in a 2,000-year-old story of a city: meetings, beatings, and cheatings; kisses, near misses, and little-boy pisses. You name it, it occurs on the streets today. Black-and-white death announcements add to the clutter on the walls. Widows sell cigarettes from buckets. For a peek behind the scenes in the shade of wet laundry, venture down a few side streets. The neighborhood action seems best at about 18:00.

A few blocks on, at the tiny fenced-in triangle of greenery, hang out for a few minutes just to observe the crazy motorbike action and teen scene.

• *From here, veer right onto Via Forcella. You emerge into Piazza Vincenzo Calenda. Our walk has come full circle, so we must be done, right? Hungry? Turn right here, on Via Pietro Colletta, and close out the walk with three typical Neapolitan...*

Eateries: Step into the North Pole at the recommended **Polo Nord Gelateria** (at #41). The oldest *gelateria* in Naples has had four generations of family working here since 1931. Before you order, sample a few flavors, including their *bacio,* or "kiss," flavor (chocolate and hazelnut)—all are made fresh daily.

Two of Napoli's most competitive **pizzerias** are nearby. **Trianon da Ciro** (across the street from Polo Nord) has been serving them up hot and fast for almost a century. A half-block farther, on the right, is the place where some say pizza was born—at **Antica Pizzeria da Michele.** (For more on both, see "Eating in Naples," later).

• *Our walk is over. It's easy to return to Centrale Station. Continue straight ahead, downhill, until you hit the grand boulevard, Corso Umberto I. Turn left here, and it's a straight 15-minute walk to Centrale Station. (Or cross the street and hop on a bus; they all go to the station.) You'll pass a gauntlet of purse/CD/sunglasses salesmen and shady characters hawking stolen mobile phones. You'll soon reach the vast Piazza Garibaldi, with a shiny new modern canopy in the middle. On the far side is the station. You made it.*

More Sights

Churches on or near Spaccanapoli

▲CHURCH OF GESÙ NUOVO

This Baroque church's unique pyramid-grill facade survives from a fortified 15th-century noble palace. Step inside for a brilliant Neapolitan Baroque interior. The second chapel on the right features a much-adored **statue of St. Giuseppe Moscati** (1880-1927), a Christian doctor famous for helping the poor. In 1987, he became the first modern doctor to be canonized.

Continue on to the third chapel and enter **Sale Moscati.** Look high on the walls of this long room to see hundreds of "Ex Votos"—tiny red-and-silver plaques of thanksgiving for prayers answered with the help of St. Moscati (each has a symbol of the ailment cured). As you leave Sale Moscati, notice the big bomb casing that hangs high in the left corner. It fell through the church's dome in 1943, but caused almost no damage...yet another miracle.

Cost and Hours: Free, daily 6:45-13:00 & 16:00-19:30, Piazza del Gesù Nuovo, www.gesunuovo.it.

CHURCH OF SANTA CHIARA

Dating from the 14th century, this Gothic church is from a period of French royal rule under the Angevin dynasty. Inside, look for the faded Trinity on the back wall, which shows a dove representing the Holy Spirit between the heads of God the Father and Christ (c. 1414). The altar is adorned with four finely carved Gothic tombs of Angevin kings. A chapel stacked with Bourbon royalty is just to the right. Its tranquil cloistered courtyard, around back, is not worth its €6 entry fee.

Cost and Hours: Free, daily 7:30-13:00 & 16:30-20:00, Piazza del Gesù Nuovo, www.monasterodisantachiara.com.

▲▲CAPPELLA SANSEVERO

This small chapel is a Baroque explosion mourning the body of Christ, who lies on a soft pillow under an incredibly realistic veil. It's also the personal chapel of Raimondo de Sangro, an eccentric inventor, patron of the arts, and a grand master of the Freemasons. The chapel, filled with Masonic symbolism, contains his tomb and the tombs of his family. Study the remarkable **Veiled Christ** in the center. Carved out of marble by Giuseppe ("Howdeedoodat") Sammartino in 1753, it combines a Christian message (Jesus died for our salvation) with Masonic philosophy (the veil represents how the body and ego are obstacles to real spiritual freedom). As you walk from Christ's feet to his head, his expression goes from suffering to peace. Downstairs are two mysterious skeletons—some of the mad inventor's work, with artificial veins to illustrate the circulatory system.

Good English explanations are posted throughout; when you buy your ticket, pick up the free floor plan, which indentifies each of the statues lining the nave.

Cost and Hours: €7, buy tickets at office at the corner—or skip the long ticket-buying line by reserving ahead online (€2 fee) and printing out a voucher; open Wed-Mon 9:30-18:30, closed Tue, Via de Sanctis 19, tel. 081-551-8470, www.museosansevero.it.

▲DUOMO

Naples' historic cathedral, built by imported French Anjou kings in the 14th century, boasts a breathtaking Neo-Gothic facade. Step into the vast interior to see the mix of styles along the side chapels—from pointy Gothic arches to rounded Renaissance ones to gilded Baroque decor. Explore the two largest side-chapels (flanking the nave, about halfway to the transept), each practically a church in its own right. On the left, the

Naples Duomo

Chapel of St. Restituta stands on the site of the original, early-Christian church that predated the cathedral. On the right is the **Chapel of San Gennaro**—dedicated to the patron saint of Naples—decorated with silver busts of bishops, and seven paintings on bronze. The cathedral's **main altar** at the front is ringed by carved wooden seats, which are filled three times a year by clergy to witness (they hope) the Miracle of the Blood, when two tiny vials of the dried blood of St. Gennaro temporarily liquefy before their eyes. Thousands of Neapolitans cram into the church to watch. They believe that if the blood remains solid, it's terrible luck for the city. The stairs beneath the altar lead to a **crypt** with the relics of St. Gennaro.

Cost and Hours: Free, Mon-Sat 8:30-13:30 & 14:30-20:00, Sun 8:30-13:30 & 16:30-19:30, Via Duomo.

In the City Center

This cluster of important sights can be found between the big ceremonial square, Piazza del Plebiscito, and the cruise ship terminal. If touring the entire neighborhood, I'd see it in this order:

▲PIAZZA DEL PLEBISCITO

This square celebrates the 1861 vote (*plebiscito,* plebiscite) in which Naples chose to join Italy. Dominating the top of the square is the Church of San Francesco di Paola, with its Pantheon-inspired dome and broad, arcing colonnades. If it's open, step inside to ogle the vast interior—a Neoclassical re-creation of one of ancient Rome's finest buildings.

• *Opposite is the...*

ROYAL PALACE (PALAZZO REALE)

From the square in front of the palace, look for eight kings in the niches, each from a different dynasty (left to right): Norman, German, French, Spanish, Spanish, Spanish, French (Napoleon's brother-in-law), and, finally, Italian—Victor Emmanuel II, King of Savoy. The statues were made at the request of V. E. II's son, so his dad is the most dashing of the group. As far as palaces go, the interior is unimpressive.

Cost and Hours: €4, includes painfully dry audioguide, Thu-Tue 9:00-20:00, closed Wed, last entry one hour before closing, tel. 848-082-408, www.palazzorealenapoli.it.

Royal Palace

• *Continue 50 yards past the Royal Palace (toward the trees) to enjoy a...*

FINE HARBOR VIEW

While boats busily serve Capri and Sorrento, Mount Vesuvius smolders ominously in the distance. Look back to see the vast "Bourbon red" palace—its color inspired by Pompeii. The hilltop above Piazza del Plebiscito is San Martino, with its Carthusian monastery-turned-museum (the Centrale funicular to the top is just across the square and up Via Toledo). The promenade you're on continues to Naples' romantic harborfront—the fishermen's quarter (Borgo Marinaro)—a fortified island connected to the mainland by a stout causeway, with its fanciful, ancient Castel dell'Ovo (Egg Castle) and trendy harborside restaurants.

• *Head back through the piazza and pop into...*

GRAN CAFFÈ GAMBRINUS

This coffee house, facing the piazza, takes you back to the elegance of 1860. It's a classic place to sample a crispy *sfogliatella* pastry, or perhaps the rum-soaked cakes called *babà*. Stand at the bar *(banco)*, pay double to sit *(tavola)*, or just wander around as you imagine the café buzzing with intellectuals, journalists, and artsy types during Naples' 19th-century heyday (daily 7:00-24:00, Piazza del Plebiscito 1, tel. 081-417-582).

• *A block away, tucked behind the palace, you can peek inside the Neoclassical...*

TEATRO DI SAN CARLO

Built in 1737, this is Europe's oldest opera house and Italy's second-most-respected (after La Scala, built in Milan 41 years later). The theater burned down in 1816, and was rebuilt within the year. Guided 35-minute visits in English just show you the fine auditorium with its 184 boxes—each with a big mirror to reflect the candlelight (€6; tours Mon-Sat at 10:30, 11:30, 12:30, 14:30, 15:30, and 16:30; Sun at 10:30, 11:30, and 12:30; tel. 081-797-2468, www.teatrosancarlo.it).

• *Beyond Teatro di San Carlo and the Royal Palace is the huge, harborfront...*

CASTEL NUOVO

This imposing castle now houses government bureaucrats and the Civic Museum. It's a mostly empty shell, with a couple of dusty halls of Neapolitan art, but the views over the bay from the upper terraces are impressive (€6, Mon-Sat 9:00-19:00, closed Sun, last entry one hour before closing, tel. 081-795-7722, www.comune.napoli.it).

• *Head back to Teatro di San Carlo, cross the street, and go through the tall yellow arch into...*

▲GALLERIA UMBERTO I

This Victorian iron-and-glass shopping mall was built in 1892 to reinvigorate the district after a devastating cholera epidemic occurred here. Gawk up, then walk left to bring you back out on Via Toledo.

• *Just up the street and behind Piazza del Plebiscito is an interesting subterranean experience.*

▲GALLERIA BORBONICA

Beneath Naples' Royal Palace was a vast underground network of caves, aqueducts, and cisterns that originated as a quarry in the 15th century. In the mid-1800s, when popular revolutions were threatening royalty across Europe, the understandably nervous king of Naples, Ferdinand II, had this underground world expanded to create an escape tunnel from the palace to his military barracks nearby. In World War II, it was used as an air raid shelter; after the war, the police used it to store impounded cars and motorcycles. Today, enthusiastic guides take the curious on a fascinating 70-minute, 500-yard-long guided walk through this many-layered world littered with disintegrating 60-year-old vehicles upon which Naples sits.

Cost and Hours: €10 English-language tours leave Fri-Sun at 10:00, 12:00, 15:30, and 17:30, tel. 081-764-5808. The most convenient entry is just behind Piazza del

Plebiscito—up Via Gennaro Serra and down Vico del Grottone to #4 (to avoid that entrance's 90 steep steps, enter at Via Morelli 61).

South of Spaccanapoli

PORTA NOLANA OPEN-AIR FISH MARKET

Of Naples' many boisterous outdoor markets, its fish market will net you the most photos, memories—and smells. It's been located for centuries under Porta Nolana (a gate in the city wall), immediately in front of the Napoli Porta Nolana Circumvesuviana station and four long blocks from Centrale Station. From Piazza Nolana, wander under the medieval gate and take your first left down Vico Sopramuro to enjoy an edible scavenger hunt (Tue-Sun 8:00-14:00, closed Mon).

▲▲HARBORSIDE PROMENADE: THE LUNGOMARE *PASSEGGIATA*

Each evening, relaxed and romantic Neapolitans in the mood for a scenic harborside stroll do their *vasche* (laps) along the inviting Lungomare harborside promenade and beyond. To join in this elegant people-watching scene (best after 19:00), stroll down to the waterfront from Piazza del Plebiscito and then along Via Nazario Sauro to the beginning of a delightful series of harborside promenades that stretches romantically all the way out of the city. Along the way, you'll enjoy views of Mount Vesuvius and the Bay of Naples. The entire route is crowded on weekends and lively any evening of the week with families, amorous couples, friends hanging out, and lots of hustlers.

Porta Nolana fish market

On San Martino

The ultimate view overlooking Naples, its bay, and the volcano is from the hill called San Martino, just above (and west of) the city center. Up top you'll find a mighty fortress (which charges for entry but offers the best views from its ramparts) and the adjacent monastery-turned-museum. While neither of these sights is exciting, the views are. And the surrounding neighborhood (especially Piazza Fuga) is classy compared to the gritty streets below. Enjoy the views for free from the benches on the square in front of the monastery.

Getting There: From Via Toledo, the Spanish Quarter gradually climbs up San Martino's lower slopes, before steep paths take you up the rest of the way. But the easiest way to ascend San Martino is by funicular. Three different funicular lines lead from lower Naples to the hilltop: The Centrale line runs from the Spanish Quarter, just near Piazza del Plebiscito and the Toledo Metro stop; the Montesanto line from the Montesanto Metro stop and Via Pignasecca market zone (near the top of Via Toledo); and the Chiaia line from farther out, near the Piazza Amadeo Metro stop. Each is covered by the regular local transit ticket. Ride any of the three up to the end of the line; they converge within a few blocks at the top of the hill—Centrale and Chiaia wind up at opposite ends of the charming Piazza Fuga, while Montesanto terminates a bit closer to the fortress and museum.

Leaving any of the funiculars, head uphill, carefully tracking the brown signs for *Castel S. Elmo* and *Museo di San Martino* (escalators make the climb easier).

Regardless of where you come up, you'll pass the Montesanto funicular station—angle right (as you face the station) down Via Pirro Ligorio, and then continue following the signs. First you'll reach the castle (containing a decent modern art museum, closed Tue), and then the monastery/museum (both are about 10 minutes' walk from Piazza Fuga).

Another convenient—if less scenic—approach is via the Metro's line 1 to the Vanvitelli stop, which is near the upper funicular terminals.

▲SAN MARTINO CARTHUSIAN MONASTERY AND MUSEUM

The monastery, founded in 1325 and dissolved in the early 1800s, is now a sprawling museum. The church is a beautiful Baroque explosion. Around the humble cloister are a variety of museum exhibits, including an excellent collection of *presepi* (Nativity scenes), both life-size and miniature, including the best I've seen, by Michele Cucinello. The square out front has views nearly as good as the ones from inside.

Cost and Hours: €6, Thu-Tue 8:30-19:30, closed Wed, last entry one hour before closing, audioguide-€5, Largo San Martino 8, tel. 081-229-4502, http://cir.campania.beniculturali.it/museosanmartino/.

Eating

Naples is the birthplace of pizza. Its pizzerias bake just the right combination of fresh dough (soft and chewy, as opposed to Roman-style, which is thin and crispy), mozzarella, and tomatoes in traditional wood-burning ovens. The famous, venerable places can have lines stretching out the door and half-hour waits for a table. If you want to skip the hassle, ask your hotel for directions to the neighborhood pizzeria. An average one-person pie (usually the only size available) costs €4-8; most places offer both take-out and eat-in, and pizza is often the only thing on the menu.

Pizza was born in Naples.

The most famous pizzerias are both a few long blocks from the train station, and at the end of my self-guided Naples walk. **$ Antica Pizzeria da Michele** is for pizza purists. It serves just two varieties: *margherita* (tomato sauce and mozzarella) and *marinara* (tomato sauce, oregano, and garlic, no cheese). Arrive early or late to get a seat. If there's a mob, head inside to get a number (Mon-Sat 10:30-24:00, closed Sun; look for the vertical red *Antica Pizzeria* sign at the intersection of Via Pietro Colletta and Via Cesare Sersale at #1; tel. 081-553-9204). If it's just too crowded, **$ Pizzeria Trianon da Ciro,** across the street and left a few doors, offers more choices, higher prices, air-conditioning, and a cozier atmosphere (daily 11:00-15:30 & 19:00-23:00, Via Pietro Colletta 42, tel. 081-553-9426).

$$ Trattoria Campagnola is a classic family place with a daily home-cooking-style chalkboard menu on the back wall, mama busy cooking in the back, and wine on tap. Here you can venture away from pastas, be experimental with a series of local dishes, and not go wrong (daily 12:30-16:00 & 19:30-23:00, between the famous pizzerias at Via Tribunali 47, tel. 081-459-034 but no reservations).

$$ La Stanza del Gusto, two blocks downhill from the Archaelogical Museum, tackles food creatively and injects crusty Naples with a little modern color and irreverence. The ground floor is casual, trendy, and playful, while the upstairs is more refined yet still polka-dotted (weekday lunch specials,

Tue-Sat 12:00-15:30 & 19:30-23:30, closed Sun-Mon, Via Santa Maria di Constantinopoli 100, tel. 081-401-578).

Sleeping

As an alternative to intense Naples, most travelers prefer to sleep in mellow Sorrento, just over an hour away. But here are a few good local options. Prices are soft during the slow summer months (July-Sept).

$$$ Decumani Hotel de Charme is a classy oasis in the very heart of the city, just off Spaccanapoli. While the street is Naples-dingy, the hotel is an inviting retreat, filling an elegant 17th-century palace with 42 rooms and a gorgeous breakfast room (air-con, elevator, Via San Giovanni Maggiore Pignatelli 15, Metro: Università; if coming from Spaccanapoli, this lane is one street toward the train station from Via Santa Chiara, tel. 081-551-8188, www.decumani.com, info@decumani.com).

$$$ Art Resort Galleria Umberto has 15 rooms in two different buildings inside the Umberto I shopping gallery at the bottom of Via Toledo. This genteel-feeling place gilds the lily, with an aristocratic setting but older bathrooms. Consider paying €20 extra for a room overlooking the gallery (air-con, elevator, Galleria Umberto 83, fourth floor—ask at booth for coin to operate elevator if needed, Metro: Toledo, tel. 081-497-6224, www.artresortgalleriaumberto.it, info@artresortgalleriaumberto.it).

$ Grand Hotel Europa, across the seedy street right next to Centrale station, has 89 decent rooms whimsically decorated. Though a bit worn, the hotel is a decent value, and its 1970s-era tackiness (including the Kool-Aid and canned fruit at breakfast) is good for a laugh (RS%, family rooms, air-con, elevator, restaurant, Corso Meridionale 14, across street from station's north exit near track 5, tel. 081-267-511, www.grandhoteleuropa.com, info@grandhoteleuropa.com).

Transportation

Getting Around Naples

Naples' entire public transportation system—Metro, buses, funicular railways, and the single tramline—uses the same tickets, which must be stamped as you enter (in the yellow or blue machines). A €1 single ticket *(corsa singola)* covers any ride on most modes of transportation (bus, tram, funicular, or Metro line 1), with no transfers; for Metro line 2 you need the €1.20 version (it's considered a "suburban" line). If you need to transfer, buy the €1.50 *90 minuti* ticket. Tickets are sold at *tabacchi* stores, some newsstands, clunky machines at Metro stations (coins and small bills only), and occasionally at station windows. A *giornaliero* day pass costs €3.50 (or €4.50 including Metro line 2), and pays for itself quickly, but can be hard to find; many *tabacchi* stores don't sell them. Several versions of the Campania ArteCard cover public transit. Always be wary of pickpockets when using public transportation.

For general info, maps, and fares in English, visit www.unicocampania.it, though schedules are on the Italian-only site www.anm.it. For journey planning, use maps.google.com.

By Metro: Naples' subway, the *Metropolitana,* has three main lines *(linea).* Station entrances and signs to the Metro are marked by a red square with a white *M.*

Line 1 is very useful for tourists. Starting from the train station (stop name: Garibaldi), it heads to Università (the university), Municipio (at Piazza Municipio, just above the harbor and cruise terminal), Toledo (south end of Via Toledo, near Piazza del Plebiscito), Dante (Piazza Dante), and Museo (Archaeological Museum). Four stops beyond Museo is the Vanvitelli stop, near the hilltop San Martino sights. Many of line 1's new stations are huge, elaborate, and designed by prominent architects; proud locals are excited to tell you about their favorite.

Line 2 (part of the Italian national rail system) is most useful for getting quickly from

Naples Transportation

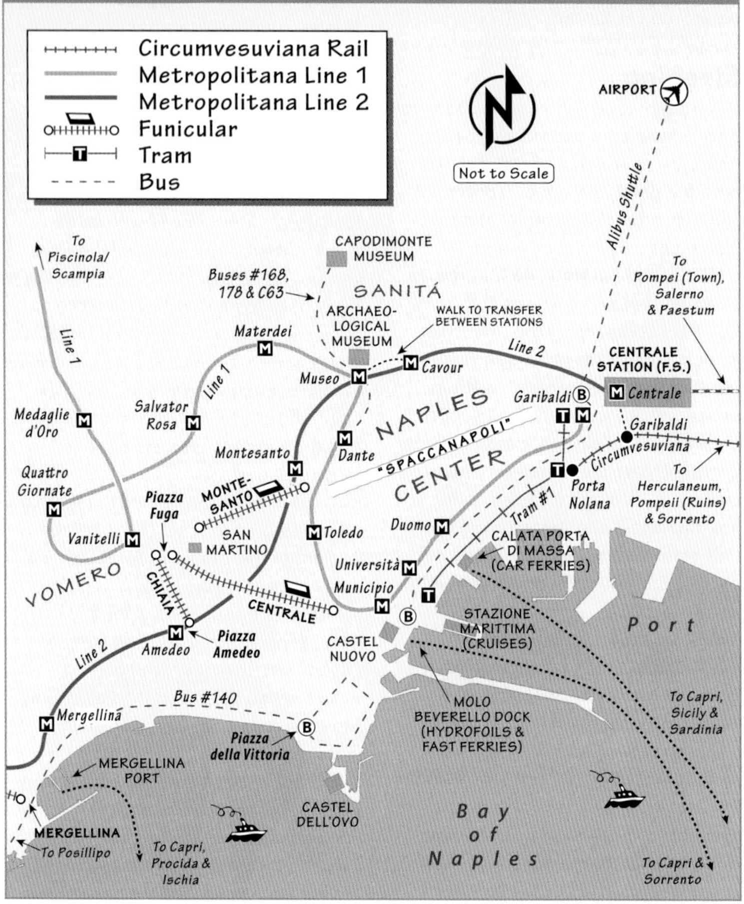

the train station to Piazza Cavour (a 5-minute walk from the Archaeological Museum) or Montesanto (the top of the Spanish Quarter and Spaccanapoli street, and base of one funicular up to San Martino).

The new, under-construction **line 6** will begin at Municipio and head west to Mergellina and beyond—unlikely to be of much use to tourists.

By Funicular: Naples' three funiculars *(funicolare)* carry commuters and sightseers into the hilly San Martino neighborhood just west of downtown. All three converge near Piazza Fuga, a short walk from the monastery/museum, hilltop castle, and marvelous views (see San Martino listing on page 416).

By Bus: Buses are crowded and poorly signed, and aren't a user-friendly option for uninitiated newcomers.

By Tram: Tramline #1 runs along Corso Garibaldi (at the other end of the big square from Centrale Station) and down to the waterfront, terminating by the ferry and cruise terminals (direction: *Stazione Marittima*). It's useful if you're connecting from boat to train, but it may be closed for repairs during your visit.

By Taxi: A short ride in town should cost €10-12. Ask for the *tariffa predeterminata* (a fixed rate). Your hotelier or a TI can tell you what a given ride should cost. You can also ask the driver to use the meter—for metered rides there are some legitimate extra charges (baggage fees, €2.50 supplement after 22:00 or all day Sun and holidays). Radio Taxi 8888 is one reputable company (tel. 081-8888).

Arriving and Departing

BY TRAIN

There are several Naples train stations, but all trains coming into town stop at either Napoli Centrale or Garibaldi—which are essentially the same place, with Centrale on top of Garibaldi. Stretching in front of this station complex is the vast Piazza Garibaldi, with a new underground shopping mall and Metro entrance. Be alert for pickpockets in the station and the surrounding neighborhood.

Centrale, on the ground floor, is the slick, modern main station. It has a small TI (near track 23), an ATM (at Banco di Napoli near track 24), a bookstore (La Feltrinelli, near track 24), and baggage check (*deposito bagagli,* near track 5). Pay WCs are down the stairs across from track 13. Shops and eateries are concentrated in the underground level. A good supermarket (Sapori & Dintorni) is out the front door and to the left.

Rick's Tip: *At the Naples train station,* **carry your own bags;** *there are no official porters. Men will offer to help you—refuse. On the Circumvesuviana train, be ready for this common trick: A team of thieves blocks the door at a stop, pretending it's stuck. While everyone rushes to try to open it, an accomplice picks their pockets.*

Garibaldi, on the lower level of the complex, is used exclusively by the Circumvesuviana commuter train (which you'll most likely use to connect to Sorrento or Pompeii). This is not the terminus for the Circumvesuviana; that's one stop farther downtown, at the station called Porta Nolana.

Getting Downtown from the Station: Arriving at either station, the best bet for reaching most sights and hotels is either the Metro or a taxi. In the lower-level corridor (below the main Centrale hall), look for signs to **Metro** lines 1 and 2. Line 2 offers the faster route to the Archaeological Museum (ride it to the Cavour stop and walk 5 minutes). Line 1 is handy for city-center stops, including the cruise port (Municipio), the main shopping drag (Toledo and Dante), and the Archaeological Museum (Museo).

A long row of white **taxis** line up out front. Ask the driver to charge you the fixed rate (*tariffa predeterminata*), which varies from €7 for the old center to €13 for the most distant hotel I list. The TI in the station can tell you the going rate.

Train Connections from Naples to: Rome (Trenitalia: 1-4/hour, 1 hour on Frecciarossa, 2 hours on Intercity, 2.5 hours and much cheaper on regional trains; Italo: hourly, 70 minutes), **Florence** (Trenitalia: hourly, 3 hours; Italo: hourly, 3 hours), **Venice** (Trenitalia: almost hourly, 5.5 hours, some change in Bologna or Rome; Italo: 3/day, 5.5 hours). Any train listed on the schedule as leaving Napoli PG or Napoli-Garibaldi departs not from Napoli Centrale, but from the adjacent Garibaldi Station.

From Naples by Circumvesuviana to: Pompeii (2/hour, 40 minutes), then **Sorrento** (2/hour, 70 minutes total, end of the line).

Rick's Tip: *To reach the ancient site of Pompeii, make sure to take the* **Circumvesuviana** *commuter train to the* **Pompei Scavi-Villa dei Misteri** *stop (*scavi *means "excavations"). Don't take a regular train to the modern city of Pompei, which is on a separate rail line and a long, dull walk from the ruins.*

Getting Around Naples, Sorrento, and the Amalfi Coast

To connect Naples, Sorrento, and the Amalfi Coast, you can travel on land by train, bus, and taxi. Whenever possible, consider taking a boat—it's faster, cooler, and more scenic.

By Circumvesuviana Train: This useful commuter train—popular with locals, tourists, and pickpockets—links Naples, Pompeii, and Sorrento. The most important Circumvesuviana station in Naples (called "Garibaldi") is underneath Naples' Centrale station. To find it, follow the signs downstairs to *Statione Garibaldi* and then *Circumvesuviana* signs down the corridor to the Circumvesuviana ticket windows (no self-service ticket machines—line up). Buy your ticket, confirm time and track, insert your ticket at the turnstiles and head down another level to the platforms.

The Circumvesuviana is covered by the Campania ArteCard (see page 398), but not rail passes. If you're heading to **Pompeii**, take any Circumvesuviana train marked *Sorrento*—they all stop at both places (usually depart from platform 3). Sorrento-bound trains depart twice hourly, and take about 40 minutes to reach Pompei Scavi-Villa Misteri (for Pompeii ruins, €2.60 one-way), and 70 minutes to reach **Sorrento**, the end of the line (€3.60 one-way). Express trains to Sorrento marked *DD* (6/day) reach Sorrento 15 minutes sooner, and also stop at Pompeii. For schedules, see www.eavsrl.it.

On the platform in Naples, double-check with a local that the train goes to Sorrento, as the Circumvesuviana has several lines that branch out to other destinations. When returning to Naples on the Circumvesuviana, get off at the next-to-the-last station, Garibaldi (Centrale station is just up the escalator).

Perhaps your biggest risk of theft is while catching or riding the Circumvesuviana. You won't be mugged—but you may be conned or pickpocketed. Especially

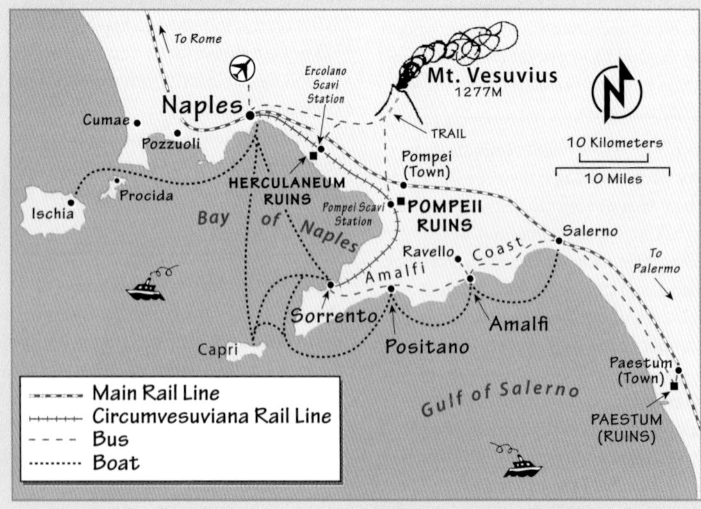

late at night, the train is plagued by ruffians. For maximum safety and peace of mind, sit in the front car, where the driver will double as your protector, and avoid riding it after dark.

By Bus: Crowded SITA buses are most useful for traversing the popular Amalfi Coast. Mondo Guide tours also cover the Amalfi Coast. For more information on both options, see pages 456 and 396.

By Taxi: For €100, you can take a 30-mile taxi ride from Naples directly to your Sorrento hotel (ask the driver for the non-metered *tariffa predeterminata*). You can hire a cab on Capri for about €70/hour. Taxis in the Amalfi Coast are generally expensive, but they can be convenient, especially with a larger group; see under "By Taxi" on page 458.

By Boat: Major companies include Caremar (www.caremar.it), SNAV (www.snav.it), Gescab (a.k.a. NLG Jet, www.gescab.it), Navigazione Libera del Golfo (www.navlib.it), Alilauro (www.alilauro.it), Travelmar (www.travelmar.it), and Alicost (www.alicost.it). Each company has different destinations and prices; some compete for the same trips. Some lines (like Sorrento-Capri) run all year; others (on the Amalfi Coast for example) only in summer. Trips can be cancelled in bad weather. Faster watercraft cost a little more than slow car ferries. A hydrofoil, sometimes called a "jet boat," skims between Naples and Sorrento—it's swifter, safer from pickpockets, more scenic, and more expensive than the train.

For schedules, check online (the best overview is at www.capritourism.com; click "Shipping Timetable"), or ask at any TI, or at Naples' Molo Beverello boat dock. Most boats charge €2 or so for luggage. If you plan to arrive at and leave a destination by boat, note the return times—the last boat usually leaves before 19:00.

The preset price for a taxi from Naples' Centrale train station to its port (Molo Beverello) is €11, or you can just hop on Metro line 1 and get off at Municipo.

BY BOAT

Naples is a ferry hub with great boat connections to Sorrento, Capri, and other nearby destinations. Cruise ships use the giant Stazione Marittima cruise terminal, hydrofoils and faster ferries use the Molo Beverello dock (to the west of the terminal), and slower car ferries leave from Calata Porta di Massa, east of the terminal. The port area is at the southeast edge of downtown Naples, near Castel Nuovo. Get to the city center by taxi, tram, Metro, or on foot; the Alibus shuttle bus runs to the airport.

The **taxi** stand is in front of the port area. There's a fixed €11 rate to the train station or to the Archaeological Museum.

As for public transit, a €1 single ticket covers either the tram or the Metro. You can buy tickets at any tobacco shop. Remember to validate your ticket as you board the tram or enter the Metro station.

Tram #1 stops at the busy road directly in front of the cruise terminal, at the corner of the big, orange brick building, and heads to Piazza Garibaldi and the train station (6/hour, 15 minutes, may be closed for repairs). If you're taking the Circumvesuviana commuter line to Pompeii or Sorrento, hop off this tram a bit earlier, at Porta Nolana, where you can catch the train at its starting point.

Straight ahead across the road from the cruise terminal (on the right side of the big fortress) is Piazza Municipio, with the handy Municipio **Metro** stop. From here, Line 1 zips you to the Archaeological Museum (Museo stop) or, in the opposite direction, to the train station (Garibaldi stop).

On foot, it's a seven-minute **walk**—past the gigantic Castel Nuovo—to Piazza del Plebiscito and the old city center.

Boat Connections from Naples to: Sorrento (6/day, more in summer, departs roughly every 2 hours starting at 9:00, 35 minutes), **Capri** (roughly hourly, more in summer, hydrofoil: 45 minutes; ferries: 50-80 minutes; for timetables, visit www.capritourism.com and click "Shipping Timetable."

BY PLANE

Naples International Airport is located a few miles outside of town (a.k.a. Capodichino, code: NAP; handy info desk just outside baggage claim, tel. 081-789-6767, www.gesac.it). **Alibus** shuttle buses whisk you from the airport to Piazza Garibaldi (by Naples' Centrale train station) in 20 minutes, and then head to the port/Piazza Municipio for boats to Capri and Sorrento (buses run daily 6:00-23:00, 4/hour, 30 minutes to the port, €4 on board, stops at train station and port only). If taking a **taxi** from the airport, ask the driver for the fixed price (€16 to the train station, €19 to the port, €23 to the Chiaia district near the waterfront).

To reach **Sorrento** from Naples Airport, take the direct Curreri bus (see page 447). A taxi to Sorrento costs about €100.

POMPEII

A once-thriving commercial port of 20,000, Pompeii (worth ▲▲▲) grew from Greek and Etruscan roots to become an important Roman city. Then, on August 24, A.D. 79, everything changed. Vesuvius erupted and began to bury the city under 30 feet of hot volcanic ash. For the archaeologists who excavated it centuries later, this was a shake-and-bake windfall, teaching them volumes about daily Roman life. Pompeii was accidentally rediscovered in 1599; excavations began in 1748.

Pompeii offers the best look anywhere at what life in Rome must have been like around 2,000 years ago. It's easily reached from Naples on the Circumvesuviana commuter train. Vesuvius, still smoldering ominously, rises up on the horizon.

Rick's Tip: *Up to* **15,000 visitors crowd the Pompeii site on the first Sunday of the month** *when it's free. Avoid visiting on that day.*

Orientation

Cost: €13, possibly more during special exhibits, free first Sun of each month. If you plan to eat or sightsee outside of the archaeological site, ask for an entrance/exit bracelet that allows you to reenter the site up to three times on the same day. Also consider the Campania ArteCard (see page 398) if visiting other sights in the region.

Hours: Daily April-Oct 9:00-19:30, Nov-March 8:30-17:00, last entry 1.5 hours before closing.

Closures: Some buildings and streets are bound to be closed for restoration when you visit. Make a point to use your map and numbers to find your way. Street names and building numbers are very clearly marked throughout the site.

Getting There: Pompeii is roughly midway between Naples and Sorrento on the Circumvesuviana train line (2/hour, 40 minutes from Naples, 30 minutes from Sorrento, either trip costs about €2.60 one-way, not covered by rail passes). Get off at the Pompei Scavi-Villa dei Misteri stop; from Naples, it's the stop after Villa Regina. The DD express trains (6/day) bypass several stations but do stop at Pompei Scavi, shaving 10 minutes off the trip from Naples. From the Pompei Scavi train station, it's just a two-minute walk to the Porta Marina entrance: Leaving the station, turn right and walk down the road about a block to the entrance (on your left).

Parking: Parking is available at Camping Zeus, next to the Pompei Scavi train station (€2.50/hour, €10/12 hours, 10 percent discount with this book); several other campgrounds/parking lots are nearby.

Information: Ignore the "info point" kiosk at the station, which is a private agency selling tours. At the site, pick up the free map and English guide-booklet at the entrance—be sure to get and use this (ask for it when you buy your ticket, or check at the info window to the left of the WCs—the maps aren't available within the walls of Pompeii). Tel. 081-857-5347, www.pompeiisites.org.

Rick's Tip: **Parents** *should note that Pompeii's ancient brothel contains* **sexually explicit frescoes;** *if you're on a tour, let your guide know if you'd rather skip that stop.*

Tours: Simply follow the self-guided tour in this chapter (or, better, enjoy the audio version with my free 🎧 Rick Steves Audio Europe app). Both cover the basics

The Forum at Pompeii

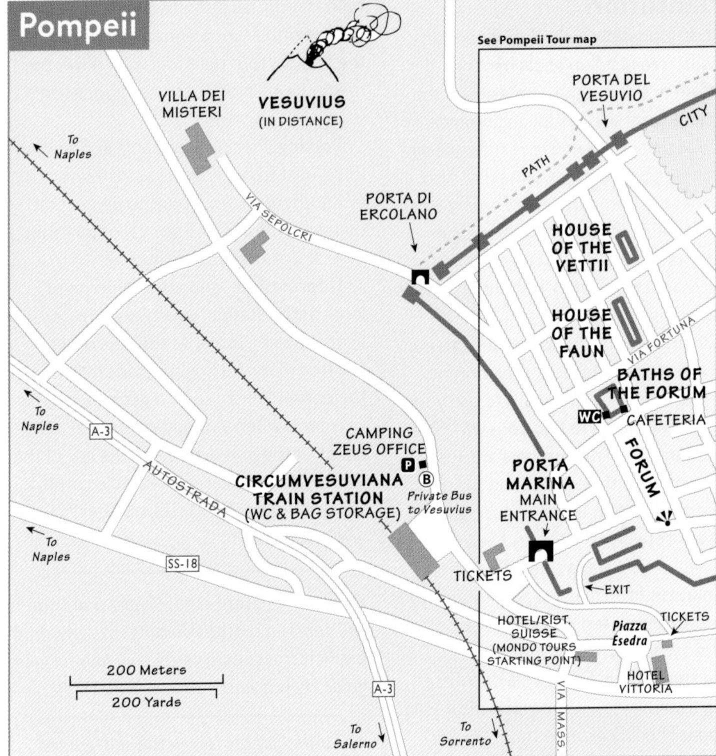

and provide a good framework for exploring the site on your own. Combined with the fine booklet and map included with your entry fee, these provide plenty of information for do-it-yourselfers.

Mondo Guide offers shared tours for Rick Steves readers. This is your best budget bet for a tour with an actual guide (€15, doesn't include €13 Pompeii entry, daily at 11:00, reservations required; meet at Hotel/Ristorante Suisse, just down the hill from the Porta Marina entrance; tel. 081-751-3290, www.sharedtours.com, info@mondoguide.com). Or hire guide **Antonio Somma** for a private or shared tour. Antonio and his team of guides offer good two-hour tours of Pompeii (€120 for up to 6 people, mobile 393-406-3824, tel. 081-850-1992, www.tourspompeiiguide.com, info@pompeitour.com).

Audioguides are available from a kiosk near the ticket booth at the Porta Marina entrance (€8, €13/2 people, ID required), but they offer basically the same info as your free booklet.

Length of This Tour: Allow two hours, or three to visit the theater and amphitheater. With less time, focus on the Forum, House of the Vettii, House of the Faun, and brothel.

Baggage Check: Use the free baggage check near the turnstiles at the site entrance (just yards from the station). The train station also offers pay luggage storage (downstairs, by the WC).

Services: A pay WC is at the train station. The Pompeii site has three WCs—one near the entrance, one in the cafeteria, and another near the end of this tour, uphill from the theaters.

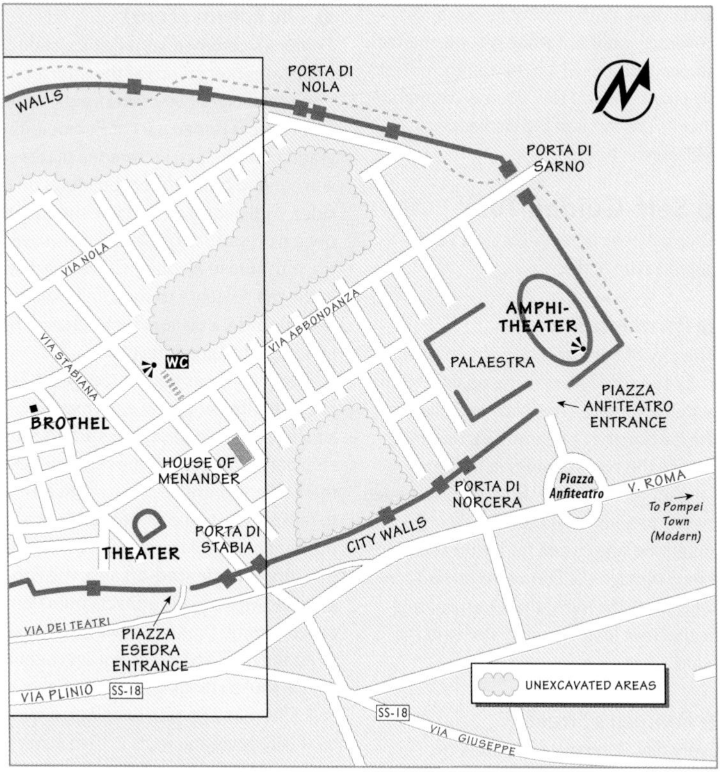

Eating: The **$ Ciao** cafeteria within the site serves good sandwiches, pizza, and pasta. You're welcome to picnic here if you buy a drink. **$ Bar Sgambati**, the café/restaurant in the train station, has air-conditioning, Wi-Fi, and reasonably priced pastas and pizzas (tel. 081-861-0966). Your cheapest bet may be a discreet picnic.

Background

Pompeii, founded in 600 B.C., eventually became a booming Roman trading city. Not rich, not poor, it was middle class—a perfect example of typical Roman life. Streets would have been lined with stalls and jammed with customers from sunup to sundown. Chariots vied with shoppers for street space. Two thousand years ago, Rome controlled the entire Mediterranean—making it a kind of free-trade zone—and Pompeii was a central and bustling port.

Rich and poor mixed it up as elegant houses existed side by side with simple homes. Pompeii served an estimated 20,000 residents with more than 40 bakeries, 30 brothels, and 130 bars, restaurants,

A typical Pompeiian street

and hotels. With most of its buildings covered by brilliant white ground-marble stucco, Pompeii in A.D. 79 was an impressive town. As you tour Pompeii, remember that its best art is in the Archaeological Museum in Naples.

Self-Guided Tour

• *Just past the ticket-taker, start your approach up to the...*

❶ *Porta Marina*

The city of Pompeii was born on the hill ahead of you. This was the original town gate. Before Vesuvius blew and filled in the harbor, the sea came nearly to here. Notice the two openings in the gate (ahead, up the ramp). Both were left open by day to admit major traffic. At night, the larger one was closed for better security.

• *Pass through the Porta Marina and continue up to the top of the street, pausing at the three large stepping-stones in the middle.*

❷ *Pompeii's Streets*

Every day, Pompeiians flooded the streets with gushing water to clean them. These stepping-stones let pedestrians cross without getting their sandals wet. Chariots traveling in either direction could straddle the stones. A single stepping-stone in a road means it was a one-way street, a pair indicates an ordinary two-way, and three (like this) signifies a major thoroughfare. The basalt stones are the original Roman pavement. The sidewalks (elevated to hide the plumbing) were paved with bits of broken pots (an ancient form of recycling) and studded with reflective bits of white marble. These "cats' eyes" helped people get around after dark, either by moonlight or with the help of lamps.

• *Continue straight ahead and enter the city as the Romans once did. The road opens up into the spacious main square—the Forum. Stand at the right end of this rectangular space and look toward Mount Vesuvius.*

❸ *The Forum (Foro)*

Pompeii's commercial, religious, and political center stands at the intersection of the city's two main streets. While it's the most ruined part of Pompeii, it's grand nonetheless. Picture the piazza surrounded by two-story buildings on all sides. The pedestals that line the square once held statues (now safely displayed in the museum in Naples). Citizens gathered in the main square to shop, talk politics, and socialize. Business took place in the buildings that lined the piazza.

The Forum was dominated by the **Temple of Jupiter,** at the far end (marked by a half-dozen ruined columns atop a stair-step base). Jupiter was the supreme god of the Roman pantheon—you might be able to make out his little white marble head at the center-rear of the temple. To the left of the temple is a fenced-off area, the **Forum granary,** where many artifacts from Pompeii are stored (and which we'll visit later).

At the near end of the Forum (behind where you're standing) is the **curia,** or city hall. Like many Roman buildings, it was built with brick and mortar, then covered with marble walls and floors. To your left (as you face Vesuvius and the Temple of Jupiter) is the **basilica,** or courthouse.

Pompeii had the same layout that you would find in any Roman city at the time. All power converged at the Forum: religious (the temple), political (the curia), judicial (the basilica), and commercial (this square was the main marketplace). Even the power of the people was expressed here, since this is where they gathered to vote.

Look beyond the Temple of Jupiter. Five miles to the north looms the ominous backstory to this site: **Mount Vesuvius.** Mentally draw a triangle up from the two remaining peaks to reconstruct the mountain before the eruption. When it blew, Pompeiians had no idea that they were living under a volcano, as Vesuvius hadn't erupted for 1,200 years. Imagine the wonder—then the horror—as a col-

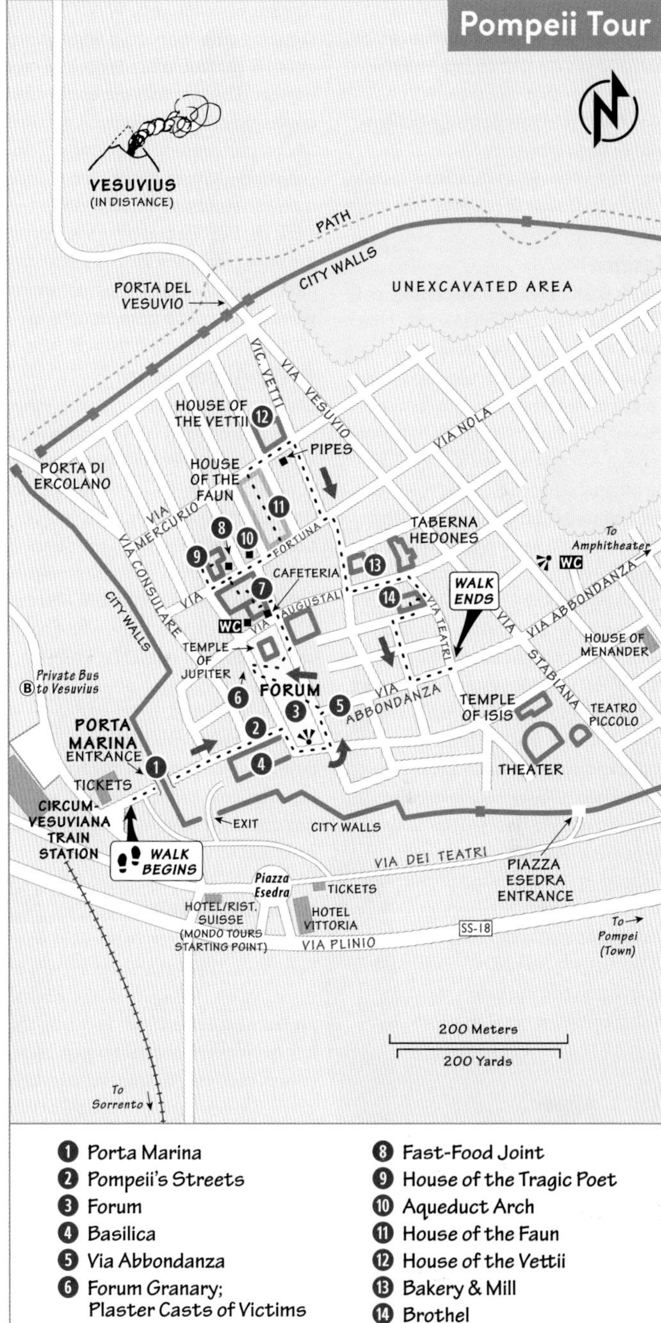
Pompeii Tour
VESUVIUS
(IN DISTANCE)
PATH
CITY WALLS
UNEXCAVATED AREA
PORTA DEL VESUVIO
VIC. VETTI
VIA VESUVIO
HOUSE OF THE VETTII
PIPES
VIA NOLA
PORTA DI ERCOLANO
HOUSE OF THE FAUN
VIA MERCURIO
FORTUNA
TABERNA HEDONES
To Amphitheater
WC
VIA CONSULARE
CITY WALLS
CAFETERIA
VIA AUGUSTALI
WALK ENDS
VIA ABBONDANZA
VIA TEATRI
VIA STABIANA
WC
TEMPLE OF JUPITER
HOUSE OF MENANDER
Private Bus to Vesuvius
FORUM
VIA ABBONDANZA
TEMPLE OF ISIS
TEATRO PICCOLO
PORTA MARINA ENTRANCE
THEATER
TICKETS
CIRCUM-VESUVIANA TRAIN STATION
EXIT
CITY WALLS
WALK BEGINS
VIA DEI TEATRI
PIAZZA ESEDRA ENTRANCE
Piazza Esedra
TICKETS
HOTEL/RIST. SUISSE (MONDO TOURS STARTING POINT)
HOTEL VITTORIA
SS-18
VIA PLINIO
To Pompei (Town)
200 Meters
200 Yards
To Sorrento
1 Porta Marina
2 Pompeii's Streets
3 Forum
4 Basilica
5 Via Abbondanza
6 Forum Granary; Plaster Casts of Victims
7 Baths of the Forum
8 Fast-Food Joint
9 House of the Tragic Poet
10 Aqueduct Arch
11 House of the Faun
12 House of the Vettii
13 Bakery & Mill
14 Brothel

umn of pulverized rock roared upward, and then ash began to fall. The weight of the ash and small rocks collapsed Pompeii's roofs later that day, crushing people who had taken refuge inside buildings instead of fleeing the city.

• *As you face Vesuvius, the basilica is to your left, lined with stumps of columns. Step inside.*

❹ *Basilica*

Pompeii's basilica was a first-century palace of justice. This ancient law court has the same floor plan later adopted by many Christian churches (also called basilicas). The big central hall (or nave) is flanked by rows of columns marking off narrower side aisles. Along the sidewalls are traces of the original stucco imitating marble.

The columns—now stumps all about the same height—were not ruined by the volcano. Rather, they were left unfinished when Vesuvius blew. Pompeii had been devastated by an earthquake in A.D. 62, and was in the process of rebuilding the basilica when Vesuvius erupted 17 years later. The half-built columns show the technology of the day. Uniform bricks were stacked around a cylindrical core. Once finished, they would have been coated with marble dust stucco to simulate marble columns—an economical construction method found throughout the Roman Empire.

Besides the earthquake and the eruption, Pompeii's buildings have suffered other ravages over the years, including Spanish plunderers (c. 1800), 19th-century souvenir hunters, WWII bombs, creeping and destructive vegetation, another earthquake in 1980, and modern neglect. The fact that the entire city was covered by the eruption of A.D. 79 actually helped preserve it, saving it from the sixth-century barbarians who plundered many other towns into oblivion.

Pompeii's Basilica

• *Exit the basilica and cross the short side of the square, to where the city's main street hits the Forum. Stop at the three white stones that stick up from the cobbles.*

❺ *Via Abbondanza*

Glance down Via Abbondanza, Pompeii's main street. Lined with shops, bars, and restaurants, it was a lively, pedestrian-only zone. The three "beaver-teeth" stones are traffic barriers that kept chariots out. On the corner at the start of the street (just to the left), look at the dark travertine column standing next to the white one. The marble drums of the white column are not chiseled entirely round—another construction project left unfinished when Vesuvius erupted.

• *Our tour will eventually end a few blocks down Via Abbondanza after making a big loop. But now, head toward Vesuvius, cutting across the Forum. To the left of the Temple of Jupiter is the...*

❻ *Forum Granary*

A substantial stretch of the west side of the Forum was the granary and ancient produce market. Today, it houses thousands of artifacts excavated from Pompeii. You'll see lots of crockery, pots, pans, jugs, and containers used for transporting oil and wine. You'll also see casts of a couple of victims (and a dog) of the eruption. These casts show Pompeiians, eerily captured in their last moments, hands covering their mouths as they gasped for air. They were quickly suffocated by a superheated avalanche of gas and ash, and their bodies were encased in volcanic debris. While excavating, modern archaeologists detected hollow spaces underfoot, created when the victims' bodies decomposed. By gently filling the holes with plaster, the archaeologists created molds of the Pompeiians who were caught in the disaster.

A few steps to the left of the granary is a tiny alcove that contained the Mensa Ponderaria, a counter where standard units (such as today's liter or gallon) were used to measure the quantities of liquid and solid food that were sold. And just to the right of the granary is the remains of a public toilet. You can imagine the many seats, lack of privacy, and constantly flushing stream running through the room.

• *Exit the Forum by crossing it again in front of the Temple of Jupiter and turning left. Go under the arch. In the road are more "beaver-teeth" traffic blocks. On the pillar to the right, look for the pedestrian-only road sign (two guys carrying an amphora, or ancient jug; it's above the* REG VII INS IV *sign). The modern cafeteria is the only eatery inside the archaeological site. Twenty yards past the cafeteria, on the left-hand side at #24, is the entrance to the...*

❼ *Baths of the Forum (Terme del Foro)*

Pompeii had six public baths, each with a men's and a women's section. You're in the men's zone. The leafy courtyard at the entrance was the gymnasium. After working out, clients could relax with a hot bath *(caldarium)*, warm bath *(tepidarium)*, or cold plunge *(frigidarium)*.

The first room you enter served as the **dressing room.** Holes on the walls were for pegs to hang clothing. High up, the window (with a faded Neptune underneath) was originally covered with a less-translucent Roman glass. Walk over the nonslip mosaics into the next room.

The ***tepidarium*** is ringed by mini—statues or *telamones* (male caryatids, figures used as supporting pillars), which divided the lockers. Clients would undress and warm up here, perhaps relaxing on one of the bronze benches near the bronze heater while waiting for a massage. Look at the ceiling—half crushed by the eruption and half intact, with its fine blue-and-white stuccowork.

Next, admire the engineering in the steam-bath room, or ***caldarium.*** The double floor was heated from below—so nice for bare feet (look into the grate across from where you entered to see the brick support towers). The double walls with brown terra-cotta tiles held the heat. Romans soaked in the big tub, which was filled with hot water. Opposite the big tub is a fountain, which spouted water onto the hot floor, creating steam. The lettering on the fountain reminded those enjoying the room which two politicians paid for it...and how much it cost. (On the far right, the Roman numerals indicate they paid 5,250 *sestertii.*) To keep condensation from dripping from the ceiling, ribbing was added to carry water down the walls.

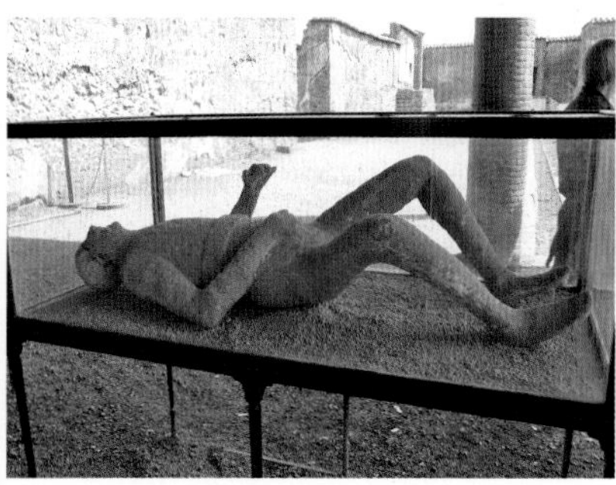

Plaster cast of victim

Baths of the Forum

• *Today's visitors exit the baths through the original entry (at the far end of the dressing room). Immediately across the street is an ancient...*

❽ Fast-Food Joint

After a bath, it was only natural to want a little snack. Just across the street is a fast-food joint, marked by a series of marble counters. Most ancient Romans didn't cook for themselves in their tiny apartments, so to-go places like this were commonplace. The holes in the counters held the pots for food. Each container was like a thermos, with a wooden lid to keep the soup hot, the wine cool, and so on. Notice the groove in the front doorstep and the holes out on the curb. The holes likely accommodated cords for stretching awnings over the sidewalk to shield the clientele from the sun, while the grooves were for the shop's folding accordion doors. Look at the wheel grooves in the pavement, worn down through centuries of use.

• *Just a few steps uphill from the fast-food joint, at #5 (with a locked gate), is the...*

The Eruption of Vesuvius

At about 1:00 in the afternoon on August 24, A.D. 79, Mount Vesuvius erupted, sending a mushroom cloud of ash, dust, and rocks 12 miles into the air. It spewed for 18 hours straight, as winds blew the cloud southward. The white-gray ash settled like heavy snow on Pompeii, its weight eventually collapsing roofs and floors, but leaving the walls intact. Although most of Pompeii's 20,000 residents fled that day, about 2,000 stayed behind.

That night, the type of eruption changed. The mountain let loose superheated avalanches of ash, pumice, and gas eastward (away from Pompeii). These red-hot "pyroclastic flows" sped down the side of the mountain at nearly 100 miles per hour, engulfing everything in their path. Around 7:30 in the morning, a pyroclastic flow headed south and struck Pompeii, snuffing out all life.

❾ House of the Tragic Poet (Casa del Poeta Tragico)

This house is typical Roman style. The entry is flanked by two family-owned shops (each with a track for a collapsing accordion door). The home has an atrium (with skylight and pool to catch the rain), den (where deals were made by the shopkeeper), and garden (with rooms facing it and a shrine to remember both the gods and family ancestors). In the entryway is the famous "Beware of Dog" *(Cave Canem)* mosaic.

When it's open, today's visitors enter the home by the back door (circle around to the left). Inside the house, the grooves on the marble well-head in the entry hall (possibly closed) were formed by generations of inhabitants dragging up the bucket by rope. The frescoed dining room is off the garden. Diners lounged on their couches (the Roman custom) and enjoyed frescoes with fake "windows," giving the illusion of a bigger and airier room. Next to the dining room is a humble BBQ-style kitchen with a little closet for the toilet (the kitchen and bathroom shared the same plumbing).

• *Return to the fast-food place and continue about 10 yards downhill to the big intersection. From the center of the intersection, look left to see a giant arch, framing a nice view of Mount Vesuvius.*

❿ Aqueduct Arch— Running Water

This arch was part of Pompeii's water—delivery system. A 100-mile-long aqueduct carried fresh water down from the hillsides to a big reservoir perched at the highest point of the city wall. Since overall water pressure was disappointing, Pompeiians built arches like the brick one you see here (originally covered in marble) with hidden water tanks at the top. Located just below the altitude of the main tank, these smaller tanks were filled by gravity and provided each neighborhood with reliable pressure. Look closely at the arch and you'll see 2,000-year-old pipes (made of lead imported all the way from Cornwall in Britannia) embedded deep in the brick.

If there was a water shortage, democratic priorities prevailed: First the baths were cut off, then the private homes. The last to go were the public fountains, where all citizens could get drinking and cooking water.

• *If you're thirsty, fill your water bottle from the modern fountain. Then continue straight downhill one block (50 yards) to #2 on the left.*

⓫ *House of the Faun (Casa del Fauno)*

Stand across the street and marvel at the grand entry with *"HAVE"* (hail to you) as a welcome mat. Go in. Notice the two shrines above the entryway—one dedicated to the gods, the other to this wealthy family's ancestors. (Contemporary Neapolitans still follow this practice; you'll notice little shrines embedded in walls all over Naples.)

House of the Faun

You're standing in Pompeii's largest home, where you're greeted by the delightful small bronze statue of the *Dancing Faun,* famed for its realistic movement and fine proportion. (The original is in Naples' Archaeological Museum.) With 40 rooms and 27,000 square feet, the House of the Faun covers an entire city block. The next floor mosaic, with an intricate diamond-like design, decorates the homeowner's office. Beyond that, at the far end of the first garden, is the famous floor mosaic of the *Battle of Alexander.* (The original is also at the museum in Naples.) In 333 B.C., Alexander the Great beat Darius and the Persians. Romans had great respect for Alexander, the first great emperor before Rome's. While most of Pompeii's nouveau riche had bad taste, stuffing their palaces with over-the-top, mismatched decor, this guy had class. Both the faun (an ancient copy of a famous Greek statue) and the Alexander mosaic show an appreciation for history.

The house's back courtyard leads to the exit in the far-right corner. The courtyard is lined with pillars rebuilt after the A.D. 62 earthquake. Take a close look at the brick, mortar, and fake-marble stucco veneer.

• *Leave the House of the Faun through its back door in the far-right corner, past a tiny guard's station. (If closed, exit out the front and walk around to the back.) Turn right and walk about a block until you see metal cages over the sidewalk protecting exposed stretches of ancient lead water pipes. Continue east and take your first left, walk about 20 yards to the entrance (on your left) to the...*

⓬ *House of the Vettii*

This is Pompeii's best-preserved home, retaining many of its mosaics and frescoes. The House of the Vettii was the bachelor pad of two wealthy merchant brothers. In the entryway, it's hard to miss the huge erection. This was not pornography. This

Fresco in the House of the Vettii

Fresco in the Brothel

was a symbol of success: The penis and sack of money balance each other on the goldsmith scale above a fine bowl of fruit. Translation? Only with a balance of fertility and money can you enjoy true abundance.

Step into the atrium with its replica wooden ceiling open to the sky and a lead pipe to collect water for the house cistern. The pool was flanked by two large moneyboxes (one survives, the footprint of the other shows how it was secured to the ground). The brothers wanted all who entered to know how successful they were. A variety of rooms give an intimate peek at elegant Pompeiian life. The dark room to the right of the entrance (as you face out) is filled with exquisite frescoes. Notice more of those white "cat's eye" stones embedded in the floor. Imagine these glinting like little eyes as the brothers and their friends wandered around by oil lamp late at night, with their sacks of gold, bowls of fruit, and enormous...egos.

• *Our next stop, the Bakery, is located about 150 yards south (downhill) from here. To get there, return to the street in front of the House of the Vettii. Walk downhill along Vicolo dei Vetti. Go one block, to where you dead-end at a T-intersection with Via della Fortuna. Go a few steps left and then right at the first corner. Continue down this gently curving road to #22.*

⓭ *Bakery and Mill*

The stubby stone towers are flour grinders. Grain was poured into the top and donkeys or slaves, treading in a circle, pushed wooden bars that turned the stones that ground the grain. The powdered grain dropped out the bottom as flour—flavored with tiny bits of rock. Nearby, the thing that looks like a modern-day pizza oven was...a brick oven. Each neighborhood had a bakery just like this.

• *Continue down the curvy road to the next intersection. As you walk consider the destructive power of all the plants and vines that you see around. Also, notice the chariot grooves worn into the pavement. When the curvy road reaches the intersection with Via degli Augustali, turn left. Ahead, in 50 yards, at #44, is the Taberna Hedones, an ancient tavern with an original floor mosaic still intact. A few steps past that, turn right and walk downhill to #18—one of many Pompeii brothels.*

⓮ *Brothel* (Lupanare)

You'll find the biggest crowds in Pompeii at a place that was likely also quite popular 2,000 ago—the brothel. Prostitutes were nicknamed *lupe* (she-wolves), alluding to the call they made when attracting business. The brothel was a simple place, with beds and pillows made of stone and then covered with mattresses. The ancient graffiti includes tallies and exotic names of the women, indicating the prostitutes came from all corners of the Mediterranean (it also served as feedback from satisfied customers). The faded frescoes above the cells may have been a kind of menu for services offered. Note the idealized women (white, which was considered beautiful; one wears an early bra) and the rougher men (dark, considered horny). The bed legs came with little disk-like barriers to keep critters from crawling up, the tiny rooms had curtains for doors, and the prostitutes provided sheepskin condoms.

• *Leaving the brothel, go right, then take the first left, and continue going downhill two blocks to return to Via Abbondanza. This walk is over. The Forum—and exit—are to the right. If you exit now, you'll be routed through the exhibition rooms (with a scale model of the city, an interesting video, and some artifacts) and the gift shop.*

But before you leave, consider these extra stops—all worth the time and energy (if you have any left). To locate them, refer to your map.

Temple of Isis

This temple served Pompeii's Egyptian community. The little white stucco shrine with the modern plastic roof housed holy water from the Nile. Isis, from Egyptian myth, was one of many foreign gods adopted by the eclectic Romans. Pompeii must have had a synagogue, too, but it has yet to be excavated.

Theater

Originally a Greek theater (Greeks built theirs with the help of a hillside), this was the birthplace of the Greek port here in 470 B.C. During Roman times, the theater sat 5,000 people in three sets of seats, all with different prices: the five marble terraces up close (filled with romantic wooden seats for two), the main section, and the cheap nosebleed section (surviving only on the high end, near the trees). The square stones above the cheap seats once supported a canvas rooftop. Take note of the high-profile boxes, flanking the stage, for guests of honor. From this perch, you can see the gladiator barracks—the colonnaded courtyard beyond the theater. They lived in tiny rooms, trained in the courtyard, and fought in the nearby amphitheater. Check out the adjacent and well-preserved smaller theater, Teatro Piccolo.

House of Menander (Casa di Menandro)

Once owned by a wealthy Pompeiian, this house takes its current name from a fresco of the Greek playwright Menander on one of the walls. Admire the grand atrium (with frescoes depicting scenes from Homer's *Iliad* and *Odyssey*, and an altar to the family gods in the corner), the wall frescoes, and the mosaics. The cloister-like back courtyard leads to a room with skeletons (not plaster casts) of eruption victims from this house. Farther back, a passage leads to the servants' quarters.

Viewpoint

You're at ground level—post-eruption. To the right (inland), the farmland shows how locals lived on top of the ruins for centuries without knowing what was underneath. To the left, you can see the entire ancient city of Pompeii spread out in front of you and appreciate the magnitude of the excavations.

Amphitheater

If you can, climb to the upper level of the amphitheater (though the stairs are often blocked). Mentally replace the tourists below with gladiators and wild animals locked in combat. Walk along the top of the amphitheater and look down into the grassy rectangular area surrounded by columns. This is the **Palaestra,** once used for athletic training. (If you can't get to the top of the amphitheater, you can see the Palaestra from outside—in fact, you can't miss it, as it's right next door.) Facing the other way, look for the bell tower that tops the roofline of the modern city of Pompei, where locals go about their daily lives in the shadow of the volcano, just as their ancestors did 2,000 years ago.

• *If it's too crowded to bear hiking back along uneven lanes to the entrance, you can slip out the site's "back door," which is next to the amphitheater. Exiting, turn right and follow the site's wall all the way back to the entrance.*

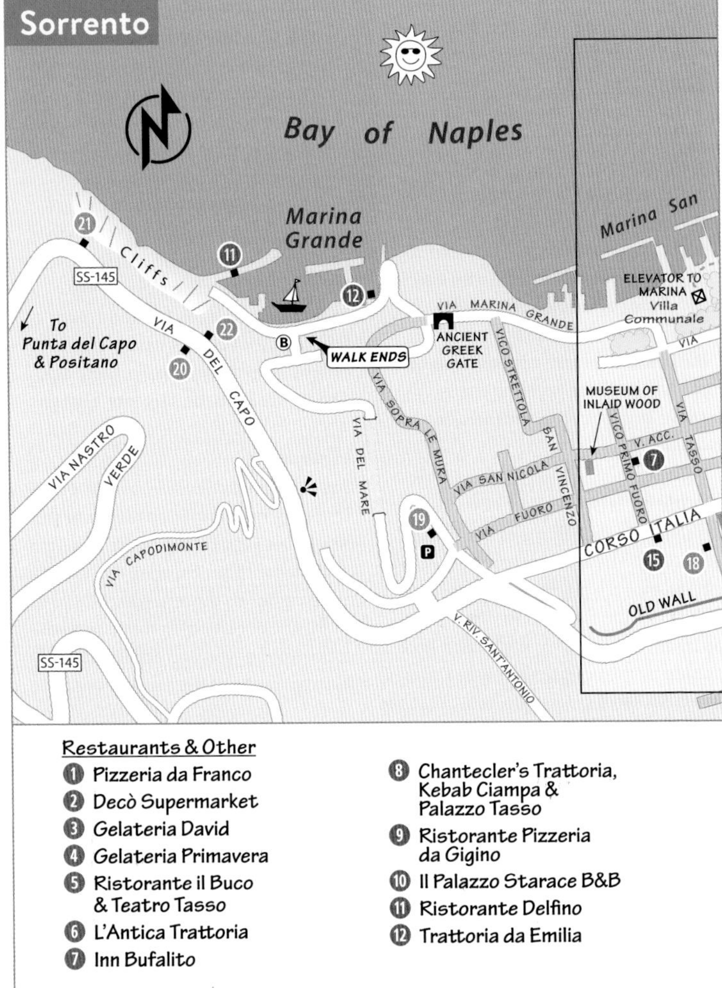

SORRENTO

Spritzed by lemon and olive groves, Sorrento is an attractive resort of 20,000 residents—and, in summer, just as many tourists. Just an hour south of Naples but without a hint of big-city chaos, serene Sorrento makes an ideal home base for exploring the entire region. This gateway to the Amalfi Coast has an unspoiled old quarter, a lively shopping street, and a spectacular cliffside setting above the Mediterranean. The town's economy is based on tourism, so everyone seems to speak fluent English and work for the Chamber of Commerce.

Orientation

Downtown Sorrento is long and narrow. Piazza Tasso marks the town's center. The congested main drag, Corso Italia, runs parallel to the sea, passing 50 yards below the train station, through Piazza Tasso, and then out toward the cape,

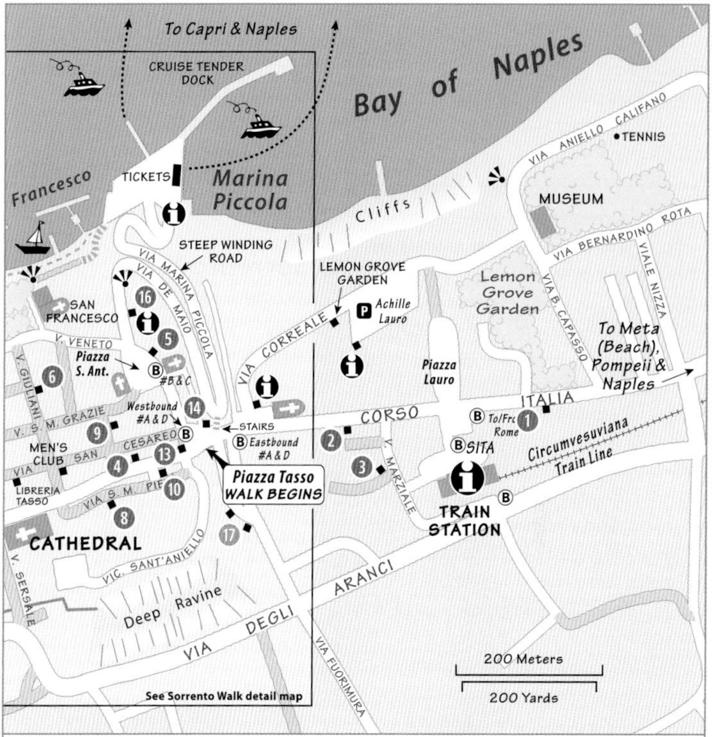

Nightlife

13 Fauno Bar
14 Daniele's Club
15 The English Inn
16 Foreigners' Club

Hotels

17 Hotel Antiche Mura (Mondo meeting point) & Plaza Sorrento
18 Hotel Mignon
19 Ulisse Deluxe Hostel
20 Hotel Minerva
21 Hotel La Tonnarella & Hotel Désirée
22 Albergo Settimo Cielo

where the road's name becomes Via Capo. Nearly everything mentioned here (except Marina Grande and the hotels on Via Capo) is within a 10-minute walk of the station. The town is perched on a cliff (some hotels have elevators down to sun-decks on the water); the best real beaches are a couple of miles away.

Sorrento has two separate port areas: Marina Piccola, below Piazza Tasso, is a functional harbor with boats to Naples and Capri, as well as cruise-ship tenders. Marina

Serene Sorrento

Grande, below the other end of downtown, is a little fishing village, with recommended restaurants and more charm.

Sorrento is busiest in summer and hibernates in winter (Nov-March), when many places close down.

Rick's Tip: *Sorrento makes a great home base because all of the* **key destinations are within an hour or so:** *Naples (by train or boat), Pompeii (by train), the Amalfi Coast (by bus), and the island of Capri (by boat).*

Tourist Information: The helpful regional TI (labeled *Azienda di Soggiorno*)—located inside the Foreigners' Club—hands out the free city map and schedules of boats and buses (Mon-Sat 9:00-19:00, Sun until 18:00 except closed Sun April-May; Nov-March Mon-Fri 8:30-16:00, closed Sat-Sun; Via Luigi de Maio 35, tel. 081-807-4033, www.sorrentotourism.com).

Small "Info Points" are conveniently located around town, where you can get answers to basic questions (open in warm months only). Find them just outside the **train station** in the green; near **Piazza Tasso** at the corner of Via Correale (under the yellow church); at **Marina Piccola**; and at the Achille Lauro **parking garage.**

Tours: Naples-based **Mondo Guide** offers affordable shared tours from Sorrento—an Amalfi Coast drive (see page 458) and a boat trip to Capri (see page 450; tel. 081-751-3290, www.mondoguide.com, info@mondoguide.com).

Sorrento Walk

This lazy stroll through town ends down by the waterside at the small-boat harbor, Marina Grande.

• *Begin on the main square. Stand under the flags between the sea and the town's main square.*

1 PIAZZA TASSO

This piazza is Sorrento's living room. Noisy and congested, it's where the action is. The most expensive apartments and top cafés are on or near this square. City buses stop at or close to the square on their way to Marina Piccola and Via Capo. The train station is a five-minute walk to the left. A statue of St. Anthony, patron of Sorrento, faces north to greet arrivals from Naples (he's often equipped with an armload of fresh lemons and oranges).

Piazzo Tasso

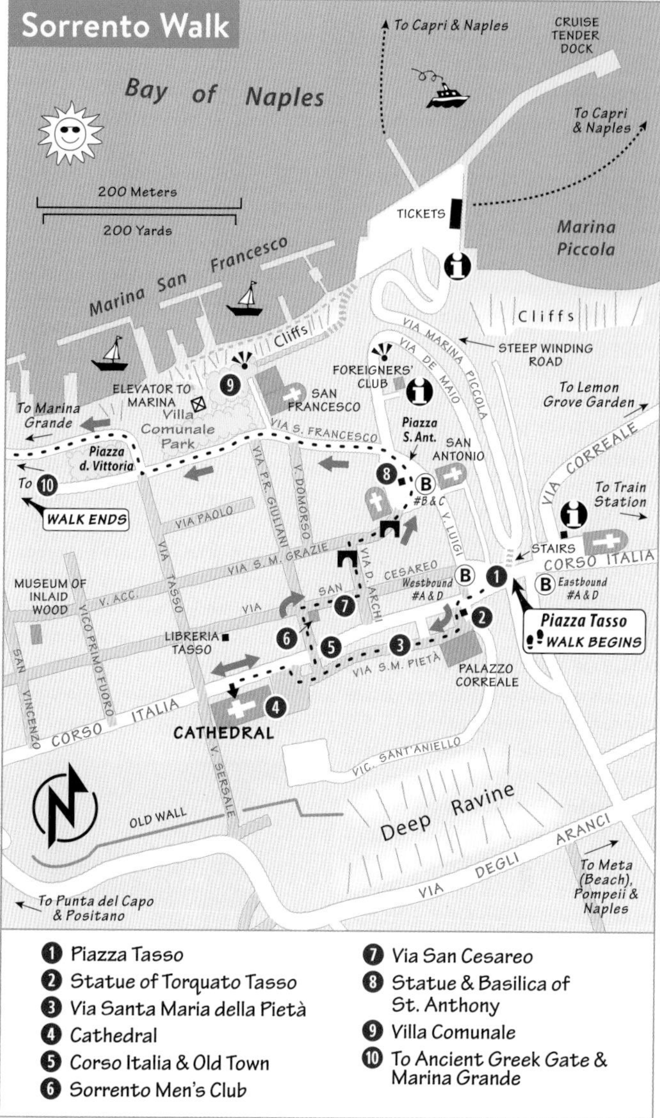

This square spans a gorge that divides downtown Sorrento. The newer section (to your left) was farm country just two centuries ago. The older part is to your right, with an ancient Greek gridded street plan.

For a better glimpse of the gorge-gouged landscape, take a quick detour: With the water to your back, carefully cross through the square and walk straight ahead a block inland, under a canopy of trees and past a long taxi queue. Belly up to the green railing in front Hotel Antiche Mura and look down to see steps that were carved centuries before Christ. The combination of the gorge and the seaside cliffs made Sorrento easy to defend. A small section of wall closed the landward gap in the city's defenses (you can still see a surviving piece of it a few blocks away, near Hotel Mignon).

Sorrento's name may come from the Greek word for "siren," the legendary half-bird, half-woman who sang an intoxicating lullaby. According to Homer, the sirens lived on an island near here. No one had ever sailed by the sirens without succumbing to their musical charms...and to death. But Homer's hero Ulysses was determined to hear the song and restrain his manhood. He put wax in his oarsmen's ears and had himself lashed to the mast of his ship. Oh, it was nice. The sirens, thinking they had lost their powers, threw themselves into the sea. Ulysses' odyssey was about the westward expansion of Greek culture; to the ancient Greeks, Sorrento was the wild west.

• *Back at Piazza Tasso, face the sea and head to the far-left inland corner of the square. You'll find a...*

❷ STATUE OF TORQUATO TASSO

The square's namesake, a Sorrento native, was a Renaissance poet—but today seems only to wonder which restaurant to choose. Directly behind the statue, pop into the **Fattoria Terranova** shop, one of many fun, family-run, and touristy boutiques that sell regional goodies and offers free biscuits and tastes of liqueurs. This one makes all organic products on its own *agriturismo* farm outside the city.

The gifty edibles spill into the courtyard of **Palazzo Correale**, which gives you a feel for an 18th-century aristocratic palace's courtyard, its walls lined with characteristic tiles from 1772.

• *As you're leaving the courtyard, on your immediate left you'll see the narrow...*

❸ VIA SANTA MARIA DELLA PIETÀ

Here, just a few yards off the busy main drag, is a street that goes back centuries before Christ. About 100 yards down the lane, at #24 (on the left), find a 13th-century palace (no balconies back then, for security reasons), now an elementary school. A few steps farther on, you'll see a tiny shrine across the street. Typical of southern Italy, it's where the faithful pray to their saint, who contacts Mary, who contacts Jesus, who contacts God. This shrine is more direct—it starts right with Mary.

• *Continue down the lane, which ends at the delightful...*

❹ CATHEDRAL

Walk alongside this long church (free, daily 8:00-12:30 & 16:30-21:00) until you reach the doors facing the street, halfway down. Step inside the outer door and examine the impressive *intarsio* (inlaid-wood) interior doors. They show scenes of the town and its industry, as well as an old-town map (find Piazza Tasso, trace the fortified walls, and notice the Greek street-grid plan). These doors were made to celebrate Pope John Paul II's visit in 1992. Now enter the church for a cool stroll around the ambulatory, checking out the intricate inlaid Stations of the Cross. Notice the fine inlaid marble seat of the bishop and how the church's elegance matches that of the town. Work your way toward the back

Sorrento Cathedral

door. Before exiting, on the right find the *presepe* (manger scene) with its lovingly painted terracotta figures, each with an expressive face. This takes Bethlehem on that first Christmas and sets it in Naples—with pasta, mozzarella, salami, and even Mount Vesuvius in the background. Exiting through the back door, notice that these doors are also finely inlaid wood.

• *Backtrack 10 yards down Via Santa Maria della Pietà, turn left at the passage under the covered arcade, and cross busy Corso Italia.*

❺ CORSO ITALIA AND THE OLD TOWN

In the summer, this stretch of road is closed to traffic each evening, when it hosts a wonderful *passeggiata* and everyone is out strolling. Look back at the bell tower, with the scavenged ancient Roman columns at its base. Now go straight down Via P. Reginaldo Giuliani, following the old Greek street plan. Locals claim the ancient Greeks laid out the streets east-west for the most sunlight and north-south for the prevailing and cooling breeze. Pause at the poster board on your right to see who's died lately.

• *One block ahead, on your right, the 14th-century loggia is home to the...*

❻ SORRENTO MEN'S CLUB

Once the meeting place of the town's nobles, it's now a retreat for retired working-class men. Strictly no women—and no phones.

Italian men venerate their mothers. (Italians joke that Jesus must have been a southern Italian because his mother believed her son was God, he believed his mom was a virgin, and he lived at home with her until he was 30.) But Italian men have also built into their culture ways to be on their own. Here, men play cards under a historic emblem of the city and a frescoed 16th-century dome, with marvelous 3-D scenes.

Sorrento Men's Club

• *Turn right for a better view of the Men's Club and a historical marker describing the building. Then continue along...*

❼ VIA SAN CESAREO

This pedestrian-only shopping street leads back to Piazza Tasso. It's lined with shops where you can sample lemon products. Notice the huge ancient doorways with their tiny doors—to let only the right people in, during a more dangerous age.

• *After a block, take a left onto Via degli Archi, go under the arch, and then hang a right (under another arch) to the square with the...*

❽ STATUE AND BASILICA OF ST. ANTHONY

Sorrento's town saint humbly looms among the palms, facing the basilica of St. Anthony. Step inside and descend into the crypt (free, stairs beside main altar) where you'll find a chapel and reliquary containing a few of Anthony's bones surrounded by lots of votives. Locals have long turned to St. Anthony when faced with challenges and hard times. Exploring the room, you'll find countless tokens of appreciation to the saint for his help. Before tourism, fishing was the big employer. The back walls feature paintings of storms with Anthony coming to the rescue. Circle behind the altar with Anthony's relics and study the shiny ex-votos (religious offerings) thanking the saint for healthy babies, good employment, surviving heart attacks and lung problems, and lots of strong legs.

• *Exit the square at the bottom-left (following the* **Lift to the Port** *signs; don't go down the street with the line of trees and* **Porto** *signs). Watch on the left for* **The Corner**

Shop, *where Giovanni sells a wide variety of wines, limoncello, pastas, and other foods. Soon after, on the right you'll see the trees in front of Imperial Hotel Tramontano, and to their right a path leading to the...*

❾ VILLA COMUNALE

This fine public park overlooks the harbor. Belly up to the banister to enjoy the view of Marina Piccola and the Bay of Naples. Notice Naples' skyline and the boats that commute from here to there in 35 minutes. Imagine the view in A.D. 70 when Vesuvius blew its top and molten mud flowed down the mountain, burying Pompeii. From here, steps zigzag down to the harbor, where lounge chairs, filled by vacationers working on tans, line the sundecks (there's also the elevator to the harbor). The Franciscan church fronting this square faces a fine modern statue of Francis across the street.

Next to the church is a dreamy little cloister. Pop inside to see local Gothic—a 13th-century mix of Norman, Gothic, and Arabic styles, all around the old pepper tree. This is an understandably popular spot for weddings and concerts.

At the far side of the cloister, stairs lead to a **photo exhibit:** *The Italians* shows off the work of local photographer Raffaele Celentano, who artfully captures classic Italian scenes from 1990 to 2016 in black and white (€2.50, daily 10:00-22:00, great prints for sale, fun photo-op through the grand tree on their deck, adjacent music box exhibit is free).

The view from Villa Comunale

Lemons

Around here, *limoni* are ubiquitous: screaming yellow painted on ceramics, dainty bottles of *limoncello,* and lemons the size of softballs at fruit stands.

The Amalfi Coast and Sorrento area produce several different kinds of lemons. The gigantic, bumpy "lemons" are actually citrons, called *cedri,* and are more for show—they're pulpier than they are juicy, and make a good marmalade. The juicy *sfusato sorrentino,* grown only in Sorrento, is shaped like an American football, while the *sfusato amalfitano,* with knobby points on both ends, is less juicy but equally aromatic. These two kinds of luscious lemons are used in sweets such as *granita* (shaved ice doused in lemonade), *limoncello* (a candy-like liqueur with a big kick, called *limoncino* on the Cinque Terre), *delizia* (a dome of fluffy cake filled and slathered with a thick whipped lemon cream), *spremuta di limone* (fresh-squeezed lemon juice), and, of course, gelato or *sorbetto alla limone.*

• *From here, you can quit the walk and stay in the town center, or continue another few minutes downhill to the waterfront at Marina Grande. To continue to Marina Grande, return to the road and keep going downhill. At the next square (Piazza della Vittoria, with a dramatic WWI memorial and another grand view), cut over to the road closest to the water. After winding steeply down for a few minutes, it turns into a wide stairway, then makes a sharp and steep switchback (take the right fork to continue downhill). Farther down, just before reaching the waterfront, you pass under an...*

❿ ANCIENT GREEK GATE

This gate fortified the city of Sorrento. Beyond it was Marina Grande, technically a separate town with its own proud residents—it's said that even their cats look different.

• *Now go all the way down the steps into Marina Grande, Sorrento's "big" small-boat harbor.*

MARINA GRANDE

Until recently, this community was traditional, with its economy based on fishing. Locals recall when women wore black when a relative died (1 year for an uncle, aunt, or sibling; 2-3 years for a husband or parent). Men got off easy, just wearing a black memorial button.

Two recommended restaurants are on the harbor. **Trattoria da Emilia** has an old newspaper clipping, tacked near the door, about Sophia Loren filming here. On the far side of the harbor, **Ristorante Delfino** boasts a delightful sundeck for a lazy drink before or after lunch (free access for those with this book).

• *From here, where the road hits the beach, buses return to the center at Piazza Tasso every hour (pay the driver). Or you can walk back up.*

Sights

▲LEMON GROVE GARDEN (AGRUMINATO)

This lemon-and-orange grove, lined with shady, welcoming paths, was rescued from development by the city of Sorrento and turned into a park. The family that manages it has seasoned green thumbs and descend from the family that started working here decades ago, when the grove was still in private hands. The garden is dotted with benches, tables, and an inviting little tasting (and buying) stand. You'll get a chance to sniff and taste the varieties of lemons and enjoy free samples of *limoncello* along with other homemade liqueurs made from mandarins, licorice, or fennel. Check out how they've grafted orange-tree branches onto a lemon tree so that both fruits grow on the same tree.

Cost and Hours: Free, daily 10:00-sunset, closed in rainy weather, tel. 081-878-1888, www.igiardinidicataldo.it. Enter the garden either on Corso Italia (100 yards north of the train station—where painted tiles show lemon fantasies) or at the intersection of Via Capasso and Via Rota (next to Hotel La Meridiana).

Nearby: The entrepreneurial family's small "factory"—where you can see how they use the lemons and buy a tasty gelato, *granita,* or lemonade—is just past the parking garage along the road below the garden (Via Correale 27). They also have a small shop across from the Corso Italia entrance (at #267).

Experiences

▲▲CORSO ITALIA *PASSEGGIATA*

Each balmy evening Sorrento offers one of Italy's most enchanting *passeggiata* scenes. Take time to explore the surprisingly pleasant old city between Corso Italia and the sea. Views from Villa Comunale,

Lemon Grove Garden

Corso Italia passeggiata

the public park next to Imperial Hotel Tramontano, are worth the detour. Each night in summer (May-Oct at 19:30; Nov-April weekends only), the police close off Corso Italia to traffic, and Sorrento's main drag becomes a thriving people scene. The *passeggiata* peaks at about 22:00.

▲SWIMMING AND SUNBATHING

There are no great beaches in Sorrento—the gravelly, jam-packed private beaches of **Marina Piccola** are more for partying than pampering, and there's just a tiny spot for public use. The elevator in Villa Comunale city park (next to the Church of San Francesco) gets you down for €1. Another humble beach is at **Marina Grande**, and Ristorante Delfino has a pier lined with rentable lounge chairs (€10 but free for those with this book).

A classic, sandy beach two miles away at **Meta** is generally overrun by teenagers from Naples. Bus #A goes directly from Piazza Tasso to Meta beach (last stop, schedule posted for hourly returns; you can also get there on the Circumvesuviana but the Meta stop is a very long walk from the beach). At Meta, you'll find pizzerias, snack bars, and a little free section of beach, but the place is mostly dominated by several sprawling private-beach complexes—if you go, pay for a spot in one of these, such as Lido Metamare (lockable changing cabins, lounge chairs, tel. 081-532-2505). It's a very Italian scene—locals complain that it's "too local" (i.e., inundated with riffraff)—with light lunches, a playground, a manicured beach, loud pop music...and no international tourists.

More relaxing beaches are west of Sorrento. Tarzan might take Jane to the wild and stony beach at **Punta del Capo,** a 15-minute bus ride west from Piazza Tasso (the same bus #A explained above, but in the opposite direction from Meta; 2/hour, get off at stop in front of the American Bar, then walk 10 minutes past ruined Roman Villa di Pollio).

Tiny fishing **Marina di Puolo** is popular in the summer for its sandy beach, surfside restaurants, and beachfront disco (to get here, stay on bus #A a bit farther—ask driver to let you off at Marina di Puolo—then follow signs and hike down about 15 minutes).

FOOD TOUR

Tamara Whiteside, a foodie from San Diego, offers an information-filled, fast-paced food tour. She dishes up a parade of local edibles interspersed with lots of food history, stopping at eight places in three hours (€75, 15 percent discount for Rick Steves readers, use code "ricksteves"; departures at 10:30 and 16:00 with demand, maximum 12 people; mobile 331-304-5666, www.sorrentofoodtours.com).

SNORKELING AND DIVING

To go snorkeling or scuba diving in the Mediterranean, contact **Futuro Mare** for a one-hour boat ride out to the protected marine zone that lies between Sorrento and Capri with options for snorkelers, beginners, and experienced certified divers (about 3 hours round-trip, call 1-2 days in advance to reserve, tel. 349-653-6323, www.sorrentodiving.it, info@futuromare.it).

BOATING

You can rent motorboats big enough for four people at Marina Piccola (with your back to the ferry-ticket offices, it's to the left around the corner at Via Marina Piccola 43; tel. 081-807-2283, www.nauticasicsic.com).

NIGHTLIFE

Sorrento is a fun place to enjoy a drink or some dancing after dinner.

Fauno Bar dominates Piazza Tasso with tables spilling onto the square.

Daniele's Club is run by DJ Daniele, who tailors music to the audience (including karaoke). The scene, while sloppy, is generally comfortable for the 30- to 60-year-old crowd. If you're alone, there's a pole you can dance with (no cover charge, no food, nightly from 21:30, down the steps from the flags at Piazza Tasso).

The English Inn offers both a streetside sports pub and a more refined garden out back—at least until evening, when the music starts. The menu includes fish-and-chips, all-day English breakfast, baked beans on toast, and draft beer (daily, Corso Italia 55, tel. 081-878-2570).

The **Foreigners' Club,** which has a sprawling terrace and some of the best sea views in town, offers live music—Neapolitan songs and Sinatra-style classics—nightly at 20:00 (May-mid-Oct). The **$$$** meals are affordable yet uninspired, but it's a good spot for dessert or an after-dinner *limoncello* (daily, Via Luigi de Maio 35, tel. 081-877-3263).

THEATER

At **Teatro Tasso,** a hardworking troupe puts on *The Sorrento Musical,* a folk-music show that treats visitors to a schmaltzy dose of Neapolitan Tarantella music and dance—complete with "Funiculì Funiculà" and "Santa Loo-chee-yee-yah." The 75-minute Italian-language extravaganza features a cast of 14 playing guitar, mandolin, saxophone, and tambourines, and singing operatically from Neapolitan balconies. Your €25 ticket (€50 with 4-course dinner) includes a drink before and after the show (3-5 nights/week mid-April-Oct at 21:30, bar opens 30 minutes before show, dinner starts at 20:00 and must be reserved in advance—in person or by email, box office open virtually all day long, facing Piazza Sant'Antonino in the old town, tel. 081-807-5525, www.teatrotasso.com, info@teatrotasso.com).

Eating

In a town proud to have no McDonald's, consider eating well for a few extra bucks (I've listed two splurges on the next page).

Budget Eating: $ Pizzeria da Franco is the place for basic, casual pizza in a fun, untouristy atmosphere. There's nothing fancy about this place—just locals on benches eating hot sandwiches and great pizzas (takeout possible, daily 8:00-late, just across from Lemon Grove Garden on busy Corso Italia at #265, tel. 081-877-2066). **$ Kebab Ciampa** is your best cheap, non-Italian meal in town. Choose beef or chicken—locals don't go for pork—and garnish with fries and/or salad (Thu-Tue from 17:00, closed Wed, off Via Santa Maria della Pietà, at Vico il Traversa Pietà 23, tel. 081-807-4595). Get groceries at the **Decò supermarket** (Mon-Sat 8:30-20:00, shorter hours on Sun, Corso Italia 223).

Gelato: Near the train station, **Gelateria David** has many repeat customers. Before choosing a flavor, sample *Profumi di Sorrento* (an explosive sorbet of mixed fruits), "Sorrento moon" (white almond with lemon zest), or lemon crème (daily 9:00-24:00, shorter hours off-season, closed Dec-Feb, a block below the train station at Via Marziale 19, tel. 081-807-3649). At **Gelateria Primavera,** Antonio and Alberta whip up 70 exotic flavors...and still have time to make pastries for the pope and other celebrities—check out the nostalgic photos in their inviting back room, proving this is a Sorrento institution (daily 9:00-24:00, just west of Piazza Tasso at Corso Italia 142, tel. 081-807-3252).

Gourmet Splurges Downtown

$$$$ Ristorante il Buco is a small, dressy restaurant that serves delightfully presented, playful, and creative modern Mediterranean dishes. Peppe holds a Michelin star, and he and his staff love to explain exactly what's on the plate. Reserve ahead (extravagant-tasting €75-100 fixed-price meal, 10 percent discount when you show this book, good vegetarian selection, Thu-Tue 12:30-14:30 & 19:30-22:30, closed Wed and Jan; just off Piazza Sant'Antonino—facing the basilica, go under the grand arch on the left and immediately enter the restaurant at II Rampa Marina Piccola 5; tel. 081-878-2354, www.ilbucoristorante.it).

$$$$ L'Antica Trattoria enjoys a sedate, romantico, candlelit ambience. The cuisine is traditional but with modern flair, and the inviting menu is fun to peruse (though pricey). Readers who show this book can choose a 10 percent discount on a fixed-price meal or a free limoncello if ordering à la carte. Reservations are smart (good vegetarian options, daily 12:00-23:30, closed Jan-Feb, air-con, Via Padre R. Giuliani 33, tel. 081-807-1082, www.lanticatrattoria.it).

Mid-Priced Restaurants Downtown

$$$ Inn Bufalito specializes in all things buffalo: mozzarella di bufala (and other buffalo milk cheeses), steak, sausage, salami, carpaccio, and buffalo-meat pasta sauce. The space has a modern, borderline-trendy, casual atmosphere (don't miss the seasonal specialties on the blackboard, Wed-Mon 12:00-23:00, closed Tue and Jan-March, Vico I Fuoro 21, tel. 081-365-6975).

$$ Ristorante Pizzeria da Gigino, lively and congested with a sprawling interior and tables spilling onto the street, makes huge, tasty Neapolitan-style pizzas in their wood-burning oven (daily 12:00-24:00, closed Jan-Feb, just off Piazza Sant'Antonino at Via degli Archi 15, tel. 081-878-1927, Antonino).

$$ Chantecler's Trattoria is a hole-in-the-wall, family-run place with delicious food, a casual familial interior, and a long string of tables outside; it's on the narrow lane that leads to the cathedral. Their lunch menu is very affordable; at dinner, prices are slightly higher but still easy on the budget (good vegetarian dishes, take out or eat in, Tue-Sun 12:00-15:00 & 18:30-23:00, closed Mon, Via Santa Maria della Pietà 38, tel. 081-807-5868; Luigi, Francesco, and family).

Harborside in Marina Grande

For a decent dinner *con vista,* head down to the small-boat harbor, Marina Grande (follow the directions from Villa Comunale on my self-guided Sorrento walk). It's about a 15-minute stroll from downtown. You can also take minibus #D from Piazza Tasso. Be prepared to walk back (last bus leaves at 20:00) or spring for an over-priced taxi.

$$$ Ristorante Delfino serves fish in big portions to hungry locals in a quiet and bright, pier restaurant. The cooking, service, and setting are all top-notch. Show this book for a free glass of *limoncello* to cap the meal. If you're here for lunch, take advantage of the sundeck—travelers with this book are welcome to relax and digest on the lounge chairs for free (daily 12:00-14:30 & 18:30-21:30, closed Nov-March, reservations recommended for dinner; at Marina Grande, facing the water, go all the way to the left and follow signs; tel. 081-878-2038).

$$ Trattoria da Emilia, at the opposite end of Marina Grande, is considerably more rustic, less expensive, and good for straightforward, typical Sorrentine home-cooking, including fresh fish, lots of fried seafood, and *gnocchi di mamma*—potato dumplings (daily 12:00-15:00 & 19:00-22:30, closed Nov-Feb, no reservations taken, indoor and outdoor seating, tel. 081-807-2720).

Sleeping

Hotels often have beautiful views; many offer balconies. Ask for a room *"con balcone, con vista sul mare"* (with a balcony, with a sea view). *"Tranquillo"* is taken as a request for a quieter room off the street.

Hotels listed are either near the center (where balconies overlook city streets) or on cliffside Via Capo (with sea-view balconies), a 20-minute walk—or short bus ride—from the station.

In August, the town is jammed with Italians and prices often rise above the regular high-season rates. Rates are soft in April and October, and drop by about a third from November to March. Always contact hotels directly, mention this book, and ask for their best rate.

In the Town Center

$$$$ Hotel Antiche Mura, with 50 rooms and four stars, is sophisticated, elegant, and plush. It offers all the amenities, including an impressive breakfast buffet. Surrounded by lemon trees, the pool and sundeck are a peaceful oasis. Just a block off the main square, it's quieter than some central hotels (RS%, some rooms with balconies, family rooms, air-con, elevator, pay parking, closed in winter, a block inland from Piazza Tasso at Via Fuorimura 7, tel. 081-807-3523, www.hotelantichemura.com, info@hotelantichemura.com, Michele). Meet in front of the hotel for the Mondo Guide full-day Amalfi Coast Minibus tour (see page 458).

$$$$ Palazzo Tasso, nicely located near the center, has 11 small, sleek, fashionably designed modern rooms; there's no public space except for the breakfast room (some rooms with balconies, air-con, elevator, Via Santa Maria della Pietà 33, tel. 081-878-3579, www.palazzotasso.com, info@palazzotasso.com).

$$$$ Plaza Sorrento is a contemporary-feeling, upscale refuge in the very center of town (next door to Antiche Mura but not as elegant). Its 65 rooms mix mod decor with wood grain, and the rooftop swimming pool is inviting (RS%, some rooms with balconies, air-con, elevator, closed in winter, Via Fuorimura 3, tel. 081-878-2831, www.plazasorrento.com, info@plazasorrento.com).

$$$ Il Palazzo Starace B&B, conscientiously run by Massimo, offers seven tidy, modern rooms in a little alley off Corso Italia, one block from Piazza Tasso (RS%, use code "RS2018," some rooms with balconies, family room, air-con, lots of stairs, no elevator but a luggage dumbwaiter, ring bell around corner from Via Santa Maria della Pietà 9, tel. 081-807-2633, mobile 366-950-5377, www.palazzostarace.com, info@palazzostarace.com).

$$$ Hotel Mignon rents 22 soothing blue rooms with beautiful, tiled public spaces, a rooftop sundeck, and a small garden surrounded by a lemon grove (RS%, most rooms have balconies but no views, air-con, closed in winter; from the cathedral, walk a block farther up Corso Italia and look for the hotel up a small gated lane to your left; Via Sersale 9, tel. 081-807-3824, www.sorrentohotelmignon.com, info@sorrentohotelmignon.com, Paolo).

$ Ulisse Deluxe Hostel is the best budget deal in town. This "hostel" is actually a hotel, with 56 well-equipped, marble-tiled rooms and elegant public areas, but it also has two single-sex dorm rooms with bunks (RS%, family rooms, breakfast buffet extra, air-con, elevator, spa and pool use extra, pay parking, closed Jan-mid-Feb, Via del Mare 22, tel. 081-877-4753, www.ulissedeluxe.com, info@ulissedeluxe.com, Chiara). It's a five-minute walk from the old-town action: From Corso Italia, walk down the stairs just beyond the hospital (*ospedale*) to Via del Mare. Go downhill along the right side of the big parking lot to find the entrance.

On Via Capo

These cliffside hotels are outside of town, toward the cape of the peninsula (from the train station, go straight out Corso Italia, which turns into Via Capo—a 20-minute walk). Or you can easily get here by bus (bus #A, about 3/hour from Piazza Tasso, €1.60). If you're in Sorrento to stay put and luxuriate, especially with a car, these places are perfect.

$$$$ Hotel Minerva is like a sun-worshipper's temple. The road-level entrance (on a busy street) leads to an elevator that takes you to the fifth-floor reception. Getting off, you'll step onto a spectacular terrace with outrageous Mediterranean views. Bright common areas, a small rooftop swimming pool, and a cold-water Jacuzzi complement 60 large, tiled, colorful rooms with views, some with balconies (3-night peak season minimum, air-con, pay parking, closed Nov-March, Via Capo 30, tel. 081-878-1011, www.minervasorrento.com, info@minervasorrento.com).

$$$$ Hotel La Tonnarella is an old-time Sorrentine villa turned boutique hotel, with several terraces, stylish tiles, and indifferent service. Eighteen of its 24 rooms have views of the sea, and you can pay extra for a terrace (air-con, pay parking, small beach with private elevator access, closed Nov-March, Via Capo 31, tel. 081-878-1153, www.latonnarella.it, info@latonnarella.it).

$$$ Albergo Settimo Cielo ("Seventh Heaven") is an old-fashioned, family-run cliff-hanger sitting 300 steps above Marina Grande. The reception is just off the waterfront side of the road, and the elevator passes down through four floors with 50 clean but spartan rooms—all with grand views, and many with balconies. The rooms feel dated for the price—you're paying for the views (family rooms, air-con in summer, parking, inviting pool, sun terrace, closed Nov-March, Via Capo 27, tel. 081-878-1012, www.hotelsettimocielo.com, info@hotelsettimocielo.com; Giuseppe, sons Stefano and Massimo, and daughter Serena).

$ Hotel Désirée is a modest affair, with reasonable rates, humbler vistas, and no traffic noise. The 22 basic rooms have high, ravine-facing or partial-sea views, and half come with balconies—all the same price (family rooms, most rooms have fans, lots of stairs and no elevator, laundry services, free parking, closed early-Nov-Feb except open at Christmas, Via Capo 31, tel. 081-878-1563, www.desireehotelsorrento.com, info@desireehotelsorrento.com).

Transportation

Getting Around Sorrento

By Bus: City buses all stop near the main square, Piazza Tasso, and run until at least 20:00 (for info, see www.eavsrl.it). Bus #A (3/hour) takes a long route parallel to the coast, heading east to Meta beach or west to the hotels on Via Capo and beyond; buses #B and #C make a loop up and down, connecting the port (Marina Piccola) to the town center; and minibus #D heads to the fishing village (Marina Grande). The trip between Piazza Tasso and Marina Piccola (or Marina Grande) costs just €1.20; for other trips, tickets cost €1.60 and are valid for up to one hour (purchase at tobacco shops and newsstands). Stamp your ticket upon entering the bus. The €8, 24-hour Costiera SITA Sud pass, good for the entire Amalfi coast, also covers local buses in Sorrento.

Bus stops can be tricky to find. Buses #A and #D stop where Corso Italia passes through Piazza Tasso. If you're heading west (to Via Capo or Marina Grande), find the stop at the west end of the piazza, across from the statue of Torquato Tasso. If you're heading east (to Meta), catch the bus in front of the yellow church at the east end of the piazza. Buses #B and #C stop at the corner of Piazza Sant'Antonino, just down the hill toward the water.

By Scooter: Several places near the station rent motor scooters for about €35 per day, including **Europcar** (Corso Italia 210p, tel. 081-878-1386, www.sorrento.it) and **Autoservizi De Martino**, in Hotel Nice (Corso Italia 259, tel. 081-878-2801, www.admitaly.com). Don't rent a vehicle in summer unless you enjoy traffic jams.

Rick's Tip: *Within Sorrento,* **taxis can be a huge rip-off.** *Because of heavy traffic and the complex one-way road system, you can often walk faster than you can ride.*

By Taxi: Taxis are expensive, charging an outrageous €15 for the short ride from the station to most hotels (more for Via Capo). Even if you agree to a set price, be sure it has a meter (all official taxis have one).

Arriving and Departing

BY TRAIN

Sorrento is the last stop on the Circumvesuviana train line from Naples. In front of the Sorrento train station is the town's

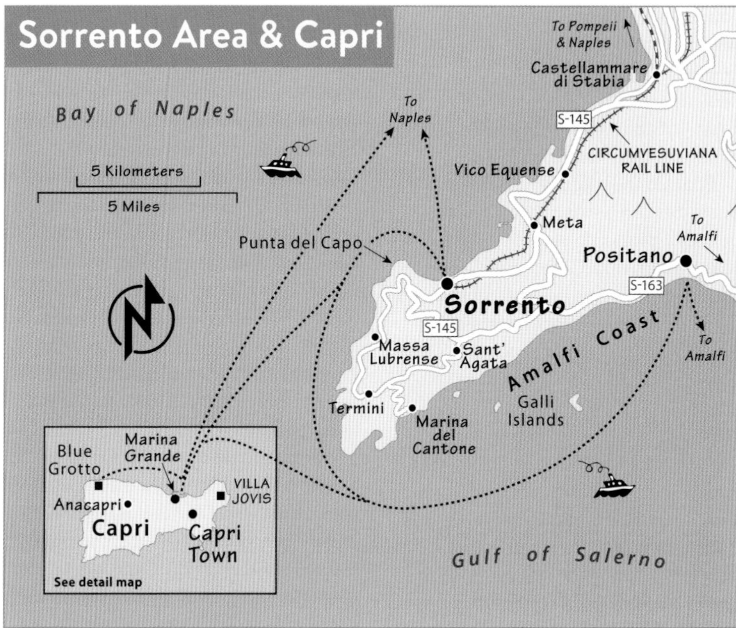

main bus stop, as well as taxis waiting to overcharge you. All recommended downtown hotels are within a 10-minute walk.

Getting to Via Capo hotels requires an uphill 20-minute walk, a €20 taxi ride, or a cheap bus ride. If you're arriving with luggage, you can wait at the train station for one of the long-distance SITA buses that stop on Via Capo on their way to Massa Lubrense (about every 40 minutes). Frequent Sorrento city buses leave from Piazza Tasso in the city center, a five-minute walk from the station (go down a block and turn left on Corso Italia; from the far side of the piazza, look for bus #A, about 3/hour). Tickets for either bus are sold at the station newsstand and tobacco shops (€1.60). Get off at the Hotel Belair stop for my recommended hotels.

Train Connections to Naples and Pompeii: The **Circumvesuviana commuter train** runs twice hourly between Naples and Sorrento (www.eavsrl.it). The schedule is available at the TI. From Sorrento, it's about 30 minutes to Pompeii (€2.20), and 70 minutes to Naples (€3.60). If there's a line at the train station, you can also buy tickets at the snack bar (across from the main ticket office) or downstairs at the newsstand.

BY BUS

Six Curreri buses run daily to and from **Naples International Airport** (€10, pay driver, leaves Sorrento daily at 6:30, 8:30, 10:30, 12:00, 14:00, and 16:30, likely 2 additional departures in summer, 1.5 hours, departs Sorrento from in front of train station, tel. 081-801-5420, www.curreriviaggi.it).

BY BOAT

Passenger boats and cruise tenders dock at Marina Piccola. To head from the marina to downtown Sorrento, go up the big staircase where the pier bends. Standing on the promenade and facing town, you'll see a TI kiosk and ticket windows for boats to Capri and Naples in the lower area to your left; and the elevator up to town to the right, about a five-minute walk along the base of the cliff (follow *lift/acensore* signs).

The elevator (€1) is a faster, cheaper, and more predictable than a bus. It takes you to the Villa Comunale city park. From there, exit through the park's gate and bear left; Piazza Tasso is about four blocks away. Buses take you directly to Piazza Tasso (city bus #B or #C, buy €1.20 ticket at newsstand or tobacco store).

Boat Connections: The number of boats that run per day varies: The frequency indicated here is for roughly mid-May through mid-October, with more boats per day in the peak of summer and fewer off-season. Check all schedules locally with the TI, your hotel, or online (use the individual boat company websites below, or www.capritourism.com). Although some ferry company websites sell tickets online. For ease, and to keep your departure options open, you can always buy tickets at the port (especially if you're watching the weather); next-day tickets typically go on sale starting the evening before. All of the boats take several hundred people each and (except for the busiest days) rarely fill up.

From Sorrento to Capri: Boats run at least hourly. Your options are a fast **ferry** (*traghetto* or *nave veloce,* 4/day, 30 minutes, Caremar, tel. 081-807-3077, www.caremar.it) or a slightly faster, pricier **hydrofoil** (*aliscafi,* up to 20/day, 20 minutes, Gescab, tel. 081-807-1812, www.gescab.it). To visit Capri when it's least crowded, it's best to buy your ticket at 8:00 and take the 8:30 hydrofoil; if you miss it, try to depart by 9:45 at the latest. If you make a reservation, it's not changable. These early boats can be jammed, but it's worth it once you reach the island.

From Sorrento to Naples: Boats depart roughly every two hours, starting at 7:20 (6/day, more in summer, 35 minutes, arrives at Molo Beverello).

BY CAR

Sorrento's Achille Lauro underground parking garage is centrally located, just a couple of blocks in front of the train station (€2/hour, €24/24 hours, on Via Correale).

CAPRI

The island of Capri is just a short cruise from Sorrento. It was the vacation hideaway of Roman emperors Augustus and Tiberius and, in the 19th century, the haunt of Romantic Age aristocrats.

About 12,000 people live on Capri (although many winter in Naples) and during any given day in high season, the island hosts another 20,000 tourists. The "Island of Dreams" is a zoo in July and August, overrun with group tourism at its worst, with nametag-wearing visitors searching for the rich and famous—and finding only their prices.

At other times of year, though still crowded, Capri can provide a relaxing, scenic break from the cultural gauntlet of Italy. Even with its crowds, commercialism, fame, and glitz, Capri is a flat-out gorgeous place: Chalky white limestone cliffs rocket boldly from the shimmering blue and green surf, and the Blue Grotto sea cave glows with reflected sunlight.

Orientation

Pronounce it right: Italians say KAH-pree, not kah-PREE like the song or the pants. The island is just four miles by two miles, separated from Sorrento by a five-mile strait. Get oriented on the boat before you dock, as you near the harbor with the island spread out before you. The port is a small community of its own, called **Marina Grande,** connected by a funicular and buses to the rest of the island. **Capri town** fills the ridge high above the harbor. The ruins of Emperor Tiberius' palace, **Villa Jovis,** cap the peak on the left. To the right, the dramatic *"Mamma mia!"* road arcs around the highest mountain on the island **(Monte Solaro),** leading up to **Anacapri** (the island's second town, just out of sight). Notice the old zigzag steps below that road. Until 1874, this was the only connection between Capri and Anacapri. The white house on the ridge above the

Scenic, relaxing Capri

zigzags is **Villa San Michele** (where you can go for a grand view).

Day Plan

Starting your day early (to avoid the day-tripping crowds) is the key to an enjoyable trip to Capri. You could take a tour (such as Mondo Guide's—see page 450), or do it on your own, as follows:

To see everything on a day trip from Sorrento, take an early hydrofoil to Capri (from Sorrento, buy a ticket at 8:00—or buy it the evening before; the boat leaves around 8:30 and arrives around 8:50). At the port, decide among three boating options: taking the scenic circle-the-island tour with a visit to the Blue Grotto (1.5-2 hours); circling the island without Blue Grotto stop (1 hour); or just visiting the Blue Grotto. (There are generally spaces available for departures every few minutes.)

Arriving back at Marina Grande, catch a bus to Anacapri, which has 2-3 hours' worth of sightseeing. In Anacapri, see the town, ride the chairlift to Monte Solaro and back (or hike down), stroll out from the base of the chairlift to Villa San Michele for the view, and eat lunch. Afterward, catch a bus to Capri town, which is worth an hour of browsing. Finally, ride the funicular from Capri town down to the harbor and laze on the free beach or wander the yacht harbor while waiting for your boat back to Sorrento.

If you're heading to Capri specifically to see the Blue Grotto, be sure to check the weather and sea conditions. If the tide is too high or the water too rough, the grotto can be closed. Ask the TI or your hotelier before going. If the Blue Grotto is closed or you're just not keen on seeing it, you can still enjoy a leisurely day on the island seeing the sights in Anacapri and Capri town. Or, for the same amount of time and less money, you can skip the Blue Grotto and enjoy circling the entire island by boat (an experience I find even more fun than the famed grotto).

If you visit Capri during July and August, it's wise to get a round-trip boat

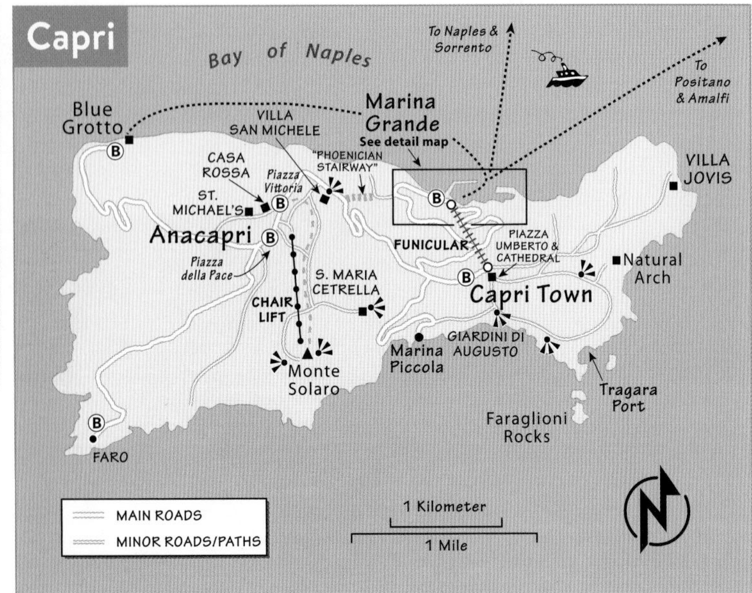

ticket (ensuring you a spot). On busy days, be 20 minutes early for the boat, or you can be bumped.

Outside of July and August, buy a one-way ticket to Capri (there's no round-trip discount anyway) to give yourself maximum schedule flexibility; then you can take any convenient hydrofoil or ferry back. Be sure to check times for the last return crossing upon arrival with any TI on Capri (or at www.capritourism.com); the last return trips usually leave between 18:30 and 19:30.

A cheap day trip to Capri is tough, as you'll pay about €20 each way just to get there and about €30 to see the Blue Grotto. That's €70 already. But if you picnic and ride buses rather than enjoying restaurants and taxis, you'll find your time on the island itself to be relatively inexpensive. Many of Capri's greatest pleasures are free.

Helpful Hints

Tourist Information: Capri's TI has branches in **Marina Grande** (near Motoscafisti Capri tour boat dock, tel. 081-837-0634), **Capri town** (on Piazza Umberto I under bell tower, WC and baggage storage downstairs behind TI, tel. 081-837-0686), and **Anacapri** (on main pedestrian/shopping street, Via Orlandi 59, tel. 081-837-1524). Their well-organized website has schedules and practical information in English (www.capritourism.com). At any TI, pick up the free map or pay for a better one if you'll be venturing to the outskirts of Capri town or Anacapri.

Baggage Storage: At the port, the fourth souvenir shop to the right of the funicular provides baggage storage (daily 9:00-18:00, look inside for *left luggage* sign on far back wall, tel. 081-837-4575). If it's closed, your best option is at the TI in Capri town (bag storage behind TI; you pay extra to take big bags up the funicular).

Tours: Naples-based **Mondo Guide** offers a no-stress, all-day shared tour for €90, which includes: pick-up at your Sorrento hotel, transportation to and from Capri on a private boat (12 people maximum), an early visit to the Blue Grotto when conditions allow (entry optional for additional fee), about four hours of free time on Capri, and a trip around the island (daily at 8:00, may be cancelled in bad weather). Reservations are required with credit card, but pay in cash only (tel. 081-751-3290, www.sharedtours.com, info@mondoguide.com); see page 396.

Tempio Travel, based at the Sorrento train station, offers a similar trip to Capri at a similar price (tel. 081-878-2103, www.tempiotravel.com).

Sights

On the Water

You have three boat-tour options: circle the island with a stop at the Blue Grotto, circle only, or Blue Grotto only.

▲▲▲CAPRI BOAT CIRCLE (GIRO DELL' ISOLA)

For me, the best experience on Capri is to take the scenic boat trip around the island. It's cheap, comes with good narration and lots of curiosities, and there are plenty of departures from Marina Grande.

Both Laser Capri and Motoscafisti Capri run trips that circle the island and pass stunning cliffs, caves, and views that most miss when they go only to the Blue Grotto (€18, no one-way discount; Motoscafisti Capri—tel. 081-837-7714, www.motoscafisticapri.com; Laser Capri—tel. 081-837-5208, www.lasercapri.com). The circular tour comes with a live guide and takes about an hour (1.5-2 hours with Blue Grotto stop). As you circle the dramatic limestone rock called Capri, you'll see quirky sights (a solar-powered lighthouse, tiny statues atop desolate rocks, holes in the cliffs with legends going back to Emperor Tiberius' times), pop into various caves and inlets, power through a tiny hole in the famed Faraglioni Rocks, hear stories of celebrity-owned villas, and marvel at a nonstop parade of staggering cliffs.

With both companies, you can combine the boat trip with a stop at the Blue Grotto at no extra charge (this adds about an hour; check schedules to find out which tours include the optional Blue Grotto stop). As the 10-minute ride just to the grotto costs €15 (no one-way discount), the island circle is well worth the extra three euros.

All boats leave daily from 9:00 until at least 13:00 (or later, depending on when the Blue Grotto rowboats stop running—likely 16:00 in summer).

▲▲BLUE GROTTO

Three thousand tourists a day visit the Blue Grotto (Grotta Azzurra). I did—early (when the light is best), without the frustration of crowds, and with choppy waves nearly making entrance impossible...and it was great.

The actual cave experience isn't much: a five-minute dinghy ride through a three-foot-high entry hole to reach a 60-yard-long cave, where the sun reflects brilliantly blue on its limestone bottom. But the experience—getting there, getting in, and getting back—is a hoot. You get a fast ride and scant narration on a 30-foot boat partway around the gorgeous island; along the way, you see bird life and limestone cliffs. Roman emperors appreciated the island's invulnerability—surrounded by cliffs, with only one good access point, it's easy to defend.

Just outside the grotto, your boat idles as you pile into eight-foot dinghies that hold up to four passengers each. Next, you'll be taken to a floating ticket counter to pay the grotto entry fee. From

Blue Grotto

there, your rower will elbow his way to the tiny hole, then pull fast and hard on the cable at the low point of the swells to squeeze you into the grotto (keep your head down and hands in the boat). Then your man rows you around, spouting off a few descriptive lines and singing "O Sole Mio." Depending upon the strength of the sunshine that day, the blue light inside can be brilliant.

The grotto was actually an ancient Roman *nymphaeum*—a retreat for romantic hanky-panky. Many believe that a tunnel led here directly from the palace; and that the grotto experience was enlivened by statues of Poseidon and company, placed half-underwater as if emerging from the sea. It was ancient Romans who smoothed out the entry hole that's still used to this day.

When dropping you off, your boatman will fish for a tip—this is optional, and €1 is sufficient.

Cost: The €14 entry fee (separate from the €15 ride from Marina Grande) includes €10 for the rowboat service plus €4 for admission to the grotto itself. Though some people swim in for free from the little dock after the boats stop running (about 17:00), it's illegal and can be dangerous.

Timing: When waves or high tide make entering dangerous, the grotto can close without notice, sending tourists home disappointed. If this happens to you, consider the one-hour boat ride around the island instead.

If you're coming from Capri's port (Marina Grande), allow 1-2 hours for the entire visit. Going with the first trip (around 9:00) will get you there at the same time as the boatmen in their dinghies—who hitch a ride behind your boat—resulting in a shorter wait at the entry point.

If you arrive on the island later in the morning—when the Blue Grotto is already jammed—try visiting about 15:00, when most of the tour groups have vacated. This may only work by bus (not boat). Confirm that day's closing time with a TI before making the trip.

Getting There: You can either take **the boat** directly from Marina Grande (either as part of a €18-circle tour, or directly for €15; described above), as most people do, or save money by taking the **bus** from Anacapri to the grotto. By bus you'll save almost €8, lose time, and see a beautiful, calmer side of the island. Anacapri-Blue Grotto buses (roughly 3/hour, 10 minutes) depart only from the Anacapri bus station at Piazza della Pace (not from the bus stop at Piazza Vittoria 200 yards away, which is more popular with tourists). If you're coming from Marina Grande or Capri town and want to transfer to the Blue Grotto buses, don't get off when the driver announces "Anacapri." Instead, ride one more stop to Piazza della Pace. If in doubt, ask the driver. At the Piazza della Pace bus station, notice the two lines: Grotta Azzurra for the Blue Grotto, and Faro for the lighthouse.

Getting Back: You can take the boat back, or ask your boatman to drop you off on the small dock next to the grotto entrance (for a small tip), from where you climb up the stairs to the stop for the bus to Anacapri (if you came by boat, you'll still have to pay the full round-trip boat fare).

Capri Town

This cute but extremely clogged and touristy shopping town is worth a brief visit. You can get here from the port (taking the funicular, which drops you just around the corner from Piazza Umberto) or by public bus from Anacapri (4/hour, 10 minutes). The **TI** is under the bell tower on Piazza Umberto.

Capri town's multi-domed Baroque **cathedral,** also on Piazza Umberto, has a multicolored marble floor dating to the 1st century A.D.—it was scavenged from Emperor Tiberius' villa.

To the left of City Hall (Municipio, lowest corner of the square), a narrow, atmospheric lane leads into the medieval part of town, which has plenty of eateries.

The lane to the left of the cathedral (past Bar Tiberio, under the wide arch) is a fashionable shopping strip, dubbed **"Rodeo Drive"** by residents. Walk a few minutes down Rodeo Drive (past Gelateria Buonocore at #35, with its fresh waffle cones) to Quisisana Hotel, the island's top old-time hotel. From there, head left for fancy shops and villas, and right for gardens and views.

Downhill and to the right, a five-minute walk leads to a lovely public garden, **Giardini di Augusto** (€1, daily 9:00-19:30, Nov-March until 17:30, free to enter off-season, no picnicking). It boasts great views—handy if you don't have the time, money, or interest to access the higher vantage points near Anacapri (Monte Solaro or Villa San Michele).

One of the most historic buildings on the island is the **Monastery of San Giacomo**—a.k.a. Certosa di San Giacomo (€4, €3 combo-ticket with Giardini di Augusto at the garden entry, Tue-Sun 10:00-17:00, later in summer, closed Mon). The stark monastery has an empty church and sleepy cloister. But the finest piece of art on Capri is over the church's front entrance: an exquisite 14th-century fresco of Mary and the baby Jesus by the Florentine Niccolo di Tommaso. Today, the monastery hosts Museo Diefenbach, a small collection of dark and moody paintings by eccentric German artist Karl Wilhelm Diefenbach.

Anacapri

Capri's second town has 2-3 hours' worth of interesting sights. Though Anacapri sits higher up on the island, there are no sea views at street level in the town center.

There are two bus stops: Piazza Vittoria, in the center of town at the base of the Monte Solaro chairlift; and 200 yards farther along at Piazza della Pace (pronounced "PAH-chay"), a larger bus station near the cemetery. Piazza Vittoria gets you a bit closer to the main sights (chairlift and Villa San Michele), while Piazza della Pace is where you transfer to or from the Blue Grotto bus.

Rick's Tip: *Buses* **leaving Anacapri** *for Capri town or Marina Grande (direction: San Costanzo), can be packed. Your best chance to get a seat is to* **catch the bus from Piazza della Pace.**

From either stop, if you're here to sightsee Anacapri, make your way to **Via Orlandi,** the town's pedestrianized main street. From Piazza Vittoria, the street is right there—just go down the lane to the right of the Anacapri statue. From Piazza della Pace, cross the street and go down the small pedestrian lane called Via Filietto. The **TI** is at Via Orlandi 59, near Piazza Vittoria.

To see the town, stroll along Via Orlandi for 10 minutes or so. Signs suggest a quick circuit that links Casa Rossa (containing four sea-worn Blue Grotto statues upstairs plus a small collection of 19th-century paintings), Church of San Michele (listed below), and peaceful side streets. Along with plenty of shops, you'll also find eateries selling quick, inexpensive pizza, *panini,* and other goodies; try **$ Sciué Sciué** (same price for informal seating or takeaway, near TI at #73, tel. 081-837-2068) or **$ Pizza e Pasta** (takeaway only, just before church at #157, tel. 328-623-8460).

▲CHURCH OF SAN MICHELE

This Baroque church in the town center has a remarkable majolica floor showing paradise on earth in a classic 18th-century Neapolitan style. The entire floor is ornately tiled, featuring an angel driving Adam and Eve from paradise and the devil wrapped around the trunk of a beautiful tree. For the best view, climb the spiral stairs from the postcard desk.

Cost and Hours: €2, daily April-Oct 9:00-19:00, Nov and mid-Dec-March

Tile floor at the Church of San Michele

usually 10:00-14:00, closed late Nov-mid Dec, in town center just off Via Orlandi—look for signs for *San Michele,* tel. 081-837-2396, www.chiesa-san-michele.com.

▲VILLA SAN MICHELE AND GRAND CAPRI VIEW

This is the 19th-century mansion of Axel Munthe, an idealistic doctor who lived here until 1946 and whose services to the Swedish royal family brought him into contact with high society. Munthe was gay at a time when that could land you in jail. He enjoyed the avant-garde and permissive scene at Capri, during an era when Europe's leading artists and creative figures could gather here and be honest about their sexual orientation.

Walk the path from Piazza Victoria past the villa to a superb viewpoint over Capri town, and—in the distance—Mount Vesuvius and Sorrento. Paying to enter the villa lets you see a few rooms with period furnishings (follow the one-way route, good English descriptions); an exhibit on Munthe; a delightful garden; and Olivetum (a tiny museum of native birds and bugs). A view café serves affordable sandwiches.

Cost and Hours: €8, May-Sept daily 9:00-18:00, closes earlier Oct-April, tel. 081-837-1401, www.villasanmichele.eu.

Getting There: From Piazza Vittoria, walk up the grand staircase and turn left onto Via Capodimonte. At the start of the shopping street, on your right, pass the deluxe Capri Palace Hotel.

▲▲CHAIRLIFT UP TO MONTE SOLARO

You can ride the chairlift *(seggiovia)* from Anacapri to the 1,900-foot summit of Monte Solaro for a commanding view of the Bay of Naples. Work on your tan as you float over hazelnut, walnut, chestnut, apricot, peach, kiwi, and fig trees, past a montage of tourists. Prospective smoochers should know that the lift seats are all single. The ride takes 13 minutes each way, and you'll want at least 30 minutes on top, where there are picnic benches and a café with WCs.

Cost and Hours: €8 one-way, €11 round-trip, daily 9:30-17:00, last run down at 17:30; March-April until 16:00, Nov-Feb until 15:30, tel. 081-837-1438, www.capriseggiovia.it. Note that the lift gets more crowded with tour groups in the afternoon.

Getting There: From the Piazza Vittoria bus stop, just climb the steps and look right.

At the Summit: Enjoy the panorama of lush cliffs. Find the iconic Faraglioni Rocks. The pink building nearest the rocks was an American R&R base during World War II. On the peak closest to Cape Sorrento are the ruins of Emperor Tiberius' palace. The

Chairlift to Monte Solaro

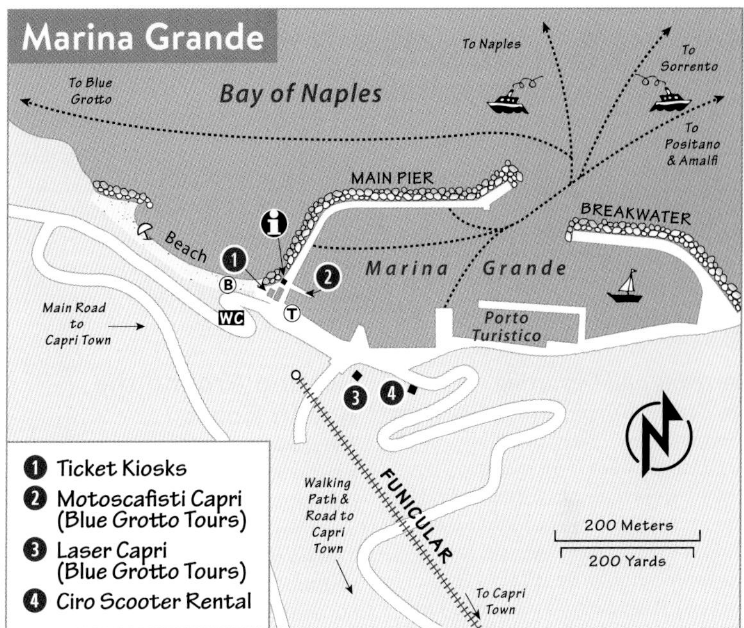

Galli Islands mark the Amalfi Coast in the distance. Cross the bar terrace for views of Mount Vesuvius and Naples.

Hiking Down: A highlight for hardy walkers (provided you have strong knees and good shoes) is the 40-minute downhill hike from the top of Monte Solaro, through lush vegetation and ever-changing views, with an optional detour to the 14th-century Chapel of Santa Maria Cetrella (at the trail's only intersection, it's a 10-minute walk to the right), and back into Anacapri. The trail starts down the stairs, past the WCs (last chance). Down two more flights of stairs, look for the sign to *Anacapri e Cetrella*—you're on your way. While the trail is well-established, you'll encounter plenty of uneven steps, loose rocks, and few signs.

Transportation

Getting Around Capri

By Public Transportation: Tickets for the island's **buses** and **funicular** cost €2 per ride and are available at newsstands, tobacco shops, official ticket offices, or from the driver. Validate your ticket when you board. The €10 all-day pass (available only at official ticket offices) isn't a good value for most visitors.

Schedules are clearly posted at all bus stations. Public buses are orange, while the gray-and-blue buses are for private tour groups. Public buses from the port to Capri town, and from Capri town to Anacapri, are frequent (4/hour, 10 minutes). The direct bus between the port and Anacapri runs less often (2/hour, 25 minutes). From Anacapri, branch bus lines run to the parking lot above the Blue Grotto and to the Faro lighthouse (3/hour each). Buses are teeny (because of the island's narrow roads) and often packed, the aisles filled with people standing. At most stops, you'll see ranks for passengers to line up in (locals feel free to cut the line). If the driver changes the bus's display to read *completo* (full), you just have to wait for the next one.

By Taxi: Taxis have fixed rates, listed at www.capritourism.com (Marina Grande to Capri town-€17; Marina Grande to Anacapri-€28). You can hire a taxi for about €70 per hour—negotiate.

By Scooter: Capri Scooter rents bright-yellow scooters with 50cc engines—strong enough to haul couples. Rental includes a map and instructions with parking tips and other helpful info (€15/hour, €55/day, includes helmet, gas, and insurance; daily April-Oct 9:30-18:00, may open in good weather off-season, at Via Don Giobbe Ruocco 55, Marina Grande, mobile 338-360-6918, www.capriscooter.com). Capri's steep and narrow roads aren't a good place for novice riders to learn.

Arriving and Departing

By Boat from Capri's Marina Grande to: Sorrento (ferry: 4/day, 30 minutes, www.caremar.it; hydrofoil: up to 20/day, 20 minutes, www.gescab.it), **Naples** (roughly hourly, more in summer, hydrofoil: 45 minutes, arrives at Molo Beverello; ferries: 50-80 minutes, arrive at Calata Porta di Massa), **Positano** (mid-April-mid-Oct, 4-6/day, 30-60 minutes; less off-season, www.gescab.it), **Amalfi** (mid-April-mid-Oct, 4-6/day, 1.5 hours). Confirm the schedule carefully at TIs or www.capritourism.com—the last boats back to the mainland usually leave around 18:00-20:00. For a steep price, you can always hire a water taxi (weather permitting).

THE AMALFI COAST

With stunning scenery, cliff-hugging towns, and historic ruins, Amalfi is Italy's coast with the most. The trip from Sorrento to Salerno is one of the world's great bus or taxi rides. Cantilevered garages, hotels, and villas cling to the vertical terrain, and beautiful sandy coves tease from far below and out of reach. As you hyperventilate, notice how the Mediterranean, a sheer 500-foot drop below, really twinkles. Over the centuries, this landscape has lured Roman Emperor Tiberius, Richard Wagner, Sophia Loren, and Gore Vidal to enjoy *la dolce vita.*

Amalfi Coast towns are pretty, but they're also touristy, congested, and overpriced. Most beaches here are private—and pebbly—and access is expensive. Check and understand your bills in this greedy region.

Three towns along the coast are popular stops: picturesque, romantic Positano; the workaday but lively Amalfi town; and the view-strewn hill town of Ravello.

The drive takes a long, full day by bus, car, or tour, and is best done as a round-trip from Sorrento. If you'd rather stay overnight on the coast, Positano is a good choice.

Getting Around the Amalfi Coast

The scenic Amalfi drive is thrilling, but treacherous; even if you have a car, consider taking the bus or hiring a driver out of Sorrento.

Many travelers take a round-trip bus tour, though you could go one way by bus and return by boat. For example, take the bus along the coast from Sorrento to Positano and/or Amalfi, then catch the ferry back. This works best in summer, because ferries run less often in spring and fall; some don't run at all off-season (mid-Oct-mid-April); and they don't run in stormy weather at any time of year. If boats aren't running between Amalfi and Sorrento, you can change boats in Capri.

By Bus

From Sorrento: SITA buses to Amalfi, via Positano, are the most common, inexpensive way to see the coast (for schedules, see www.sitabus.it or—easier to read—www.positano.com). In Sorrento, buses depart from in front of the train station beginning at 6:30; from 8:30 they run roughly every half hour until 16:00, then hourly until 22:00 in summer, until 19:00 in winter (50-minute trip to Positano; another 50 minutes to Amalfi). To reach Ravello (the hill town beyond Amalfi) or Salerno (at the far end of the coast), transfer in Amalfi.

Individual tickets are inexpensive (€2-4). All rides are covered by the 24-hour

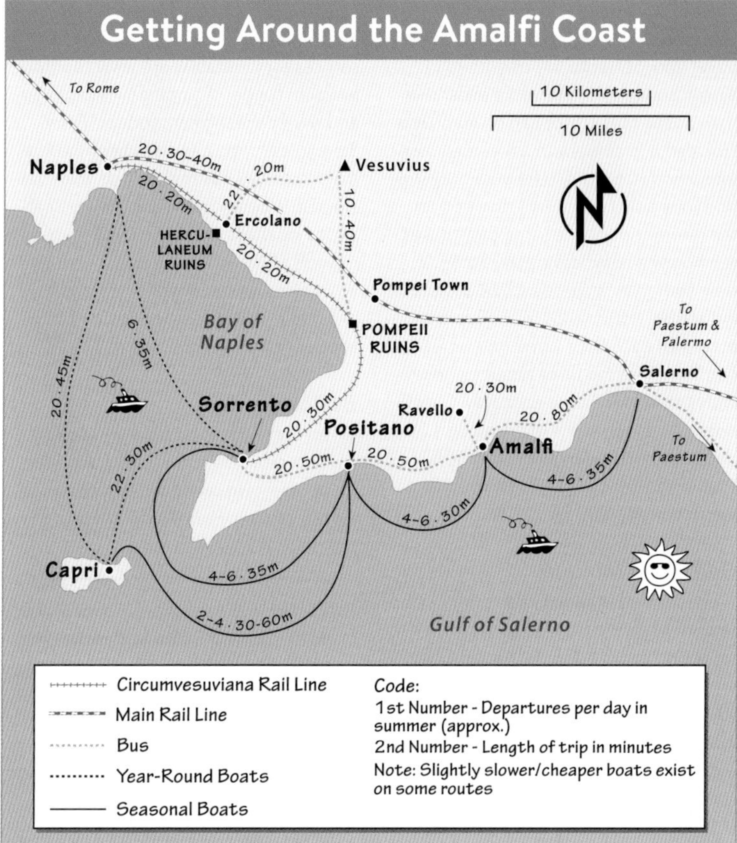

Costiera SITA Sud pass (€8), which may not save you money but does save time buying tickets. Tickets are sold at tobacco shops and newsstands, not by drivers; in Sorrento, buy them at an outdoor stand by the bus stop or in train station shops.

Line up under the *Bus Stop SITA* sign across from the train station. A schedule is posted on the wall; lettered codes indicate which days a particular bus runs. *Giornaliero* (*G*) means daily; *Feriale* (*F*) denotes Monday-Saturday departures; and *Festivo* (*H*) is for Sundays and holidays.

Avoiding Crowded Buses: Amalfi Coast public buses are routinely unable to handle the demand during summer months and holidays. But generally, if you don't get on one bus, you're well-positioned to catch the next one (in 20 minutes). From Sorrento, aim to leave on the 8:30 bus at the latest, and earlier if possible. Departures between 9:00 and 11:00 can be frustratingly crowded.

Rick's Tip: *Summer congestion can be so bad that return buses don't even stop in Positano (because they filled up in Amalfi). Those trying to get back from Positano to Sorrento are stuck with taking an extortionist taxi or hopping a boat...if one's running. If touring the coast by bus,* **stop in Positano first and come home from Amalfi**, *where the bus originates.*

From April through October, **City-Sightseeing Sorrento**'s bright red buses travel from Sorrento to Positano to Amalfi and back. While more expensive than public buses, they can be much less crowded and come with a recorded commentary. You'll pay €10 for your outgoing ride (buy tickets onboard), then €6 for the return trip (on the same day). Buses run hourly all day, leaving the Sorrento train station at :45 past each hour starting at 8:45. Return trips from Amalfi leave at :15 past each hour (until 19:15—but confirm). The trip takes about 1.5 hours, with a stop in Positano each way. Check out www.sorrento.city-sightseeing.it (but don't be confused by their "two bays" tour of the Cape of Sorrento, which is not worth considering).

By Shared Minibus

Naples-based **Mondo Guide** offers a nine-hour minibus trip that departs from Sorrento and heads down the Amalfi Coast, with brief stops in Positano, Amalfi, and Ravello, before returning to Sorrento. Lunch isn't included; to save time for exploring, just grab a quick lunch in one of the towns. Reserve in advance (€50, daily at 9:00; meet in front of Sorrento's Hotel Antiche Mura, at Via Fuorimura 7, a block inland from Piazza Tasso, tel. 081-751-3290, www.sharedtours.com, info@mondoguide.com); see page 396.

By Boat

A few passenger boats a day link Positano and Amalfi with Sorrento, Capri, and Salerno; they generally run from April through October (no service off-season). The last daily departure can be as early as midafternoon and is never much later than 18:00. Check schedules carefully: Frequency varies from month to month, and boats may be suspended without notice in bad weather (especially at Positano, where there's no real pier). The specific companies operating each route change frequently, compete for passengers, and usually claim to know nothing about their rivals' services. The best sources for timetables are www.capritourism.com (under "Shipping Timetable") and www.positano.com (under "Ferry Schedules"). You can also check individual company websites (such as www.travelmar.it, www.alicost.it, and www.gescab.it). It's smartest to confirm locally—the region's TIs hand out current schedules. Buy tickets on the dock. For a summary of sample routes, frequencies, and travel times, see the map on page 457.

By Taxi

Given the challenging drive, impossible parking, crowded public buses, consider hiring your own car and driver for an Amalfi day trip. Payment for most of these car services is by cash only.

Rick's Tip: *If you can organize a small group, an* **eight-seater minibus with driver is a good deal** *(about €300; €40 per person).*

The Monetti family and their car-and-driver service have taken excellent care of my readers' transit needs for decades. Sample trips and rates: all-day Amalfi Coast (Positano, Amalfi, Ravello), 8 hours, €280; Amalfi Coast and Paestum, 10 hours, €400; transfer to Naples airport or train station to Sorrento, €110. These prices are for up to four people, more for a larger eight-seater van. Though Sorrento-based, they also offer trips from Naples. Don't hop into any taxi claiming to be a Monetti—call first. Their reservation system is simple and reliable (English-speaking office 338-946-2860, mobile 335-602-9158, www.monettitaxi17.it, monettitaxi17@libero.it).

Francesco del Pizzo is another good, honest Sorrento-based driver, who offers commentary in English (9 hours or so in a car with up to 4 passengers, €280; up to 8 passengers in a minibus, €320; mobile 333-238-4144, francescodelpizzo@yahoo.it).

Anthony Buonocore, based in Amalfi,

specializes in cruise shore excursions, as well as transfers anywhere in the region in his eight-person Mercedes van (rates vary, tel. 349-441-0336, www.amalfitransfer.com, buonocoreanthony@yahoo.it).If you're hiring a **cabbie** off the street for a ride and not a tour, here are sample fares from Sorrento to Positano: up to four people in a car one-way for about €80 (or up to six people for €90 in a minibus); figure on paying 50 percent more to Amalfi. While taxis must use a meter within a city, a fixed rate is OK otherwise. Negotiate—ask about a round-trip.

Amalfi Coast Tour

The wildly scenic Amalfi Coast drive from Sorrento to Salerno, worth ▲▲▲, is one of the all-time great white-knuckle rides, whether you tackle it by bus, taxi, or shared minibus. Traffic is so heavy that private tour buses are only allowed to go in one direction (southbound from Sorrento). Summer traffic is infuriating. Fluorescent-vested police are posted at tough bends during peak hours to help fold in side-view mirrors and keep things moving. This loose self-guided tour is organized from west to east.

Rick's Tip: *For the* **best views of the Amalfi Coast,** *sit on the right when leaving from Sorrento and on the left returning to Sorrento. Sit toward the front to* **minimize carsickness.**

➲ *Self-Guided Tour*

Leaving **Sorrento,** the road winds up into the hills past lemon groves and hidden houses. The gray-green trees are olives. (Notice the green nets slung around the trunks; these are unfurled in October and November, when the ripe olives drop naturally, for an easy self-harvest.) Dark, green-leafed trees planted in dense groves are the source of the region's lemons. The black nets over the orange and lemon groves create a greenhouse effect, trapping warmth and humidity for maximum tastiness, while offering protection from extreme weather.

Atop the ridge outside of Sorrento, look to your right: The two small islands after Sorrento are the **Galli Islands.** Once owned by the famed ballet dancer Rudolf Nureyev, these islands mark the boundary between the Bay of Naples and the Bay of Salerno. Technically, the Amalfi Coast drive begins here.

One of the islands has the first of many stony watchtowers you'll see all along the coast. These were strategically placed within sight of each other, so that a relay of rooftop bonfires could quickly spread word of a pirate attack.

The limestone cliffs that plunge into the sea were traversed by a hand-carved trail that became a modern road in the mid-19th century. Limestone absorbs the heat and rainwater, making this south-facing coastline a fertile suntrap, with temperatures 10 degrees higher than in nearby Sorrento. The chalky, reflective limestone, which extends below the surface, accounts for the uniquely colorful blues and greens of the water. Bougainvillea, geraniums, oleander, and wisteria grow like weeds. Notice the nets pulled tight against the cliffs—they're designed to catch rocks that often tumble loose after absorbing heavy rains.

As you approach **Positano,** you know you've reached the scenic heart of the Amalfi Coast. This colorful, pretty town is built on a series of manmade terraces, carefully carved out of the steep rock, then filled with fertile soil carried here from Sorrento on the backs of donkeys.

If you're getting off here, stay on through the first stop by the round-domed yellow church (Chiesa Nova), which is a long walk above town. Get off at the second stop, Sponda, then head downhill toward the start of my self-guided Positano Walk (described later). Sponda is also the best place to catch the

Positano overview

Marina di Praia

onward bus to Amalfi. If you're coming on a smaller minibus, you'll twist all the way down—seemingly going in circles—to the start of the walk.

The next town you'll see is **Praiano.** Less ritzy or charming than Positano or Amalfi, it's notable for its huge Cathedral of San Genarro, with a characteristic majolica-tiled roof and dome. Most of the homes are accessible only by tiny footpaths and staircases. Near the end of town, just before the big tunnel, watch on the left for the big *presepi* (manger scene) embedded into the cliff face. This Praiano-in-miniature was carved by one local man over several decades. At Christmas-time, each house is filled with little figures and twinkle lights.

Just past the tunnel, look below and on the right to see another watchtower. Yet another caps the little point on the horizon.

A bit farther along, look down to see the fishing hamlet of **Marina di Praia** tucked into the gorge between two tunnels. If you're driving, consider a detour here for a coffee break or meal. This serene nook has its own little pebbly beach with great views of the stout bluffs and watchtower that hem it in. A seafront walkway curls around the bluff all the way to the tower.

Just after going through the next tunnel, watch for a jagged rock formation on its own little pedestal. Locals see the face of the Virgin Mary in this natural feature, and say that she's holding a flower (the tree growing out to the right). Also notice several caged, cantilevered parking pads sticking out from the road. This stretch of coastline is popular for long-term villa rentals.

Don't blink or you'll miss the fishing village of **Fiordo** ("fjord"), down and on the left, filling yet another gorge. Humble homes are tucked so far into the gorge that they're entirely in shadows for much of the year. Today these are rented out to vacationers; the postage-stamp beach is uncrowded and inviting.

After the next tunnel is another hamlet. Keep an eye out for donkeys with big baskets on their backs; they're the only way to make heavy deliveries to homes high in the rocky hills.

Soon you'll pass the parking lot of **Grotta dello Smeraldo** (Emerald Grotto), a cheesy roadside attraction that wrings the most it can out of a pretty, seawater-filled cave. Passing tourists park here and pay to take an elevator down to sea level, pile into big rowboats, and get paddled around a genuinely impressive cavern. Unless you've got time to kill, skip it.

Now you're approaching what might be the most dramatic watchtower on the coast, which guarded the harbor of the Amalfi navy until the fleet was destroyed in 1343 by a tsunami, which led to Amalfi's decline.

Around the next bend you're treated to stunning views of the coastline's namesake: **Amalfi.** The white villa sitting on the low point between here and there

Positano, on the Amalfi Coast

(with another watchtower at its tip) once belonged to Sophia Loren. Now pan up to the top of the steep, steep cliffs overhead to see the hulking former Monastery of Santa Rosa. Locals proudly explain that the beloved *sfogliatella* dessert was first created there. Today, it's a luxury resort, where you can pay a premium to sleep in a former monk's tiny cell.

The most striking stretch of coastline ends where the bus pulls to a halt—at the end of the line, the waterfront of Amalfi town. Spend some time enjoying the city.

From Amalfi, you can transfer to another bus to either head up to **Ravello** (described later), capping a cliff just beyond Amalfi, or onward to the big city of **Salerno** (which is on a direct train line to Naples). Alternatively, buses and boats take you back to Positano and/or Sorrento.

Positano

Specializing in scenery and sand, Positano hangs halfway between Sorrento and Amalfi town on the most spectacular stretch of the coast.

The town flourished as a favorite under the Bourbon royal family in the 1700s, when many of its fine mansions were built. Until the late 1800s, the only access was by donkey path or by sea. In the 20th century, Positano became a haven for artists and writers escaping Communist Russia and Nazi Germany. In 1953, American writer John Steinbeck's essay on the town popularized Positano among tourists, and soon after it became a trendy Riviera stop. The town gave the world "Moda-Positano"—a leisurely *dolce vita* lifestyle of walking barefoot, wearing colorful clothes, and sporting skimpy bikinis.

Today, it's a pleasant gathering of cafés and expensive stores draped over a steep hillside. Terraced gardens and historic houses cascade down to a stately cathedral and a broad, pebbly beach. The "skyline" looks like it did a century ago. Notice the town's characteristic rooftop domes.

There's little to do here but eat, window-shop, and enjoy the beach and views...hence the town's popularity. While

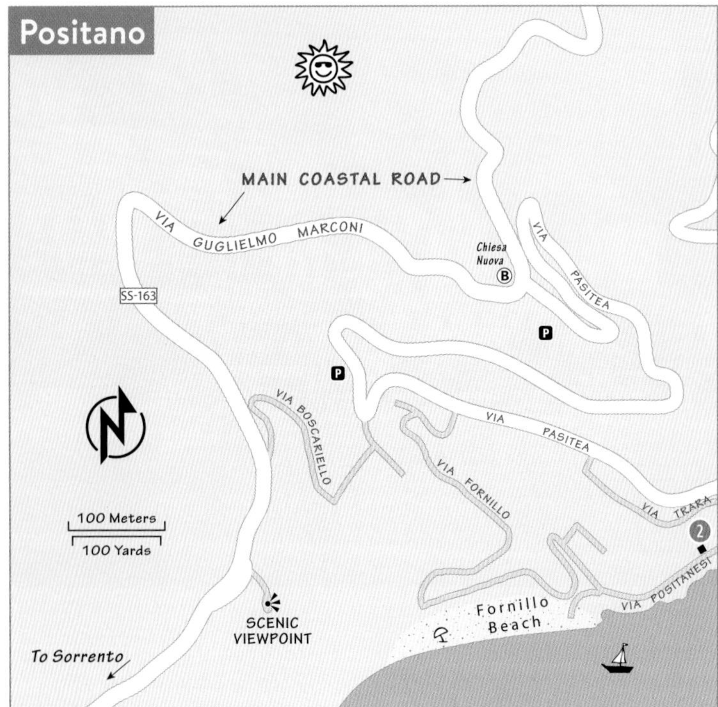

Positano has 4,000 residents, an average of 12,000 tourists visit daily from Easter through October. But because hotels don't take large groups (bus access is too difficult), this town—unlike Sorrento—has been spared the worst ravages of big-bus tourism.

Consider seeing Positano as a day trip from Sorrento: Take the bus out and the afternoon ferry home, but be sure to check the boat schedules when you arrive—the last ferry often leaves before 18:00, and doesn't always run in spring and fall.

Orientation

Squished into a ravine, with narrow alleys that cascade down to the harbor, Positano requires you to stroll, whether you're going up or heading down. Endless staircases are a way of life. Only one street allows motorized traffic; the rest are narrow pedestrian lanes. The center of town has no main square, unless you count the beach.

Tourist Information: The **TI** is a block from the beach, in the red building a half-block beyond the bottom of the church steps (Mon-Sat 9:00-19:00, Sun until 14:00, shorter hours off-season, Via Regina Giovanna 13, tel. 089-875-067, www.aziendaturismopositano.it).

Baggage Storage: Neither bus stop has baggage storage. **Blu Porter** can meet you at the Sponda bus stop and watch your bags for €5 apiece; call in advance (tel. 089-811-496).

Private Guide: Lucia Ferrara is a Positano native who leads food and evening walking tours (departs at 17:00, 3 hours, €30/person) as well as hiking tours (mobile 339-272-0971, www.zialucy.com).

➲ *Positano Walk*

This short, self-guided stroll downhill will help you get your bearings.

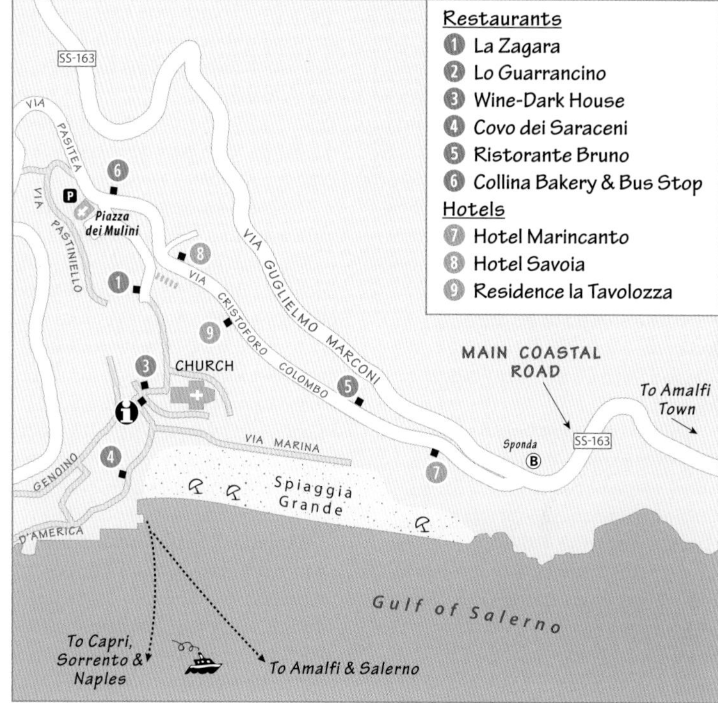

Start at...

Piazza dei Mulini: This is the lower stop for the little orange-and-white shuttle bus—and as close to the beach as vehicles can get. Older people gather inside **Collina Bakery,** while the younger crowd congregates on the wisteria-draped terrace across the street, which shades the best *granita* (lemon slush) stand in town.

Dip into the little yellow **Church of the Holy Rosary** (by the road), with a serene 12th-century interior. Up front, to the right of the main altar, find the delicately carved fragment of a Roman sarcophagus (first century B.C.). As we walk, we'll see a few reminders that Positano sits upon the site of a sprawling Roman villa.

Continue downhill into town, passing shops selling linen and ceramics. These industries boomed when tourists discovered Positano in the 1970s. The beach-inspired Moda Positano fashion label was born as a break from the rigid dress code of the 1950s. You'll also see many galleries featuring local art.

• *Wander downhill to the "fork" in the road (stairs to the left, road to the right). You've reached...*

Midtown: At **Enoteca Cuomo** (#3), butchers Pasquale and Rosario stock fine local red wines and make homemade sausages, salami, and *panini*—good for a quick lunch. The smaller set of stairs leads to the Delicatessen grocery store, where Emilia can fix you a good picnic.

La Zagara (across the lane from the steps, at #10) is a pricey pastry shop by day and a cocktail bar by night (music starts around 21:00, summers only). Tempting pastries such as the rum-drenched *babà* fill the window display. A bit farther downhill, **Brunella** (on the right, at #24) is respected for fine linens.

Across the street, **Hotel Palazzo Murat** fills what was once a grand 12th-century

Benedictine monastery. Napoleon, fearing the power of the Church, had many such monasteries closed during his rule here. This one became a private palace, named for his brother-in-law, who was briefly the King of Naples. Step into the plush courtyard to enjoy the scene, with great views of the cathedral's majolica-slathered dome. Continuing on, under a fragrant wisteria trellis, you'll pass "street merchants' gulch," where artisans display their goodies.

• *Continue straight down. You'll run into a fork at the big church. For now, turn right and go downstairs to Piazza Flavio Gioia, facing the big...*

Church of Santa Maria Assunta: Set atop Roman ruins, this was once the abbey of the Benedictine monastery. Originally Romanesque, it was given a Baroque makeover in the 18th century. Inside, in the first chapel on the left is a fine manger scene *(presepe)*. Its original 18th-century figurines give you an idea of the folk costumes of the age. Above the main altar is the Black Madonna, a Byzantine painting, likely brought here from Constantinople by monks in the 12th century. To the right of the altar, a small freestanding display case holds a silver and copper bust of St. Vitus—the town patron, who brought Christianity here in about A.D. 300. In the adjacent niche (on the right) is a rare 1599 painting of Baby Jesus by Fabrizio Santafede.

Back outside, you'll see the **bell tower,** dating from 1707. Above the door, it sports a Romanesque relief scavenged from the original church. The scene—a wolf mermaid with seven little fish—was a reminder how integral the sea was to the town's livelihood.

• *Backtrack up the steps, circling around the church. You'll likely see the entry to an underground Roman exhibit.*

The entire town center—from this cathedral all the way up to the Piazza dei Mulini, where we started this walk—sits upon the site of a huge **Roman villa complex,** buried when Mount Vesuvius erupted in A.D. 79. Positano recently excavated part of the villa; a small museum exhibits a surviving fragment of a Roman fresco.

• *Continue climbing down the steps arcing to the right (following* beach/spiaggia *signs). You'll eventually come to the square, with concrete benches, facing the beach.*

Piazzetta: This square is a gathering point in the evening, as local boys hustle tourist girls into the nearby nightclub. Step down to beach level. Residents traded their historic baptistery font with Amalfi town for the two iron lions you see facing the beach. Around the staircase, you'll also see some original Roman columns, scavenged from the buried villa. Look up to admire the colorful majolica tiles so typical of church domes in this region.

Big Beach: Called **Spiaggia Grande,** it's colorful with umbrellas. It's half public (straight ahead) and half private (to the left, behind the little fence). The nearest WC is beneath the steps to the right. The kiosks offer rowboat rentals and excursions to Capri and elsewhere.

Church of Santa Maria Assunta

Spiaggia Grande Beach, Positano

From the beach you can see three of the **watchtowers** built centuries ago to protect the Amalfi Coast from pirates: one on the far-left horizon, just below Praiano; one on the Galli Islands, straight ahead; and one far to the right, marking the end of Fornillo Beach. (The round tower in the foreground is modern.)

Defenders used these towers—situated within sight of each other—to relay smoke signals. In more recent times, artists holed up inside the tower on the right (near Fornillo Beach) for inspiration.

As you face out to sea, on the far-left side of the beach (below Rada Restaurant) is **Music on the Rocks,** the only remaining piece of the chic 1970s scene. While it's dead until very late, you're welcome to peek in at the cool troglo-disco interior, or go upstairs to the Fly Bar for the priciest cocktails in town. This and La Zagara (mentioned earlier on the walk) are your best nightlife options.

• *Now turn right and wander across the beach to a nearby beach. Behind the kiosks that sell boat tickets, find the steps up to the path that climbs up and over, past a 13th-century lookout fort from pirate days, to the next beach. It's a worthwhile five-minute walk through a shady ravine to...*

Fornillo Beach: This is where locals go to swim (and escape tourists). It's less crowded and chair/umbrella rentals are cheaper. There are a few snack bars and lunch eateries here.

• *Our walk is over. Time to relax.*

Shopping

Linen garments are popular items. To find a good-quality piece, look for "Made in Positano" (or at least "Made in Italy") on the label, and check the percentage of linen; 60 percent or more is good quality and 100 percent is best. **Brunella** and **Pepito's** have top reputations and multiple outlets throughout town.

For handmade **sandals** crafted to your specifications while you wait (at prices starting about €50), try **La Botteguccia,** facing the tranquil little square just up from the TI, or **Carmine Todisco,** around the corner.

Eating

At the waterfront, restaurants with view terraces leave people fat and happy, albeit with skinnier wallets. All are scenic, convenient, and overpriced (figure €15-20 pastas and *secondi,* plus pricey drinks and sides, and a cover charge).

$$$ Lo Guarracino, hidden on the path to Fornillo Beach, is a local favorite for its great views and good food at prices similar to the beachfront places (daily 12:00-15:30 & 19:00-23:00, closed Nov-Easter, follow path behind the boat-ticket kiosks 5 minutes to Via Positanesi d'America 12, tel. 089-875-794).

$$ Wine-Dark House, tucked around the corner from the beach (and the TI), fills a cute little *piazzetta* at the start of Via del Saraceno. They serve good pastas and *secondi,* have a respect for wine (several local wines), and are popular with Positano's youngsters for their long list of sandwiches (closed Tue, Via del Saraceno 6, tel. 089-811-925).

$$$ Covo dei Saraceni offers the best value on the beach, with good pizza and tables overlooking the action (daily, on the far right as you face the sea, where Via Positanesi d'America starts, tel. 089-875-400).

The unassuming, family-run **$$$** Ristorante Bruno is handy to my listed hotels. While expensive, it is worth considering if you want a meal without hiking down into the town center (daily 12:30-23:00, closed Nov-Easter, near the top of Via Cristoforo Colombo at #157, tel. 089-875-179).

Sleeping

These hotels are all on Via Cristoforo Colombo, which leads from the Sponda bus stop down into the village. They close in the winter (Dec-Feb or longer). Expect to pay more than €20 a day to park.

$$$$ Hotel Marincanto is a recently restored, somewhat impersonal four-star hotel with 32 beautiful rooms and a bright breakfast terrace practically teetering on a cliff (air-con, elevator, pool, stairs down to a private beach, pay parking, closed Nov-March, Via Cristoforo Colombo 50, tel. 089-875-130, www.marincanto.it, info@marincanto.it).

$$$ Hotel Savoia, run by the friendly D'Aiello family, has 39 sizeable, breezy, bright, simple, tiled rooms (RS%, some cheaper nonview rooms, some rooms with balcony or terrace, air-con, elevator, closed Nov-March, Via Cristoforo Colombo 73, tel. 089-875-003, www.savoiapositano.it, info@savoiapositano.it).

$$ Residence la Tavolozza is an attractive six-room hotel. Each cheerily tiled room comes with a view, a terrace, and silence (lavish à la carte breakfast extra, families can ask for "Royal Apartment," air-con, confirm by phone if arriving late, Via Cristoforo Colombo 10, tel. 089-875-040, www.latavolozzapositano.it, info@latavolozzapositano.it).

Transportation

The main coast highway winds above the town of Positano. Regional SITA buses stop at two scheduled bus stops located at either end of town: **Chiesa Nuova** (at Bar Internazionale, near the Sorrento end of town) and **Sponda** (nearer Amalfi town). Although both stops are near roads leading downhill through the town to the beach, Sponda is closer and less steep; from this stop, it's a scenic 20-minute downhill stroll to the beach (and TI).

The SITA bus **from Positano** leaves from the Sponda stop, sometimes up to five minutes before the printed departure time. In case the driver is early, you should be, too. Buy **tickets** at the tobacco shop in the town center (on Piazza dei Mulini) or just below the Sponda bus stop at the Li Galli Bar or Total gas station (across from Hotel Marincanto).

The local red-and-white **shuttle bus** (marked *Interno Positano*) connects the lower town with the highway's two bus stops (2/hour, €1.30 at tobacco shop on Piazza dei Mulini, €1.70 on board, convenient stop at the corner of Via Colombo and Via dei Mulini, heads up to Sponda). Collina Bakery, located off Piazza dei Mulini, is just across from the shuttle bus stop, with a fine, breezy terrace to enjoy while you wait.

Drivers must go with the one-way flow, entering the town only at the Chiesa Nuova bus stop (closest to Sorrento) and exiting at Sponda. Driving is a headache here. Parking is even worse.

Amalfi Town

After Rome fell, the Amalfi Coast's namesake town was one of the first to trade goods—coffee, carpets, and paper—between Europe and points east. In its 10th- and 11th-century heyday, it was a powerful maritime republic that rivaled Venice. Amalfi established "rules of the sea"—the basics of which survive today.

In 1343, this little powerhouse was suddenly destroyed by a tsunami. That disaster, compounded by devastating plagues, left Amalfi a humble town. Today, its 5,000 residents live off tourism. Amalfi is not as picturesque as Positano or as well-connected as Sorrento, but it has a real-city feel and a vivacious bustle.

Amalfi's one main street runs up from the waterfront through a deep valley, with stairways to courtyards and houses on either side. It's worth walking uphill to the workaday upper end of town. Narrow, stepped side lanes squeeze between hulking old buildings.

Orientation

Amalfi's waterfront is the coast's biggest transport hub. Right next to each other are the bus station, ferry docks, and a parking lot (€5/hour). Venture into the town and you'll quickly come to Piazza Duomo, the main square (sporting a statue of St. Andrew), and the cathedral.

Tourist Information: The **TI** is about 100 yards from the bus station and ferry

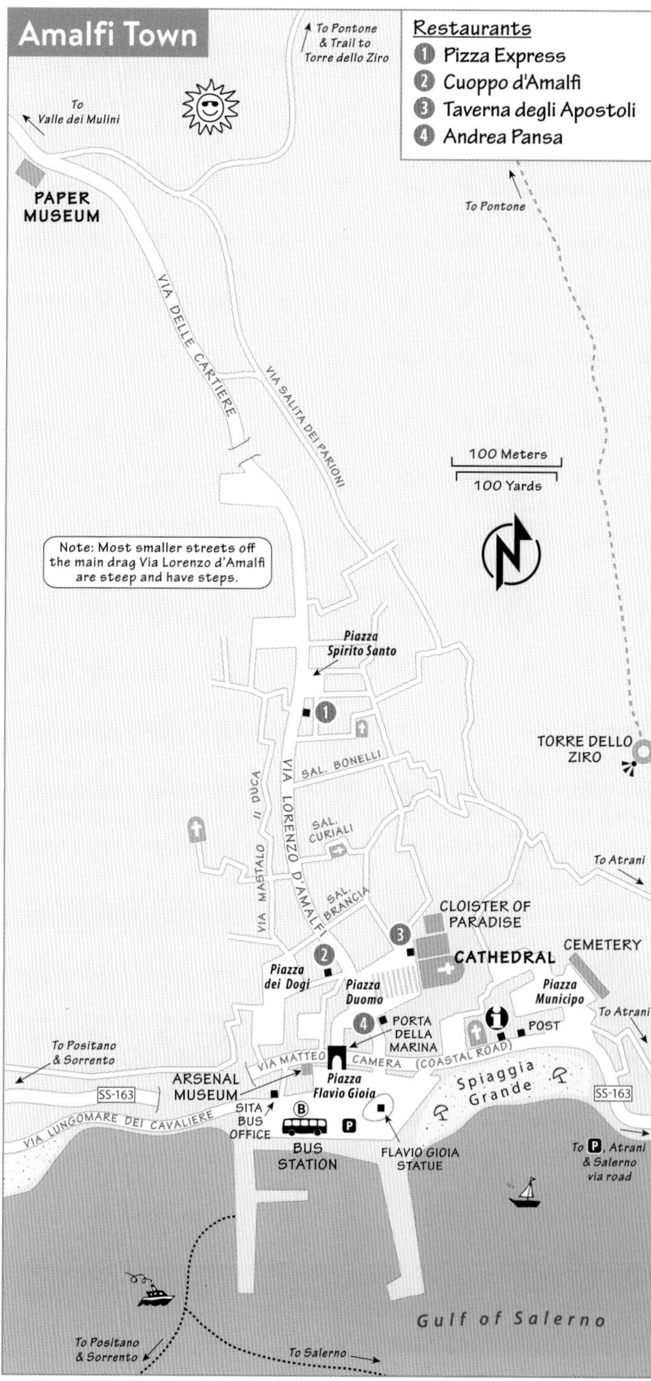
Amalfi Town
To Pontone & Trail to Torre dello Ziro
Restaurants
1 Pizza Express
2 Cuoppo d'Amalfi
3 Taverna degli Apostoli
4 Andrea Pansa
To Valle dei Mulini
PAPER MUSEUM
To Pontone
VIA DELLE CARTIERE
VIA SALITA DEI PARIONI
100 Meters
100 Yards
Note: Most smaller streets off the main drag Via Lorenzo d'Amalfi are steep and have steps.
Piazza Spirito Santo
TORRE DELLO ZIRO
SAL. BONELLI
VIA LORENZO D'AMALFI
VIA MASTALO II DUCA
SAL. CURIALI
To Atrani
SAL. BRANCIA
CLOISTER OF PARADISE
CEMETERY
CATHEDRAL
Piazza dei Dogi
Piazza Duomo
Piazza Municipo
To Atrani
PORTA DELLA MARINA
POST
To Positano & Sorrento
VIA MATTEO CAMERA (COASTAL ROAD)
ARSENAL MUSEUM
Piazza Flavio Gioia
Spiaggia Grande
SS-163
SS-163
VIA LUNGOMARE DEI CAVALIERE
SITA BUS OFFICE
BUS STATION
FLAVIO GIOIA STATUE
To P, Atrani & Salerno via road
Gulf of Salerno
To Positano & Sorrento
To Salerno

dock, next to the post office (Mon-Sat 8:30-13:00 & 14:00-18:00, Nov-March Mon-Sat 8:30-13:00, closed Sun year-round, pay WC in same courtyard, Corso della Repubbliche Marinare 27, tel. 089-871-107, www.amalfitouristoffice.it).

Baggage Storage: You can store your bag safely for €5 at **Divina Costiera Travel Office** facing the waterfront square, across from the bus parking lot (daily 8:00-13:00 & 14:00-19:00, closed mid-Nov-March, tel. 089-872-467).

Speedboat Charters: Consider **Charter La Dolce Vita** (mobile 335-549-9365, www.amalficoastyacht.it).

Rick's Tip: **Don't get stranded!** *The* **last bus from Amalfi back to Sorrento** *leaves in the evening (in winter this can be as early as 19:00). Don't plan to leave on the last bus of the day; if that bus is full, your only option might be a €100 taxi ride.*

Sights

CATHEDRAL

This church, built c. 1000-1300, is a mix of Moorish and Byzantine flavors. Its imposing stairway functions as a hangout zone and outdoor theater. The 1,000-year-old bronze door at the top was given to Amalfi by a wealthy local merchant who had it made in Constantinople. The courtyard of 120 graceful columns—the "Cloister of Paradise"—was the cemetery for nobles in the 13th century. Don't miss the fine view of the bell tower and its majolica tiles. The original ninth-century church, known as the Basilica of the Crucifix, named for its fine 13th-century wooden crucifix, is today a museum filled with art treasures. Down the stairs to the right of the altar is the Crypt of St. Andrew. Under the huge bronze statue, you'll see a reliquary holding what are believed to be Andrew's remains (€3, daily in summer 9:00-19:45, shorter hours off-season, tel. 089-871-324, www.parrocchiaamalfi.com). A free WC is at the top of the steps (through unmarked green door, just a few steps before ticket booth, ask for key at desk).

Amalfi Cathedral

▲PAPER MUSEUM

Paper has been a vital industry here since Amalfi's glory days in the Middle Ages. At this cavernous, cool 13th-century paper mill-turned-museum, a guide recounts the history and process of papermaking and demonstrates vintage machinery (€4; daily 10:00-18:30; Nov-Feb Tue-Wed and Fri-Sun until 15:30, closed Mon and Thu; a 10-minute walk up the main street from the cathedral, look for signs to *Museo della Carta;* tel. 089-830-4561, www.museodellacarta.it).

Eating

To grab a fast bite, walk five minutes up the main drag; on the right, past the first archway, is **$ Pizza Express,** with honest pies, calzones, and sandwiches to go (Mon-Sat 9:00-21:00, closed Sun, Via Capuano 46, mobile 339-581-2336). The **Cuoppo d'Amalfi** fried-fish shop at Piazza dei Doge fills cardboard cones with all manner of deep-fried sea life.

$$ Taverna degli Apostoli, with colorful outdoor tables and cozy upstairs dining room in what was once an art gallery. The menu is brief but thoughtful, going beyond the old standbys, and everything is well-executed (daily 12:00-16:00 & 19:00-24:00, Supportico San Andrea 6, tel. 089-872-991). For dessert, the Andrea Pansa pastry shop and café, to the right as you face the cathedral steps, is the most venerable place in town—a good spot to try *sfogliatella* (the delicate pastry invented at a nearby monastery) and other desserts popular in southern Italy.

Ravello

Ravello sits atop a lofty perch 1,000 feet above the sea, with breathtaking views that have attracted celebrities for generations. Richard Wagner, D. H. Lawrence, M. C. Escher, Henry Wadsworth Longfellow, Greta Garbo, and Gore Vidal have all called it home.

The town is like a lush and peaceful garden floating in a world all its own, with nothing but stones, old villas-turned-luxury hotels, cafés, tourists, and grand views. Ravello feels like a place to convalesce.

Sights

The town's entry tunnel deposits you on the main square, **Piazza Duomo,** with the Duomo. The **TI** is down the street past the cathedral (TI open daily 10:00-18:00, closes earlier off-season, 100 yards from the square—follow signs to Via Roma 18, tel. 089-857-096, www.ravellotime.it).

The **Duomo,** which overlooks the main square, feels stripped-down and Romanesque. Its key features are its 12th-century bronze doors, the carved marble pulpit supported by six lions, and the relic of holy blood (left of main altar). The front door is locked; enter through the humble cathedral museum on Viale Wagner, around the left side (€3, daily 9:00-19:00, Nov-April until 18:00).

Villa Rufolo, also on Piazza Duomo, has wistful gardens with spectacular views. Enter the villa through the stout watchtower to buy your ticket and pick up the English booklet explaining the sight. Then walk through part of the sprawling villa ruins. Check out the short video in the tiny theater at the base of the tower and the exhibit upstairs. The palace itself has little to show, but the gardens and views are magnificent and invite exploration (€7, daily 9:00-21:00, Oct-April until sunset, tel. 089-857-621, www.villarufolo.it). You can enjoy the same view, sans the entry fee, from the bus parking lot below the villa.

Eating

Several no-brainer, interchangeable restaurants face Piazza Duomo and line the surrounding streets. To enjoy this fine setting, just take your pick. You can also grab a takeaway lunch at one of the little groceries and sandwich shops that line Via Roma (between Piazza Duomo and the TI). Enjoy your meal at the panoramic benches at the far end of Piazza Duomo (facing the cathedral).

Transportation

Ravello and the town of **Amalfi** are connected by bus along a very windy road. Coming from Amalfi town, buy your bus ticket at the bar on the waterfront, and ask where the stop for Ravello is (normally by the statue on the waterfront, just to the statue's left as you face the water). When returning from Ravello, line up early, since the buses are often crowded (at least every 40 minutes, 30-minute trip, €1.20, buy ticket in tobacco shop; catch bus 100 yards off main square, at other end of tunnel).

Italian History

Italy has a lot of history, so let's get started.

Origins of Rome

(C. 753 B.C.-450 B.C.)

A she-wolf breastfed two human babies, Romulus and Remus, who grew to build the city of Rome in 753 B.C.—you buy that? Closer to fact, farmers and shepherds of the Latin tribe settled near the mouth of the Tiber River, a prime trading location. The crude settlement was sandwiched between two sophisticated civilizations—the Etruscans of Tuscany to the north, and Greek colonists to the south. Little Rome was both dominated and nourished by these societies.

In 509 B.C., the Romans drove out the Etruscan kings and replaced them with elected Roman senators and (eventually) a code of law ("Laws of the Twelve Tables," 450 B.C.). The Roman Republic was born.

The Republic Expands

(C. 509 B.C.-A.D. 1)

Located in the center of the peninsula, Rome was ideally situated for trading salt and wine. Roman businessmen, backed by an army, expanded through the Italian peninsula, establishing an infrastructure as they went. Rome soon conquered its northern Etruscan neighbors.

Next, Rome overcame the Greek colonists (c. 275 B.C.). Rome now ruled a united federation stretching from Tuscany to the southern tip of the Italian peninsula, with a standard currency, a system of roads, and an army of a half-million soldiers ready for the next challenge: Carthage (in modern-day Tunisia). Carthage and Rome fought the Punic Wars for control of the Mediterranean (264-201 B.C. and 146 B.C.). Rome emerged victorious.

The well-tuned Roman legions easily subdued cultured Greece in the Macedonian Wars (215-146 B.C.). By the first century B.C., Rome was master of the Mediterranean. Booty, cheap grain, and thousands of captured slaves poured in, transforming the economic model from small farmers to unemployed city dwellers living off tribute from conquered lands.

Civil Wars and the Transition to Empire

(FIRST CENTURY B.C.)

With easy money streaming in and traditional roles obsolete, Romans bickered among themselves over their slice of the pie. Wealthy landowners wrangled with the middle and working classes and with the growing population of slaves, who demanded a greater say in government.

Amid the chaos of class war and civil war, charismatic generals who could provide wealth and security became dictators—men such as Julius Caesar (100-44 B.C.). He was a cunning politician, riveting speaker, conqueror of Gaul, author of *The Gallic Wars,* and lover of Cleopatra, Queen of Egypt. In his four-year reign, he reformed and centralized the government around himself. Disgruntled Republicans feared that he would make himself king. At his peak of power, they surrounded Caesar on the "Ides of March" (March 15, 44 B.C.) and killed him.

Julius Caesar died, but the concept of one-man rule lived on in his adopted son, who was proclaimed Emperor Augustus (27 B.C.). Augustus outwardly followed the traditions of the Republic, while in practice he acted as a dictator with the backing of Rome's legions and the rubber-stamp approval of the Senate. He established his family to succeed him (making the family name "Caesar" a title), and set the pattern of rule by emperors for the next 500 years.

The Roman Empire

(c. A.D. 1-500)

In his 40-year reign, Augustus ended Rome's civil wars and ushered in the Pax Romana: 200 years of prosperity and peace. Rome ruled an empire of 54 million people, stretching from Scotland to Africa, from Spain to the Middle East. Conquered peoples were welcomed into the fold of prosperity, linked by roads, common laws, common gods, education, and the Latin language. The city of Rome, with more than a million inhabitants, was decorated with statues and monumental structures faced with marble. Rome was the marvel of the known world, though it prospered on a (false) economy of booty, slaves, and cheap imports.

Decline and Fall

(A.D. 200-500)

Rome peaked in the second century A.D. under the capable emperors Trajan (r. 98-117), Hadrian (r. 117-138), and Marcus Aurelius (r. 161-180). For the next three centuries, the Roman Empire declined, shrinking in size and wealth, a victim of corruption, disease, an overextended army, a false economy, and the constant pressure of "barbarian" tribes pecking away at its borders.

Trying to stall the disintegration, Emperor Diocletian (r. 284-305) split the empire into two administrative halves under two equal emperors. Constantine (r. 306-337) moved the capital of the empire from decaying Rome to the new city of Constantinople (330, present-day Istanbul). Almost instantly, the once-great city of Rome became a minor player in imperial affairs. (The eastern "Byzantine" half of the empire would thrive and live on for another thousand years.) Constantine also legalized Christianity (313), and the once-persecuted cult soon became virtually the state religion, the backbone of Rome's fading hierarchy.

By 410, "Rome" had shrunk to just the city itself. Barbarian tribes from the north and east poured in to loot and plunder. The city was sacked by Visigoths (410) and vandalized by Vandals (455), and the pope had to plead with Attila the Hun for mercy (451). Peasants huddled near lords for protection from bandits, planting the seeds of medieval feudalism.

In 476, the last emperor sold his title for a comfy pension, and Rome fell, plunging

Europe into a thousand years of darkness. For the next 13 centuries, there would be no "Italy," just a patchwork of rural dukedoms and towns, victimized by foreign powers. Italy lay in shambles, helpless.

Invasions

(A.D. 500-1000)

In 500 years, Italy suffered through a full paragraph of invasions: Lombards (568) and Byzantines (536) occupied the north. In the south, Muslim Saracens (827) and Christian Normans (1061) established thriving kingdoms. Charlemagne, king of the Germanic Franks, defeated the Lombards, and on Christmas Day, A.D. 800, he knelt before the pope in St. Peter's in Rome to be crowned Holy Roman Emperor, an empty title meant to resurrect the glory of ancient Rome united with medieval Christianity. For the next thousand years, Italians would pledge nominal allegiance to weak, distant German kings as their "Holy Roman Emperor," an empty title meant to resurrect the glory of ancient Rome united with medieval Christianity.

Through all the invasions and chaos, the glory of ancient Rome was preserved in the pomp, knowledge, hierarchy, and wealth of the Christian Church. Strong popes (Leo I, 440-461, and Gregory the Great, 590-604) ruled like small-time emperors, governing territories in central Italy called the Papal States.

Prosperity and Politics

(A.D. 1000-1300)

Sea-trading cities like Venice, Genoa, Pisa, Naples, and Amalfi grew wealthy as middlemen between Europe and the Orient. During the Crusades (e.g., First Crusade 1097-1130), Italian ships ferried Europe's Christian soldiers eastward, then returned laden with spices and highly marked-up luxury goods from the Orient. Trade spawned banking, and Italians became capitalists, loaning money at interest to Europe's royalty. The medieval prosperity of the cities laid the foundation of the future Renaissance.

Politically, the Italian peninsula was dominated by two rulers—the pope in Rome and the German "Holy Roman Emperor" (with holdings in the north). This split Italy into two warring political parties: supporters of the popes (called Guelphs, centered in urban areas) and supporters of the emperors (Ghibellines, popular with the rural nobility).

The Unlucky 1300s

In 1309, the pope—enticed by France, Europe's fast-rising power—moved from Rome to Avignon, France. At one point, two rival popes reigned, one in Avignon and the other in Rome, and they excommunicated each other. The papacy eventually returned to Rome (1377), but the schism had created a breakdown in central authority that was exacerbated by an outbreak of bubonic plague (Black Death, 1347-1348), which killed a third of the Italian population.

In the power vacuum, new powers emerged in the independent cities. Venice, Florence, Milan, and Naples were under the protection and leadership of local noble families, such as the Medici in Florence. Florence thrived in the wool and dyeing trade, which led to international banking, with branches in all of Europe's capitals. A positive side effect of the terrible Black Death was that the now-smaller population got a bigger share of the land, jobs, and infrastructure. By century's end, Italy was poised to enter its most glorious era since antiquity.

The Renaissance

(1400s)

The Renaissance—the "rebirth" of ancient Greek and Roman art styles, knowledge, and humanism—began in Italy (c. 1400), and spread through Europe over the next two centuries. Many of Europe's most famous painters, sculptors, and thinkers—such as Michelangelo, Leonardo, and Raphael—were Italian.

Influential Italians

Ancient Rome

Julius Caesar (100-44 B.C.): After conquering Gaul (France), subduing Egypt, and winning Cleopatra's heart, Caesar ruled Rome with king-like powers. In an attempt to preserve the Republic, senators killed him, but the concept of one-man rule lived on.

Augustus (born Octavian, 63 B.C.-A.D. 14): Julius' adopted son became the first of the Caesars that ruled Rome during its 500 years as a Europe-wide power. He set the tone for emperors both good (Trajan, Hadrian, Marcus Aurelius) and bad (Caligula, Nero, and dozens of others).

Constantine (c. 280-337 A.D.): Raised in a Christian home, this emperor legalized Christianity, almost instantly turning a persecuted sect into a Europe-wide religion. With the Fall of Rome, the Church was directed by strong popes and so guided Italians through the next thousand years of invasions, plagues, political decentralization, and darkness.

The Renaissance

Lorenzo the Magnificent (1449-1492): Soldier, poet, lover, and ruler of Florence in the 1400s, this Renaissance Man embodied the "rebirth" of ancient enlightenment. Lorenzo's wealthy Medici family funded Florentine artists who pioneered a realistic 3-D style.

Michelangelo Buonarroti (1475-1564): His statue of David—slaying an ignorant brute—stands as a monumental symbol of Italian enlightenment. Along with fellow geniuses **Leonardo da Vinci** and **Raphael,** Michelangelo spread the Italian Renaissance (painting, sculpture, architecture, literature, and ideas) to a worldwide audience.

Giovanni Lorenzo Bernini (1598-1680): The "Michelangelo of Baroque" kept Italy a major exporter of sophisticated trends. Bernini's ornate statues and architecture decorated palaces of the rising power in France, even as Italy was reverting to a stagnant patchwork of foreign-ruled states.

Modern Italy

Victor Emmanuel II (1820-1878): As the only Italian-born ruler on the peninsula, this King of Sardinia became the rallying point for Italian unification. Aided by the general Garibaldi, writer Mazzini, and politician Cavour (with a soundtrack by Verdi), he became the first ruler of a united, democratic Italy in 1870.

Benito Mussolini (1883-1945): An inspiration for Hitler, he derailed Italy's fledgling democracy, becoming dictator of a fascist state, leading the country into defeat in World War II. No public places honor Mussolini, but many streets and piazzas throughout Italy bear the name of Giacomo Matteotti (1885-1924), a politician whose outspoken opposition to Mussolini got him killed by Fascists.

Federico Fellini (1920-1993): Fellini's films *(La Strada, La Dolce Vita, 8½)* chronicle Italy's postwar years in gritty black and white—the poverty, destruction, and disillusionment of the war followed by the optimism, decadence, and materialism of the economic boom. He captured the surreal chaos of Italy's abrupt social change from traditional Catholic to a secular, urban world.

This cultural boom, financed by thriving trade and lucrative banking, changed people's thinking about every aspect of life. In politics, it meant an eventual rebirth of Greek ideas of democracy. In religion, it meant a move away from Church dominance and toward the assertion of man (humanism) and a more personal faith. Science and secular learning were revived after centuries of superstition and ignorance. In architecture, there was a return to the balanced columns and domes of Greece and Rome. During the Renaissance, the peninsula once again became the trendsetting cultural center of Europe.

Foreign Invasions
(1500s)

In May of 1498, Vasco da Gama of Portugal landed in India, having found a sea route around Africa. Italy's monopoly on trade with the East was broken. Portugal, France, Spain, England, and Holland—nation-states under strong central rule—began to overtake decentralized Italy. Italy's once-great maritime cities now traded in an economic backwater, as Italy's bankers (such as the Medici in Florence) were going bankrupt. While the Italian Renaissance was all the rage throughout Europe, it declined in its birthplace. Italy—culturally sophisticated but weak and decentralized—was ripe for the picking by Europe's rising powers.

Several kings of France invaded (1494, 1495, and 1515)—initially invited by Italian lords to attack their rivals—and began divvying up territory for their noble families. Italy also became a battleground in religious conflicts between Catholics and the new Protestant movement. In the chaos, the city of Rome was brutally sacked by foreign mercenaries (1527).

Foreign Rule
(1600-1800)

For the next two centuries, most of Italy's states were ruled by foreign nobles, serving as prizes for the winners of Europe's dynastic wars. Italy ceased to be a major player in Europe, politically and economically. Italian intellectual life was often cropped short by a conservative Catholic Church trying to fight Protestantism. Galileo, for example, was forced by the Inquisition to renounce his belief that the Earth orbited the sun (1633). But Italy did export Baroque art (Giovanni Lorenzo Bernini) and the budding new medium of opera.

The War of the Spanish Succession (1713)—a war in which Italy did not participate—gave much of northern Italy to Austria's ruling family, the Habsburgs (who now wore the crown of "Holy Roman Emperor"). In the south, Spain's Bourbon family ruled the Kingdom of Naples (known after 1816 as the Kingdom of the Two Sicilies), making it a culturally sophisticated but economically backward area, preserving a medieval, feudal caste system.

In 1720, a minor war (the War of Austrian Succession) created a new state at the foot of the Alps, called the Kingdom of Sardinia (a.k.a. the Kingdom of Piedmont, or Savoy). Ruled by the Savoy family, this was the only major state on the peninsula that was actually ruled by Italians. It proved to be a toehold to the future.

Italy Unites—The Risorgimento
(1800s)

In 1796, Napoleon Bonaparte swept through Italy and changed everything. He ousted Austrian and Spanish dukes, confiscated Church lands, united scattered states, and crowned himself "King of Italy" (1805). After his defeat (1815), Italy's old ruling order (namely, Austria and Spain) was restored. But Napoleon had planted a seed: What if Italians could unite and rule themselves like Europe's other modern nations?

For the next 50 years, a movement to unite Italy slowly grew. Called the Risorgimento ("rising again"), the movement promised a revival of Italy's glory. It started as a revolutionary, liberal movement, but gradually, Italians of all stripes warmed to the idea of unification.

The movement coalesced around the Italian-ruled Kingdom of Sardinia and its king, Victor Emmanuel II. In 1859, Sardinia's prime minister, Camillo Cavour, cleverly persuaded France to drive Austria out of northern Italy, leaving the region in Italian hands. A vote was held, and several central Italian states (including some of the pope's) rejected their feudal lords and chose to join the growing Kingdom of Sardinia.

After victory in the north, General Giuseppe Garibaldi (1807-1882) steamed south with 1,000 of his best soldiers *(I Mille)* and marched on the Spanish-ruled city of Naples (1860). The old order simply collapsed. In two short months, Garibaldi had achieved a seemingly impossible victory against a far superior army. Garibaldi sent a one-word telegram to the king of Sardinia: *"Obbedisco"* (I obey). Victor Emmanuel II was crowned King of Italy. Only the pope in Rome held out, protected by French troops. When the city finally fell—easily—to unification forces on September 20, 1870, the Risorgimento was complete.

The Risorgimento was largely the work of four men: Garibaldi (the sword), Mazzini (the spark), Cavour (the diplomat), and Victor Emmanuel II (the rallying point). Today, street signs throughout Italy honor them and the dates of their great victories.

Mussolini and War
(1900-1945)

Italy—now a nation-state—entered the 20th century with a progressive government (a constitutional monarchy), a collection of colonies, a flourishing northern half of the country, and an economically backward south. After World War I (1915-1918), being on the winning Allied side, the Italians were granted possession of the alpine regions. But in the postwar cynicism and anarchy, many radical political parties rose up—Communist, Socialist, Popular, and Fascist.

Benito Mussolini (1883-1945), a writer for socialist newspapers, led the Fascists. In 1922, he seized the government and began his rule as dictator for the next two decades.

Mussolini struck an agreement with the pope (Concordato, 1929), giving Vatican City to the papacy, while Mussolini ruled Italy with the implied blessing of the Catholic Church.

Mussolini allied his country with Hitler's Nazi regime, drawing an unprepared Italy into World War II (1940). Italy's lame army was never a factor in the war, and when Allied forces landed in Sicily (1943), Italians welcomed them as liberators. The Italians toppled Mussolini's government and surrendered to the Allies, but Nazi Germany sent troops to rescue Mussolini. The war raged on as Allied troops inched their way north against German resistance. Italians were reduced to poverty. In the last days of the war (April of 1945), Mussolini was killed by the Italian resistance.

Postwar Italy

At war's end, Italy was ruined and poor. The nation rebuilt in the 1950s and 1960s with Marshall Plan aid from the US. Italy regained its standing among nations, joining the United Nations, NATO, and what would later become the European Union.

However, the government remained weak, changing on average once a year, shifting from right to left to centrist coalitions (it's had 63 governments since World War II). Afraid of another Mussolini, the authors of the postwar constitution created a feeble executive branch; without majorities in both houses of parliament, nothing could get done. All Italians acknowledged that the real power lay in the hands of backroom politicians and organized crime. The country remained strongly divided between the rich, industrial north and the poor, rural south.

Italian society changed greatly in the 1960s and 1970s, spurred by the liberal reforms of the Catholic Church at the Vatican II conference (1962-1965). The once-conservative Catholic country legalized divorce and contraception, and the birth rate plummeted. In the 1970s, the economy slowed due to inflation, strikes, organized crime, terrorist attacks, and the worldwide energy crisis. A series of coalition governments in the 1980s brought some stability to the economy.

Italy Today

In the early 1990s, the judiciary launched a campaign to rid politics of corruption and Mafia ties. Though still ongoing, the investigation sent a message that Italy would no longer tolerate evils that were considered normal just a generation earlier.

Over the last decade, the Great Recession hit the Italian economy hard. Like other European nations, Italy had run up big deficits by providing comfy social benefits without sufficient tax revenue, forcing the Italian government to tighten its belt. By the end of 2011, Italy's debt load was the second worst in the euro zone, behind only Greece.

A caretaker government imposed severe austerity measures, leading to high rates of unemployment, particularly among youth. Italy wanted change, and got it when Matteo Renzi took over as prime minister in early 2014—at age 39, he was the youngest prime minister in modern Italian history. For a time, the dynamic Renzi was immensely popular. Later, though, he was dogged by a persistently sluggish economy, repeated corruption scandals, and an immigration crisis brought on by the influx of people streaming from across the Mediterranean seeking a better life in Europe. In late 2016, Renzi resigned after Italians rejected his far-reaching constitutional reforms.

The new prime minister is Paolo Gentiloni--a former mayor of Rome--who served as minister of foreign affairs under Renzi and is a member of the same political party. Some observers say the 62-year-old Gentiloni is just a placeholder until Renzi returns to power in the next elections.

As you travel through Italy today, you'll encounter a fascinating country with a rich history and a per-capita income that comes close to its neighbors to the north. Despite its ups and downs, Italy remains committed to Europe...yet it's as wonderfully Italian as ever.

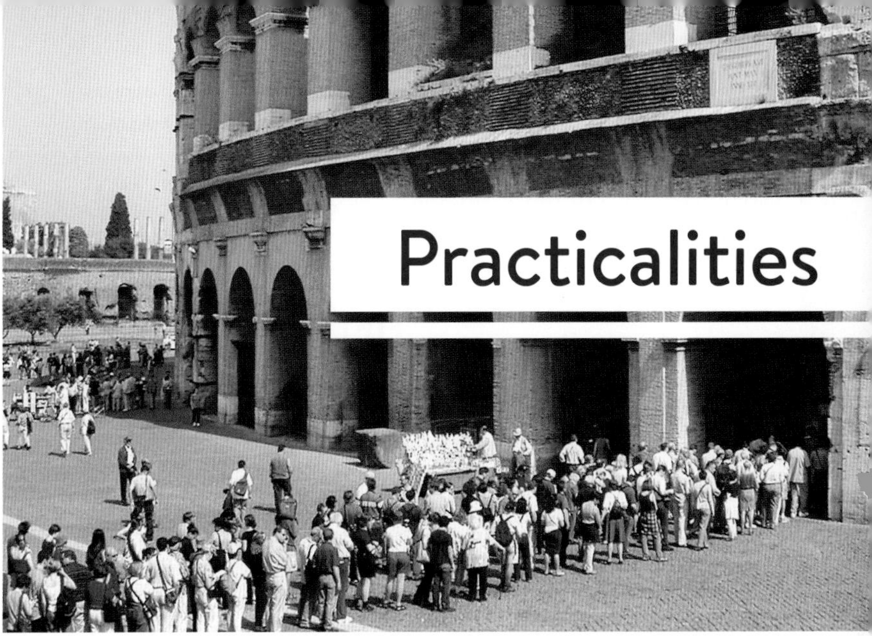

Practicalities

TOURIST INFORMATION

Before your trip, scan the website of the Italian national tourist office (www.italia.it) for a wealth of travel information. If you have a specific question, try contacting one of their US offices (New York: Tel. 212/245-5618, newyork@enit.it; Chicago: Tel. 312/644-9335, chicago@enit.it; Los Angeles: Tel. 310/820-1898, losangeles@enit.it).

In Italy, a good first stop in every town is the tourist information office (abbreviated TI in this book). Prepare a list of questions and a proposed plan to double-check. Pick up a city map, confirm opening hours of sights, and get information on public transit (including bus and train schedules), walking tours, special events, and nightlife.

TRAVEL TIPS

Time Zones: Italy, like most of continental Europe, is generally six/nine hours ahead of the East/West Coasts of the US. The exceptions are the beginning and end of Daylight Saving Time: Europe "springs forward" the last Sunday in March (two weeks after North America), and "falls back" the last Sunday in October (one week before North America). For an online converter, try www.timeanddate.com/worldclock.

Business Hours: Some businesses respect the afternoon siesta; when it's 90 degrees in the shade, you'll understand why. Shops are generally open from 9:00 to 13:00 and from 16:00 to 19:30, daily except Sunday, though in touristy places many stores stay open throughout the day and on Sunday, too. Most museums stay open all day; smaller ones may close for a siesta.

Watt's Up? Bring an adapter with two round prongs (sold at travel stores in the US) to plug into Europe's outlets. You won't need a converter, because newer electronics—such as tablets, laptops, and battery chargers—are dual voltage and convert automatically to Europe's 220-volt system. If your old hair dryer isn't dual voltage, buy a cheapie in Europe.

Discounts: This book lists only the full adult price for sights. However, many sights offer discounts for youths (up to age 18), students (with proper identification cards, www.isic.org), families, and seniors (loosely defined as retirees or those willing to call themselves seniors). Always ask. Italy's national museums generally offer free admission to anyone under 18, though some discounts are only available for citizens of the European Union.

Tobacco Shops: Tobacco shops (*tabacchi,* often indicated with a big *T* sign) are ubiquitous across Italy as handy places to get stamps, pay for street parking, and buy tickets for city buses and subways.

Online Translation: Google's Chrome browser instantly translates websites. You can also paste text or the URL of a foreign website into the translation window at Translate.google.com. The Google Translate app converts spoken English into most European languages (and vice versa).

HELP!

Emergency and Medical Help

Dial 113 for English-speaking police help. To summon an ambulance, call 118. Or ask at your hotel for help—they'll know the nearest medical and emergency services. If you get a minor ailment, do as the locals do and go to a pharmacist for advice.

Theft or Loss

To replace a passport, you'll need to go in person to an embassy or consulate office (listed below). If your credit and debit cards disappear, cancel and replace them. If your things are lost or stolen, file a police report, either on the spot or within a day or two; you'll need it to submit an insurance claim for rail passes and travel gear, and it can help with replacing your passport and credit and debit cards. For more information, see www.ricksteves.com/help.

Damage Control for Lost Cards

If you lose your credit or debit card, report the loss immediately to your card company. Call these 24-hour US numbers collect: Visa (tel. 303/967-1096), MasterCard (tel. 636/722-7111), and American Express (tel. 336/393-1111). In Italy, to make a collect call to the US, dial 800-172-444; press zero or stay on the line for an English-speaking operator.

If you report your loss within two days, you typically won't be responsible for unauthorized transactions on your account, although many banks charge a liability fee of $50. You can generally receive a

Avoiding Theft and Scams

With sweet-talking con artists at the train station, pickpockets on buses, and thieving gangs of children roving ancient sites, tourists face a gauntlet of rip-offs. Fortunately, violent crime is rare. Pickpockets don't want to hurt you; they just want your money and gadgets.

My recommendations: Stay alert and wear a money belt (tucked under your clothes) to keep your cash, debit card, credit card, and passport secure; carry only the money you need for the day in your front pocket.

Treat any disturbance (e.g., someone bumps into you or spills something on you) as a smoke screen for theft. Be on guard while boarding and leaving crowded buses and subways. Thieves target tourists overloaded with bags or distracted with smartphones.

The sneakiest thieves pose as well-dressed businessmen or even tourists. The scruffy beggars on the street are easy to spot: fast-fingered moms with babies, and gangs of scruffy children holding up newspapers or cardboard signs to confuse their victims. They'll scram like stray cats if you're on to them.

Scams abound. When paying for something, be aware of how much cash you're handing over (even state the denomination of the bill when paying a cabbie), demand clear and itemized bills at restaurants, and count your change. If self-proclaimed "police" on the street warn you about counterfeit (or drug) money, and ask to see your cash, don't give them your wallet. Just say no to locals who want to "help" you use self-service machines that require your credit card for payment (for train tickets, parking, and so on). For advice on using cash machines smartly, read "Security Tips" under "Cash," later.

There's no need to be scared; just be smart and prepared.

temporary replacement card within two or three business days in Europe.

Embassies and Consulates

US Embassy in Rome: Tel. 06-4674-2420, 24-hour emergency tel. 06-46741 (visit by appointment only, Via Vittorio Veneto 121, http://it.usembassy.gov).

US Consulates: in Milan—tel. 02-290-351 (Via Principe Amedeo 2/10, http://milan.usconsulate.gov); in Florence—tel. 055-266-951 (Lungarno Vespucci 38, http://florence.usconsulate.gov); in Naples—tel. 081-583-8111 (Piazza della Repubblica, http://naples.usconsulate.gov)

Canadian Embassy in Rome: Tel. 06-854-442-911 (Via Zara 30, www.italy.gc.ca).

Canadian Consulate in Milan: Tel. 02-626-94238 (Piazza Cavour 3, www.italy.gc.ca)

MONEY

This section offers advice on how to pay for purchases on your trip (including getting cash from ATMs and paying with plastic), VAT (sales tax) refunds, and tipping.

What to Bring

Bring both a credit card and a debit card. You'll use the debit card at cash machines (ATMs) to withdraw local cash for most purchases, and the credit card to pay for larger items. Some travelers carry a third card as a backup, in case one gets demagnetized or eaten by a rogue machine.

Exchange Rate

1 euro (€) = about $1.20

To convert prices in euros to dollars, add about 20 percent: €20 = about $24; €50 = about $60. (Check www.oanda.com for the latest exchange rates.) Just like the dollar, one euro is broken down into 100 cents. Coins range from €0.01 to €2, and bills from €5 to €500 (though bills over €50 are rarely used).

What NOT to Bring: Resist the urge to buy **euros** before your trip or you'll pay the price in bad stateside exchange rates. Wait until you arrive to withdraw money. I've yet to see a European airport that didn't have plenty of ATMs.

Plastic versus Cash: Although credit cards are widely accepted in Europe, day-to-day spending is generally more cash-based than in the US. I find cash is the easiest—and sometimes only—way to pay for cheap food, bus fare, taxis, tips, and local guides. Some businesses (especially smaller ones, such as B&Bs and mom-and-pop cafés and shops) may charge you extra for using a credit card—or might not accept credit cards at all.

I use my credit card to book hotel reservations, to buy advance tickets for events or sights, and to cover major expenses (such as car rentals or plane tickets). It can also be smart to use plastic near the end of your trip, to avoid another visit to the ATM.

Using Credit Cards: European cards use chip-and-PIN technology, while most cards issued in the US use a chip-and-signature system. Most European card readers can automatically generate a receipt for you to sign, just as you would at home. If a cashier is present, you should have no problems. Some card readers will instead prompt you to enter your PIN (so it's important to know the code for each of your cards).

At self-service payment machines (transit-ticket kiosks, parking, etc.), results are mixed, as US chip-and-signature cards aren't configured for unattended transactions. If your card won't work, look for a cashier who can process your card manually—or pay in cash.

Using Cash Machines: European cash machines have English-language instructions and work just like they do at home—except they spit out local currency instead of dollars, calculated at the day's standard bank-to-bank rate. In most places, ATMs are easy to locate—in Italy ask for a *bancomat*.

Avoid "independent" ATMs, such as Travelex, Euronet, Moneybox, Cardpoint, and Cashzone. These have high fees, can be less secure than a bank ATM, and may try to trick users with "dynamic currency conversion" (or DCC).

Dynamic Currency Conversion: Some European merchants and hoteliers cheerfully charge you for converting your purchase price into dollars. If it's offered, refuse this "service." You'll pay extra for the expensive convenience of seeing your charge in dollars.

Security Tips: Before inserting your card into an ATM, inspect the front. If anything looks crooked, loose, or damaged, it could be a sign of a card-skimming device. When entering your PIN, carefully block other people's view of the keypad.

While traveling, be sure to use a secure connection if you need to access your accounts online (see page 493).

Pretrip Checklist

Report your travel dates. Let your bank know that you'll be using your debit and credit cards in Europe, and when and where you're headed.

Know your PIN. Make sure you know the numeric, four-digit PIN for all of your cards, both debit and credit. Request it if you don't have one and allow time to receive the information by mail.

Adjust your ATM withdrawal limit. Find out how much you can take out daily and ask for a higher daily withdrawal limit if you want to get more cash at once. Note that European ATMs will withdraw funds only from checking accounts; you're unlikely to have access to your savings account.

Ask about fees. For any purchase or withdrawal made with a card, you may be charged a currency conversion fee (1-3 percent), a Visa or MasterCard international transaction fee (1 percent), and—for debit cards—a $2-5 transaction fee each time you use a foreign ATM (some US banks partner with European banks, allowing you to use those ATMs with no fees).

Tipping

Tipping in Italy isn't as automatic and generous as it is in the US. For special service, tips are appreciated, but not expected. As in the US, the right amount depends on your resources and the circumstances, but some general guidelines apply.

Restaurants: In Italy, a service charge *(servizio)* is usually built into your bill, so the total you pay already includes a basic tip. It's up to you whether to tip beyond this; for details, see page 484.

Taxis: Round up your fare a bit (for instance, if the fare is €4.50, pay €5). If the cabbie hauls your bags and zips you to the airport to help you catch your flight, you might want to toss in a little more. But if you feel like you're being driven in circles or otherwise ripped off, skip the tip.

Services: In general, if someone in the service industry does a super job for you, a small tip of a euro or two is appropriate...but not required. If you're not sure whether (or how much) to tip for a service, ask a local for advice.

Getting a VAT Refund

Wrapped into the purchase price of your Italian souvenirs is a Value-Added Tax (VAT) of about 22 percent. You're entitled to get most of that tax back if you purchase more than €155 (about $170) worth of goods at a store that participates in the VAT refund scheme. Typically, you must ring up the minimum at a single retailer—you can't add up your purchases from various shops to reach the required amount.

If the store ships the goods to your US home, VAT is not assessed on your purchase. Otherwise, you'll need to:

Get the paperwork. Have the merchant completely fill out the necessary refund document. You'll have to present your passport. Get the paperwork done before you leave the store to ensure you'll have everything you need (including your original sales receipt).

Get your stamp at the border or airport. Process your VAT document at your last stop in the European Union (the airport or border) with the customs agent who deals with VAT refunds. Arrive an additional hour early before you need to check in to allow time to find the customs office—and to stand in line. Some customs desks are positioned before airport security; confirm the location before going through security. It's best to keep your purchases in your carry-on. But if they're too large or dangerous to carry on (such as knives), pack them in your checked bags and alert the check-in agent. You're not supposed to use your purchased goods before you leave. If you show up at customs wearing your new Italian leather shoes, officials might look the other way—or deny you a refund.

Collect your refund. Many merchants work with services—such as Global Blue or Premier Tax Free—that have offices at major airports, ports, or border crossings. These services, which extract a four-percent fee, can refund your money immediately in cash or credit your card (within two billing cycles). If the retailer handles VAT refunds directly, it's up to you to contact the merchant for your refund. You can mail the documents from home or from your point of departure. You'll then have to wait—it can take months.

Customs for American Shoppers

You are allowed to take home $800 worth of items per person duty-free, once every 31 days. You can take home many processed and packaged foods: vacuum-packed cheeses, dried herbs, jams, baked goods, candy, chocolate, oil, vinegar, mustard, and honey. Fresh fruits and vegetables and most meats are not allowed, with exceptions for some canned items. As for alcohol, you can bring home one liter duty-free (it can be packed securely in your checked luggage, along with any other liquid-containing items). But if you want to pack the alcohol (or any liquid-packed food) in your carry-on bag for your flight home, buy it at a duty-free shop at the airport.

For details on allowable goods, customs rules, and duty rates, visit http://help.cbp.gov.

SIGHTSEEING

Sightseeing can be hard work. Use these tips to make your visits to Italy's finest sights meaningful, fun, efficient, and painless.

Plan Ahead

Set up an itinerary that allows you to fit in all your must-see sights. For a one-stop look at opening hours, see the "At a Glance" sidebars in this book for each major destination. Most places keep stable hours, but you can confirm the latest at the local TI or by checking museum websites. Many museums are closed or have reduced hours at least a few days a year, especially on holidays such as Labor Day (May 1), Christmas, and New Year's; check online for possible museum closures during your trip. Whenever you go, don't put off visiting a must-see sight—you never know if a place will close unexpectedly for a holiday, strike, or restoration.

Several cities, including Venice, Florence, and Rome, offer sightseeing passes that cover many (but not all) museums. Do the math: Add up the entry costs of

the sights you want to see to figure out if a pass will save you money. An added bonus is that passes allow you to bypass the long ticket-buying lines at popular sights; that alone can make a pass worthwhile.

Use the suggestions in this book to avoid waiting in line to buy tickets or enter sights. Sometimes you can make reservations for an entry time (for example, at Florence's Uffizi Gallery or Rome's Vatican Museums). Some cities offer museum passes for admission to several museums (e.g., Roma Pass and Firenze Card) that let you skip ticket-buying lines. At some popular places (such as Rome's Colosseum or Venice's Doge's Palace), you can get in more quickly by buying your ticket or pass at a less-crowded sight (Rome's Palatine Hill or Venice's Correr Museum). Booking a guided tour can help you avoid lines at many popular sights. If you can't reserve a popular sight, try visiting very early or very late. When available, evening visits are usually peaceful, with fewer crowds.

Study up. To get the most out of the sight descriptions in this book, read them before you visit. That said, every sight or museum offers more than what is covered in this book. Use the information in this book as an introduction—not the final word.

At Sights

Here's what you can typically expect:

Entering: Be warned that you may not be allowed to enter if you arrive 30-60 minutes before closing time. And guards start ushering people out well before the actual closing time, so don't save the best for last.

Some important sights have a security check, where you must open your bag or send it through a metal detector. Some sights require you to check daypacks and coats.

Photography: If the museum's photo policy isn't clearly posted, ask a guard. Generally, taking photos without a flash or tripod is allowed. Some sights ban photos altogether.

Expect Changes: Artwork can be on tour, on loan, out sick, or shifted at the whim of the curator. Pick up a floor plan as you enter, and ask the museum staff if you can't find a particular item. Say the title or artist's name, or point to the photograph in this book and ask, *"Dov'è?"* (doh-VEH, meaning "Where is?").

Audioguides and Apps: Many sights rent audioguides, which generally offer excellent recorded descriptions of the art in English. If you bring your own earbuds, you can enjoy better sound. A growing number of sights offer apps (often free) that you can download to your mobile device—check their websites. I've produced free, downloadable audio tours for some of Italy's major sights; these are indicated in this book with the symbol 🎧. For more on my audio tours, see page 28.

Before Leaving: At the gift shop, scan the postcard rack or thumb through a guidebook to be sure that you haven't overlooked something that you'd like to see.

At Churches

Remember that a modest dress code (no bare shoulders or shorts for anyone, including children) is enforced at the famous churches, such as Vatican City's St. Peter's and Venice's St. Mark's, but is often relaxed in other churches. If needed, you can improvise, using maps to cover your shoulders and a jacket for your knees. (I wear a super-lightweight pair of long pants rather than shorts for my hot and muggy big-city Italian sightseeing.)

Some churches have coin-operated audioboxes that describe the art and history; just set the dial on English, put in your coins, and listen. Coin boxes near a piece of art illuminate the art, presenting a better photo opportunity. I pop in a coin whenever I can. Let there be light.

EATING

The Italians are masters of the art of fine living. That means eating long and well. Lengthy, multicourse meals and many hours sitting in outdoor cafés are the norm. Americans eat on their way to an evening event and complain if the check is slow in coming. For Italians, the meal is an end in itself, and only rude waiters would rush you.

In general, Italians eat lunch and dinner later than we do. At 7:00 or 8:00 in the morning, they have a light breakfast (coffee—usually cappuccino or espresso—and a pastry). Lunch (between 13:00 and 15:00) is traditionally the largest meal of the day. Then they eat a late, light dinner (around 20:00-21:30, or maybe earlier in winter). To bridge the gap, people drop into a bar in the late afternoon for a snack.

Breakfast

The basic, traditional version is coffee and a roll with butter and marmalade. These days, many hotels also offer yogurt and juice, and possibly also cereal, ham, cheese, and hard-boiled eggs. Small budget hotels may leave a basic breakfast in a fridge in your room (croissant, roll, jam, yogurt, coffee). In general, the pricier the hotel, the bigger the breakfast.

If you want to skip your hotel breakfast, consider browsing for a morning picnic at a local open-air market. Or do as the Italians do: Stop into a bar or café to drink a cappuccino and munch a *cornetto* (croissant) while standing at the bar.

Restaurants

When restaurant-hunting, choose a spot filled with locals. Venturing even a block or two off the main drag leads to higher-quality food for less than half the price of the tourist-oriented places. Locals eat better at lower-rent locales.

Most restaurant kitchens close down between their lunch and dinner service. Good restaurants don't reopen for dinner before 19:00. Small restaurants with a full slate of reservations for 20:30 or 21:00 often will accommodate walk-in diners willing to eat a quick, early meal, but you aren't expected to linger.

For help in ordering, get a phrase book, such as the *Rick Steves Italian Phrase Book & Dictionary,* which has a menu decoder and plenty of useful phrases for navigating the culinary scene.

Cover and Tipping

Before you sit down, look at a menu to see what extra charges a restaurant tacks on. Two different items are routinely factored into your bill: the *coperto* and the *servizio.*

The ***coperto*** (cover charge), sometimes called ***pane e coperto*** (bread and cover), offsets the overhead expenses from the basket of bread on your table to the electricity running the dishwasher. It's not negotiable, even if you don't eat the bread. Think of it as the cost of using the table for as long as you like. Most restaurants add the *coperto* onto your bill as a flat fee (€1-3.50 per person; the amount should be clearly noted on the menu).

The ***servizio*** (service charge) of about 10 percent pays for the waitstaff. At most eateries, the words *servizio incluso* are written on the menu and/or the receipt, indicating that the listed prices already include the fee. You can add on a tip, if you choose, by including €1-2 for each person in your party. While Italians don't think about tips in terms of percentages—and many don't tip at all—this bonus amount usually comes out to about 5 percent (10 percent is excessive for all but the very best service).

A few restaurants tack on a 10 percent *servizio* charge to your bill. If a menu reads *servizio 10%,* the listed prices don't include the fee; it will be added onto your bill (so you don't need to calculate it yourself and pay it separately). Rarely, you'll see the words *servizio non incluso* on the menu or bill; in this case, you're expected to add a tip of about 10 percent.

When you want the bill, mime—scribble on your raised palm or request it: *"Il conto, per favore."* You may have to ask for it more than once. If you're in a hurry, request the check when you receive the last item you order.

Courses: Antipasto, Primo, *and* Secondo

A full Italian meal consists of several courses, though you're not obliged to get it all:

Antipasto: An appetizer such as bruschetta, grilled veggies, deep-fried tasties, thin-sliced meat (such as prosciutto or carpaccio), or a plate of olives, cold cuts, and cheeses.

Primo piatto: A "first dish" generally consisting of pasta, rice, or soup. If you think of pasta when you think of Italy, you can dine well without ever going beyond the *primo.*

Secondo piatto: A "second dish," equivalent to our main course, of meat or fish/seafood. A vegetable side dish *(contorno)* may come with the *secondo* but more often must be ordered separately.

Restaurant Strategy: For most travelers, a meal with all three courses (plus *contorni,* dessert, and wine) is simply too much food—and euros can add up in a hurry. To avoid overeating and to stretch your budget, share dishes. A good rule of thumb is for each person to order any two courses. For example, a couple can order and share one antipasto, one *primo,* one *secondo,* and one dessert; or two *antipasti* and two *primi;* or whatever combination appeals.

Another good option is sharing an array of *antipasti*—either by ordering several specific dishes or, at restaurants that offer

self-serve buffets, by choosing a variety of cooked appetizers from an *antipasti* buffet spread out like a salad bar. At buffets, you pay per plate; a typical serving costs about €8. Generally Italians don't treat buffets as all-you-can-eat, but take a one-time moderate serving; watch other customers and follow their lead.

Ordering Your Food

Seafood and steak may be sold by weight (priced by the kilo—1,000 grams, or just over two pounds; or by the *etto*—100 grams). The abbreviation *s.q. (secondo quantità)* means an item is priced "according to quantity." Unless the menu indicates a fillet *(filetto)*, fish is usually served whole, with the head and tail. Sometimes, especially for steak, restaurants require a minimum order of four or five *etti* (which diners can share). Make sure you're clear on the price before ordering.

Some special dishes come in larger quantities meant to be shared by two people. The shorthand way of showing this on a menu is "X2" (for two), but the price listed generally indicates the cost per person.

In a traditional restaurant, if you order a pasta dish and a side salad—but no main course—the waiter will bring the salad after the pasta (Italians prefer it this way, believing that it enhances digestion). If you want the salad with your pasta, specify *insieme* (een-see-YEH-meh; together).

At places with counter service—such as at a bar or a freeway rest-stop diner—you'll order and pay at the *cassa* (cashier). Take your receipt over to the counter to claim your food.

Fixed-Price Meals

You can save by getting a fixed-priced meal, which is frequently exempt from cover and service charges. Avoid the cheapest ones (often called a *menù turistico*), which tend to be bland and heavy, pairing a basic pasta with reheated meat. Look instead for a genuine *menù del giorno* (menu of the day), which offers diners a choice of appetizer, main course, and dessert. It's worth paying a little more for an inventive fixed-price meal that shows off the chef's creativity.

Budget Eating

Pizzerias

Pizzerias are ubiquitous and affordable, though even cheaper is a hole-in-the-wall takeout pizza shop. Some shops sell takeout Naples-style pizza whole or by the slice *(al taglio)*. Others offer *pizza rustica* (thick pizza baked in a big rectangular pan) by the weight, in which case you indicate how much you want: 100 grams, or *un etto*, is a hot and cheap snack; 200 grams, or *due etti*, makes a light meal. Or show the size with your hands—*tanto così* (TAHN-toh koh-ZEE; this much).

Bars/Cafés

Italian "bars" are not taverns, but inexpensive cafés. These neighborhood hangouts serve coffee, mini pizzas, sandwiches, and drinks from the cooler. This budget choice is the Italian equivalent of English pub grub.

Many bars are small—if you can't find a table, you'll need to stand or find a ledge to sit on outside. Most charge extra for table service. To get food to go, say, *"da portar via"* (for the road). All bars have a WC *(toilette, bagno)* in the back, and customers—and the discreet public—can use it.

Prices and Paying: Bars have a two- or three-tiered pricing system. Drinking a cup of coffee while standing at the bar is cheaper than drinking it at an indoor table; you'll pay still more at an outdoor table. Many places have a *lista dei prezzi* (price list) with two columns—*al bar* and *al tavolo* (table)—posted somewhere by the bar or cash register. If you're on a budget, don't sit down without first checking out the financial consequences. You can ask, "Same price if I sit or stand?" by saying, *"Costa uguale al tavolo o al banco?"* (KOH-stah oo-GWAH-lay ahl TAH-voh-loh oh ahl BAHN-koh).

If the bar isn't busy, you can probably

just order and pay when you leave. Otherwise: 1) Decide what you want; 2) find out the price by checking the prices posted near the food, the price list on the wall, or by asking the barista; 3) pay the cashier; and 4) give the receipt to the barista (whose clean fingers handle no dirty euros) and tell him or her what you want.

Cafeterias, Rosticcerie, *and* Tavola Calda *Bars*

For a fast, cheap meal, these options offer the point-and-choose basics without add-on charges. Self-service cafeterias are as predictable in Italy as they are in your hometown.

Or try the Italian version of the corner deli: a *rosticceria* (specializing in roasted meats and accompanying *antipasti*) or a *tavola calda* bar (a "hot table" buffet spread of meat and vegetables). Belly up to the bar, and with a pointing finger, you can assemble a fine meal, such as lasagna, rotisserie chicken, and sides like roasted potatoes and spinach. If something's a mystery, ask for *un assaggio* (oon ah-SAH-joh) to get a taste. To have your choices warmed up, ask for them to be heated (*scaldare;* skahl-DAH-ray). You can sometimes eat at tables or counters provided, or just get the food to go for a classy, filling picnic.

Wine Bars

Wine bars *(enoteche)* are popular, fast, and affordable for lunch. Surrounded by the office crowd, you can get a salad, a plate of cold cuts and cheeses, and a glass of good wine (see blackboards for the day's selection and price per glass). A good *enoteca* aims to impress visitors with its wine, and will generally choose excellent-quality ingredients for the simple dishes it offers with the wine. Be warned: Prices add up—keep track of what you're ordering to keep this a budget choice.

Aperitivo *Buffets*

The Italian term *aperitivo* means a before-dinner drink, but it's also used to describe their version of what we might call happy hour: a light buffet that many bars serve to customers during the pre-dinner hours (typically around 18:00 or 19:00 until 21:00). The drink itself may not be cheap (typically around €8-12), but bars lay out an array of meats, cheeses, grilled vegetables, and other *antipasti*-type dishes, and you're welcome to nibble to your heart's content while you nurse your drink.

Groceries and Markets

Picnicking saves lots of euros. Drop by a neighborhood grocery *(alimentari), a supermercato* (such as Conad, Despar, or Co-op), or an open-air market to pick up meats, cheeses, fresh rolls, and other picnic treats. Ordering 100 grams *(un etto)* of cheese or meat is about a quarter-pound, enough for two sandwiches. Yogurt is cheap and healthful.

Shopkeepers will sell small quantities of produce (like a couple of apples or some carrots), but it's customary to let the merchant choose for you; watch locals and imitate. To get ripe fruit, say *"per oggi"* (pehr OH-jee; for today). Either say or indicate by gesturing how much you want. The word *basta* (BAH-stah; enough) works as a question or as a statement. Items can be sold by weight, or per slice *(fetta)*, piece *(pezzi)*, portion *(porzione)*, or takeout container *(contenitore)*.

Gelato

Most *gelaterie* clearly display prices and sizes. Even if you order the smallest size cup or cone, you can generally pick out two flavors. A key to gelato appreciation is sampling liberally. Ask, as Italians do, for a taste: *"Un assaggio, per favore?"*

The best *gelaterie* display signs reading *artiginale, nostra produzione,* or *produzione propia,* indicating the gelato is made on the premises. Seasonal flavors are also a good sign, as are mellow hues (avoid colors that don't appear in nature). Gelato stored in covered metal tins (rather

than white plastic) is more likely to be homemade.

Gelato variations or alternatives include *sorbetto* (sorbet—made with fruit, but no milk or eggs); *granita* or *grattachecca* (a cup of slushy ice with flavored syrup); and *cremolata* (a gelato-*granita* float).

Beverages

Water, Juice, and Cold Drinks

Italians are notorious water snobs. At restaurants, your server just can't understand why you wouldn't want good water to go with your good food. It's customary and never expensive to order a *litro* or *mezzo litro* (half-liter) of bottled water. *Acqua leggermente effervescente* (lightly carbonated water) is a meal-time favorite. Or simply ask for *con gas* if you want fizzy water and *senza gas* if you prefer still water. You can ask for *acqua del rubinetto* (tap water) in restaurants, but your server may give you a funny look.

Chilled bottled water—still *(naturale)* or carbonated *(frizzante)*—is sold cheap in stores. Half-liter mineral-water bottles are available everywhere for about €1 (I refill my water bottle with tap water).

Juice is *succo,* and *spremuta* means freshly squeezed. Order *una spremuta* (don't confuse it with *spumante,* sparkling wine). In grocery stores, you can get a liter of O.J. for the price of a Coke or coffee. Look for *100% succo* or *senza zucchero* (without sugar) on the label—or be surprised by something diluted and sugary sweet. To save money, buy juice in cheap liter boxes, drink some, and pour (and store) the excess in an empty water bottle.

Tè freddo (iced tea) is usually from a can—sweetened and flavored with lemon or peach. Lemonade is *limonata.*

Coffee and Other Hot Drinks

Espresso was born in Italy. If you ask for *"un caffè,"* you'll get a shot of espresso in a little cup—the closest thing to American-style drip coffee is a *caffè americano.* Most Italian coffee drinks begin with espresso, to which they add varying amounts of hot water and/or steamed or foamed milk. Milky drinks, like cappuccino or *caffè latte,* are served to locals before noon and to tourists any time of day (to an Italian, cappuccino is a morning drink; they believe having milk after a big meal or anything with tomato sauce impairs digestion). If they add any milk after lunch, it's just a tiny bit, in a *caffè macchiato.* Italians like their coffee only warm—to get it very hot, request *"Molto caldo, per favore"* (MOHL-toh KAHL-doh pehr fah-VOH-ray). Any coffee drink is available decaffeinated—ask for it *decaffeinato* (deh-kah-feh-NAH-toh). *Cioccolato* is hot chocolate. *Tè* is hot tea.

Experiment with a few of the options:

Cappuccino: Espresso with foamed milk on top (*cappuccino freddo* is iced cappuccino).

Caffè latte: Espresso mixed with hot milk, no foam, in a tall glass (if you order just a "latte," you'll get only warm milk).

Caffè macchiato: Espresso "marked" with a splash of milk, in a small cup.

Latte macchiato: Layers of hot milk and foam, "marked" by an espresso shot, in a tall glass (if you order simply a *"macchiato,"* you'll probably get a *caffè macchiato*).

Caffè lungo: Concentrated espresso diluted with a tiny bit of hot water, in a small cup.

Caffè americano: Espresso diluted with even more hot water, in a larger cup.

Caffè corretto: Espresso "corrected" with a shot of liqueur (normally grappa, *amaro,* or *sambuca*).

Ordering Wine

To order a glass of red or white wine, say, *"Un bicchiere di vino rosso / bianco."* House wine comes in a carafe; choose from a quarter-liter pitcher (8.5 oz, *un quarto*), half-liter pitcher (17 oz, *un mezzo*), or one-liter pitcher (34 oz, *un litro*). *Salute!*

English	Italian
wine	*vino* (VEE-noh)
house wine	*vino della casa* (VEE-noh DEH-lah KAH-zah)
glass	*bicchiere* (bee-kee-EH-ree)
bottle	*bottiglia* (boh-TEEL-yah)
carafe	*caraffa* (kah-RAH-fah)
red	*rosso* (ROH-soh)
white	*bianco* (bee-AHN-koh)
rosé	*rosato* (roh-ZAH-toh)
sparkling	*spumante / frizzante* (spoo-MAHN-tay / freed-ZAHN-tay)
dry	*secco* (SEH-koh)
earthy	*terroso* (teh-ROH-zoh)
fruity	*fruttato* (froo-TAH-toh)
full-bodied	*corposo / pieno* (kor-POH-zoh / pee-EH-noh)
mature	*maturo* (mah-TOO-roh)
sweet	*dolce* (DOHL-chay)

Marocchino: "Moroccan" coffee with espresso, foamed milk, and cocoa powder; the similar *mocaccino* has chocolate instead of cocoa.

Caffè freddo: Sweet and iced espresso.

Caffè hag: Instant decaf.

Alcoholic Beverages

Beer: While Italy is traditionally considered wine country, in recent years there's been a huge and passionate growth in the production of craft beer *(birra artigianale)*. Beer on tap is *alla spina*. Get it *piccola* (33 cl, 11 oz), *media* (50 cl, about a pint), or *grande* (a liter). Italians drink mainly lager beers. A *lattina* (lah-TEE-nah) is a can and a *bottiglia* (boh-TEEL-yah) is a bottle.

Cocktails and Spirits: Italians appreciate both *aperitivi* (palate-stimulating cocktails) and *digestivi* (after-dinner drinks designed to aid digestion). Popular *aperitivo* options include Campari (dark-colored bitters with herbs and orange peel), *Americano* (vermouth with bitters, brandy, and lemon peel), and *Punt e Mes* (sweet red vermouth and red wine).

Digestivo choices are usually either a strong herbal bitters (such as *amaro*—popular commercial brands are Fernet Branca and Montenegro) or something sweet, such as *amaretto* (almond-flavored), Frangelico (hazelnut), *limoncello* (lemon), and *nocino* (walnut). Grappa is a strong brandy; *stravecchio* is an aged, mellower variation.

Wine: Wine is part of the Italian culinary trinity—grape, olive, and wheat. (I'd add gelato.) Ideal conditions for grapes (warm climate, well-draining soil, and an abundance of hillsides) make the Italian peninsula a paradise for grape growers, winemakers, and wine drinkers. Italy makes and consumes more wine per capita than any other country.

In general, Italy designates its wines by one of four official categories (check the label):

Vino da Tavola (VDT) is table wine, the lowest grade, made from grapes grown anywhere in Italy. It's inexpensive and quite good. Restaurants are often proud of their *vino della casa* (house wine).

Denominazione di Origine Controllata (DOC), which meets national standards for high-quality wine, is made from grapes grown in a defined area; it's usually affordable and surprisingly good.

Denominazione di Origine Controllata e Guarantita (DOCG) is the highest grade; it's just like DOC, though its quality is guaranteed. *Riserva* indicates a DOC or DOCG wine matured for a longer time.

Indicazione Geographica Tipica (IGT) is a broad group of wines that range from basic to some of the best. They're not limited to Italian grapes, but give vintners creative license.

SLEEPING

Book your accommodations well in advance, particularly if you'll be traveling during holidays or peak season (May-Oct in northern Italy, and May-June and Sept-Oct in southern Italy). See page 509 for a list of major holidays and festivals in Italy; for tips on making reservations, see page 491.

Rates and Deals

I've described my recommended accommodations using a Sleep Code (see sidebar). The price ranges suggest an estimated cost for a one-night stay in a standard double room with a private toilet and shower in high season, include breakfast, and assume you're booking directly with the hotel (not through a booking site).

Once your dates are set, check the specific price for your preferred stay at several hotels. You can do this either by comparing prices online on the hotels' own websites, or by emailing several hotels directly and asking for their best rate. Even if you start your search on a booking site such as TripAdvisor or Booking.com, you'll usually find the best deal through a hotel's own website.

Sleep Code

Hotels are classified based on the average price of a standard double room with breakfast in high season.

$$$$	**Splurge:** Most rooms over €170
$$$	**Pricier:** €130–170
$$	**Moderate:** €90–130
$	**Budget:** €50–90
¢	**Backpacker:** Under €50
RS%	Rick Steves discount

Unless otherwise noted, credit cards are accepted, hotel staff speak basic English, and free Wi-Fi is available. For the best deal, book directly with the hotel. Ask for a discount if paying in cash; if the listing includes RS%, request a Rick Steves discount.

Types of Accommodations

Hotels

Italians usually use the word hotel, but you might also see *albergo* or *pensione*. English works in all but the cheapest places.

If you're heading south in summer, opt for a place with air-conditioning. It's not always available in spring and fall. To conserve energy, the government enforces limits on air-conditioning and heating: There's a one-month period each spring and fall when neither is allowed.

Most listed hotels have rooms for any size group, from one to five people. Some hotels can add an extra bed (for a small charge) to turn a double into a triple; some offer larger rooms for four or more people (I call these "family rooms" in the listings). If there's space for an extra cot, they'll cram it in for you.

Arrival and Check-In: When you check in, the receptionist will normally ask for your passport and keep it for anywhere from a couple of minutes to a couple of hours. Hotels are legally required to register each guest with the police. Relax. Americans are notorious for making this chore more difficult than it needs to be. If you're

Making Hotel Reservations

Requesting a Reservation: For family-run hotels, it's generally cheaper to book your room direct via email or a phone call. For business-class hotels, or if you'd rather book online, reserve directly through the hotel's official website (not a booking agency's site). For complicated requests, send an email. Almost all of my recommended hotels take reservations in English.

Here's what the hotelier wants to know:

- type(s) of rooms you need and size of your party
- number of nights you'll stay
- your arrival and departure dates, written European-style as day/month/year (for example, 18/06/19 or 18 June 2019);
- special requests (such as en suite bathroom vs. down the hall, cheapest room, twin beds vs. double bed, quiet room)
- applicable discounts (such as a Rick Steves reader discount, cash discount, or promotional rate)

Confirming a Reservation: Most places will request a credit-card number to hold your room. If you're using an online reservation form, look for the *https* or a lock icon at the top of your browser. If you book direct, you can email, call, or fax this information.

Canceling a Reservation: If you must cancel, it's courteous—and smart—to do so with as much notice as possible, especially for smaller family-run places (which describes many of the hotels I list). Cancellation policies can be strict; read the fine print or ask about these before you book. Many discount deals require prepayment, with no cancellation refunds.

Reconfirming a Reservation: Always call or email to reconfirm your room reservation a few days in advance. For B&Bs or very small hotels, I call again on my day of arrival to tell my host what time to expect me (especially important if arriving late—after 17:00).

Phoning: For tips on calling hotels overseas, see page 494.

arriving in the morning, your room probably won't be ready. Drop your bag safely at the hotel and dive right into sightseeing.

In Your Room: Hotel bathrooms often include a bidet (which Italians use for quick sponge baths). The cord that dangles over the tub or shower is not a clothesline. You pull it when you've fallen and can't get up.

More pillows and blankets are usually in the closet or available on request. Towels and linens aren't always replaced every day. Some hotels use lightweight "waffle," or very thin, tablecloth-type towels; these are preferred by many Italians.

Checking Out: While it's customary to pay for your room upon departure, it can be a good idea to settle your bill the day before, when you're not in a hurry and while the manager's in. That way you'll have time to discuss and address any points of contention.

Hotelier Help: Hoteliers can be a great help and source of advice. Most know their cities well, and can assist you with everything from public transit and airport connections to finding a good restaurant, the nearest launderette, or a Wi-Fi hotspot.

The Good and Bad of Online Reviews

User-generated review sites and apps such as Yelp, Booking.com, and TripAdvisor can give you a consensus of opinions about everything from hotels and restaurants to sights and nightlife. If you scan reviews of a hotel and see several complaints about noise or a rotten location, it tells you something important that you'd never learn from the hotel's own website.

But as a guidebook writer, my sense is that there is a big difference between the uncurated information on a review site and a guidebook. A user-generated review is based on the experience of one person, who likely stayed at one hotel in a given city and ate at a few restaurants there (and who doesn't have much of a basis for comparison). A guidebook is the work of a trained researcher who, year after year, visits many alternatives to assess their relative value. I recently checked out some top-rated user-reviewed hotel and restaurant listings in various towns; when stacked up against their competitors, some were gems, while just as many were duds.

Both types of information have their place, and in many ways, they're complementary. If a place or activity is well-reviewed in a guidebook, and also gets good ratings on one of these sites, it's likely a winner.

Hotel Hassles: Even at the best places, mechanical breakdowns occur: Air-conditioning malfunctions, sinks leak, hot water turns cold, and toilets gurgle and smell. Report your concerns clearly and calmly at the front desk.

To guard against theft in your room, keep valuables out of sight. Some rooms come with a safe, and other hotels have safes at the front desk. I've never bothered using one.

If you find that night noise is a problem (if, for instance, your room is over a nightclub), ask for a quieter room in the back or on an upper floor.

Hostels

A hostel provides cheap beds in dorms where you sleep alongside strangers for about €25-30 per night. Travelers of any age are welcome if they don't mind dorm-style accommodations and meeting other travelers. Most hostels offer kitchen facilities, guest computers, Wi-Fi, and a self-service laundry. Hostels almost always provide bedding, but the towel's up to you (although you can usually rent one for a small fee). Family and private rooms are often available.

Independent hostels tend to be easygoing, colorful, and informal (no membership required; www.hostelworld.com). You may pay slightly less by booking direct with the hostel. **Official hostels** are part of Hostelling International (HI) and share a booking site (www.hihostels.com). HI hostels typically require that you be a member or pay extra per night.

Other Accommodation Options

Renting an apartment, house, or villa can be a fun and cost-effective way to go local. Websites such as Booking.com, Airbnb, VRBO, and FlipKey let you browse properties and correspond directly with European property owners or managers. If you prefer to work from a curated list of accommodations, consider using a rental agency such as InterhomeUSA.com or RentaVilla.com. Or try Cross-Pollinate, a booking service for private rooms and apartments in the old centers of Rome, Venice, and Florence; rates start at €30 per person (www.cross-pollinate.com).

STAYING CONNECTED

Staying connected in Europe gets easier and cheaper every year. The simplest solution is to bring your own device—mobile phone, tablet, or laptop—and use it just as you would at home (following the tips below, such as connecting to free Wi-Fi whenever possible). Another option is to buy a European SIM card for your mobile phone—either your US phone or one you buy in Europe. Or you can use European landlines and computers to connect. Each of these options is described below, and you'll find even more details at www.ricksteves.com/phoning.

Using a Mobile Phone in Europe

Here are some budget tips and options.

Sign up for an international plan. Using your cellular network in Europe on a pay-as-you-go basis can add up. To stay connected at a lower cost, sign up for an international service plan through your carrier. Most providers offer a simple bundle that includes calling, messaging, and data. Your normal plan may already include international coverage (T-Mobile's does).

Before your trip, call your provider or check online to confirm that your phone will work in Europe, and research your provider's international rates. Activate the plan a day or two before you leave, then remember to cancel it when your trip's over.

Use free Wi-Fi whenever possible. Unless you have an unlimited-data plan, you're best off saving most of your online tasks for Wi-Fi. You can access the Internet, send texts, and even make voice calls over Wi-Fi.

Most accommodations in Europe offer free Wi-Fi, but some—especially expensive hotels—charge a fee. Many cafés (including Starbucks and McDonald's) have free hotspots for customers. You'll also often find Wi-Fi at TIs, city squares, major museums, public-transit hubs, airports, highway rest stops (Autogrills), and aboard trains and buses.

Minimize the use of your cellular network. Even with an international data plan, wait until you're on Wi-Fi to Skype, download apps, stream videos, or do other megabyte-greedy tasks. Using a navigation app such as Google Maps can take lots of data, so use this sparingly.

Limit automatic updates. By default, your device is constantly checking for a data connection and updating apps. It's smart to disable these so they'll only update when you're on Wi-Fi.

Use Wi-Fi calling and messaging apps. Skype, Viber, FaceTime, and Google+

Tips on Internet Security

Make sure that your device is running the latest versions of its operating system, security software, and apps. Next, ensure that your device and key programs (like email) are password- or passcode-protected. On the road, use only secure, password-protected Wi-Fi hotspots. Ask the hotel or café staff for the specific name of their Wi-Fi network, and make sure you log on to that exact one.

If you must access your financial info online, use a banking app rather than accessing your account via a browser. A cellular connection is more secure than Wi-Fi. Avoid logging onto personal finance sites on a public computer.

Never share your credit-card number (or any other sensitive information) online unless you know that the site is secure. A secure site displays a little padlock icon, and the URL begins with *https* (instead of the usual *http*).

How to Dial

International Calls

Whether phoning from a US landline or mobile phone, or from a number in another European country, here's how to make an international call. I've used one of my recommended Florence hotels as an example (tel. 055-213-154).

Initial Zero: Drop the initial zero from international phone numbers—except when calling Italy.

Mobile Tip: If using a mobile phone, the "+" sign can replace the international access code (for a "+" sign, press and hold "0").

US/Canada to Europe

Dial 011 (US/Canada international access code), country code (39 for Italy), and phone number.

- To call the Florence hotel from home, dial 011-39-055-213-154.

Country to Country Within Europe

Dial 00 (Europe international access code), country code, and phone number.

- To call the Florence hotel from Germany, dial 00-39-055-213-154.

Europe to the US/Canada

Dial 00, country code (1 for US/Canada), and phone number.

- To call from Europe to my office in Edmonds, Washington, dial 00-1-425-771-8303.

Domestic Calls

To call within Italy (from one Italian landline or mobile phone to another), simply dial the phone number, including the initial 0 if there is one.

- To call the Florence hotel from Rome, dial 055-213-154.

More Dialing Tips

Italian Phone Numbers: Italian phone numbers vary in length; a hotel can have, say, an eight-digit phone number and a nine-digit fax number. Italy's landlines start with 0; mobile lines start with 3 and cost substantially more to dial.

Hangouts are great for making free or low-cost voice and video calls over Wi-Fi. With an app installed on your phone, tablet, or laptop, you can log on to a Wi-Fi network and contact friends or family members who use the same service. If you buy credit in advance, with some of these services you can call any mobile phone or landline worldwide for just pennies per minute. Many of these apps also allow you to send messages over Wi-Fi to any other person using that app.

Using a European SIM Card

With a European SIM card, you get a European mobile number and access to cheaper rates than you'll get through your US carrier. This option works well if you

Toll and Toll-Free Calls: Italy's toll-free lines, called *numero verde* (green number), begin with 800 or 803. They can be dialed free from Italian phones without using a phone card but don't work from the US. Any Italian phone number that starts with 8 but isn't followed by a 0 is a toll call (generally costing €0.10-0.50/minute). International rates apply to US toll-free numbers dialed from Italy—they're not free.

More Phoning Help: See www.howtocallabroad.com.

European Country Codes	
Austria	43
Belgium	32
Bosnia-Herzegovina	387
Croatia	385
Czech Republic	420
Denmark	45
Estonia	372
Finland	358
France	33
Germany	49
Gibraltar	350
Great Britain	44
Greece	30
Hungary	36
Iceland	354
Ireland & N. Ireland	353 / 44
Italy	39
Latvia	371
Montenegro	382
Morocco	212
Netherlands	31
Norway	47
Poland	48
Portugal	351
Russia	7
Slovakia	421
Slovenia	386
Spain	34
Sweden	46
Switzerland	41
Turkey	90

want to make a lot of voice calls or need faster connection speeds than your US carrier provides. Fit the SIM card into a cheap phone you buy in Europe (about $40 from phone shops anywhere), or swap out the SIM card in an "unlocked" US phone (check with your carrier about unlocking it).

SIM cards are sold at mobile-phone shops, department-store electronics counters, some newsstands, and vending machines. Costing about $5-10, they usually include prepaid calling/messaging credit, with no contract and no commitment. To get the best rates, buy a new SIM card whenever you arrive in a new country (although the EU caps the roaming fees that local providers can charge).

Public Phones and Computers

It's possible to travel in Europe without a mobile device. You can make calls from your hotel (or the increasingly rare public phone).

Most **hotels** charge a fee for placing calls—ask for rates before you dial. You can use a prepaid international phone card (*carta telefonica prepagata internazionale*—available at post offices, newsstands, street kiosks, tobacco shops, and train stations) to call out from your hotel. Dial the toll-free access number, enter the card's PIN code, then dial the number.

You'll see **public pay phones** in a few Metro and train stations. The phones generally come with multilingual instructions and take coins and credit cards (as well as hard-to-find Telecom Italia phone cards, which may be sold at newsstands).

Most hotels have **public computers** in their lobbies for guests to use; otherwise you may find them at Internet cafés and public libraries (ask your hotelier or the TI for the nearest location). On a European keyboard, use the "Alt Gr" key to the right of the space bar to insert the extra symbol that appears on some keys. Italian keyboards are a little different from ours; to type an @ symbol, press the "Alt Gr" key and the key that shows the @ symbol. If you can't locate a special character, simply copy it from a Web page and paste it into your email message.

Mail

You can mail one package per day to yourself worth up to $200 duty-free from Europe to the US (mark it "personal purchases"). If you're sending a gift to someone, mark it "unsolicited gift." For details, visit www.cbp.gov and search for "Know Before You Go."

The Italian postal service works fine, but for quick transatlantic delivery (in either direction), consider services such as DHL (www.dhl.com).

TRANSPORTATION

Considering the convenience and affordability of Italy's trains and buses, I'd do most of Italy by public transportation. A car is a worthless, expensive headache in big cities and along the Cinque Terre. If you want to drive, consider taking the train between the big, intense cities (Rome, Naples area, Florence, and Venice), and renting a car for exploring the hill-town region. My recommended hill towns can be done by train and/or bus, but if you have time to putter through the countryside, stopping here and there for photo ops and wineries, a car is a good way to go. For covering long distances in Europe, look into flying.

Taxis and Uber

Most European taxis are reliable and cheap. In many cities, couples can travel short distances by cab for little more than two bus or subway tickets. Taxis can be your best option for getting to the airport for an early morning flight or to connect two far-flung destinations. If you like ride-booking services like Uber, these apps usually work in Europe just like they do in the US: You request a car on your mobile device (connected to Wi-Fi or a data plan), and the fare is automatically charged to your credit card.

Trains

Train tickets are a good value in Italy. To travel economically, you can simply buy tickets as you go. Taking fast trains costs more than slow trains, but all are cheaper per mile than their northern European counterparts.

In general, if you're on a tight budget, compare the different options (see "Types of Trains" next) before buying. Assume you'll need to make reservations for fast trains.

Types of Trains

Most trains in Italy are operated by the state-run Trenitalia company (a.k.a. Fer-

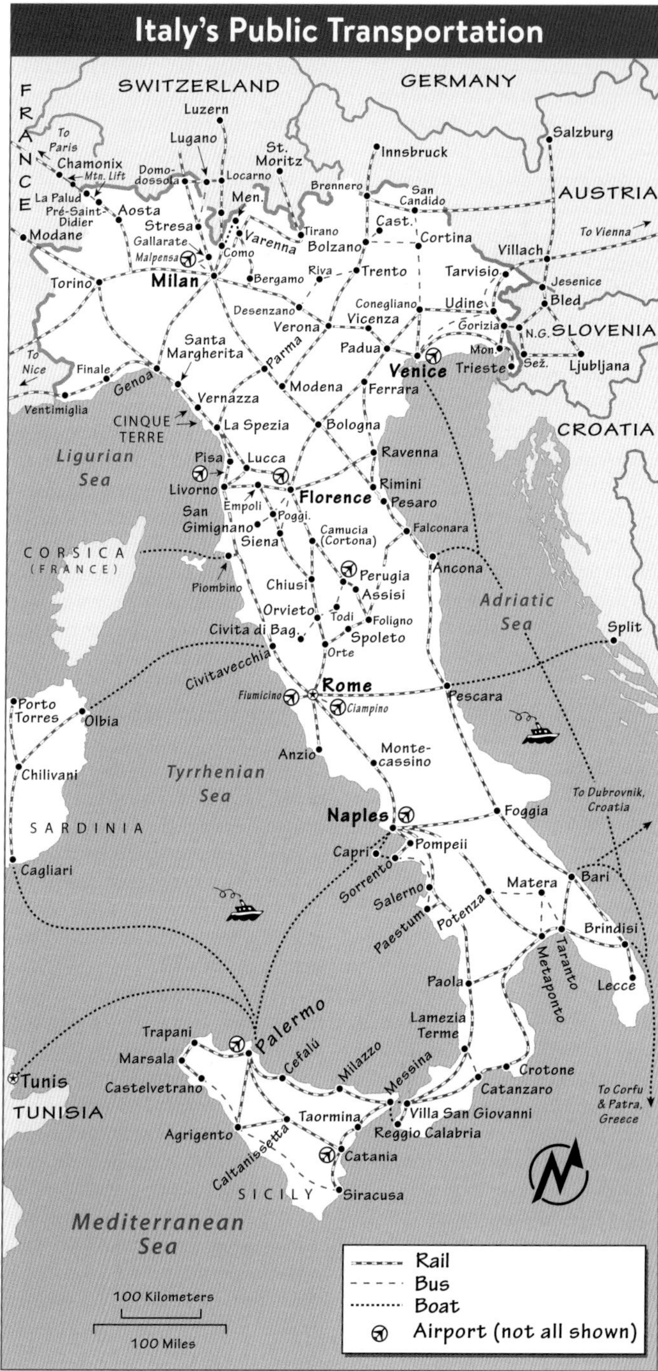
Italy's Public Transportation
SWITZERLAND
GERMANY
FRANCE
AUSTRIA
SLOVENIA
CROATIA
Luzern
Lugano
St. Moritz
Innsbruck
Salzburg
To Paris
Chamonix
Mtn. Lift
Domodossola
Locarno
Brennero
San Candido
La Palud
Pré-Saint-Didier
Aosta
Men.
Cast.
Cortina
To Vienna
Modane
Stresa
Gallarate
Malpensa
Varenna
Como
Tirano
Bolzano
Villach
Torino
Milan
Bergamo
Riva
Trento
Tarvisio
Jesenice
Bled
Desenzano
Conegliano
Udine
Verona
Vicenza
Gorizia
N.G.
Santa Margherita
Parma
Padua
Mon.
To Nice
Finale
Genoa
Venice
Trieste
Sež.
Ljubljana
Ventimiglia
Vernazza
Modena
Ferrara
CINQUE TERRE
La Spezia
Bologna
Ligurian Sea
Pisa
Lucca
Ravenna
Livorno
Florence
Rimini
Pesaro
San Gimignano
Empoli
Poggi.
Camucia (Cortona)
Falconara
Siena
CORSICA (FRANCE)
Ancona
Perugia
Piombino
Chiusi
Assisi
Adriatic Sea
Orvieto
Todi
Foligno
Civita di Bag.
Spoleto
Split
Orte
Civitavecchia
Rome
Fiumicino
Ciampino
Pescara
Porto Torres
Olbia
Anzio
Montecassino
Chilivani
Tyrrhenian Sea
To Dubrovnik, Croatia
Naples
Foggia
SARDINIA
Capri
Pompeii
Cagliari
Sorrento
Matera
Bari
Salerno
Paestum
Potenza
Brindisi
Taranto
Metaponto
Paola
Lecce
Lamezia Terme
Palermo
Trapani
Marsala
Cefalù
Milazzo
Messina
Crotone
Tunis
Castelvetrano
Catanzaro
To Corfu & Patra, Greece
TUNISIA
Taormina
Villa San Giovanni
Agrigento
Reggio Calabria
Caltanissetta
Catania
SICILY
Siracusa
Mediterranean Sea
100 Kilometers
100 Miles
Rail
Bus
Boat
Airport (not all shown)

rovie dello Stato Italiane, abbreviated *FS* or *FSI*, www.trenitalia.com).

Since ticket prices depend on the speed of the train, it helps to know the different types of trains: The fastest trains are the Frecce trains: Frecciabianca, Frecciargento, and so on. Frecce trains may be marked on schedules as ES, AV, or EAV. Other fast trains (though not as fast as Frecce) are IC (InterCity) and EC (EuroCity). Medium-speed trains are RV *(regionale veloce)*, IR (InterRegio), D *(diretto)*, and E *(espresso)*. Pokey trains are R or REG *(regionali)*.

If you're traveling with a rail pass, note that seat reservations are required for EC, IC, international, and Frecce trains. You can't make reservations for regional trains, such as most Pisa-Cinque Terre connections.

A private train company called Italo runs fast trains on these two major routes: Venice-Padua-Bologna-Florence-Rome and Turin-Milan-Bologna-Florence-Rome-Naples. They charge about the same rates as Trenitalia, and they also offer discounts for advance purchase. In Rome and Naples, some Italo departures use secondary stations—if taking an Italo train, pay attention to which station you need. Italo does not accept rail passes, but they're a worthy alternative for point-to-point tickets.

Schedules

At the station, large printed schedules are posted (departure—*partenzi*—posters are always yellow; the white posters show arrivals); these list both Trenitalia and Italo routes when applicable.

You can also check schedules at ticket machines (marked Trenitalia or Italo—each company maintains their own machines). Enter the desired date, time, and destination to see your options.

Online, you can visit www.trenitalia.it and www.italotreno.it (domestic journeys only); for international trips, use www.bahn.com (Germany's excellent all—Europe schedule website). For train information, you can call Trenitalia (tel. 06-6847-5475, daily 7:00-24:00) or Italo (tel. 06-8937-1892, daily 6:00-23:00). If you encounter a language barrier, ask your hotelier to call for you.

Be aware that Trenitalia and Italo don't cooperate. If you buy a ticket for one train line, it's not valid on the other. Even if you're just looking for schedule information, the company you ask will most likely ignore the other's options.

Buying Train Tickets

You have several options for buying train tickets: at the station (easy at machines for domestic trips), a travel agency (a good choice for booking international trips), or online (ideal for getting advance-purchase discounts). Because most Italian trains run frequently, you can keep your travel plans flexible by purchasing tickets as you go. You can buy tickets for several trips at one station when you are ready to commit.

At the Station: If you go to the train station to buy your ticket, avoid ticket-office lines whenever possible by using the ticket machines in station halls. You'll be able to easily purchase tickets for travel within Italy, make seat reservations, and even book a *cuccetta* (koo-CHEH-tah; overnight berth). Pay all ticket costs in the station before you board, or you'll pay a penalty on the train.

Trenitalia's ticket machines (new ones are red, old ones are green-and-white; marked *Trenitalia/Biglietti*) are user-friendly and found in all but the tiniest stations in Italy. You can pay with cash (change given when indicated) or by debit or credit card (even for small amounts, but you may need to enter your PIN). Select English, then your destination. You can choose from first- and second-class seats, request tickets for more than one traveler, and (on the high-speed Frecce trains) choose an aisle or window seat. Don't select a discount rate with-

Deciphering Italian Train Schedules

At the station, look for the big yellow posters labeled *Partenze—Departures* (white posters show arrivals). Departures are listed chronologically, hour by hour, showing the trains leaving the station throughout the day.

Reading from the left, the schedule lists the time of departure *(ora),* the type of train *(treni),* and service classes offered *(classi servizi)*—first- and second-class cars, dining car, *cuccetta* berths, and, more important, whether you need reservations (usually denoted by an R in a box). All Frecce trains, many EuroCity (EC) and InterCity (IC) trains, and most international trains require reservations.

The next column lists the train's destination *(principali fermate destinazioni),* often showing intermediate stops (with arrival times in parentheses). Note that your destination may be listed in fine print as an intermediate stop. For example, if you're going from Milan to Florence, scan the schedule and you'll notice that virtually all trains that terminate in Rome stop in Florence en route. Travelers who read the fine print end up with a far greater choice of trains. You may also see pertinent notes about the train, such as "also stops in..." *(ferma anche a...),* "doesn't stop in..." *(non ferma a...),* "stops in every station" *(ferma in tutte le stazioni),* "delayed..." *(ritardo...),* and so on.

The last column gives the track *(binario)* from which the train departs. Confirm the *binario* with a ticket seller or railway official, the electronic board that lists immediate departures, or monitors on the platform.

For any odd symbols on the poster, look at the key at the end. Some phrasing can be deciphered easily, such as *servizio periodico* (periodic service—doesn't always run). For the trickier ones, ask a local or railway official, or try your *Rick Steves Italian Phrase Book & Dictionary.*

You can also check schedules for trains anywhere in Italy at ticket machines. Enter the date and time of your departure (to or from any Italian station), and view all your options.

out being sure that you meet the criteria (for example, Americans are not eligible for certain EU or resident discounts). Rail-pass holders can use the machines to make seat reservations. If you need to validate your ticket, you can do it in the same machine if you're boarding your train right away.

To buy tickets **for Italo** trains, look for a dedicated service counter (in most major rail stations), or a red ticket machine labeled *Italo.*

To buy **international tickets,** or anything else that requires a real person, you must go to a ticket window. Be sure you're in the correct line. Key terms are: *biglietti* (general tickets), *prenotazioni* (reservations), *nazionali* (domestic), and *internazionali.*

Travel Agencies: Local travel agencies sell domestic and international tickets and make reservations. They charge a small fee, but the language barrier (and the lines) can be smaller than at the station's ticket windows.

Advance Tickets: For travelers ready to lock in dates and times weeks or months in advance, buying nonrefundable tickets online can cut costs in half. It also makes sense to reserve ahead for busy weekends or holiday travel. For Trenitalia, see www.trenitalia.com. You can book Italo tickets online (www.italotreno.it) or by phone (tel. 06-0708). Regional trains

Rail Passes and Train Travel in Italy

A Eurail **Italy Pass** lets you travel by train in Italy for three to eight days (consecutively or not) within a one-month period. Discounted rates are offered for two or more people traveling together.

Italy can also be included in a Eurail **Select Pass,** which allows travel in two to four neighboring countries over two months, and it's covered (along with most of Europe) by the classic Eurail **Global Pass.**

Rail passes are sold only outside Europe (through travel agents or Rick Steves' Europe). For more on the ins and outs of rail passes, including prices, download my **free guide to Eurail Passes** (www.ricksteves.com/rail-guide) or go to www.ricksteves.com/rail.

If you're taking just a couple of train rides, look into buying individual **point-to-point tickets,** which may save you money over a pass. Use this map to add up approximate pay-as-you-go fares for your itinerary, and compare that to the price of a rail pass. Keep in mind that significant discounts on point-to-point tickets may be available with advance purchase.

Map shows approximate costs, in US$, for one-way, second-class tickets on faster trains.

don't offer advance discounts or seat assignments, so there's little need to buy those tickets in advance.

Family Discounts: Families with young kids can get discounts on some trips—kids ages 4 and under travel free; ages 4-11 at half-price. Ask for the "Offerta Familia" deal at a ticket counter (or, at a ticket machine, choose "Yes" at the "Do you want ticket issue?" prompt, then choose "Familia").

Validating Train Tickets

If your ticket includes a seat reservation on a specific train *(biglietto con prenotazione),* you're all set and can just get on

Understanding Your Train Ticket

Open or Non-Reserved Ticket—Need to Validate

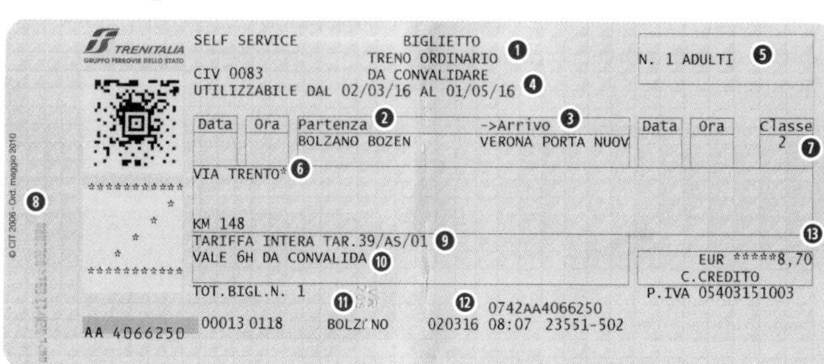

TRENITALIA
GRUPPO FERROVIE DELLO STATO
SELF SERVICE BIGLIETTO
TRENO ORDINARIO
CIV 0083 DA CONVALIDARE
UTILIZZABILE DAL 02/03/16 AL 01/05/16
N. 1 ADULTI
Data Ora Partenza ->Arrivo Data Ora Classe
BOLZANO BOZEN VERONA PORTA NUOV 2
VIA TRENTO*
KM 148
TARIFFA INTERA TAR.39/AS/01
VALE 6H DA CONVALIDA
EUR *****8,70
C.CREDITO
P.IVA 05403151003
TOT.BIGL.N. 1
0742AA4066250
AA 4066250 00013 0118 BOLZANO 020316 08:07 23551-502

1. Open ticket for non-express train, must be validated
2. Point of departure
3. Destination
4. Period in which ticket is valid
5. Number of passengers
6. Route
7. Class of travel (1st or 2nd)
8. Validation stamp
9. Full fare for non-express train
10. Ticket good for 1 trip within 6 hours after validation
11. Location of ticket sale
12. Date of ticket purchase
13. Ticket cost

Reserved Ticket (Fast Train)—Need Not Validate

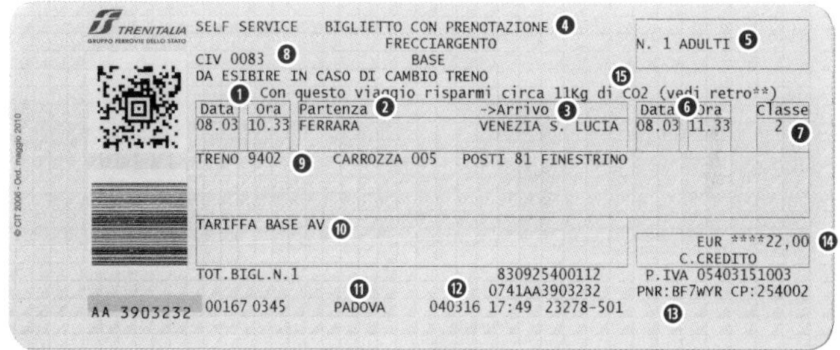

TRENITALIA
GRUPPO FERROVIE DELLO STATO
SELF SERVICE BIGLIETTO CON PRENOTAZIONE
FRECCIARGENTO
CIV 0083 BASE
N. 1 ADULTI
DA ESIBIRE IN CASO DI CAMBIO TRENO
Con questo viaggio risparmi circa 11Kg di CO2 (vedi retro**)
Data Ora Partenza ->Arrivo Data Ora Classe
08.03 10.33 FERRARA VENEZIA S. LUCIA 08.03 11.33 2
TRENO 9402 CARROZZA 005 POSTI 81 FINESTRINO
TARIFFA BASE AV
EUR ****22,00
C.CREDITO
TOT.BIGL.N.1 830925400112 P.IVA 05403151003
0741AA3903232 PNR:BF7WYR CP:254002
AA 3903232 00167 0345 PADOVA 040316 17:49 23278-501

1. Departure date & time
2. Point of departure
3. Destination
4. "Ticket with reservation"
5. Number of passengers
6. Arrival date & time
7. Class of travel (1st or 2nd)
8. "Present to official if changing trains"
9. Train, car & seat numbers (*finestrino* = window seat)
10. Fast-train fare
11. Location of ticket sale
12. Date of ticket purchase
13. Booking ID
14. Ticket cost
15. Amount of CO_2 usage reduced by this train trip

board. An open ticket with no seat reservation (generally for a *regionali* train) must always be validated. Before you board, stamp your ticket (it may say *da convalidare* or *convalida*) in the machine near the platform (usually marked *convalida biglietti* or *vidimazione*). Once you validate a ticket, you must complete your trip within the timeframe shown on the ticket. If you forget to validate your ticket, go right away to the train conductor—before he comes to you—or you'll pay a fine.

Tickets purchased online are prevalidated, meaning that they can be used only for the date and time that you select (or within a four-hour window for unreserved regional trains).

Rail Passes

The single-country Eurail Italy Pass may save you money if you take several long train rides or prefer first-class travel, but for most people it's not a good value. Most train travelers in Italy take relatively short rides on the Milan-Venice-Florence-Rome circuit. For these trips, it can be cheaper to buy point-to-point tickets instead. Remember that rail passes are valid only on the Italian state railway, not on Italo-brand trains.

Furthermore, a rail pass doesn't offer much hop-on convenience in Italy, since many trains, such as Le Frecce, EuroCity, and InterCity, require paid seat reservations (€5-10 each). Most regional trains (such as Florence-Pisa-Cinque Terre service) don't require (or offer) reservations. Reservations for berths on overnight trains cost extra and aren't covered by rail passes. All Eurail passes allow up to two kids (ages 4-11) to travel free with an adult.

For more detailed advice on figuring out the smartest rail-pass options for your train trip, visit www.ricksteves.com/rail.

Train Tips

Seat Reservations: Trains can fill up, even in first class. If you're on a tight schedule, you'll want to reserve a few days ahead for fast trains.

If you're taking an unreserved *regionali* train that originates at your departure point (e.g., you're catching the Rome-Assisi train in Rome), arriving at least 15 minutes before the departure time will help you snare a seat.

Baggage Storage: Many Italian stations have *deposito bagagli* where you can safely leave your bag for a standardized but rather steep price (€6/5 hours, €12/12 hours, €17/24 hours, double-check closing hours). Due to security concerns, no Italian stations have lockers.

Theft Concerns: In big cities, exercise caution and prudence at train stations to avoid thieves and con artists. If someone helps you to find your train or carry your bags, be aware that they are not an official porter; they are simply hoping for some cash. And if someone other than a uniformed railway employee tries to help you use the ticket machines, politely refuse.

Italian trains are famous for their thieves. Never leave a bag unattended. Police do ride the trains, cutting down on theft. Still, for an overnight trip, I'd feel safe only in a *cuccetta* (a bunk in a special sleeping car with an attendant who keeps track of who comes and goes while you sleep—approximately €40 or more).

Strikes: Strikes, which are common, generally last a day (often a Friday). But in actuality, "essential" main-line service is maintained (by law) during strikes. If I need to get somewhere and know a strike is imminent, I leave early (before the strike, which often begins at 9:00), or I just go to the station with extra patience in tow and hop on anything rolling in the direction I want to go. See www.trenitalia.com, choose English, then "Information and Contacts," and then "In Case of Strike."

Buses

You can usually get anywhere you want to in Italy by bus, as long as you're not in a hurry and plan ahead using bus schedules (pick up at local TIs or bus stations). For reaching small towns, buses are sometimes the only option if you don't have a car.

Long-distance buses are catching on in Italy as an alternative to the train. They are usually cheaper, modern, and often (unlike trains) have free Wi-Fi. They're especially useful on routes poorly served by train. Some of the operators you'll see are Eurolines/Baltour (www.baltour.it), Megabus (www.megabus.com), Flixbus (www.flixbus.com), and Marozzi (www.marozzivt.it).

Larger towns have a (usually chaotic) long-distance bus station *(stazione degli autobus)*, with ticket windows and several stalls. Smaller towns—where buses are more useful—often have a central bus stop *(fermata)*, likely along the main road or on the main square, and maybe several more scattered around town. In small towns, buy bus tickets at newsstands or tobacco shops (with the big *T* signs). When buying your ticket, confirm the departure point *("Dov'è la fermata?")*.

Before boarding, confirm the destination with the driver. You are expected to stow big backpacks underneath the bus (open the luggage compartment yourself if it's closed). Upon arrival, double-check that the posted schedule lists your next destination and departure time.

Sundays and holidays are problematic; even from large cities, schedules are sparse, departing buses are jam-packed, and ticket offices are often closed. Plan ahead and buy your ticket in advance. Most travel agencies book bus (and train) tickets for a small fee.

Renting a Car

If you're renting a car in Italy, bring your driver's license. You're also technically required to have an International Driving Permit—an official translation of your driver's license (sold at your local AAA; see www.aaa.com). While that's the letter of the law, I generally rent cars without having this permit.

Figure on paying roughly $250 for a one-week rental. Allow extra for supplemental insurance, fuel, tolls, and parking.

Research car rentals before you go. It's cheaper to arrange most car rentals from the US. Consider several companies to compare rates. Most of the major US rental agencies (including Avis, Budget, Enterprise, Hertz, and Thrifty) have offices throughout Europe. Also consider the two major Europe-based agencies, Europcar and Sixt. It can be cheaper to use a consolidator, such as Auto Europe/Kemwel (www.autoeurope.com—or the often cheaper www.autoeurope.eu).

Always read the fine print or query the agent carefully for add-on charges—such as one-way drop-off fees, airport surcharges, or mandatory insurance policies—that aren't included in the "total price."

For the best deal, rent by the week with unlimited mileage. To save money on fuel, request a diesel car. I normally rent

the smallest, least-expensive model with a stick shift (generally cheaper than an automatic). Almost all rentals are manual by default, so if you need an automatic, request one in advance. You'll do yourself a favor by renting the smallest car that meets your needs.

Picking Up Your Car: Compare pickup costs (downtown can be less expensive than the airport) and explore drop-off options. Always check the hours of the location you choose: Many rental offices close from midday Saturday until Monday morning and, in smaller towns, at lunchtime.

When you pick up the rental car, check it thoroughly and make sure any damage is noted on your rental agreement. Rental agencies in Europe tend to charge for even minor damage, so be sure to mark everything. Before driving off, find out how your car's gearshift, lights, turn signals, wipers, radio, and fuel cap function, and know what kind of fuel the car takes (diesel vs. unleaded). When you return the car, make sure the agent verifies its condition with you. Some drivers take pictures of the returned vehicle as proof of its condition.

Car Insurance Options

When you rent a car, you're liable for a very high deductible, sometimes equal to the entire value of the car. Limit your financial risk in case of an accident by choosing one of these two options: Buy Collision Damage Waiver (CDW) coverage from the car-rental company (figure roughly 30-40 percent extra), or get coverage through your credit card (free, but more complicated).

In Italy, most car-rental companies' rates automatically include CDW coverage. Even if you try to decline CDW when you reserve your Italian car, you may find when you show up at the counter that you must buy it after all.

While each rental company has its own variation, basic CDW costs $15–30 a day and reduces your liability, but does not eliminate it. When you pick up the car, you'll be offered the chance to "buy down" the deductible to zero (for an additional $10–30/day; this is sometimes called "super CDW" or "zero-deductible coverage").

If you opt for credit-card coverage, there's a catch. You'll technically have to decline all coverage offered by the car-rental company, which means they can place a hold on your card for up to the full value of the car. In case of damage, it can be time-consuming to resolve the charges with your credit-card company. Before you decide on this option, quiz your credit-card company about how it works.

For more on car-rental insurance, see www.ricksteves.com/cdw.

Theft Insurance: Note that theft insurance (separate from CDW insurance) is mandatory in Italy. It usually costs about $15-20 a day, payable when you pick up the car.

Leasing

For trips of three weeks or more, consider leasing (which automatically includes zero-deductible collision and theft insurance); you'll save lots of money on tax and insurance. Leasing provides you a new car with unlimited mileage and a 24-hour emergency assistance program. You can lease for as little as 21 days to as long as five and a half months. Car leases must be arranged from the US. Auto Europe is one of many companies offering affordable lease packages.

Driving

Italian drivers can be aggressive: They drive fast and tailgate as if it were required. They pass where Americans are taught not to—on blind corners and just before tunnels. Roads have narrow shoulders or none at all. Driving in the countryside can be less stressful than driving through urban areas or on busy highways, but stay alert.

Road Rules: Stay out of restricted urban traffic zones or you'll risk huge fines. Car traffic is restricted in many city centers. Don't drive or park in any area that has a sign reading *Zona Traffico Limitato* (*ZTL*, often shown above a red circle). If you do, your license plate will likely be photographed and a hefty (€100-plus) ticket mailed to your home without your ever having met a cop. If your hotel is within a restricted area, it's best to ask your hotelier to direct you to parking outside the zone.

Be aware of typical European road rules. For example, many countries require headlights to be turned on at all times, and nearly all forbid talking on your mobile phone without a hands-free headset. Seatbelts are mandatory, and children under age 12 must ride in child-safety

or booster seats. In Europe, you're not allowed to turn right on a red light, unless there is a sign or signal specifically authorizing it, and on expressways it's illegal to pass drivers on the right. For more rules, check the US State Department website (www.travel.state.gov, search for your country in the "Learn about your destination" box, then click on "Travel and Transportation").

Navigation Maps and Apps: A big, detailed regional road map (buy one at a newsstand, gas station, or bookstore) and a semiskilled navigator are helpful.

When driving in Europe, you can use the mapping app on your phone as long as you have an international data plan. Without a data plan (or to conserve data), you can rely on offline maps (via a mapping app or by downloading Google maps). As an alternative, you could rent a GPS device or bring your own GPS device from home (but you'll need to buy and download European maps before your trip).

A number of well-designed offline mapping apps offer much of the convenience of online maps without any costly data demands. Google Maps, Here WeGo, and Navmii provide turn-by-turn voice directions and recalibrate even when they're offline.

Signage: Learn the universal road signs. Although roads are numbered on maps, actual road signs give just a city name (for example, if you were heading west out of Venice, the map would be marked "route S-11"—but you'd follow signs to *Padua,* the next town along this road). The signs can be inconsistent: They may direct you to the nearest big city or simply the next town along the route.

Freeways and Tolls: Italy's freeway system, the autostrada, is as good as our interstate system, but you'll pay a toll (for costs, use the trip-planning tool at www.autostrade.it or search "European Tolls" on www.theaa.com). When approaching a tollbooth, skip lanes marked *Telepass;* if you want a staffed booth, choose a lane with a sign that shows a hand.

Fuel: Fuel is expensive—often about $8 per gallon. Diesel cars are common in Europe, so be sure you know what type of fuel your car takes before you fill up. Gas pumps are color-coded: green for unleaded *(senza piombo),* black for diesel *(gasolio).* Diesel costs only a bit less. *Autostrada* rest stops are self-service stations open daily without a siesta break. Many 24-hour-a-day stations are entirely automated. Small-town stations are usually cheaper and offer full service but shorter hours.

Theft: Cars are routinely vandalized and stolen. Thieves easily recognize rental cars and assume they're filled with a tourist's gear. Be sure all of your valuables are out of sight and locked in the trunk, or even better, with you or in your room.

Parking: White lines painted on the street generally mean parking is free. Yellow lines mean that parking is reserved only for residents (who have permits). Blue lines

mean you'll have to pay—usually around €1.50 per hour (use machine, leave time-stamped receipt on dashboard). Study the signs. Often the free zones have a 30- or 60-minute time limit.

Zona disco has nothing to do with dancing. Italian cars come equipped with a time disc (a cardboard clock), which you can use in a *zona disco*—set the clock to your arrival time and leave it on the dashboard. (If your rental car doesn't come with a *disco,* pick one up at a tobacco shop or just write your arrival time on a piece of paper and place it on the dashboard.)

Garages are safe, save time, and help you avoid the stress of parking tickets. Take the parking voucher with you to pay the cashier before you leave.

Flights

The best comparison search engine for both international and intra-European flights is www.kayak.com. An alternative is Google Flights, which has an easy-to-use system to track prices. For inexpensive flights within Europe, try Skyscanner.com.

Flying to Europe: Start looking for international flights four to six months before your trip, especially for peak-season travel. Off-season tickets can be purchased a month or so in advance. Depending on your itinerary, it can be efficient to fly into one city and out of another.

Flying within Europe: If you're considering a train ride that's more than five hours long, a flight may save you both time and money. When comparing your options, factor in the time it takes to get to the airport and how early you'll need to arrive to check in.

These days you can fly within Europe on major airlines affordably for around $100 a flight. If you go instead with a budget airline such as Easyjet or Ryanair, be aware of the potential drawbacks and restrictions: nonrefundable and nonchangeable tickets, minimal or nonexistent customer service, pricey and time-consuming treks to secondary airports, and stingy baggage allowances with steep overage fees. To avoid unpleasant surprises, read the small print before you book.

Flying to the US: Because security is extra tight for flights to the US, be sure to give yourself plenty of time at the airport (see www.tsa.gov for the latest rules).

Resources from Rick Steves

Begin Your Trip at www.RickSteves.com

My mobile-friendly **website** is *the* place to explore Europe. You'll find thousands of fun articles, videos, photos, and radio interviews; a wealth of money-saving tips for planning your dream trip; my travel talks and blog; and guidebook updates (www.ricksteves.com/update).

Our **Travel Forum** is an immense collection of message boards, where our travel-savvy community answers questions and shares personal travel experiences—and our well-traveled staff chimes in when they can help.

Our **online Travel Store** offers bags and accessories designed to help you travel smarter and lighter. These include my popular bags (which I live out of four months a year), money belts, totes, toiletries kits, adapters, guidebooks, planning maps, and more.

Choosing the right **rail pass** for your trip can drive you nutty. Our website will help you find the perfect fit for your itinerary and your budget: We offer easy, one-stop shopping for rail passes, seat reservations, and point-to-point tickets.

Guidebooks, Video, Audio Europe, and Tours

Books: *Rick Steves Best of Italy* is just one of many books in my series on European travel, which includes country and city guidebooks, Snapshot guides (excerpted chapters from my country guides), Pocket Guides (full-color little books on big cities, including Rome, Florence, and Venice), and my budget-travel skills handbook, *Rick Steves Europe Through the Back Door*. My phrase books—including one for Italian—are practical and budget-oriented. A more complete list of my titles appears near the end of this book.

TV Shows: My public television series, *Rick Steves' Europe,* covers Europe from top to bottom with over 100 half-hour episodes. To watch full episodes online for free, see www.ricksteves.com/tv. Or to raise your travel I.Q. with video versions of our popular classes (including my talks on travel skills, packing smart, most European countries, and European art), see www.ricksteves.com/travel-talks.

Audio: My weekly public radio show, *Travel with Rick Steves,* features interviews with travel experts from around the world. A complete archive is available at www.soundcloud.com/rick-steves, and much of this audio content is available for free, along with my audio tours of Europe's (and Italy's) top sights, through my **Rick Steves Audio Europe** app (see page 28).

Small Group Tours: Want to travel with greater efficiency and less stress? We organize **tours** with more than three-dozen itineraries reaching the best destinations in this book...and beyond. You'll find European adventures to fit every vacation length, and you'll enjoy great guides and a fun but small group of travel partners. For all the details, and to get our tour catalog, visit www.ricksteves.com or call us at 425/608-4217.

HOLIDAYS AND FESTIVALS

This list includes selected festivals in major cities, plus national holidays. Before planning a trip around a festival, verify its dates by checking the festival's website or TI sites (www.italia.it).

In Italy, hotels get booked up on Easter weekend (from Good Friday through Easter Monday), April 25 (Liberation Day), May 1 (Labor Day), November 1 (All Saints' Day), and on Fridays and Saturdays year-round.

Jan 1	New Year's Day
Jan 6	Epiphany
Jan	Fashion convention, Florence
Late Jan-early Feb	Carnevale, Venice (Mardi Gras, www.carnevale.venezia.it)
Feb	Carnevale Celebrations / Mardi Gras, Florence
March or April	Easter Sunday (and Scoppio del Carro fireworks in Florence)
After Easter	Easter Monday
Early April	Vinitaly, Verona (wine festival)
April 25	Italian Liberation Day
April / May	Italy's Cultural Heritage Week (www.beniculturali.it)
May 1	Labor Day
May 5	Feast of the Ascension Day
Mid-May	Cricket Festival, Florence (music, entertainment, and food)
Late May-early June	Fashion convention, Florence
Late May-early June	Vogalonga Regatta, Venice
June 1-30	Annual Flower Display, Florence (flowers on main square)
June 2	Anniversary of the Republic
June 16-17	Festival of St. Ranieri, Pisa
June 24	St. John the Baptist Day, celebrated in Rome and Florence (parades, dances, costumed soccer game)
June 29	Sts. Peter and Paul's Day, most fervently celebrated in Rome
June-Aug	Verona Opera season
July 2	Palio horse race, Siena
Mid-July	Feast and Regatta of the Redeemer, Venice (third weekend)
Aug 10	St. Lawrence Day, Rome
Aug 15	Feast of the Assumption (called Ferragosto)
Aug 16	Palio horse race, Siena
Early Sept	Historical Regatta, Venice (first weekend)
Oct	Musica dei Popoli Festival, Florence (folk music and dances)

Nov 1	All Saints' Day
Nov 21	Feast of Our Lady of Good Health, Venice
Dec	Christmas Market, Rome, Piazza Navona
Dec 8	Feast of the Immaculate Conception
Dec 25	Christmas
Dec 26	St. Stephen's Day

CONVERSIONS AND CLIMATE

Numbers and Stumblers

- Europeans write a few of their numbers differently than we do. 1= 1, 4 = 4, 7 = 7.
- In Europe, dates appear as day/month/year. Christmas is always 25/12.
- Commas are decimal points and decimals are commas. A dollar and a half is $1,50, and one thousand is 1.000.
- When counting with fingers, start with your thumb. If you hold up your first finger to request one item, you'll probably get two.
- What Americans call the second floor of a building is the first floor in Europe.
- On escalators and moving sidewalks, Europeans keep the left "lane" open for passing. Keep to the right.

Clothing and Shoe Sizes

Shoppers can use these US-to-European comparisons as general guidelines, but note that no conversion is perfect. For info on VAT refunds, see page 479.

Women: For pants, dresses, and shoes, add 30 (US 10 = European 40). For blouses and sweaters, add 8 (US 32 = European 40).

Men: For shirts, multiply by 2 and add about 8 (US 15 = European 38). For jackets and suits, add 10. For shoes, add 32-34.

Children: Clothing is sized by height—in centimeters (2.5 inches = 1 cm), so a US size 8 roughly equates to 132-140. For shoes up to size 13, add 16-18, and for sizes 1 and up, add 30-32.

Metric Conversions

A kilogram equals 1,000 grams and about 2.2 pounds. One hundred grams (a common unit of sale at markets) is about a quarter-pound.

One liter is about a quart, or almost four to a gallon.

A kilometer is six-tenths of a mile. To convert kilometers to miles, cut the kilometers in half and add back 10 percent of the original (120 km: 60 + 12 = 72 miles). One meter is 39 inches.

Using the Celsius scale, 0°C equals 32°F. To roughly convert Celsius to Fahrenheit, double the number and add 30. For weather, 28°C is 82°F—perfect. For health, 37°C is just right. At a launderette, 30°C is cold, 40°C is warm (default setting), and 60°C is hot.

Italy's Climate

First line, average daily high; second line, average daily low; third line, average days without rain. For more detailed weather statistics for destinations in this book (as well as the rest of the world), check www.wunderground.com.

Rome

J	F	M	A	M	J	J	A	S	O	N	D
52°	55°	59°	66°	74°	82°	87°	86°	79°	71°	61°	55°
40°	42°	45°	50°	56°	63°	67°	67°	62°	55°	49°	44°
13	19	23	24	26	26	30	29	25	23	19	21

Florence

J	F	M	A	M	J	J	A	S	O	N	D
40°	46°	56°	65°	74°	80°	84°	82°	75°	63°	51°	43°
32°	35°	43°	49°	57°	63°	67°	66°	61°	52°	43°	35°
25	21	24	22	23	21	25	24	25	23	20	24

Venice

J	F	M	A	M	J	J	A	S	O	N	D
42°	46°	53°	62°	70°	76°	81°	80°	75°	65°	53°	46°
33°	35°	41°	49°	56°	63°	66°	65°	61°	53°	44°	37°
25	21	24	21	23	22	24	24	25	24	21	23

Packing Checklist

Clothing

- ❑ 5 shirts: long- & short-sleeve
- ❑ 2 pairs pants or skirt
- ❑ 1 pair shorts or capris
- ❑ 5 pairs underwear & socks
- ❑ 1 pair walking shoes
- ❑ Sweater or fleece top
- ❑ Rainproof jacket with hood
- ❑ Tie or scarf
- ❑ Swimsuit
- ❑ Sleepwear

Money

- ❑ Debit card
- ❑ Credit card(s)
- ❑ Hard cash ($20 bills)
- ❑ Money belt or neck wallet

Documents & Travel Info

- ❑ Passport
- ❑ Airline reservations
- ❑ Rail pass/train reservations
- ❑ Car-rental voucher
- ❑ Driver's license
- ❑ Student ID, hostel card, etc.
- ❑ Photocopies of all the above
- ❑ Hotel confirmations
- ❑ Insurance details
- ❑ Guidebooks & maps
- ❑ Notepad & pen
- ❑ Journal

Toiletries Kit

- ❑ Toiletries
- ❑ Medicines & vitamins
- ❑ First-aid kit
- ❑ Glasses/contacts/sunglasses (with prescriptions)
- ❑ Earplugs
- ❑ Packet of tissues (for WC)

Miscellaneous

- ❑ Daypack
- ❑ Sealable plastic baggies
- ❑ Laundry soap
- ❑ Clothesline
- ❑ Sewing kit
- ❑ Travel alarm/watch

Electronics

- ❑ Smartphone or mobile phone
- ❑ Camera & related gear
- ❑ Tablet/ereader/media player
- ❑ Laptop & flash drive
- ❑ Earbuds or headphones
- ❑ Chargers
- ❑ Plug adapters

Optional Extras

- ❑ Flipflops or slippers
- ❑ Mini-umbrella or poncho
- ❑ Travel hairdryer
- ❑ Belt
- ❑ Hat (for sun or cold)
- ❑ Picnic supplies
- ❑ Water bottle
- ❑ Fold-up tote bag
- ❑ Small flashlight
- ❑ Small binoculars
- ❑ Small towel or washcloth
- ❑ Inflatable pillow
- ❑ Tiny lock
- ❑ Address list (to mail postcards)
- ❑ Postcards/photos from home
- ❑ Extra passport photos
- ❑ Good book

Italian Survival Phrases

English	Italian	Pronunciation
Good day.	*Buon giorno.*	bwohn **jor**-noh
Do you speak English?	*Parla inglese?*	**par**-lah een-**gleh**-zay
Yes. / No.	*Si. / No.*	see / noh
I (don't) understand.	*(Non) capisco.*	(nohn) kah-**pees**-koh
Please.	*Per favore.*	pehr fah-**voh**-ray
Thank you.	*Grazie.*	**graht**-see-ay
You're welcome.	*Prego.*	**preh**-go
I'm sorry.	*Mi dispiace.*	mee dee-spee-**ah**-chay
Excuse me.	*Mi scusi.*	mee **skoo**-zee
(No) problem.	*(Non) c'è un problema.*	(nohn) cheh oon proh-**bleh**-mah
Good.	*Va bene.*	vah **beh**-nay
Goodbye.	*Arrivederci.*	ah-ree-veh-**dehr**-chee
one / two	*uno / due*	**oo**-noh / **doo**-ay
three / four	*tre / quattro*	tray / **kwah**-troh
five / six	*cinque / sei*	**cheeng**-kway / **seh**-ee
seven / eight	*sette / otto*	**seh**-tay / **oh**-toh
nine / ten	*nove / dieci*	**noh**-vay / dee-**ay**-chee
How much is it?	*Quanto costa?*	**kwahn**-toh **koh**-stah
Write it?	*Me lo scrive?*	may loh **skree**-vay
Is it free?	*È gratis?*	eh **grah**-tees
Is it included?	*È incluso?*	eh een-**kloo**-zoh
Where can I buy / find...?	*Dove posso comprare / trovare...?*	**doh**-vay **poh**-soh kohm-**prah**-ray / troh-**vah**-ray
I'd like / We'd like...	*Vorrei / Vorremmo...*	voh-**reh**-ee / voh-**reh**-moh
...a room.	*...una camera.*	**oo**-nah **kah**-meh-rah
...a ticket to ____.	*...un biglietto per ____.*	oon beel-**yeh**-toh pehr ____
Is it possible?	*È possibile?*	eh poh-**see**-bee-lay
Where is...?	*Dov'è...?*	doh-**veh**
...the train station	*...la stazione*	lah staht-see-**oh**-nay
...the bus station	*...la stazione degli autobus*	lah staht-see-**oh**-nay **dehl**-yee **ow**-toh-boos
...tourist information	*...informazioni per turisti*	een-for-maht-see-**oh**-nee pehr too-**ree**-stee
...the toilet	*...la toilette*	lah twah-**leh**-tay
men	*uomini / signori*	**woh**-mee-nee / seen-**yoh**-ree
women	*donne / signore*	**doh**-nay / seen-**yoh**-ray
left / right	*sinistra / destra*	see-**nee**-strah / **deh**-strah
straight	*sempre dritto*	**sehm**-pray **dree**-toh
What time does this open / close?	*A che ora apre / chiude?*	ah kay **oh**-rah ah-**pray** / kee-**oo**-day
At what time?	*A che ora?*	ah kay **oh**-rah
Just a moment.	*Un momento.*	oon moh-**mehn**-toh
now / soon / later	*adesso / presto / tardi*	ah-**deh**-soh / **preh**-stoh / **tar**-dee
today / tomorrow	*oggi / domani*	**oh**-jee / doh-**mah**-nee

In an Italian Restaurant

English	Italian	Pronunciation
I'd like...	*Vorrei...*	voh-**reh**-ee
We'd like...	*Vorremmo...*	vor-**reh**-moh
...to reserve...	*...prenotare...*	preh-noh-**tah**-ray
...a table for one / two.	*...un tavolo per uno / due.*	oon **tah**-voh-loh pehr **oo**-noh / **doo**-ay
Is this seat free?	*È libero questo posto?*	eh **lee**-beh-roh **kweh**-stoh **poh**-stoh
The menu (in English), please.	*Il menù (in inglese), per favore.*	eel meh-**noo** (een een-**gleh**-zay) pehr fah-**voh**-ray
service (not) included	*servizio (non) incluso*	sehr-**veet**-see-oh (nohn) een-**kloo**-zoh
cover charge	*pane e coperto*	**pah**-nay ay koh-**pehr**-toh
to go	*da portar via*	dah **por**-tar **vee**-ah
with / without	*con / senza*	kohn / **sehnt**-sah
and / or	*e / o*	ay / oh
menu (of the day)	*menù (del giorno)*	meh-**noo** (dehl **jor**-noh)
specialty of the house	*specialità della casa*	speh-chah-lee-**tah** **deh**-lah **kah**-zah
first course (pasta, soup)	*primo piatto*	**pree**-moh pee-**ah**-toh
main course (meat, fish)	*secondo piatto*	seh-**kohn**-doh pee-**ah**-toh
side dishes	*contorni*	kohn-**tor**-nee
bread	*pane*	**pah**-nay
cheese	*formaggio*	for-**mah**-joh
sandwich	*panino*	pah-**nee**-noh
soup	*zuppa*	**tsoo**-pah
salad	*insalata*	een-sah-**lah**-tah
meat	*carne*	**kar**-nay
chicken	*pollo*	**poh**-loh
fish	*pesce*	**peh**-shay
seafood	*frutti di mare*	**froo**-tee dee **mah**-ray
fruit / vegetables	*frutta / legumi*	**froo**-tah / lay-**goo**-mee
dessert	*dolce*	**dohl**-chay
tap water	*acqua del rubinetto*	**ah**-kwah dehl roo-bee-**neh**-toh
mineral water	*acqua minerale*	**ah**-kwah mee-neh-**rah**-lay
milk	*latte*	**lah**-tay
(orange) juice	*succo (d'arancia)*	**soo**-koh (dah-**rahn**-chah)
coffee / tea	*caffè / tè*	kah-**feh** / teh
wine	*vino*	**vee**-noh
red / white	*rosso / bianco*	**roh**-soh / bee-**ahn**-koh
glass / bottle	*bicchiere / bottiglia*	bee-kee-**eh**-ray / boh-**teel**-yah
beer	*birra*	**bee**-rah
Cheers!	*Cin cin!*	cheen cheen
More. / Another.	*Di più. / Un altro.*	dee pew / oon **ahl**-troh
The same.	*Lo stesso.*	loh **steh**-soh
The bill, please.	*Il conto, per favore.*	eel **kohn**-toh pehr fah-**voh**-ray
Do you accept credit cards?	*Accettate carte di credito?*	ah-cheh-**tah**-tay **kar**-tay dee **kreh**-dee-toh
tip	*mancia*	**mahn**-chah
Delicious!	*Delizioso!*	day-leet-see-**oh**-zoh

For more user-friendly Italian phrases, check out *Rick Steves' Italian Phrase Book & Dictionary* or *Rick Steves' French, Italian, and German Phrase Book*.

INDEX

D

INDEX

Q

R

T

U

V

W

Z

MAP INDEX

NAPLES, SORRENTO, AND THE AMALFI COAST

PRACTICALITIES

Start your trip at

Our website enhances this book and turns

Explore Europe

At ricksteves.com you can browse through thousands of articles, videos, photos and radio interviews, plus find a wealth of money-saving travel tips for planning your dream trip. And with our mobile-friendly website, you can easily access all this great travel information anywhere you go.

TV Shows

Preview the places you'll visit by watching entire half-hour episodes of Rick Steves' Europe (choose from all 100 shows) on-demand, for free.

ricksteves.com

your travel dreams into affordable reality

Radio Interviews

Enjoy ready access to Rick's vast library of radio interviews covering travel tips and cultural insights that relate specifically to your Europe travel plans.

Travel Forums

Learn, ask, share! Our online community of savvy travelers is a great resource for first-time travelers to Europe, as well as seasoned pros. You'll find forums on each country, plus travel tips and restaurant/hotel reviews. You can even ask one of our well-traveled staff to chime in with an opinion.

Travel News

Subscribe to our free Travel News e-newsletter, and get monthly updates from Rick on what's happening in Europe.

Rick Steves has

Experience maximum Europe

Save time and energy
This guidebook is your independent-travel toolkit. But for all it delivers, it's still up to you to devote the time and energy it takes to manage the preparation and logistics that are essential for a happy trip. If that's a hassle, there's a solution.

Rick Steves Tours
A Rick Steves tour takes you to Europe's most

great tours, too!

with minimum stress

interesting places with great guides and small groups of 28 or less. We follow Rick's favorite itineraries, ride in comfy buses, stay in family-run hotels, and bring you intimately close to the Europe you've traveled so far to see. Most importantly, we take away the logistical headaches so you can focus on the fun.

Join the fun

This year we'll take thousands of free-spirited travelers—nearly half of them repeat customers—along with us on four dozen different itineraries, from Ireland to Italy to Athens.

Is a Rick Steves tour the right fit for your travel dreams? Find out at ricksteves.com, where you can also request Rick's latest tour catalog.

Europe is best experienced with happy travel partners. We hope you can join us.

See our itineraries at ricksteves.com

A Guide for Every Trip

BEST OF GUIDES

Full-color easy-to-scan format, focusing on Europe's most popular destinations and sights.

Best of England
Best of Europe
Best of France
Best of Germany
Best of Ireland
Best of Italy
Best of Spain

COMPREHENSIVE GUIDES

City, country, and regional guides with detailed coverage for a multi-week trip exploring the most iconic sights and venturing off the beaten track.

Amsterdam & the Netherlands
Barcelona
Belgium: Bruges, Brussels, Antwerp & Ghent
Berlin
Budapest
Croatia & Slovenia
Eastern Europe
England
Florence & Tuscany
France
Germany
Great Britain
Greece: Athens & the Peloponnese
Iceland
Ireland
Istanbul
Italy
London
Paris
Portugal
Prague & the Czech Republic
Provence & the French Riviera
Rome
Scandinavia
Scotland
Spain
Switzerland
Venice
Vienna, Salzburg & Tirol

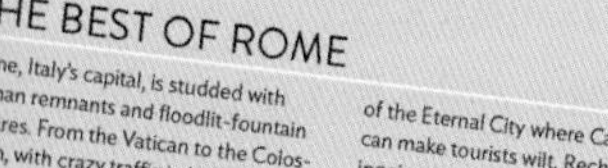
HE BEST OF ROME

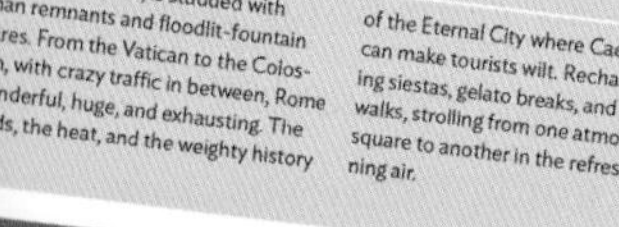
me, Italy's capital, is studded with nan remnants and floodlit-fountain ares. From the Vatican to the Colos- n, with crazy traffic in between, Rome nderful, huge, and exhausting. The ds, the heat, and the weighty history of the Eternal City where Caesars walked can make tourists wilt. Recharge by taking siestas, gelato breaks, and after-dark walks, strolling from one atmospheric square to another in the refreshing evening air.

Rick Steves guidebooks are published by Avalon Travel, an imprint of Perseus Books, a Hachette Book Group company.

POCKET GUIDES

Compact, full-color city guides with the essentials for shorter trips.

Amsterdam
Athens
Barcelona
Florence
Italy's Cinque Terre
London
Munich & Salzburg
Paris
Prague
Rome
Venice
Vienna

SNAPSHOT GUIDES

Focused single-destination coverage.

Basque Country: Spain & France
Copenhagen & the Best of Denmark
Dublin
Dubrovnik
Edinburgh
Hill Towns of Central Italy
Krakow, Warsaw & Gdansk
Lisbon
Loire Valley
Madrid & Toledo
Milan & the Italian Lakes District
Naples & the Amalfi Coast
Normandy
Northern Ireland
Norway
Reykjavik
Sevilla, Granada & Southern Spain
St. Petersburg, Helsinki & Tallinn
Stockholm

Rick Steves books are available from your favorite bookseller. Many guides are available as ebooks.

CRUISE PORTS GUIDES

Reference for cruise ports of call.

Mediterranean Cruise Ports
Scandinavian & Northern European Cruise Ports

Complete your library with...

TRAVEL SKILLS & CULTURE

Study up on travel skills before visiting "Europe through the back door" or gain insight on European history and culture.

Europe 101
European Christmas
European Easter
European Festivals
Europe Through the Back Door
Postcards from Europe
Travel as a Political Act

PHRASE BOOKS & DICTIONARIES

French
French, Italian & German
German
Italian
Portuguese
Spanish

PLANNING MAPS

Britain, Ireland & London
Europe
France & Paris
Germany, Austria & Switzerland
Ireland
Italy
Spain & Portugal

PHOTO CREDITS

Dominic Arizona Bonuccelli (www.azphoto.com): 1 top middle, 1 top right, 2 top left, 3 top left, 3 bottom left, 6, 9 left, 10 top right, 10 center right, 10 bottom, 11 bottom, 13 top left, 13 top right, 13 middle right, 13 middle left, 15 middle, 17 middle right, 18 top, 19 top right, 19 middle left, 19 middle right, 22 middle, 23 middle right, 25, 26, 29 left, 32, 37 left, 56 right, 58, 59 bottom, 70, 71, 74, 75, 114, 115, 120 bottom right, 122, 135, 140 top, 151 left, 152, 153, 167 right, 196 top, 212, 220, 223 top, 223 bottom left, 223 top right, 224, 270, 275, 284, 287, 304, 313 right, 321, 329, 333, 342 right, 363, 369, 370 left, 374, 470, 477 bottom, 482, 483, 485, 488, 490, 502 left, 502 right, 507

1 top left © Birute Vijeikiene | Dreamstime.com, 1 bottom © Tomas Marek | Dreamstime.com, 2 bottom left © Stian Olsen | Dreamstime.com, 10 top left © Bilderpool| Dreamstime.com, 11 middle © Jennifer Barrow | Dreamstime.com, 14 top © Lornet | Dreamstime.com, 15 top © Ermess | Dreamstime.com, 16 top © minnystock | Dreamstime.com, 17 center left © M. Rohana | Dreamstime.com, 24 © Raluca Tudor | Dreamstime.com, 36 © Beatrice Preve | Dreamstime.com, 37 top right © Tinamou | Dreamstime.com, 43 © Beatrice Preve | Dreamstime.com, 59 top © Anna Hristova | Dreamstime.com, 102 left © Marco Clarizia | Dreamstime.com, 116 © Nickolay Stanev | Dreamstime, 120 top © Razvanjp | Dreamstime.com, 120 bottom left © Elenaphotos | Dreamstime.com, 128 bottom © Krylon80 | Dreamstime.com, 129 © FreeSurf69 | Dreamstime.com, 146 © Stian Olsen | Dreamstime.com, 150 © Sung Choi | Dreamstime.com, 157 left © Zaramira | Dreamstime.com, 160 © Spectral-design | Dreamstime.com, 164 © Nicknickko | Dreamstime.com, 175 right © Skif55 | Dreamstime.com, 180 © Natalia Volkova | Dreamstime.com, 223 bottom right © Krisztian Miklosy | Dreamstime.com, 243 © M. Rohana | Dreamstime.com, 302 © minnystock | Dreamstime.com, 308 © Skaliger | Dreamstime.com, 312 © F11photo | Dreamstime.com, 315 left © Olga Shtytlkova | Dreamstime.com, 324 © Volgariver | Dreamstime.com, 330 © Natalaiya Hora | Dreamstime.com, 347 © Emircristea | Dreamstime.com, 394 © Jennifer Barrow | Dreamstime.com, 454 left © Antonio Gravante | Dreamstime.com, 460 right © Gigavisual | Dreamstime.com

372 © Hedda Gjerpen/istockphoto.com

357 © tupungato/123rf.com

72 left © Elena Bauer

367 © Scala / Art Resource, NY

Public Domain via Wikimedia Commons: 15 bottom, 22 top, 59 middle left, 59 middle right, 61 bottom, 65, 67 right, 188, 235 top, 240, 274, 278

Additional photography by Ben Cameron, Mary Ann Cameron, Cameron Hewitt, Michaelanne Jerome, Suzanne Kotz, Gene Openshaw, Michael Potter, Robyn Stencil, Jennifer Schutte, Rick Steves, Gretchen Strauch, Laura VanDeventer, Ian Watson, and Robert Wright. All photos used by permission and are the property of the copyright holders.

Avalon Travel
Hachette Book Group
1700 Fourth Street
Berkeley, CA 94710

Printed in China by RRD Shenzhen
Second Edition
ISBN 978-1-63121-807-1
Third printing June 2019

For the latest on Rick's talks, guidebooks, tours, public radio show, and public television series, contact Rick Steves' Europe, 130 Fourth Avenue North, Edmonds, WA 98020, 425/771-8303, www.ricksteves.com, rick@ricksteves.com.

RICK STEVES' EUROPE
Special Publications Manager: Risa Laib
Managing Editor: Jennifer Madison Davis
Project Editor: Suzanne Kotz
Editors: Glenn Eriksen, Tom Griffin
Editorial & Production Assistant: Jessica Shaw
Graphic Content Director: Sandra Hundacker
Maps & Graphics: David C. Hoerlein, Lauren Mills, Mary Rostad

AVALON TRAVEL
Editorial Director: Kevin McLain
Senior Editor and Series Manager: Madhu Prasher
Editor: Jamie Andrade
Associate Editor: Sierra Machado
Copy Editor: Kelly Lydick
Proofreader: Patrick Collins
Indexer: Stephen Callahan
Production & Typesetting: Tabitha Lahr
Cover Design: Kimberly Glyder Design
Maps & Graphics: Kat Bennett, Mike Morgenfeld

Front Cover Photos: Top left: Venice; gondola; palazzi; canal grande © Schaffer | Dreamstime. Top middle: interiors and architectural details of the duomo, Siena cathedral © Photogolfer | Dreamstime. Top right: Pantheon and the Fountain by night on Piazza della Rotonda in Rome in Italy © Dariusz Szwangruber | Dreamstime. Bottom: Manarola village at sunset. Cinque Terre National Park, Liguria Italy © Sorin Colac | Dreamstime
Back Cover Photos: Left: Amalfi Coast from Villa Rufolo gardens in Ravello, Campania, Italy © minnystock | Dreamstime. Middle: espresso machine pouring coffee © Seubsai Koonsawat | Dreamstime. Right: Italy, rome. piazza navona. four rivers fountain © Ginasanders | Dreamstime.